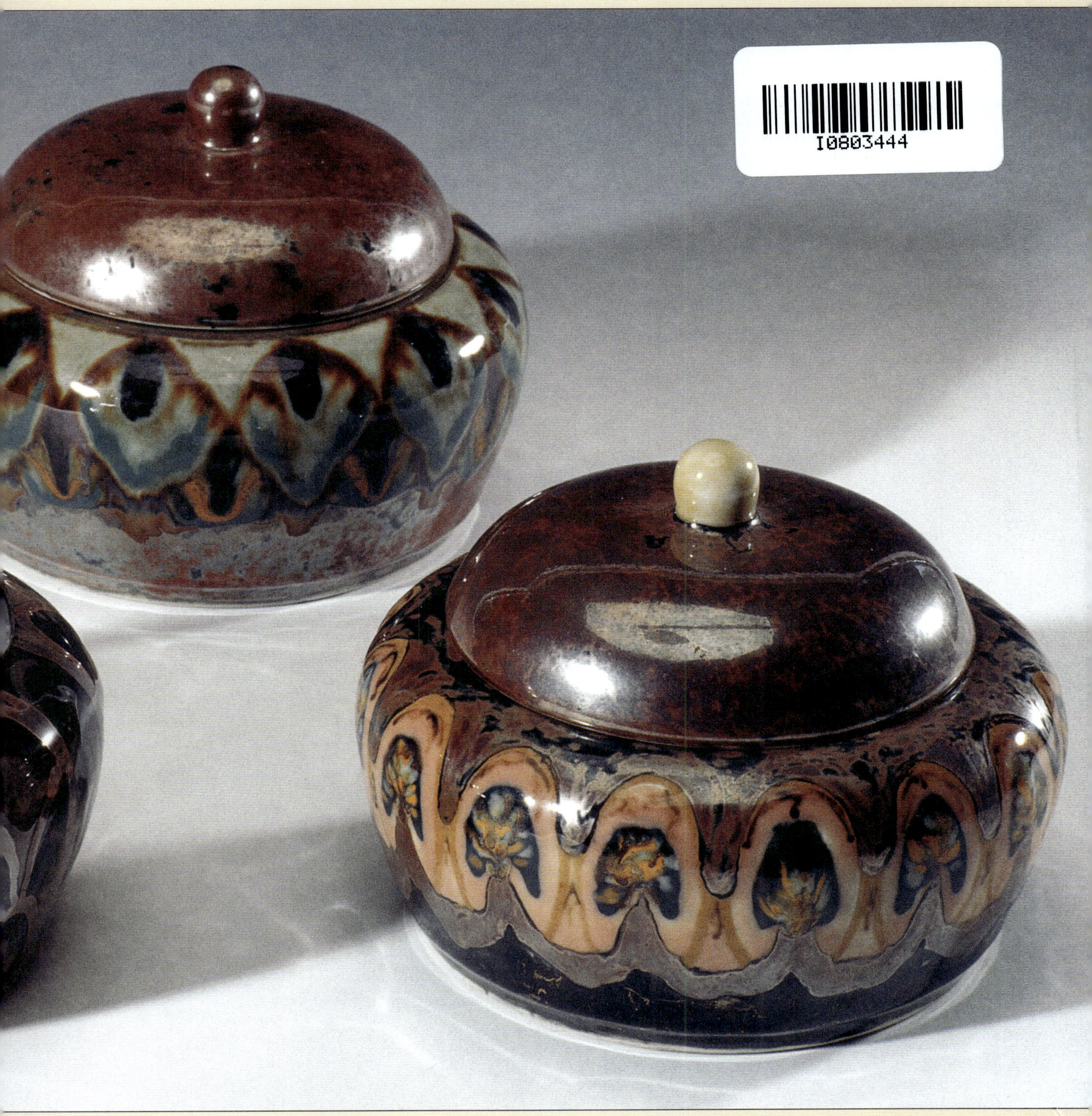

I0803444

Art Deco Limoges
Camille Tharaud and Other Ceramists

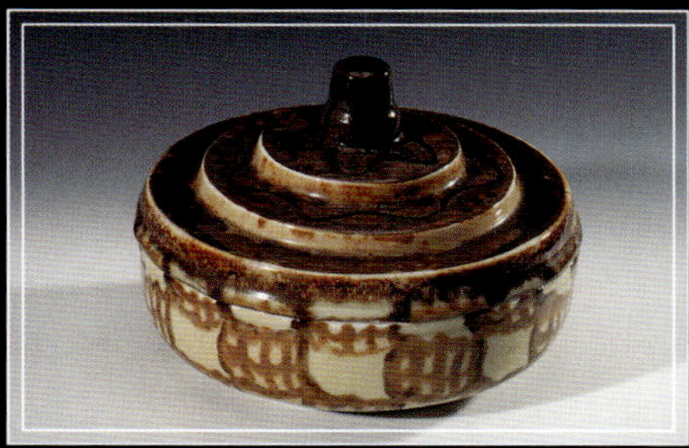
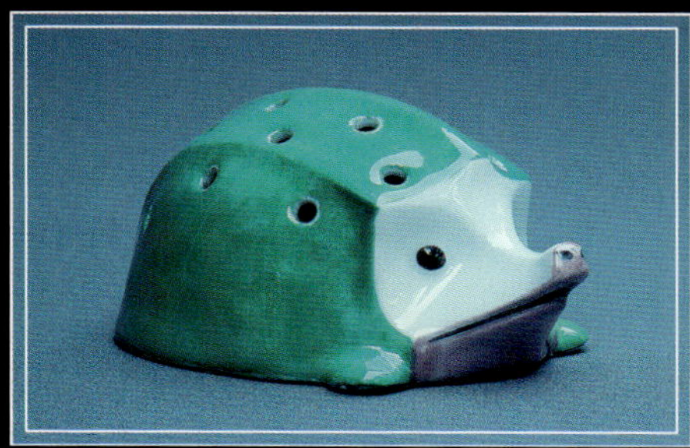
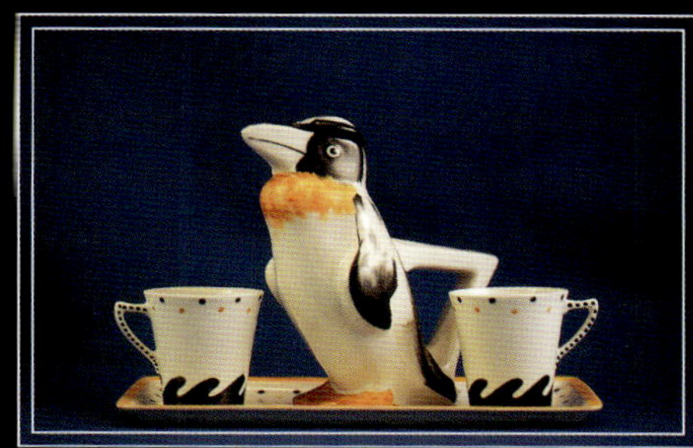
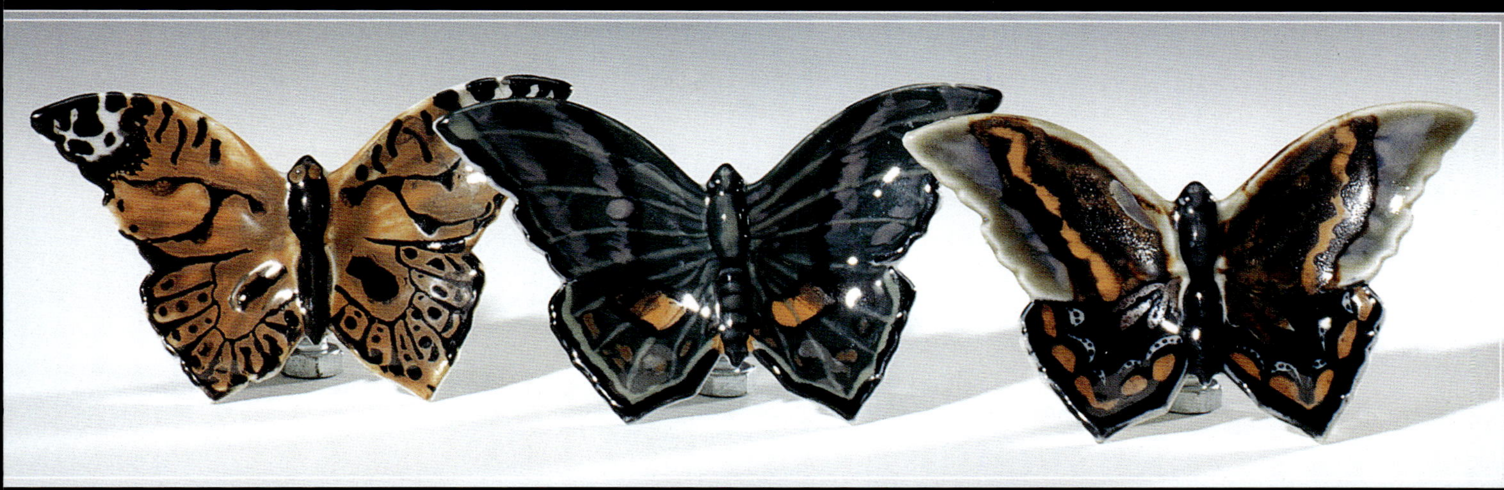

Keith & Thomas Waterbrook-Clyde

Schiffer® Publishing Ltd

4880 Lower Valley Road, Atglen, PA 19310 USA

Thanks

To our friends, Laurence de la Grange and Sol Brien, who also did a lot of work on this book behind the scenes.

Dedication

Monsieur Albert Goumot-Labesse died in August 2003 during the time we were working on this book and three months after we met with him and his wife, Odette [Tharaud], in their home in Limoges. He and his wife were incredibly generous with us in sharing information about Camille Tharaud and in allowing us to photograph their personal collection of Tharaud pieces. We will never forget Mr. Goumot-Labesse's jolly and infectious laughter and the personal experiences which he happily shared with us.

Mr. Goumot-Labesse was a major figure in the history of Limoges porcelain. He worked for Camille Tharaud in 1942 and later in 1954 built and started his own factory in Panazol. He bought the shapes and patterns of the Charles Ahrenfeldt manufacturer when it closed in 1959. In 1978, the Goumot-Labesse company took back the Tharaud name. During the forty years of the factory's existence, it had the highest productivity of any of the Limoges porcelain manufacturers.

With this book, we want to acknowledge his contributions to porcelain and extend our condolences to his wife, Odette Goumot-Labesse, and their families.

Library of Congress Cataloging-in-Publication Data

Waterbrook-Clyde, Keith.
Art deco Limoges : Camille Tharaud and other ceramists / By Keith & Thomas Waterbrook-Clyde.
p. cm.
ISBN 0-7643-2178-1 (hardcover)
1. Tharaud, Camille, 1878-1956. 2. Limoges porcelain. 3. Decoration and ornament—Art deco. I. Waterbrook-Clyde, Thomas. II. Title.

NK4210.T45A4 2005
738.2'0944'6624—dc22
2004025678

Designed by Mark David Bowyer
Type set in Bernhard Modern BT/Humanist 521 BT

ISBN: 0-7643-2178-1
Printed in China
1 2 3 4

Published by Schiffer Publishing Ltd.
4880 Lower Valley Road
Atglen, PA 19310
Phone: (610) 593-1777; Fax: (610) 593-2002
E-mail: Info@schifferbooks.com

In Europe, Schiffer books are distributed by
Bushwood Books
6 Marksbury Ave.
Kew Gardens
Surrey TW9 4JF England
Phone: 44 (0) 20 8392-8585; Fax: 44 (0) 20 8392-9876
E-mail: info@bushwoodbooks.co.uk
Free postage in the U.K., Europe; air mail at cost.

Contents

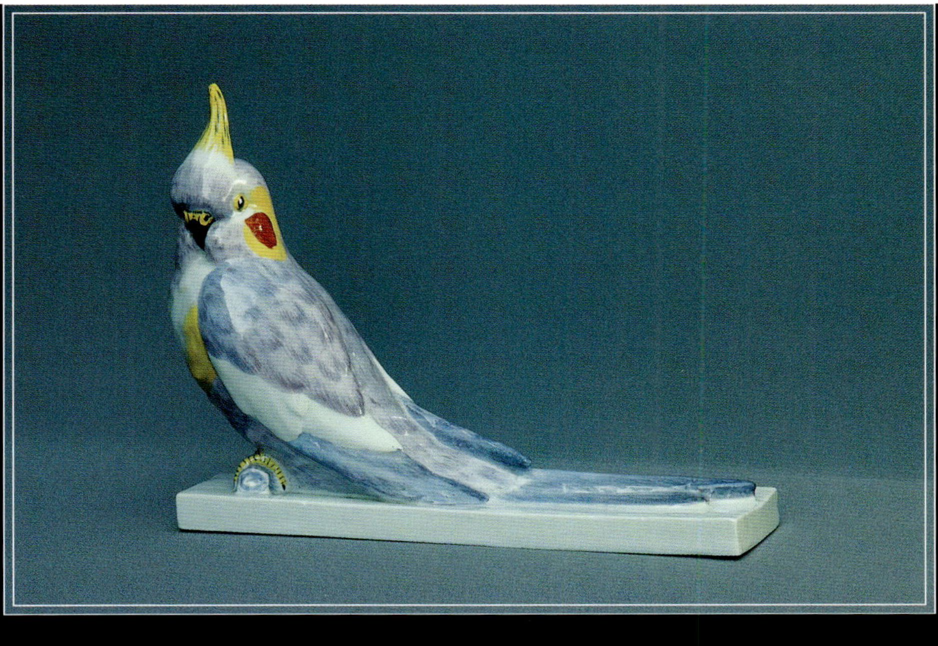

Acknowledgments

The preparation of this book was a long but enjoyable experience. We had the opportunity once again to work with Laurence de la Grange, the director of Atelier Le Tallec in Paris. She is a recognized expert on European porcelain decoration, is a world-class creator of porcelain designs, and is happily a friend. She made sure that we covered all the bases in Limoges, France, the home of Camille Tharaud. She planned two separate trips for us—accompanied us and translated for us—introduced us to many people in the porcelain business in Limoges, shared with us her own expertise and insights, and upon our return translated several pieces written in French. She is a great teacher and a good friend, and she helped us begin and end this project with a bang. She also gained, by this experience, a new sense of appreciation for the works of Camille Tharaud, whose decorating technique and style is different from that of Atelier Le Tallec. We were delighted to be able to introduce a new ceramist to our teacher and friend.

One of the most exciting moments of this project was the opportunity to meet Odette and Albert Goumot-Labesse, both of whom are prominent figures in the great history of Limoges porcelain. Mrs. Goumot-Labesse is the daughter of Mr. Tharaud and was a notable figure in design and painting in her father's studio. Likewise, Mr. Goumot-Labesse also worked in Mr. Tharaud's factory where he was head chemist and responsible for the high temperature firings and later went on to establish his own Limoges factory. The Goumot-Labesses opened their home to us for two days—to photograph their personal collection of Limoges porcelain and to explain to us some of the history and techniques of Mr. Tharaud. They gladly shared insights with us that gave us a much richer feel for the genius of Mr. Tharaud. It was an honor to meet them both.

Sol Brien of Montréal, herself a porcelain painter, helped us not only with this book on Mr. Tharaud but also with our previous book on Atelier Le Tallec. We would be totally lost without her aesthetics and insight into the decoration of porcelain. She has patiently helped us with numerous translations, some of which were very lengthy. This book would have taken at least another year if it had not been for her help, which was literally only a mouse click away.

Harry Root of Chicago, who is one of the world's experts on eighteenth century English ceramics, also came to our rescue. He tapped one of his colleagues, Rebecca Tilles, at The Chicago Art Institute, who did a wonderful job of translating a very technical piece on Mr. Tharaud's technique.

We want to thank Art and Karen Levin for letting us photograph their Tharaud porcelain collection. The representation of Tharaud's work in this book is much more complete because of the pieces in their collection. They were kind and helpful hosts. We also want to thank Lionel Delaygue, president of Royal Limoges, and Thierry de Merindol, president of Artoria Limoges and the grandson of Mr. Tharaud, for letting us photograph their Tharaud pieces. Mr. Delaygue also welcomed us back to Limoges for a second visit a year later to photograph Art Deco pieces in the Royal Limoges museum, which we have also included in this book.

Two other important collectors shared pieces of their Art Deco collections for this book. Jeffrey Sanfilippo took a day to let us photograph many of his significant Robj pieces, and JoAnn Williams sent us photographs of important Suzanne Lalique and Édouard Sandoz pieces, which were made by Haviland. With the help of Lionel Delaygue, Jeffrey Sanfilippo, and JoAnn Williams, we were able to expand the number of photographs of Art Deco pieces produced by a number of different companies.

We had two outstanding photographers. R. Godrant, well known for his fine work in the Limoges region, photographed all of the Tharaud pieces in Limoges; and Rick Aguilar of Chicago, an equally fine photographer, photographed the two Tharaud collections in this city.

In addition to the information provided by the Goumot-Labesses, we have relied heavily on the information provided by Jean-Marc Ferrer in his definitive book on Camille Tharaud. We have tried to be careful to give attribution to Monsieur Ferrer when we have used him as a source; but inevitably, because we used his research extensively, we may have inadvertently from time to time left out attributions to him as a source. We also want to thank Gérard Tatin for sending us copies of material on Camille Tharaud.

This book was a multidisciplinary effort. We are indebted to many people for their contributions.

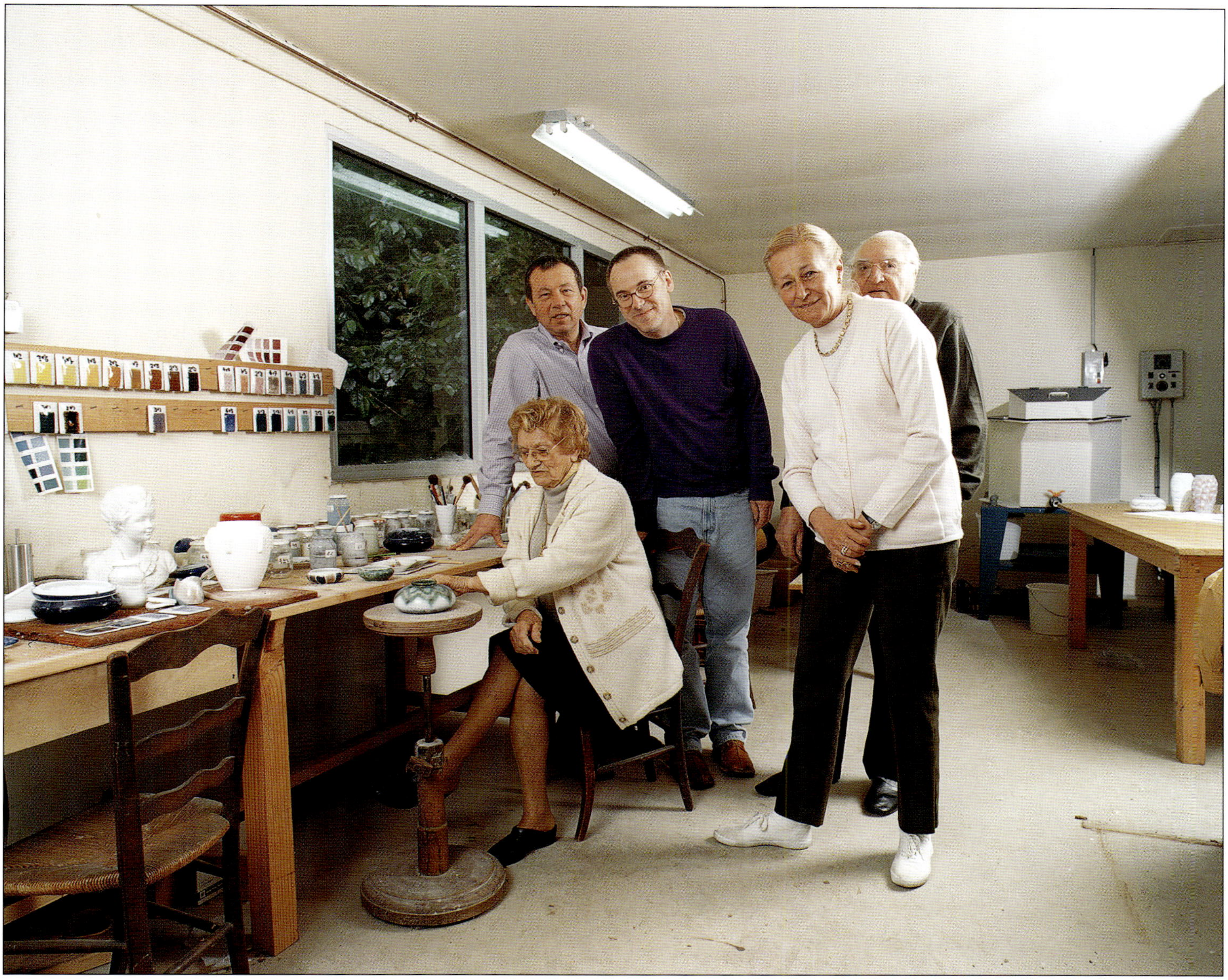

At the home of the Goumot-Labesses, from right to left, Albert Goumot-Labesse, Laurence de la Grange, Thomas Waterbrook-Clyde, Keith Waterbrook-Clyde, Odette [Tharaud] Goumot-Labesse (seated).

Odette and Albert Goumot-Labesse

Odette Goumot-Labesse, the daughter of Camille Tharaud, was one of the prominent artists and painters in her father's studio. She started going to the studio at the age of four, and she would later manage thirty-five decorators and painters. She attended design school in Limoges and later worked at the studio from 1937-1944. Mrs. Goumot-Labesse did not often mark her own pieces—she wanted to keep them for herself—and those that are marked with her initials are rare and command very high prices. She started out as a designer only, and then at the age of fifteen she started painting. Mrs. Goumot-Labesse had a sister, but she did not work in the studio.

Albert Goumot-Labesse's introduction to porcelain in Limoges came as a prerequisite to his marriage to Odette Tharaud. Mr. Tharaud said that Mr. Goumot-Labesse could only marry his daughter, Odette, if he resigned from the air force and joined Mr. Tharaud's porcelain factory. This is just what Mr. Goumot-Labesse did in 1942. Knowing nothing about porcelain, Mr. Goumot-Labesse learned everything about the porcelain business from his father-in-law. He soon took over the responsibilities for the laboratory and the firing process from start to finish. In 1944, he started his own factory, Goumot-Labesse, where his wife assumed the responsibilities for all of the shipping.

After his retirement, Mr. Goumot-Labesse set up a kiln in his garage. Located throughout the garage are different colored porcelain tiles and several vases decorated with layered but unfired enamels. The color palettes in his garage are recreations of the colors used by Mr. Tharaud. Because Mr. Goumot-Labesse used a gas-fired kiln, the pieces were fired at 1300° Celsius instead of 1410°. Mr. Goumot-Labesse ended his experimentations with colors and firings in 2001.

The Goumot-Labesse family still has all of the original molds of the Tharaud factory.

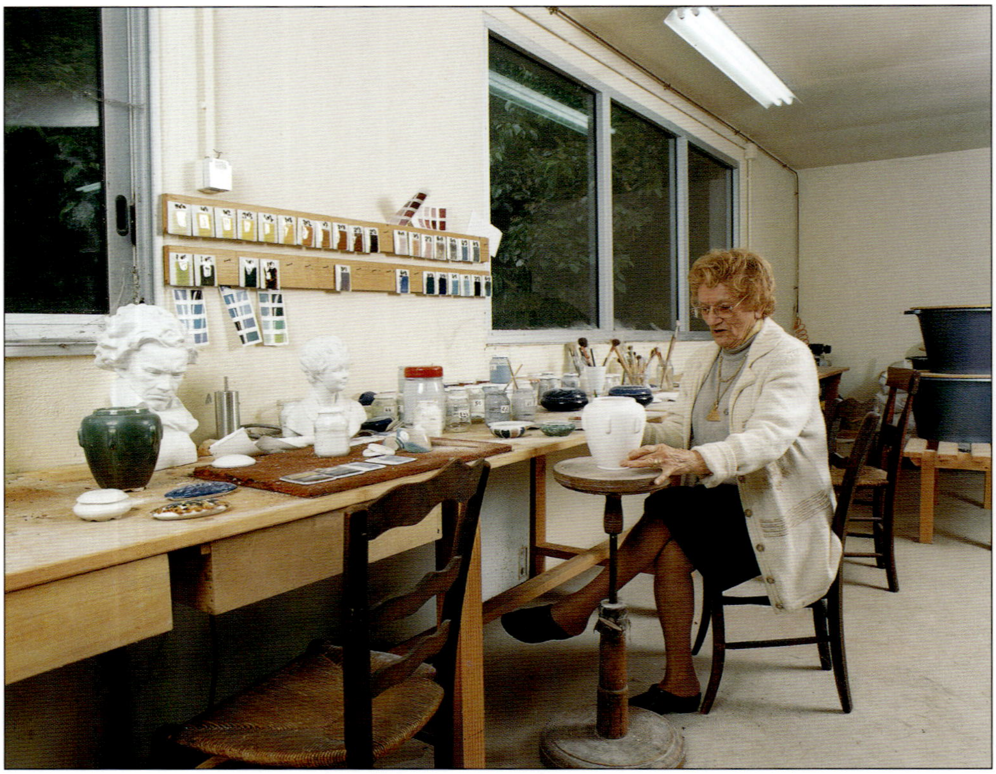

Odette Goumot-Labesse in their home workshop.

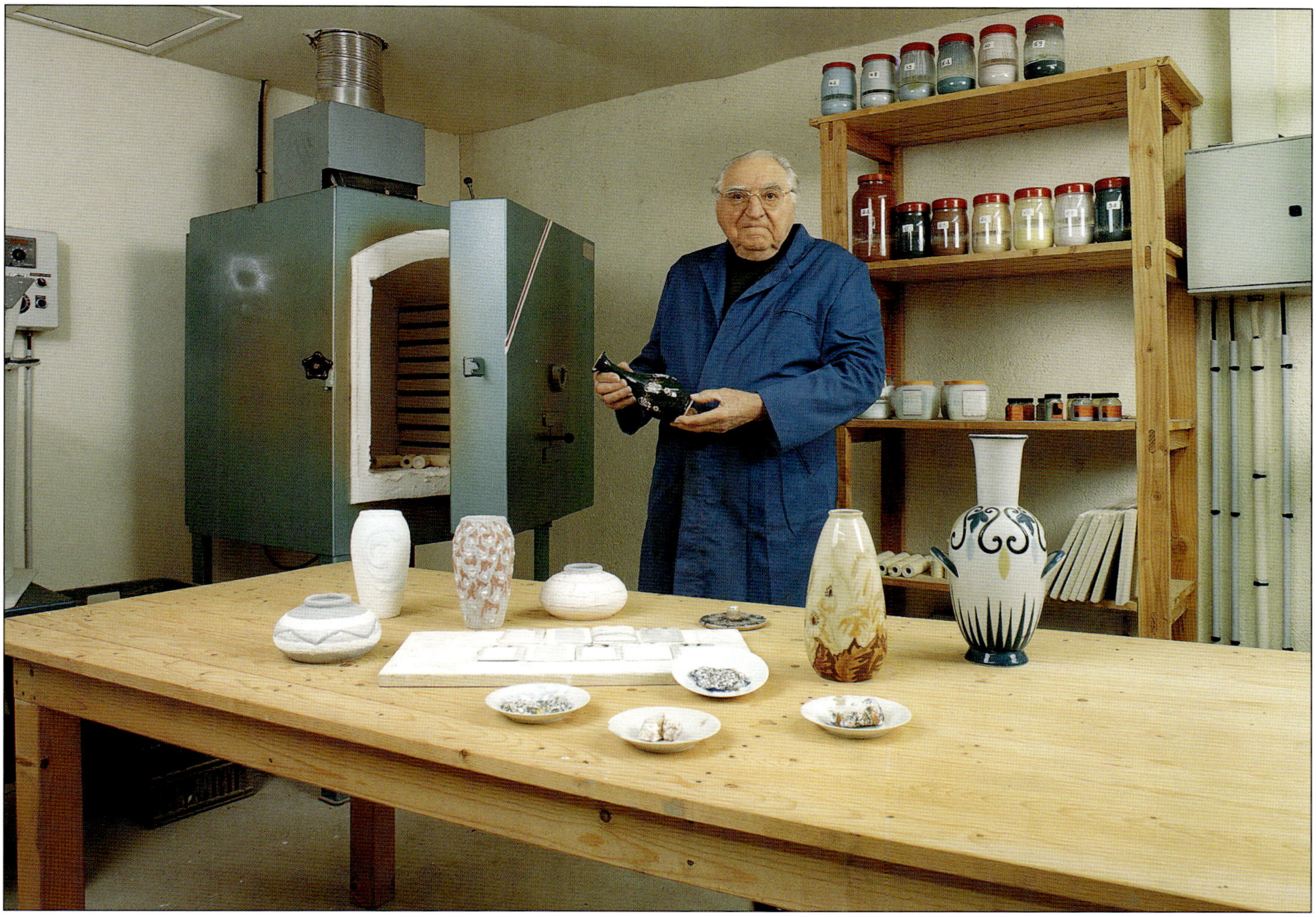

Albert Goumot-Labesse in their home workshop.

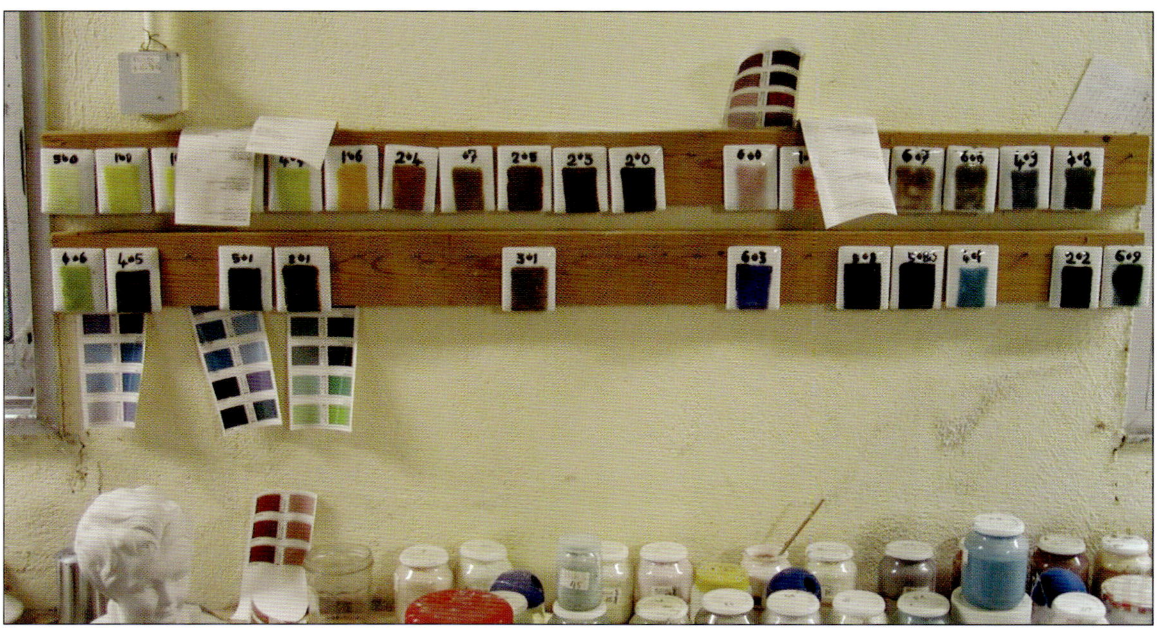

Albert Goumot-Labesse's recreations of Tharaud's colors.

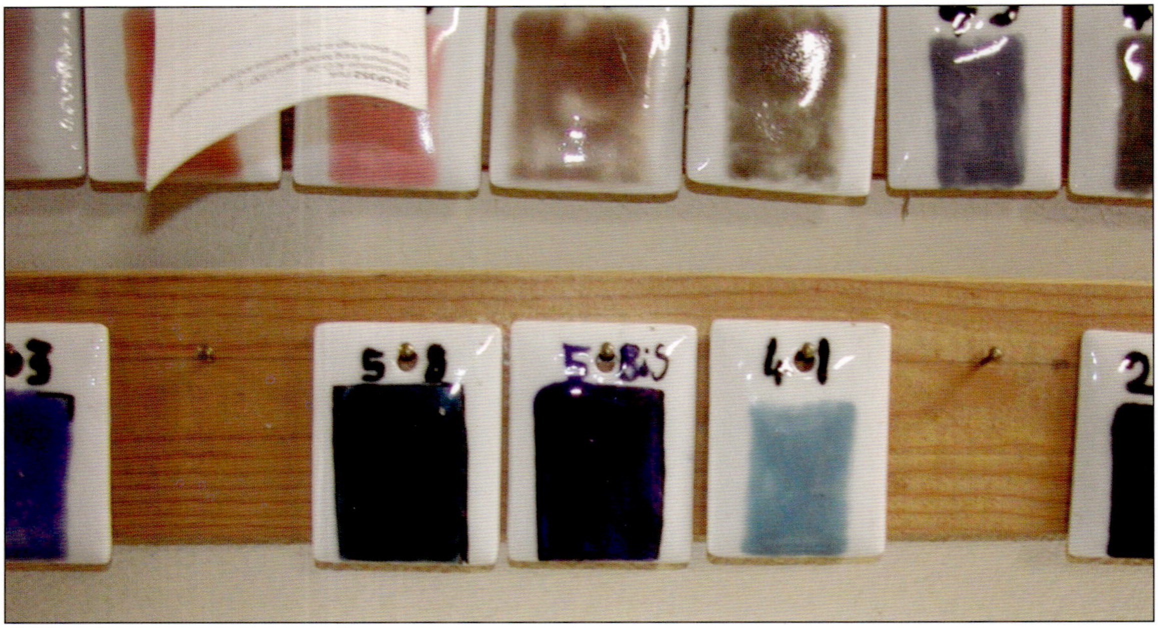

Close up of color tiles.

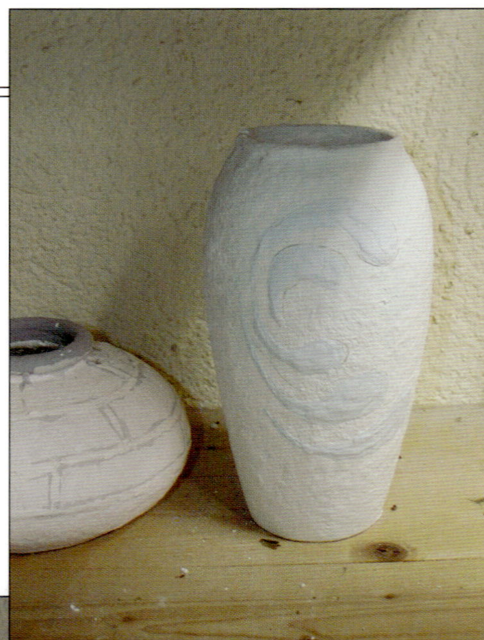

Unfired enamel decorations in the manner of Tharaud. Because Albert Goumot-Labesse used gas instead of wood to fire the kiln, the firing temperature was 1300° Celsius instead of 1410° used by Tharaud.

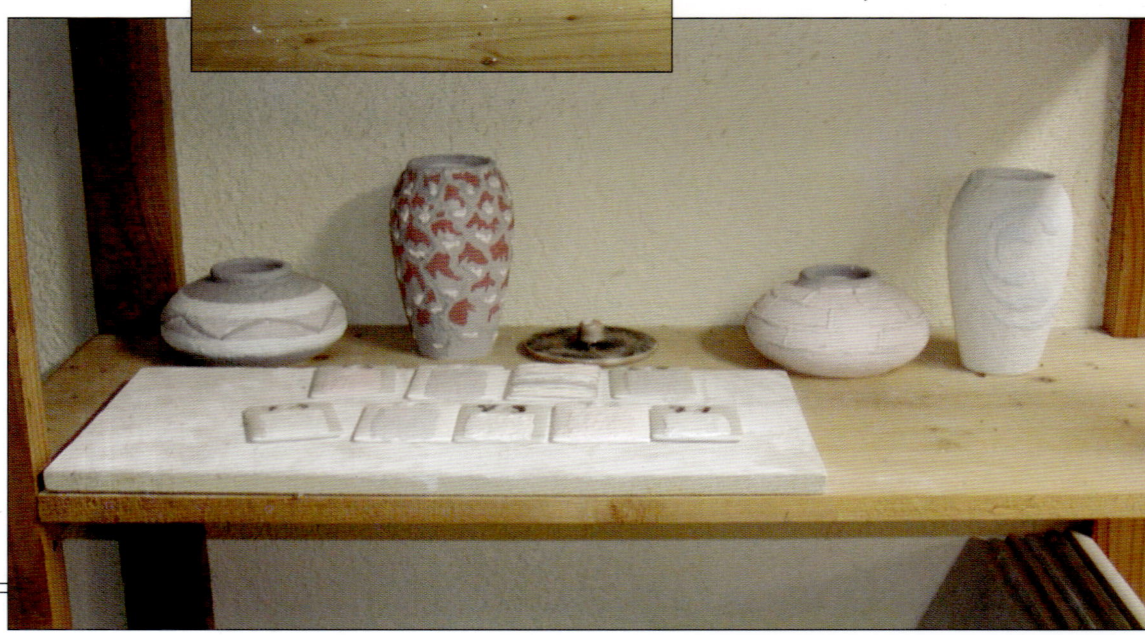

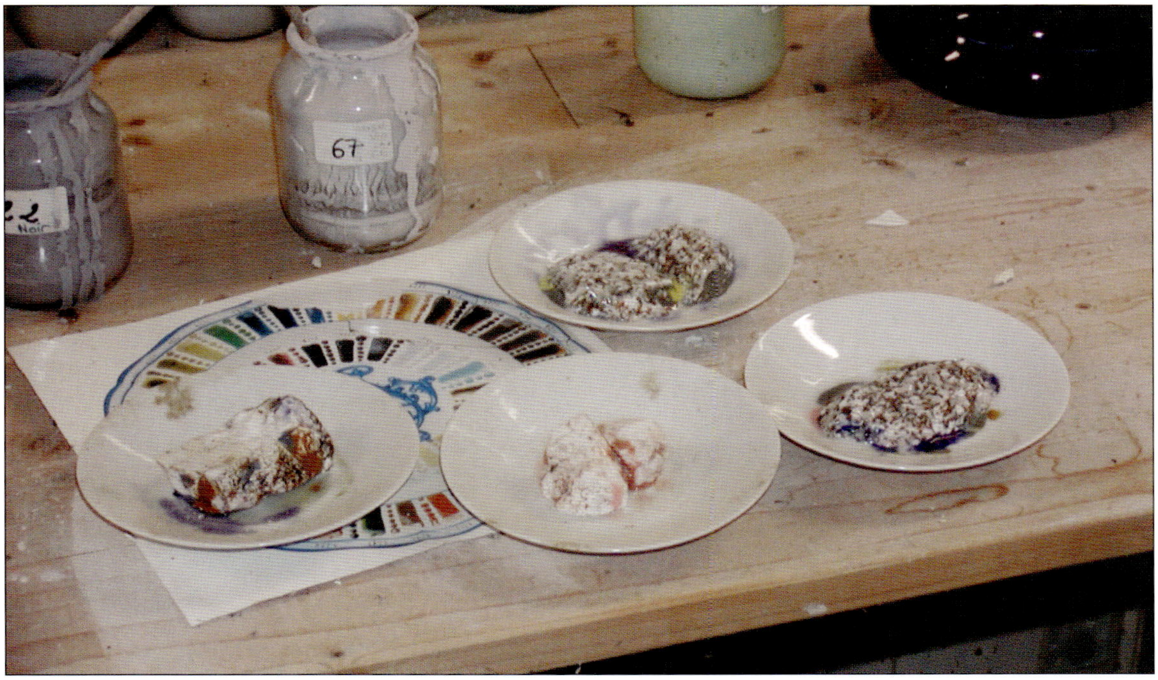

Dishes with granite, mica feldspar, and quartz.

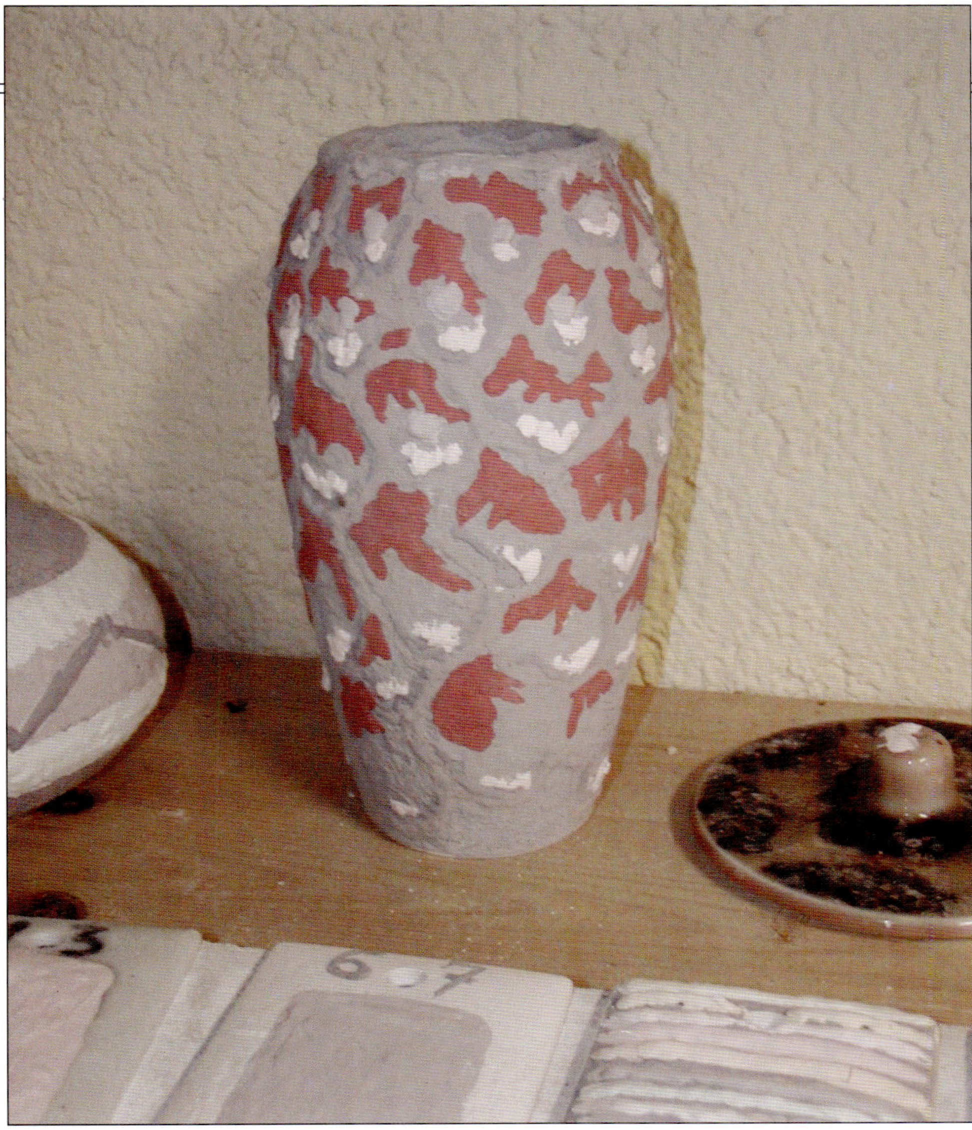

Values

The values in this book reflect a mature collectors market in France in particular and in Europe generally for Camille Tharaud porcelain, while they also reflect the significantly growing popularity of Tharaud pieces sold on eBay. In fact, many of the art dealers and auctions in France are now reporting that a large number of Tharaud pieces are being purchased by Americans. Even though the U.S. was for several years the major export market for Tharaud's work, the majority of the pieces imported into the U.S. were mass-produced and reflect the American taste for cobalt blue and decorations with flowers. Few of the unique and rare pieces were exported to the U.S.

What is missing in the American collectors market for Tharaud is an understanding of the mechanics of the decorating and firing processes for porcelain, which are central to Mr. Tharaud's genius. Many of Tharaud's pieces were unique because of his combination of the layering of many enamels and a single high firing process for the decoration—a combining of the technical and artistic processes. Americans have not had a cultural history of porcelain decoration like many of the European countries, so therefore lack an understanding of the difficulties of Tharaud's techniques. There is a shift occurring, however, as a result of articles published in American antique newspapers and the influence of eBay.

Tharaud pieces are also sought by Art Deco collectors. Tharaud was one of the most prominent Art Deco ceramists in Europe, and his work was heavily influenced by many of the notable Art Deco artists in France, many of his pieces actually being collaborations between himself and these other artists.

We expect that the increased awareness of Tharaud in the U.S. will have a significant impact on the values of his work worldwide.

The values of the other Art Deco pieces in this book reflect a mature collectors market. Like Tharaud, pieces sold by the retailer Robj during the 1920s are also very popular in the US.

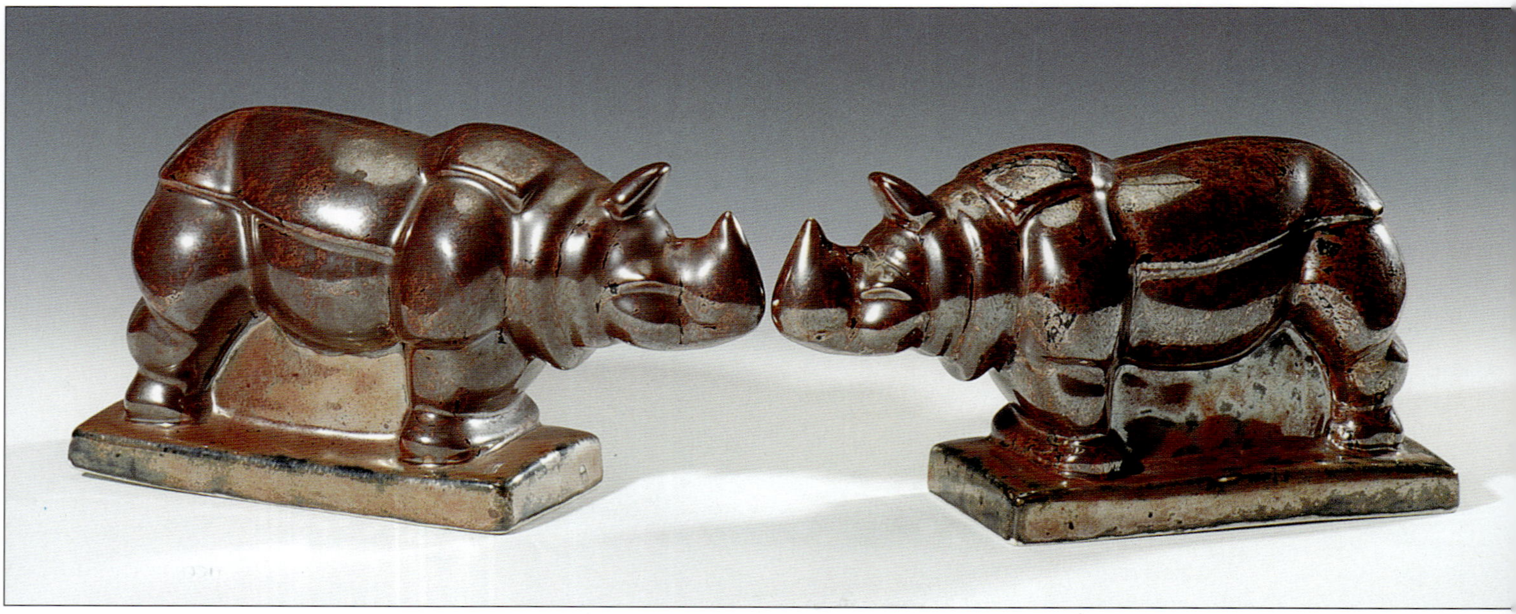

Introduction to Camille Tharaud and Art Deco Ceramics

This book is divided into two main sections: the works of Camille Tharaud and the Art Deco works of other companies, primarily those in Limoges, France. While Tharaud's works are not confined to Art Deco patterns and designs, many of his pieces are outstanding examples of this style. The works of the other Limoges companies, in the second section of this book, are limited to the Art Deco style. Nearly all of the ceramists in France were influenced by what later was called the Art Deco style. Perhaps the most pronounced Art Deco styles and designs are reflected in the pieces sold by Robj, a retailer in Paris, from 1921-1931. Since Robj did not manufacture its own ceramics, they bought their porcelain from other companies, many from the companies in Limoges. Because Robj is so synonymous with Art Deco, we have included many ceramic pieces sold by this retailer.

Secondly, Haviland & Co. made many pieces that reflect the influence of the Art Deco style. As a result, we have included several photographs of works designed by Suzanne Lalique and Édouard Sandoz for Haviland, which are true representations of this style. Finally, we were able to photograph many pieces from Gérard, Dufraisseix, Abbot (GDA), and A. Lanternier, which are part of Royal Limoges. What is particularly interesting is the large number of photographs of patterns used by GDA during this period, and which are now included in one of the company's old pattern books. While it would probably be impossible to find actual porcelain examples of all of these patterns, we were able instead to photograph the Art Deco style patterns which were used by the company and the names the company gave to these patterns.

We have finally included other miscellaneous examples of the Art Deco style from some of the other Limoges companies. Taken as a whole, the breadth of the Art Deco style in France is fully presented in the photographs in both sections of this book.

The Art Deco Period

Art Deco is a modern, twentieth century style that started around 1910, gained momentum during World War I, reached its peak and started its decline in 1925, and lasted through the 1930s. It was a period of dramatic technological change and political and economic crises. The Art Deco style was revealed and exalted at the 1925 Exposition internationale des arts décoratifs industriels et modernes in Paris. (The term, Art Deco, gained currency in the 1960s.) This style was rapidly adapted to all forms of artistic expression in clothing, jewelry, furniture, silverware, ceramics, appliances, buildings, and fine arts.

The movement drew on a range of ancient and exotic sources, including among others, African, Egyptian, Chinese, Japanese, Pre-Columbian, and Middle Eastern cultures. These influences, originating in nineteenth century colonialism, were incorporated into mass culture and were suggestive of an exciting and sensual future. Exotic materials such as tropical woods, ebony, sharkskin, and lacquers were often used. The designers also embraced naturalism and abstraction, and the effects of light and transparency with bright colors and muted grays and browns. Primary colors and stark contrasts replaced pastels. Broken and interrupted contours were common designs. Participating in this movement were French designers such at Lalique, Christofle, and Baccarat; and two famous schools in Paris, École Boulle and École Estienne, were the first to promote these ideas to their students.

Naturally, this same movement was evident in the ceramics, sculpture, enamels, and stained glass in Limoges and the rest of France. There was a preoccupation with glazes, which were richly colored, crackled, and "jewel like." The Art Deco preoccupation with naturalism, the effects of light and transparency with bright colors, the emphasis on glazes, and the African, Egyptian, Mexican, Eastern, and Middle Eastern influences are all brought together in many of the works of Camille Tharaud. The French were the leaders in Art Deco ceramics.

Camille Tharaud collaborated with many of the French leaders in the Art Deco movement—Camille Fauré, René Barlaud, Henry Rapin, Marcel Goupy, Jules Sarlandie, Léon Jouhaud, and Georges Papault. Many of Tharaud's collaborators were men who worked in enamels, influences that show up in his preoccupation with his own enamels for his porcelain. Evidences of the Art Deco style in Limoges include shapes and designs by Édouard Sandoz, Jean Dufy, and Susan Lalique for Théodore Haviland. Tharaud went a step further than both Sandoz and Dufy and incorporated a higher degree of abstractionism in many of his designs. Also, unlike many of the major porcelain manufacturers in Limoges, Tharaud never decorated with transfers.

Speaking about the use of transfers near the end of his life, Tharaud said, "A cabinet maker makes a magnificent piece of mahogany furniture, and after having carefully waxed it, covers it in a thick coat of house paint. Everyone would agree that this craftsman was crazy. But the same thing happens in the making of porcelain. Porcelain is a beautiful matter in itself. It is criminal to cover it with little drawings that have nothing to do with it." (Ferrer, translated from the original French.) In other words, the qualities of the porcelain and the qualities of the decoration needed to be complementary and each should enhance the other. Aesthetically and organically, they must fit together.

The Works of Camille Tharaud (1878-1956)

Tharaud's Early Years

During his tour of duty in World War I, Camille Tharaud came into contact with Chinese porcelain, which was to have a major influence on him throughout his career. With a background in chemistry, and before his entry into the manufacture and decorating of porcelain, Tharaud opened shops in optics and photography in Limoges. Tharaud was to later draw on this background in experimenting with the composition of his enamels and pigments.

In 1919, Camille Tharaud took over the old Limoges factory of Louis Tharaud. After starting his factory in 1920, Tharaud was generally considered an "upstart" among artists and decorators, while at the same time collaborating with a number of artists in Limoges and Paris. Yvanhoé Rambosson wrote in 1930 that Tharaud's experiments with porcelain from 1920-1923 nearly resulted in disaster, but Tharaud's memory of Bernard Palissy, an innovative sixteenth century ceramist who discovered the composition of enamels, kept him going. Tharaud had invested all of his inheritance and more in his factory, and he was frequently greeted by skeptics.

Tharaud's first major introduction into the art world in France came in 1924 when Jules Sarlandie, the most well known enameller of the period, introduced Tharaud to Georges Rouard who owned a famous gallery in Paris. At this time, Rouard was head of the ceramics section for the Exposition internationale des arts décoratifs industriels et modernes, which would open in April 1925 in Paris (later known as the Art Deco Exposition). Through Rouard, Tharaud then met Marcel Goupy, who was Rouard's artist and decorator for his ceramics factory. Goupy provided Tharaud with several watercolors, which were the basis of the decoration of several pieces for Tharaud's exhibit at the Exhibition. Later, Goupy designed several lidded jars for Tharaud.

It was at the Exposition of 1925 that Tharaud's work was first formally presented to the public. Because of his interest in Tharaud, Rouard gave Tharaud a place of honor at the Exposition, alongside other well-known Limoges ceramists. Tharaud's works earned for him a diploma of honor. Of more lasting importance, however, was his introduction to Henri Rapin who was already a renowned and respected artist. Rapin was in a position to help and influence Tharaud, since he was the inspector of artistic works for the Manufacture de Sèvres. Rapin was "surprised" at the works of Tharaud, which he saw at the Exhibition, and Rapin shared his opinions as an artist with Tharaud. The result was a fruitful artistic collaboration that lasted a lifetime. Not only did the two artists collaborate on many decorations over the years, but Rapin also designed about twenty different shapes for vases and lidded jars for Tharaud's studio. These shapes were named after flowers and operas. According to the Goumot-Labesses, Rapin would visit Tharaud in Limoges on weekends and on his vacations to make designs and paint in Tharaud's studio.

Other artists who came to collaborate with Tharaud after the 1925 Exhibition included Léon Jouhaud, an enameller and artistic advisor to Gérard, Dufraisseix & Abbot; Georges Papault, a sculptor at École Nationale des Arts Décoratifs; Lucien Crèlerot, his brother-in-law; Le Jan, the animal sculptor; and Juliette Geoffroy, painter and decorator, who created new designs and who helped him master high temperature firing. In 1930, an in depth article about Tharaud's work by Yvanhoé Rambosson was published in a special edition of *Mobilier et Décoration*, and Tharaud's place as an artist was finally established.

The Three Periods of Tharaud's Work

Ferrer has divided Tharaud's work into three different periods: first period, 1920-1927; second period, 1927-1937; and third period, 1937-1956. The information on these three periods is based on the work by Ferrer, as well as from information provided by the Goumot-Labesses.

Ferrer divides the works in the first period, 1920-1927, into two subgroups, 1920-1924 and 1924-1927. During the years 1920-1924, the studio's decoration was relatively simple. The decoration was mostly *sous email* (under the enamel), with a limited palette, with different colors, sometimes two or three, juxtaposed to each other, but never with mixed enamel oxides. Some of the decorations appear quite crude when compared with Tharaud's later works. In addition, most of the pieces were small objects—bonbonnières, knife rests, salt and egg sets, and ashtrays—which were reproduced in large numbers. Although some collectors value these early pieces, because they represent Tharaud's early works, they do not reach the levels of artistic achievement of his later works nor do the shapes of these pieces have the grandeur of the shapes later developed by Tharaud, Henri Rapin, Marcel Goupy, and others.

The 1925 Exposition was a major turning point in terms of the studio's decorations and the shapes of it pieces. Both Marcel Goupy and Henri Rapin collaborated with Tharaud and both contributed elaborate decorations as well as many new shapes. The famous lidded jar, *Manon,* designed by Rapin (see photograph on page 54) was introduced at the 1927 Salon des artistes décorateurs, Paris. In addition,

Georges Papault, Lucien Crèlerot, and Juliette Geoffroy also started their collaborations with Tharaud at this time.

The second period, 1927-1937, is characterized by much more elaborate decorations with the use of new oxides (which expanded the color palette) and the layering of enamels to achieve different effects. Additional shapes were also created by Rapin and Maurice Dufrène; and the series of animal sculptures were also introduced, the series based on shapes created by François Thomas Cartier, Francine Cartier, Robert Lemoine, and Le Jan. The worldwide economic crises of the early 1930s interrupted much of the work at the studio, as it did with other businesses; but, there was a new creative energy which emerged for the 1937 Exhibition internationale des arts et techniques with the collaboration of Tharaud, Rapin, and Tharaud's daughter, Odette Tharaud [Goumot-Labesse]. New influences became prominent, including Orientalism, Africanism, and abstractionism.

Ferrer notes that the decorations during this period were characterized by three major preoccupations:

> 1) the continuation of the tradition of pastoral landscapes. The works of Léon Jouhaud and René Barlaud were prominent and decorations by these two artists were not mass-produced and were often unique. Tharaud also collaborated with Auguste Riffaterre during this period.
>
> 2) the continuation of floral decorations. Juliette Geoffroy contributed two different variations to the traditional floral decorations. The first variation was decoration where the colored enamel became the design or pattern with an "orderly abstraction." The second variation was a strictly geometrical design, which was typically Art Deco. At this time, the first important pattern used as a series was developed, the "butterfly wings" pattern (see photograph on page 53). Other series, although mass-produced, were also started in this period. These include, among others, the wisteria, fern, and pinecone designs (see photographs on pages 92, 124, & 127). Although made in large numbers, each piece was hand painted and has its own individuality. These are the only series that were continued after World War II, and they were especially popular in the US.
>
> 3) the last preoccupation in decoration during this second period was, according to Ferrer, the most important. It was during this period that Tharaud was able to reduce to a minimum the unintended effects of his enamels. His mastery of his techniques allowed him to apply different mixtures and layering of different enamels that resulted in works of art. Tharaud referred to these results as *effets de matière*. (See covered vase on page 48.) These were exquisite pieces that were exhibited and acquired by museums and collectors.

Also during this period, Tharaud expanded the production of novelty pieces, such as bookends and small lamps, in mainly Art Deco themes, and introduced Berger lamps (see photograph on page 44). More importantly, the studio produced animal models made by François Thomas Cartier and Robert Lemoine. Ferrer comments that Cartier's shapes were often classical but also modern, while those of Lemoine were more geometrical and more modern than Cartier's. Most of these animal models were decorated *sous émail* in gray. Lastly, Tharaud introduced his successful tea and coffee services and his "architectural" ceramic works (see listing on page 143) described elsewhere.

The third period of Tharaud's work, 1937-1956, as described by Ferrer, had two important characteristics. Because of the shortage of precious metals during the war, the factory produced thousands of cameos to be worn as jewelry (see photographs on pages 112 & 137). These were designed by Lucien Crèlerot, the only artist to work with Tharaud during the war years. Secondly, during his last twenty years, Tharaud strove to perfect his work. There were six new shapes for vases and additional oxides were used to expand the number of colors. Also, beginning in 1954, two years before Tharaud's death, Tharaud began producing matt porcelain. Colored paste was superimposed over a white paste and was called double "coulee." The decorations were inspired by neoclassical designs.

According to the Goumot-Labesses, the war years were difficult for the studio. It was difficult to obtain wood to fire the kiln, it was hard to obtain pigments, and the Germans controlled the mines where Tharaud obtained many of his stones. The large kiln was only fired once a month with an average of 200 pieces. Most of the pieces produced by the factory during these years were giftware items for the French market. The Goumot-Labesses commented that Limoges one night escaped bombing by the Germans because of the large flames from Tharaud's kilns, which the Germans mistook to mean that the city had been bombed earlier.

Also in this last period, the naturalist decorations of wisteria and leaves were continued and there were many decorations, for example, of geometrical friezes, herringbones or chevrons, and other repeating patterns. At the age of seventy-six, Tharaud made his last designs on biscuit porcelain, which resembled the works of the Wedgwood factory in England.

When Tharaud died on September 8, 1956, his wife, Berthe Tharaud, continued the factory with the help of Albert and Odette Goumot-Labesse. Gemaine Dufour, manager and decorator, was the last individual to make major design contributions to the studio. The factory closed in 1968 when the city of Limoges purchased it and converted the land into a public swimming pool.

Tharaud's Art and Technique

Background on Making and Decorating Porcelain

The art of Camille Tharaud is rooted in his technical innovations in the composition and application of enamels and his firing process. To better understand Tharaud's contributions to the decoration of porcelain, it is first necessary to understand the basic and traditional techniques for making and decorating porcelain.

Following are the traditional steps for making porcelain:

The thick liquid porcelain mix, pastry, is created from a mixture of kaolin, feldspar, and quartz. This pastry, called greenware or barbotine, is poured into the mold. (Kaolin is the main ingredient, the feldspar is the enamel that gives porcelain its translucence and helps it vitrify, and the quartz is the hardening agent that also reduces the shrinkage when it is fired.)

The porcelain pastry is fired in the kiln at about 900° Celsius to dry. At this point it is call *dégourdi*.

The *dégourdi* is then placed in "dipping enamel" (also made from kaolin, feldspar, and quart). The dried porcelain absorbs the dipping enamel and comes out dry.

The piece is then fired at 1400° Celsius to become the hard paste porcelain that is familiar to us. The porcelain is fired for approximately twelve hours and then cools another twelve hours before the porcelain is removed from the kiln. During this firing, the porcelain shrinks thirteen to fifteen percent. The result is the common hard shiny white blanks that are used for decoration.

Dégourdi, which has not been placed in dipping enamel and is then fired at 1400° comes out as *bisque*. This porcelain has a dull finish and is not shiny.

Petit feu de four (low temperature firing)

Petit feu de four is the traditional method for decorating porcelain. The paint (pigments) or the transfers are applied after the 1400° firing noted above, which produces the familiar traditional undecorated white blanks. At Atelier Le Tallec in Paris, for example, there are three firings during the decorating process—the first firing, at about 800°-900°, is for "high fire" colors such as blue and purple; the second firing, about 600°-700°, is for "middle fire" colors such as reds and yellows; and the last firing at still lower temperatures is for the gold. This decorating technique is called *sur émail* (above the enamel). Each firing lasts seven hours and twenty minutes. These lower firing temperatures are referred to as *petit feu de four* (small fire). With this technique, there is a wide range of possible colors, but the heat is not hot enough to soften the porcelain, so the colors do not penetrate past the surface of the porcelain but stay on the enamel. Consequently, the colors are less transparent and scratch more easily than in the following *grand feu* method.

Grand feu de four (high temperature firing)

There are two types of *grand feu de four*. The first is the application of pigments directly onto the *dégourdi* itself or after the *dégourdi* has been placed in the dipping enamel. Once the pigments are applied, the piece is then fired at a low temperature. Once it has cooled, the piece is then placed in dipping enamel and fired at 1400° (*grand feu*). This decorating technique is call *sous émail* (under the enamel). This technique is commonly used by the Copenhagen manufacturers. The problem with this technique is that it produces pale colors because the pigments do not receive the required oxidation during the firing process, and it is difficult to reproduce identical colors. The colors, however, are permanent—they do not wear—because they are fired under the enamel, which is vitrified with the porcelain, at 1400°.

The second type of *grand feu*, which is more rare, is the technique primarily used by Tharaud. The *dégourdi* is placed in dipping enamel, and then the piece is decorated with enamels that contain different oxides, which produce different colors. The entire piece is then fired at 1400° degrees—there are no separate firings according to the colors of the enamels. All the effects of an object—color tone, depth, and translucency—occur during this one firing. This decorating technique is also called *dans l'émail* (into the glaze or enamel). Since the color is part of the enamel, the enamel with the oxides is vitrified with the porcelain; and the decoration and the porcelain become "one." The main disadvantage of this technique, as with the other type of *grand feu*, is that the color palette is poor.

Tharaud spent most of his professional career perfecting this second type of *grand feu*.

Tharaud's Colors

Tharaud experimented endlessly with the composition of the enamels and the different oxides to produce various colors. Tharaud expanded on the work of Antoine Edouard Peyrusson, who in 1891 presented his decorating technique at a public conference in Limoges. The difference between Tharaud and Peyrusson, however, was that Peyrusson decorated on porcelain that had already been fired at 1400° while Tharaud decorated on unfired porcelain. Not much attention was given to Peyrusson's methods between the time of his presentation in 1891 and the time of his death in 1909, so many of his techniques were lost. Nevertheless, Tharaud essentially began where Peyrusson ended. Tharaud significantly expanded the color palette of high-fired colors and solved many of the problems of the simultaneously firing of the porcelain and the enamels.

Like the other porcelain decorators in Limoges, Tharaud purchased colored oxides for his enamels from commercial suppliers. But he didn't stop there. Tharaud was a frequent visitor to the quarries around Limoges. He would bring stones from the surrounding quarries back to the studio and crush them to be used as oxides to color the enamels. As a scientist, he experimented with the different types of stones, discarded those which were not suitable, and labeled and classified those he kept for mixing with the enamels. He eventually had over thirty-five colors in his palette. Beginning in 1930, for example, Tharaud began using the oxides from the lava rocks of Auvergne, which produced a bright brown metallic. (Goumot-Labesse)

Although Tharaud initially had a limited color palette, in 1925 the palette included the following colors (from Ferrer):

- A range of pinks prepared from aluminum oxide.
- Magnificent cobalt blues. The blue when mixed with chrome gave a range of blues and greens. Unlike other decorators, the oxides were mixed with a thick coat of enamel, which resulted in a unique transparency and deepness. The "thickness" gave the shade. Tharaud commented that red wine appears to be deeper when in a thick bottle; he applied this same principle to his *bleu de four.*
- A range of grays resulting from the mixture of nickel and cobalt. Only platinum salts were used after 1930, and it was applied *sous émail.* According to Albert Goumot-Labesse, the platinum was applied on bisque, the piece was placed in the dipping enamel, and then fired at 1410°.
- The blacks contain a mixture of iron and cobalt and are very strong and deep.
- Browns, which Tharaud especially liked, were already important before 1930. They always have a magnesium base. After 1930, the lava from Auvergne also appears in the oxides. The result is a bright metallic and vibrant brown.

Just before World War II, Tharaud mixed new oxides, which expanded his palette of colors:

- Uranium created a magnificent black. When jasper and uranium were combined, the result was a wonderful red. Albert Goumot-Labesse told us that when the studio discovered the dangers of uranium, they quit using it.
- Wolfram taken from Puy des Vignes gave a metallic effect.
- Beryl, when mixed with wolfram, produced emerald green. It was used to decorate the friezes of the metallic pieces.

Tharaud was never interested in color for its own sake. Rather, he sought to achieve certain results by layering different enamels with different oxides that would produce unusual colors and other results, such as marbling, mosaics, spots, specks, iridescence, and metallic effects. He also tried to achieve true transparent tints, which were as fluid as watercolors. Trying for a variety of color hues, the coat of raw enamel would often be 1.5 cm thick. (Ferrer)

Since there are few existing records documenting Tharaud's use of various oxides, it is not possible to know all of the various oxides that he used and the different combinations. Oxides which would work well during a test firing would fail on subsequent firings. Equally important as the oxides was the firing process itself; something which Tharaud worked to master throughout his life.

The Role of the *Grand Feu*

Because the management of the firing process was key to Tharaud's colors and the solution to many of the other problems Tharaud encountered, he was obsessed with the firing process. As a result, his detractors early on referred to him as the "fakir with the flames." (Mannoni) He utilized two kilns—a ten cubic meter kiln used for his *sous émail* decorations and a twenty-four cubic meter kiln for his *dans l'émail* decorations. Not any wood could be used for the fire—only beech or oak which was twenty-five to thirty years old. Much of the wood was transported on the Vienne River to the factory.

The firing process had several stages. During the first stage, the kiln reached 1050° Celsius over fourteen hours to burn the impurities in the porcelain paste. Next was the stage of oxygen reduction as the temperature in the kiln reaches 1280°. Once this temperature was reached, Tharaud began his own technique of starting a very slow oxygenation process rather than continuing the reduction for another five or six hours. Tharaud himself placed the last logs and spaced them out to let more oxygen circulate. The production of the color was done at the end of the firing when the oxides came into contact with the gas oxidants. The period of maximum oxidation produced the maximum brightness of the color. (Ferrer) According to Albert Goumot-Labesse, the key to the "brightness" of Tharaud's colors, the "Tharaud trademark," was the last 10° of the 1410° firing.

During the highly productive years, Mr. Goumot-Labesses stated that there was one firing every month of about 600 pieces and that each firing lasted twenty-four hours.

According to Mannoni and others, the effects and brilliance of Tharaud's colors were due not just to the oxides and the layering of the different enamels but just as importantly to his manipulation of the firing at high temperatures.

The Problems and the Challenges

Tharaud was ridiculed by many of his contemporaries for his obsession with solving the problems associated with the *grand feu*. These problems were numerous, and he had to repeatedly address them throughout his career. These problems included cracking and crazing; limited colors, coupled with translucency and tints; dripping and running of the enamels; and fusibility, dilation, and contraction of the enamels and the porcelain in the firing process. For example, different oxides would often alter the characteristics of the enamels, so that the elasticity of the enamels would occur at different rates and the layers would separate or crack during firing. Tharaud was always searching for versatile enamel that would serve as the base for all colors.

The special effects which Tharaud often sought—marbling, mosaics, spots, specks, iridescence, mottling, and metallic—usually were the result of the layering of two or three enamels that fused differently, with the less fusible ones floating on those that were more fusible, like oil on vinegar. Often there were drippings, crystallizations, and metallic effects that produced wonderful results. (Ferrer) Sometimes the outcomes were unexpected and brilliant. When these extraordinary results were due to a combination of factors—the composition of the enamels, the layering of the enamels, the oxides and/or the firing, Tharaud referred to these results as *effets de matière*. It is unfortunate that Tharaud's notes about his oxides and enamels were destroyed by his wife, at his direction, after his death.

Although Tharaud was more interested in producing unique pieces for connoisseurs and museums, he also worked to develop techniques which would produce replicable results. We can see these in his series of pieces decorated with wisteria, pinecones, and leaves, among others, and in his last works decorating on bisque porcelain. The genius of Tharaud, however, was his vast experimentation with oxides, enamels, and firing, which are unique to the decoration of porcelain. Tharaud combined the techniques of the superb, always experimenting, craftsman with those of the artist—they are inseparable in his work. This is the genius of Camille Tharaud.

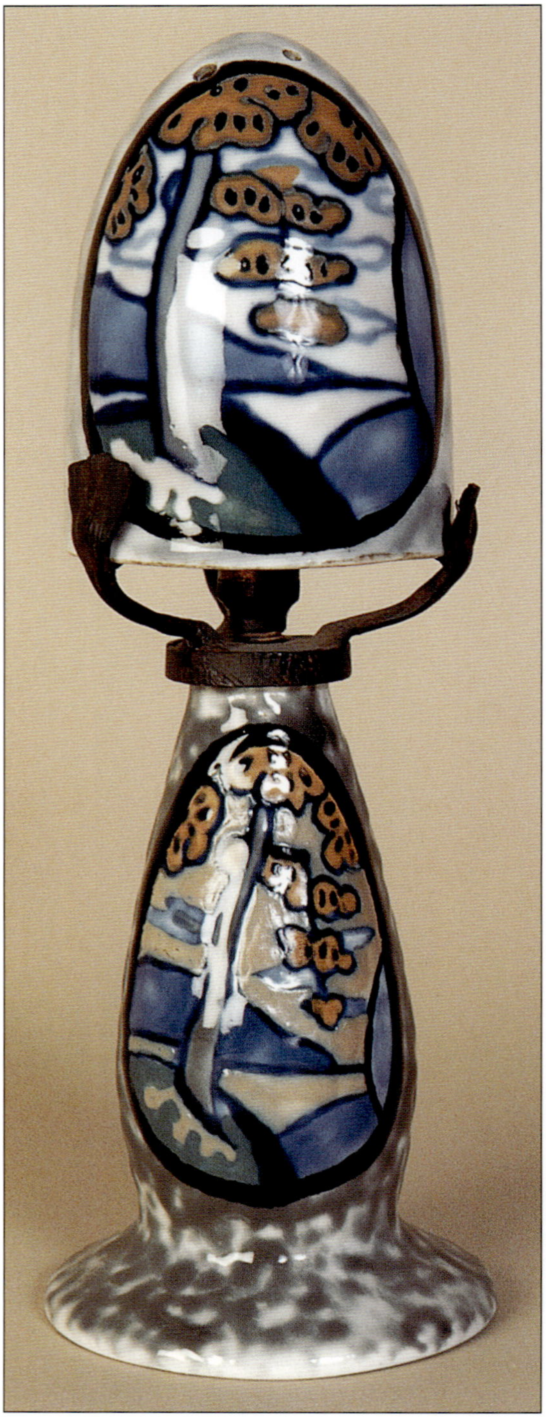

Photographs of the Works of Camille Tharaud

The photographs are organized by time period, and we used a number of factors to help us date the pieces. These factors included the decorating marks, the dates when specific painters were employed by the studio, information from our interviews with the Goumot-Labesses, the book by Ferrer, and the dates of the expositions where we know that Tharaud showed specific pieces of his work. For some pieces, we are able to provide the year they were made, although the decorating mark provides a broader range of dates. There are also a few pieces which we are unable to date.

When possible, we have identified the name of the shape (which is shown in italics after the identification of the object), the date when it was decorated, the name of the painter and/or the name of the person who designed the pattern, and sometimes additional historical or decorating information. There are times when we can identify only the first or last name of the painter.

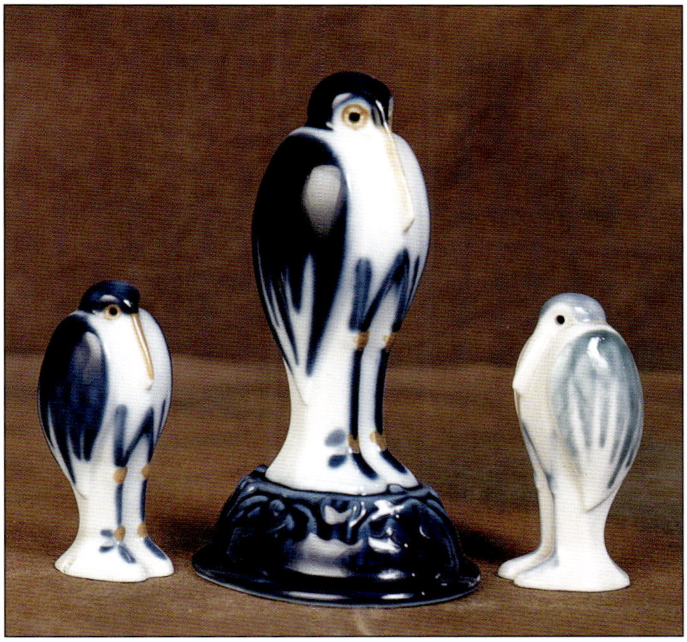

Stork nightlight and salt shakers, 5.25" high and 3.5" high respectively; nightlight, 1925-1927, and salt shakers, 1920-1924. Each less than $500.

1920-1924

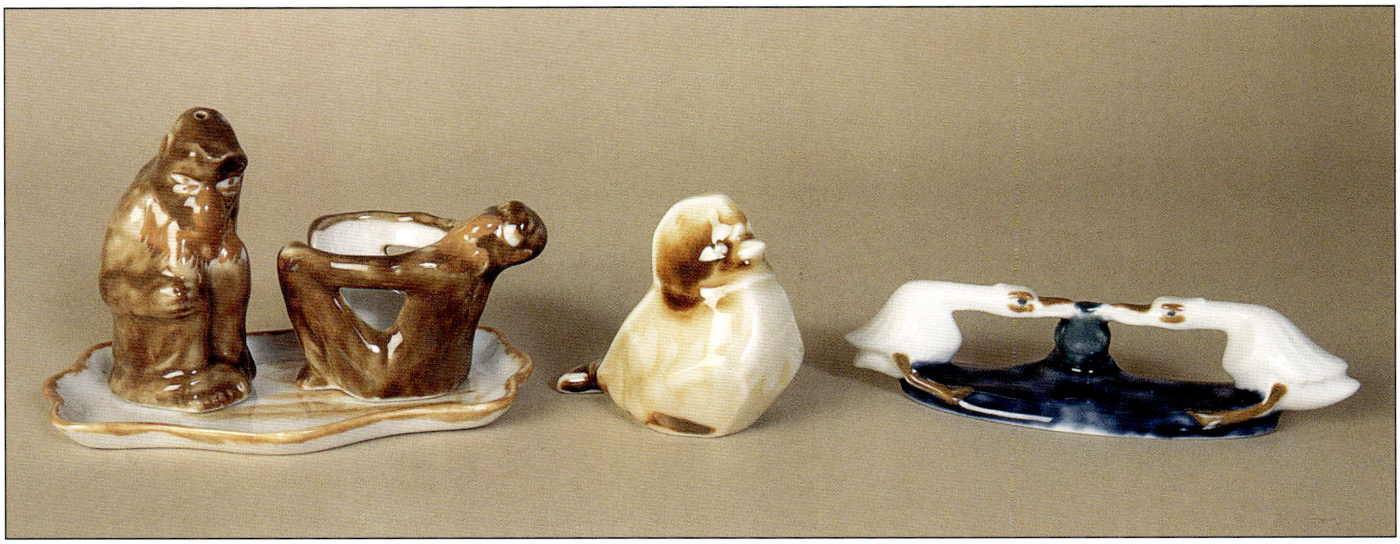

Monkey egg cup, salt, and tray, 1920-1924; bird salt shaker, 1920-1924, second from right; and knife rest, right, 5.5" wide x 1.4" high, 1928-1930 (first made 1920-1924). Each less than $500.

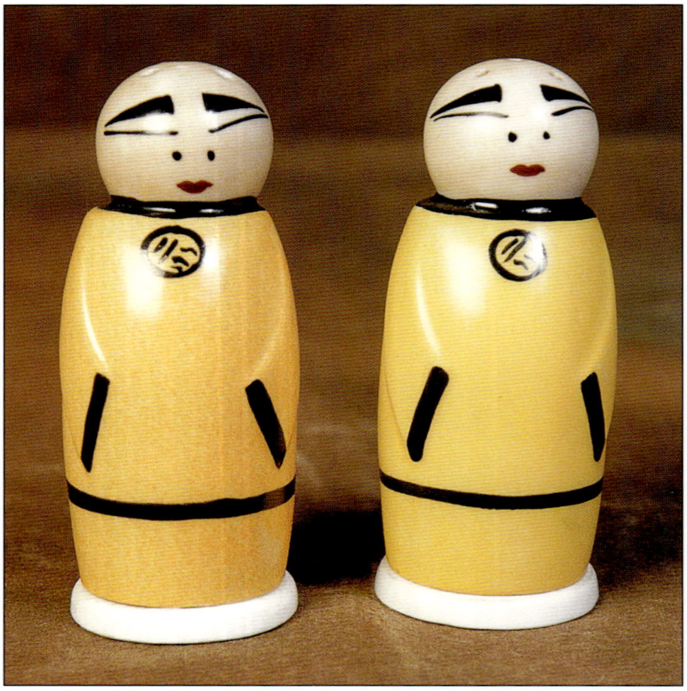

Salt and pepper shakers, 4" high, 1920-1924. Less than $500.

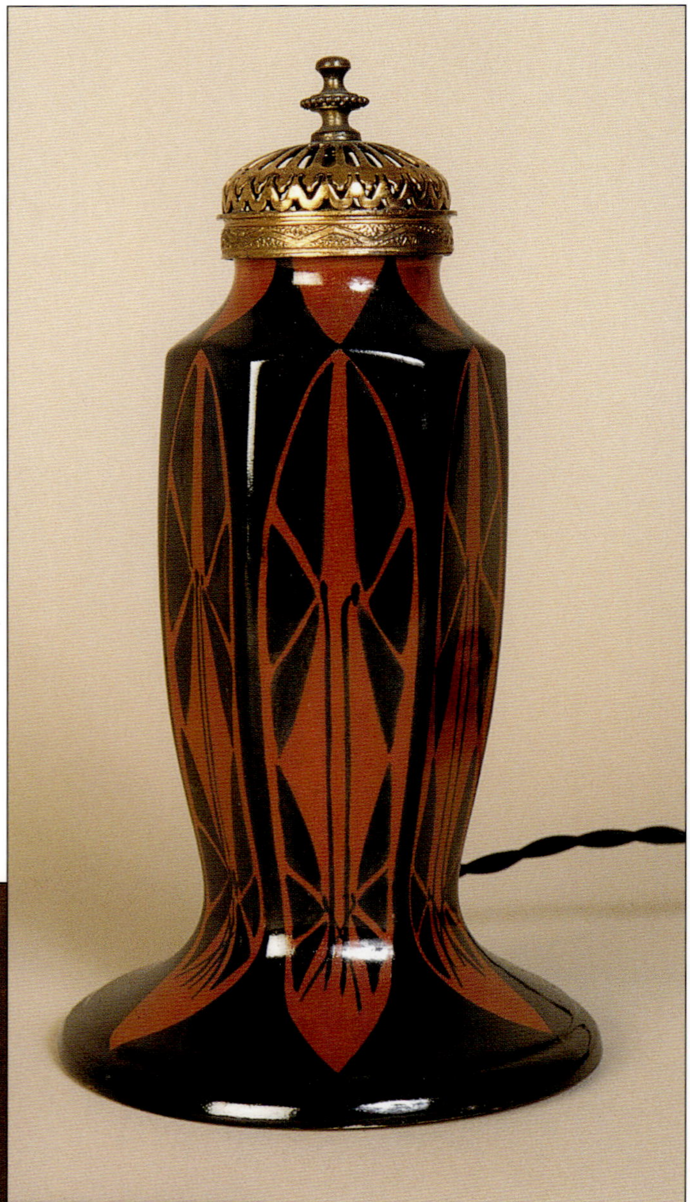

Nightlight, 8.4" high, 1920-1924. Less than $500.

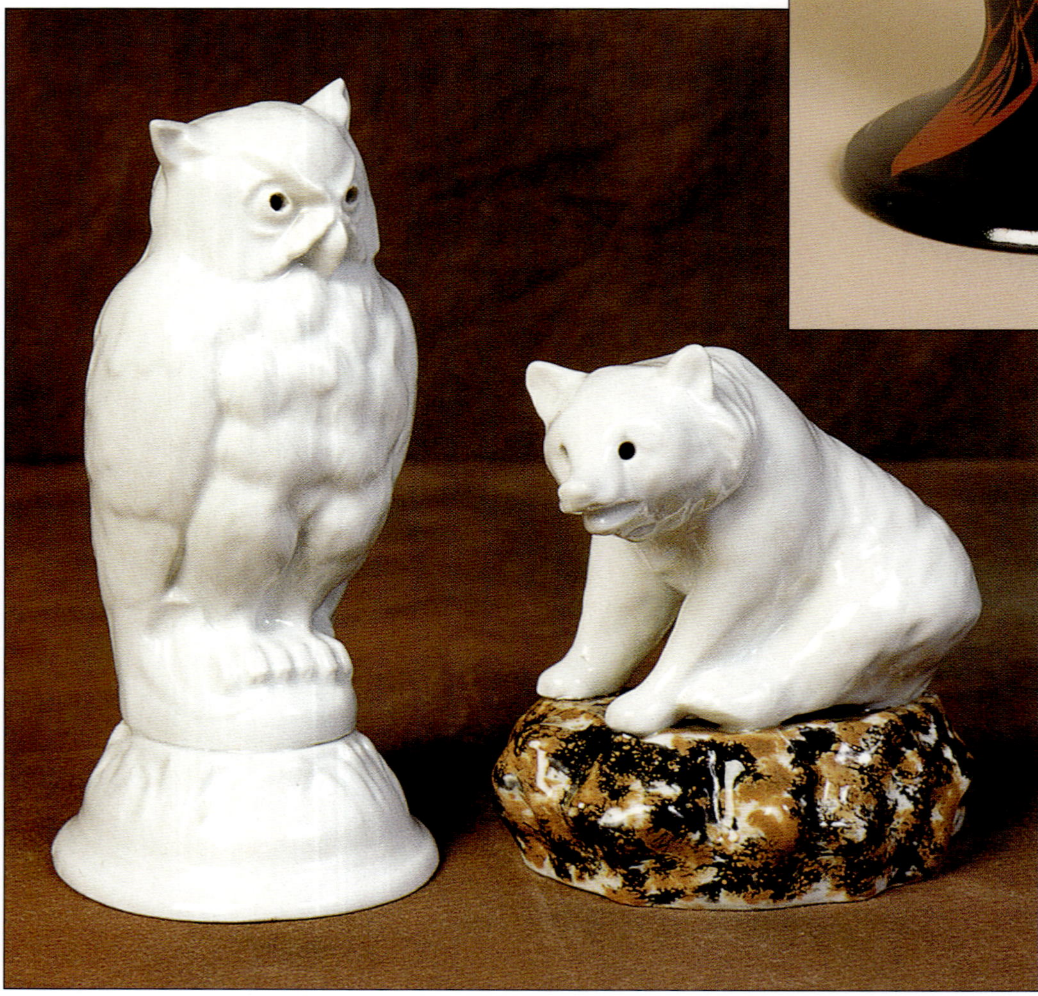

Owl and polar bear nightlights, owl, 6.5" high, 1920-1924, and polar bear, 1925-1927. Owl less than $500; bear, $500-$1,000.

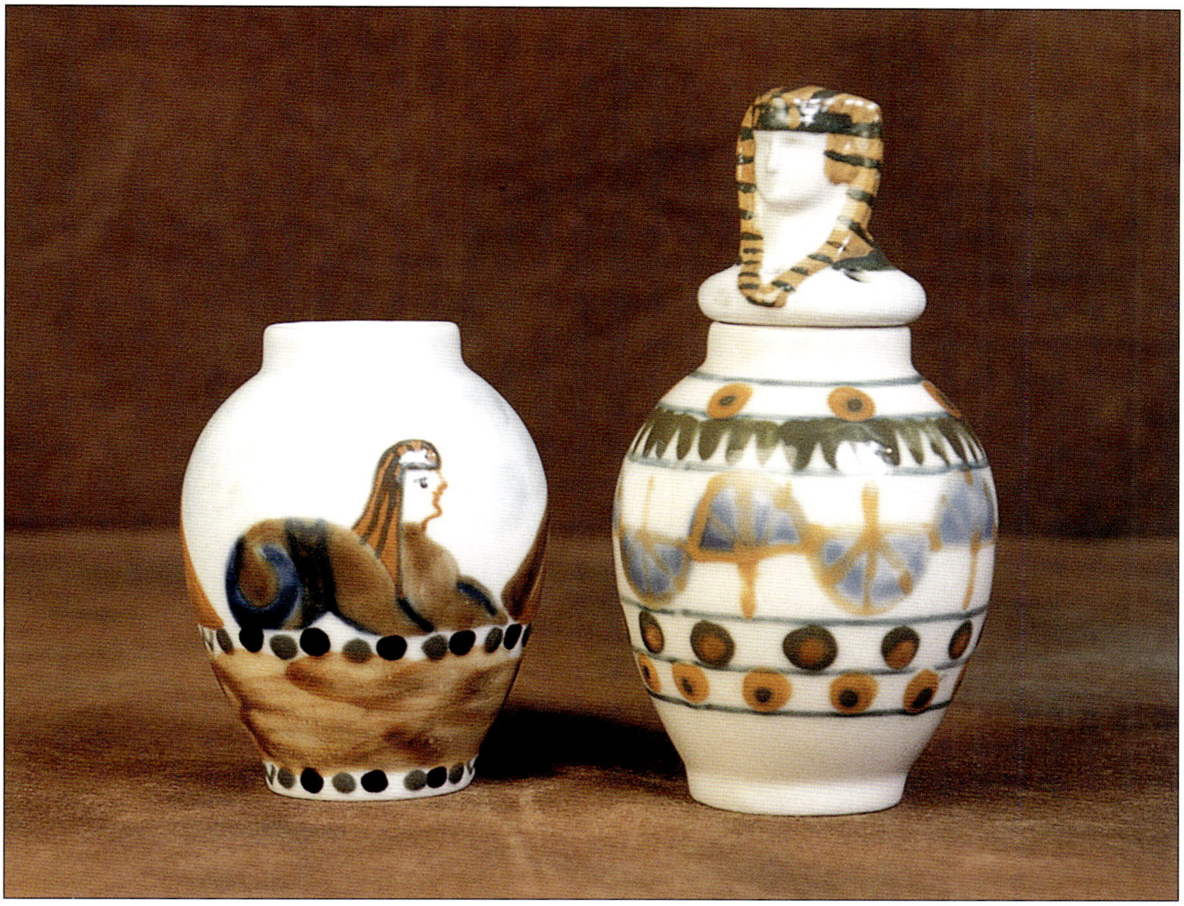

Vase, left, 3.75" high, 1925-1927, and incense holder, right, 5.75" high, 1920-1924. Each less than $500.

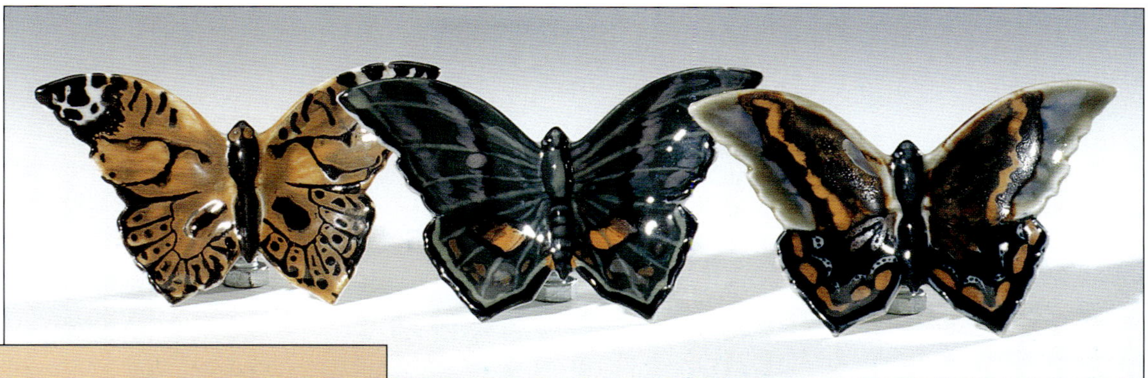

Butterflies, uncertain of date but probably between 1920-1927. Each less than $500.

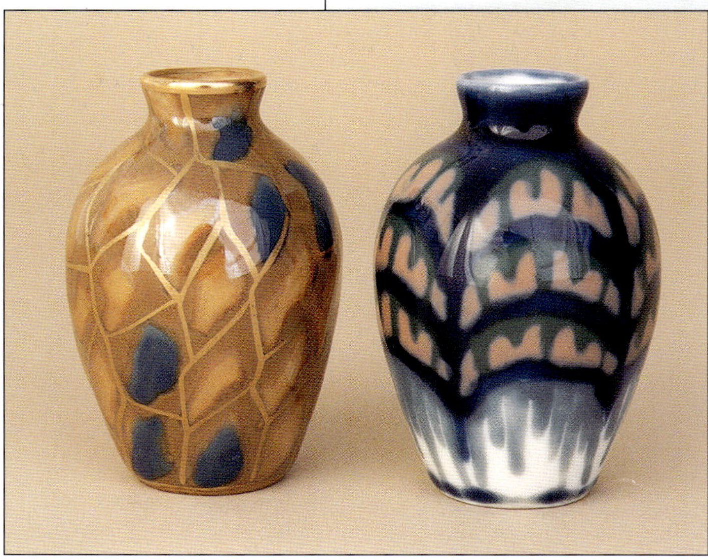

Two small vases, 3.25" high, uncertain of date, but probably between 1920-1927. Each less than $500.

1925-1927

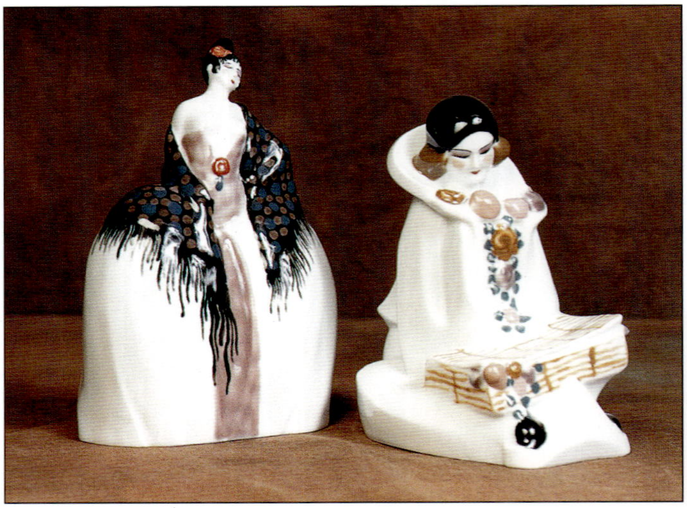

Nightlights, left, *The Gypsy*, 7.5" high, exhibited at the Exposition internationale des arts décoratifs, 1925, Paris, and right, 6.25" high, 1925-1927. Left, $500-$1,000; right, less than $500.

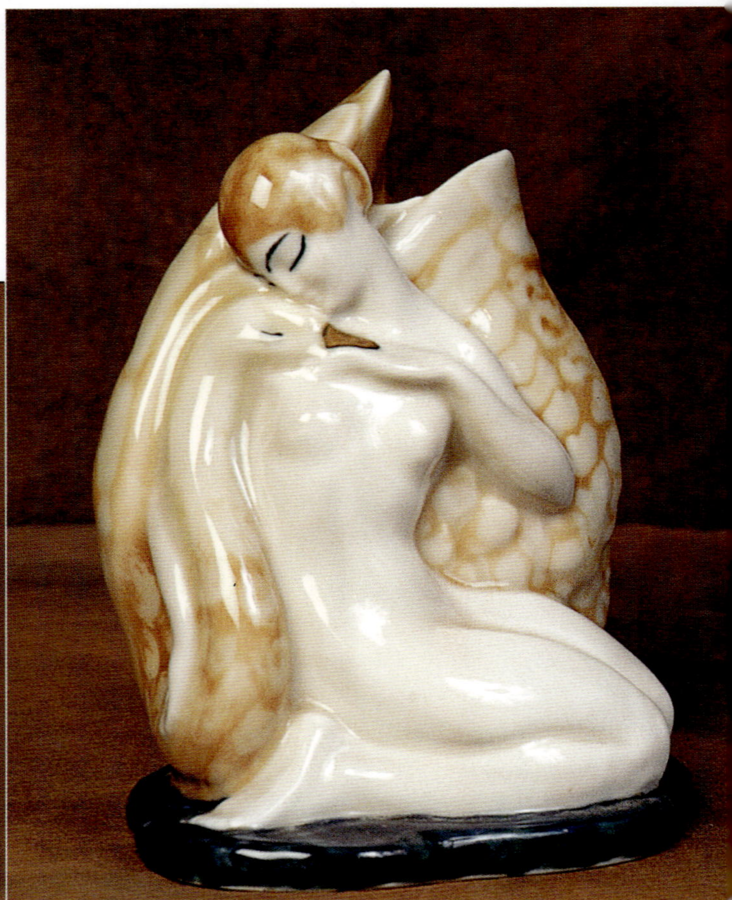

Nightlight, *Léda and the Swan*, 7.75" high, shape of Lucien Crélerot, 1926. $500-$1,000.

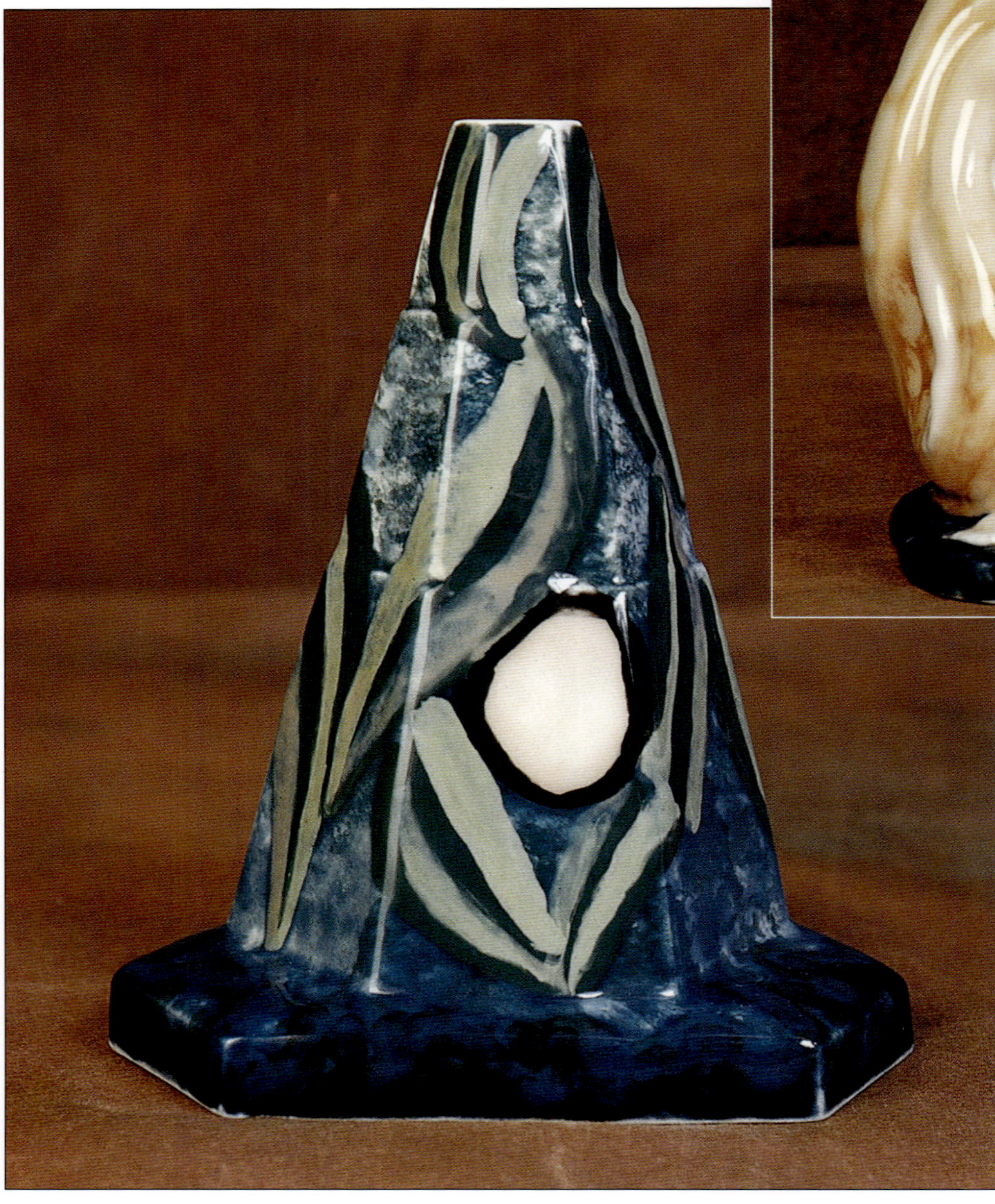

Nightlight, 7.3" high, 1925-1927. Less than $500.

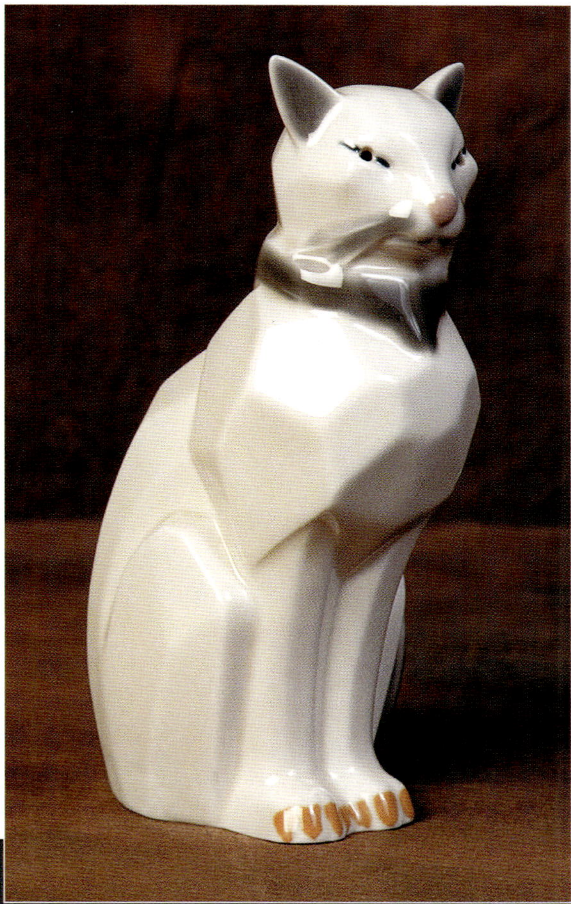

Cat nightlight, 8.5" high, about 1927, model of Georges Papault, made in three different sizes. (Ferrer) $500-$1,000.

Nightlights, *Sultan-Sultane*, 8" high, about 1930, shape created about 1927. (Ferrer) $500-$1,000.

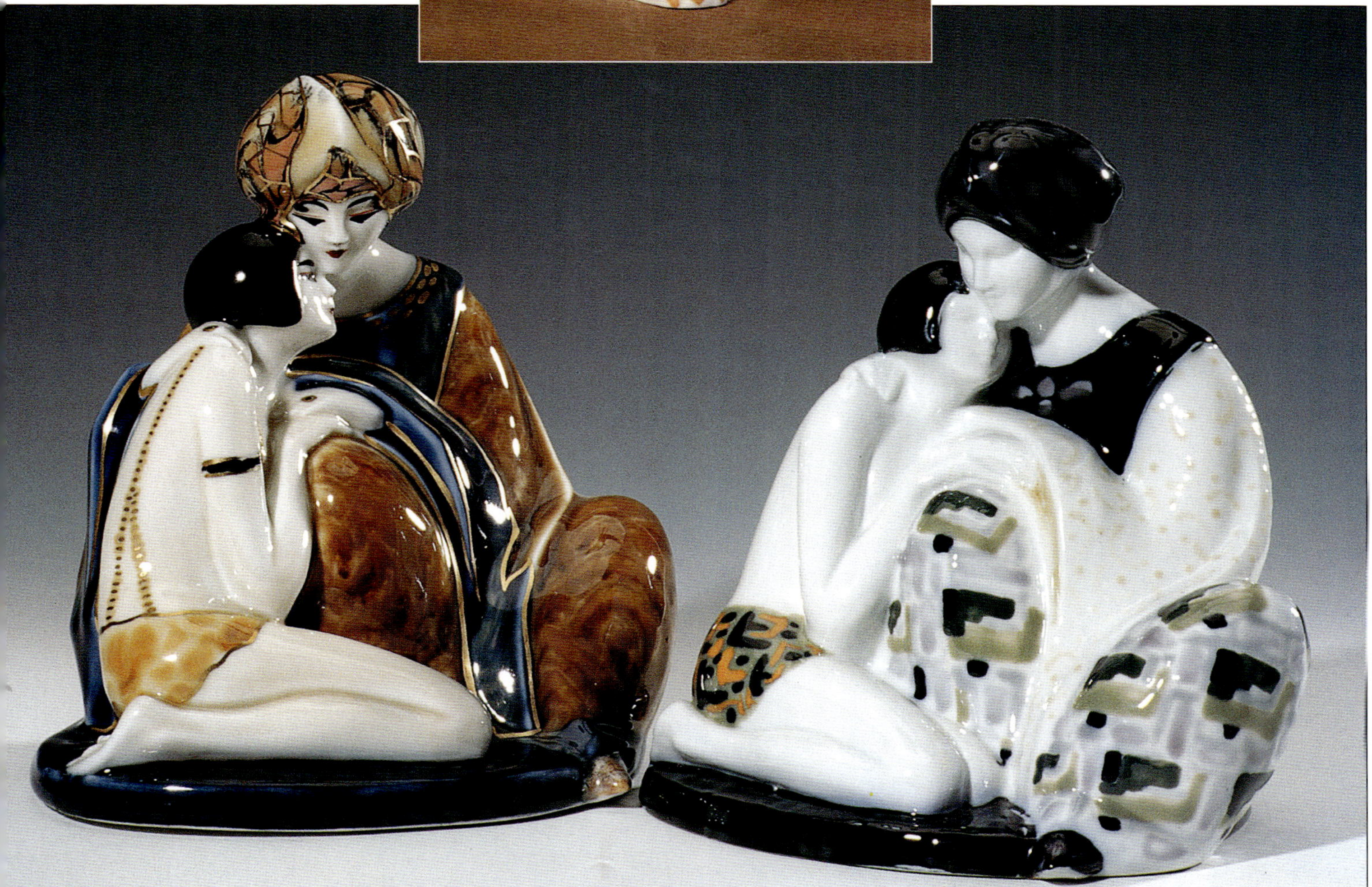

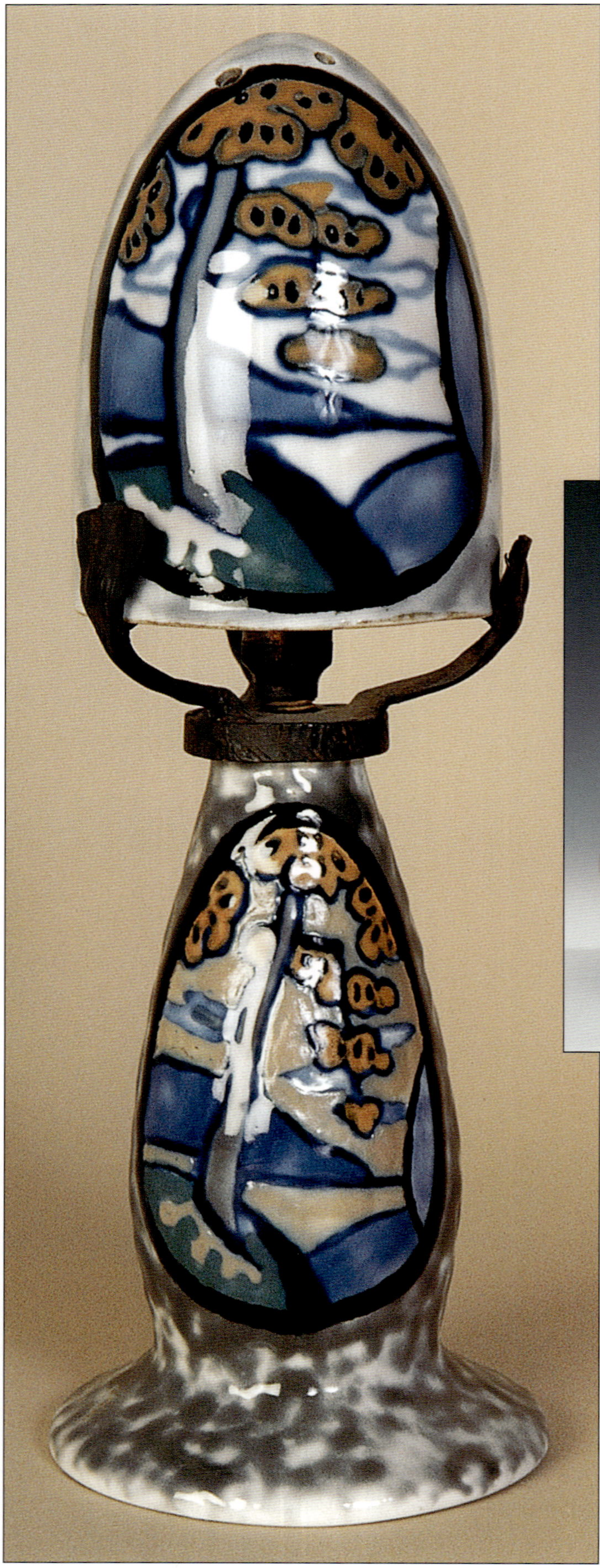

Rare scenic lamp, 10.75" high, 1925-1927. $1,000+.

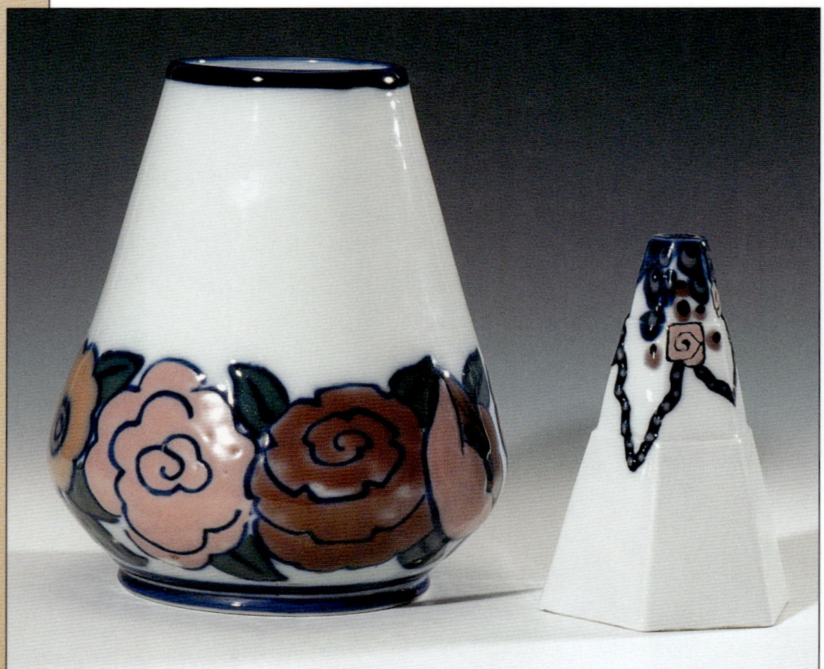

Vase and lamp shade, 1925-1927. Each less than $500.

Right:
Egg and two covered boxes, 1925-1927; egg, 10" high; small box, 2.6" in diameter; and large box, 5" in diameter. Egg, $500-$1,000; boxes, less than $500 each.

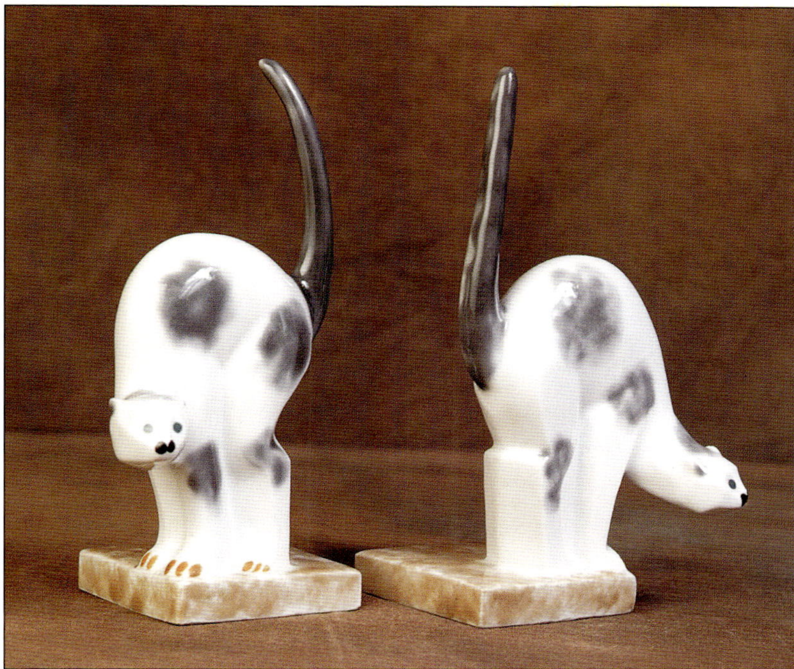

Lemur Bookends, 8.5" high, *sous émail* decoration, 1925-1927. $1,000-$1,500.

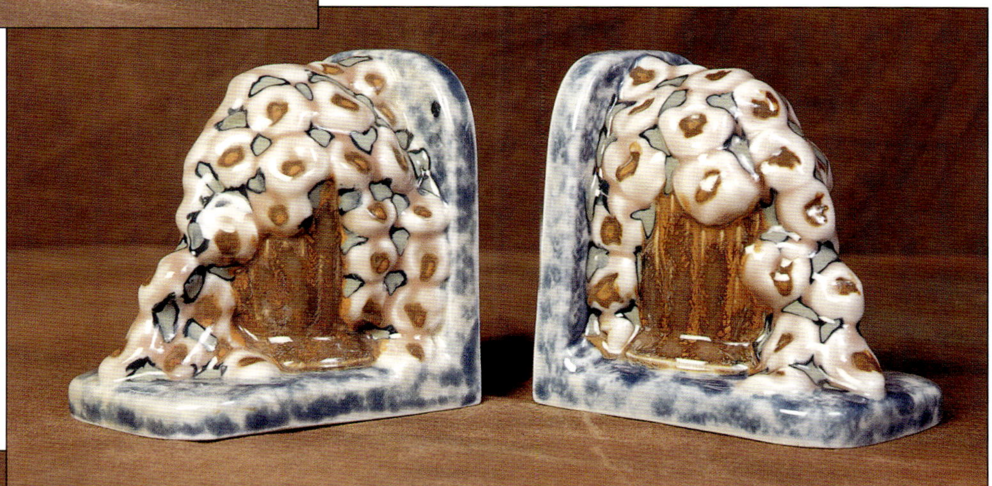

Flower bookends, 1925-1927, 5" high x 4.75" wide x 3.5" deep. $500-$1,000.

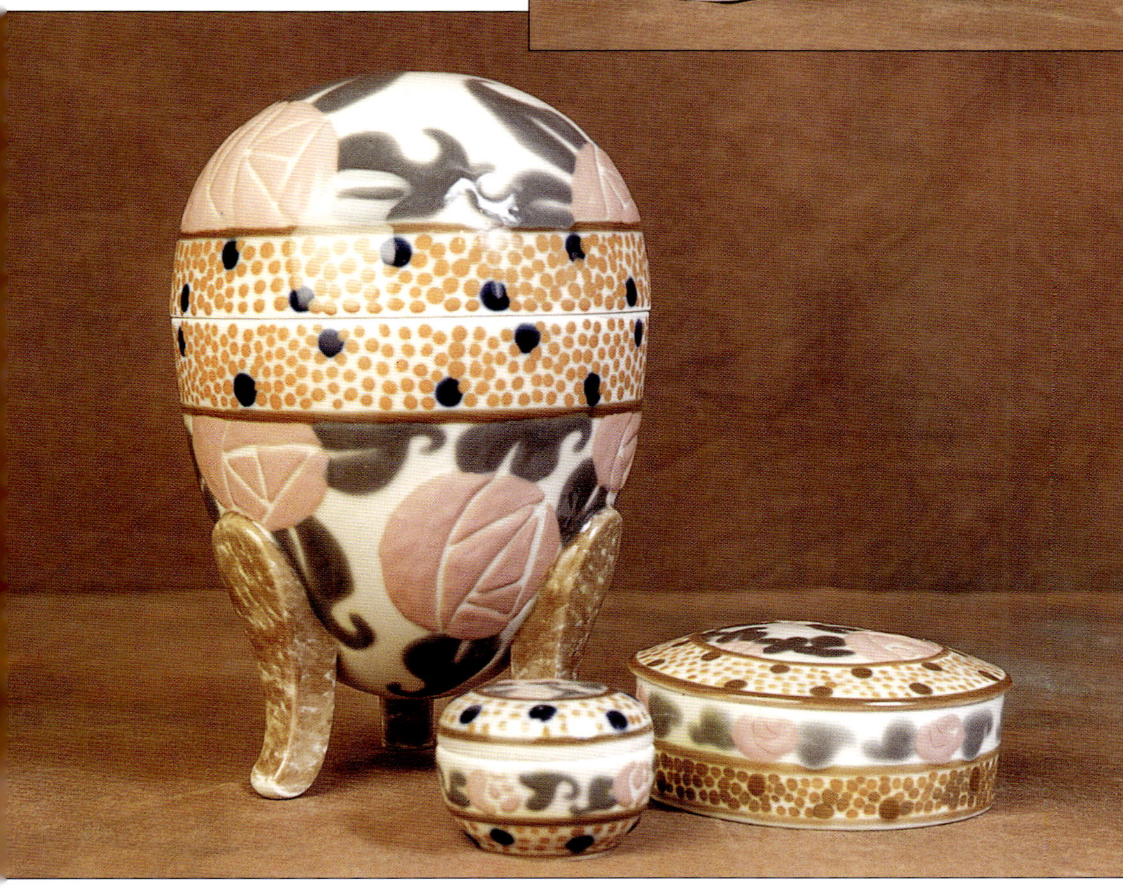

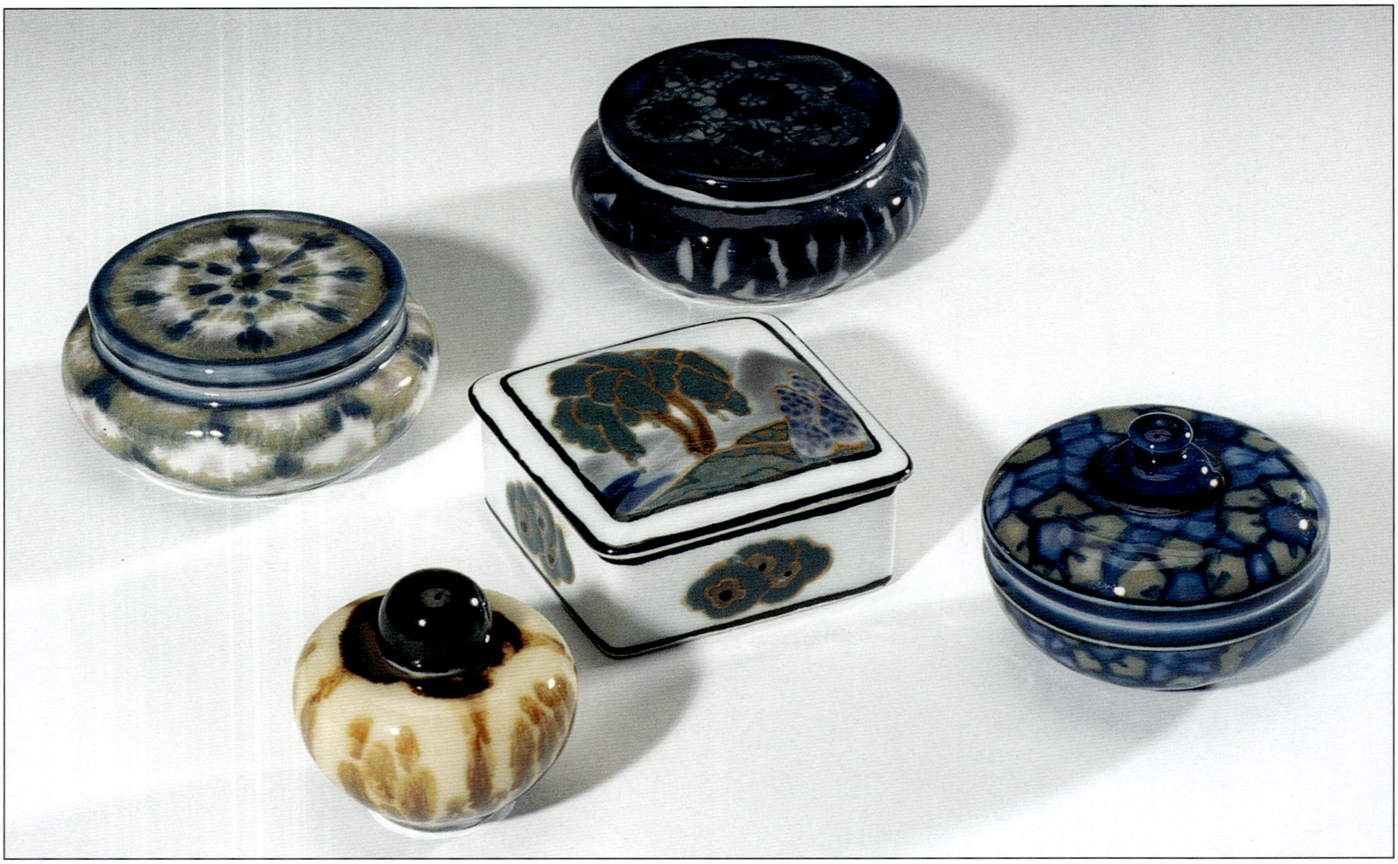

Boxes, 1925-1927, box with finial, marked *LJ* (Léon Jouhaud), an important enameller, and also a ceramist and painter in Limoges. Less than $500 each.

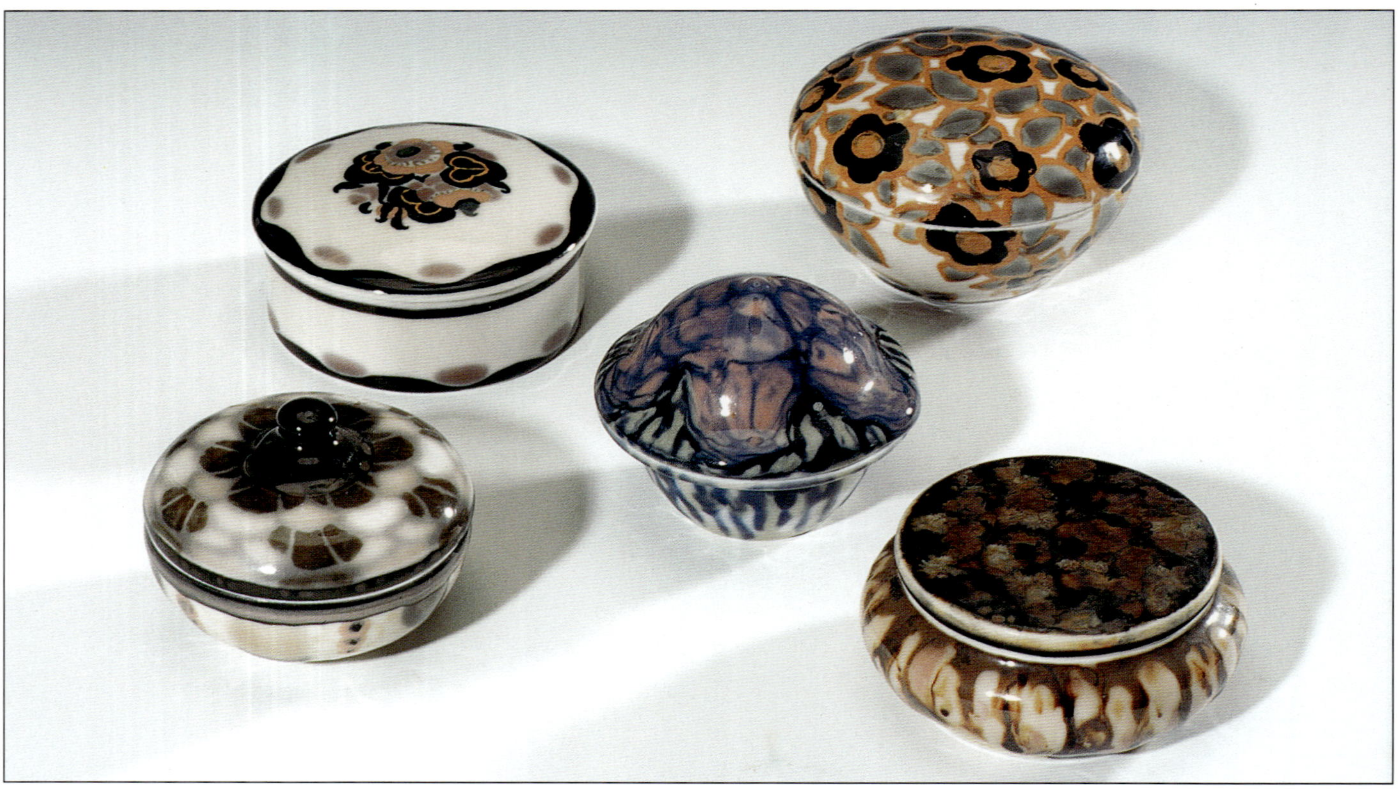

Boxes, 1925-1927, right rear, marked *LJ* (Léon Jouhaud). Each less than $500.

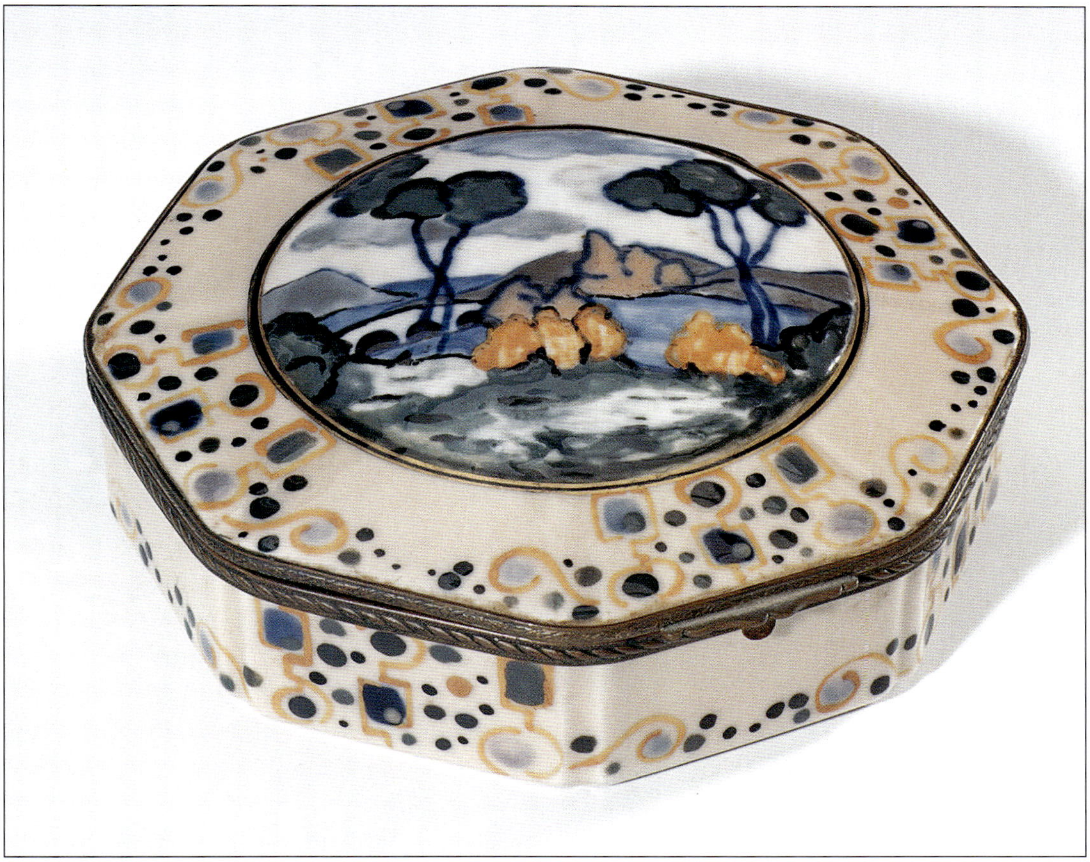

Box, 1925-1927. $500-$1,000.

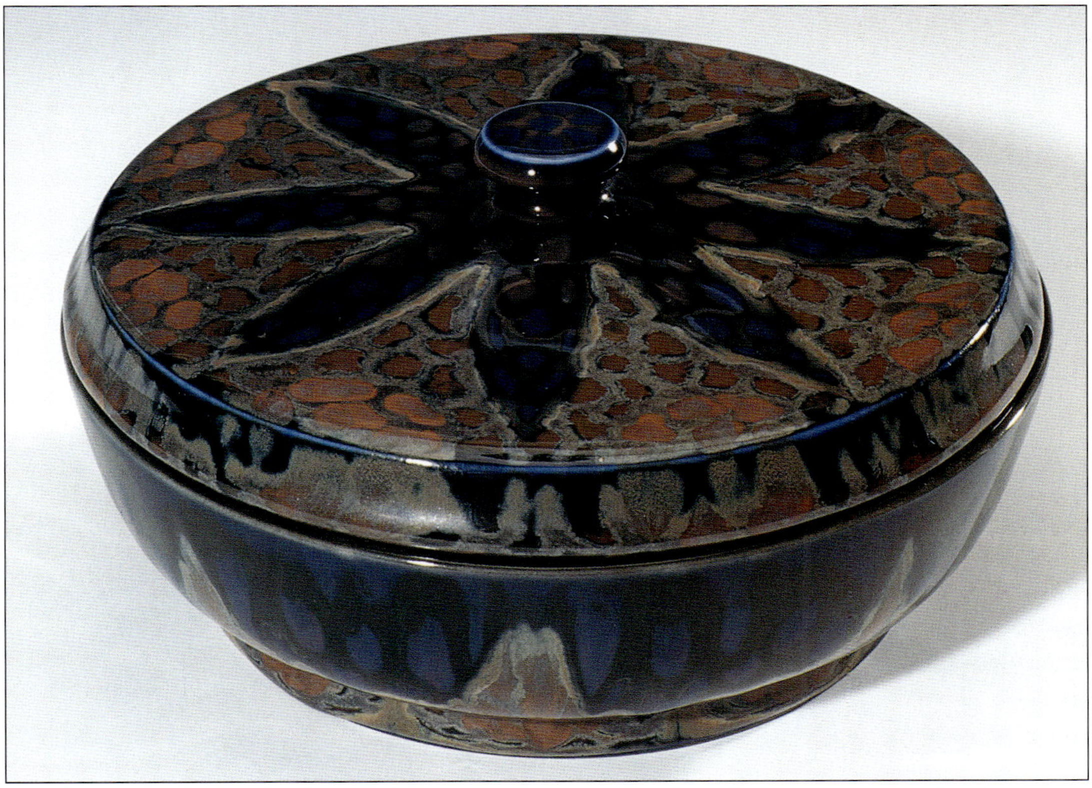

Box, 1925-1927, mark painted *Th* in blue (decoration by Camille Tharaud). $500-$1,500.

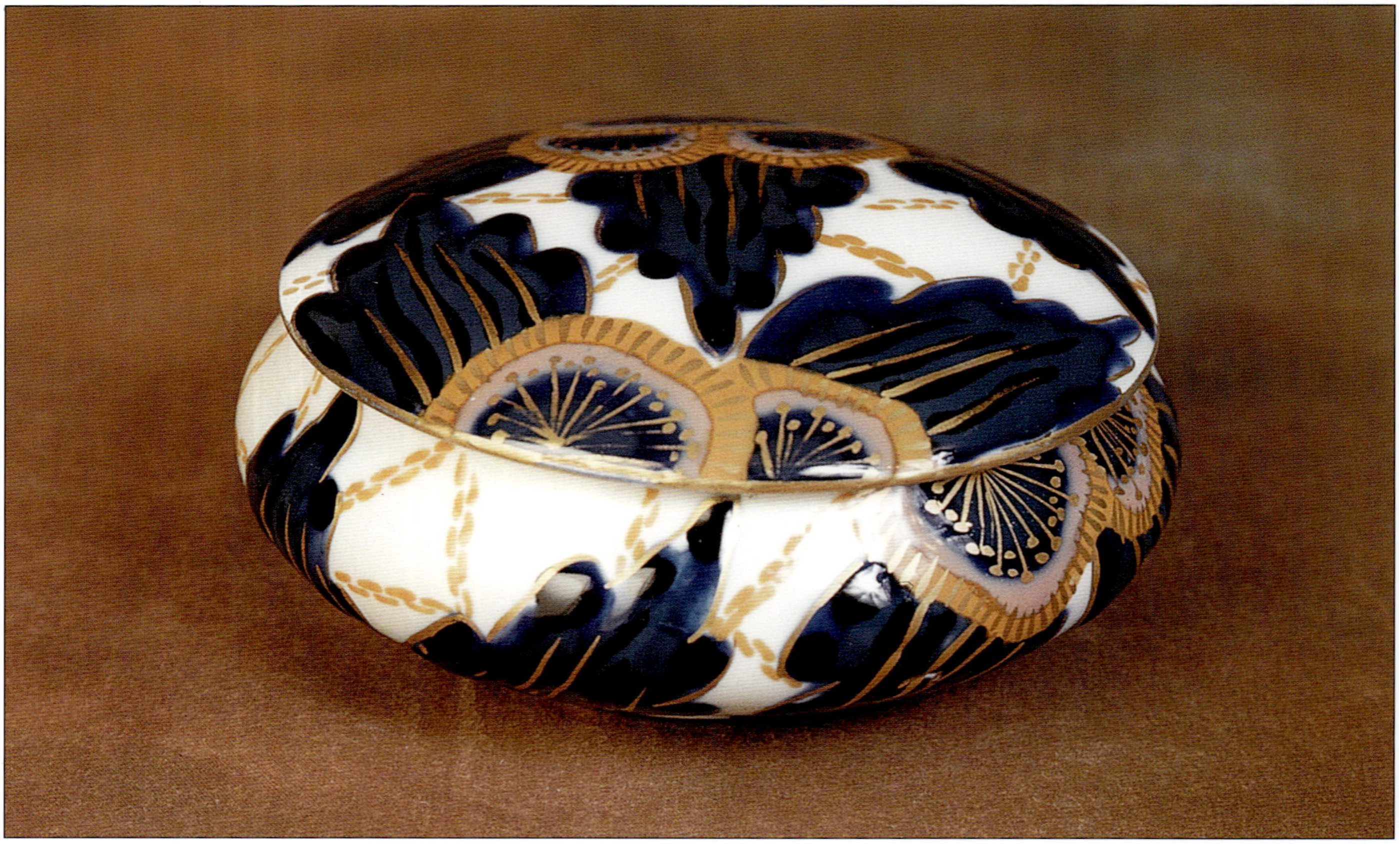

Covered Box, 6" in diameter, 1925-1927. Less than $500.

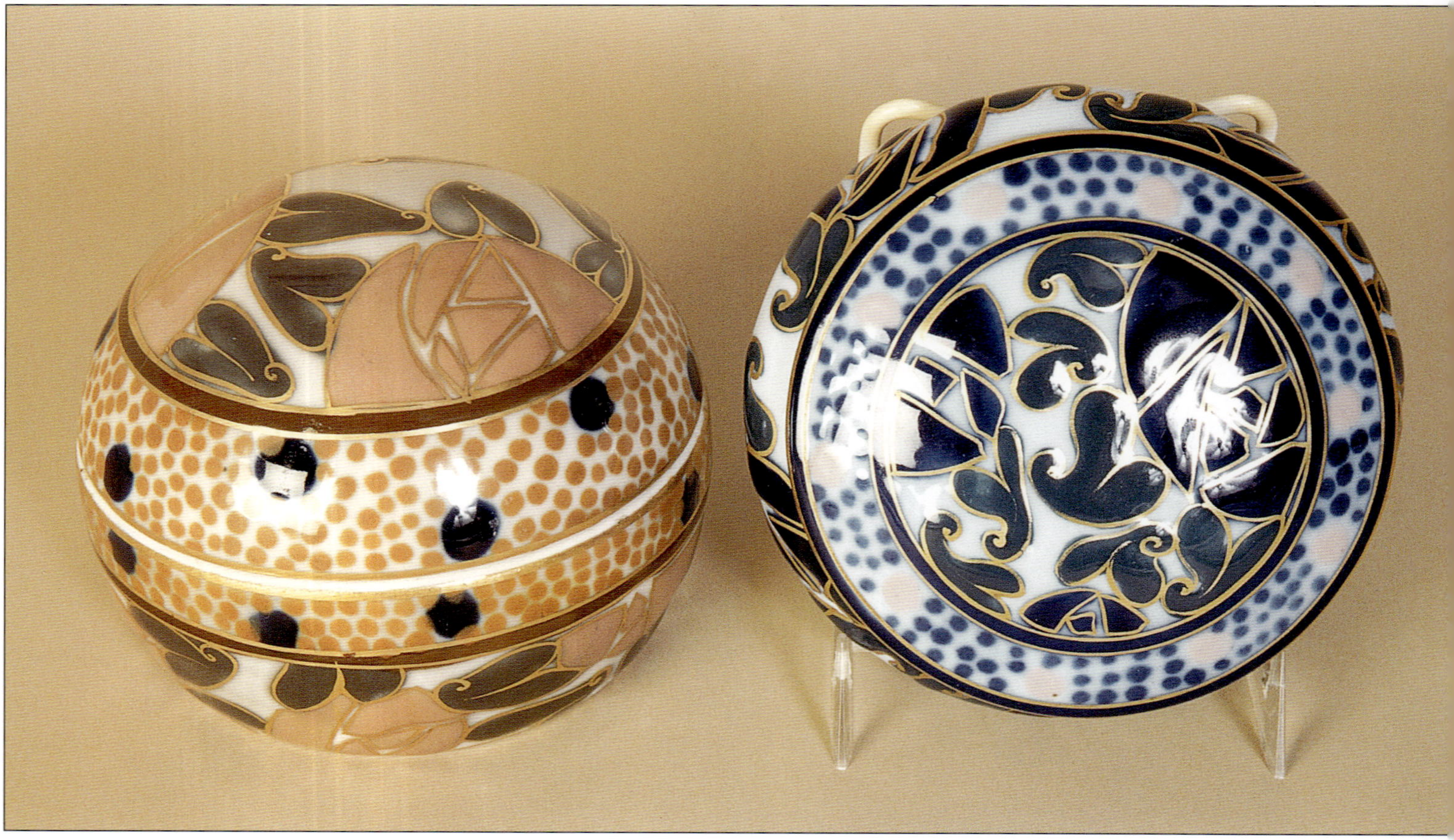

Round box, left, 4" high x 5" in diameter, 1928-1930, and covered box, right, 4.75" in diameter, 1925-1927. Each less than $500.

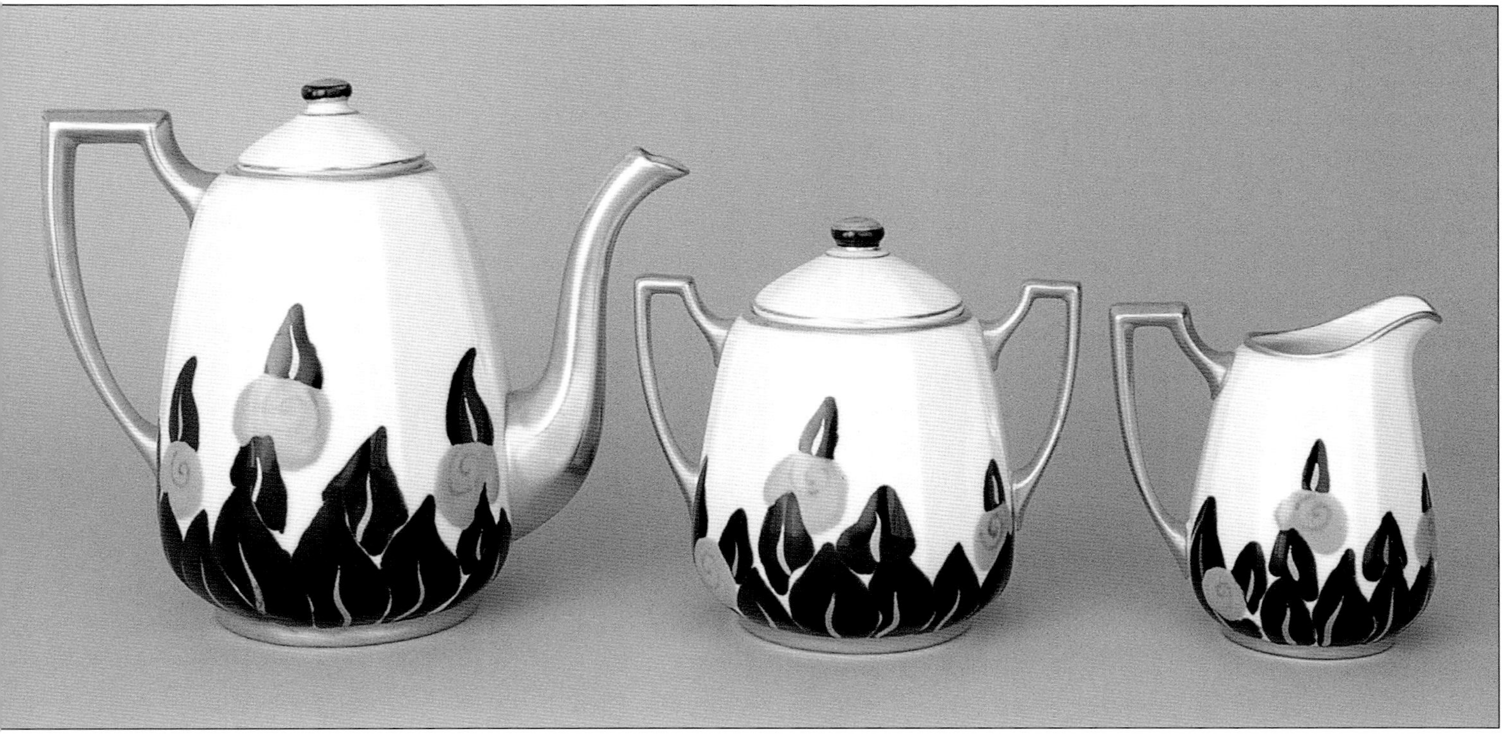

Coffee set, 1925-1927. $500-$1,000.

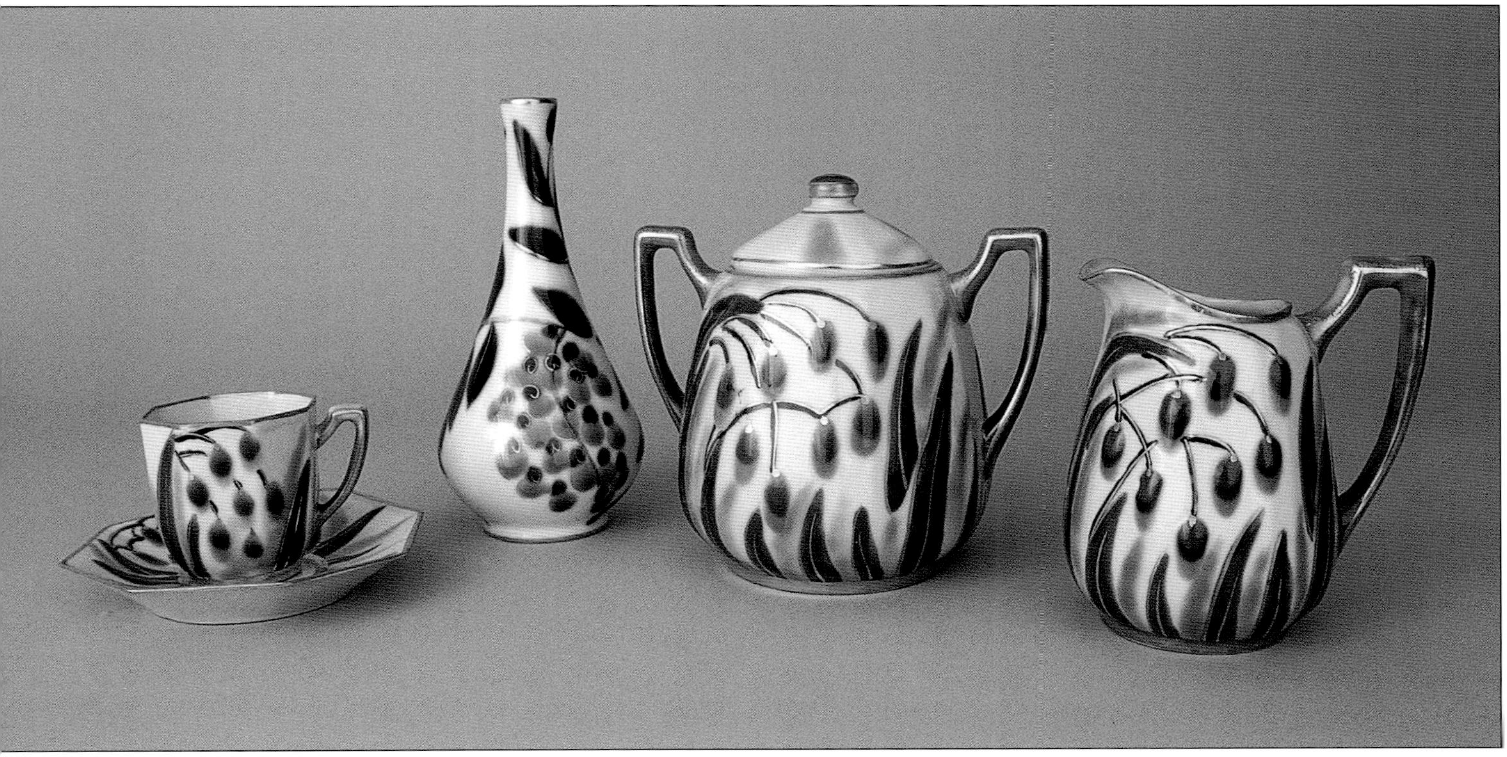

Single flower vase and sugar, creamer and demitasse, 1925-1927. Each less than $500.

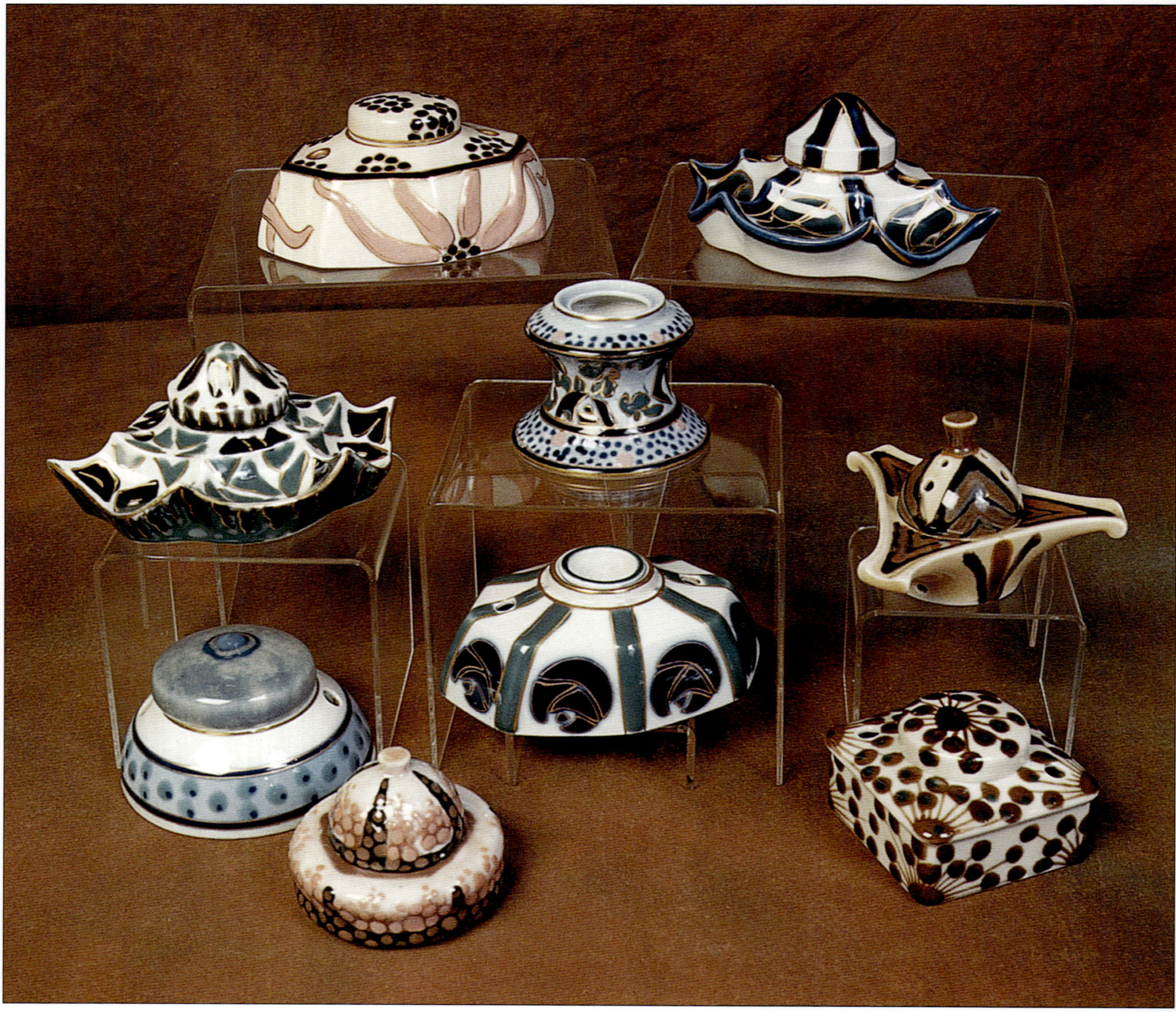

Inkwells, all 1925-1927, except for center right, 1928-1930. Each less than $500.

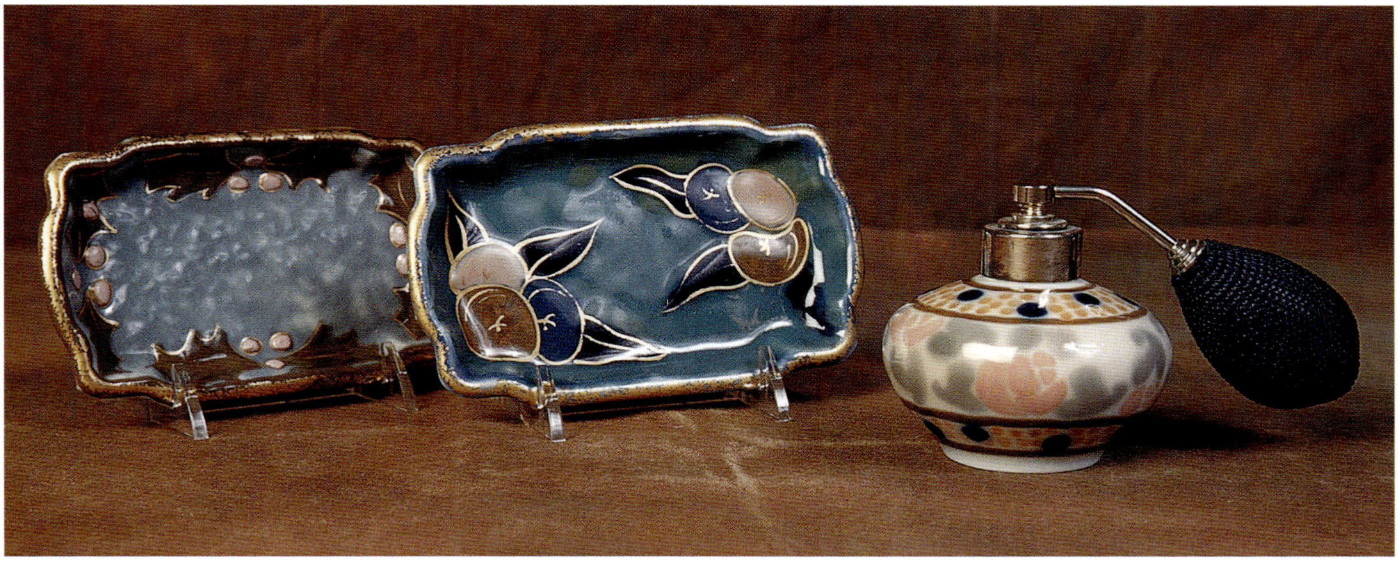

Trays and perfume bottle with atomizer, 1925-1927. Each less than $500.

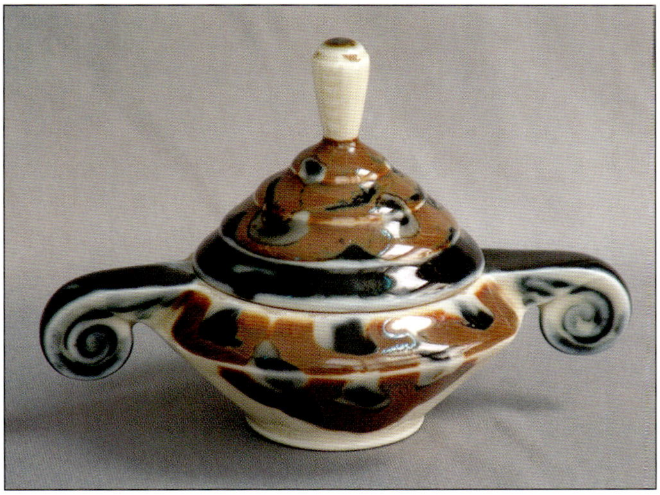

Candy dish, 3.5" high x 5.5" handle to handle. Less than $500.

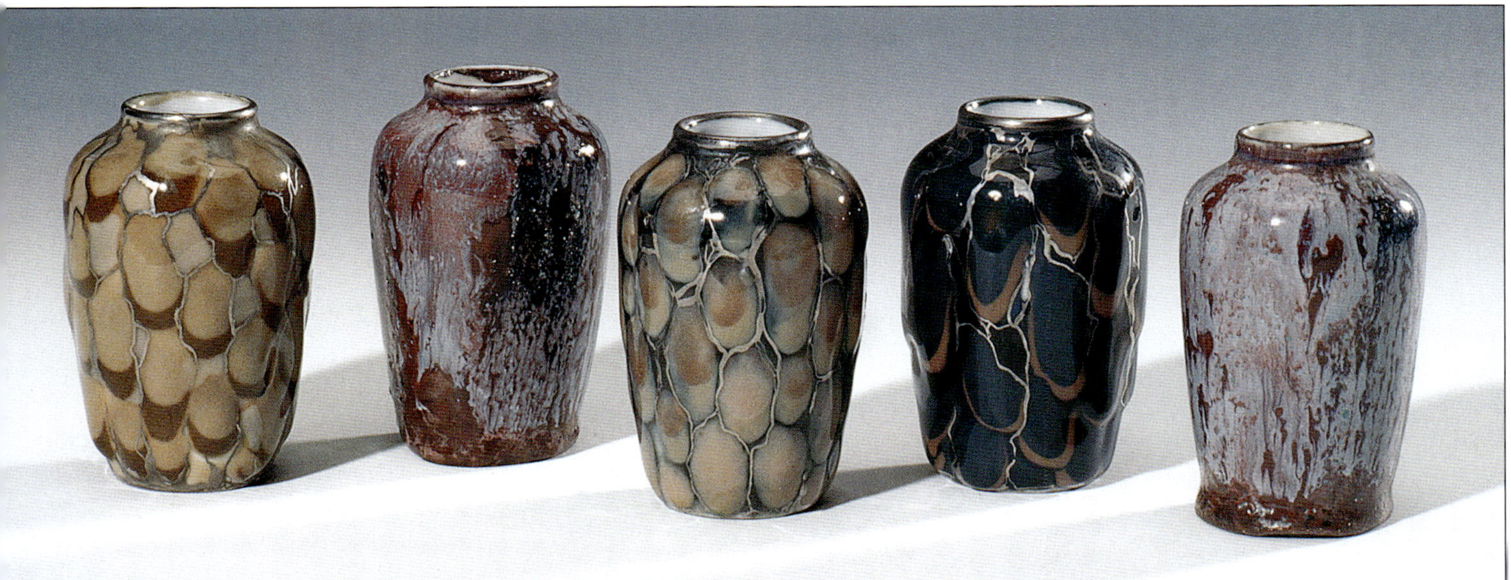

Vases, 1925-1927. Less than $500 each.

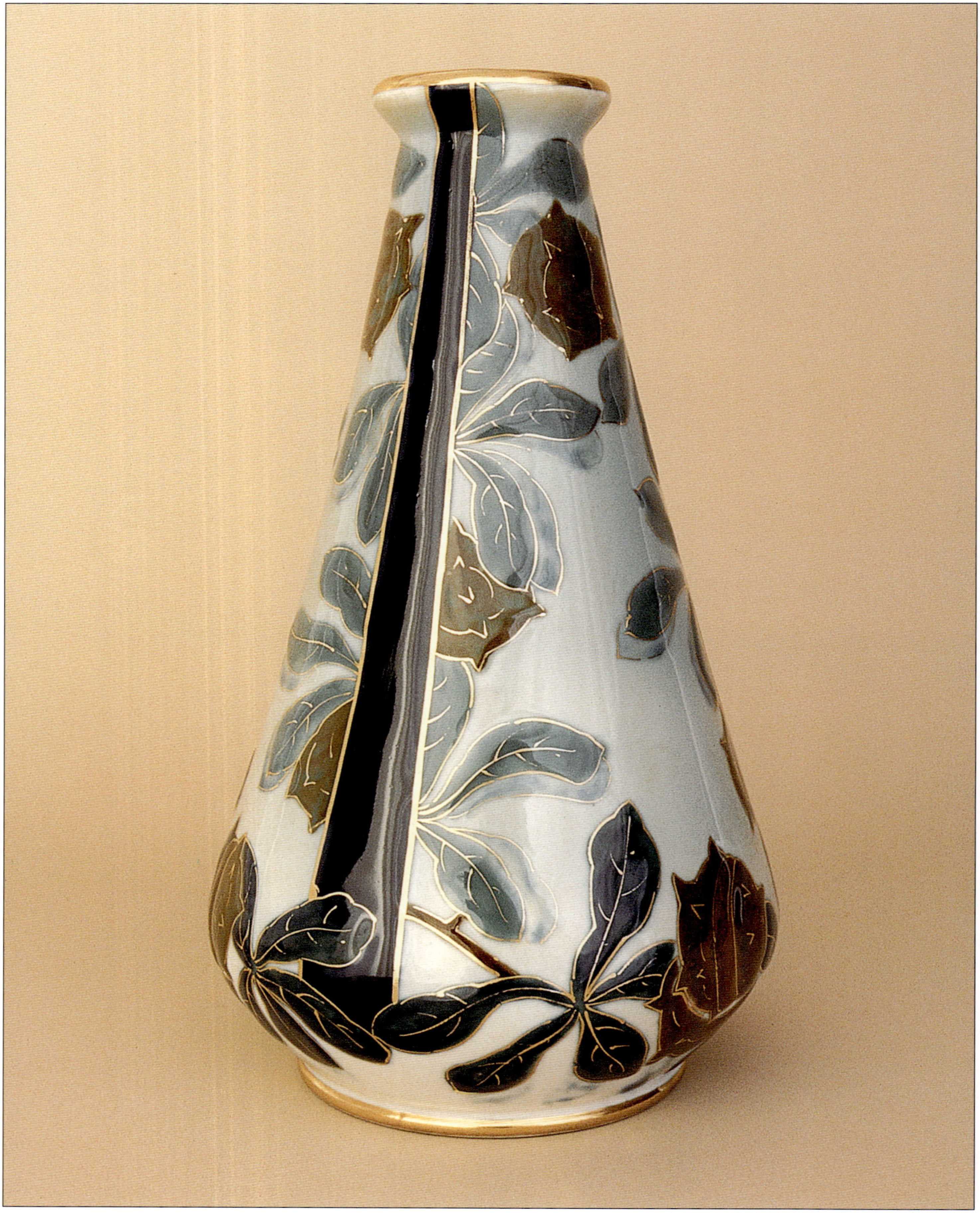

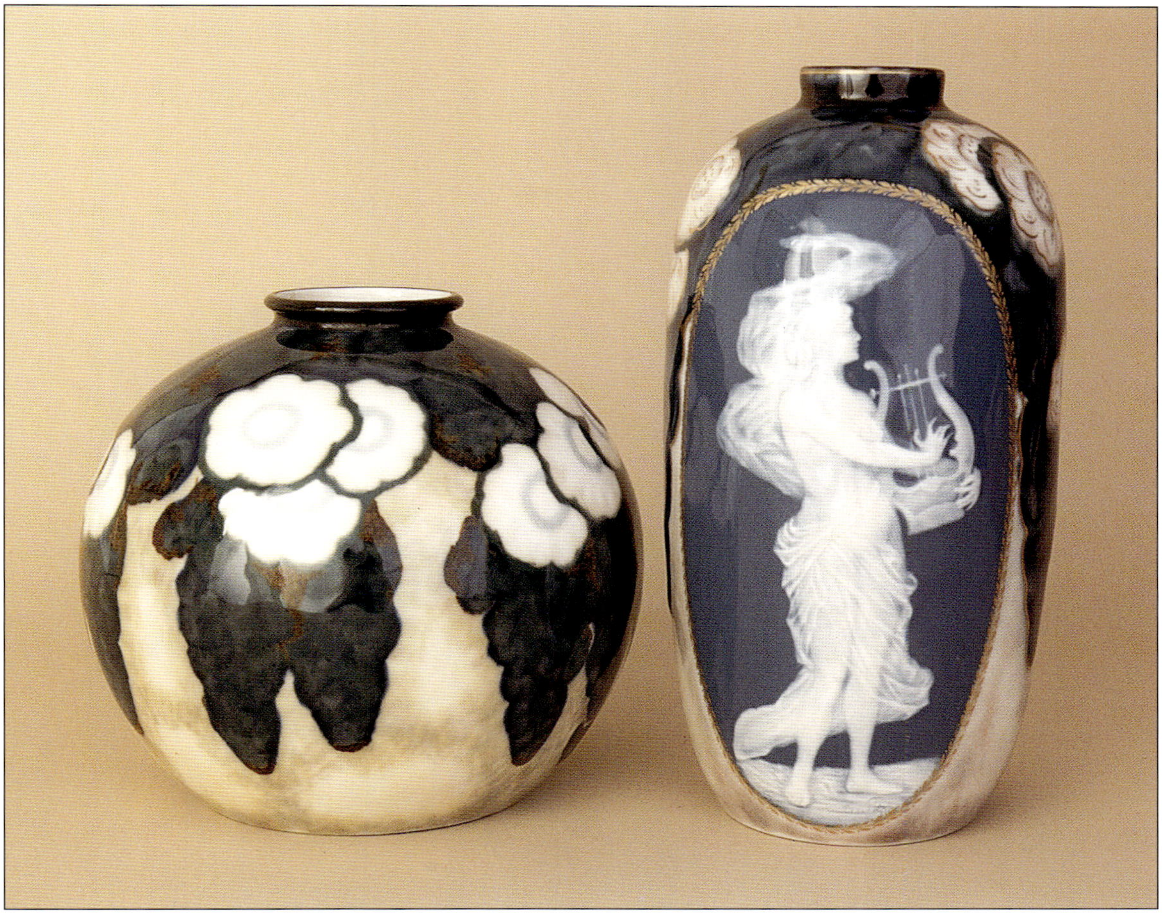

Two vases, above, 7" high, and right, "pâte sur pâte." Flowers designed by Geoffroy Juliette for the Salon des artistes décorateurs, Paris, 1927. The Art Deco style is free from repetition. (Ferrer) Each $500-$1,000.

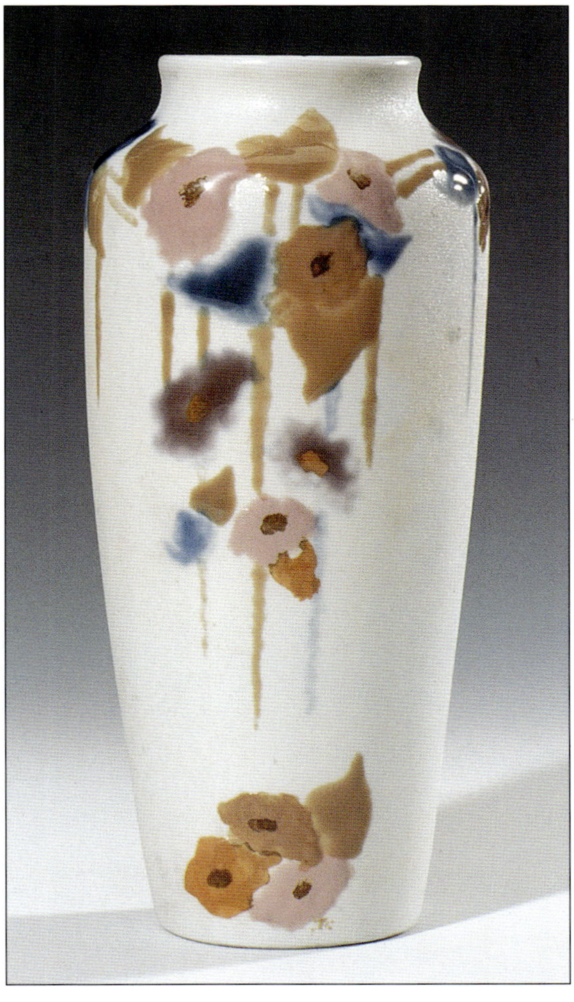

Vase, 1925-1927. $1,000-$1,500.

Opposite page:
Vase, 12" high, 1925-1927. $500-$1,000.

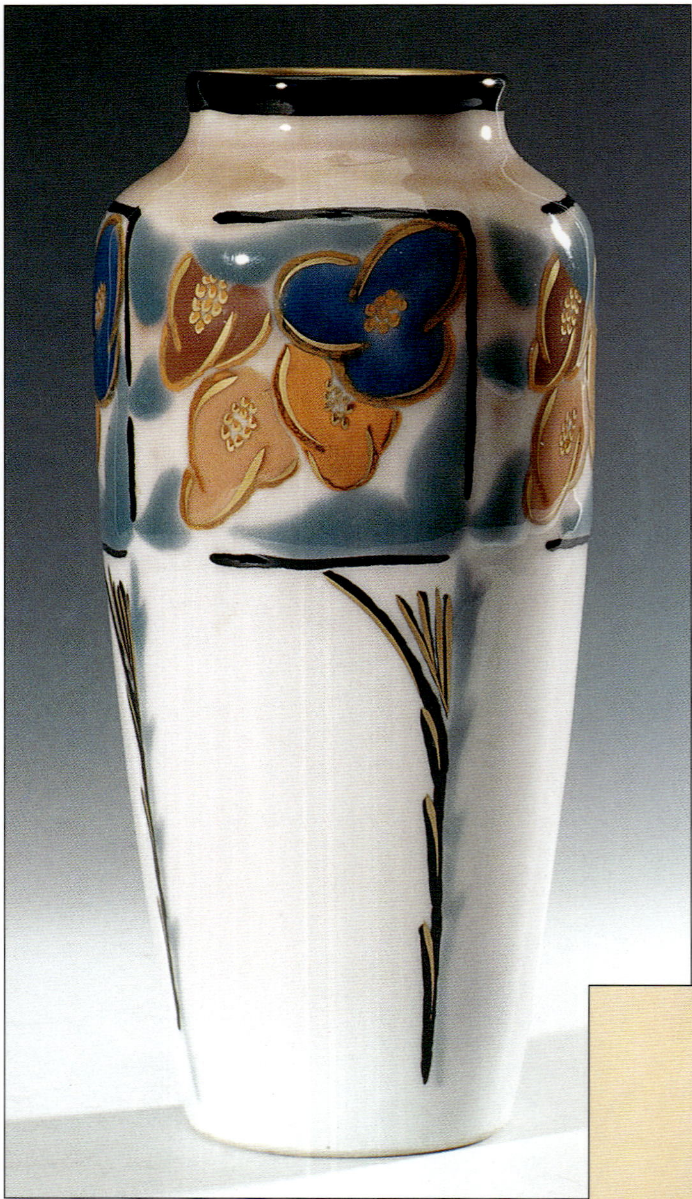

Vase, 8.75" high, based on a decoration by Marcel Goupy, the pink is made with aluminum, shown at the Exposition internationale des arts, 1925, Paris. (Ferrer) 1,000-$1,500.

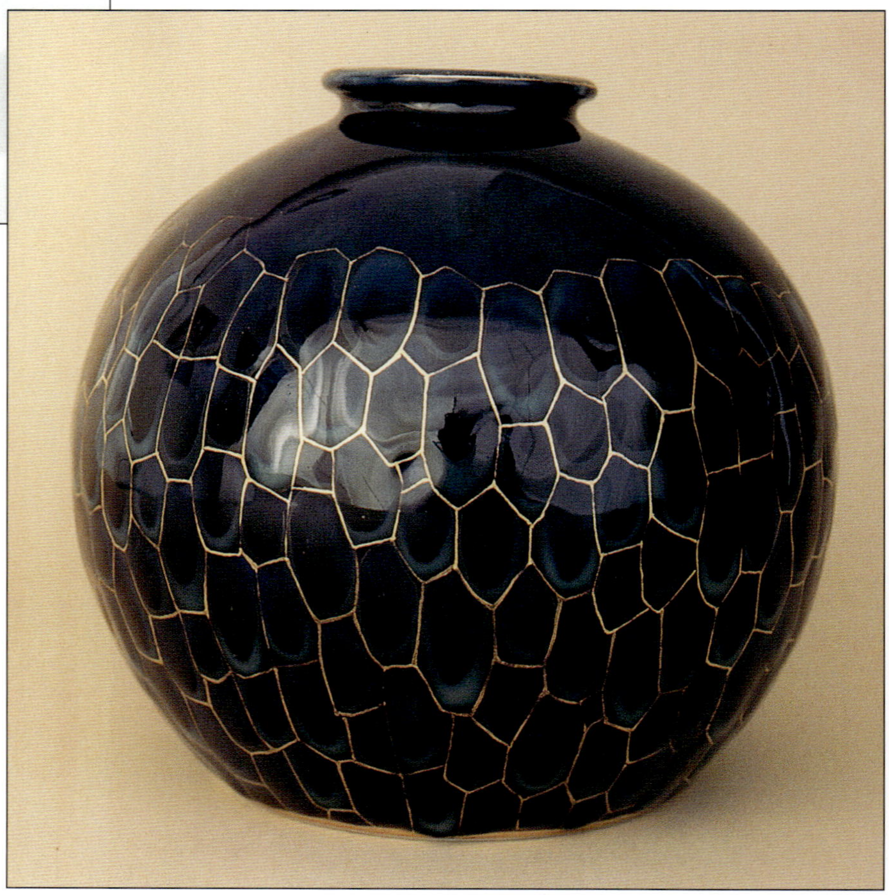

Cobalt crackled vase, 7.75" high, 1925-1927. $500-$1,000.

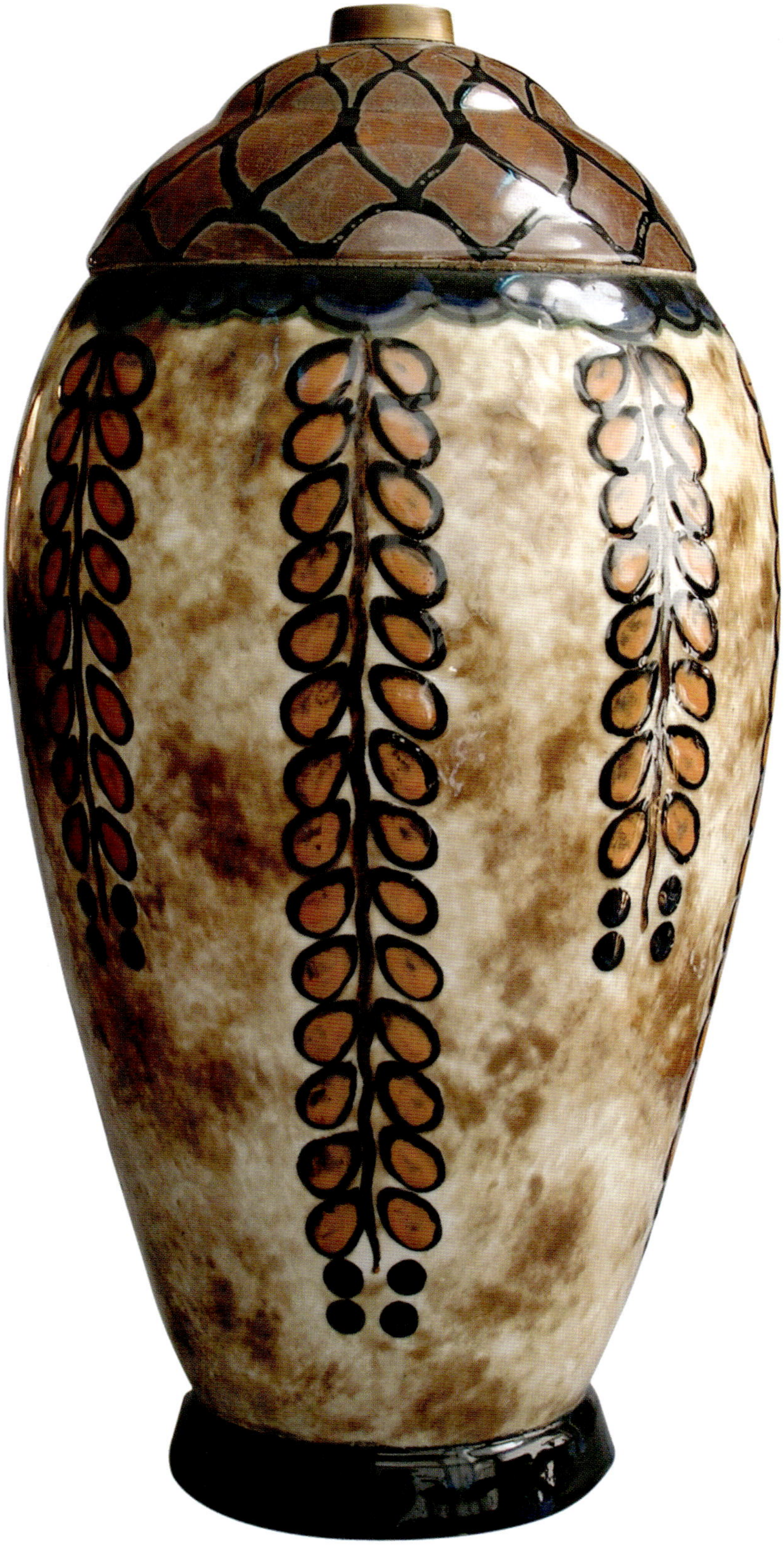

Lamp, 21" high, most probably decorated by Henri Rapin, marked on bottom with Rapin's initials in black. This piece was originally designed as a lamp and not a vase which was later converted to a lamp. $2,000+.

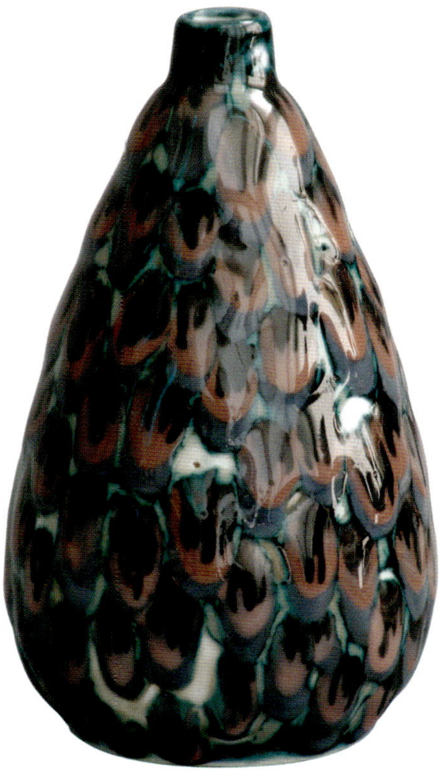

Vase, 8' high, enamel is very, very thick. Less than $500.

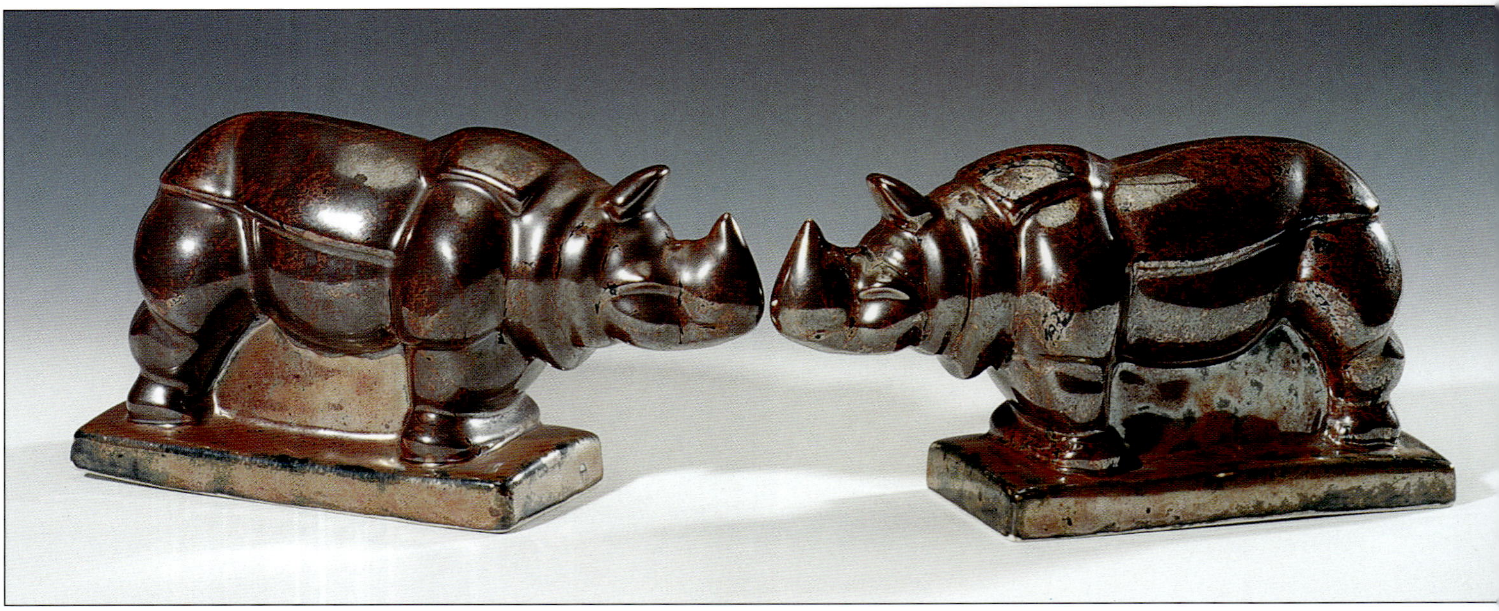

Rhinoceros, 6.25" high x 10.25", rare shape created by Robert Lemoine and exhibited at the Salon des artistes décorateurs, Paris, 1929. According to Albert Goumot-Labesse and Pierre Forestier, a respected Tharaud collector, only 100 of these pieces were created. According to Forestier, only 5-10 of the blue and brown colored rhinoceros were made. Each $3,000+.

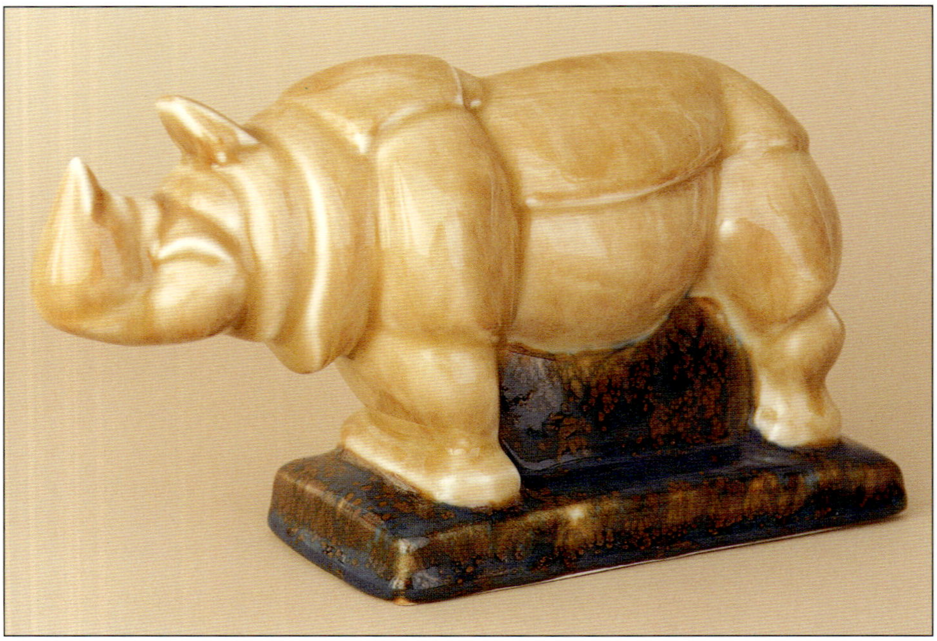

Rhinoceros, rare shape created by Robert Lemoine, 10.25" long x 6.25" high, 1929. $1,500-$2,000.

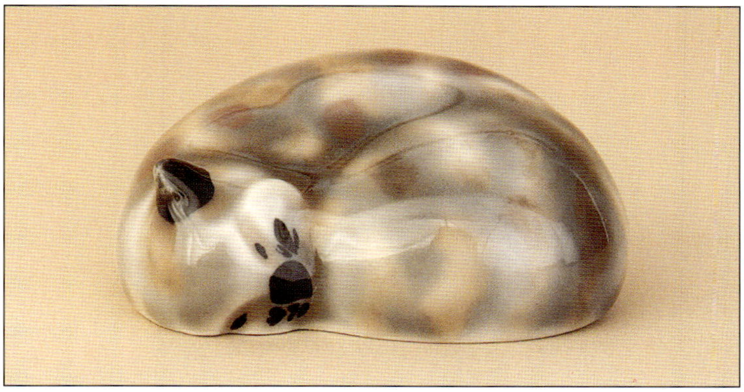

Cat, rare, 3.25" x 2.4", probably around 1928. Less than $500.

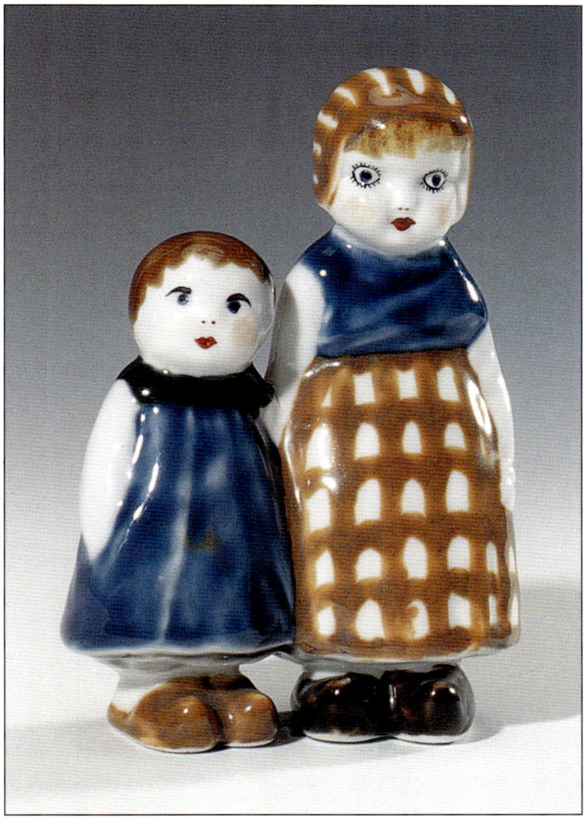

Figurines, 1928-1930.
Less than $500.

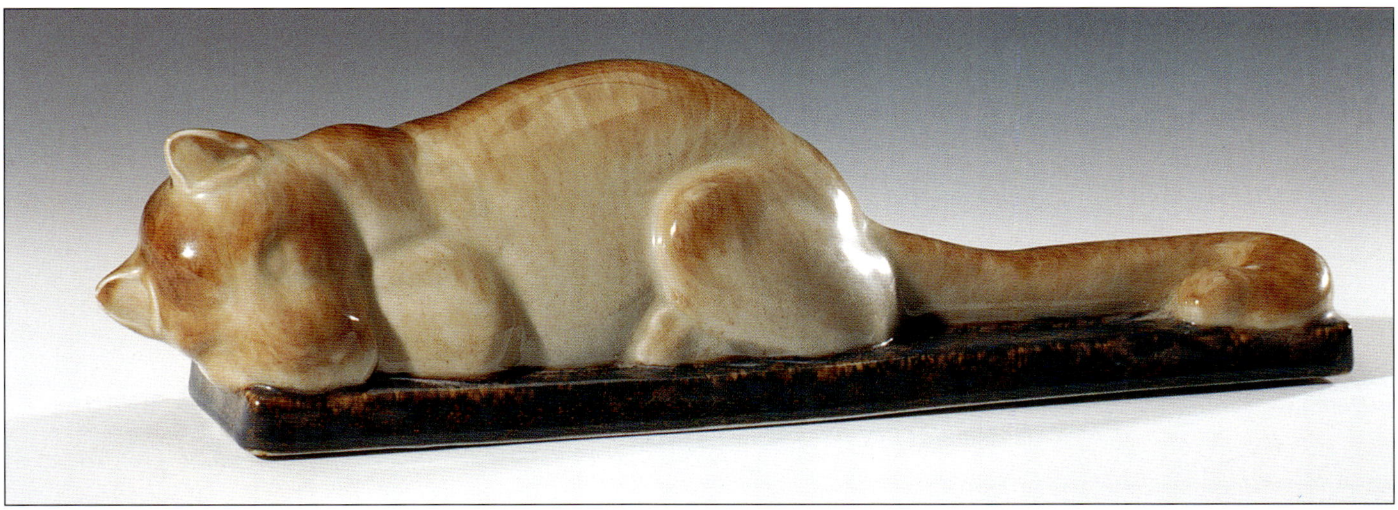

Sleeping lion, 16", shape of Robert Lemoine, about 1929. $1,500-$2,000.

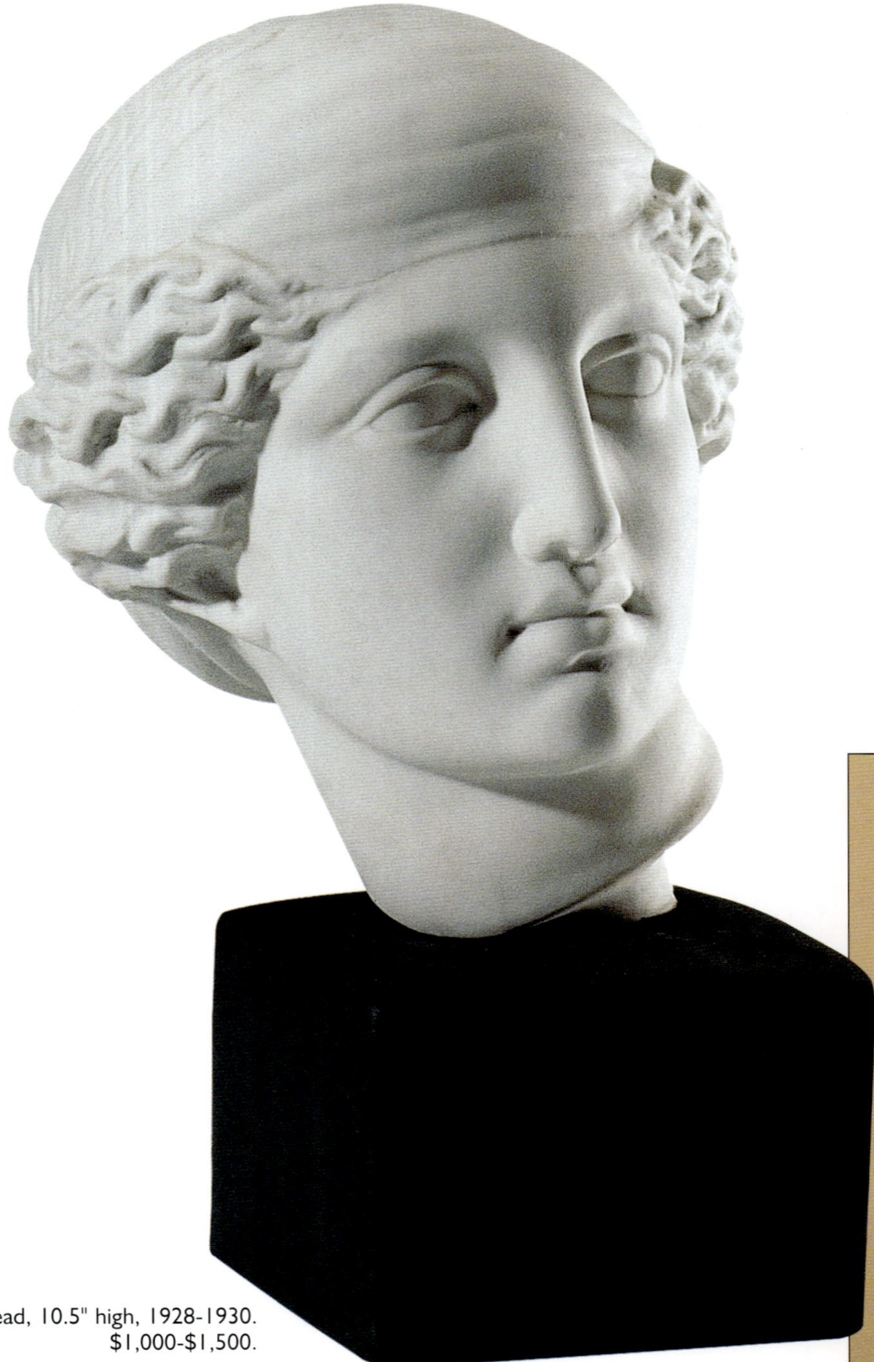

Greek head, 10.5" high, 1928-1930. $1,000-$1,500.

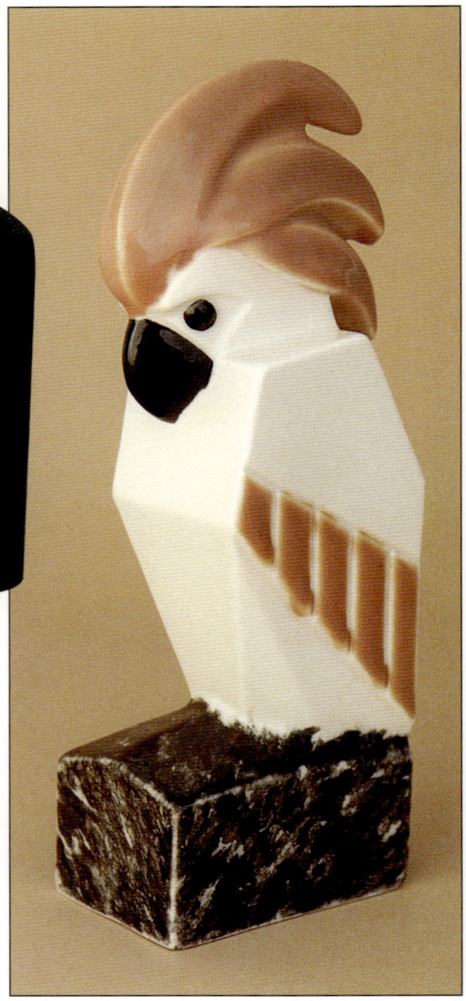

Cockatoo bookend, rare, 8.75" high, geometric style, 1928-1930. $500-$1,000.

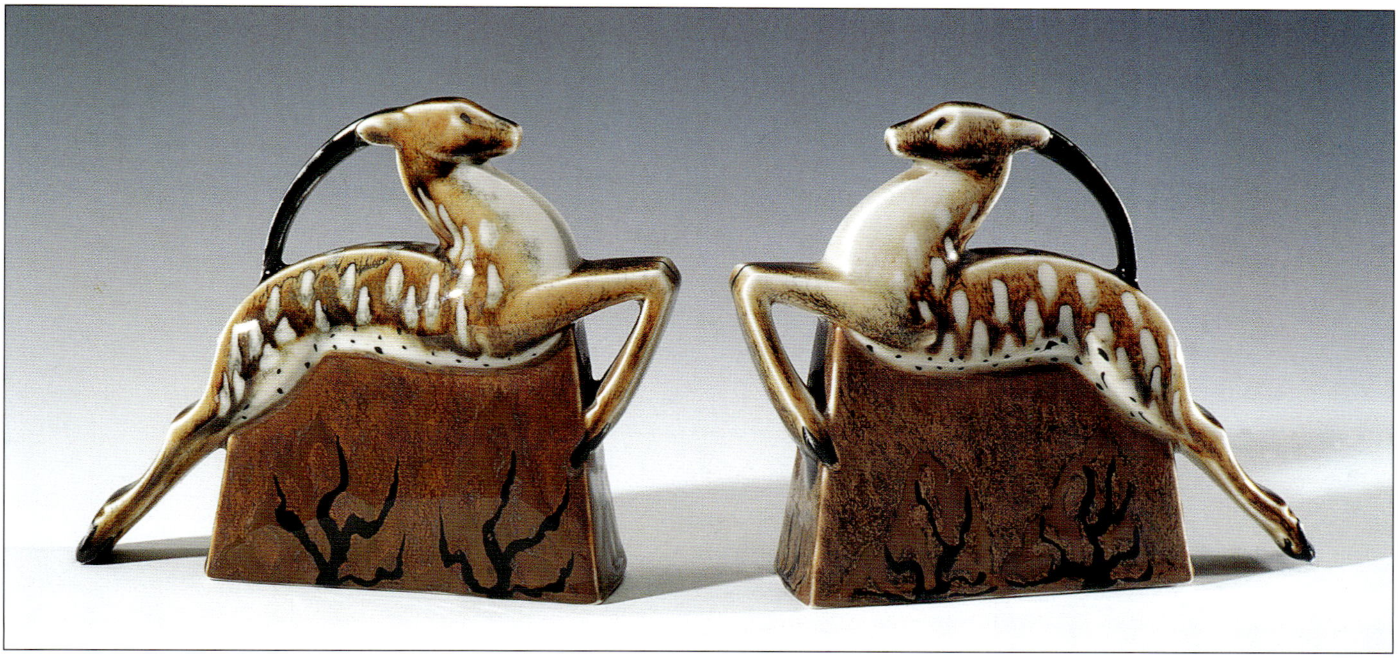

Gazelle bookends, 7.5" x 10" diagonal high, 1928-1930, part of a series of African or country animals produced by Camille Tharaud. The designs and shapes are much more original than those done by his contemporaries. One of the best decorated sets of these bookends. $1,000-$1,500.

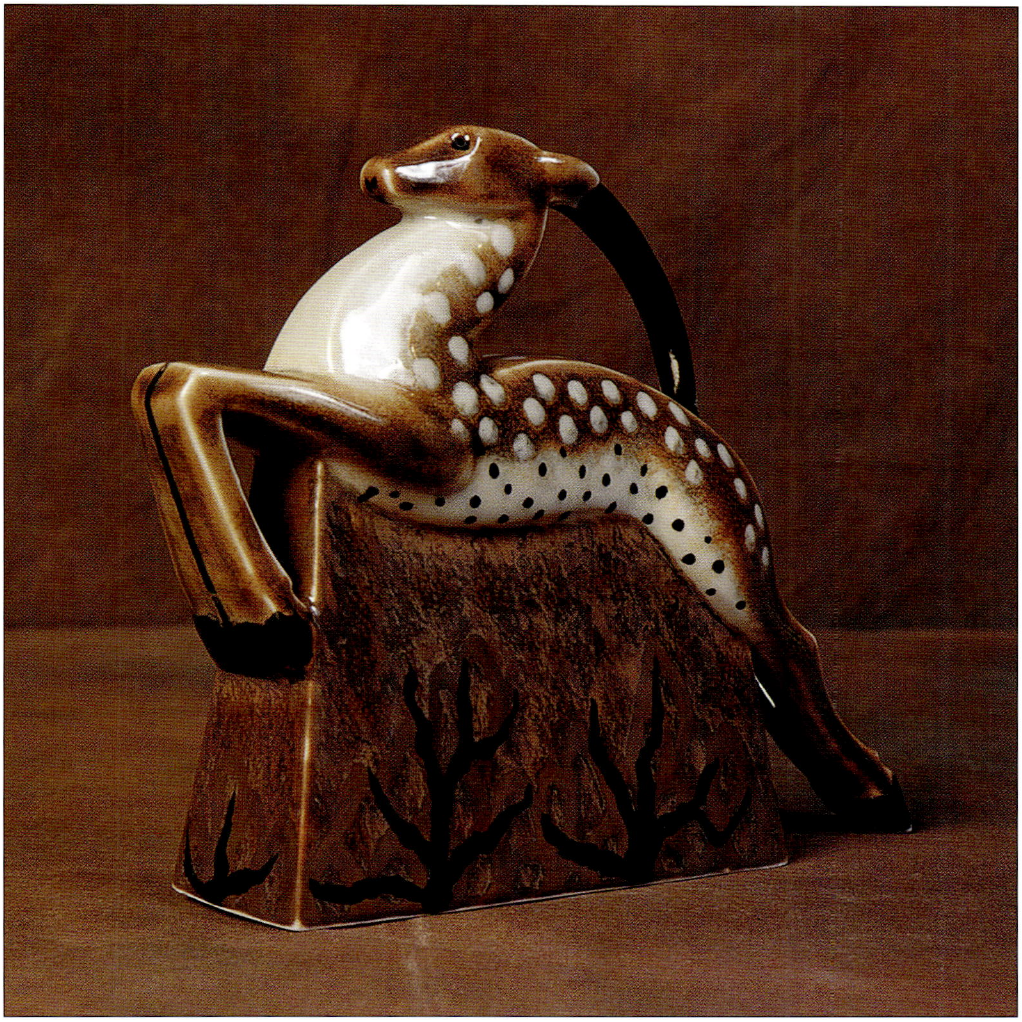

Gazelle nightlight, 7.5" high x 10" diagonal, 1928-1930, very well decorated. $500-$1,000.

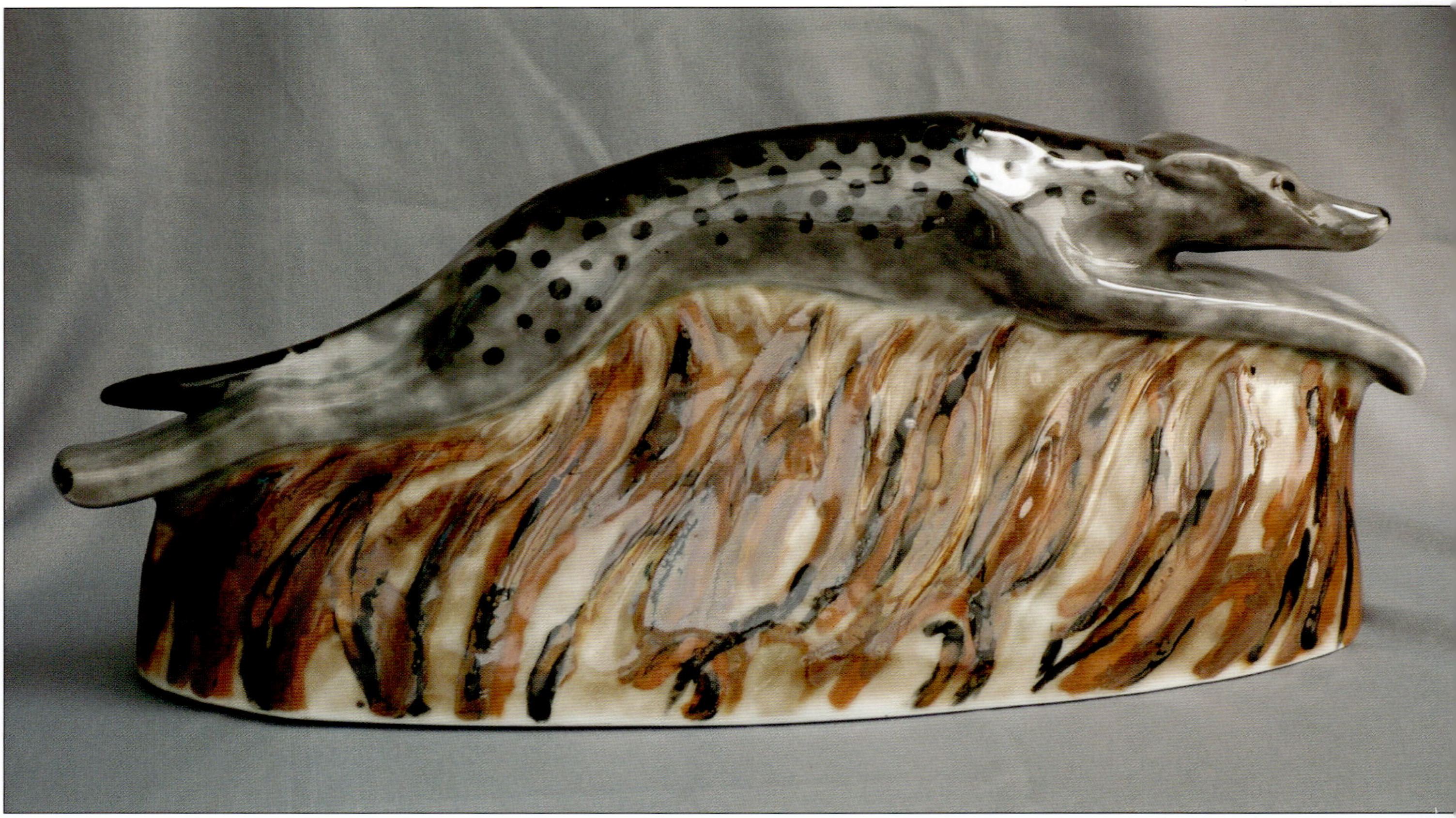

Greyhound nightlight, 13" wide, very well decorated. $1,000-$1,500.

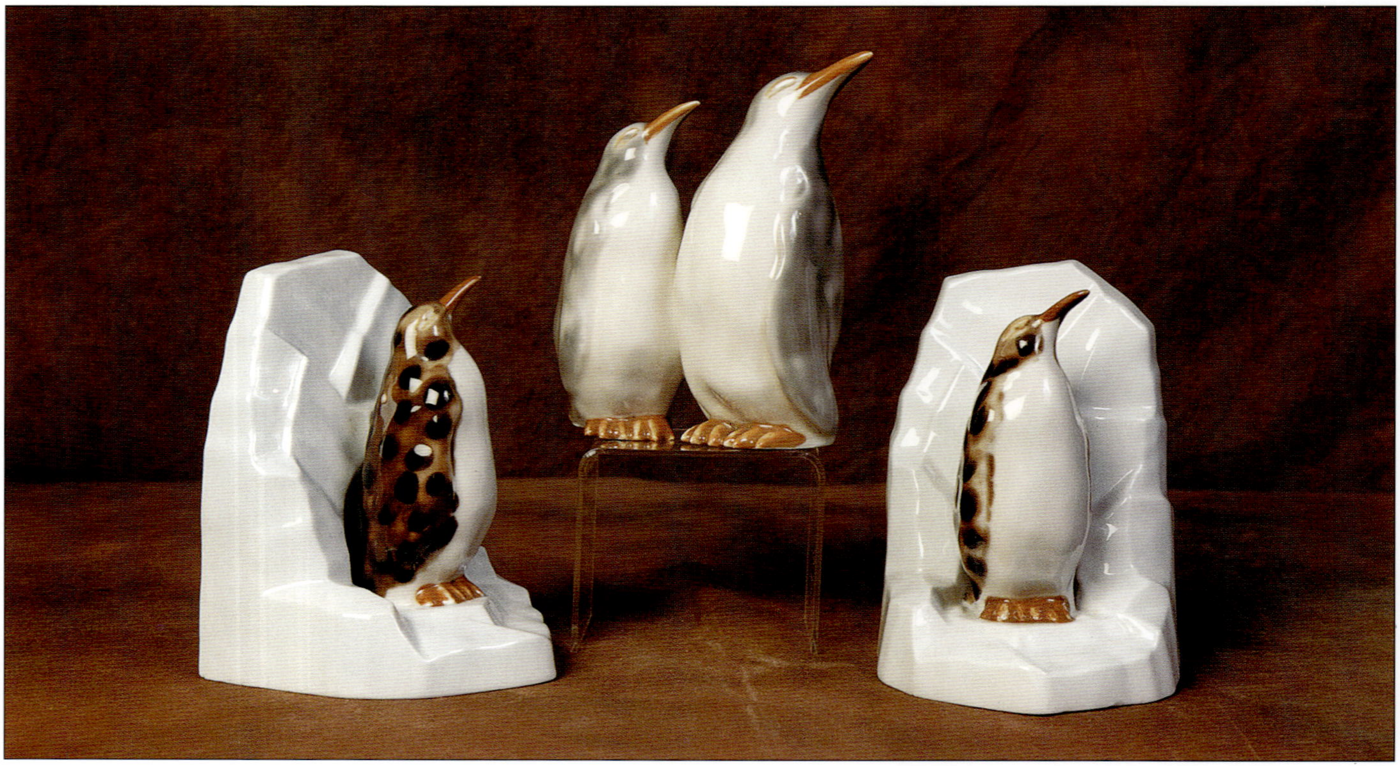

Penguin nightlight and bookends, model of Camille Tharaud (Ferrer); nightlight, 6" high, about 1927; and bookends, 6" high, 1928-1930, both *sous émail* decoration. Nightlight and set of bookends, each $500-$1,500.

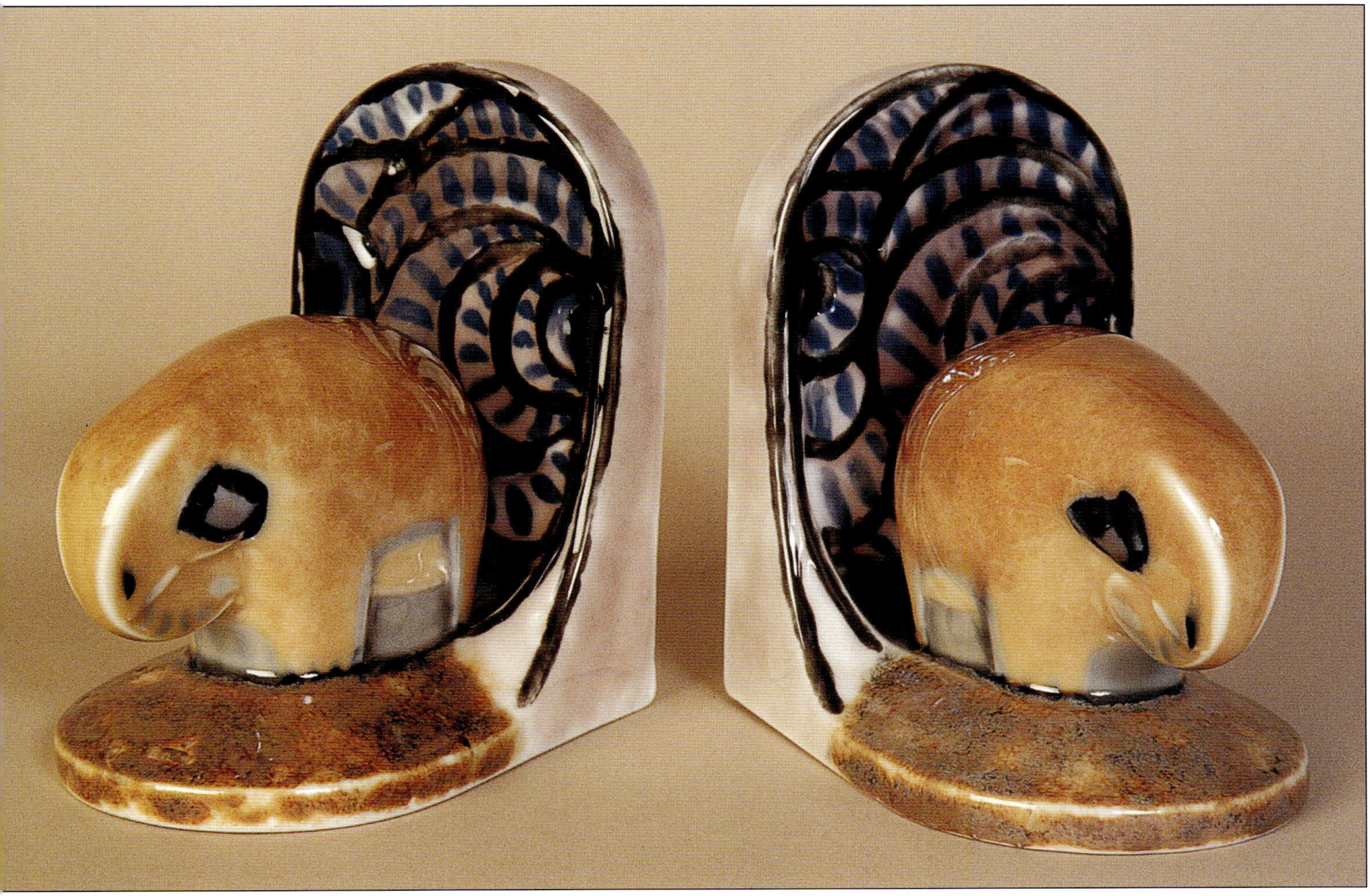

Elephant bookends, 4.75" high x 4.6" x 3.6", 1928-1930. A jungle is depicted Art Deco style behind the elephants. $500-$1,000.

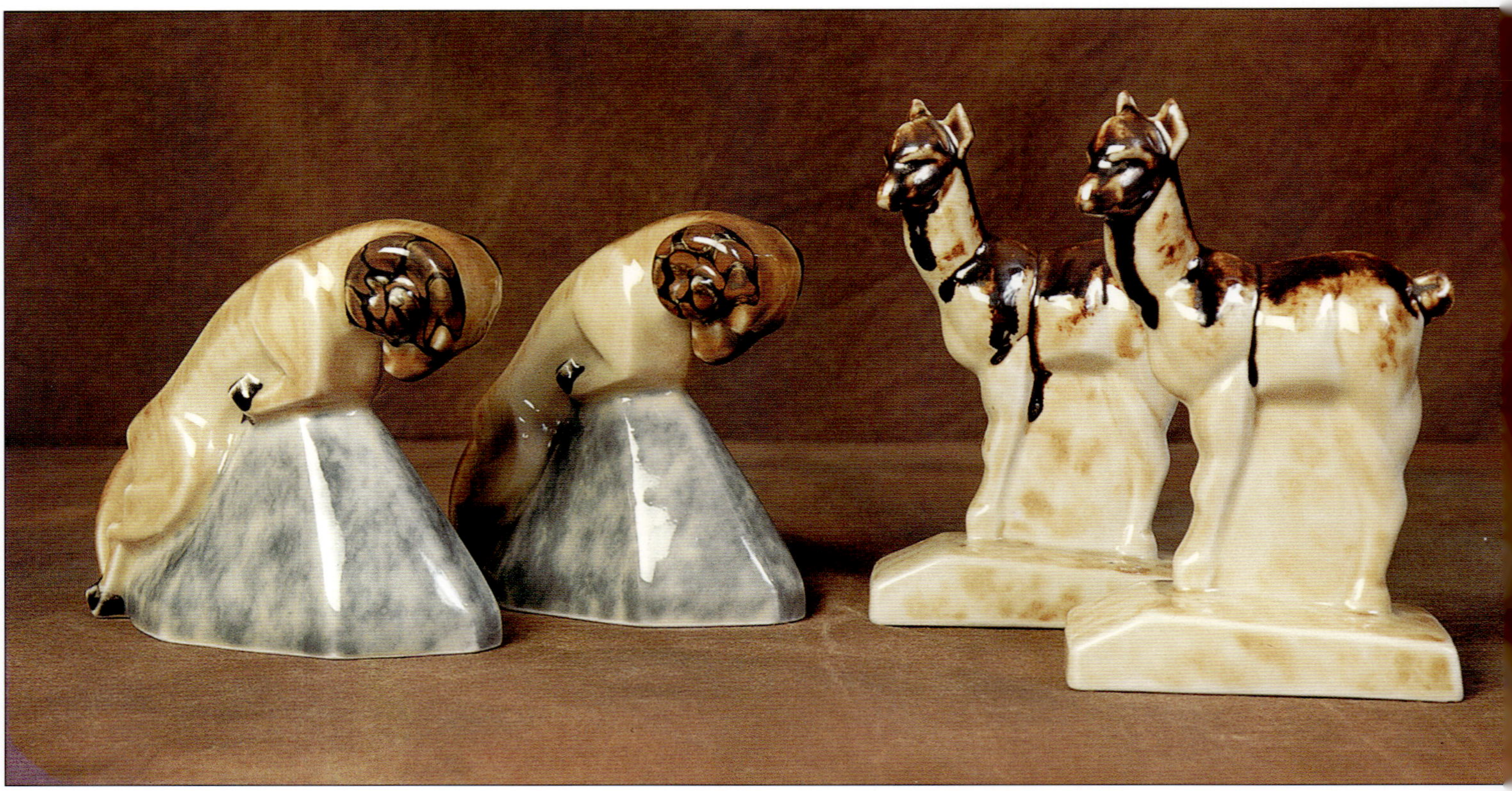

Ram and goat bookends; rams, left, 5" high x 7.25" diagonal, 1928-1930 and goats, right, 6" high, 1930-1945. Each set, $500-$1,000.

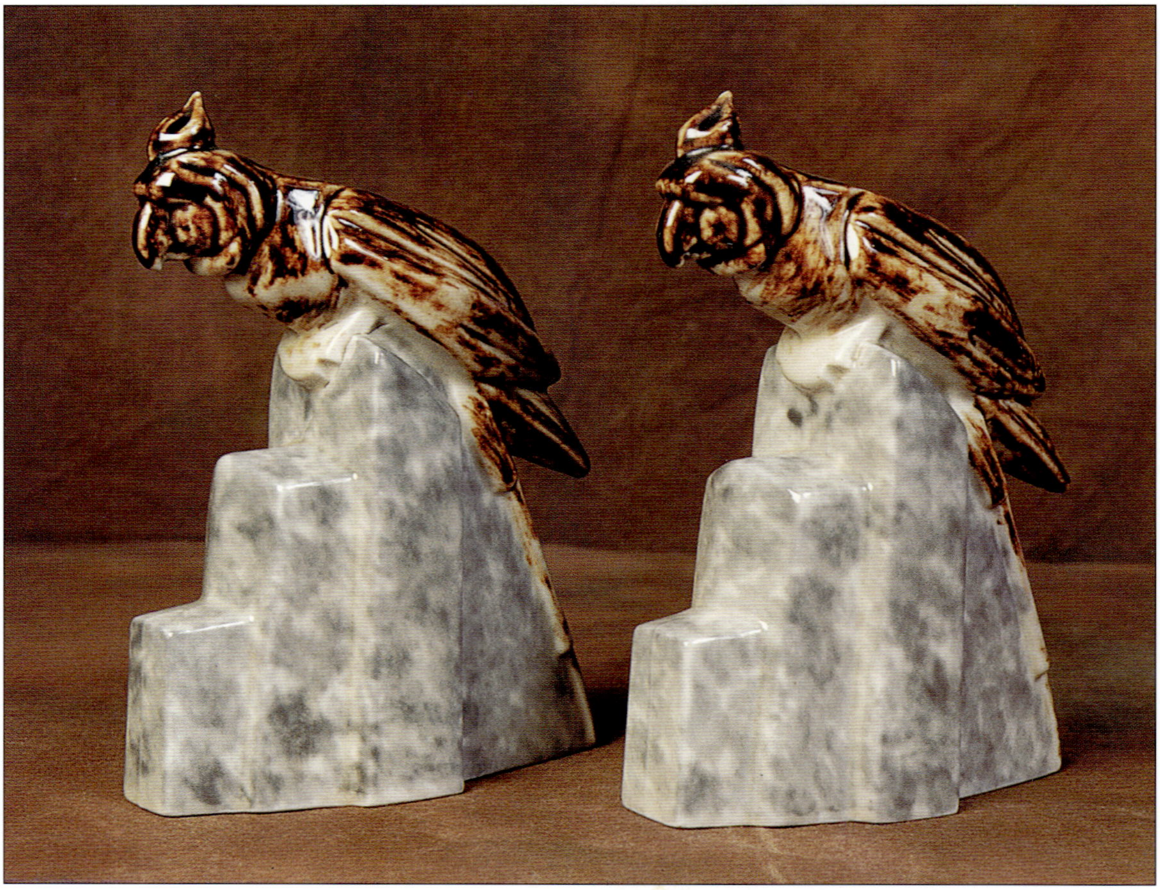

Parrot bookends, 7.5" high, about 1930. $500-$1,000.

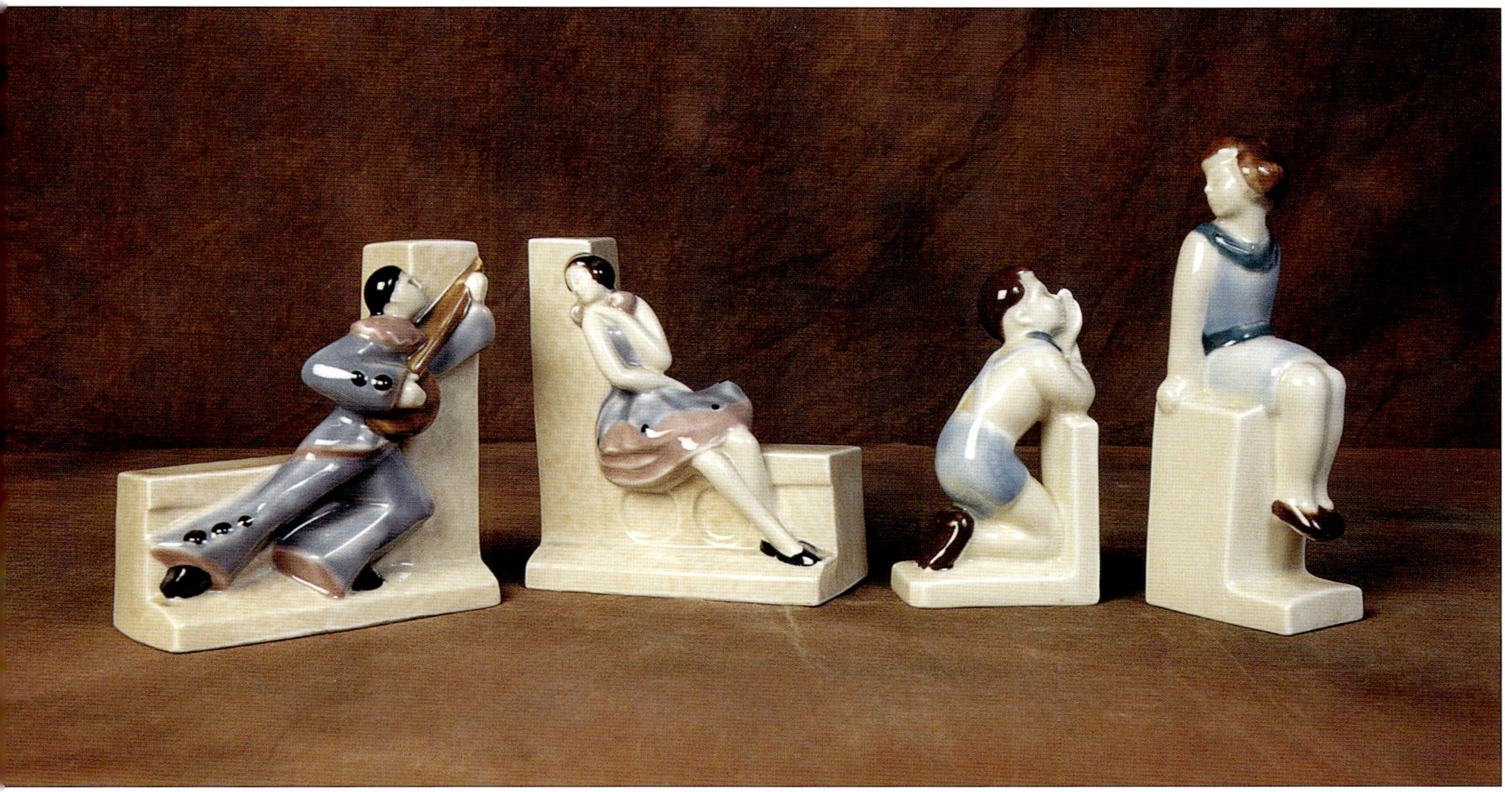

Colombin, Colombine bookends, left, about 1930, and *Confidences* bookends, right, about 1929. $500-$1,000.

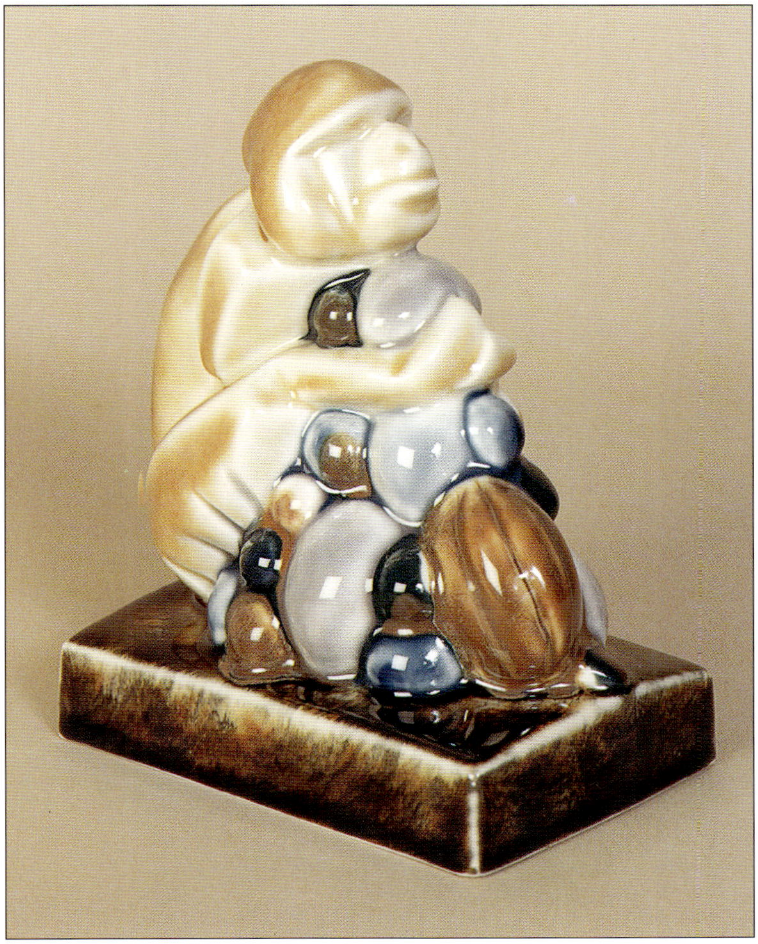

Monkey bookend, 6.6" high x 5.25", 1928-1930. $500-$1,000 for set of two.

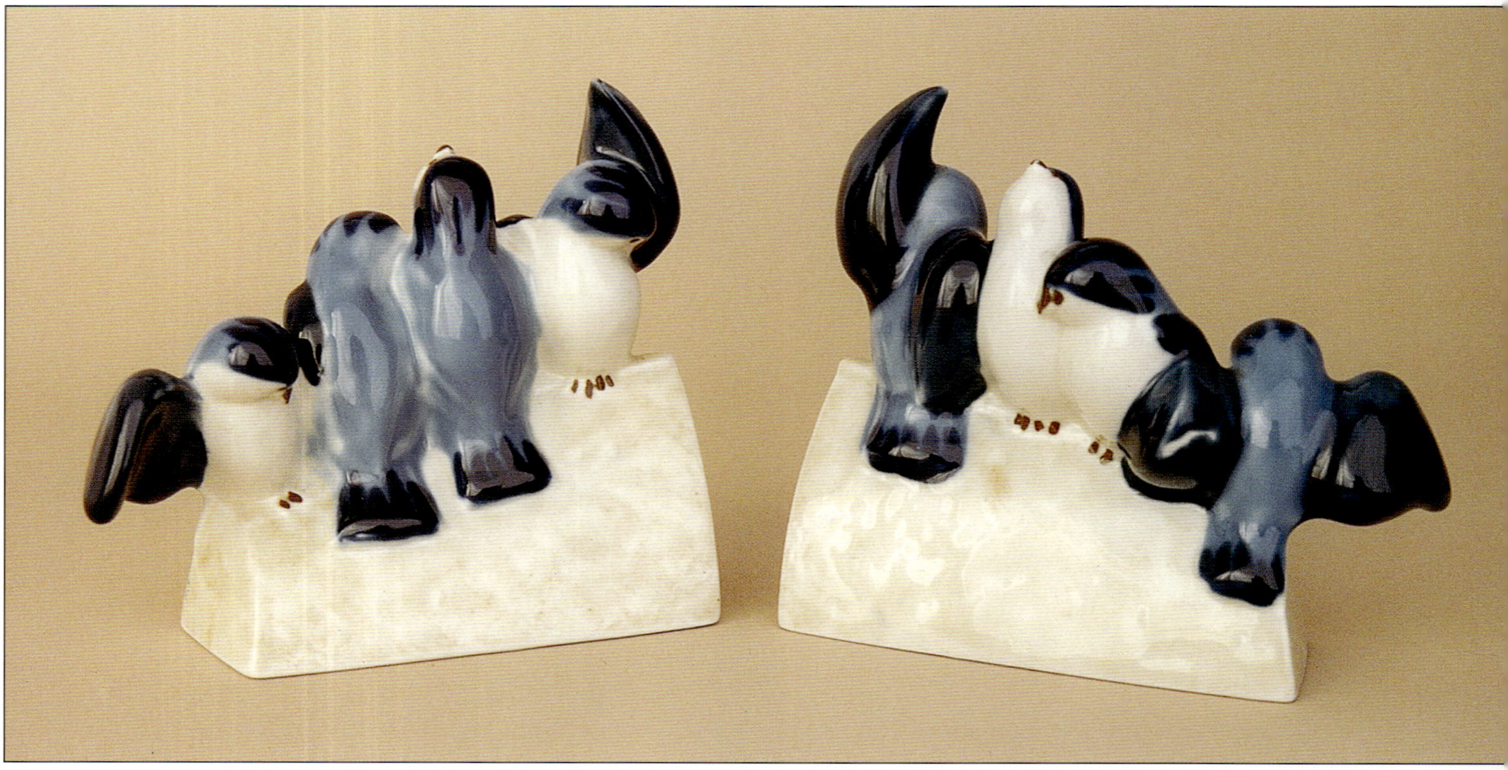

Bird bookends, 5.75" high x 6", around 1930. $500-$1,000.

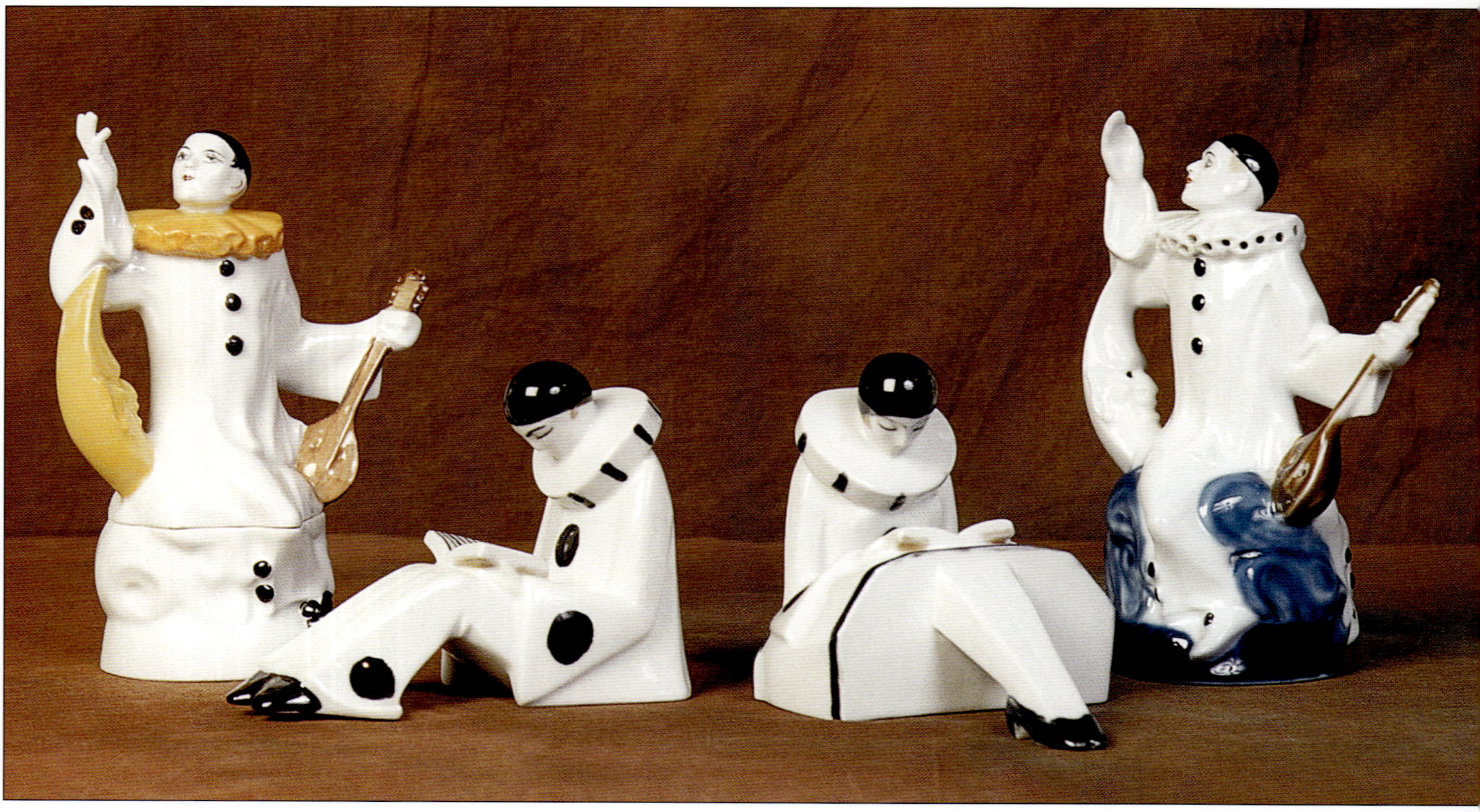

Pierrot bookends, center, 5" high x 6.75", 1928-1930; pierrot box, 8" high, after 1943; and pierrot nightlight, 8.25" high, after 1943. Box less than $500; bookends, $500-$1,000; nightlight, $500-$1,000.

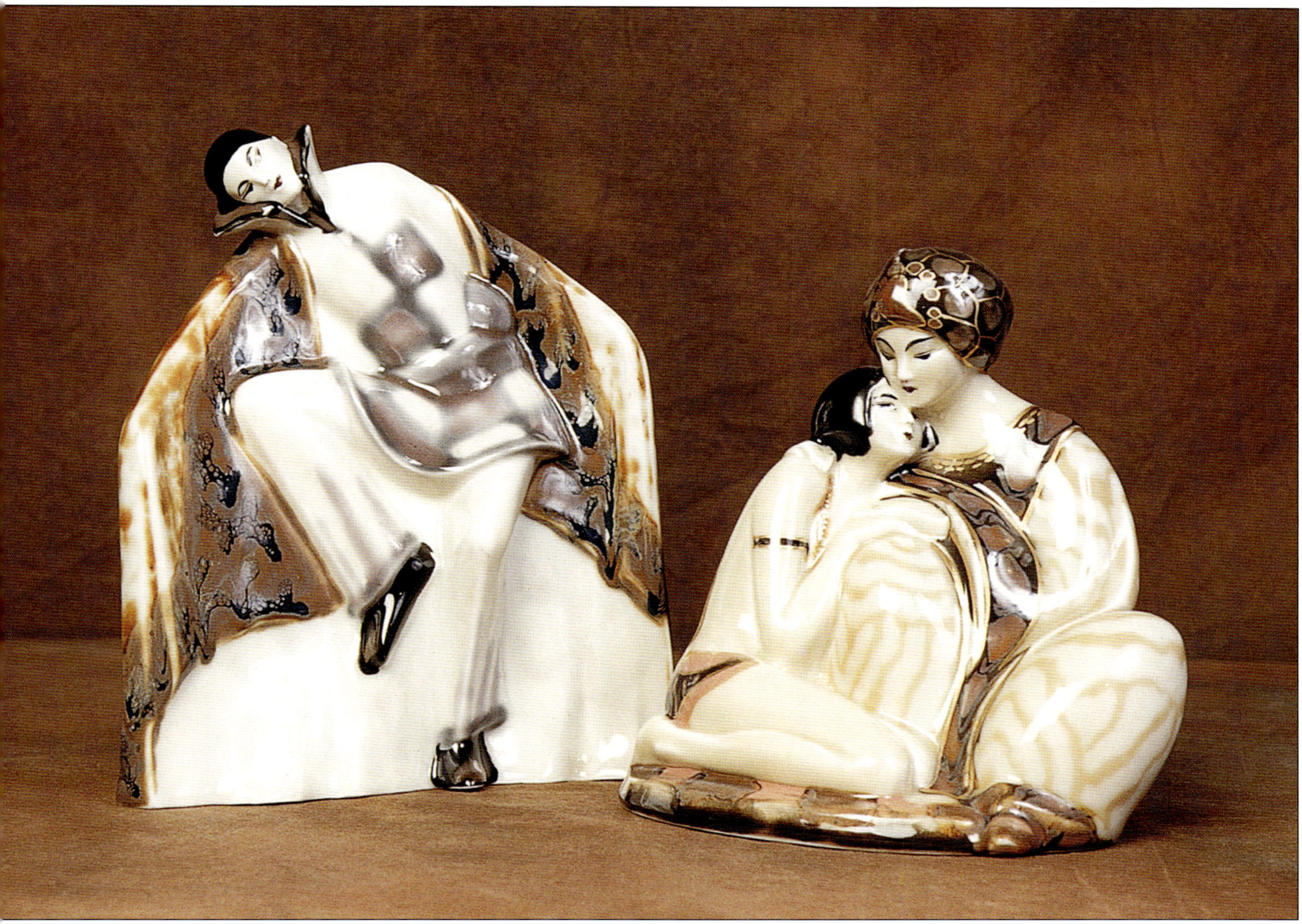

Nightlights, left, one of a set of two nightlights from *Pierrot et Colombine*, 9.25" high, about 1930 and right, *Sultan-Sultane*, 7.5" high, about 1930; the shape created about 1927. (Ferrer) Left, $500-$1,000 and right, $500-$1,000.

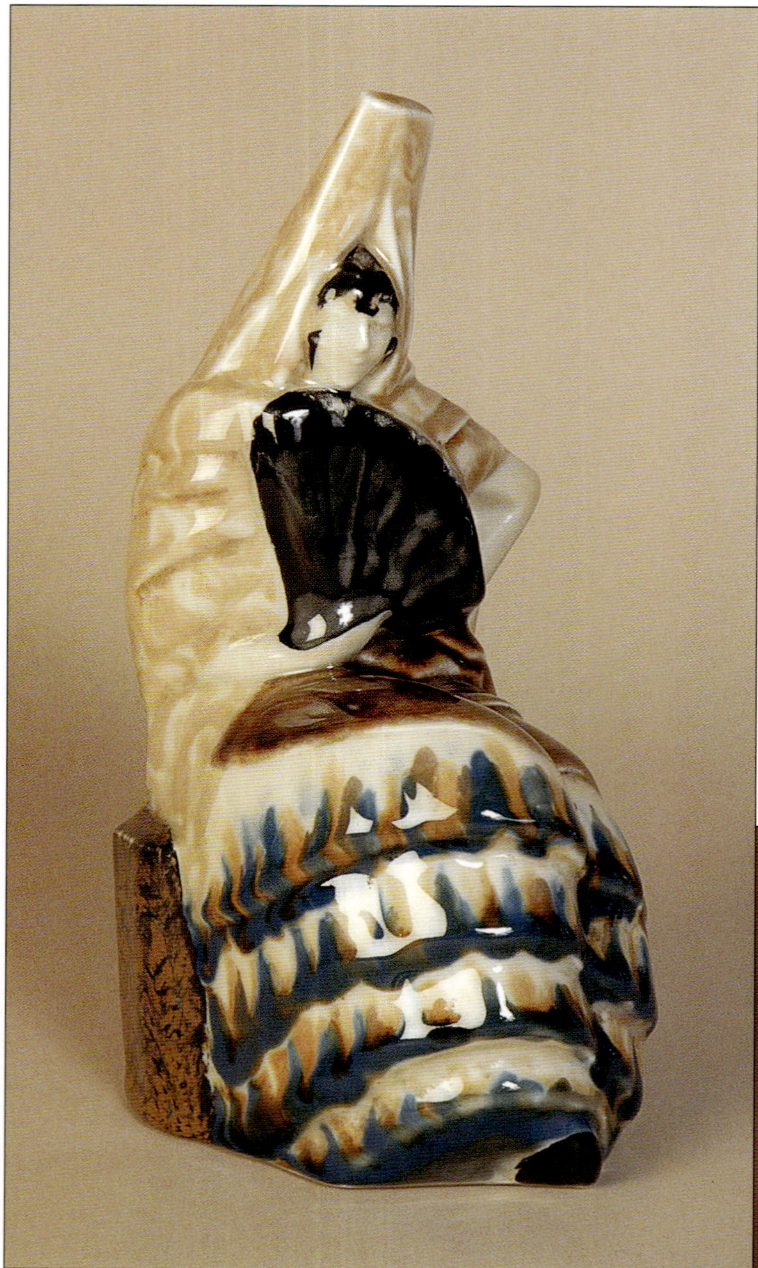

Nightlight, Spanish flamenco dancer with a mantilla, 10" high, about 1929. $500-$1,000.

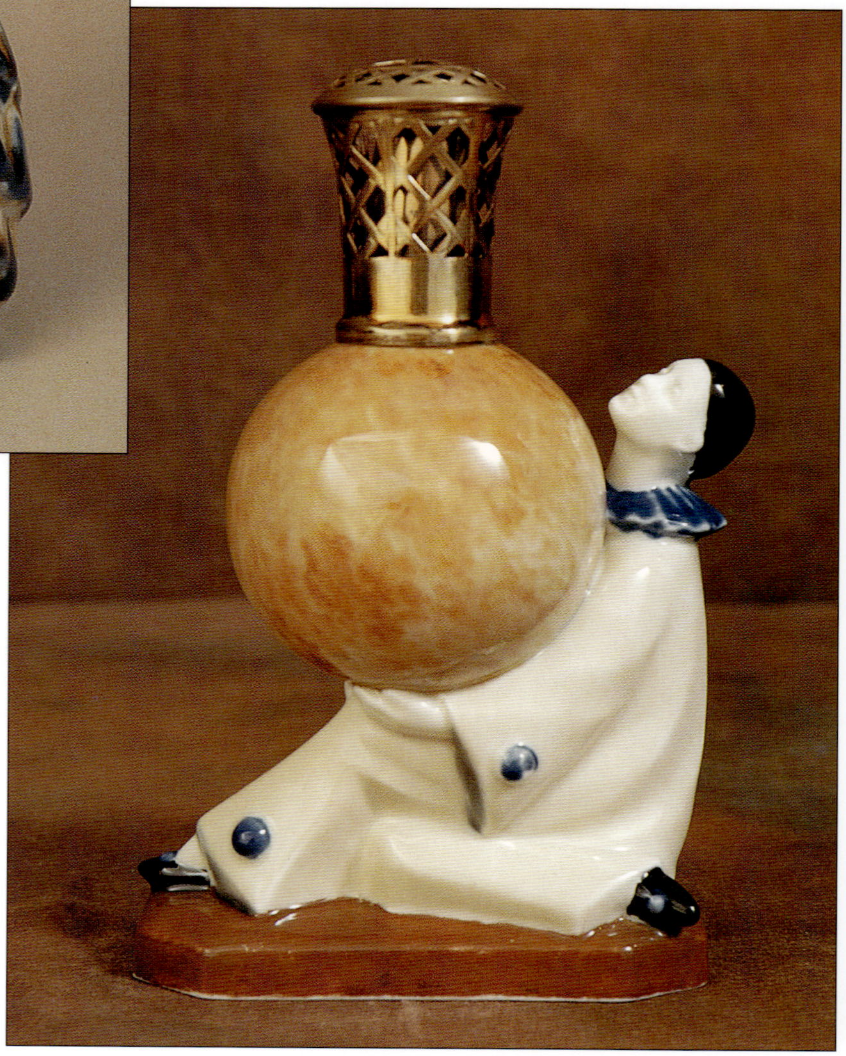

Lamp Berger *Pierrot*, 8.5" high, original lamp about 1930. This piece decorated many years later. $1,000-$1,500.

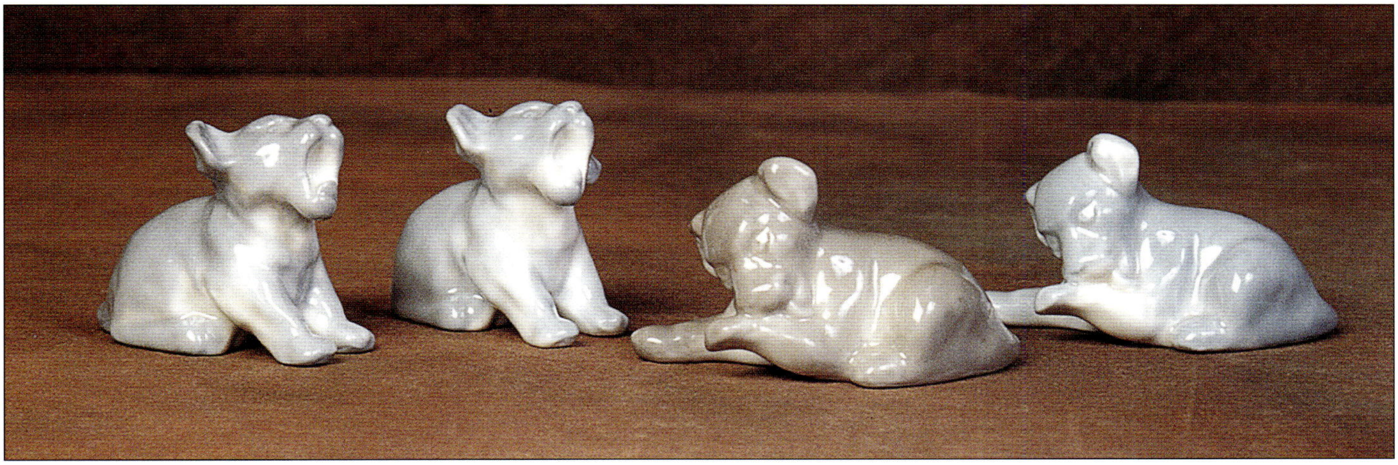

Puppies, gray and platinum *sous émail*, about 1930. Each less than $500.

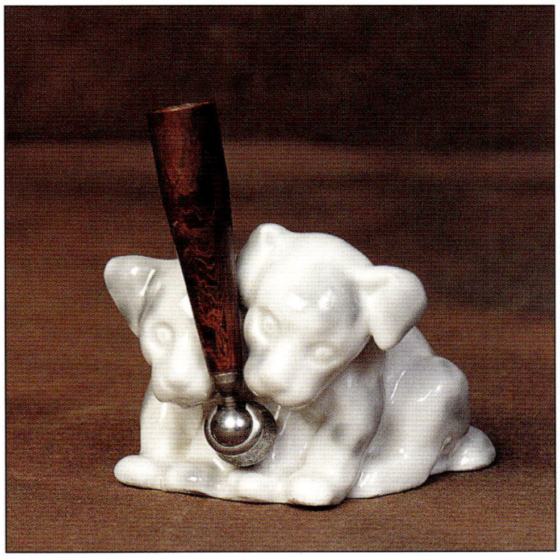

Puppies pen holder, gray *sous émail*, about 1930. Less than $500.

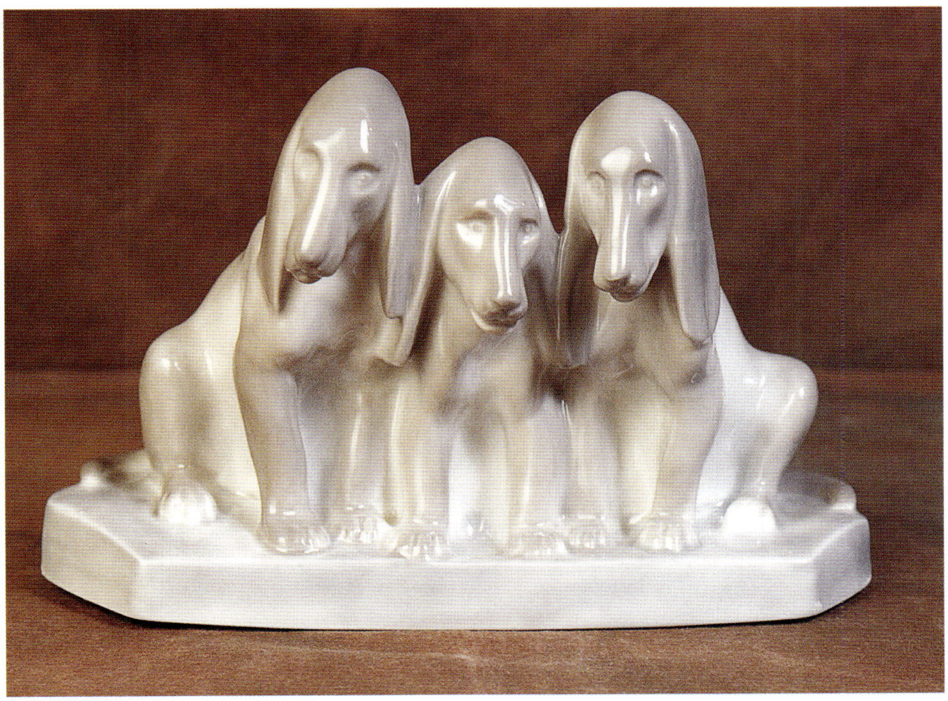

Dogs, 6.75" high x 10.5", 1928-1930, decorated *sous émail* with gray and platinum. $1,000-$1,500.

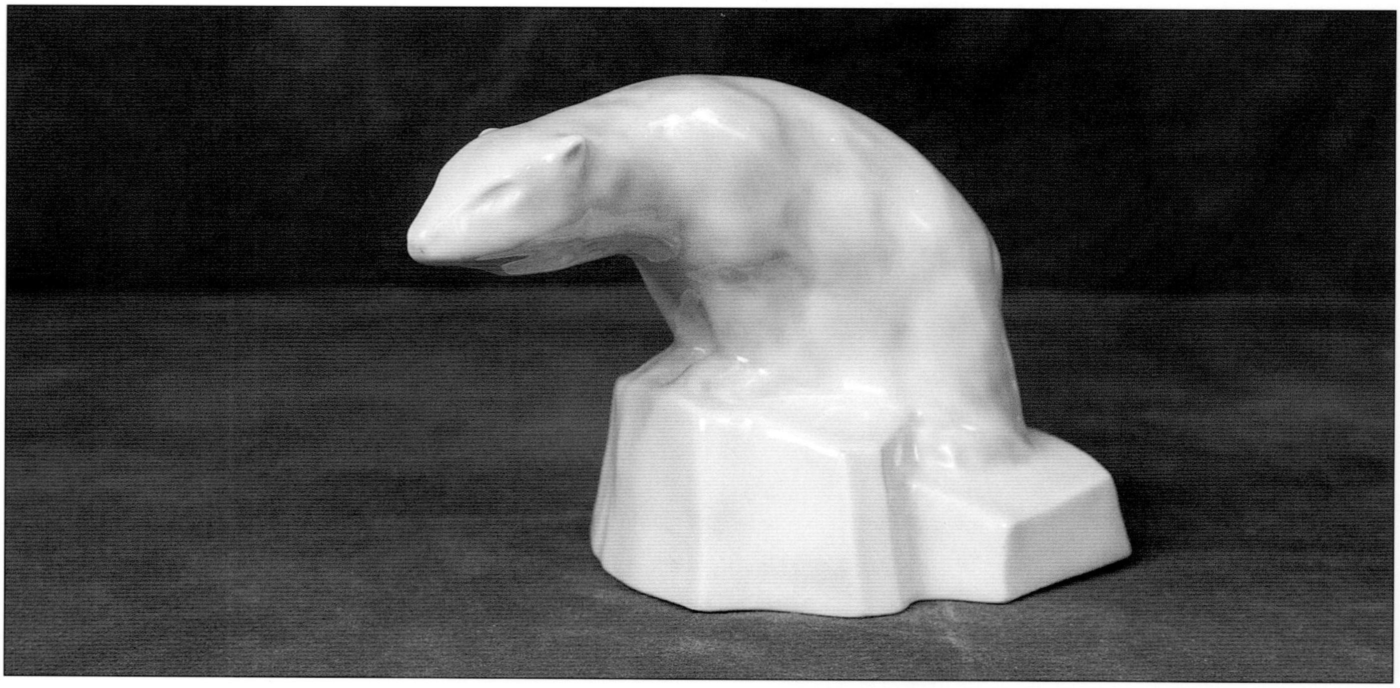

Polar bear, 5" high x 8" diagonal, probably about 1930 or before. $500-$1,000.

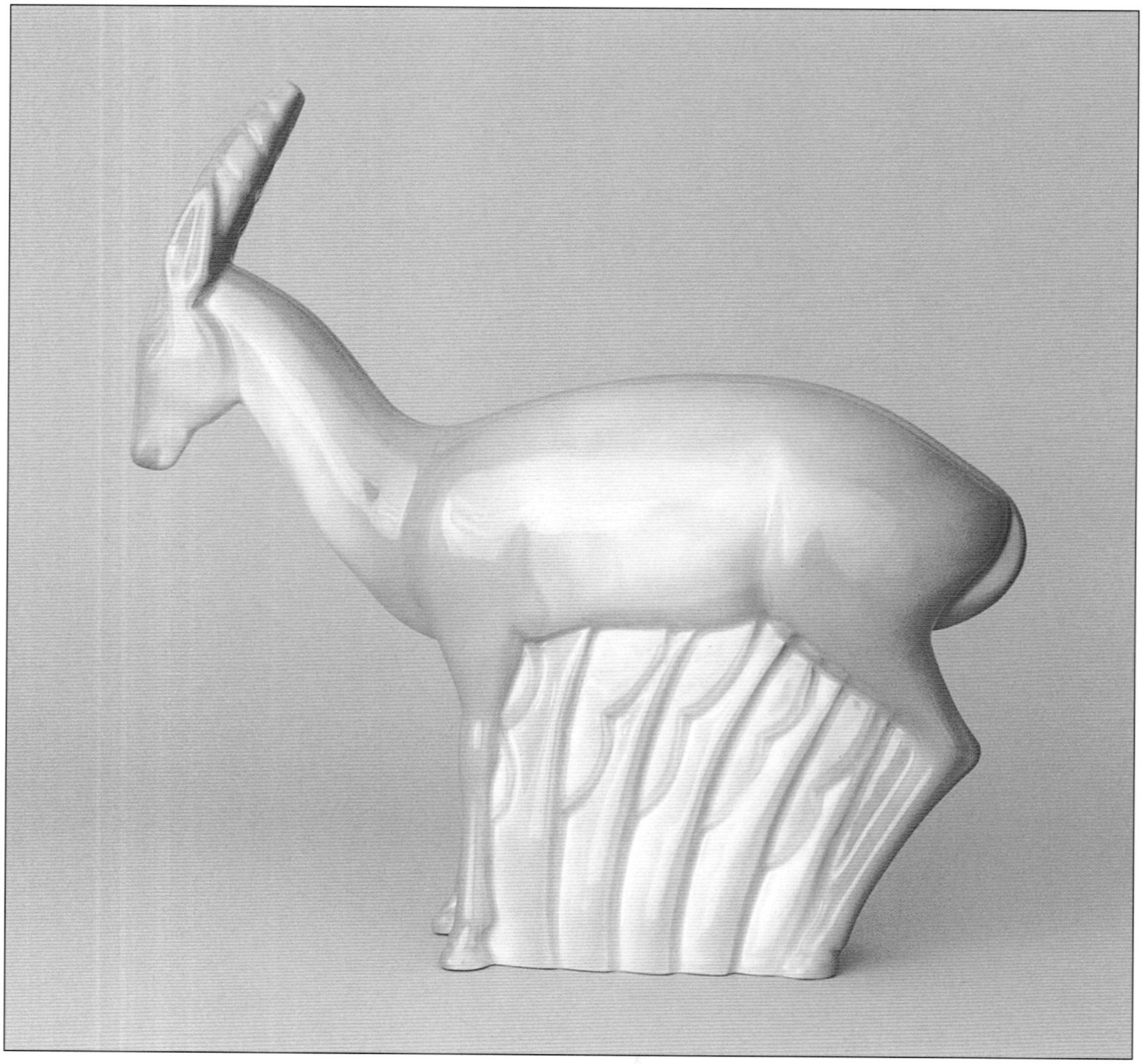

Gazelle, 6.25" high x 8", about 1930. $500-$1,000.

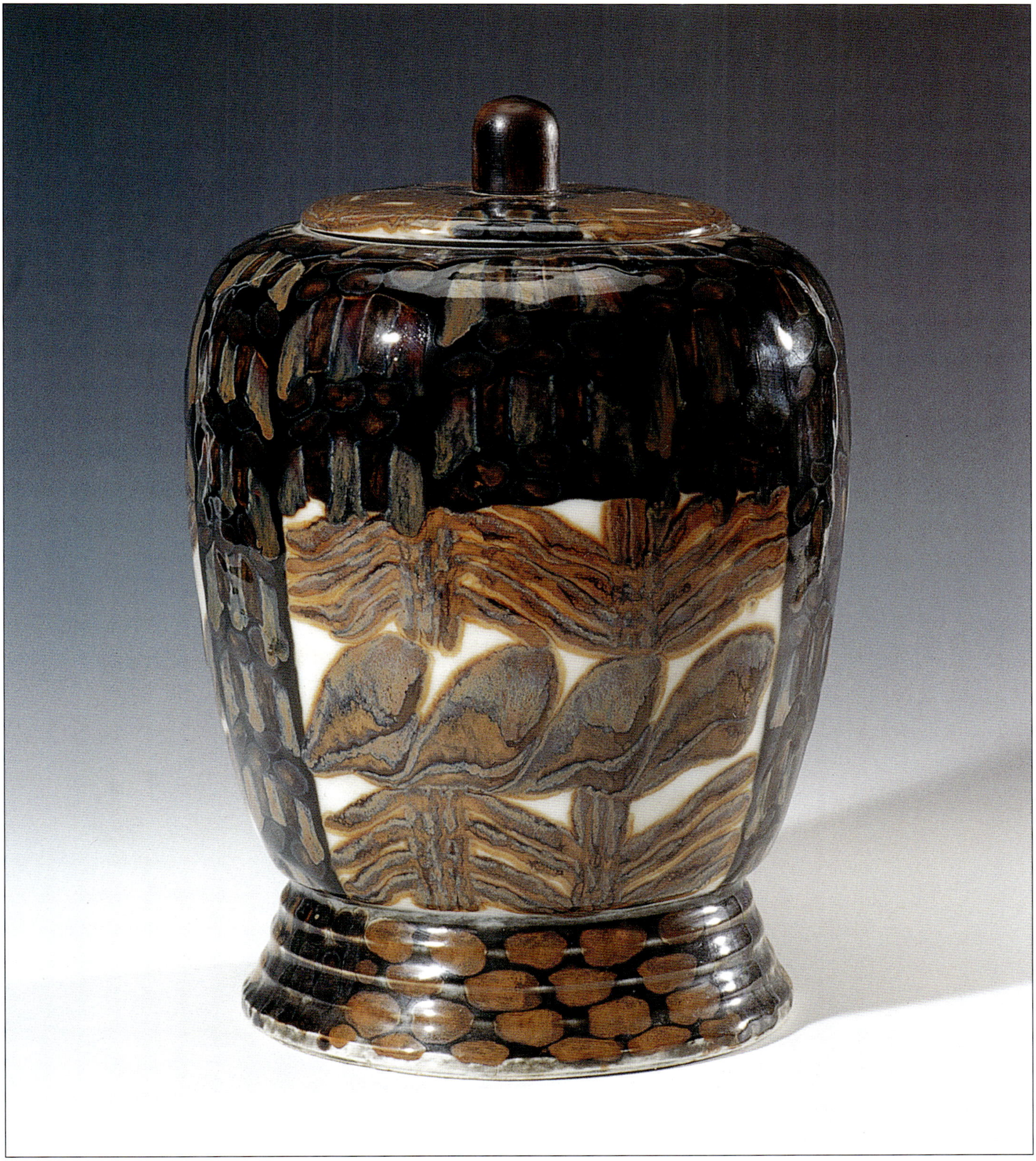

Vase with wooden finial, *Thaïs*, shape by Henri Rapin, 12.25" high, incised with the marks of Camille Tharaud for the decoration and Henri Rapin for the shape. The *Thaïs* shape was inspired by the 1884 opera of the same name by Jules Massenet and was displayed at the Salon des artistes décorateurs, Paris, 1928. It was greatly admired with the juxtaposition of the two different shades of brown. The base of the enamel is magnesium. (Ferrer) $1,000-$1,500.

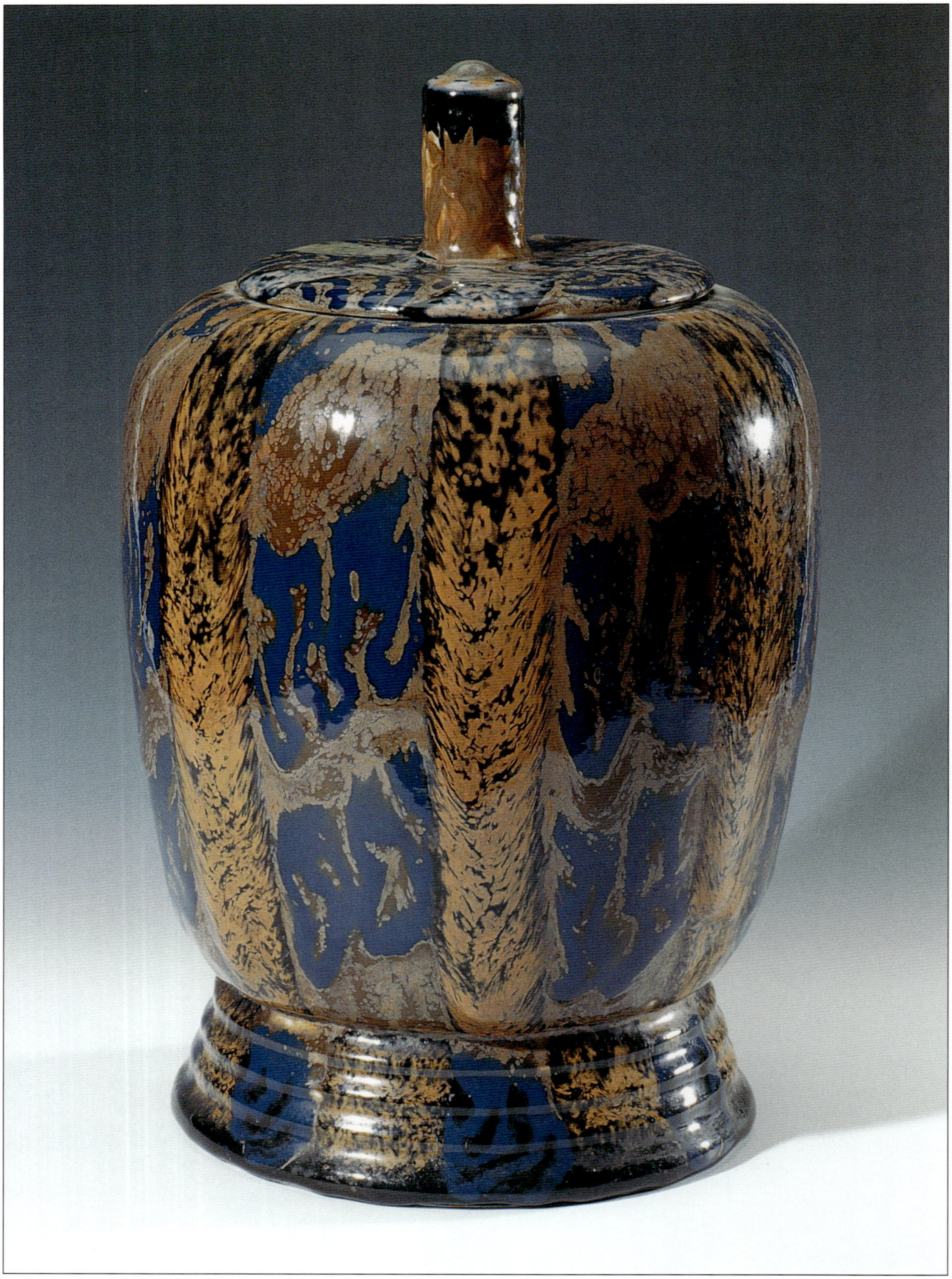

Covered vase, *Thaïs*, 16.5" high, incised marks of Camille Tharaud and Henry Rapin. Vase was decorated by Henri Rapin according to Odette [Tharaud] Goumot-Labesse and exhibited at the Salon des artistes décorateurs, Paris, 1928, where it received an "exceptional" award. The decoration is a good example of Tharaud's "effets de matière." The cobalt is painted under the glaze, *sous émail*. The enamels are painted directly on the cobalt, and the atmospheric firing altered the enamels on the surface and gave them a look of semi-precious stones. The decoration has an unexpected look from the colorations and the materials. During the firing the cobalt and the enamels mix together due to the lead in the cobalt. $1,500-$2,000.

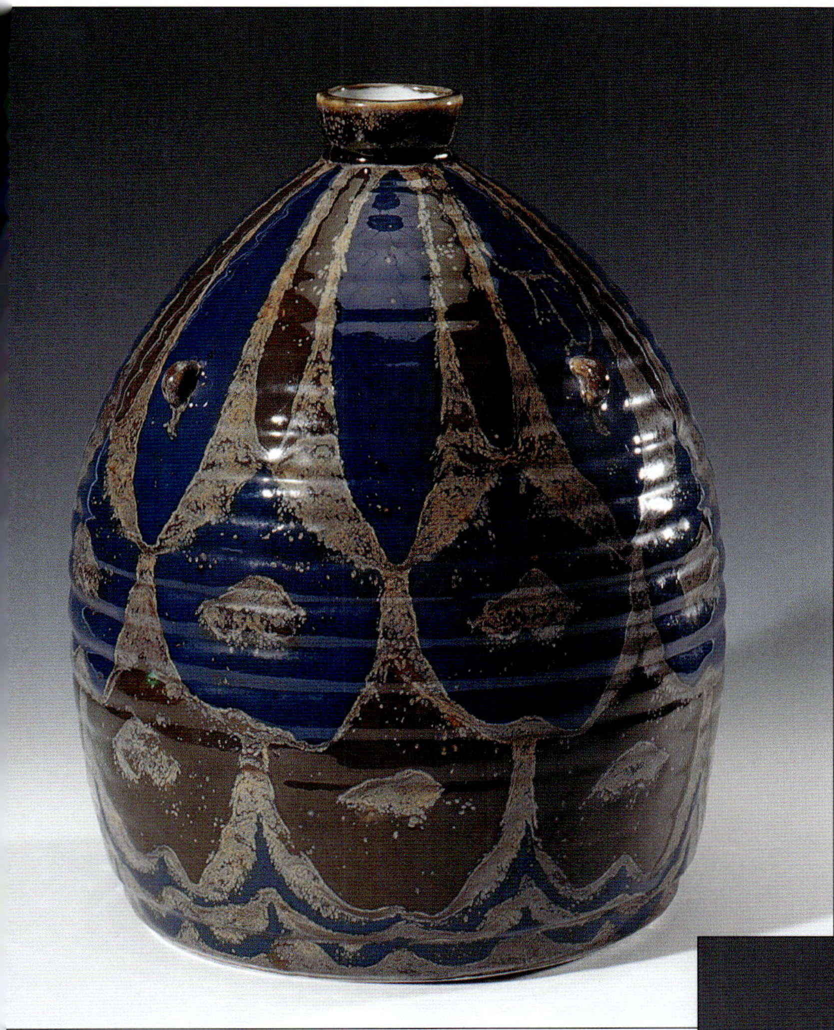

Rare vase, *Ruche*, in the shape of a hive, 14.25" high, decoration represents the collaboration between Camille Tharaud and Henri Rapin, 1929. (Ferrer) $1,000-$1,500.

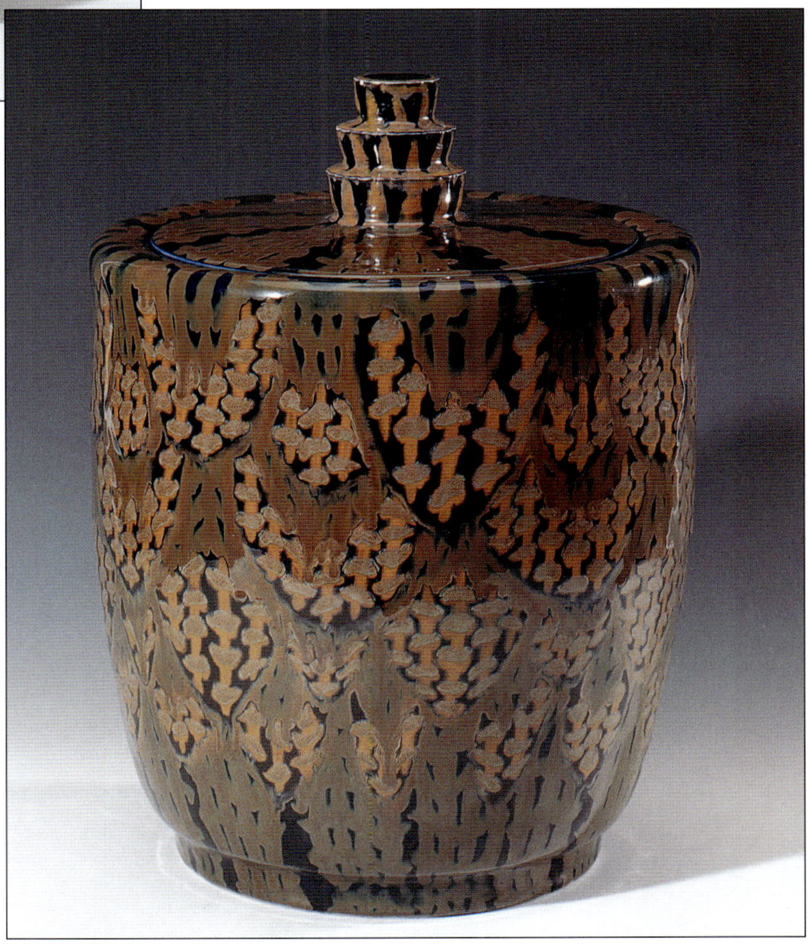

Vase, *Hérodiate*, after the same name of the opera by Jules Massenet, shape of Henri Rapin, 14.25" high, 1928. The decoration was designed by Camille Tharaud. The base is cobalt, *sous émail*, layered with brown enamels containing manganese and titanium oxide. The decoration met with high critical success at the Société d'encouragement à l'art et à l'industrie at the Salon des artistes décorateurs, Paris, 1928. The minister of the Beaux-Arts acquired this piece for the national collection. (Ferrer) $1,000-$1,500.

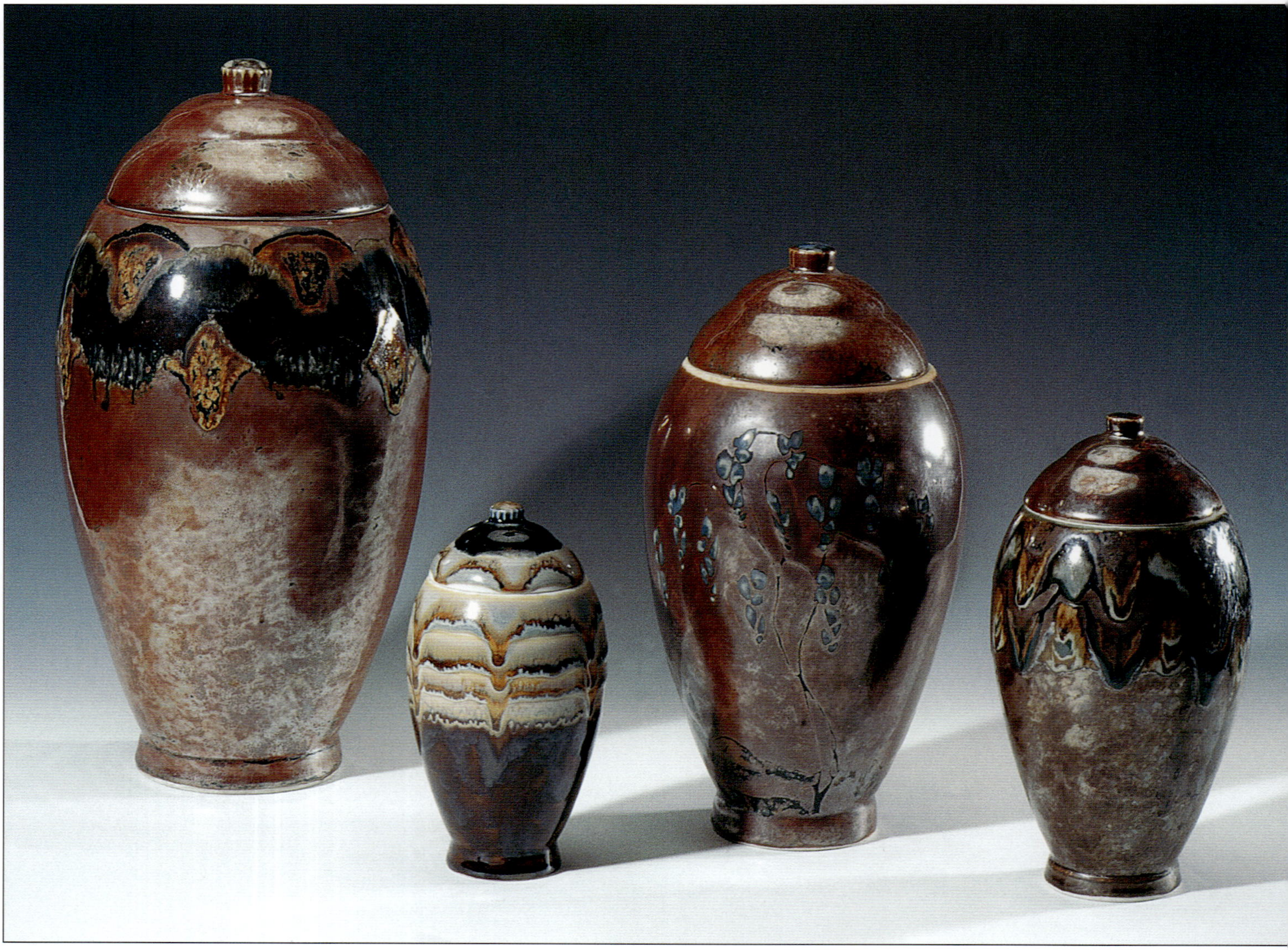

Vases, *Manon*, far left, 1928-1930; all others, 1930-1945. $500-$1,000 each.

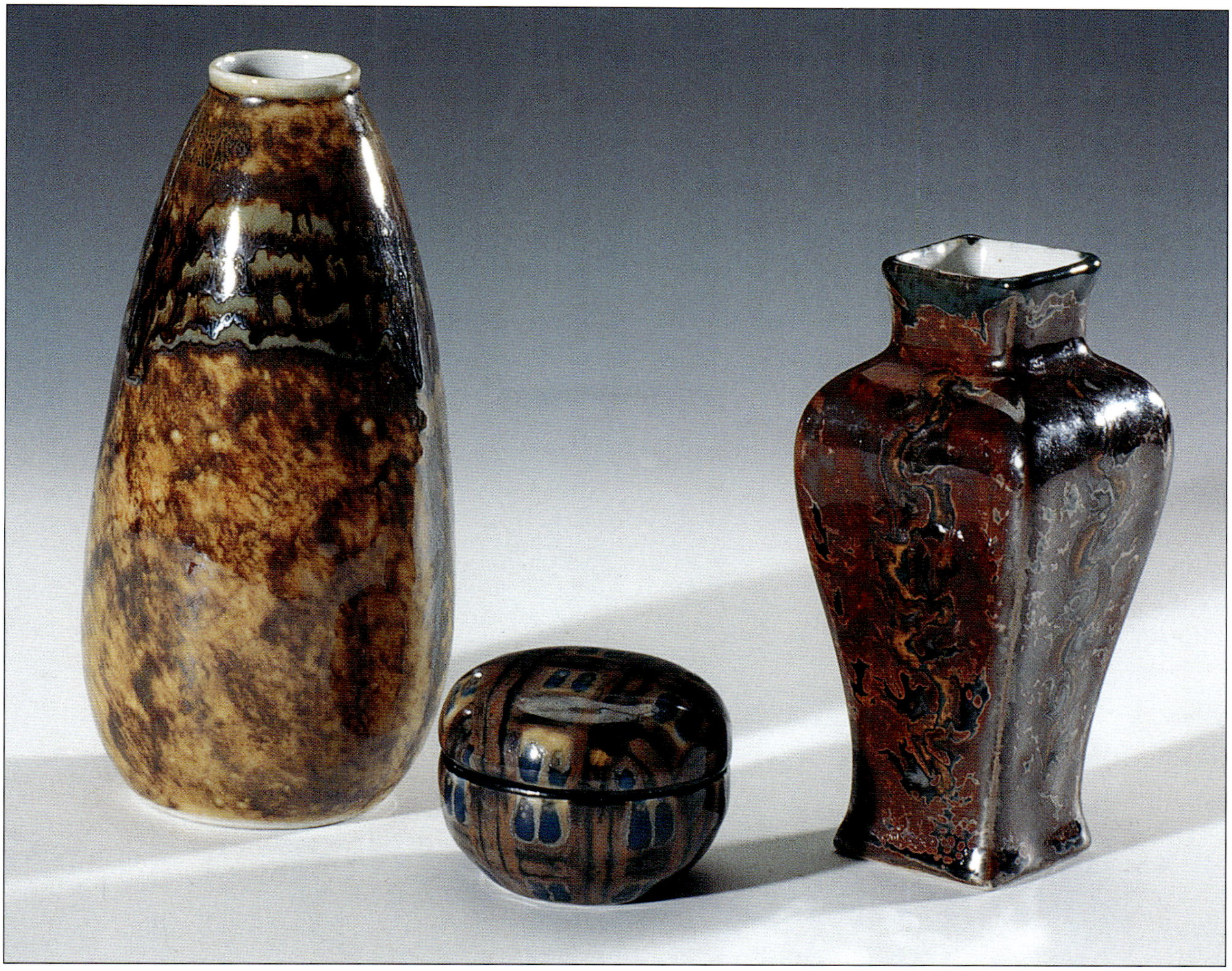

Two vases and lidded box, 6" and 5" high for vases and 2.25" in diameter for lidded box. Tallest vase, on left, 1930-1945; other vase, 1928-1930; and lidded box marked *Th* in black (decoration by Camille Tharaud), 1928-1930. Vases, less than $500 each; lidded box, less than $500.

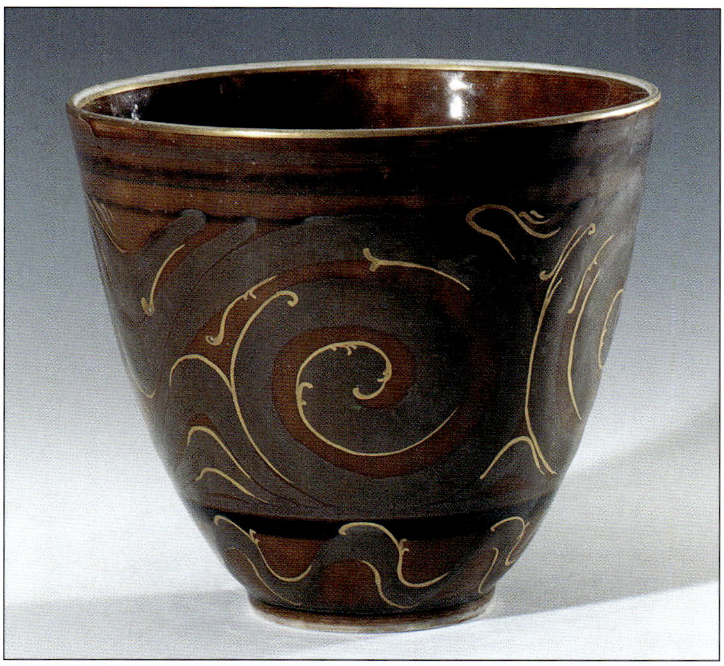

Cup, 7" high, 1928-1930, signed *L. Rav* (Léona Rav). Less than $500.

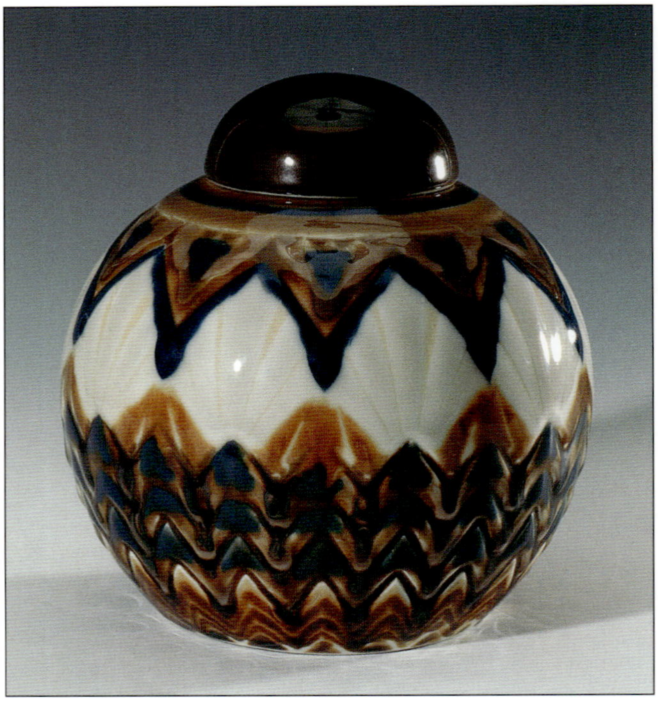

Covered vase, *Huguenot*, shape of Camille Tharaud, 1928-1930, the brown enamel contains lava. $500-$1,000.

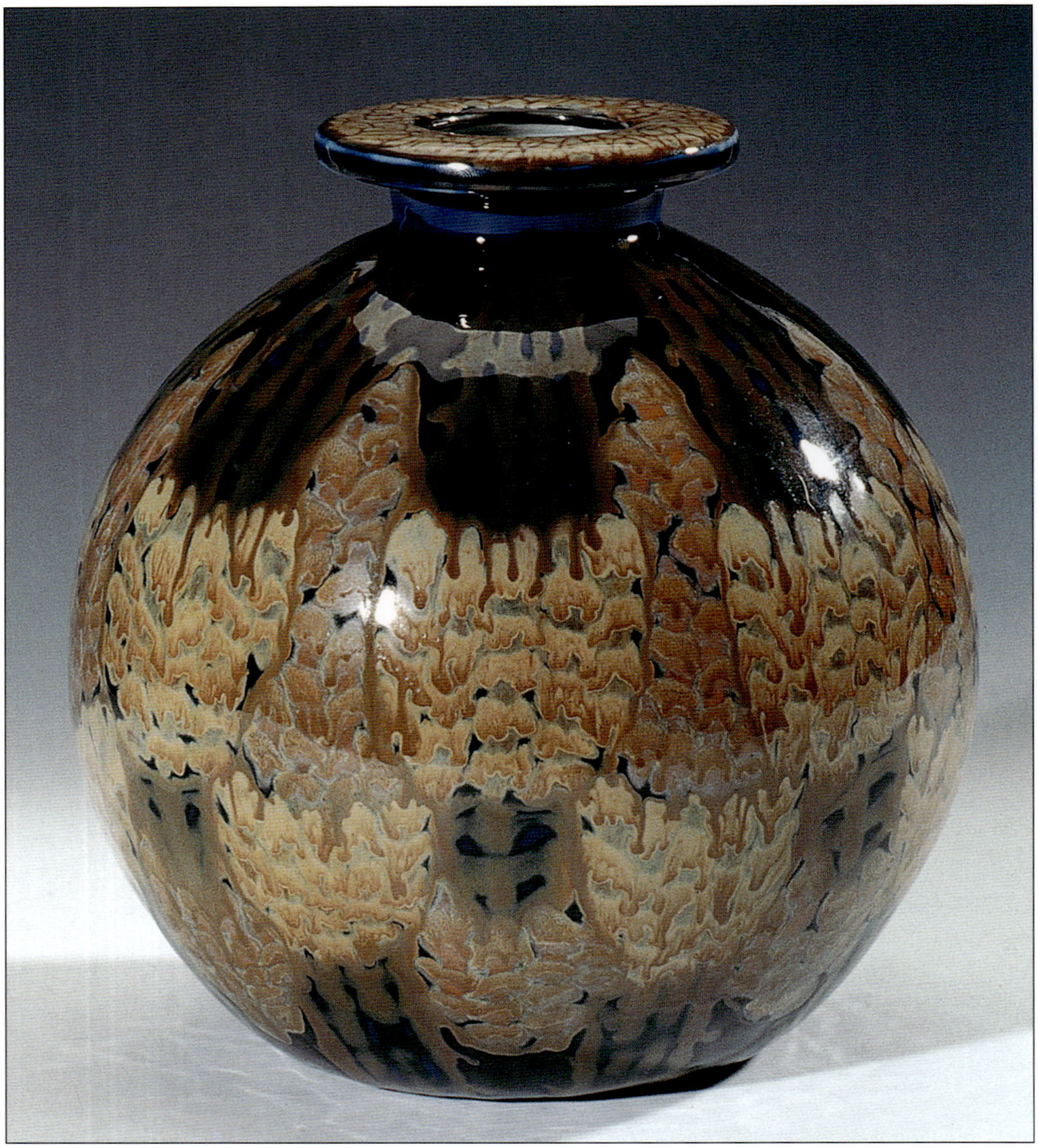

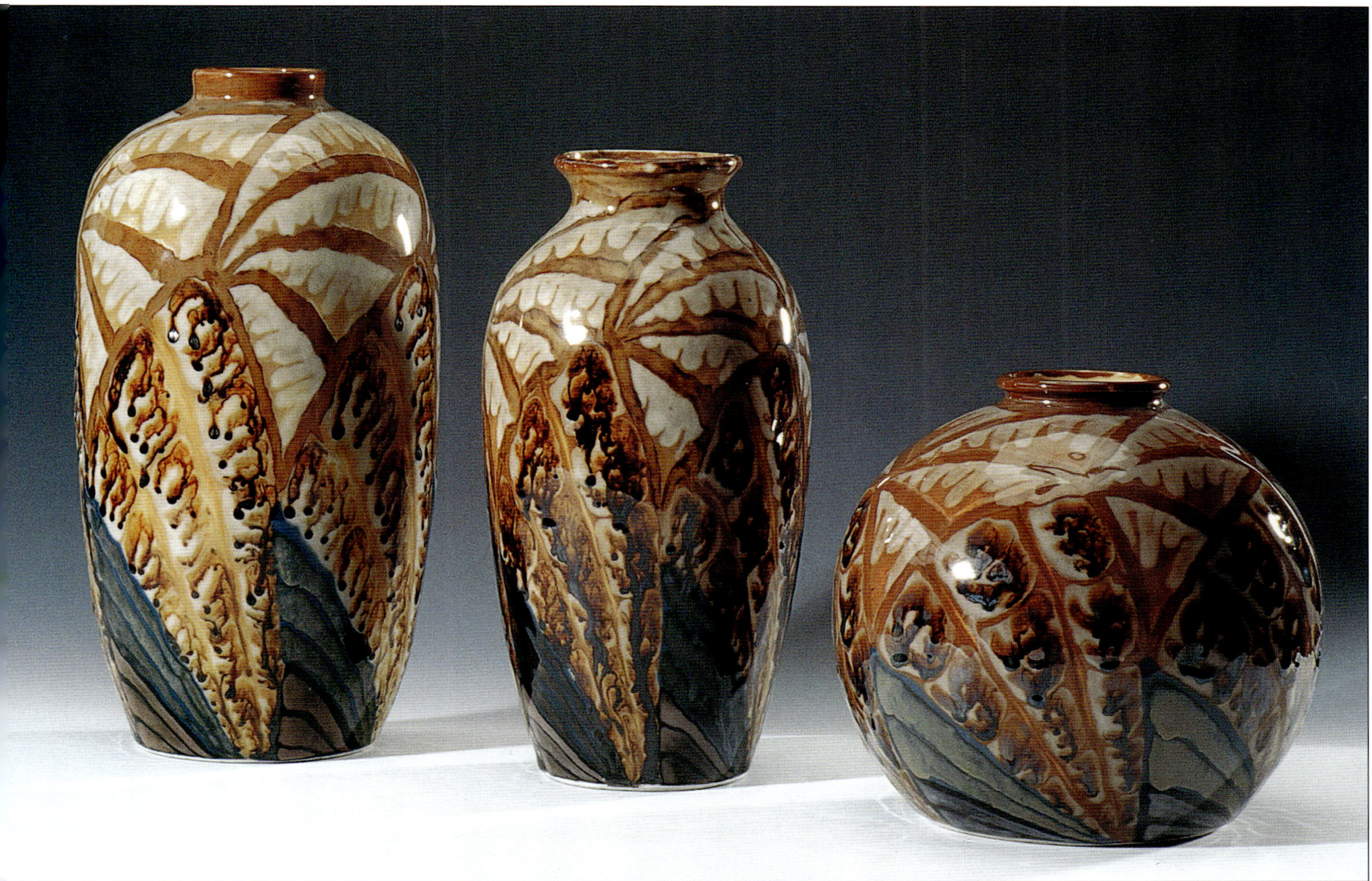

Three *Wings of Butterfly* vases, 11.5", 10.25", and 7". *Wings of Butterfly* decoration used first time in 1930, the lavas from Auvergne were used as a base for the enamels. Each $500-$1,000.

Left:
Vase, *Genêt*, 11" high, marked *M.M.* (Marguerite Mouton), one of the premier painters at the Tharaud studio, about 1930. $500-$1,000.

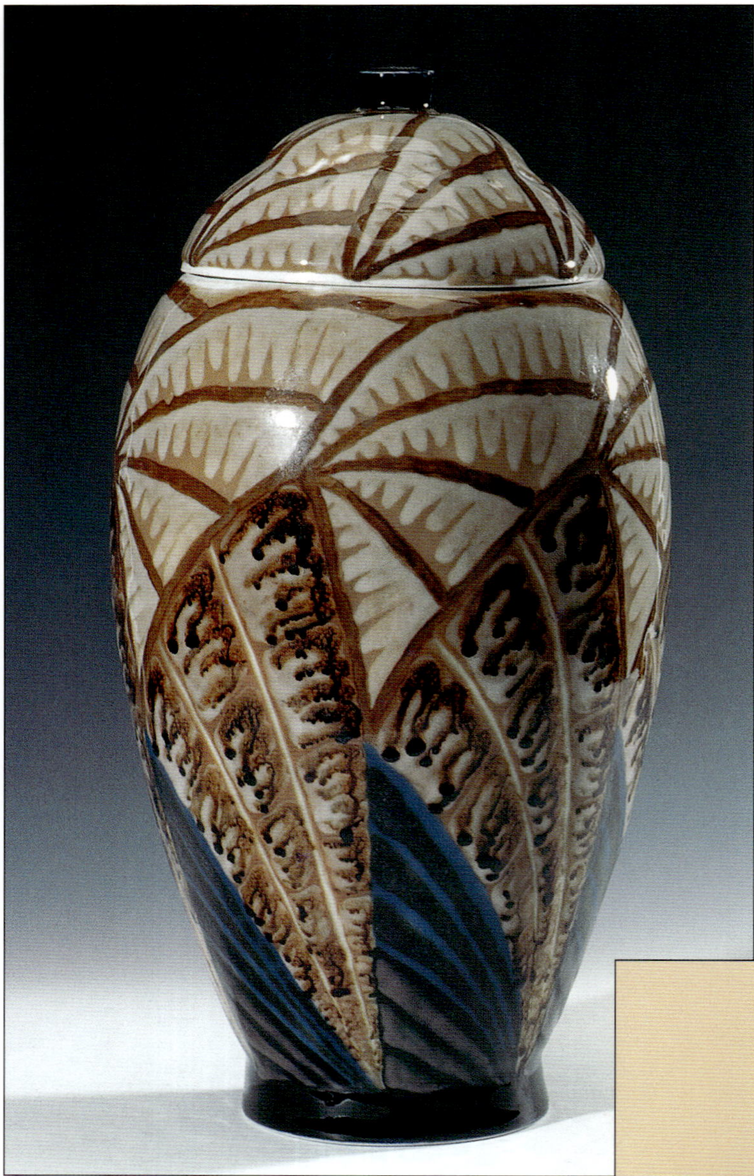

Covered vase, *Manon*, *Wings of Butterfly* decorated with enamels containing lavas from Auvergne. This piece decorated after 1943. $1,500-$2,000.

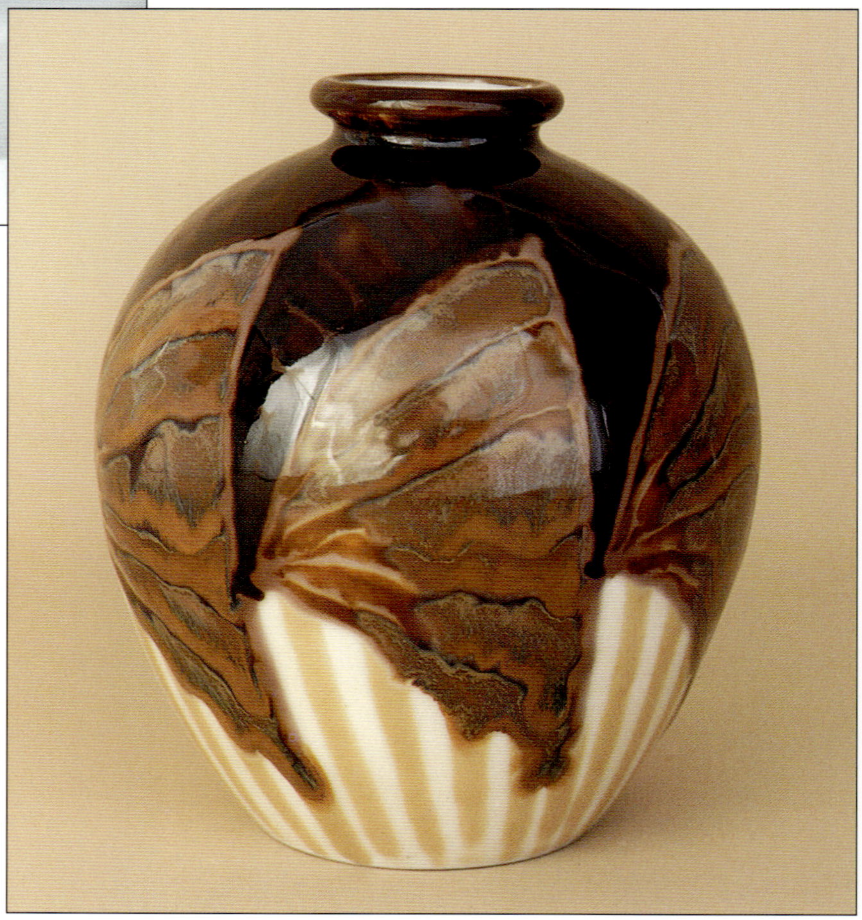

Vase, 6.25" high, 1930-1945, *Wings of Butterfly* decoration. Less than $500.

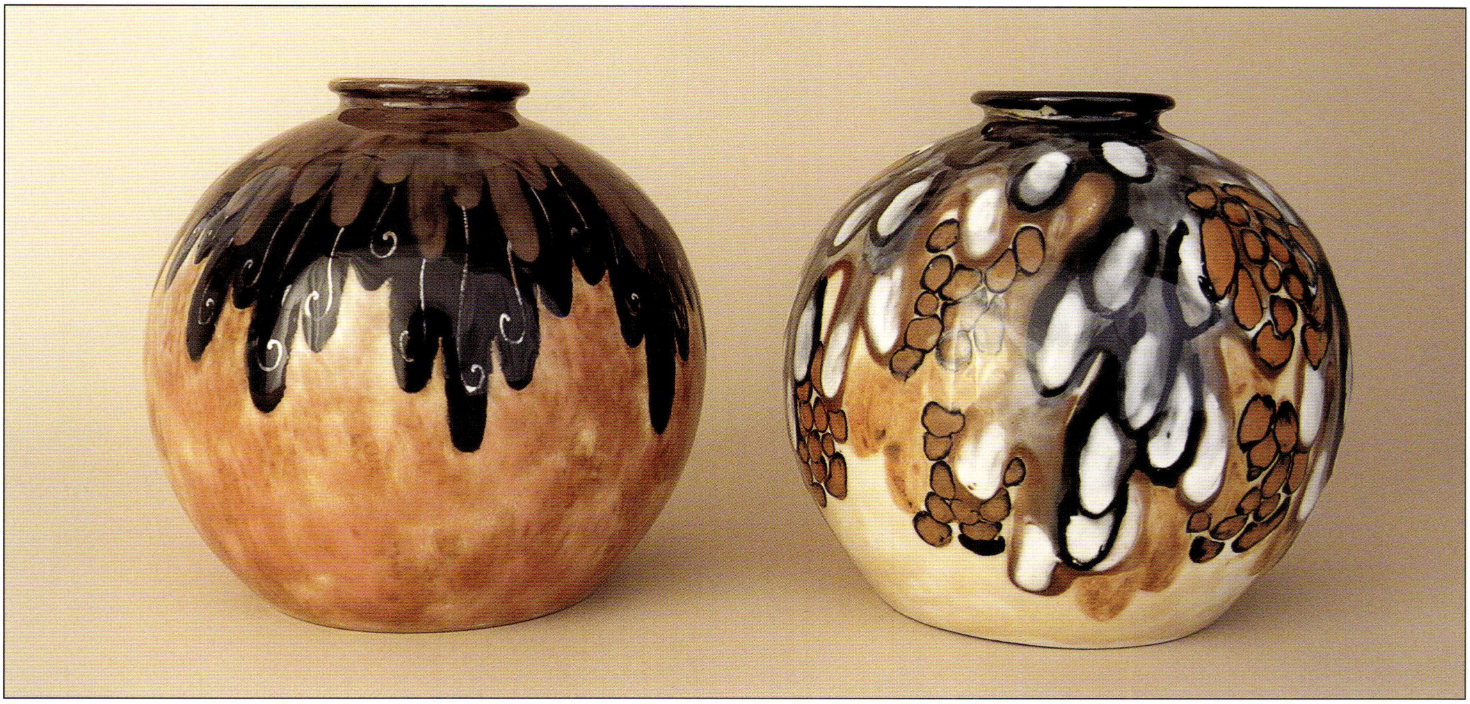

Vase, left, 7.25" high, 1928-1930, and vase, right, 7" high, the enamel in places is quite thick, 1928-1930. Each less than $500.

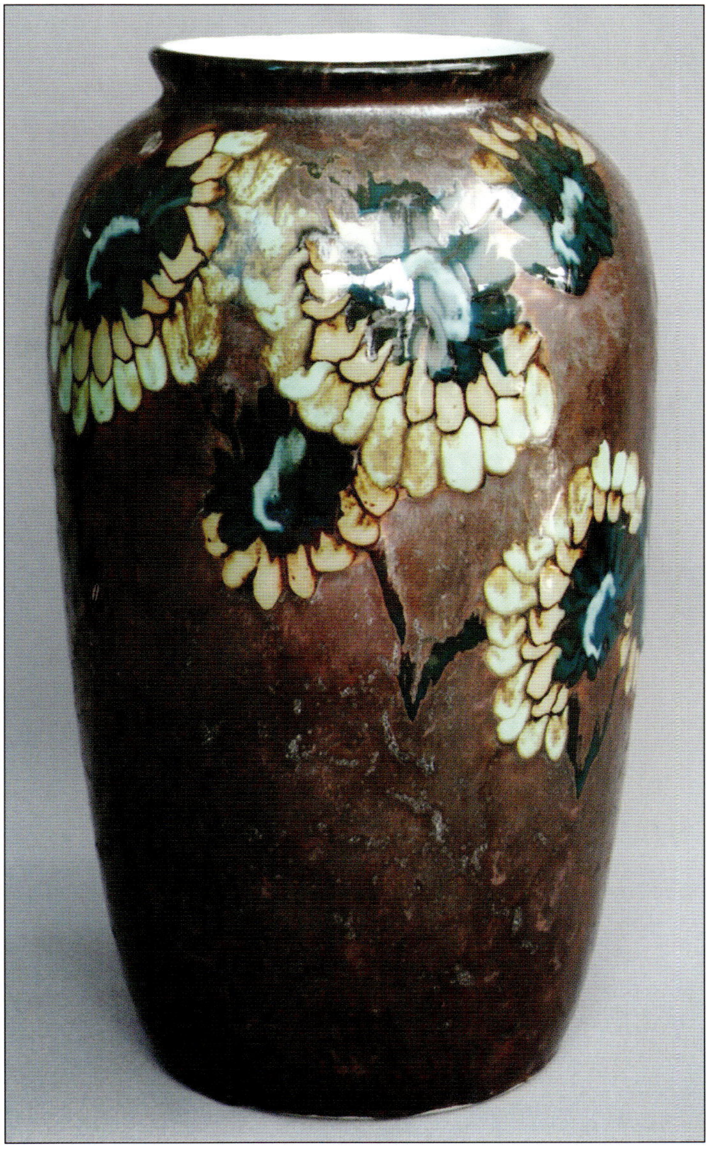

Vase, 13.5" high, 1928-1935, sticker on bottom says Porcelaine de Tha [uard]. $500-$1,000.

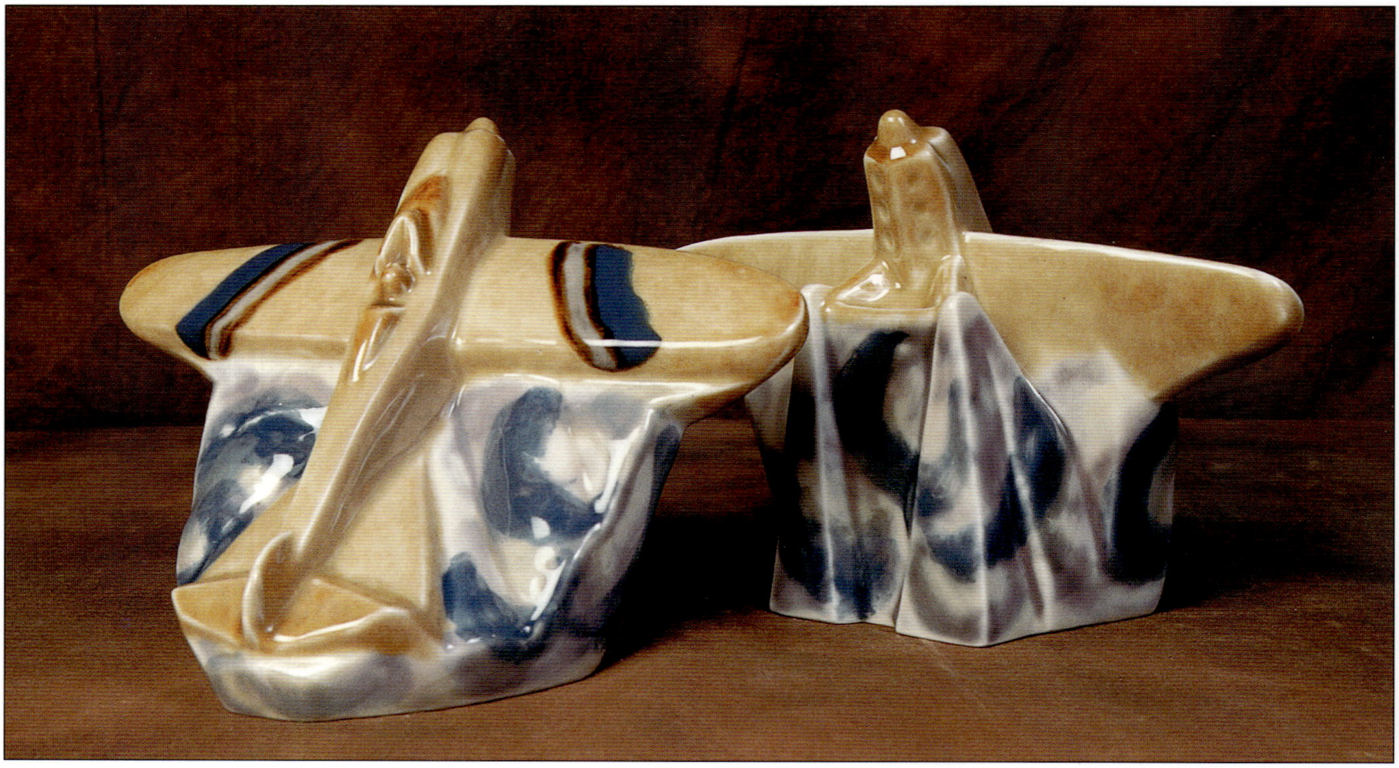

Airplane bookends, 7.25" high x 10" x 6.75", exhibited at the Exposition internationale "L'aéronautique et l'art," Paris, 1930. $1,500-$2,000.

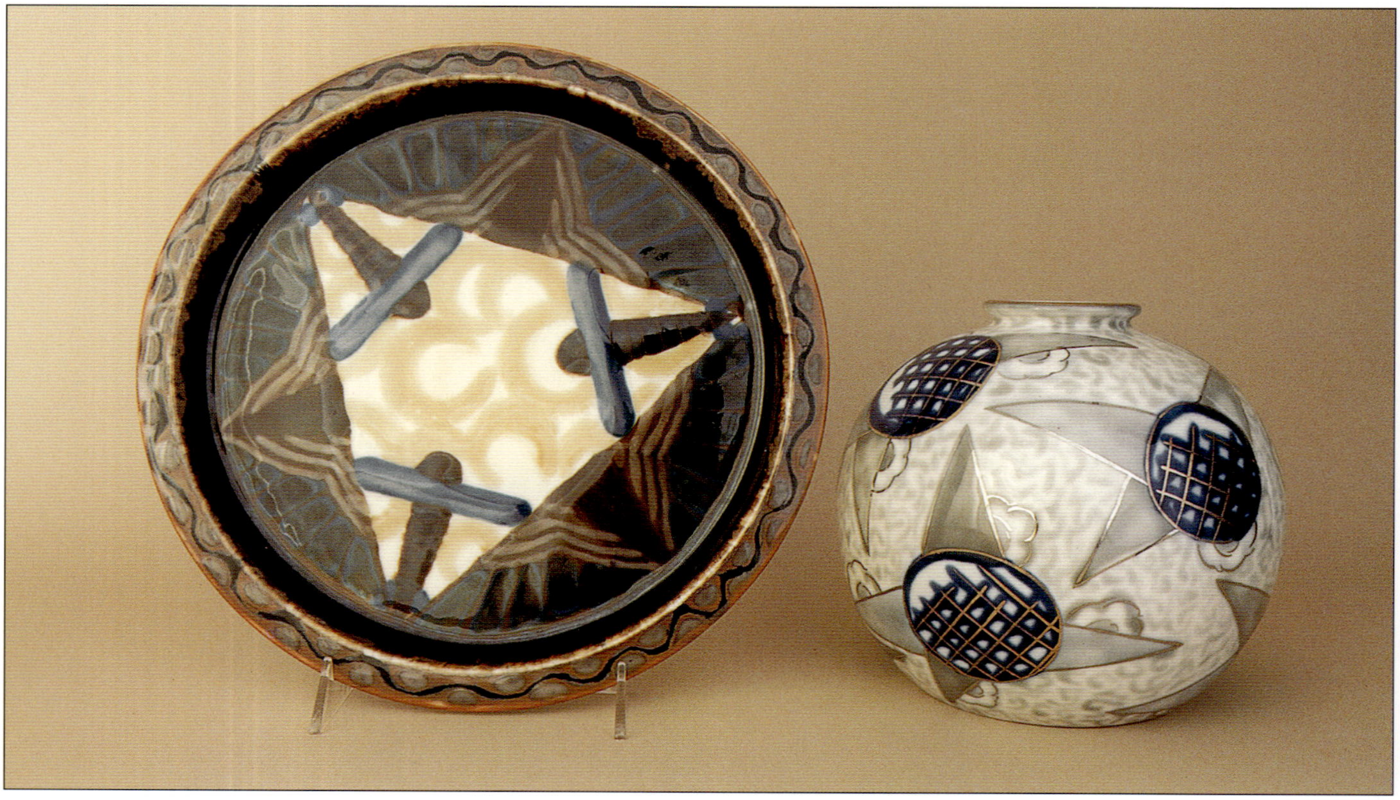

Tray, left, 11.5" in diameter, and vase, right, 7.25" high. Two designs exhibited at the Exposition internationale "L'aéronautique et l'art," Paris, 1930. Marked on the back is *assiette créé pour le Salon de l'Aviation 1930/ Acheté à Limoges*. The tray is decorated with three airplanes on a background of clouds with undulating lines representing air currents. The designs in the vase are also suggestive of air currents, with clouds and triangle shapes for the wings of airplanes. $500-$1,000.

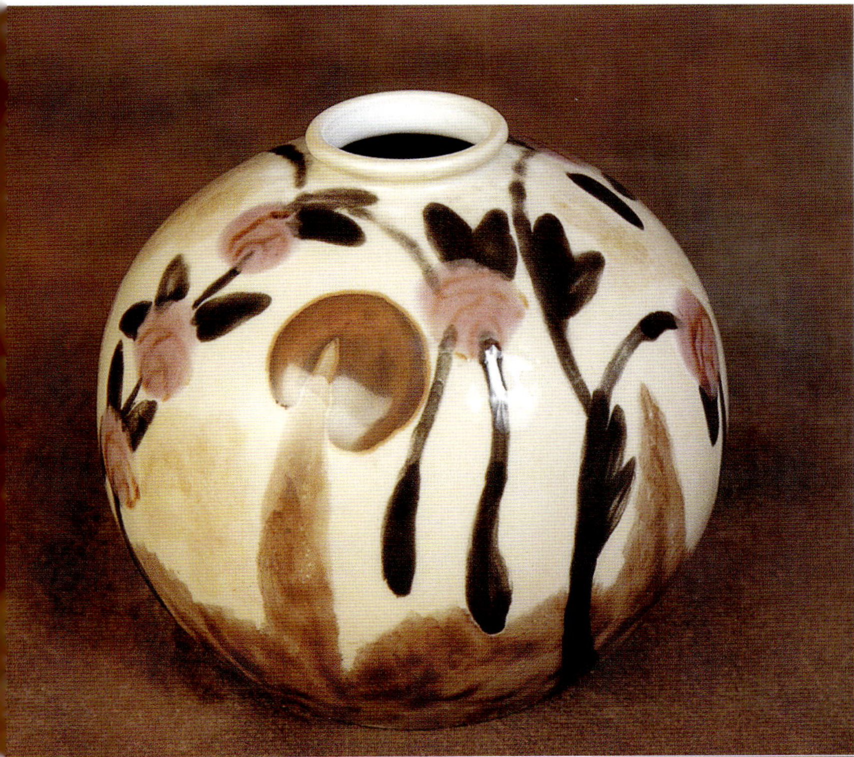

Vase, 5.25" high, decoration of mushrooms in "pure" Art Deco style, 1928-1930. $500-$1,000.

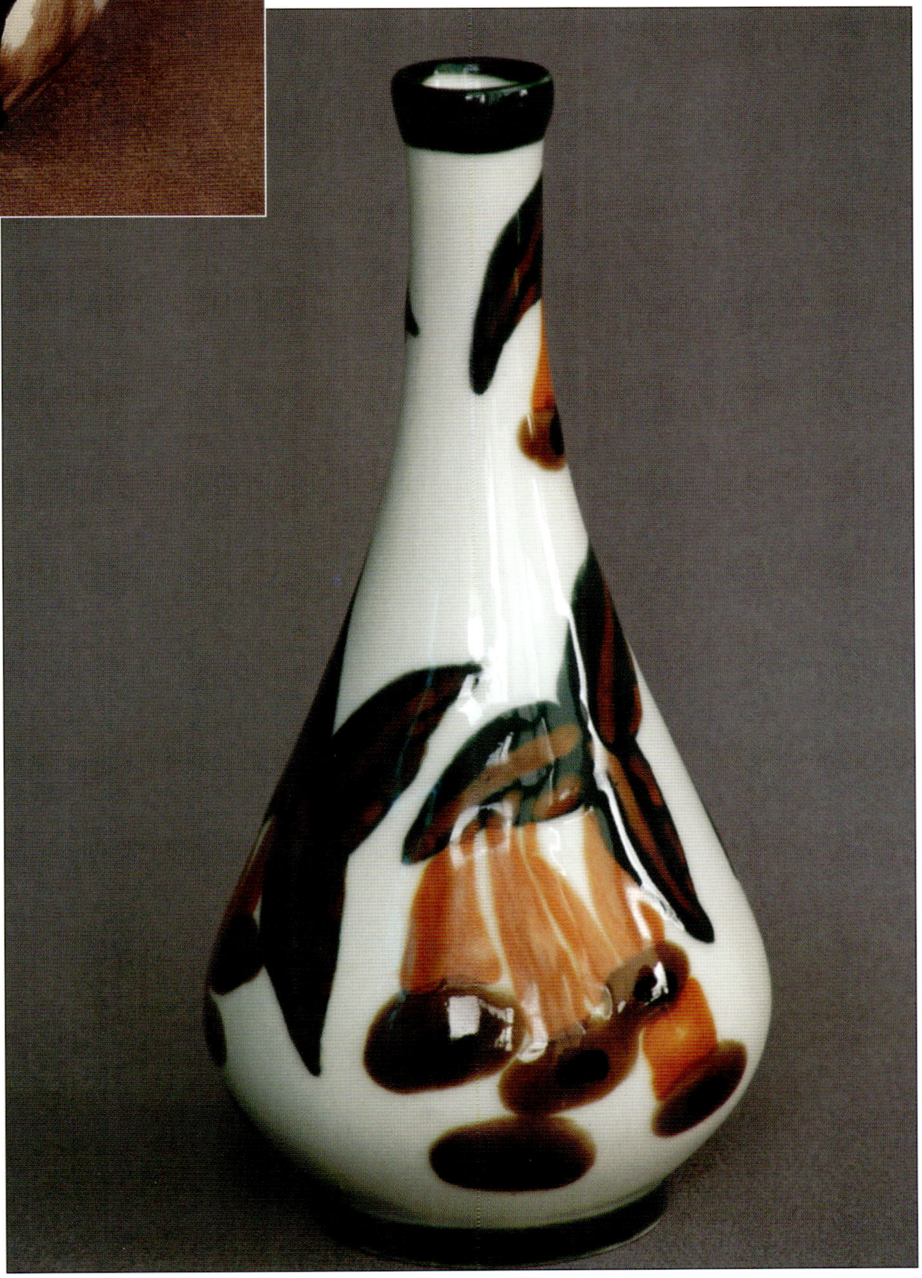

Single Flower Vase, 7" high. Less than $500.

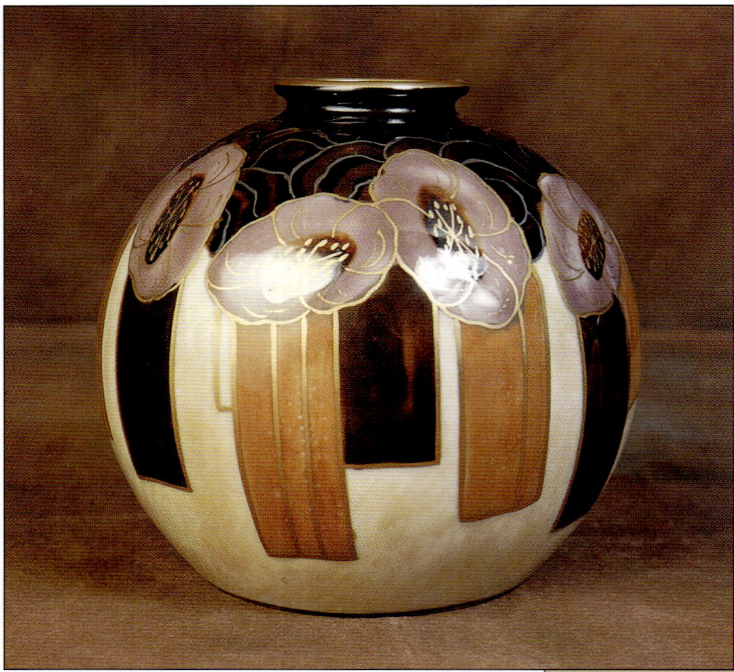

Vase, 7.5" high, "pure" Art Deco, with the layering of the enamels and *coulées* perfectly mastered (Ferrer), about 1930. $500-$1,500.

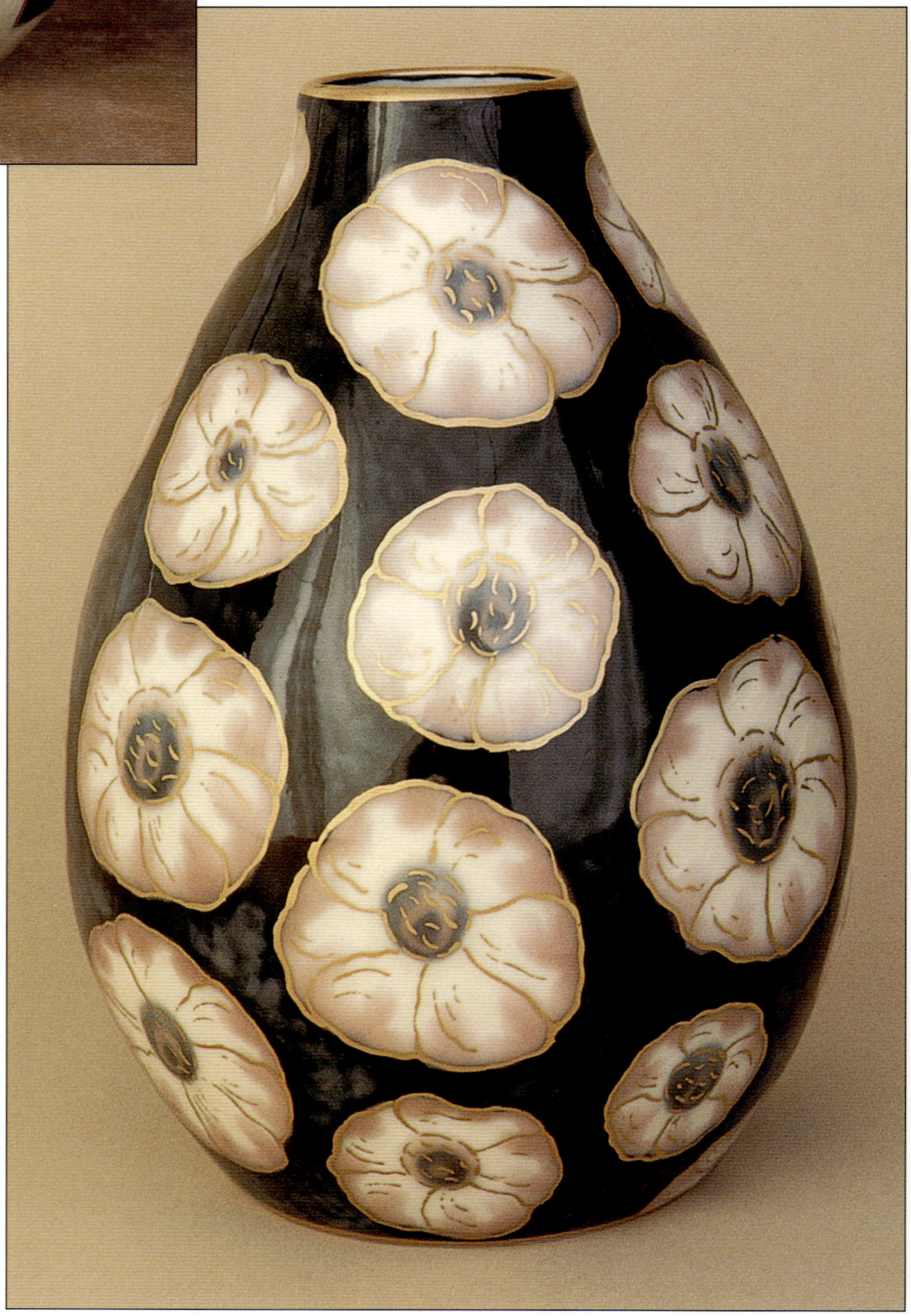

Vase, 9" high, about 1930. Decorated in "pure" Art Deco style, with perfect mastery in the layering of the enamels. (Ferrer) $500-$1,000.

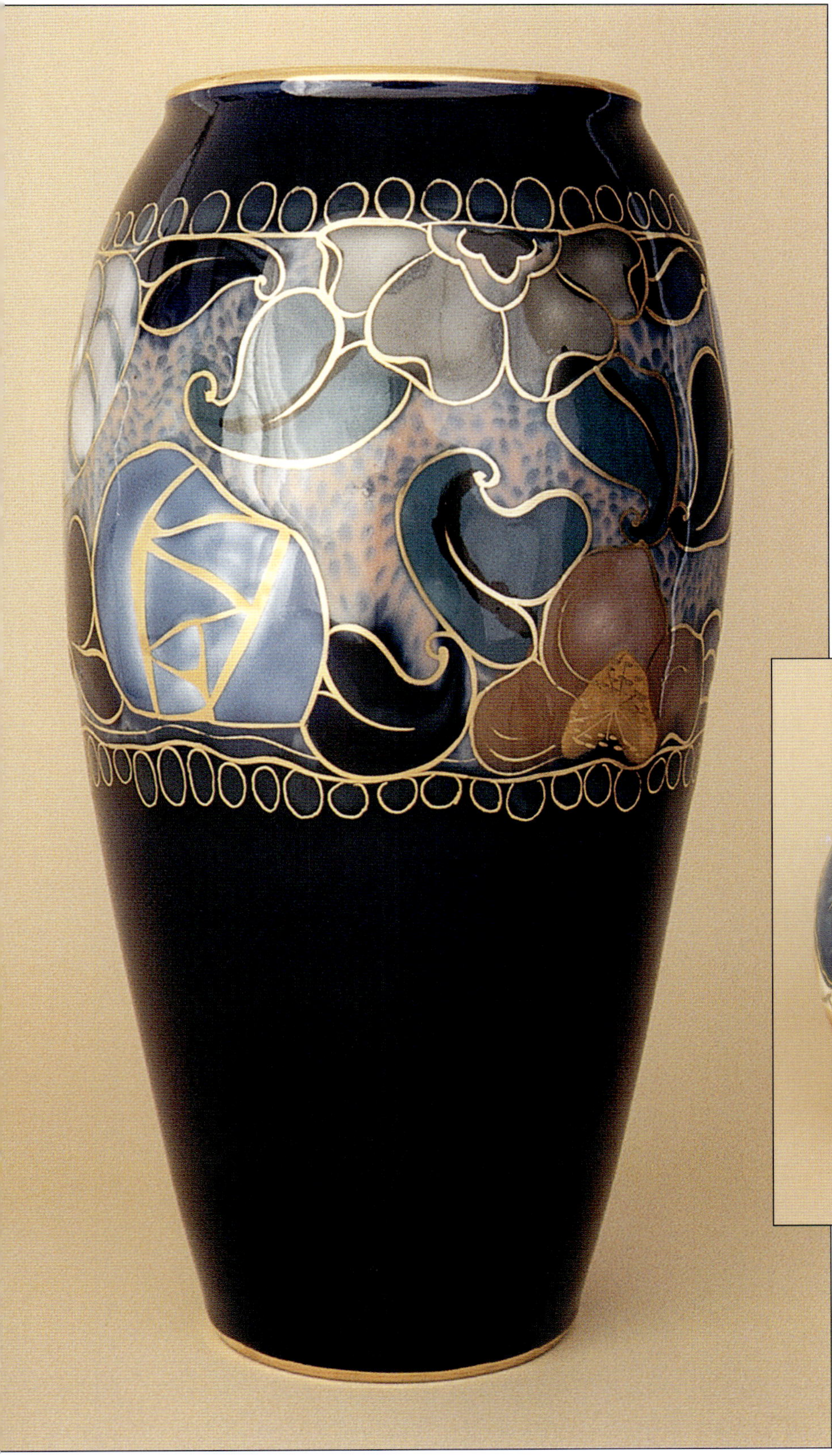

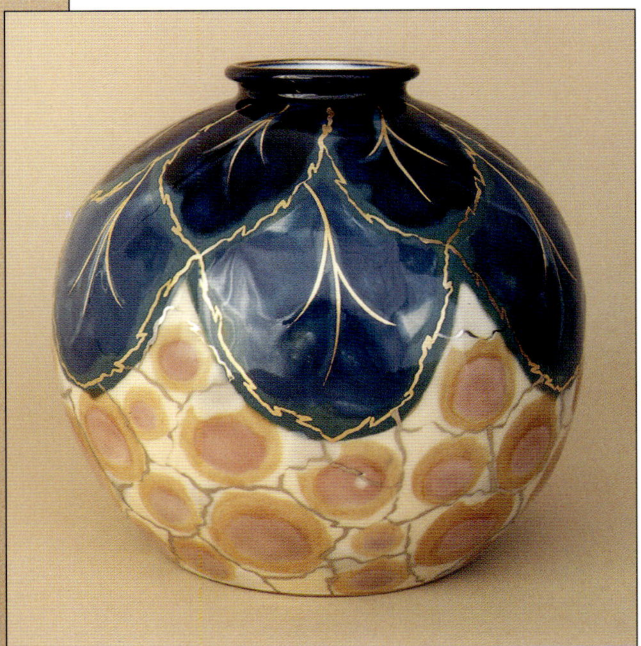

Vase, 7.5" high, 1928-1930. Falling from the collar of the vase are six *bleu de four* leaves, then six lighter blue leaves, and then seedlings. Less than $500.

Vase, 11.5" high, 1928-1930, Art Deco style with the effect of cloisonné. $500-$1,000.

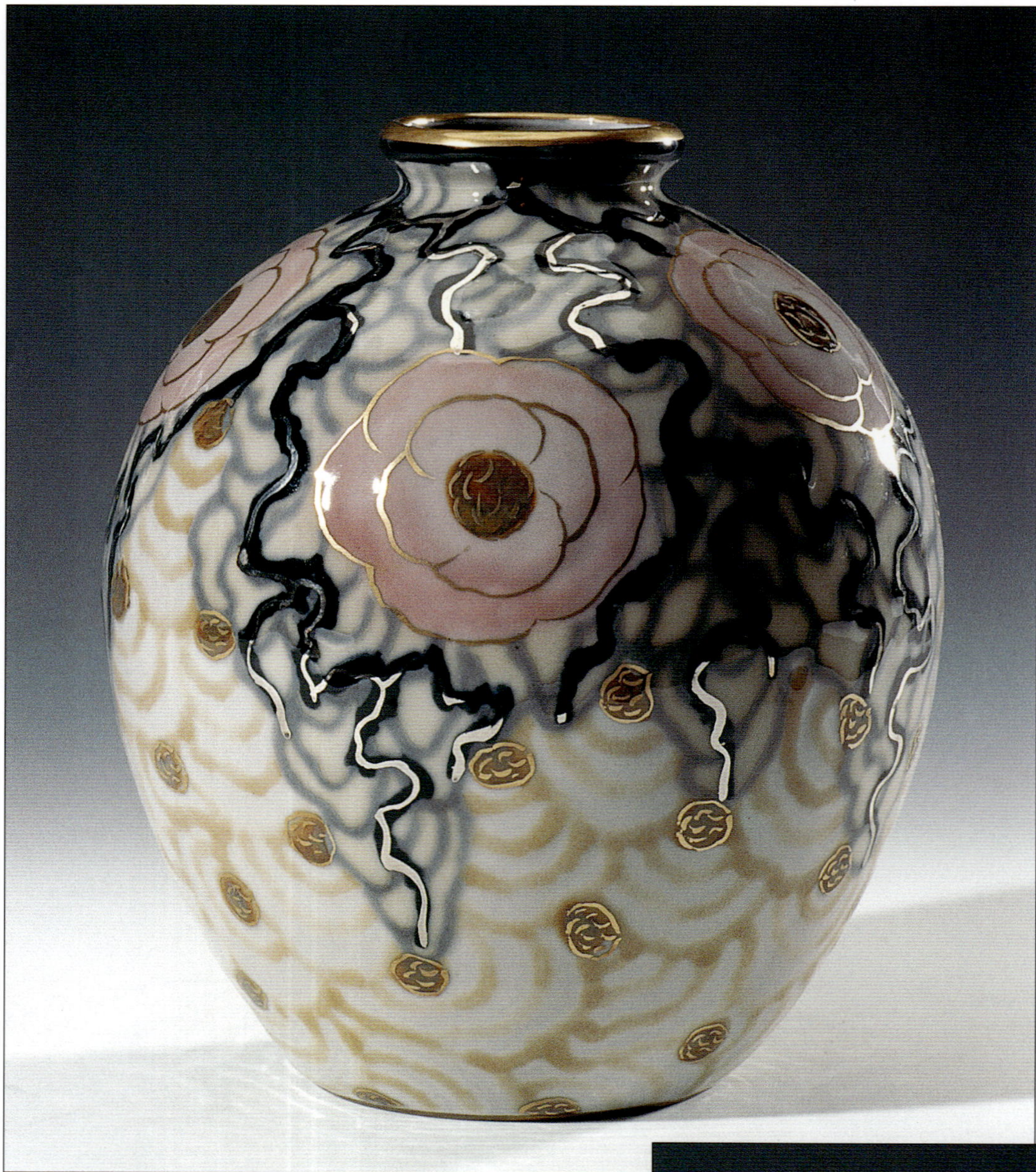

Vase, *Jasmin*, shape of Henri Rapin, 12.5" high, decorated by Aimée Lotherie, 1930. Decorated with Art Deco concentric circles. $1,000-$1,500.

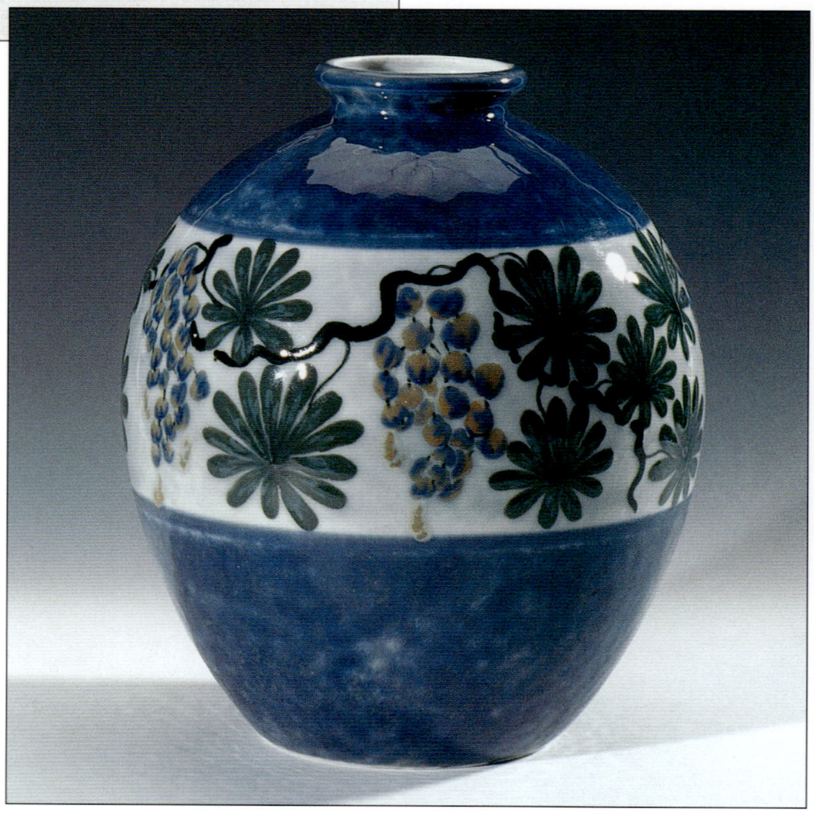

Vase, *Lilas*, 8.5" high, 1928-1930, *Th* incised (decoration of Camille Tharaud) and paper label, *Création de H. Rapin*. Less than $500.

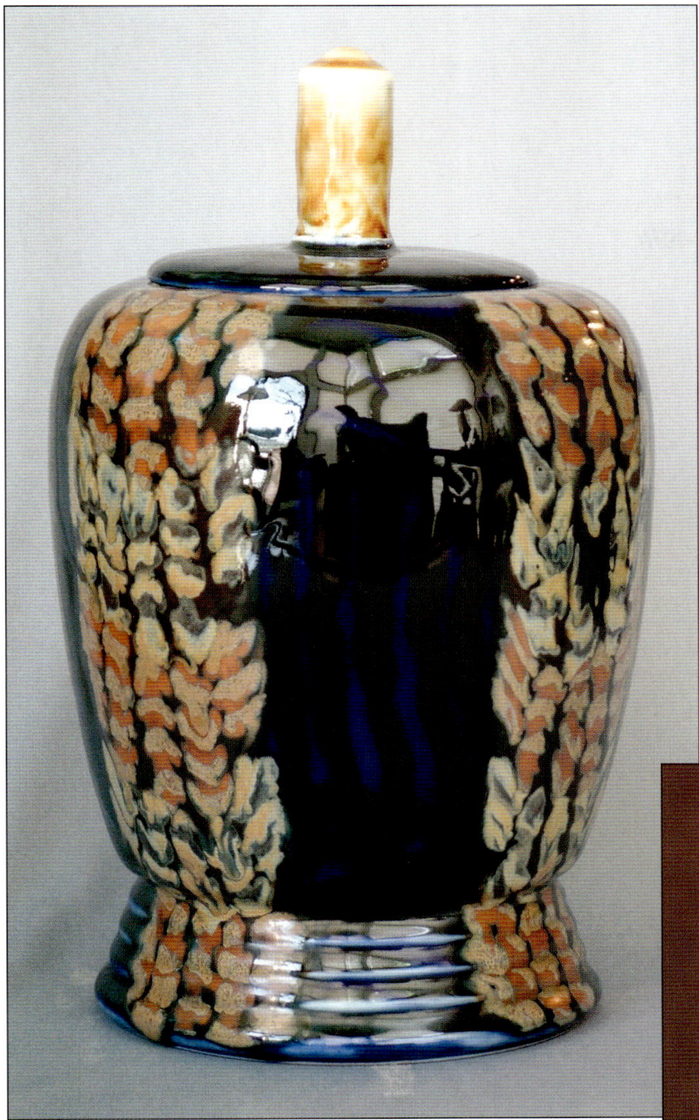

Jar, *Thaïs*, 10.5" high, the cobalt mixed with the dark emerald green has a rare and magnificent effect. $1,000-$1,500.

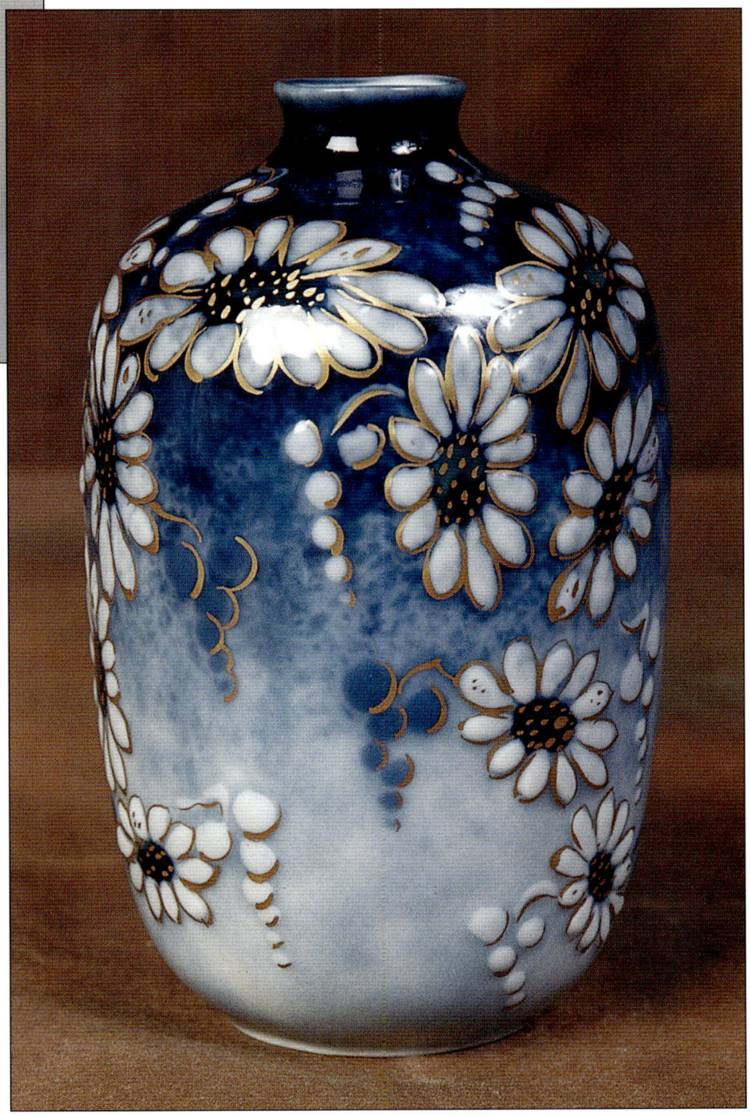

Vase, 6.25" high, 1928-1930. Less than $500.

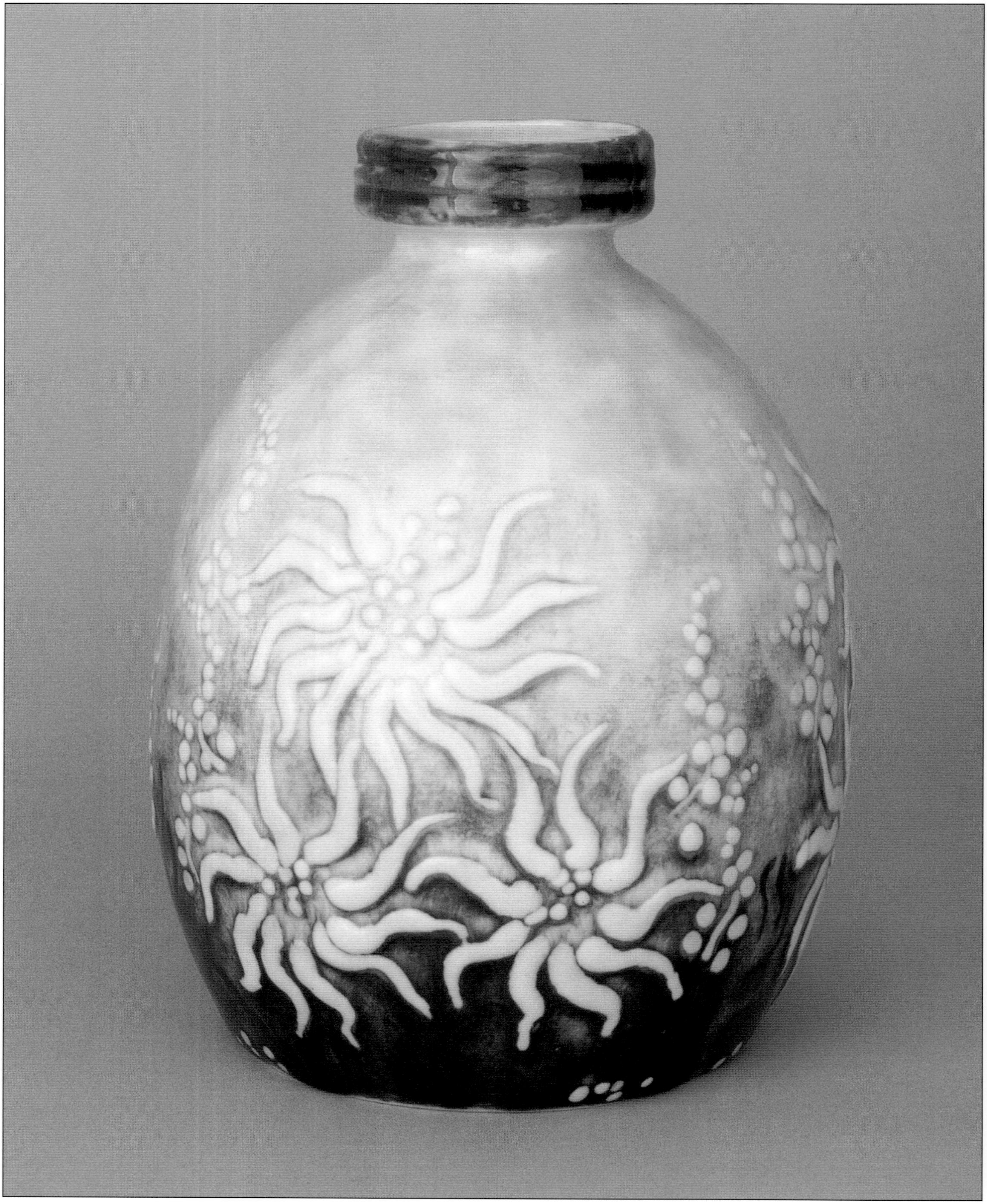

Vase, *Anthémis,* shape attributed to Henri Rapin, 10.5" high, starfish and algae in green sea water, signed MLR (Mercedes Rogé), 1928-1930. Less than $500.

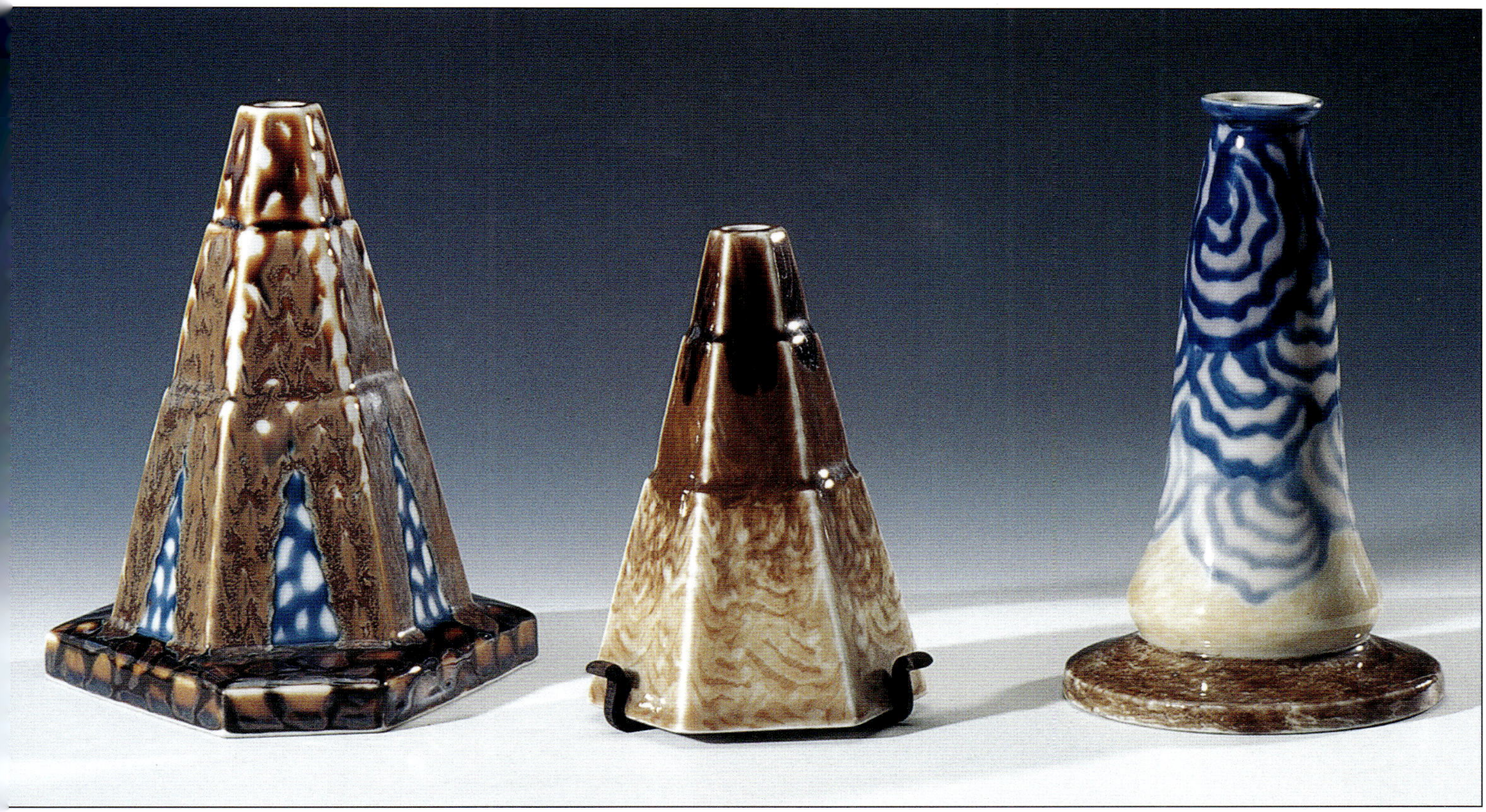

Three lamp bases, from left to right, 7.5", 5.75", and 7.25", 1930-1945 for left and center bases and 1928-1930 for base on right. Each less than $500.

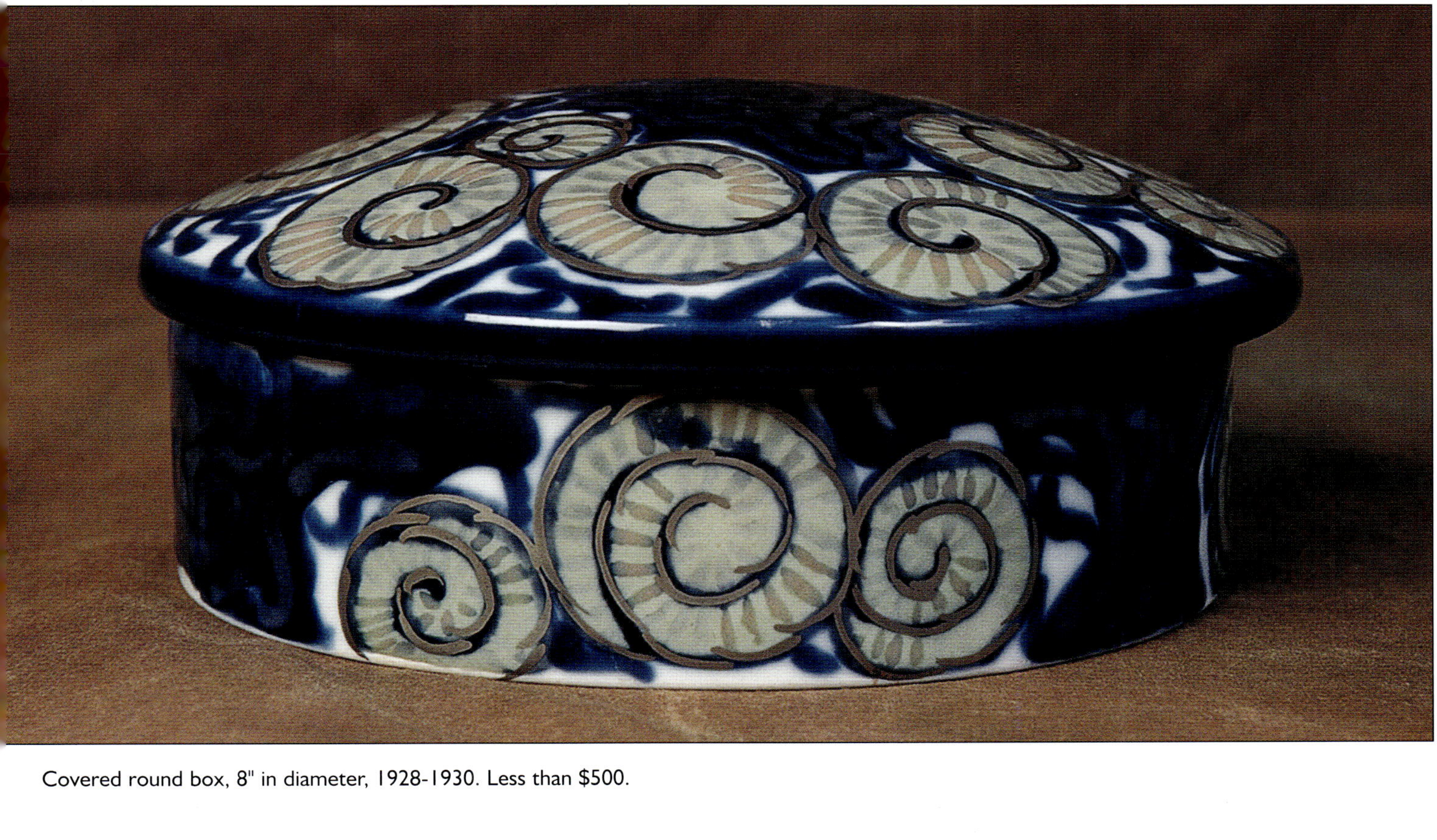

Covered round box, 8" in diameter, 1928-1930. Less than $500.

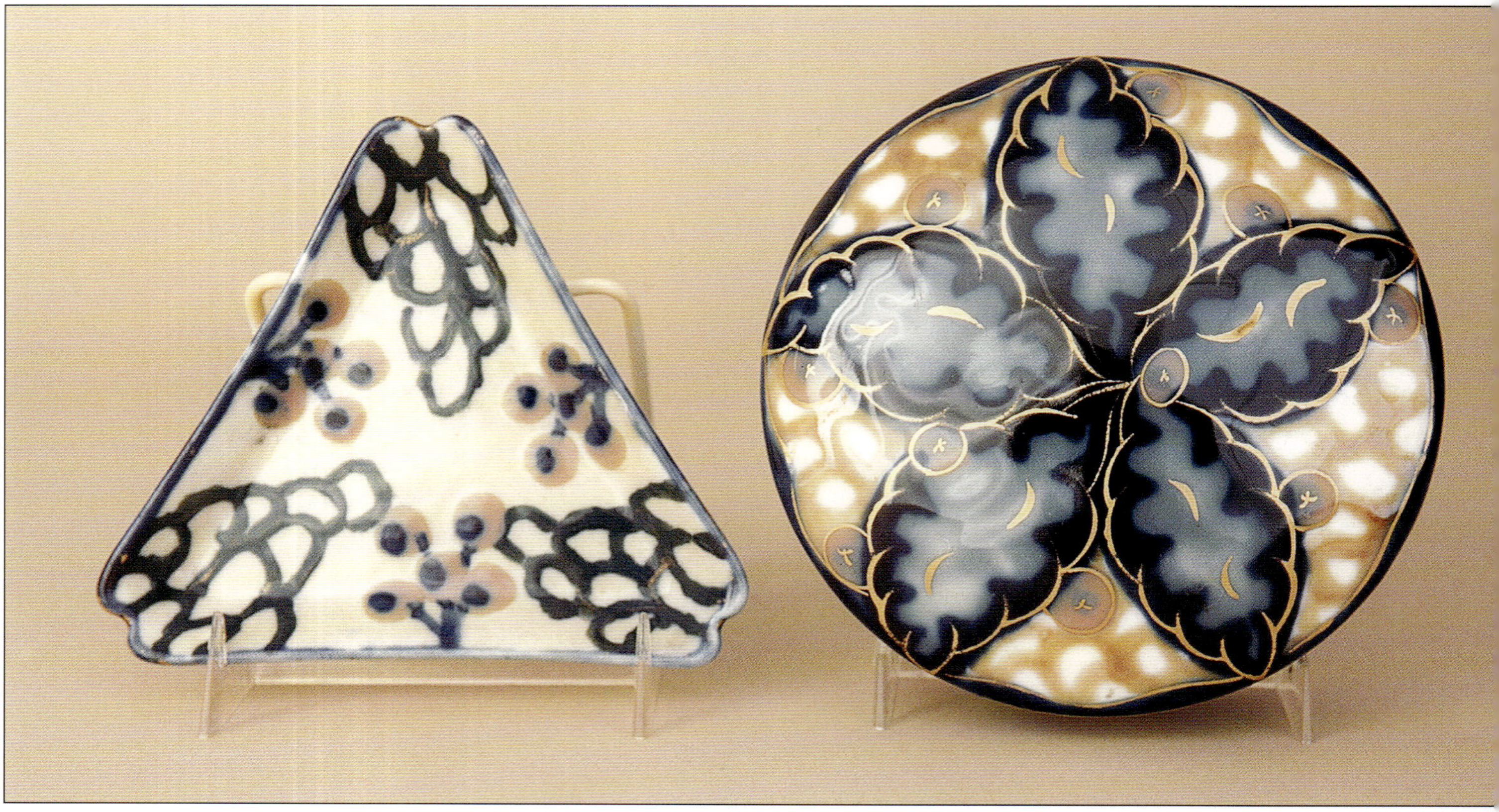

Ashtray and covered dish, right, 5.25" in diameter, both 1928-1930. Less than $500.

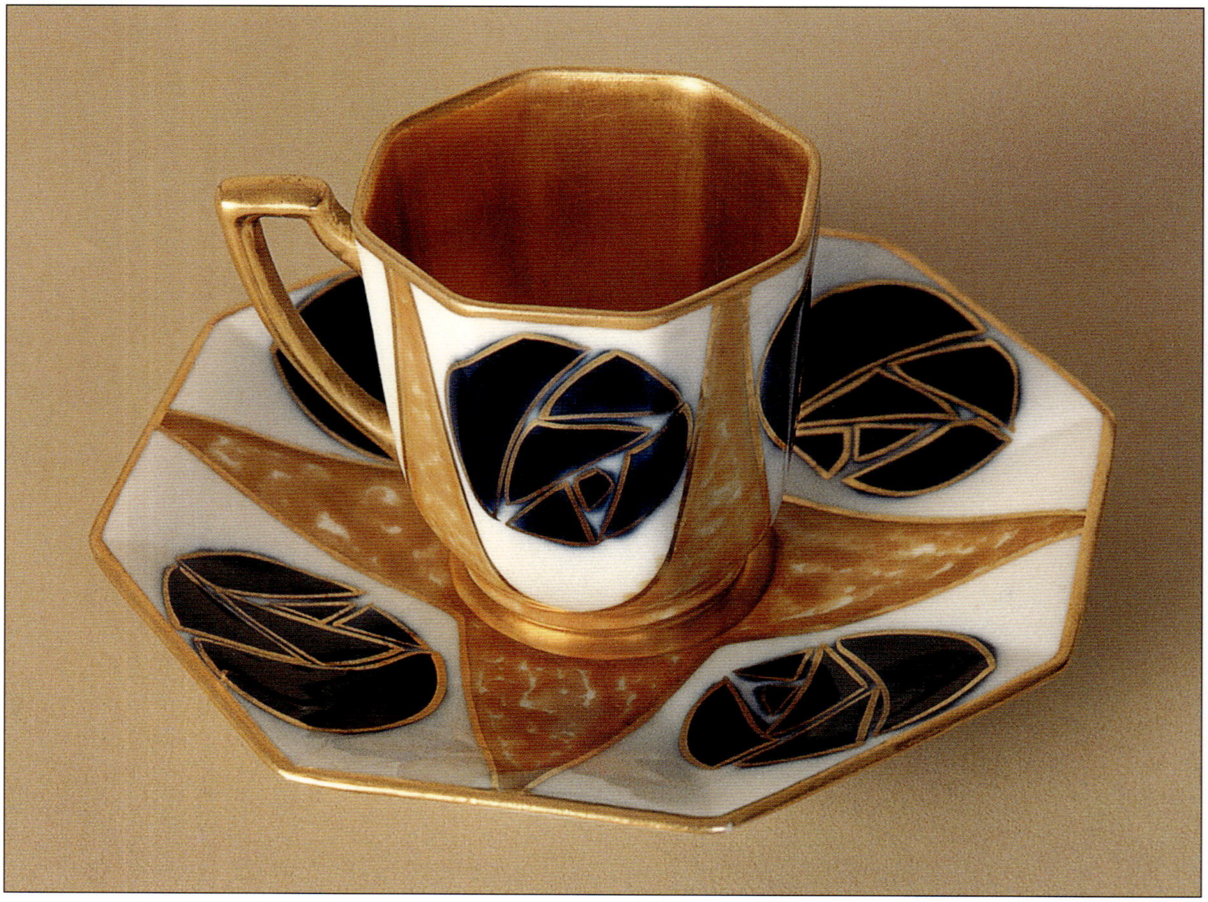

Demitasse, 1929-1930. Less than $500.

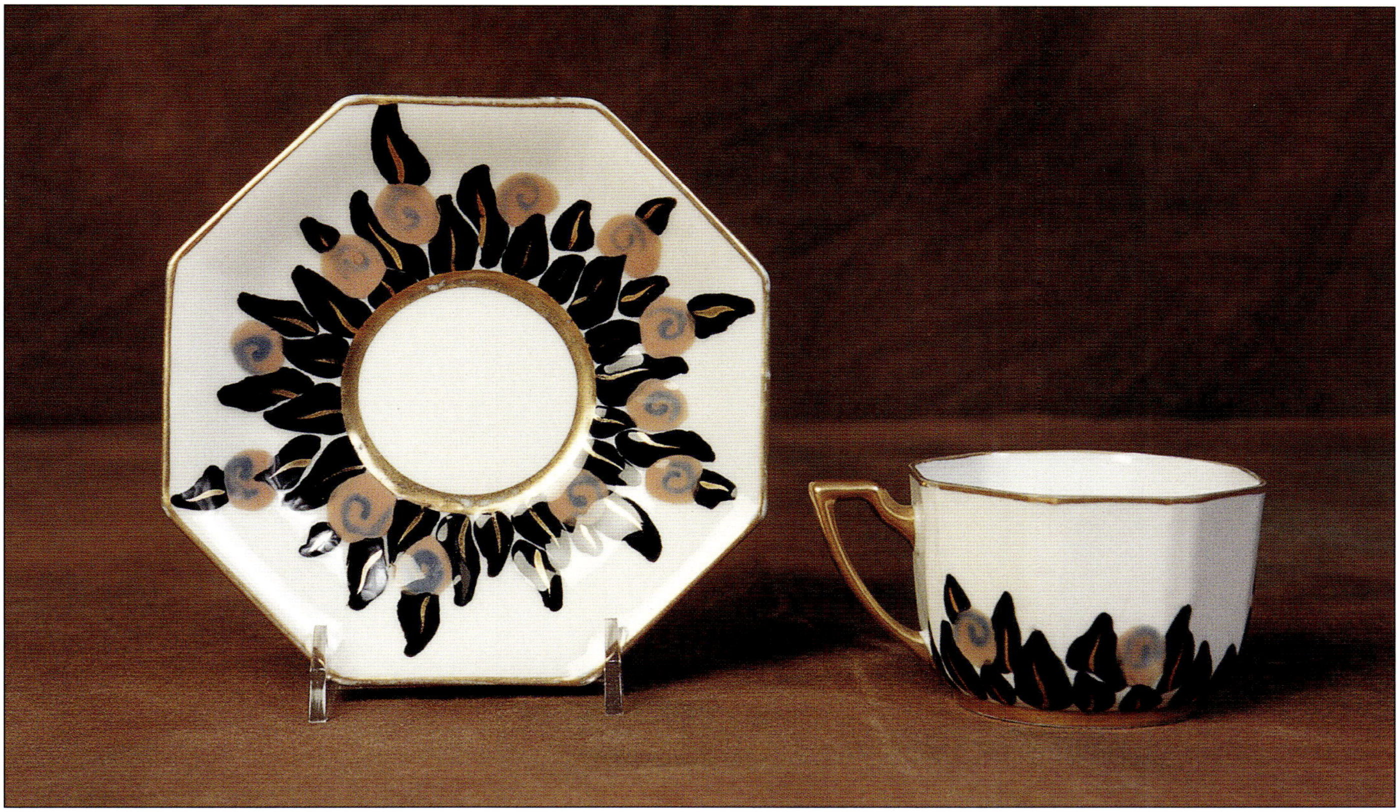

Cup and Saucer, 1928-1930. Less than $500.

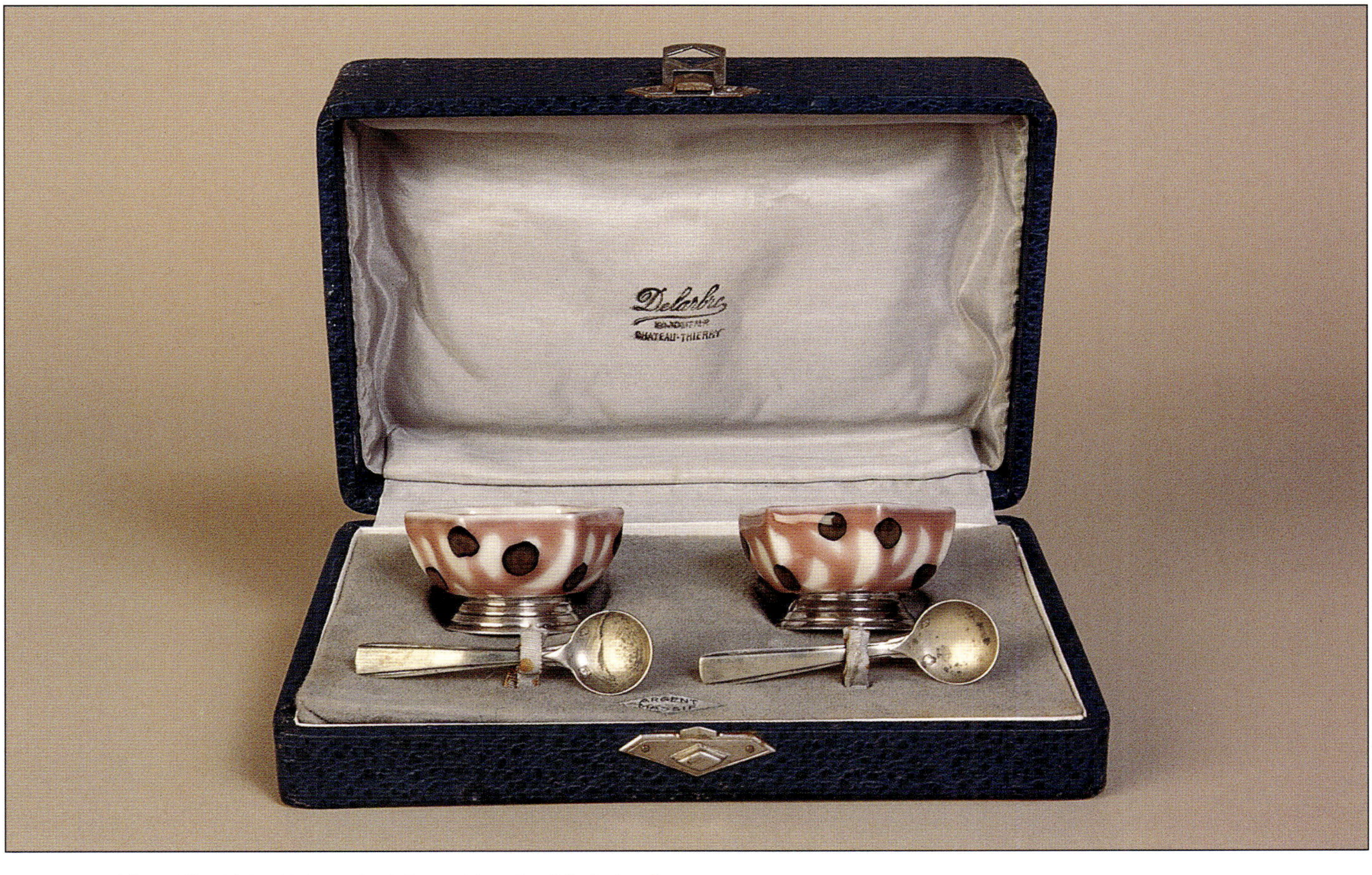

Salt cups, 1.3" x 1.9", 1928-1930, marked *Agent Massif* and *Delarbre Bijoutier Châeau-Thierry*, silver bases have the mark of Minerve. Less than $500.

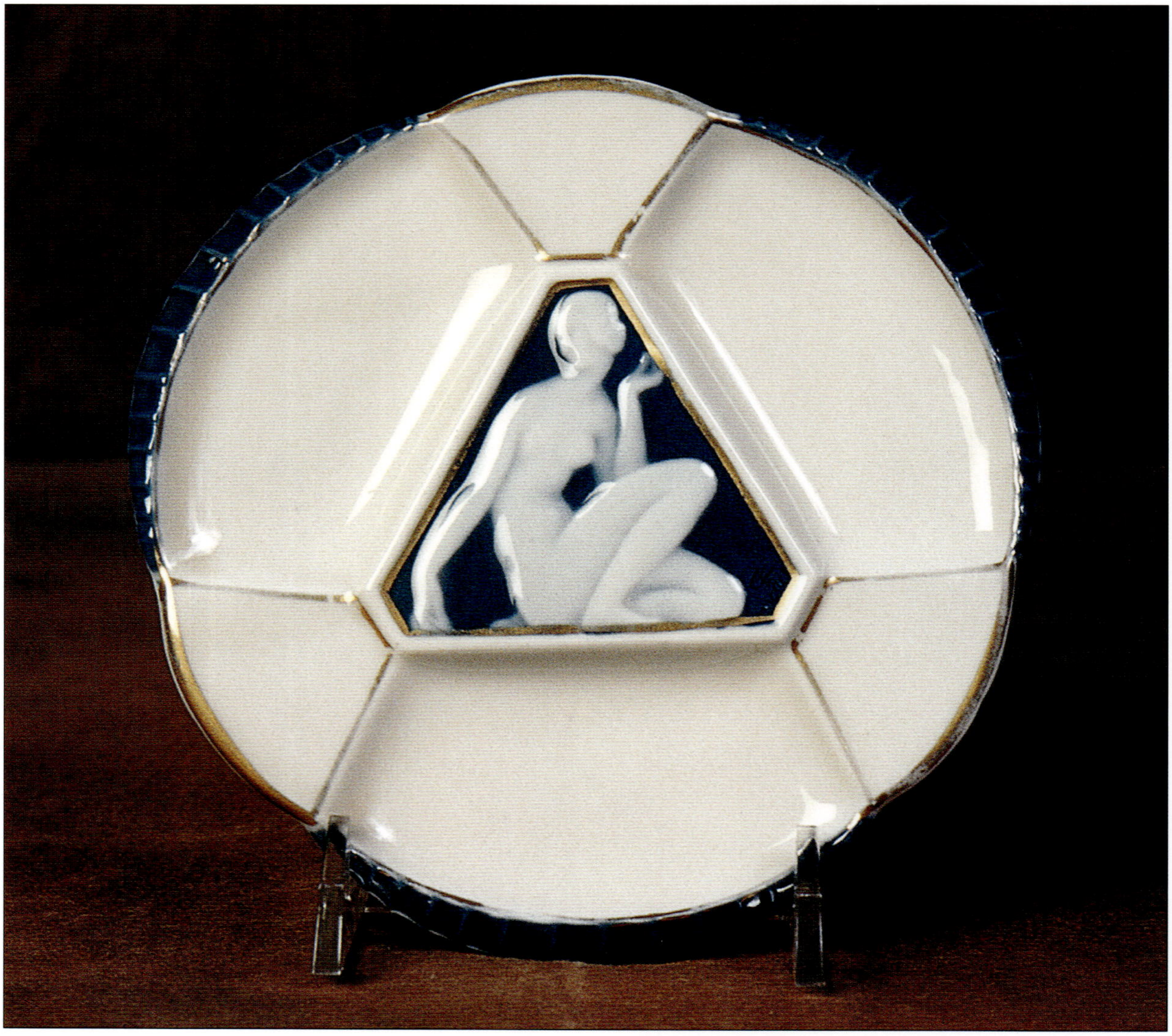

Ashtray, 5.25" in diameter, same "pâte sur pâte" same decoration as a piece signed Auguste Riffaterre, probably around 1930. (Ferrer) Less than $500.

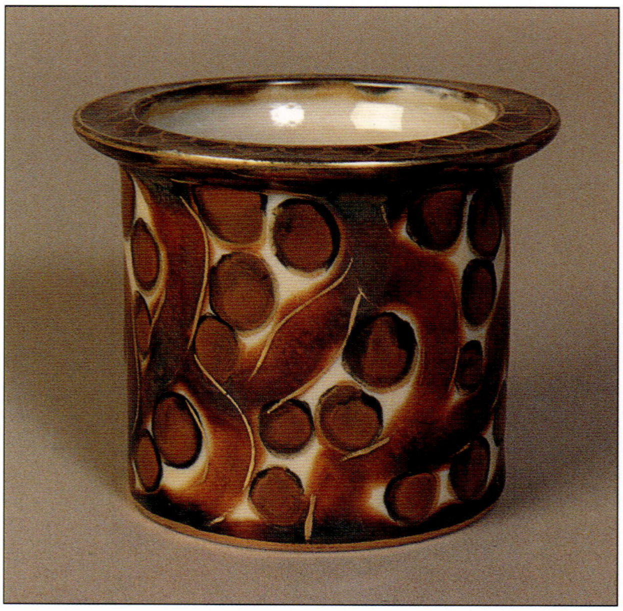

Cup shape, 2.6" high x 3" in diameter, 1928-1930. Less than $500.

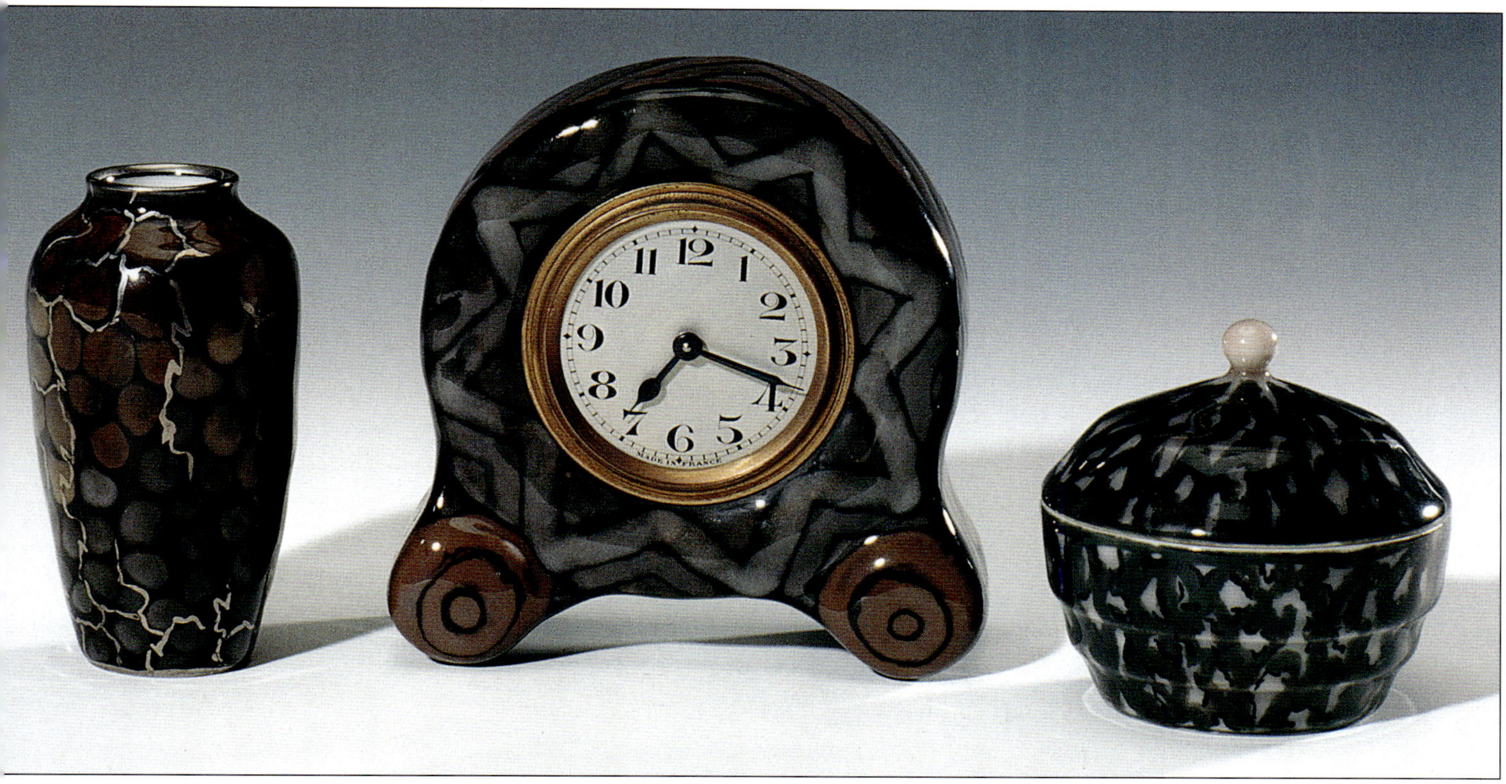

Vase, clock, covered box, all 1928-30. Each less than $500.

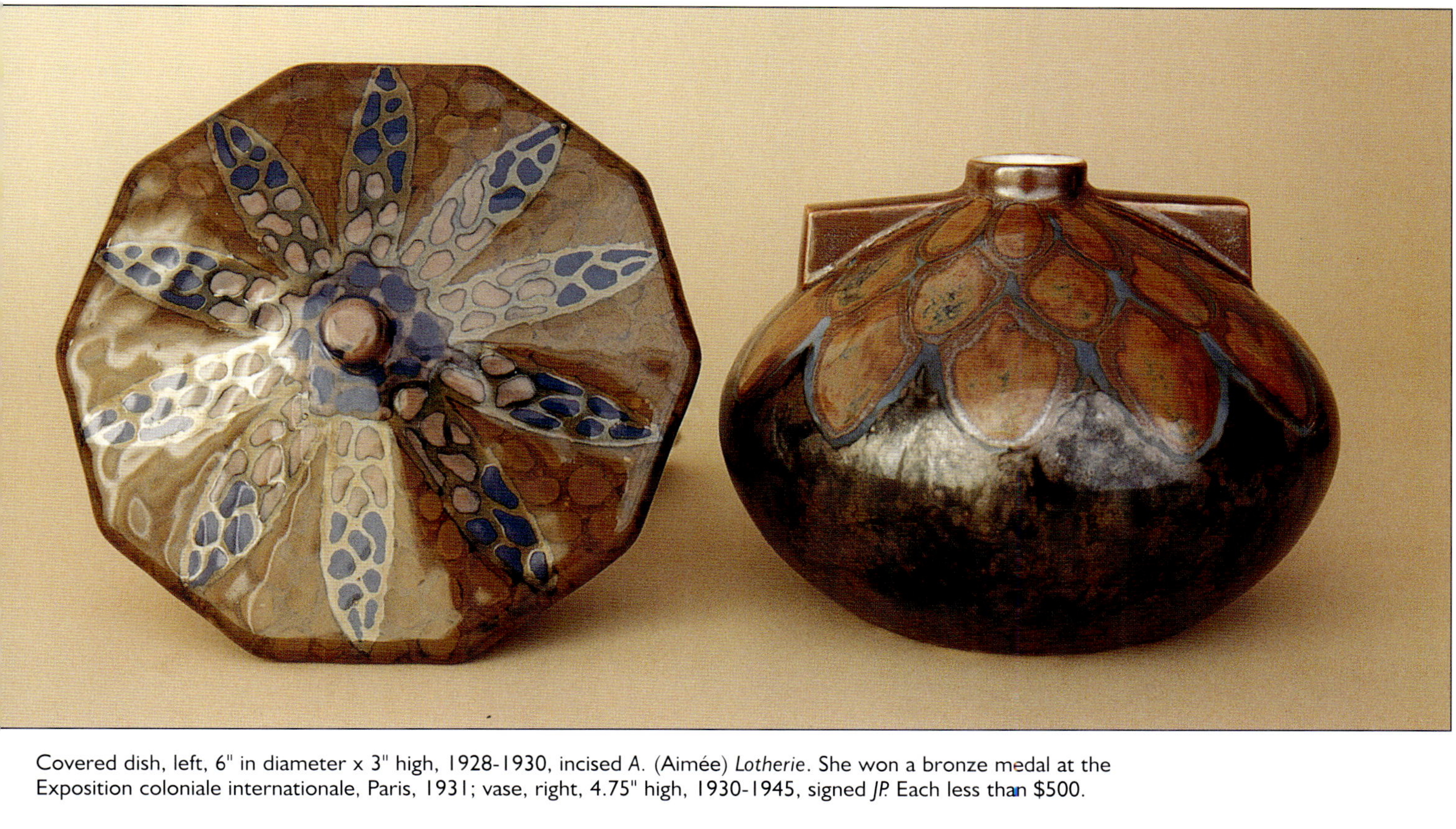

Covered dish, left, 6" in diameter x 3" high, 1928-1930, incised *A.* (Aimée) *Lotherie*. She won a bronze medal at the Exposition coloniale internationale, Paris, 1931; vase, right, 4.75" high, 1930-1945, signed *JP.* Each less than $500.

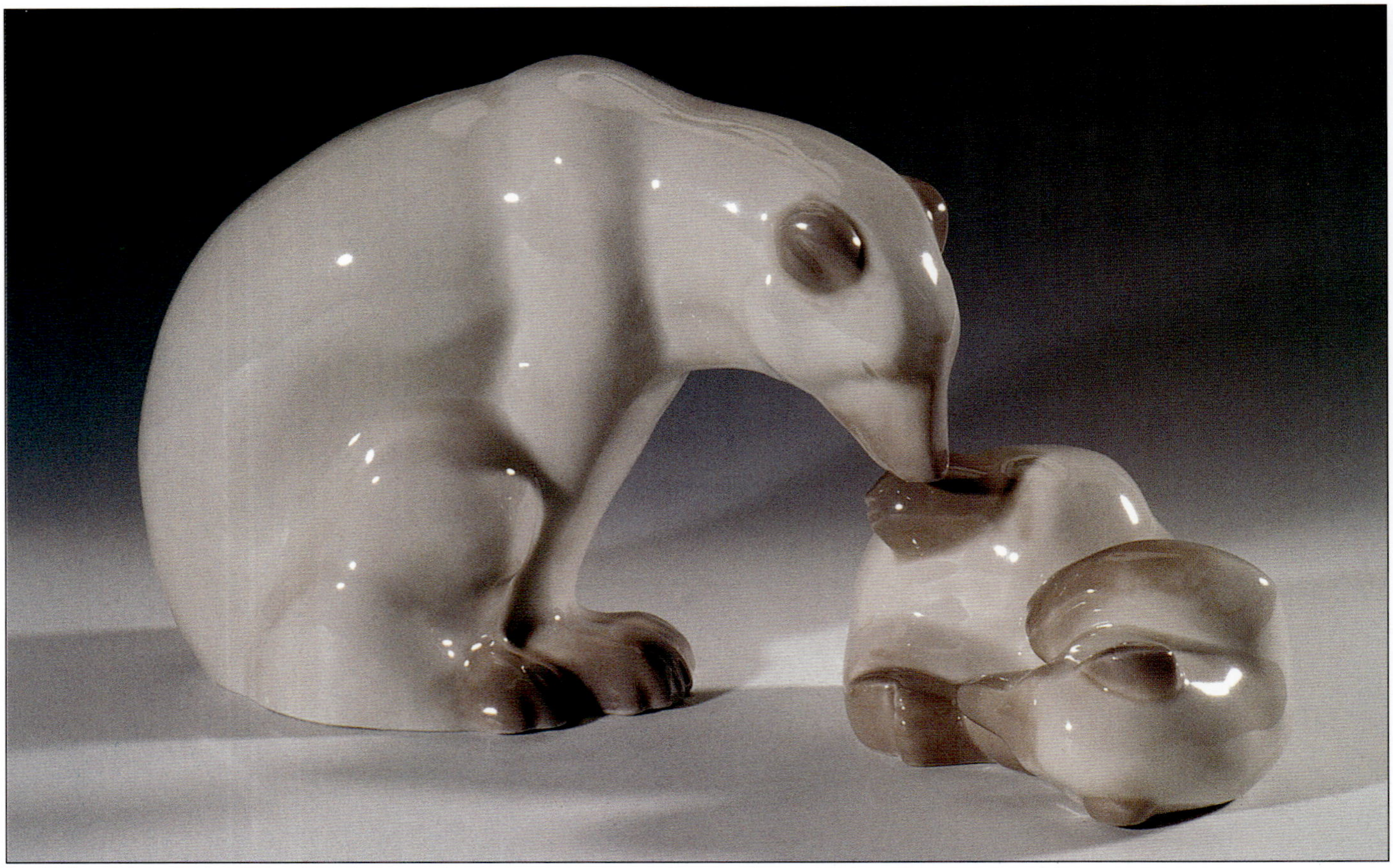

Polar Bears, mother 8.5" high x 11" and cub 7.25" x 4.5" wide, 1929, shapes of Robert Lemoine, *sous émail* gray, exhibited at the Exposition internationale des arts et techniques, Paris, 1937. $1,500-$2,000 for both.

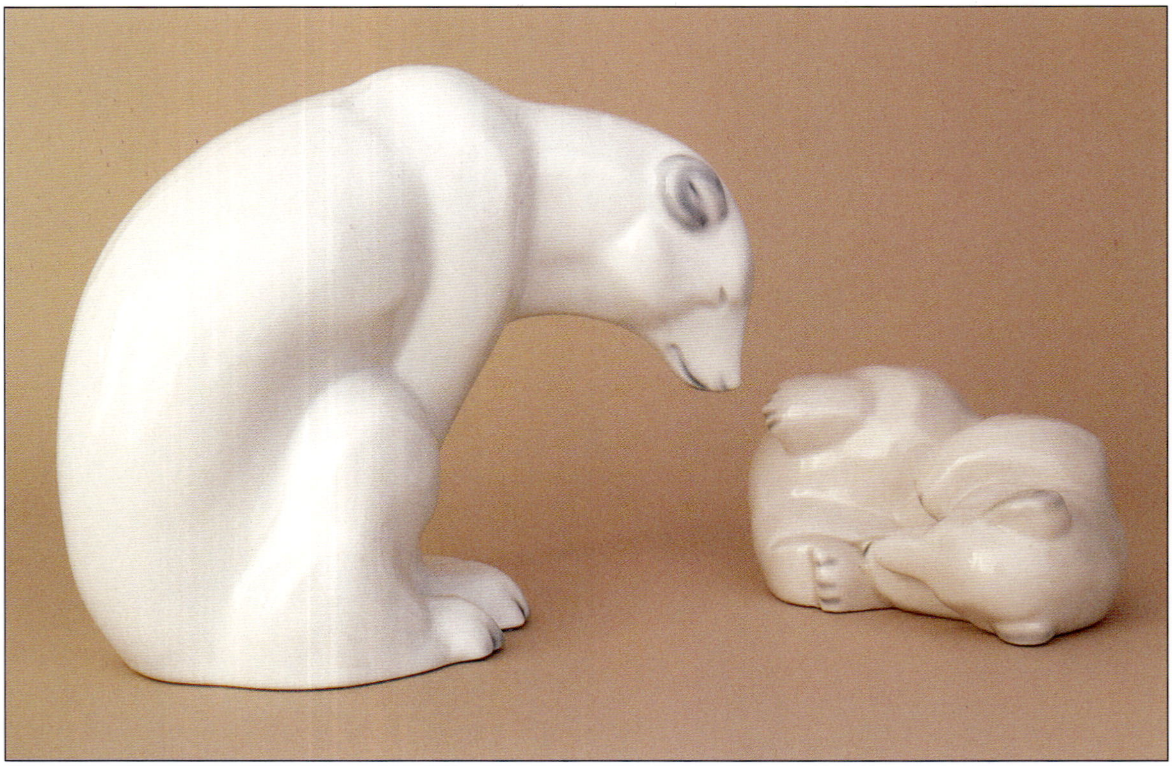

Polar Bears, mother, 11" x 8.5" and cub, 7.25" x 4.5", shapes of Robert Lemoine; adult bear in this photograph was reissued in 1970 by Goumot-Labesse and cub is original, 1929, exhibited at the Exposition internationale des arts et techniques, Paris, 1937. $1,000-$1,500.

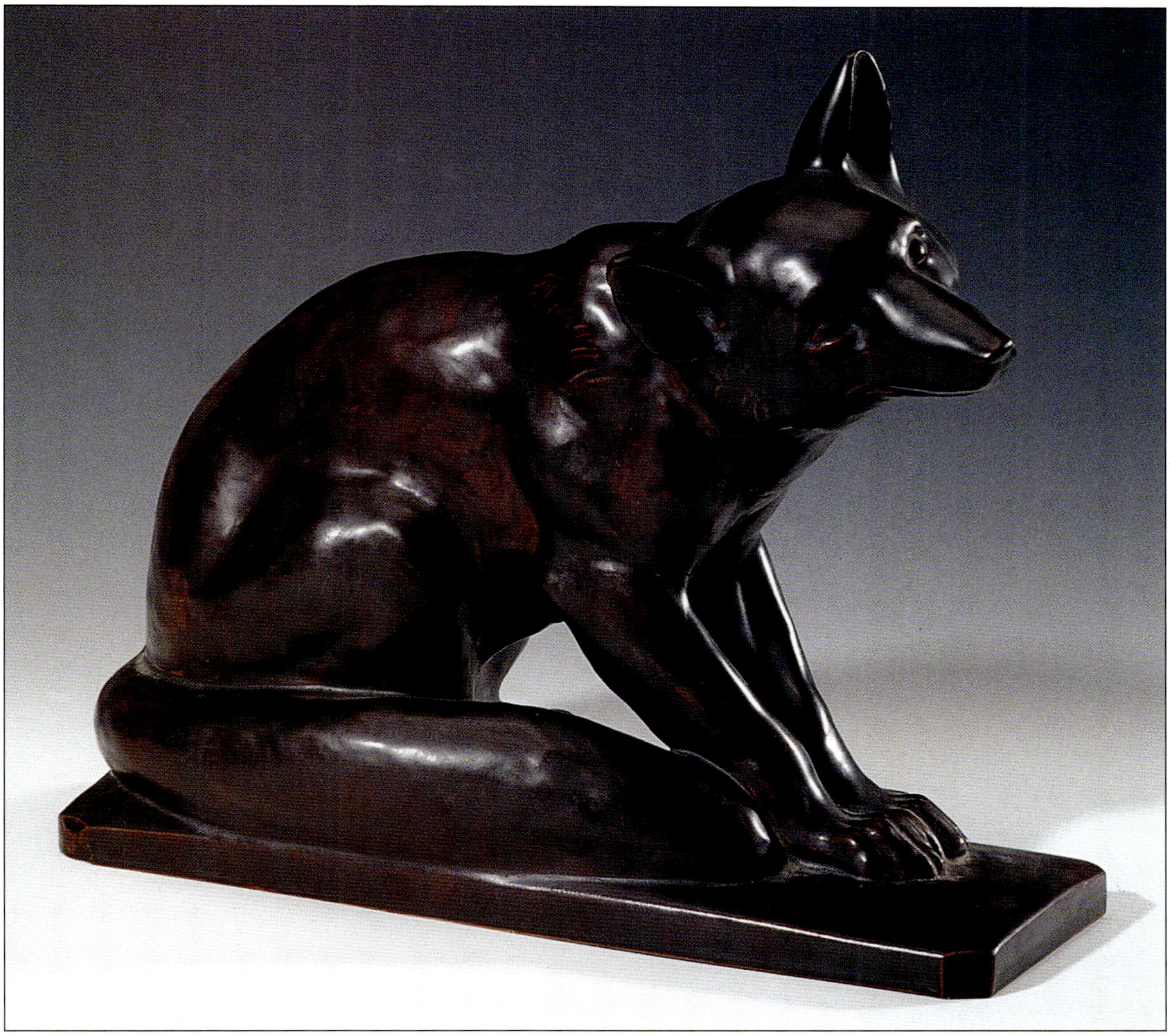

Fox, 11.5" high, marked *Th* (decoration by Camille Tharaud), shape by Robert Lemoine and exhibited at the Exposition internationale des arts et techniques, Paris, 1937. This piece was decorated with lava—"dipped in lava," according to Albert Goumot-Labesse. Other models decorated with gray jasper enamel. $1,500-$2,000.

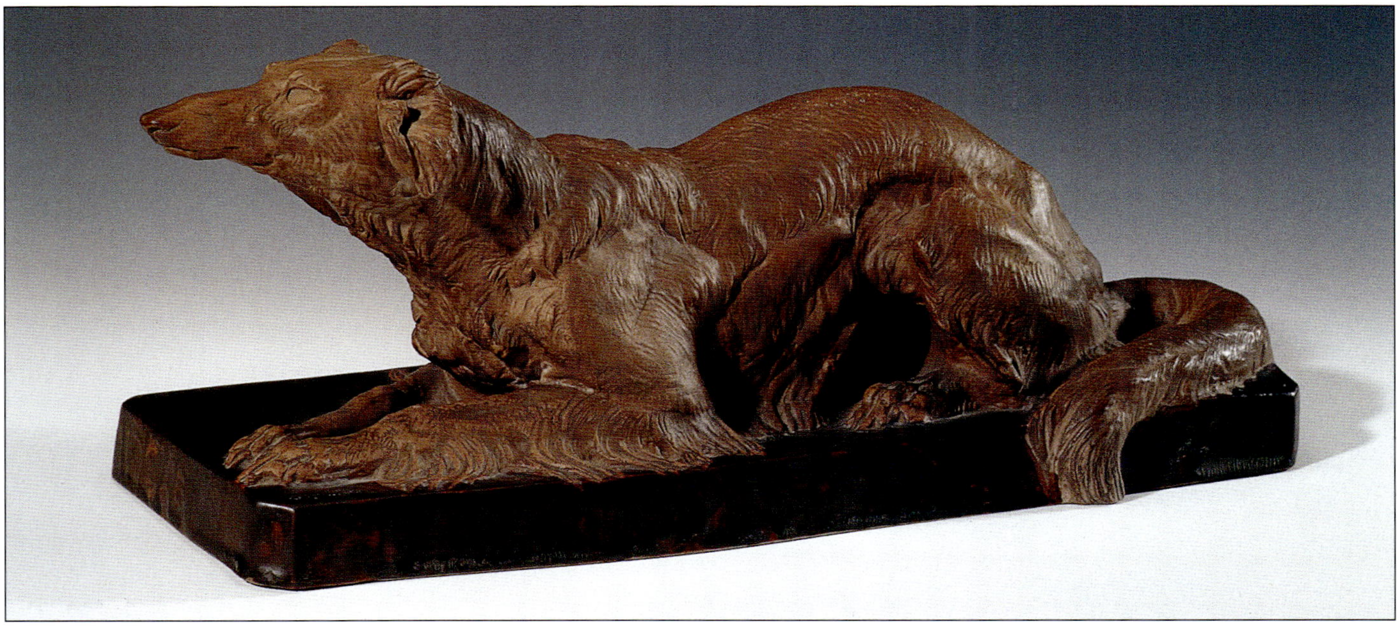

Borzoi, 17.25", about 1935, matt finish, shape attributed to François Thomas Cartier. $1,000-$1,500.

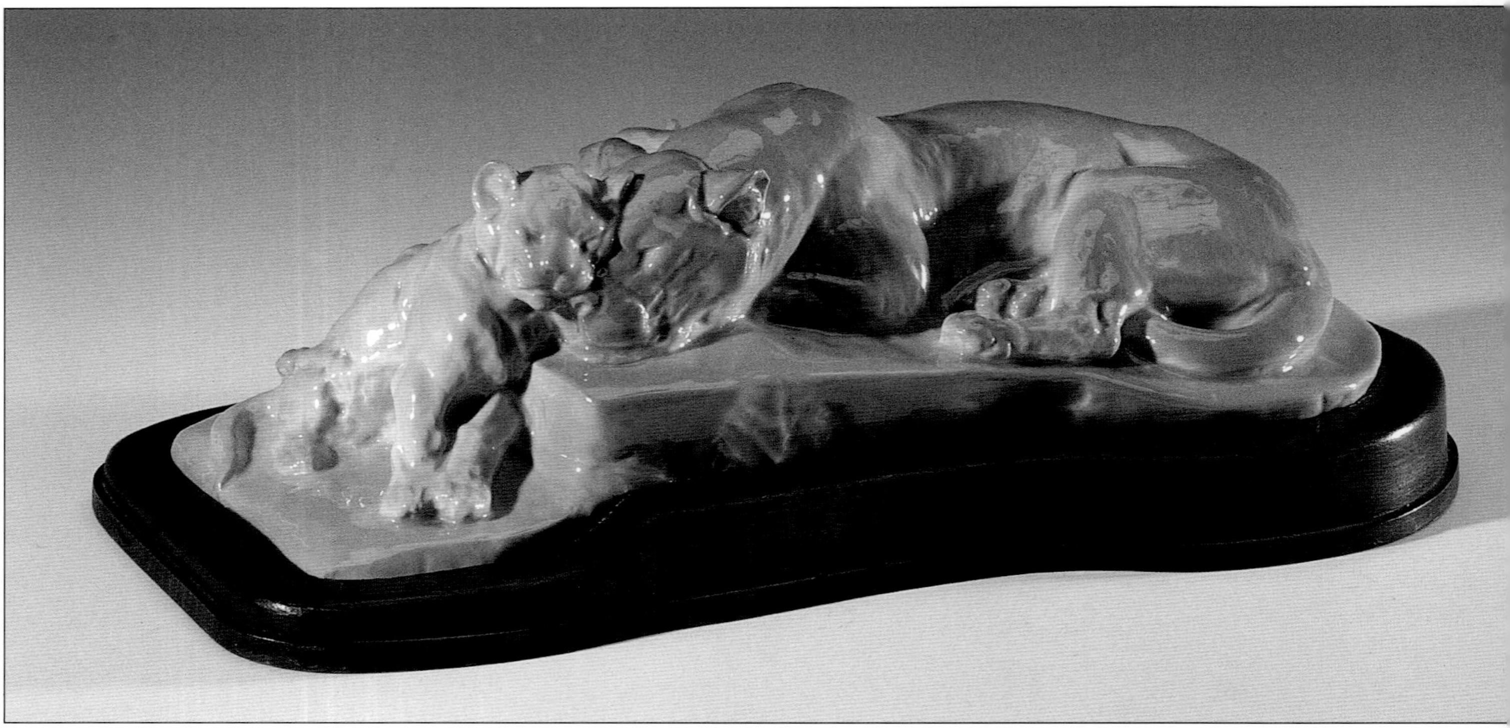

Lioness and cub on wood, 15.5", shape of François Thomas Cartier and Francine Cartier, decorated in gray *sous émail*, about 1935. $1,500-$2,000.

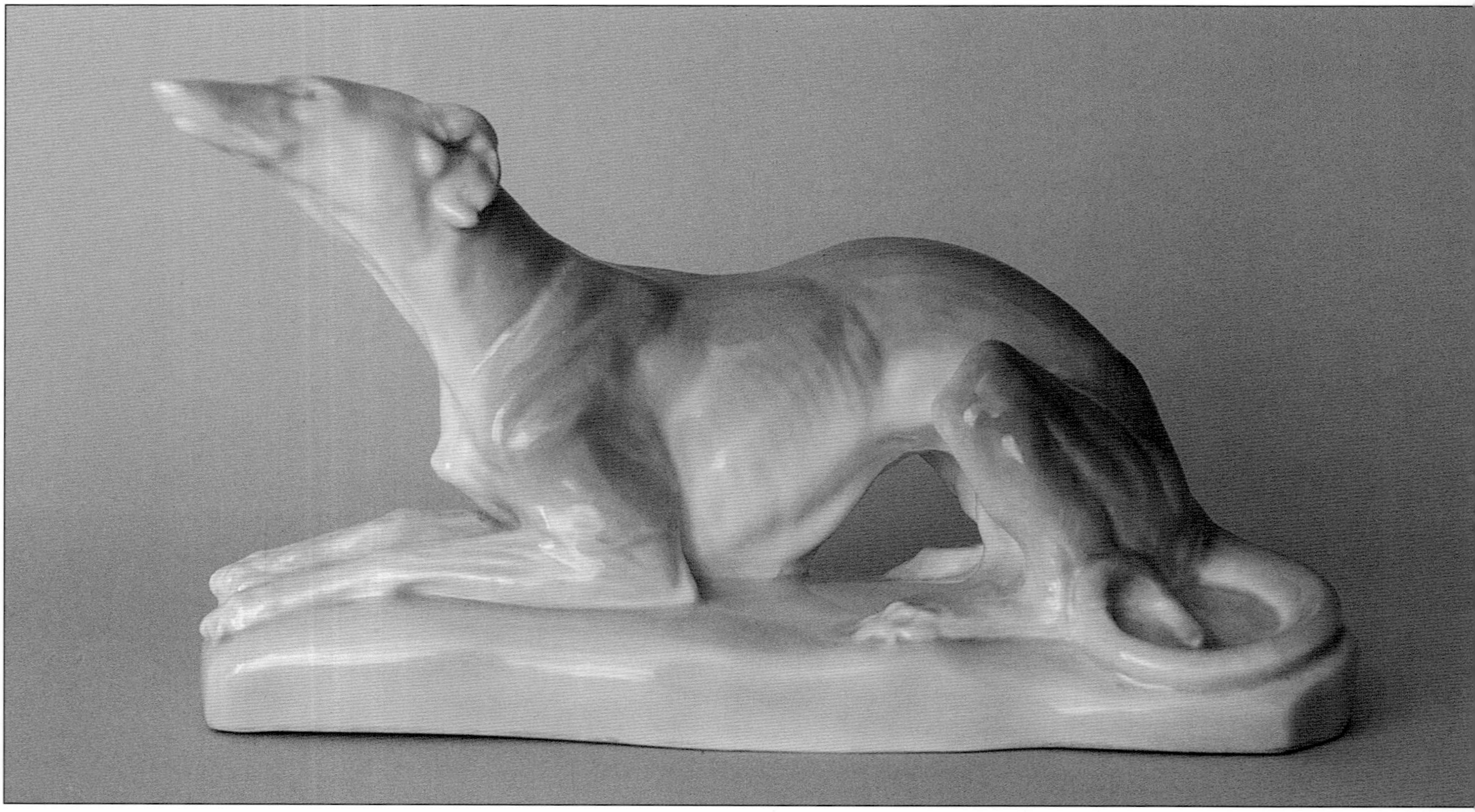

Greyhound, 6.5" high x 11", model of François Thomas Cartier, *sous émail* decoration with gray and platinum, about 1935. (Ferrer) $500-$1,000.

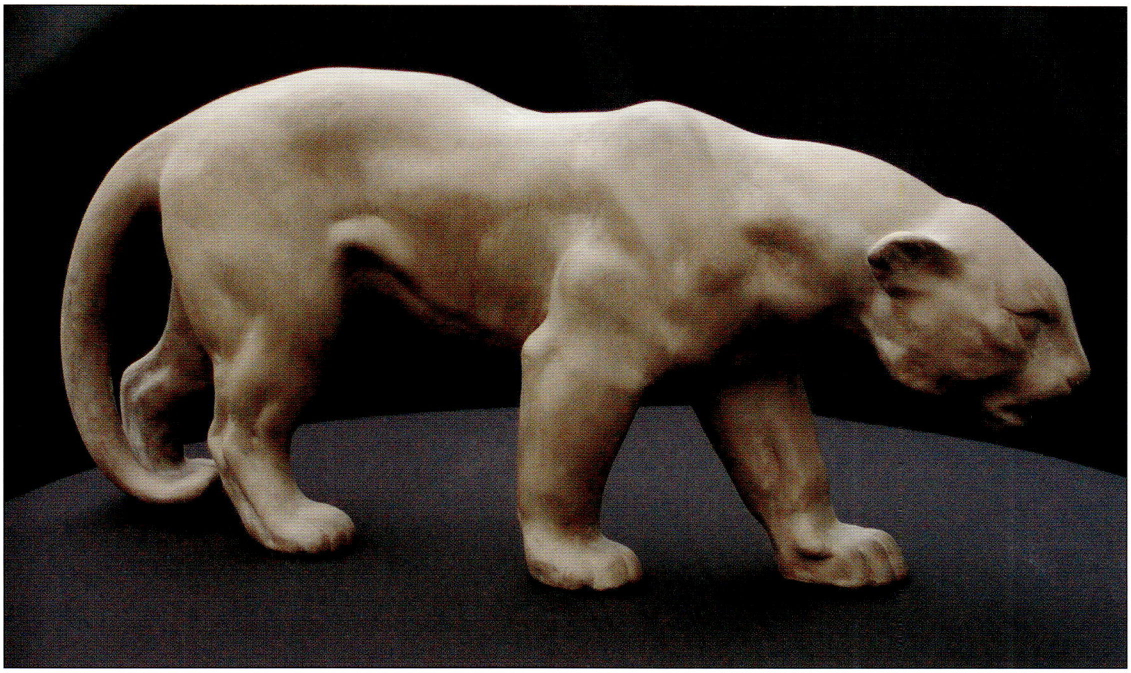

Prototype of Panther. $1,000-$1,500.

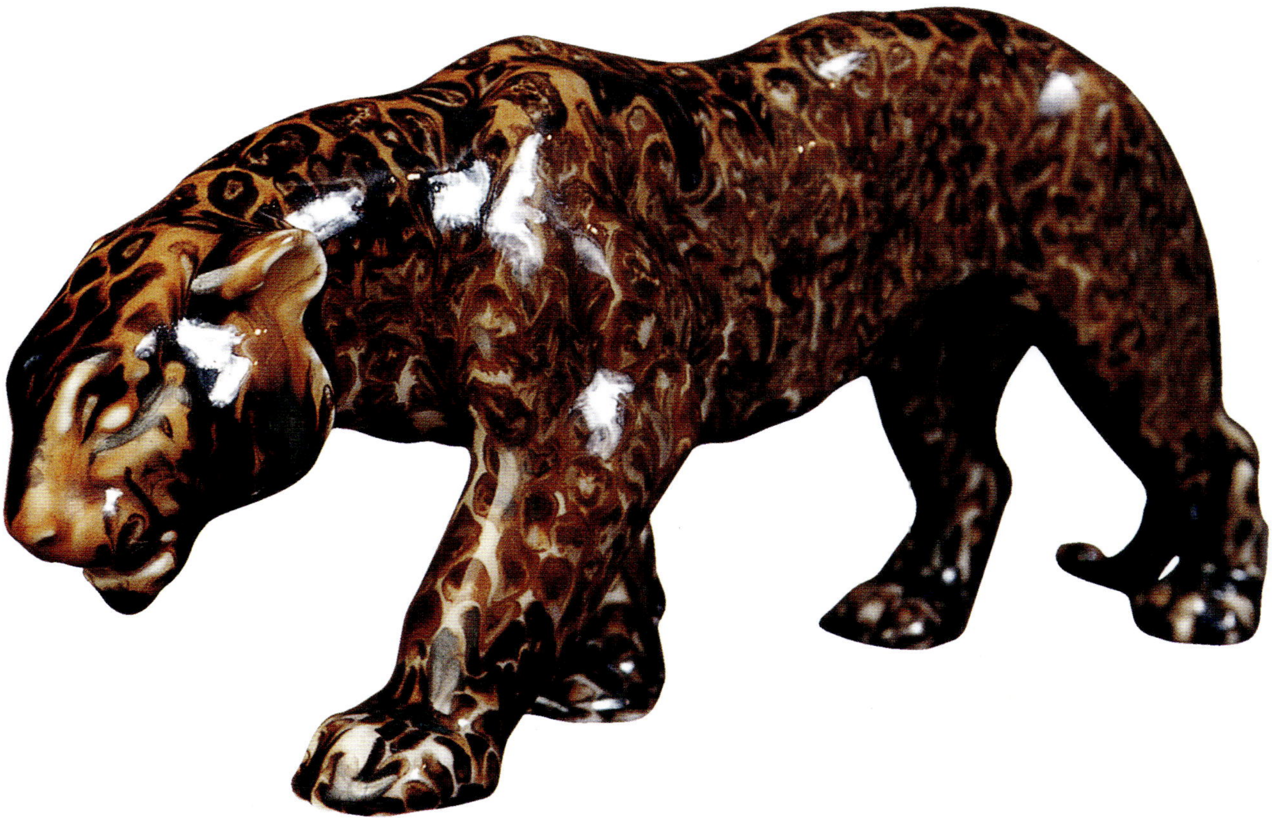

Panther, 14.5" x 6.5" high, model of Robert Lemoine, about 1933. The panthers originally exhibited at the Exposition internationale des arts et téchniques, Paris, 1937 were decorated *sous émail* with gray and platinum. $1,500-$2,000.

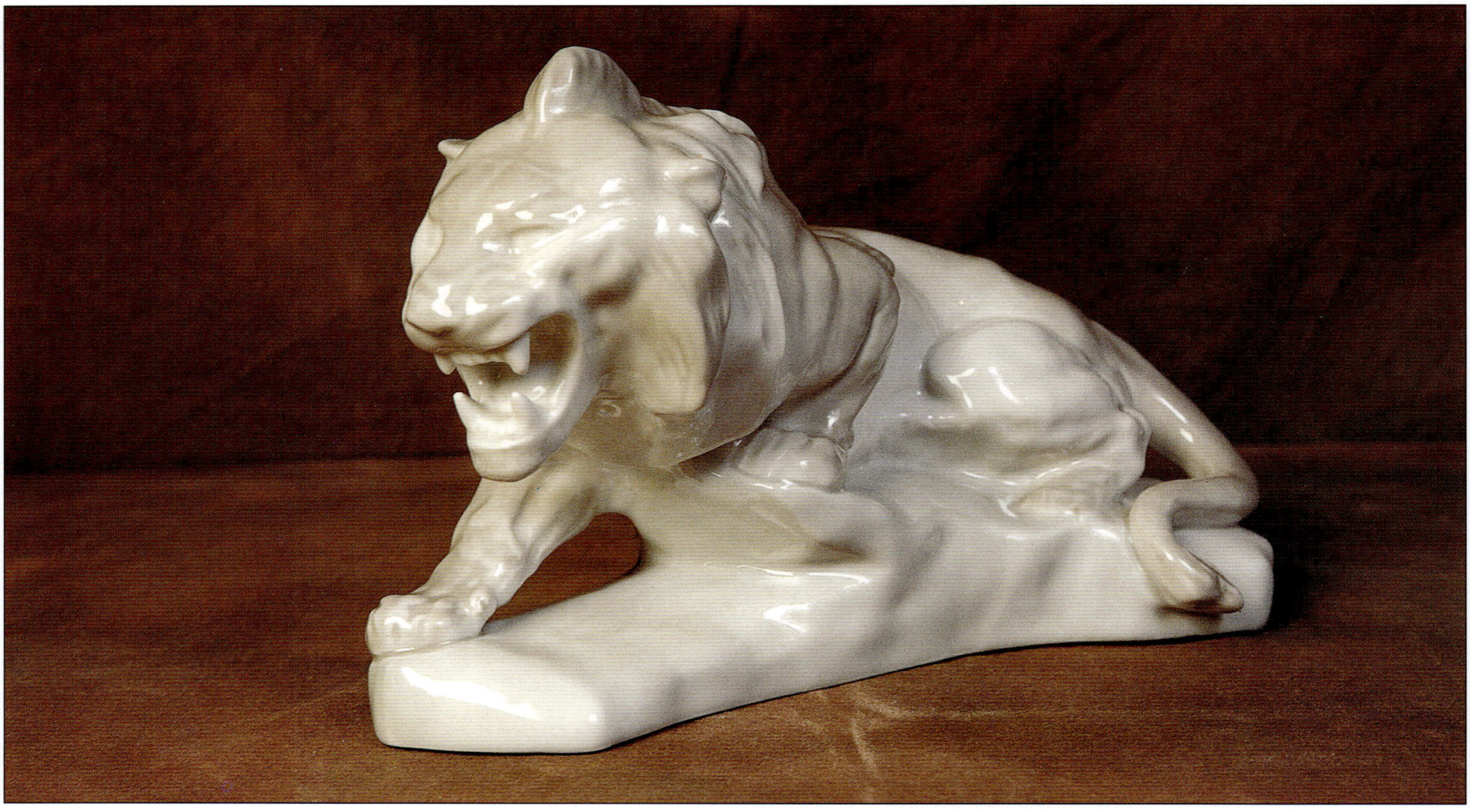

Lion, 7.5" high x 12.5", model of François Thomas Cartier, decorated *sous émail* with gray and platinum, about 1935. (Ferrer) Mark on this particular piece indicates it was decorated many years later. $1,000-$1,500.

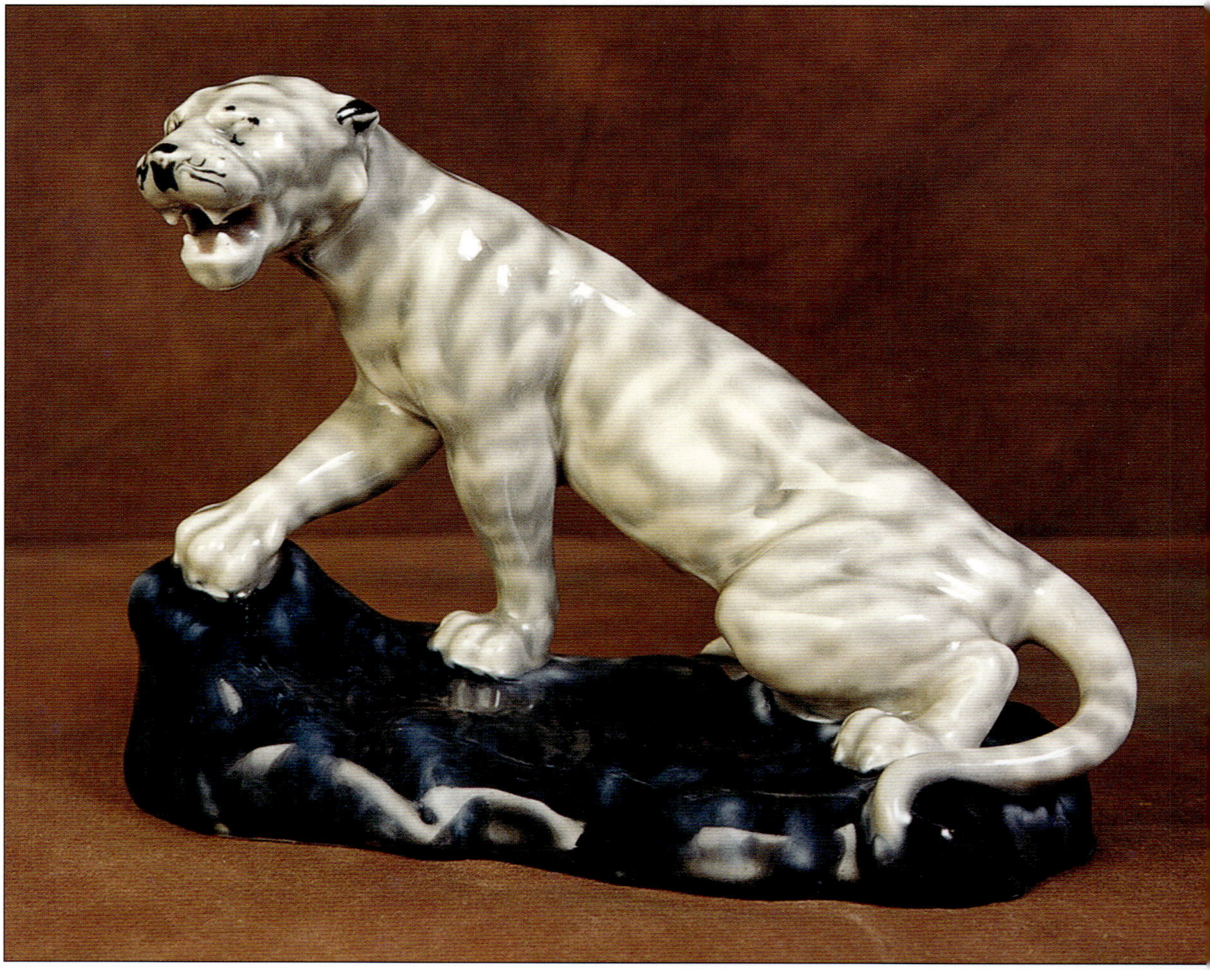

Tiger, 8" high x 10", about 1935, model created in 1935 and attributed to François Thomas Carter. (Ferrer) $500-$1,500.

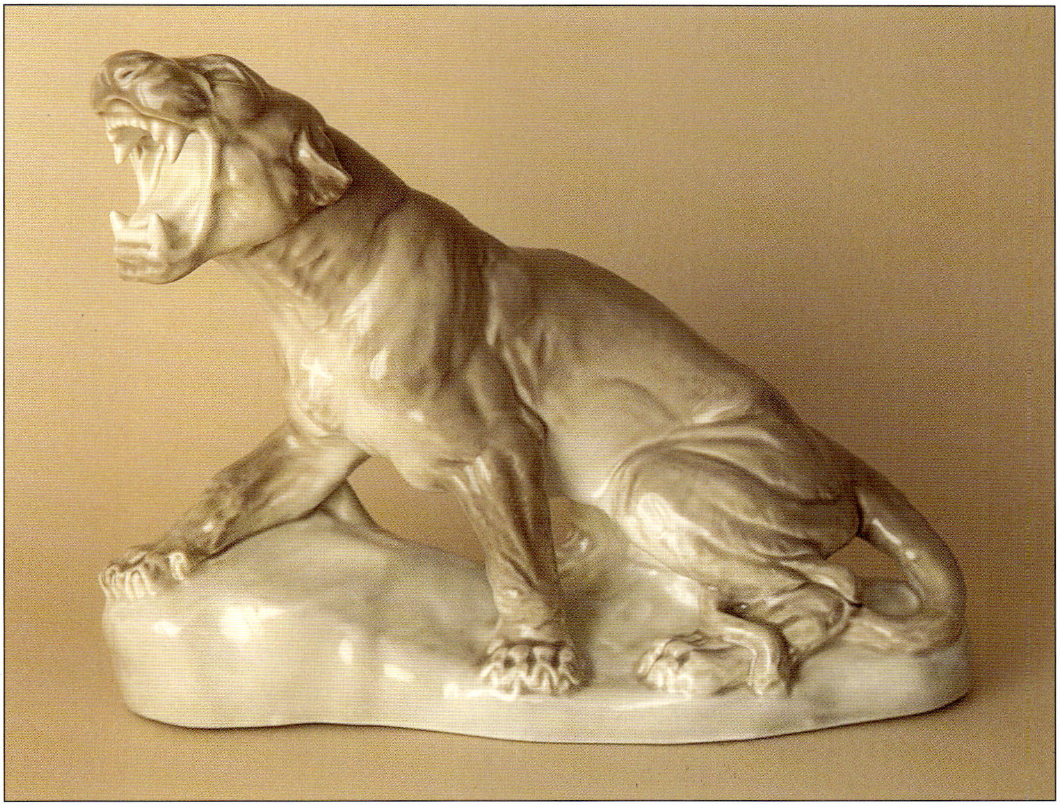

Tiger, 1.5" high x 14.5", shape attributed to François Thomas Carter, shape created in 1935. (Ferrer) $1,000-$1,500.

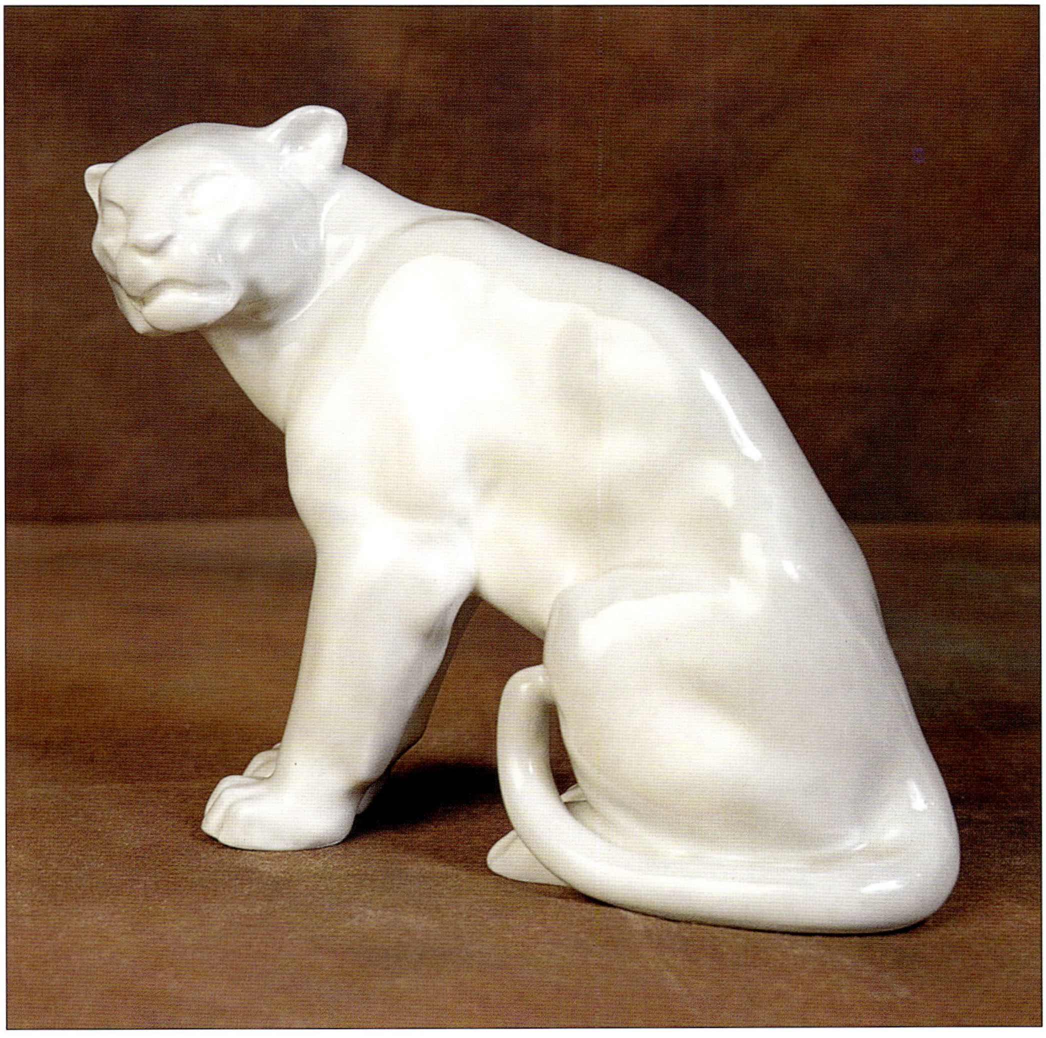

Panther, 7.5" high x 10.5" diagonal. This piece was decorated *sous émail* gray and platinum, like the piece exhibited at the Exposition internationale des arts et techniques, Paris, 1937. $500-$1,000.

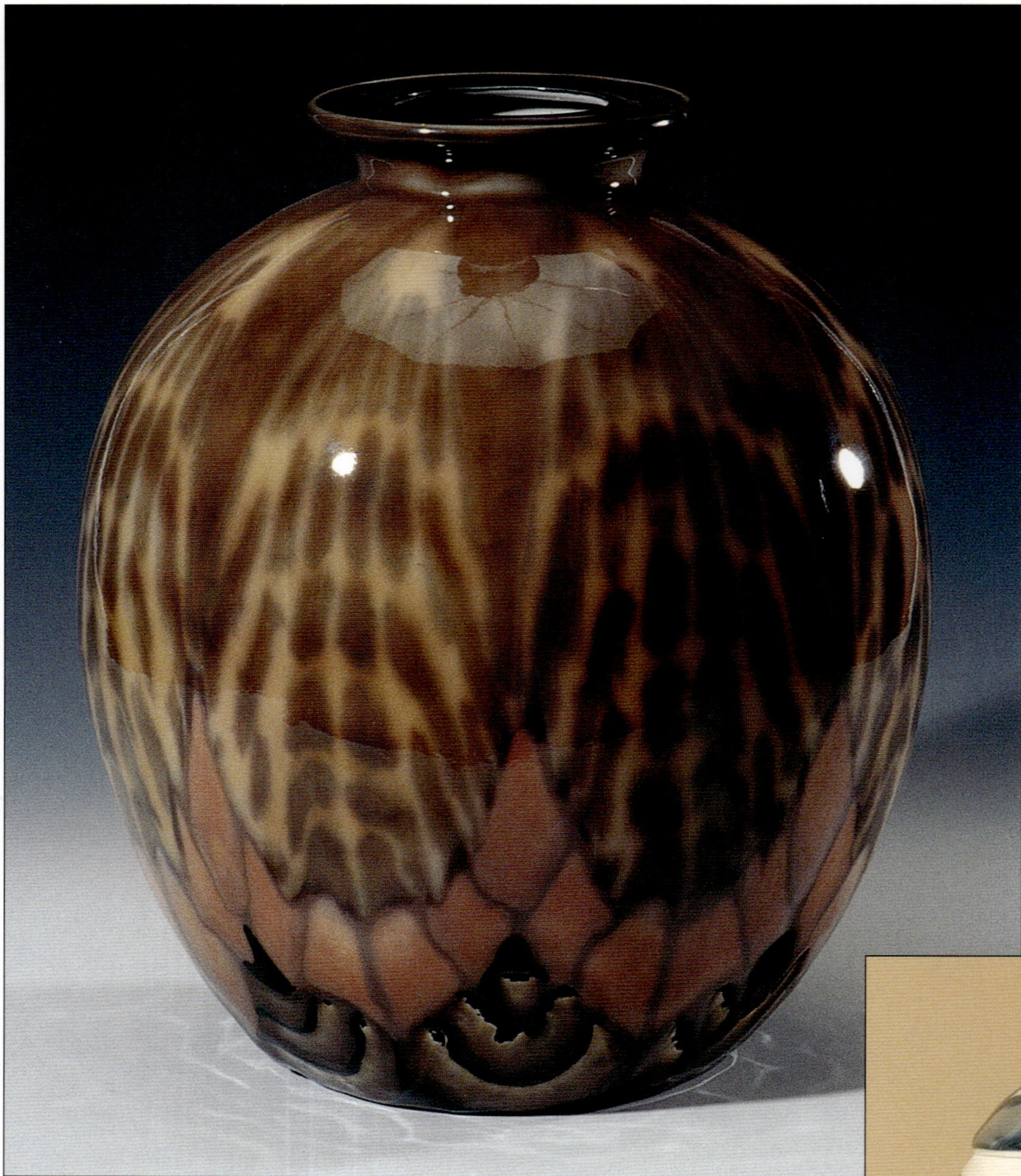

Vase, *Jasmin*, shape of Henry Rapin, 13" high. This decoration was exhibited at the Salon des artistes décorateurs, Paris, 1931. The pink color was achieved using a base of gold chloride rather than the usual pink from using alumina. (Ferrer) $500-$1,000.

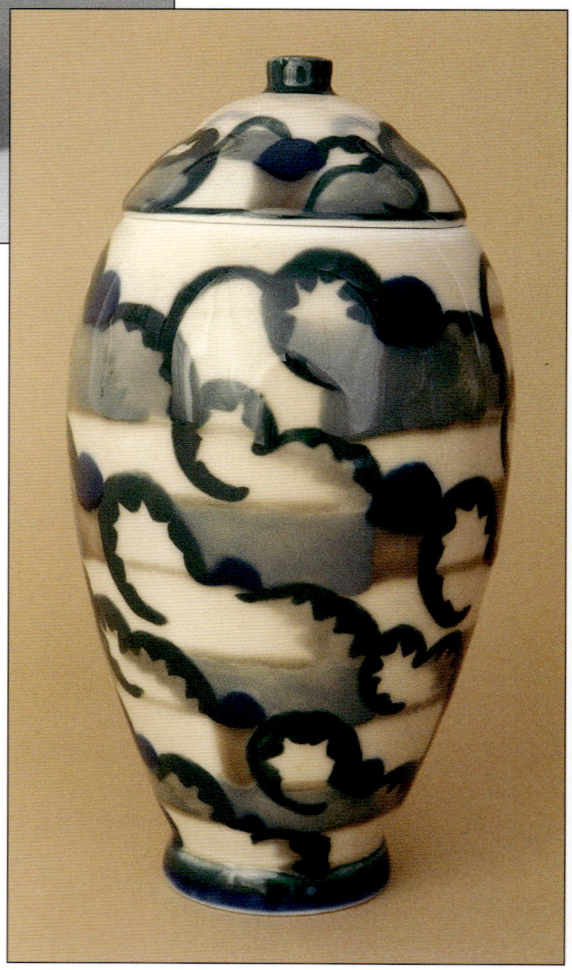

Vase, *Manon*, 9.75" high, 1933, rare decoration and signed *René Barlaud*. Barlaud was a painter and enameller who designed several Art Deco and landscape decorations for Camille Tharaud. $1,000-$1,500.

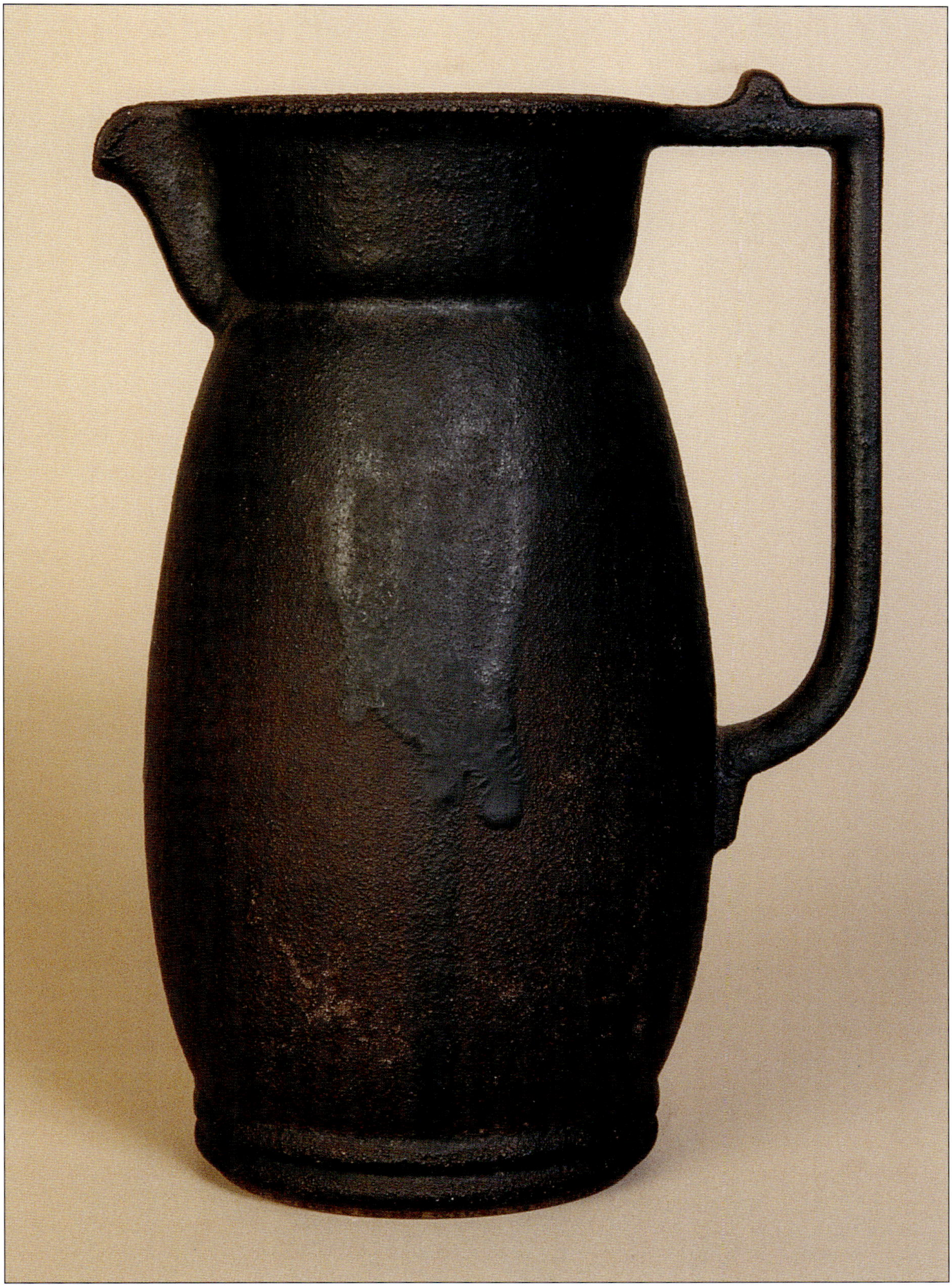

Pitcher, *Rapin*, 8.35" high, marked *5/7—36 CTharaud* in brown (July 5, 1936). Pierre Forestier, a respected and knowledgeable Tharaud collector, stated that this piece is signed by Camille Tharaud himself and was probably an experiment with an enamel. He further said that this piece was part of Tharaud's estate. $500-$1,000.

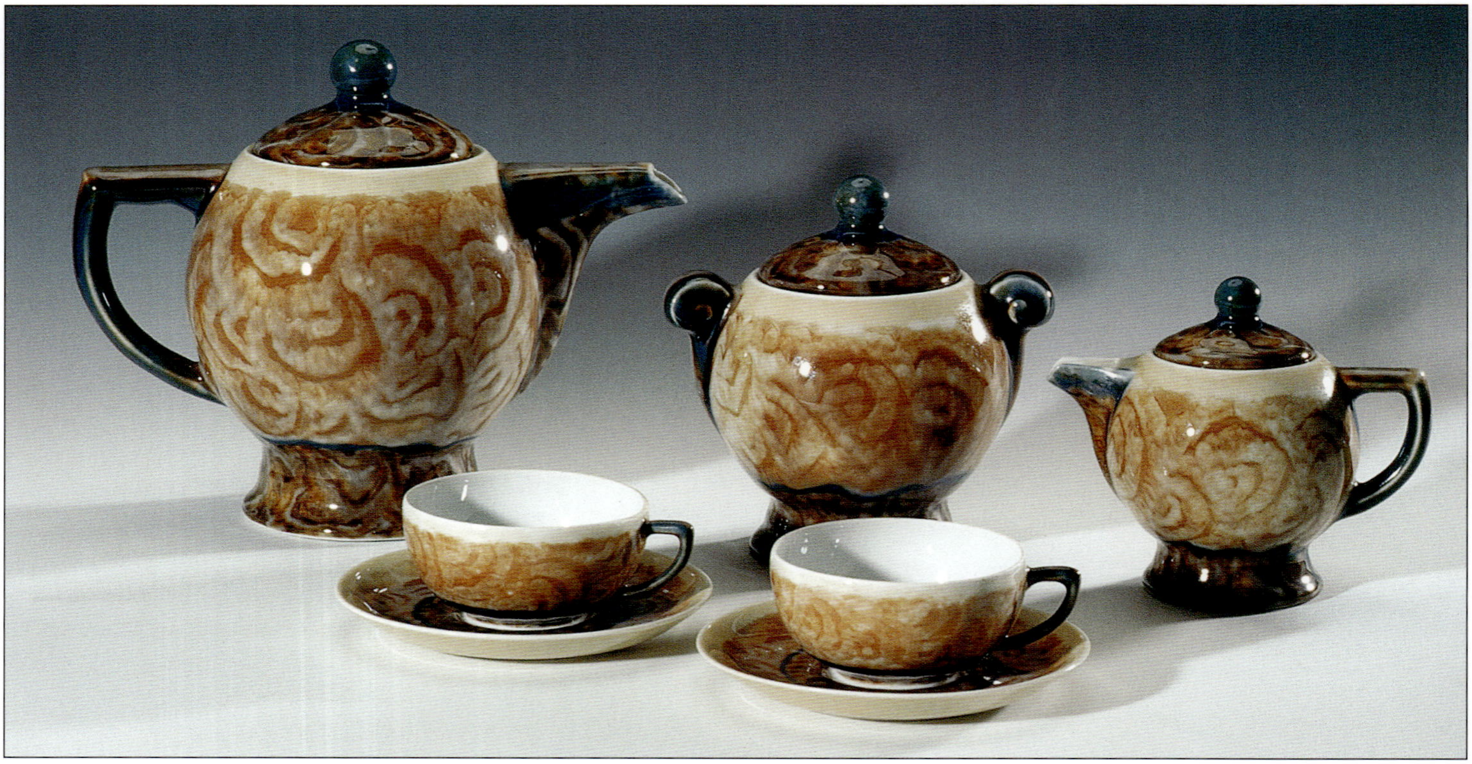

Tea Set, 1930-1945. $500-$1,000.

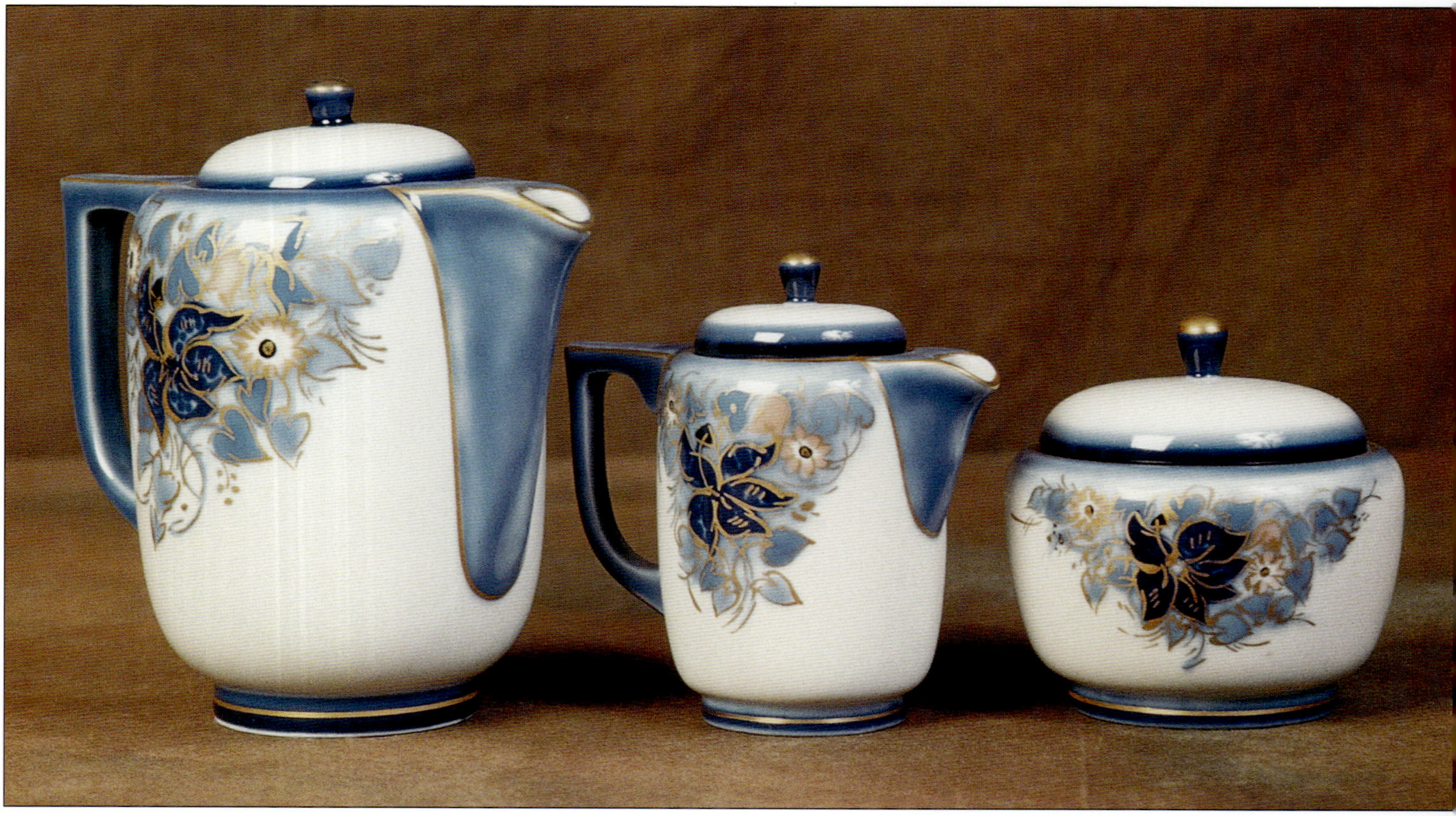

Coffee set, 1930-1945. Less than $500.

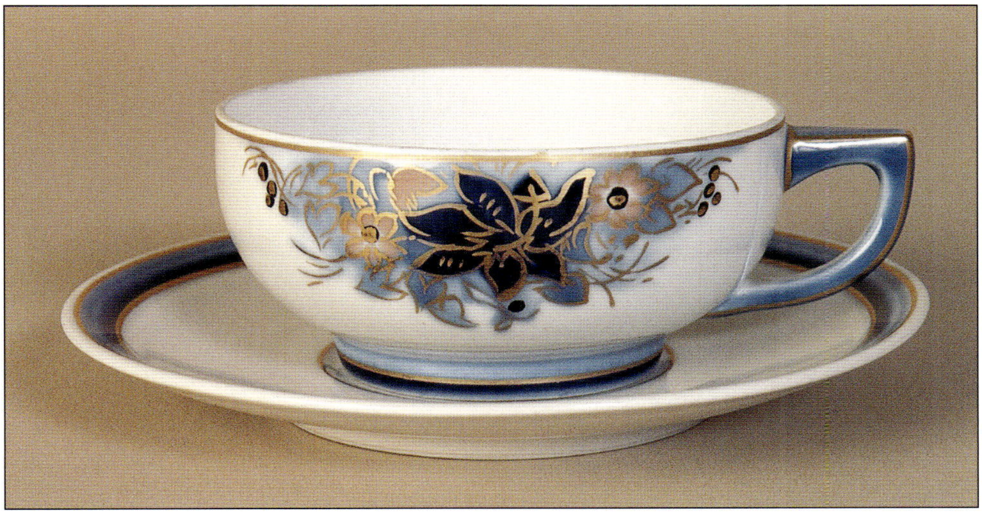

Cup and saucer, cup, 1.9" high x 3.75" in diameter, and saucer, 6" in diameter, after 1943, incised *RL* (Renée L.). Less than $500.

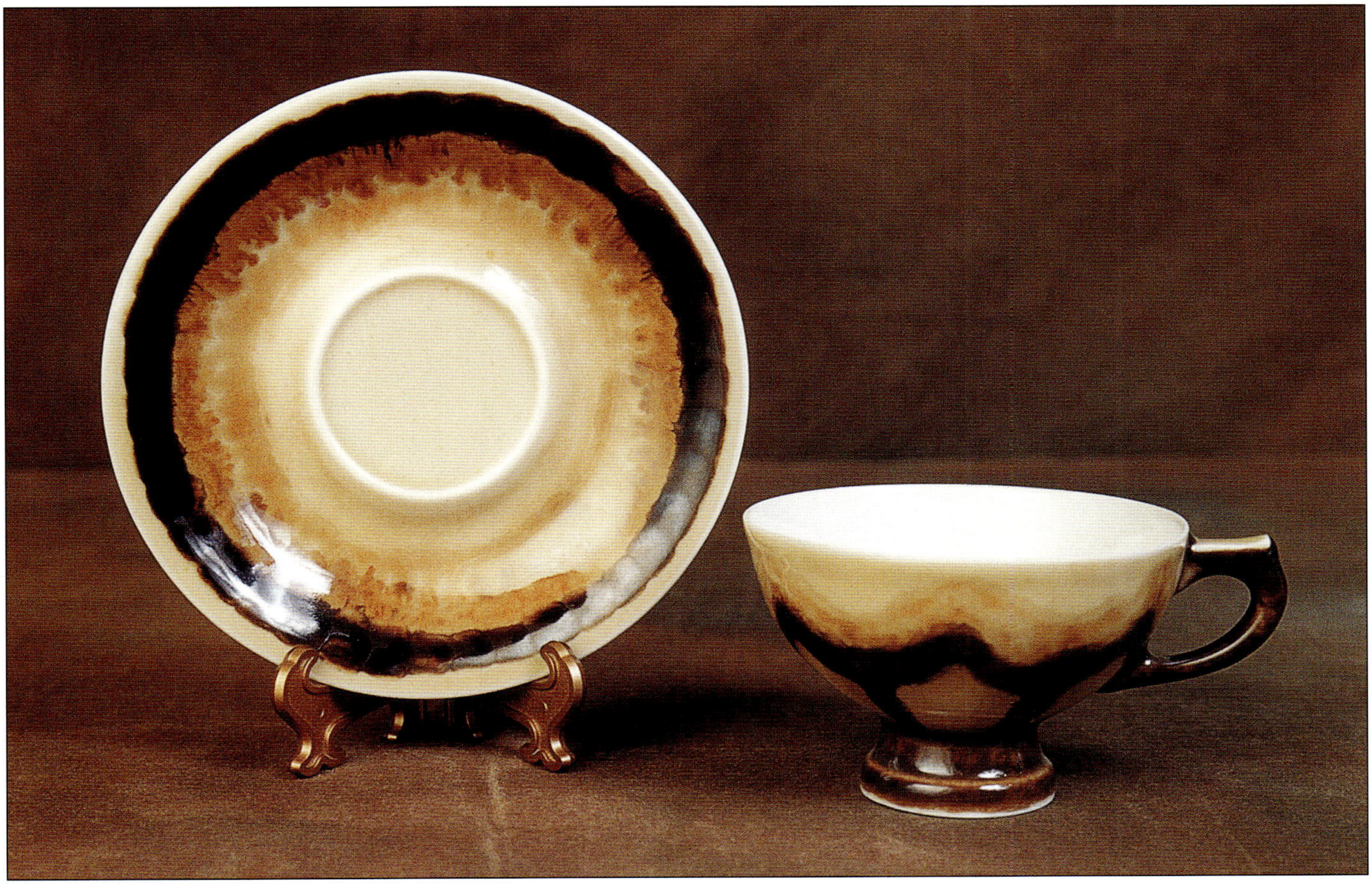

Cup and saucer, 1930-1945. Less than $500.

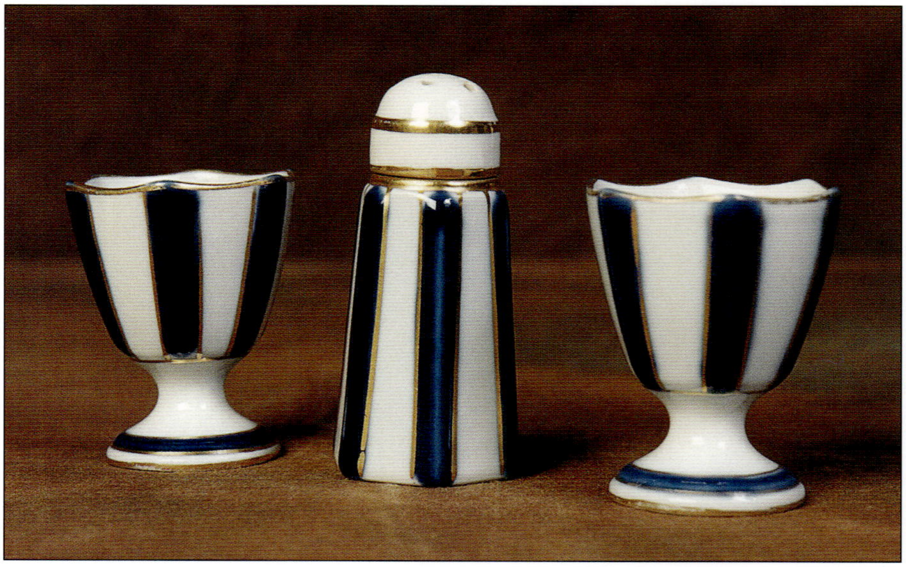

Egg set, 1930-1945. Less than $500.

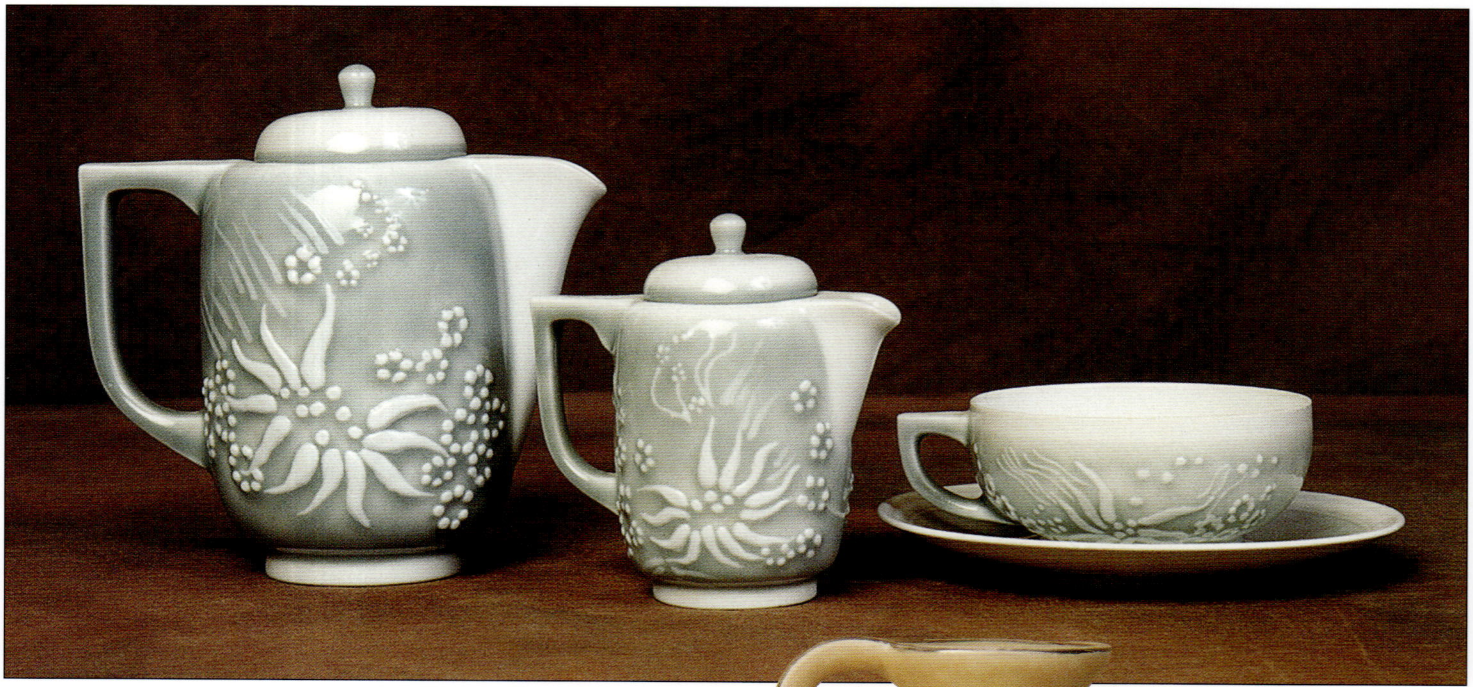

Coffee set, 1930-1945, starfish and algae. Less than $500.

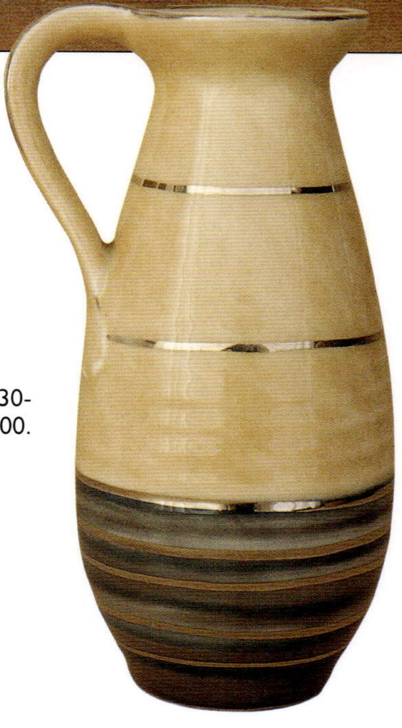

Pitcher, 6.75" high, 1930-1945. Less than $500.

Pitcher, *Rapin*, 8" high, 1930-1945. Less than $500.

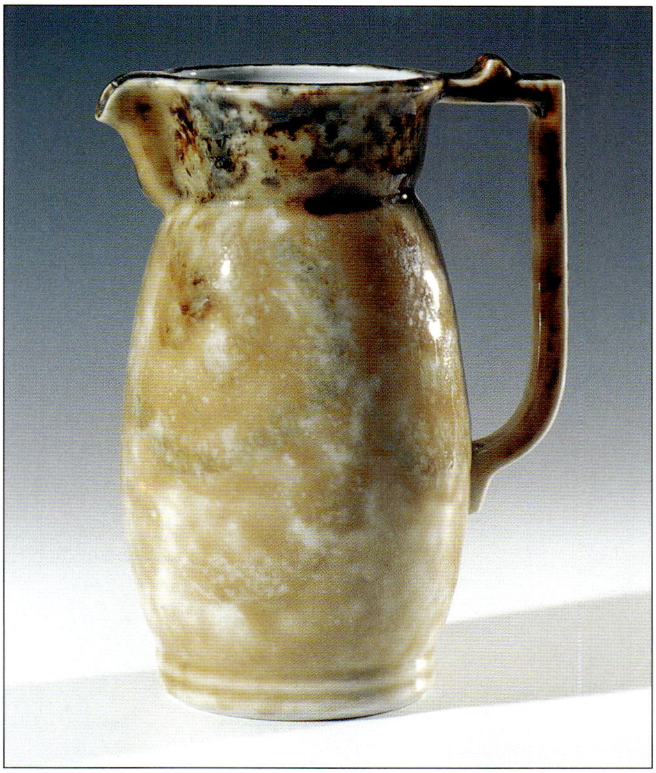

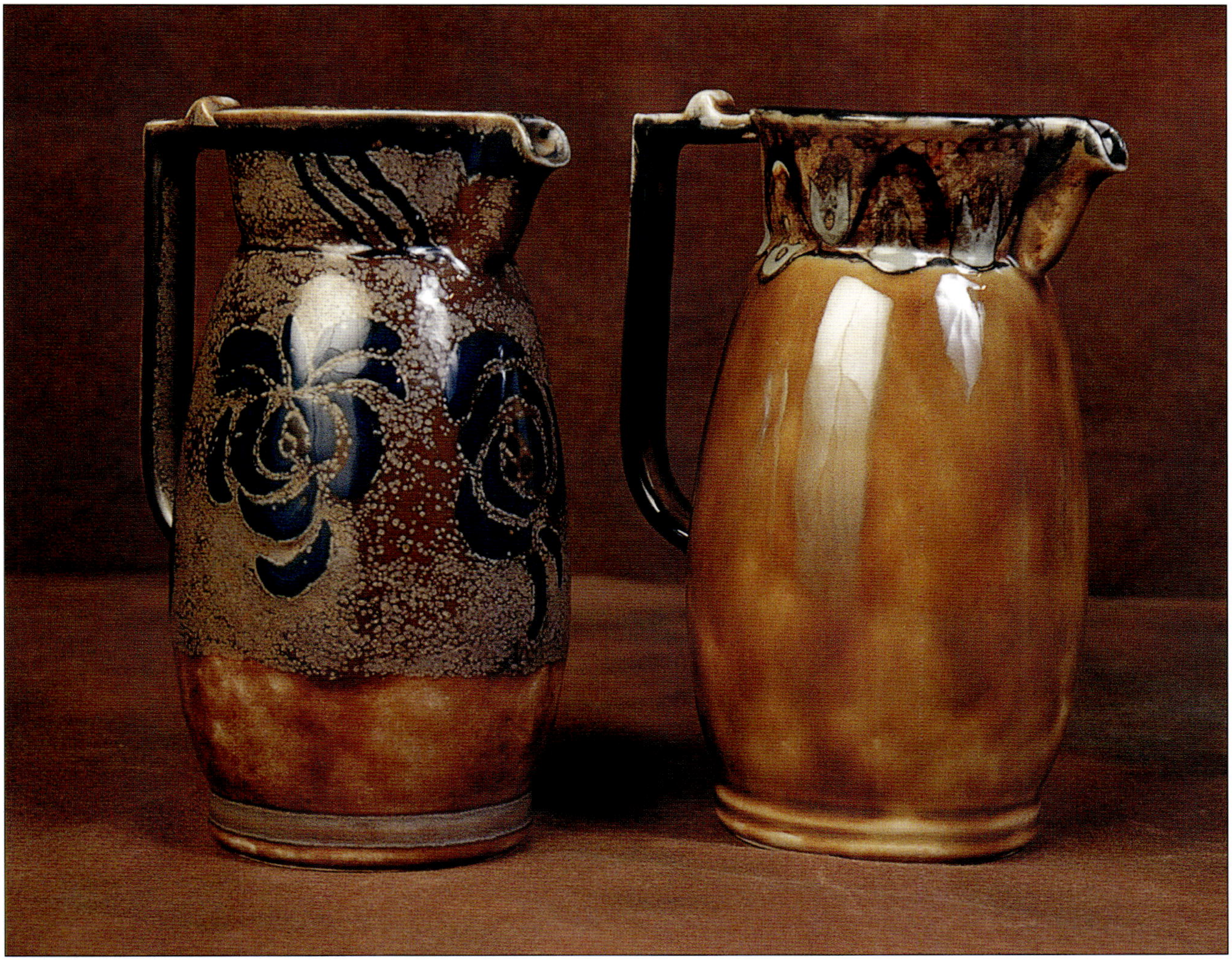

Pitchers, *Rapin*, 8.25" high, 1930-1945. Left, $500-$1,000; right, less than $500.

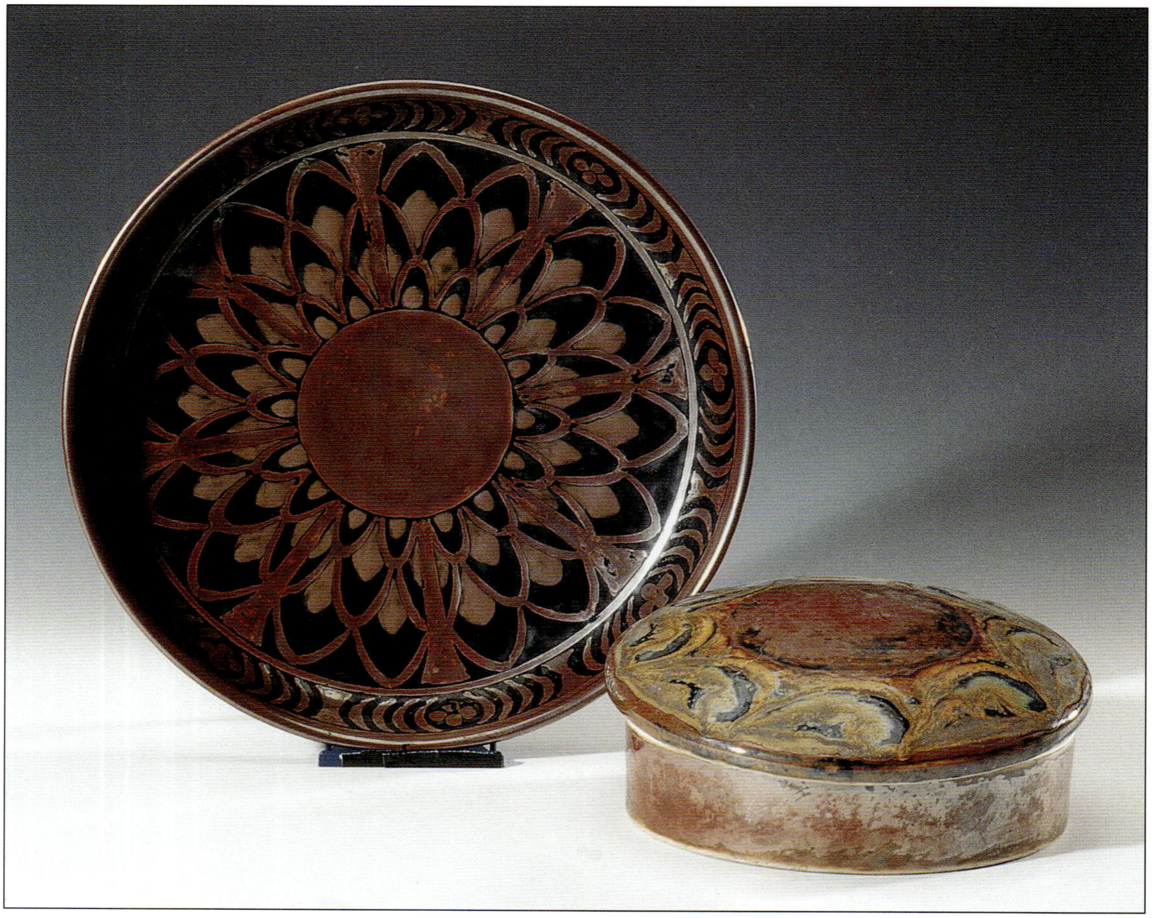

Tray and covered box, 1930-1945. The enamel of the box contains uranium. Uranium was used for a time until the studio realized that it was hazardous (Goumot-Labesses). Each less than $500.

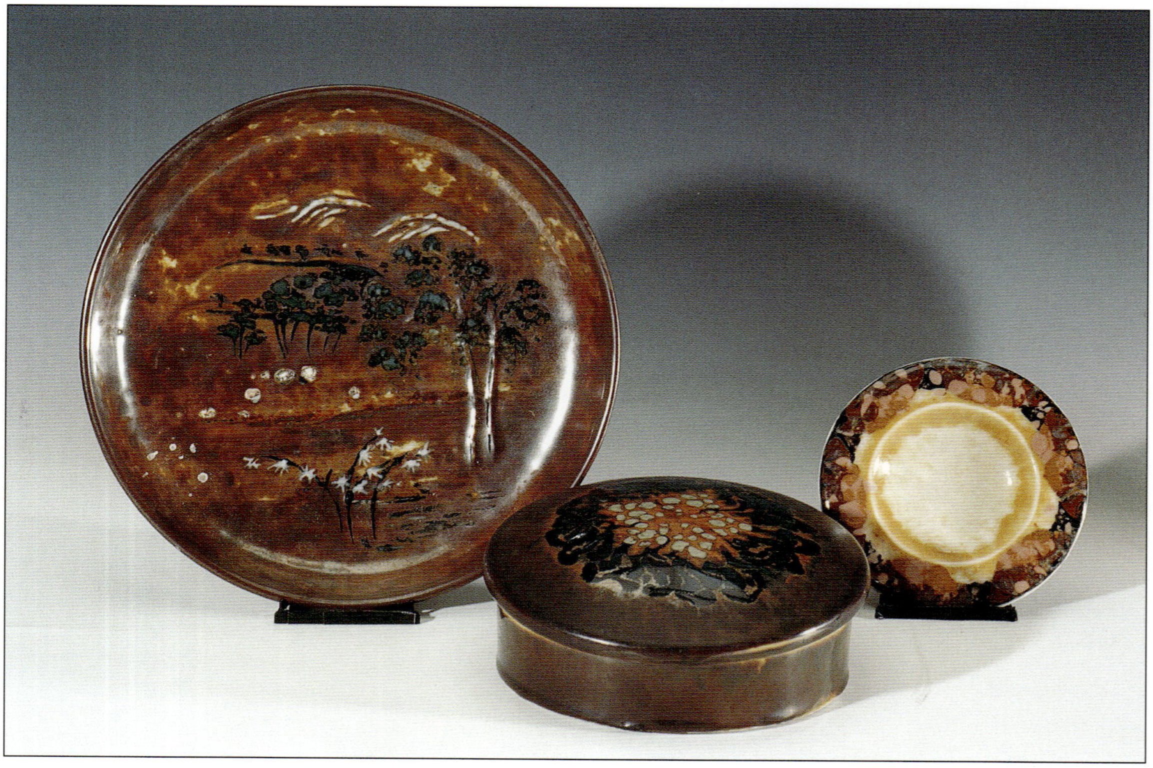

Scenic plate, marked *Th* but decorated by Odette Tharaud, according to Odette [Tharaud] Goumot-Labesse. Covered box and ashtray marked and decorated by Odette Tharaud. Each $500-$1,000.

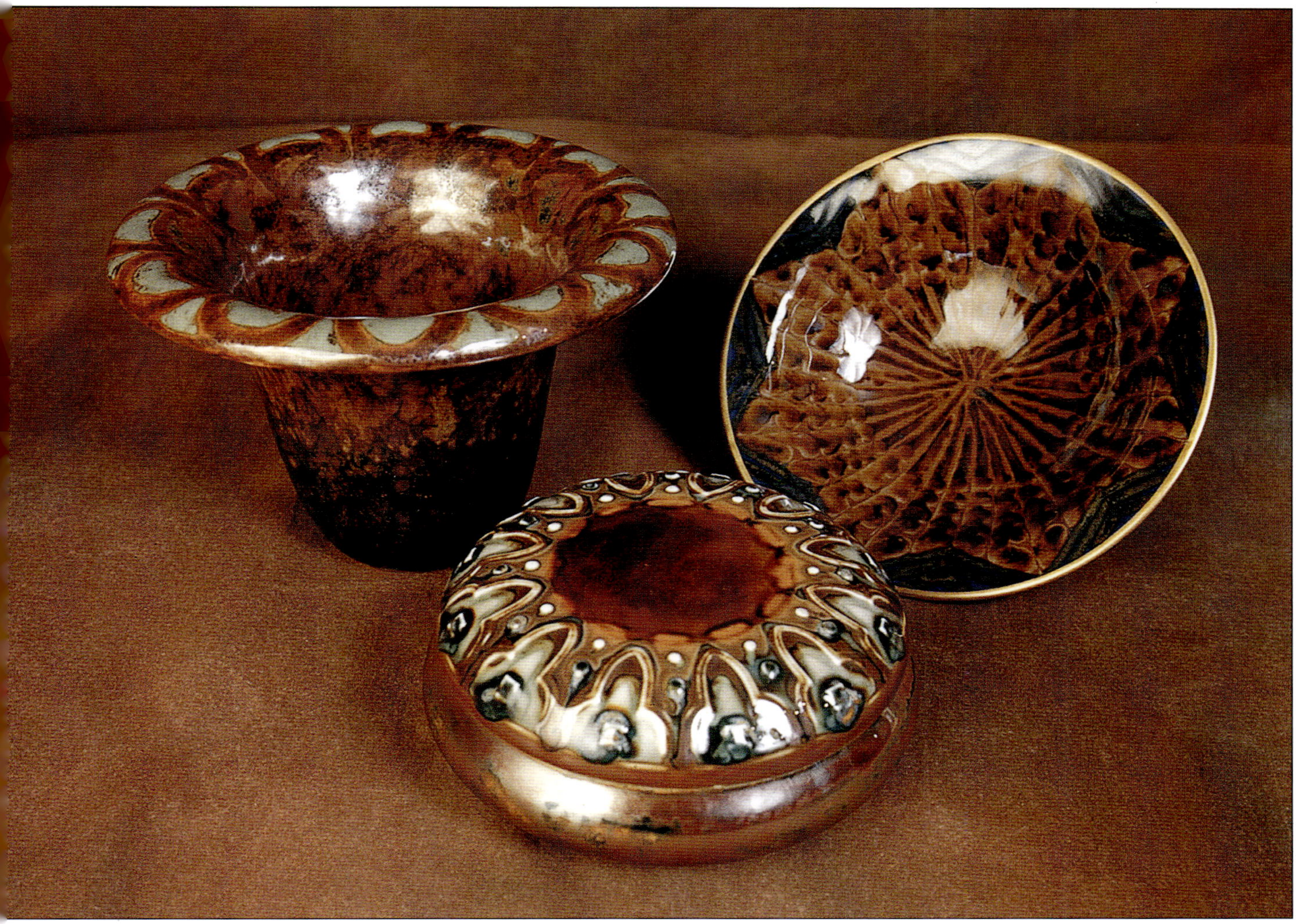

Flared vase, 5.75" high, incised *GD*, 1930-1945; covered box, 6" in diameter, signed *JP* in black, 1930-1945; and bowl, 7" in diameter, 1930-1945. Less than $500.

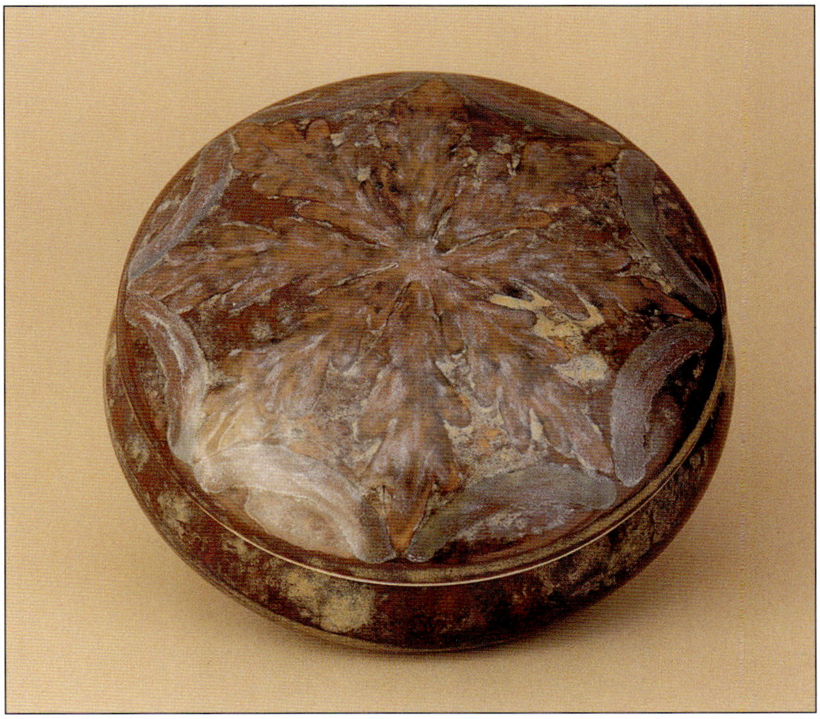

Covered box, 6" in diameter, 1930-1945. Less than $500.

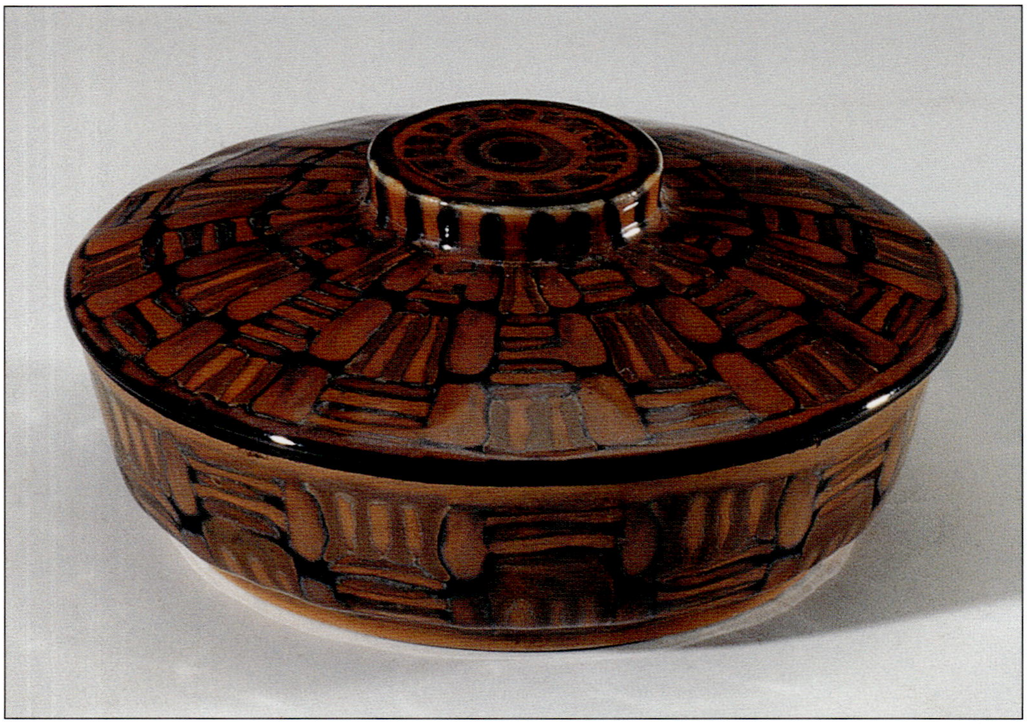

Covered dish, 5.25" in diameter, incised with the marks of Camille Tharaud and Henri Rapin. According to Odette [Tharaud] Goumot-Labesse, this piece was decorated by Henri Rapin. $500-$1,000.

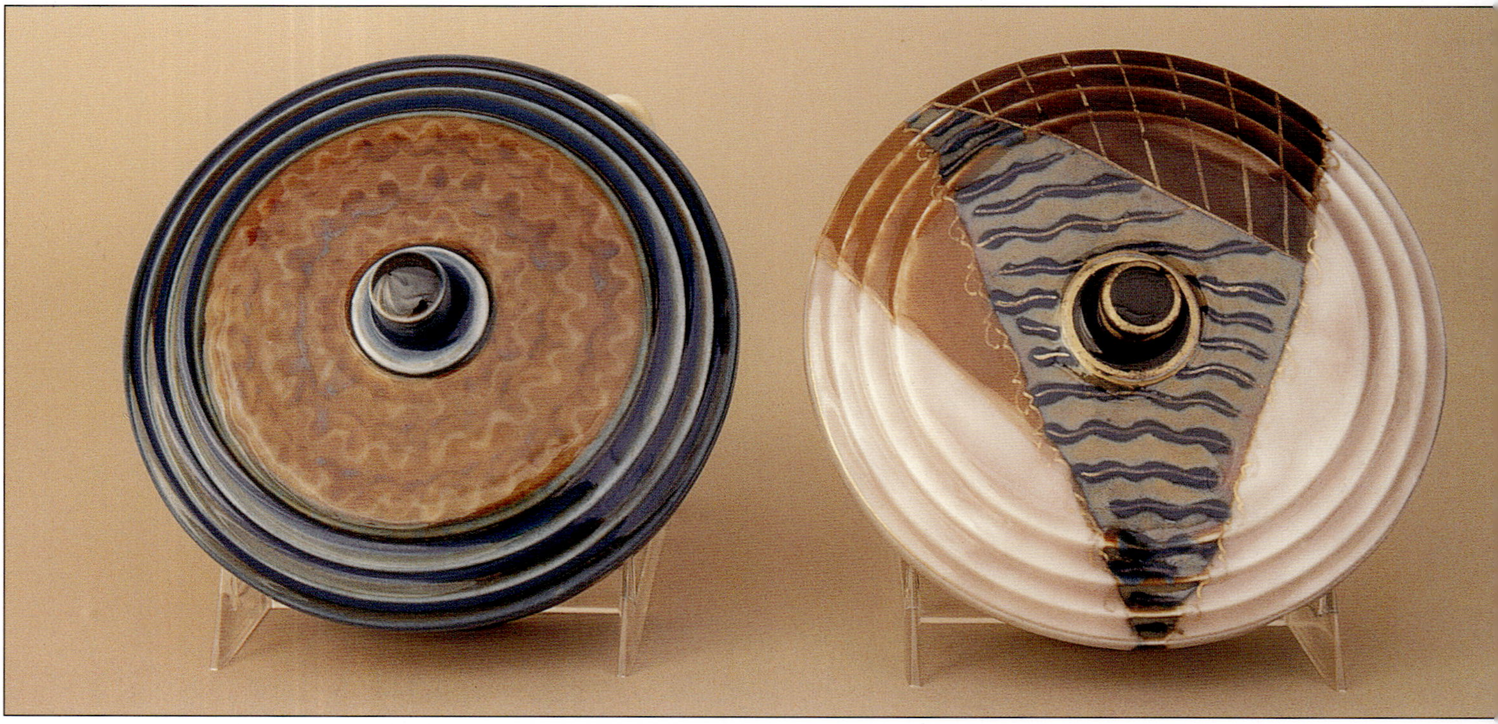

Two covered dishes with finials, 5" in diameter x 2.75" high, 1930-1945. Each less than $500.

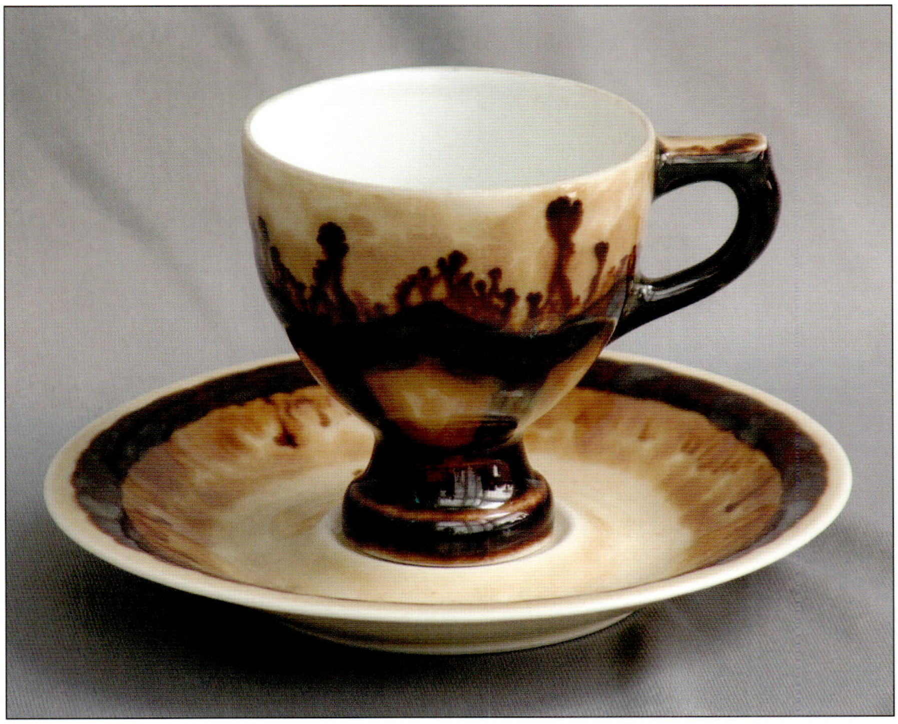

Cup and saucer. Less than $500.

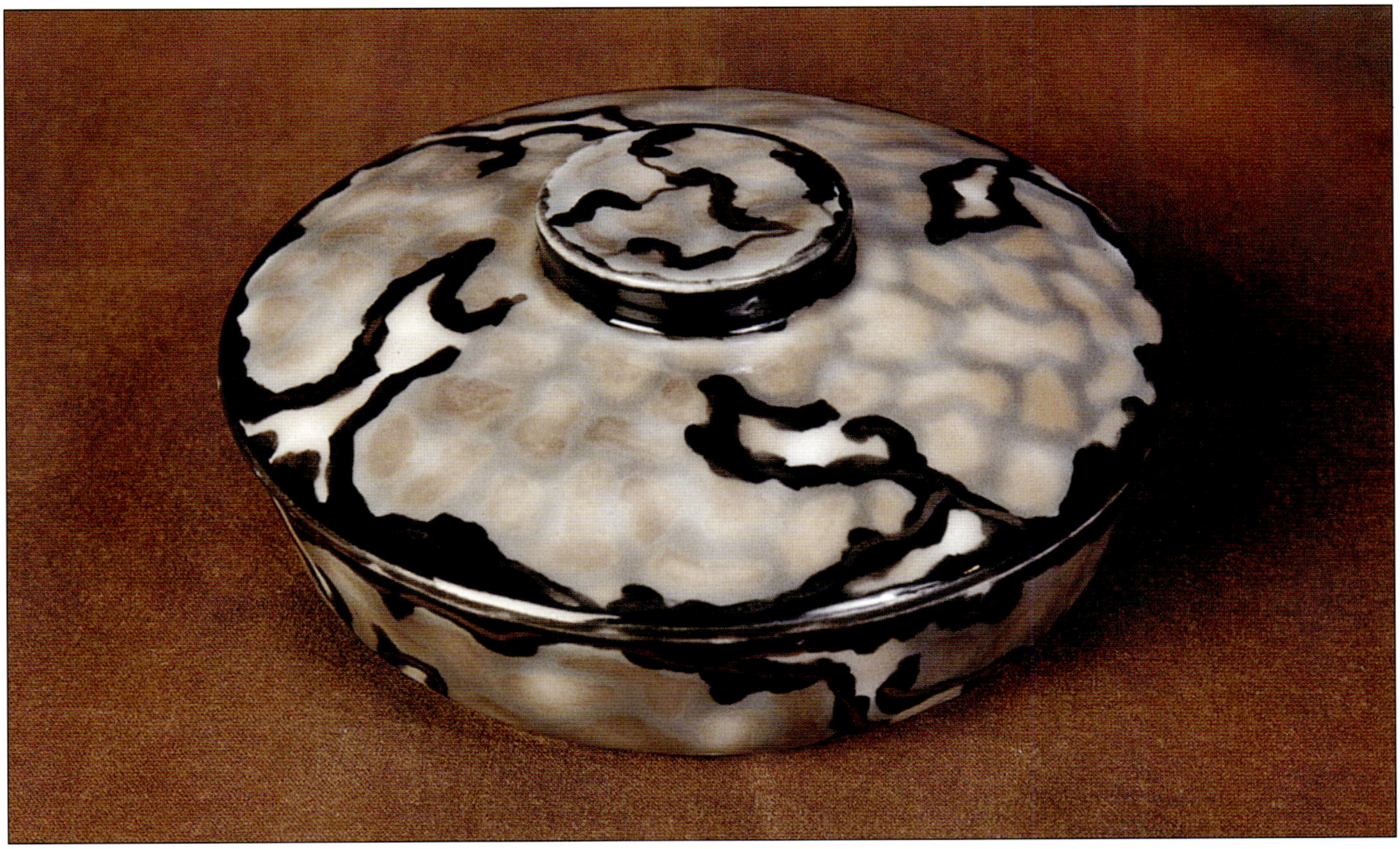

Covered dish, 5" diameter, 1930-1945. Less than $500.

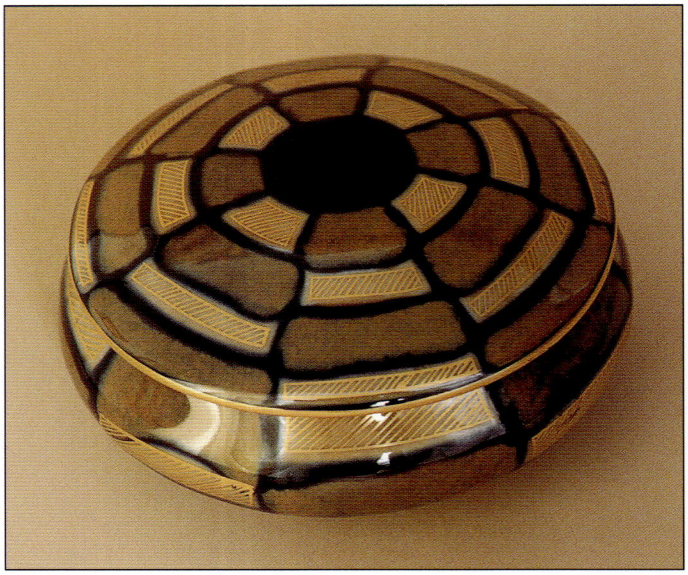

Covered box, 6" in diameter, 1930-1945. Less than $500.

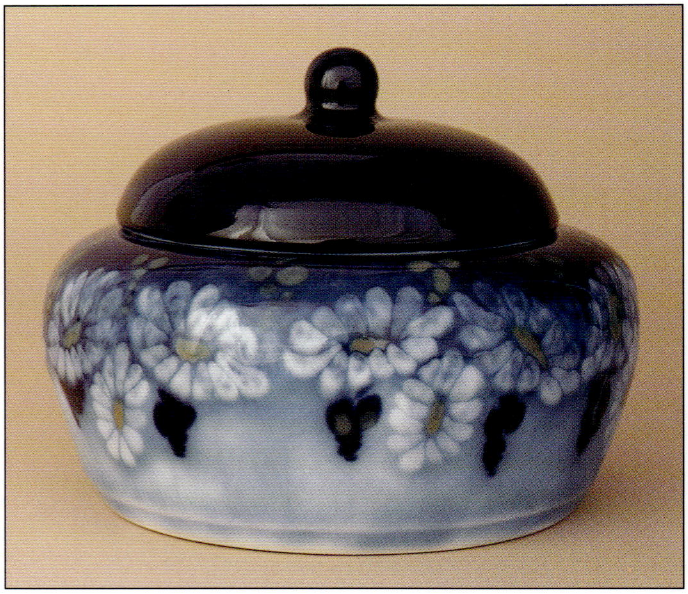

Covered dish, 5.25" high, 1930-1945, incised *R.*, cobalt with white daisies. Less than $500.

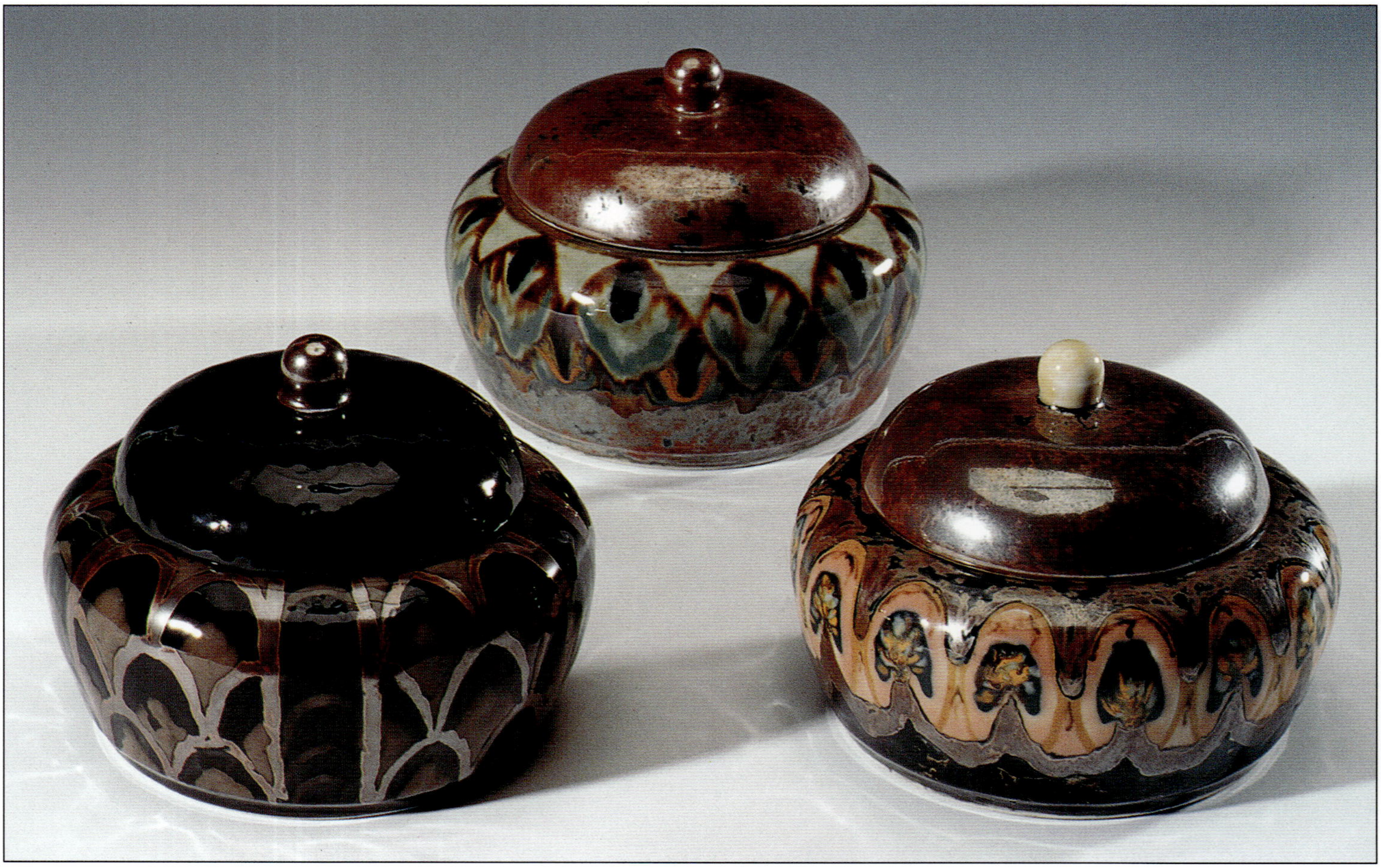

Covered bowls; bowl in center, after 1943; other bowls, 1930-1945. Each less than $500.

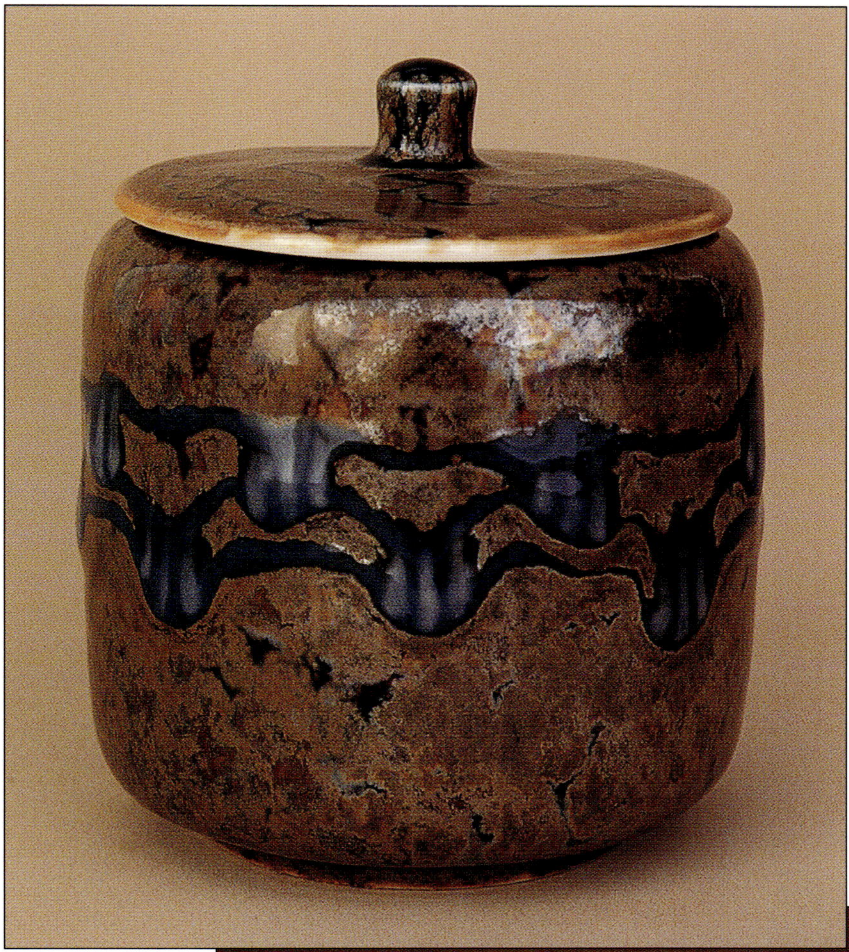

Covered pot, 4.5" high x 3.5" in diameter, 1930-1945. Less than $500.

Egg box, 6" x 3.9", 1930-1945. Less than $500.

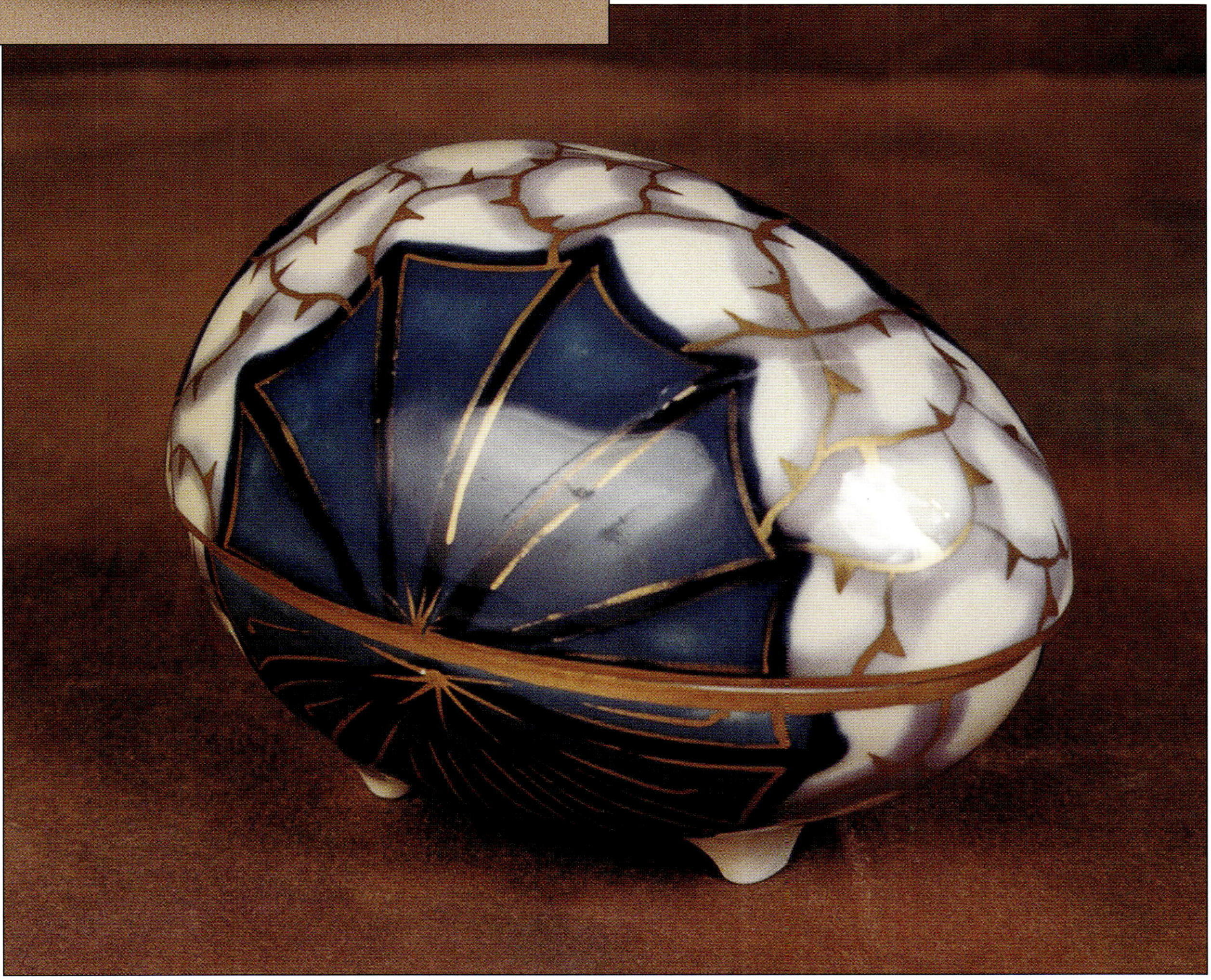

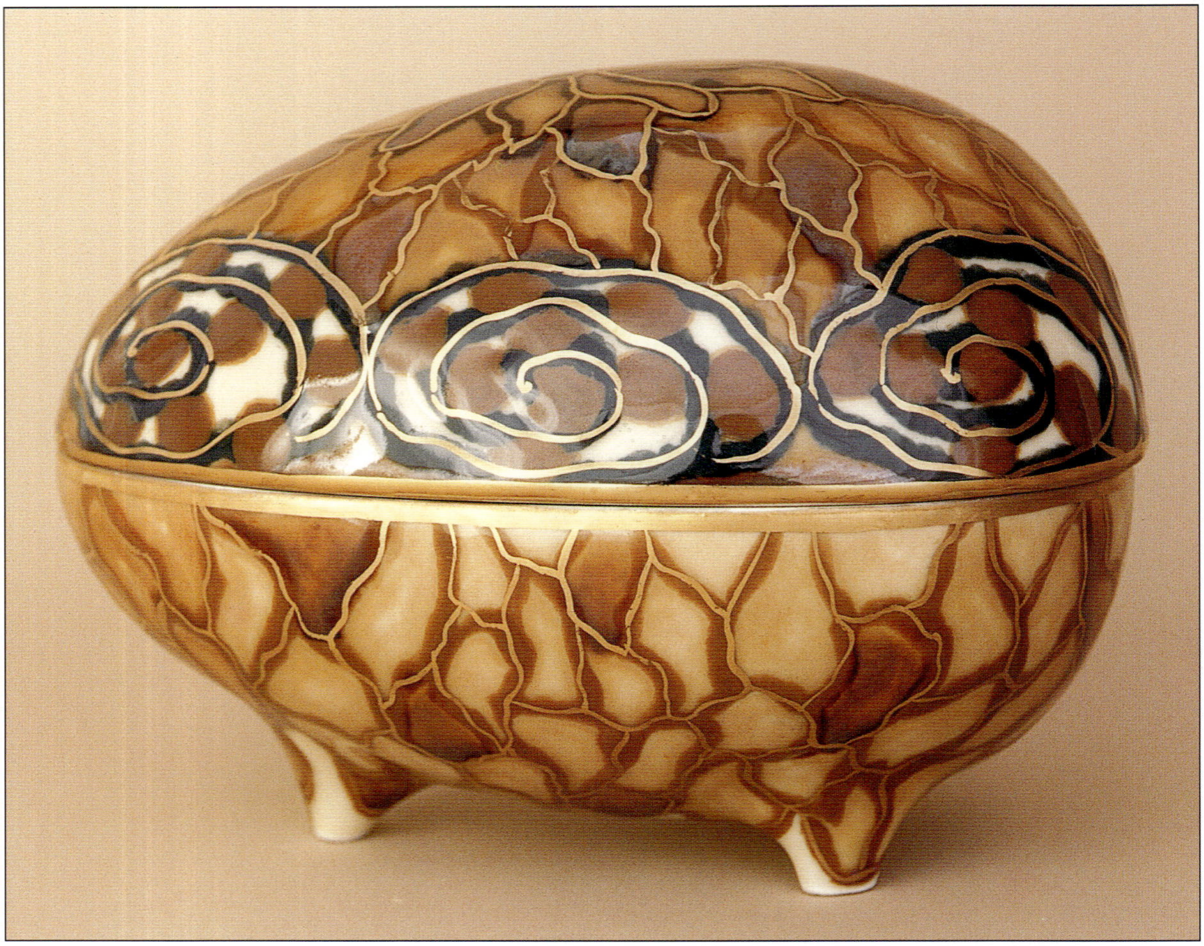

Rare egg box, 6" high x 8" x 5.75", 1940-1945. $500-$1,000.

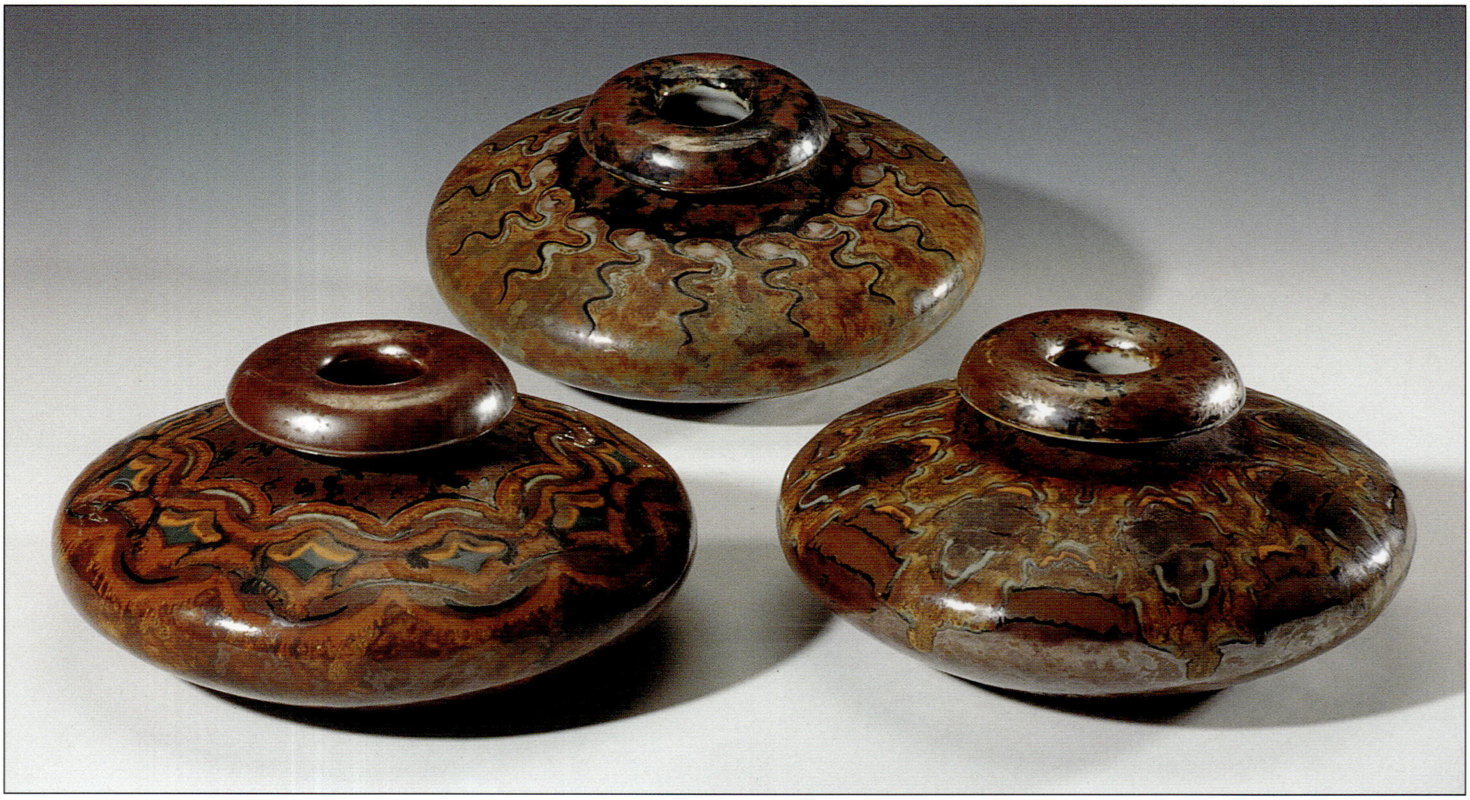

Vases, *Lentille*, 1930-1945. Each $500-$1,000.

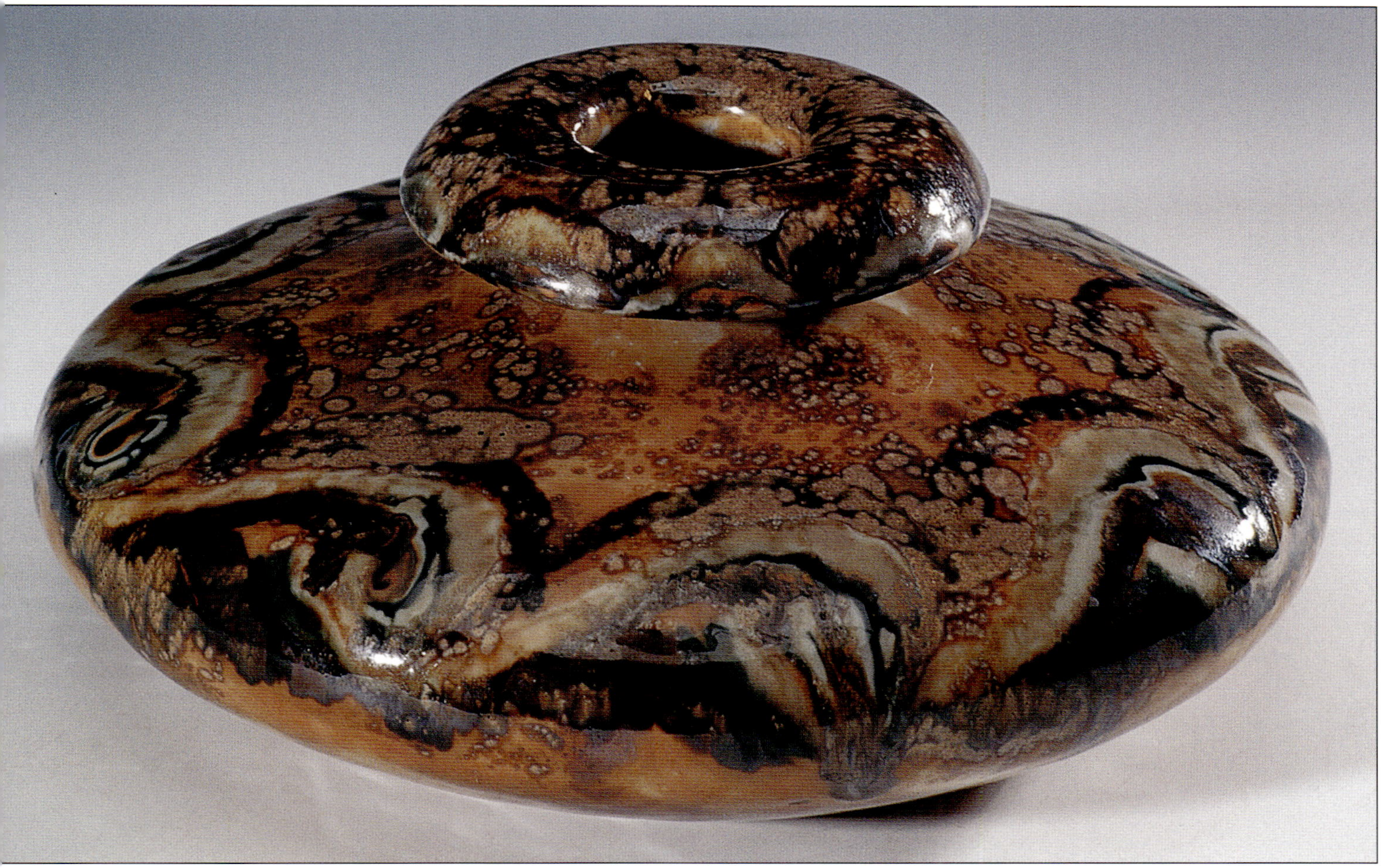
Vase, *Lentille*, 9.5" in diameter, marked *OTh* (decoration by Odette Tharaud). $500-$1,000.

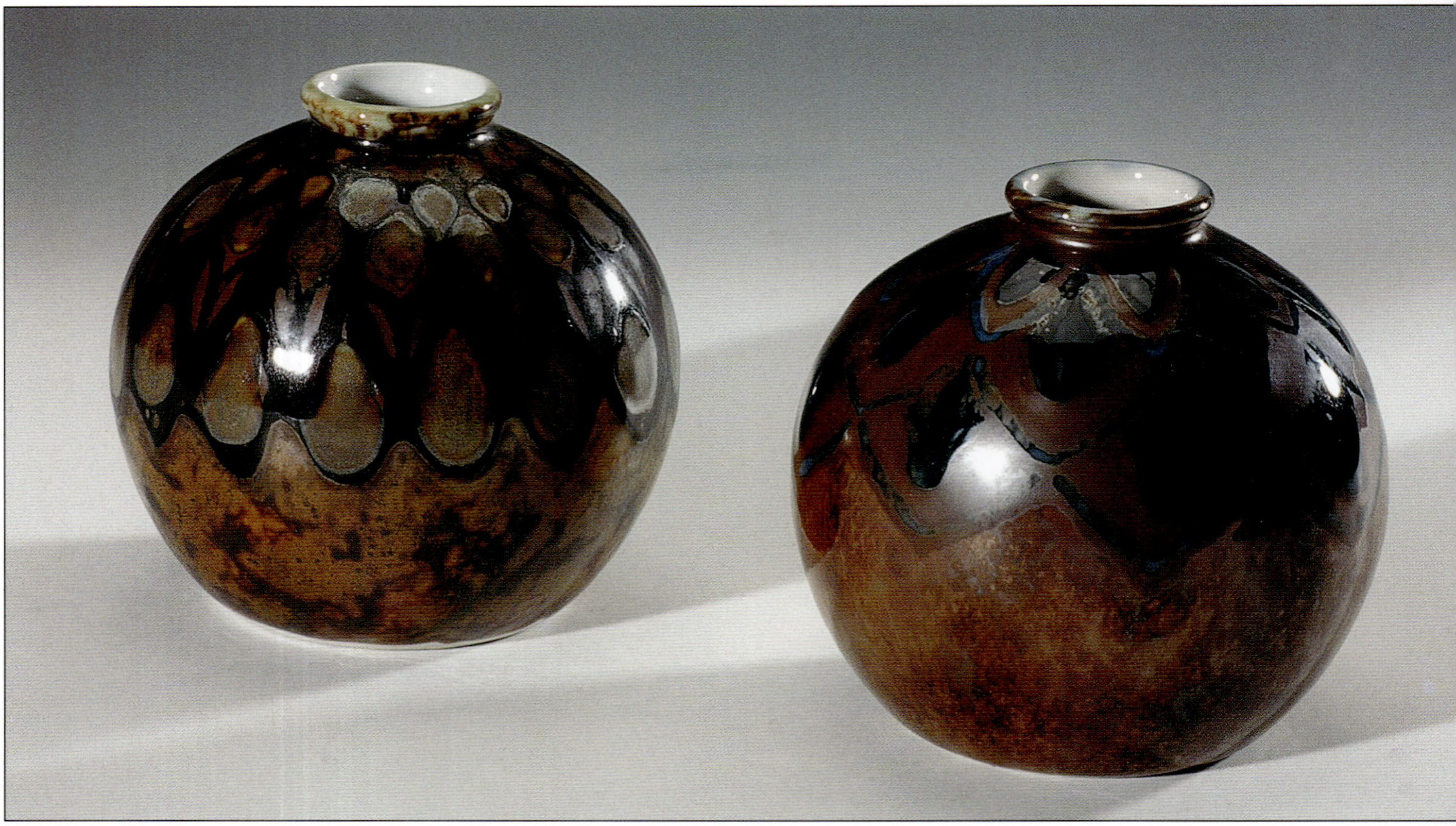

Two small vases, both 4.5" high, 1930-1945. Each less than $500.

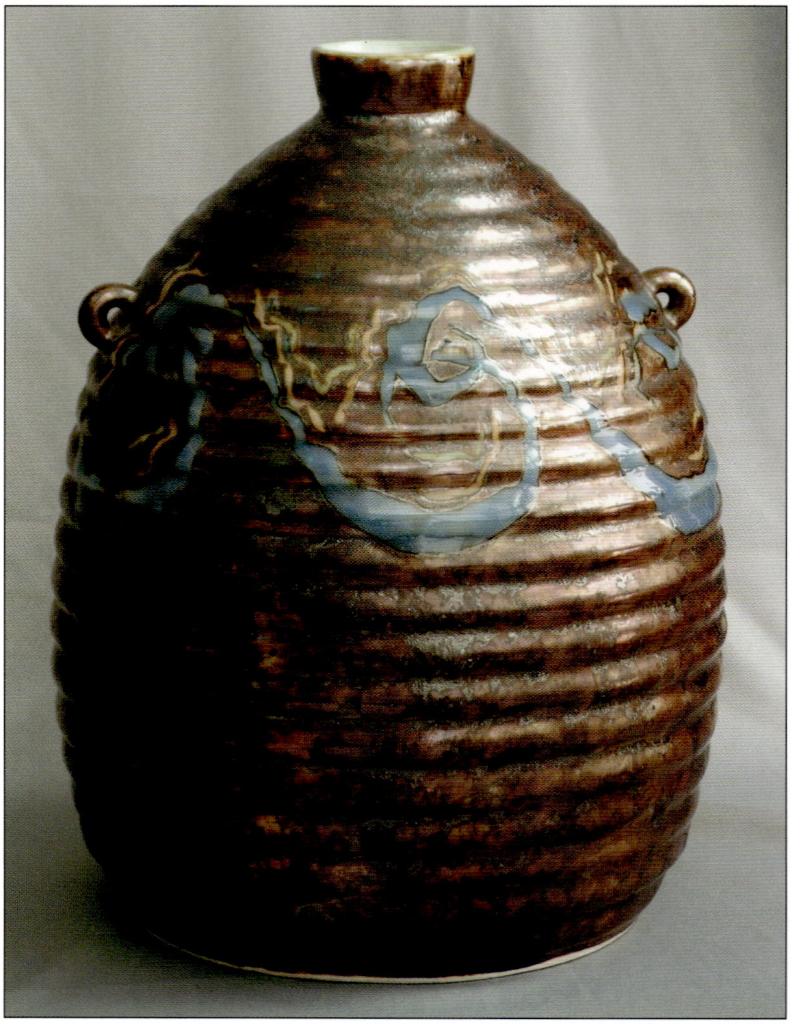

Gourd Jar, *Ruche*, very rare shape (Ferrer), 10.75" high. $1,000-$1,500.

Vase, 4.5" high, 1930-1945.
Less than $500.

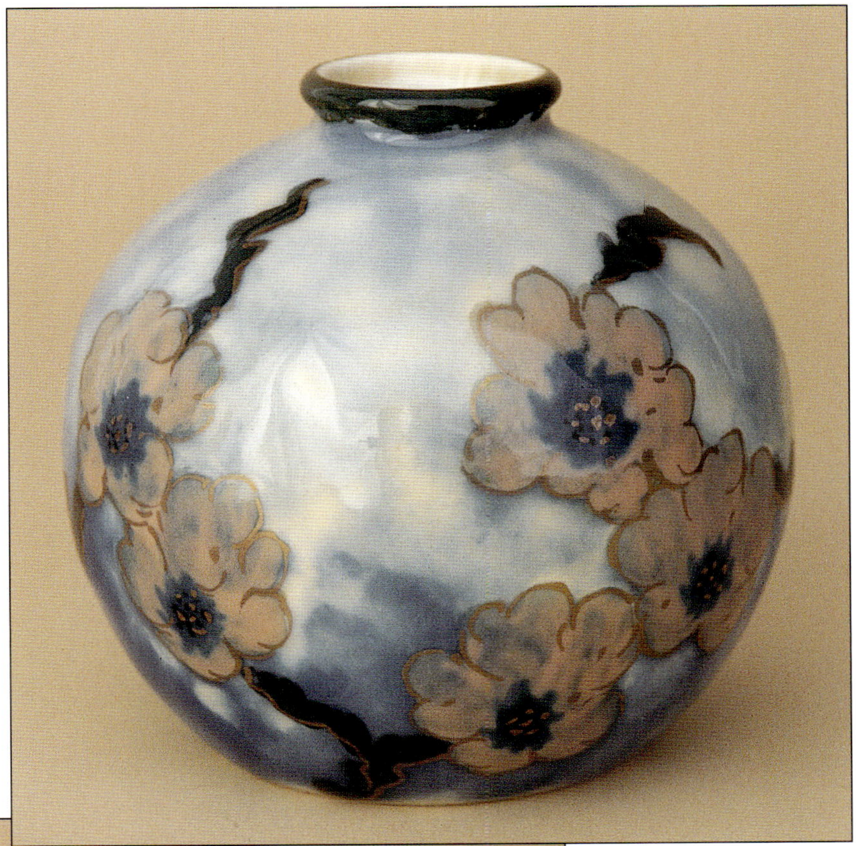

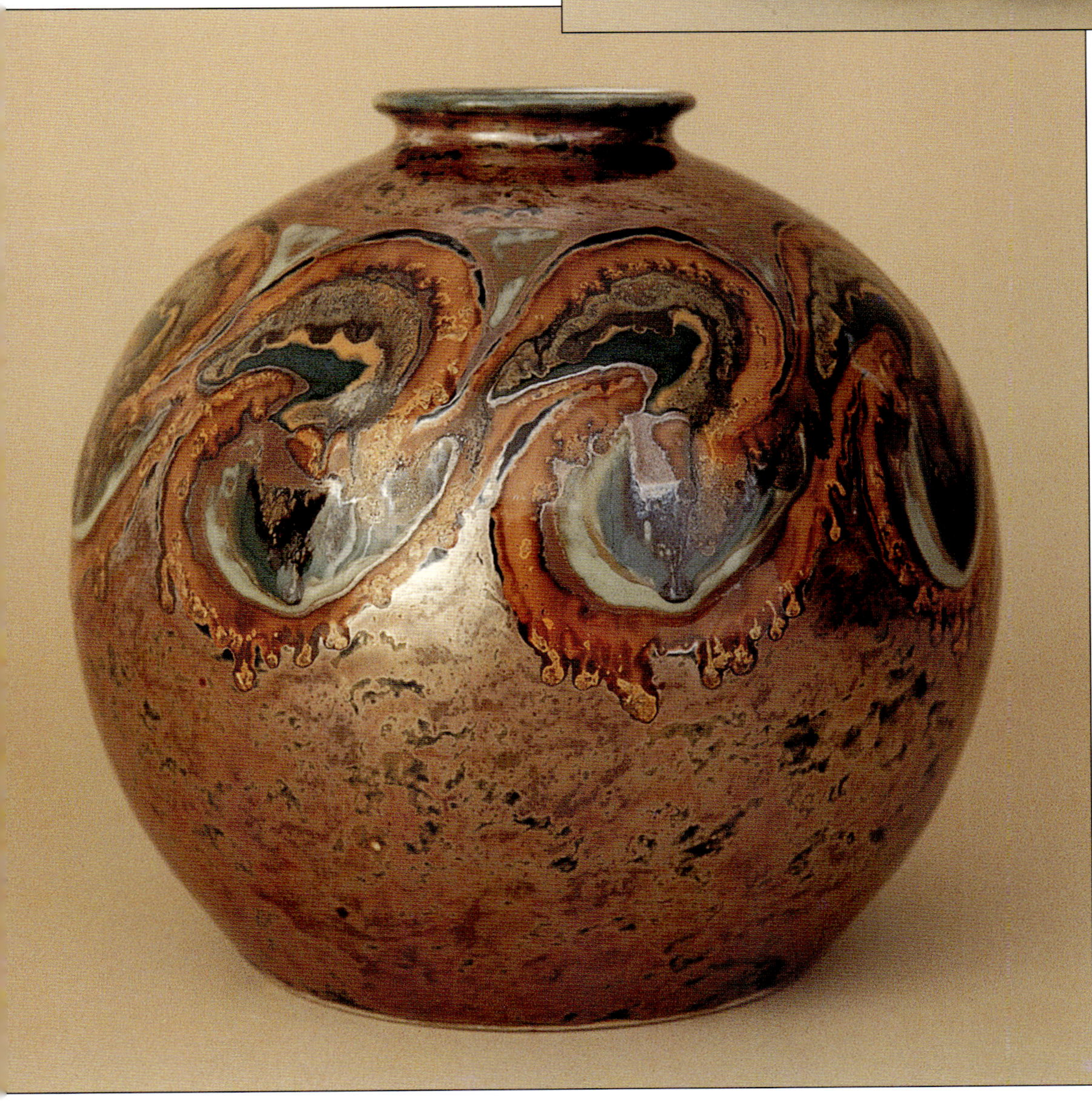

Vase, 7.5" high, 1930-1945. *DA* or *AA* incised. $500-$1,000.

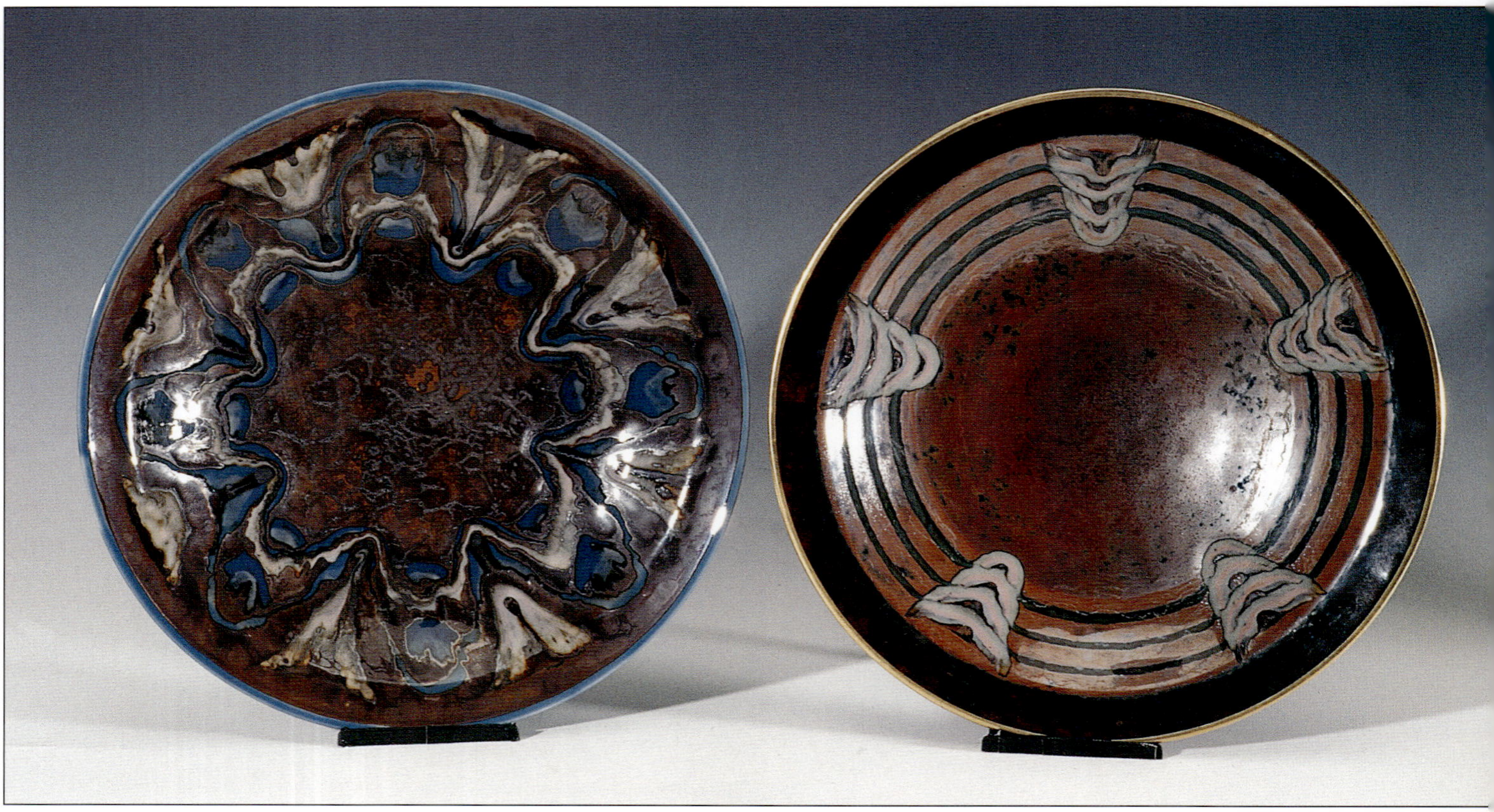

Two bowls, *Rabat*, left, 1930-1945, and right, after 1943. Each less than $500.

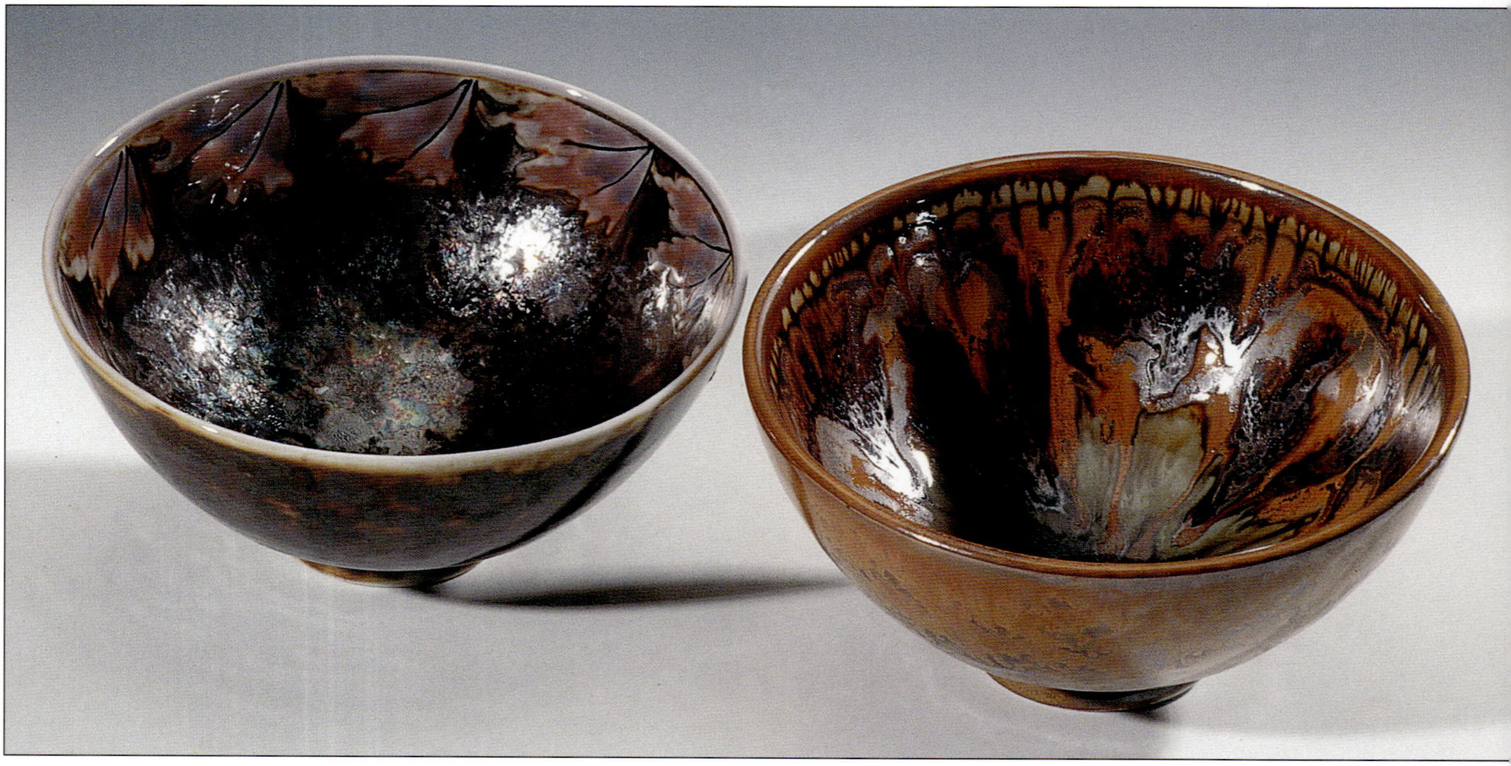

Bowls, each 7.75" in diameter and 4" high, 1930-1945. Each less than $500.

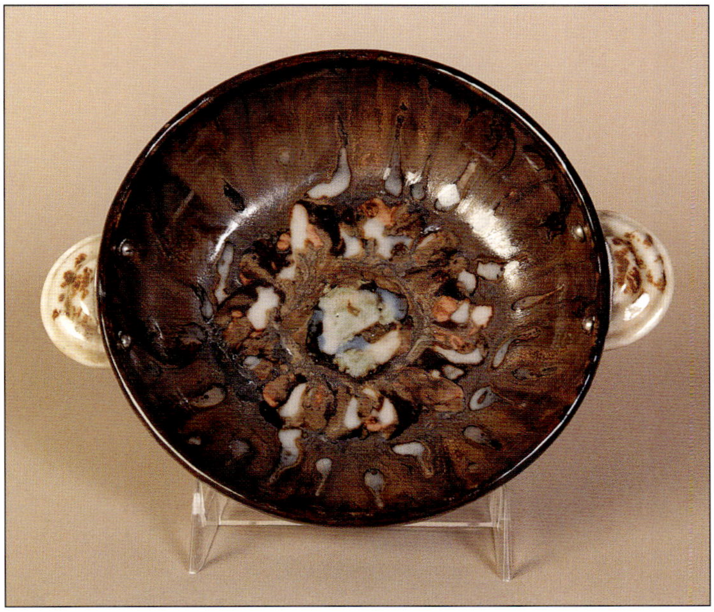

Handled bowl, 5.5" in diameter, about 1943, mark painted *OTh*, decorated by Odette Tharaud. Less than $500.

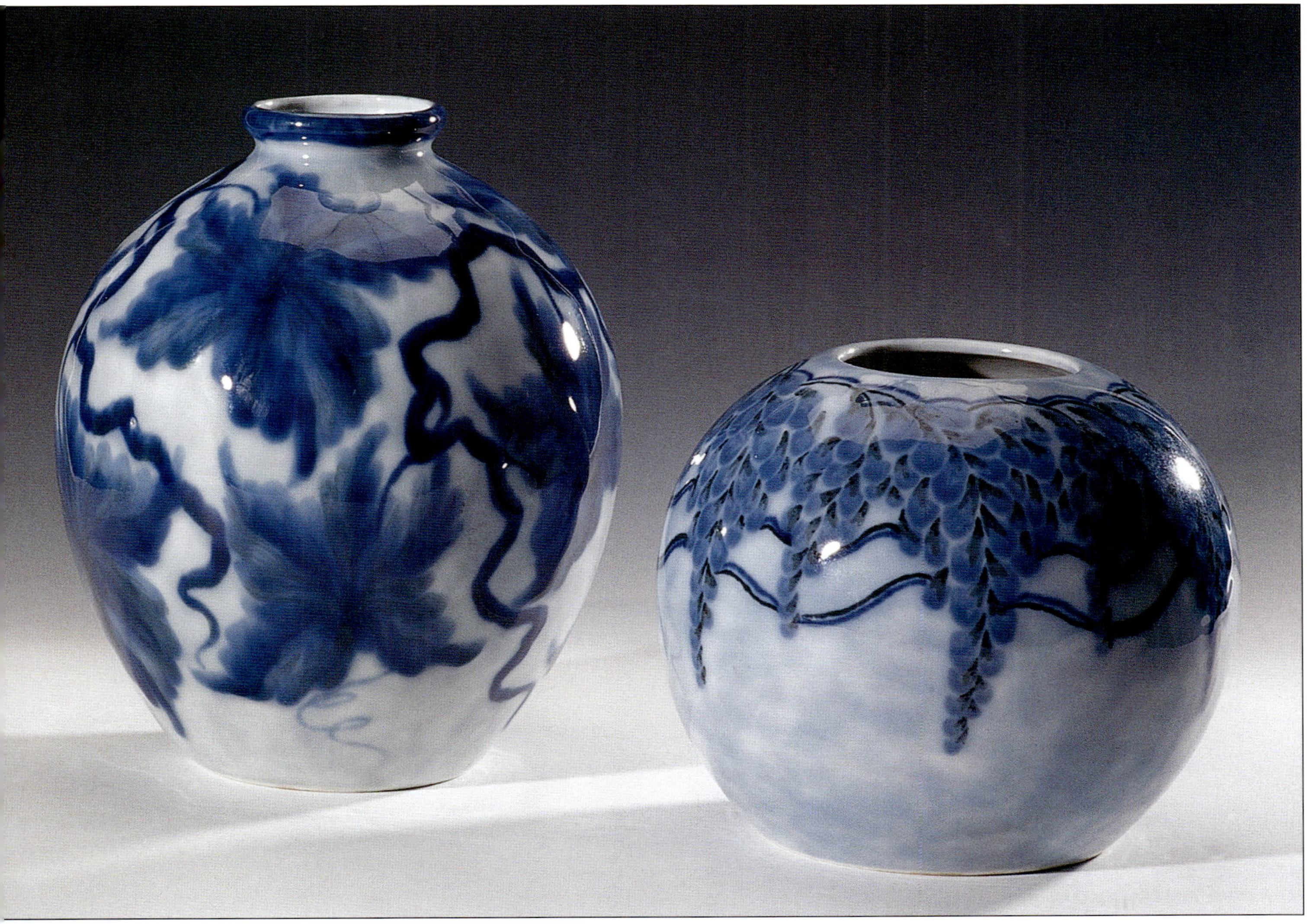

Vases, left, *Genêt,* decorated with *Feuilles de vigne*, 9.5" high and marked *A.M.* in black, and right, decorated with *Glycines* [wisteria], both 1930-1945. Each less than $500.

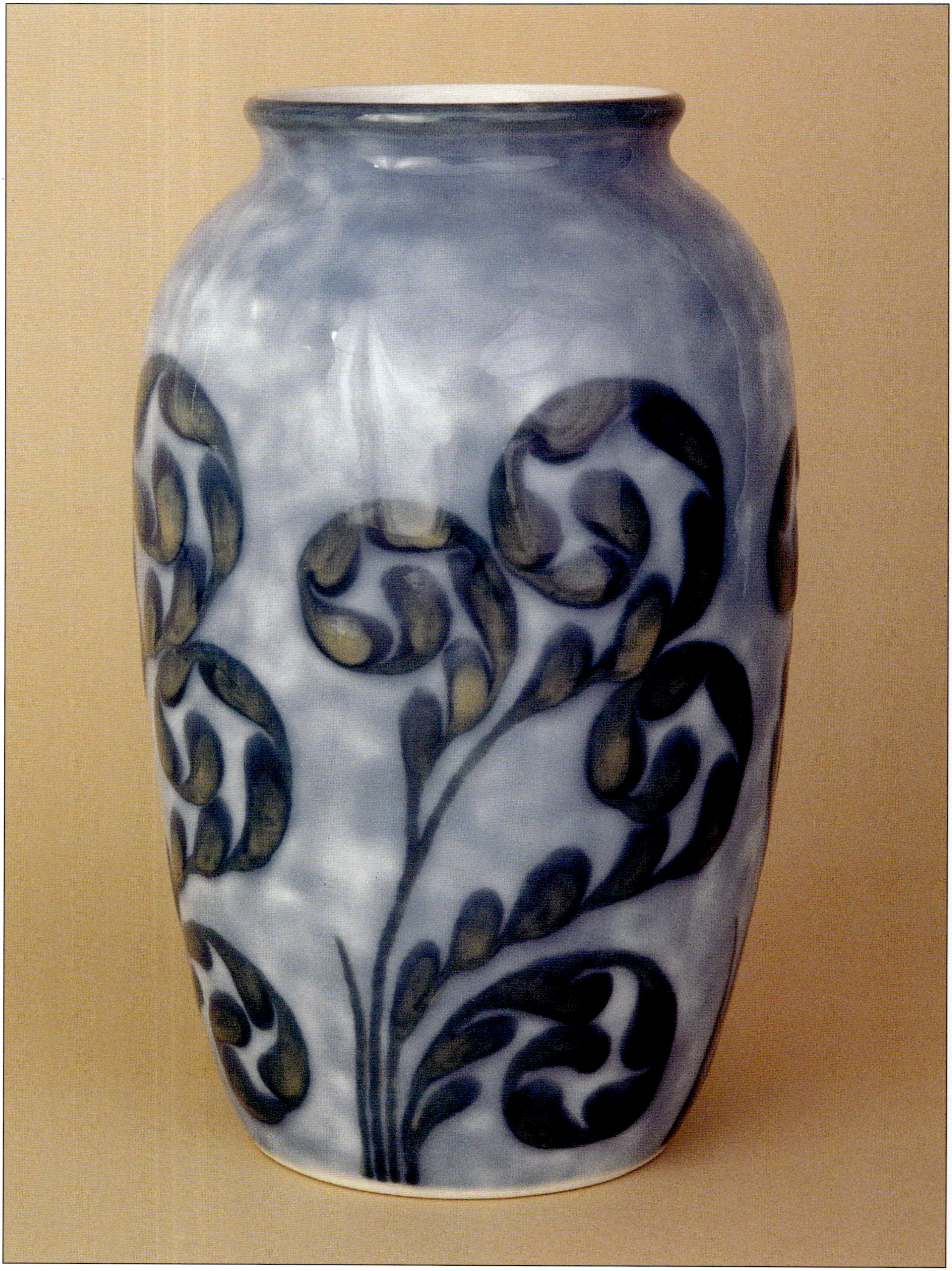

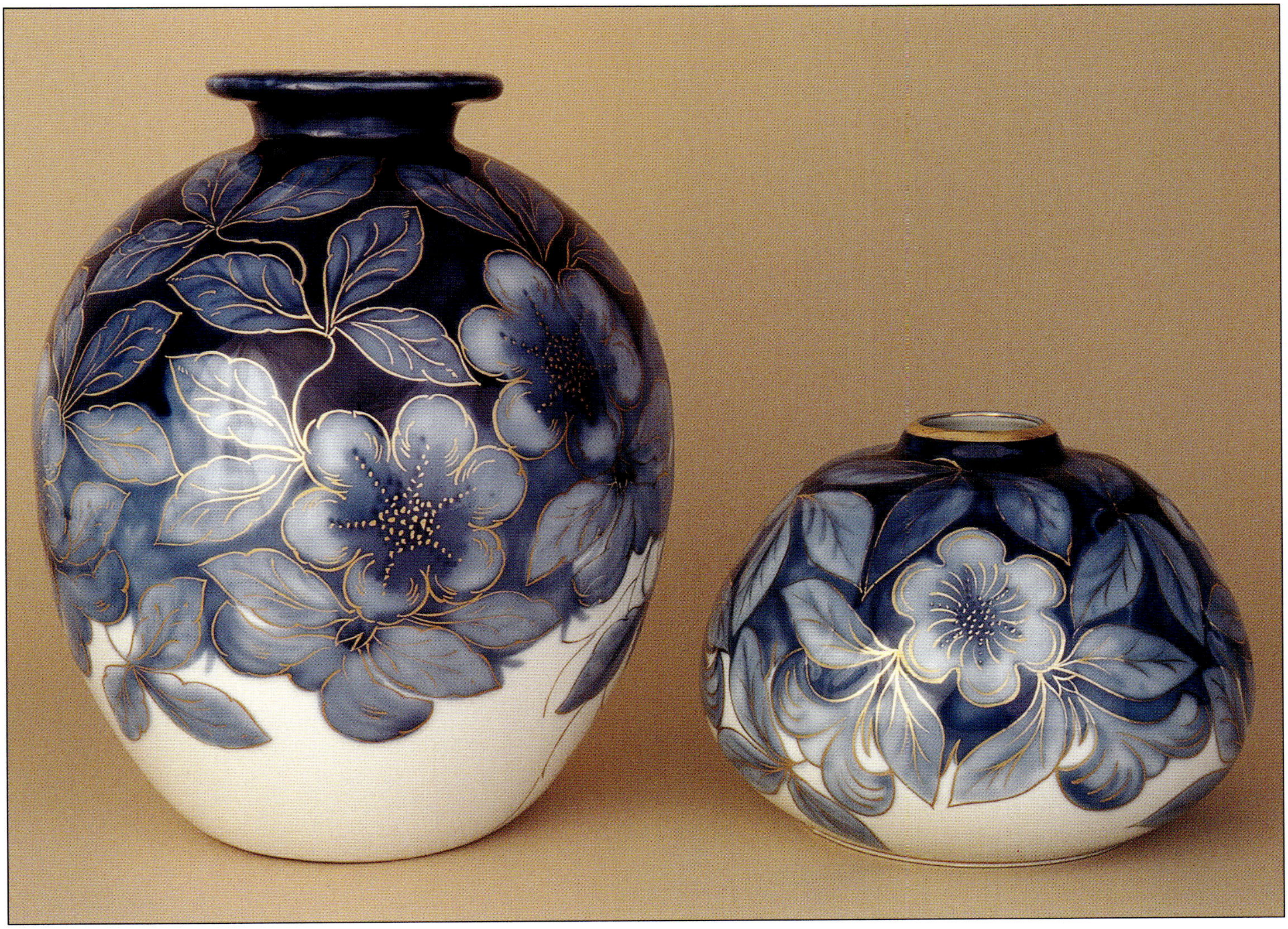

Vases, left, *Jasmin*, shape by Henri Rapin, 11" high, and vase, right, *Chardon,* 6.5" high, both decorated in shades of blue, 1930-1945. Each less than $500.

Opposite page:
Vase, 10.25" high, fronds of opened ferns, 1930-1945. Less than $500.

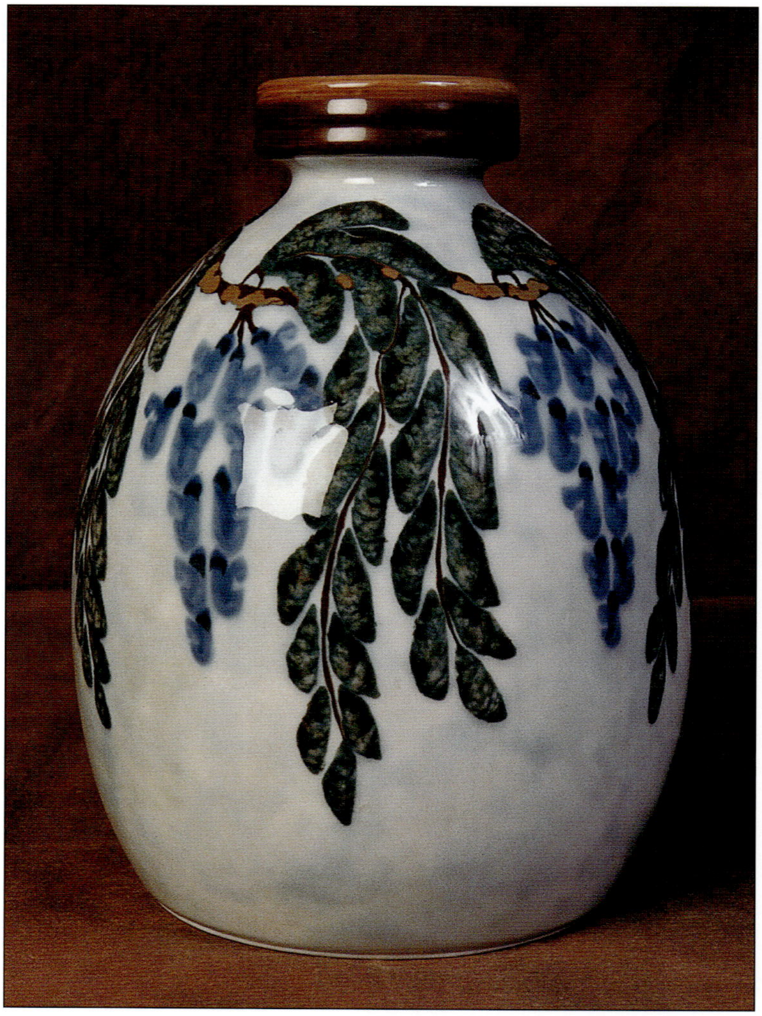

Vase, *Anthémis*, attributed to Henri Rapin, 10.5" high, 1930-1945, *YC* (Yvette C.) and *B* incised, *glycines* [wisteria] *et feuillage* decoration. Less than $500.

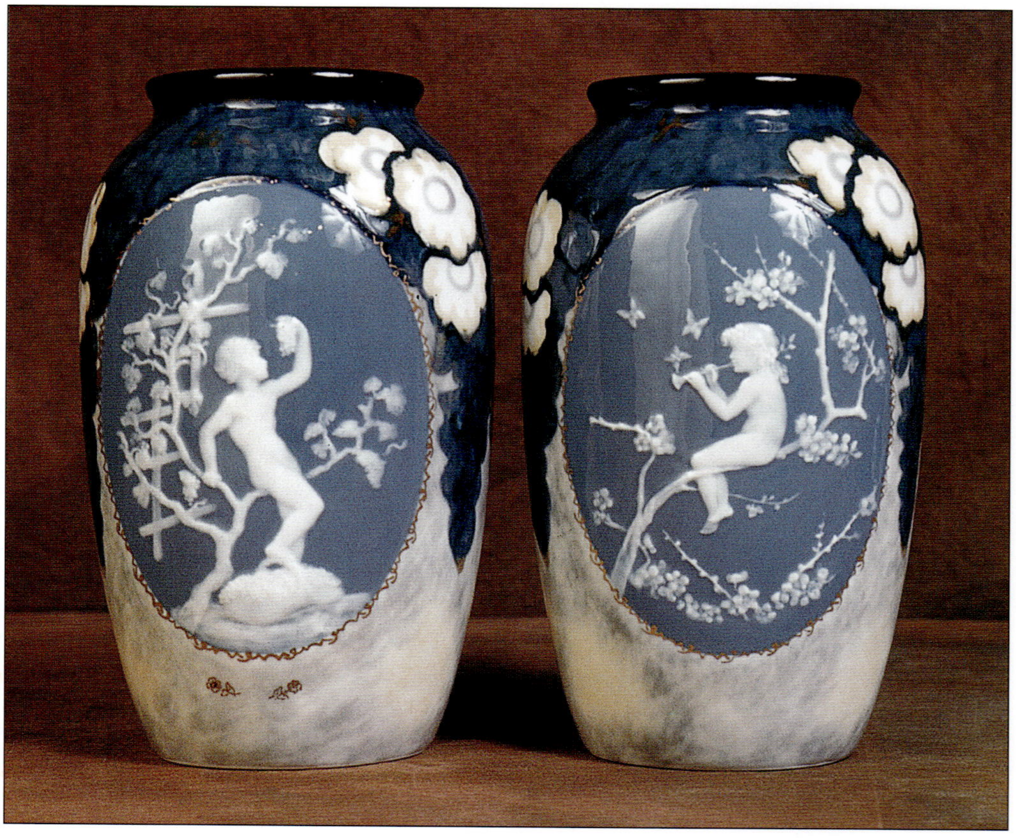

Vases, 10.5" high, 1930-1945. Each less than $500.

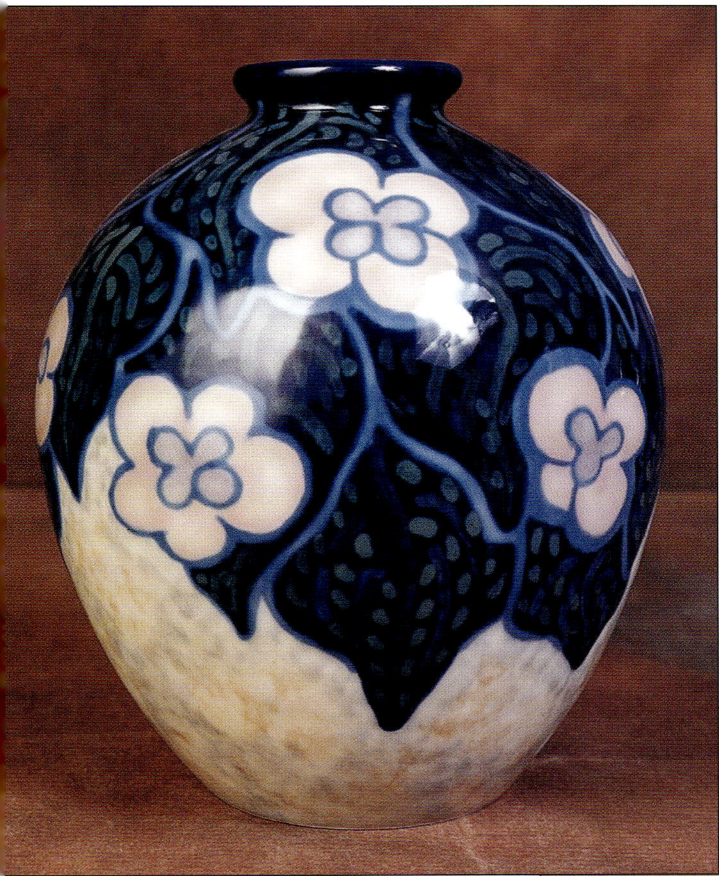

Vase, *Genêt*, 9" high, 1930-1945, good example of Art Deco style. $500-$1,000.

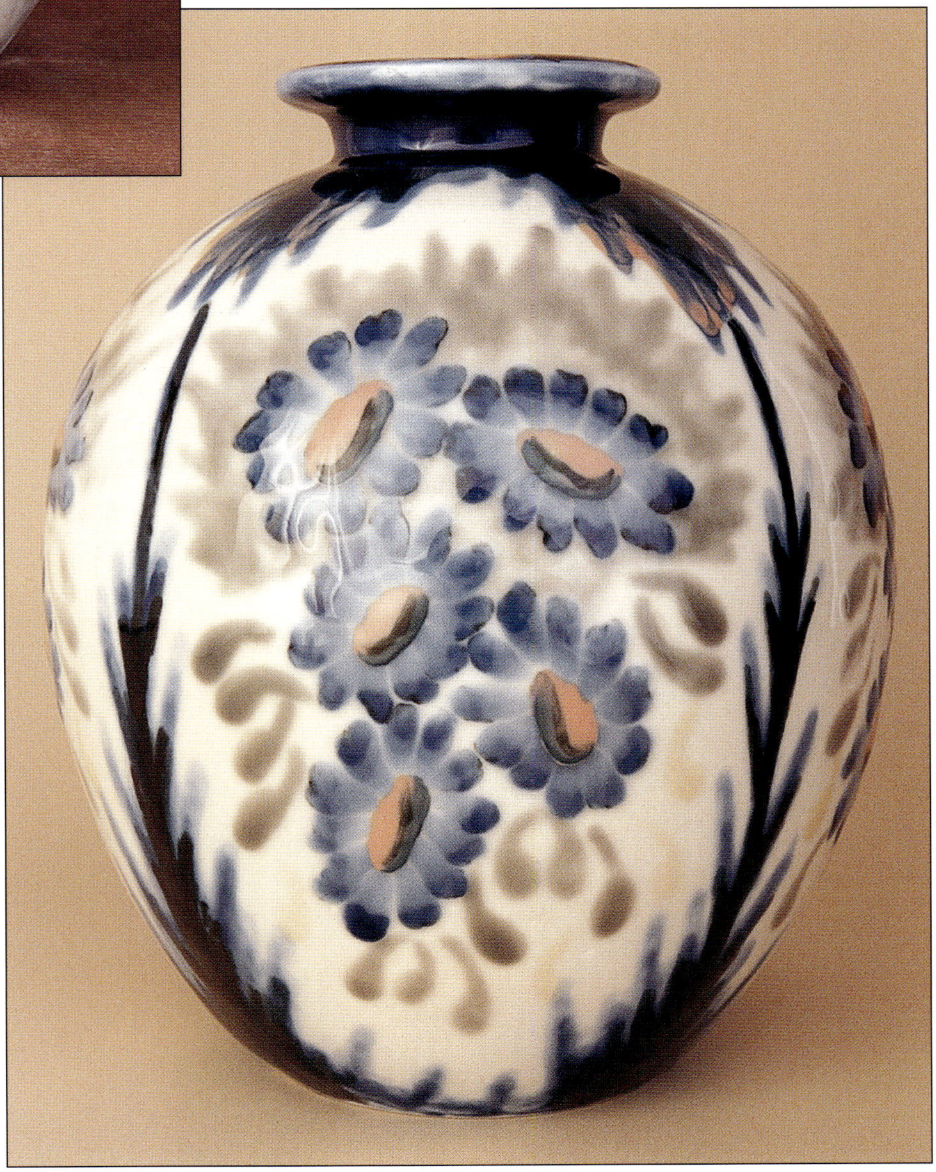

Vase, *Amarante*, 11" high, 1930-1945, decoration of five detached cineraria flowers on white base with gray accents. Cineraria are ornamental plants derived from species native to the Canary Islands and widely grown for their showy, variously colored radiating flower heads and attractive silvery foliage. $500-$1,000.

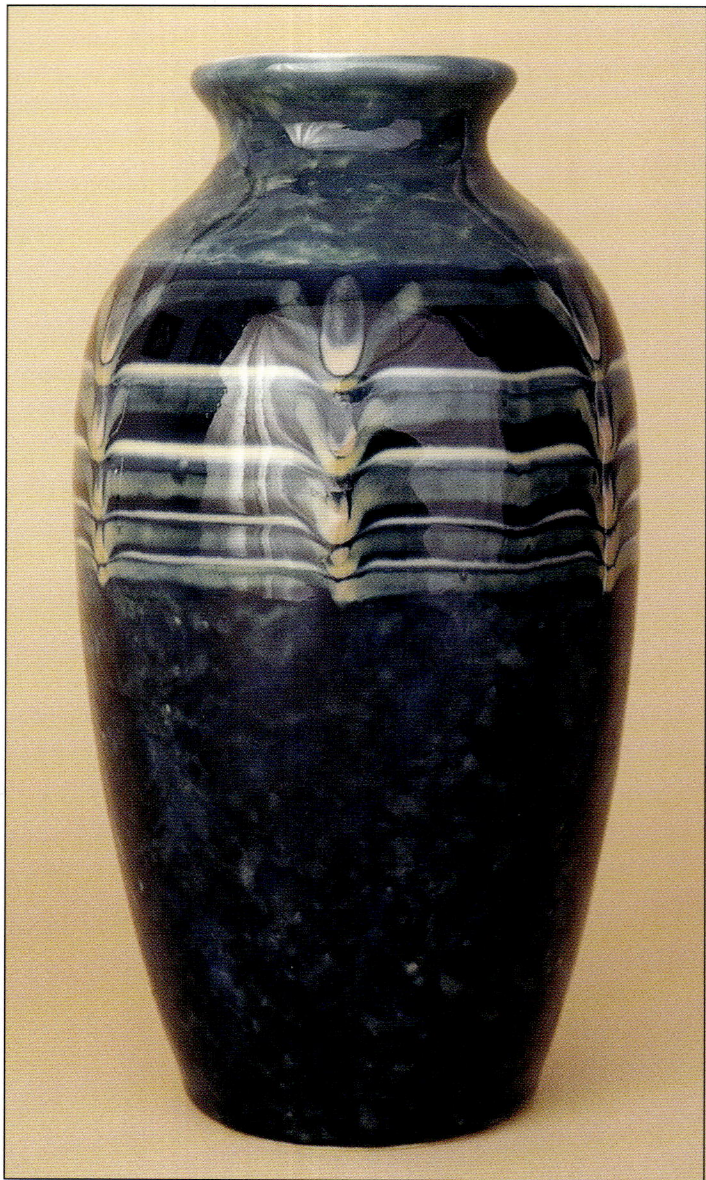

Vase, 10.4" high, 1930-1945, *Th* incised (decoration of Camille Tharaud). $500-$1,000.

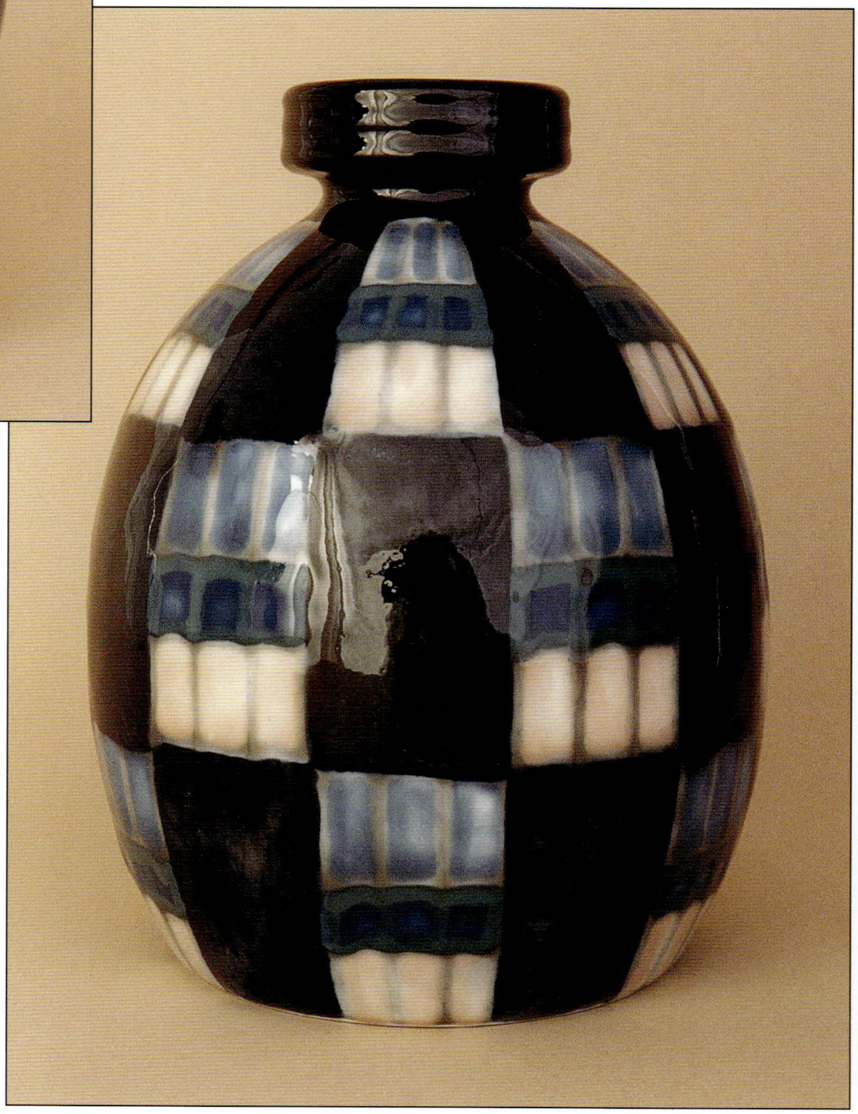

Vase, *Anthémis,* shape attributed to Henri Rapin, 10.75" high, windowpane pattern, 1930-1945. $500-$1,000.

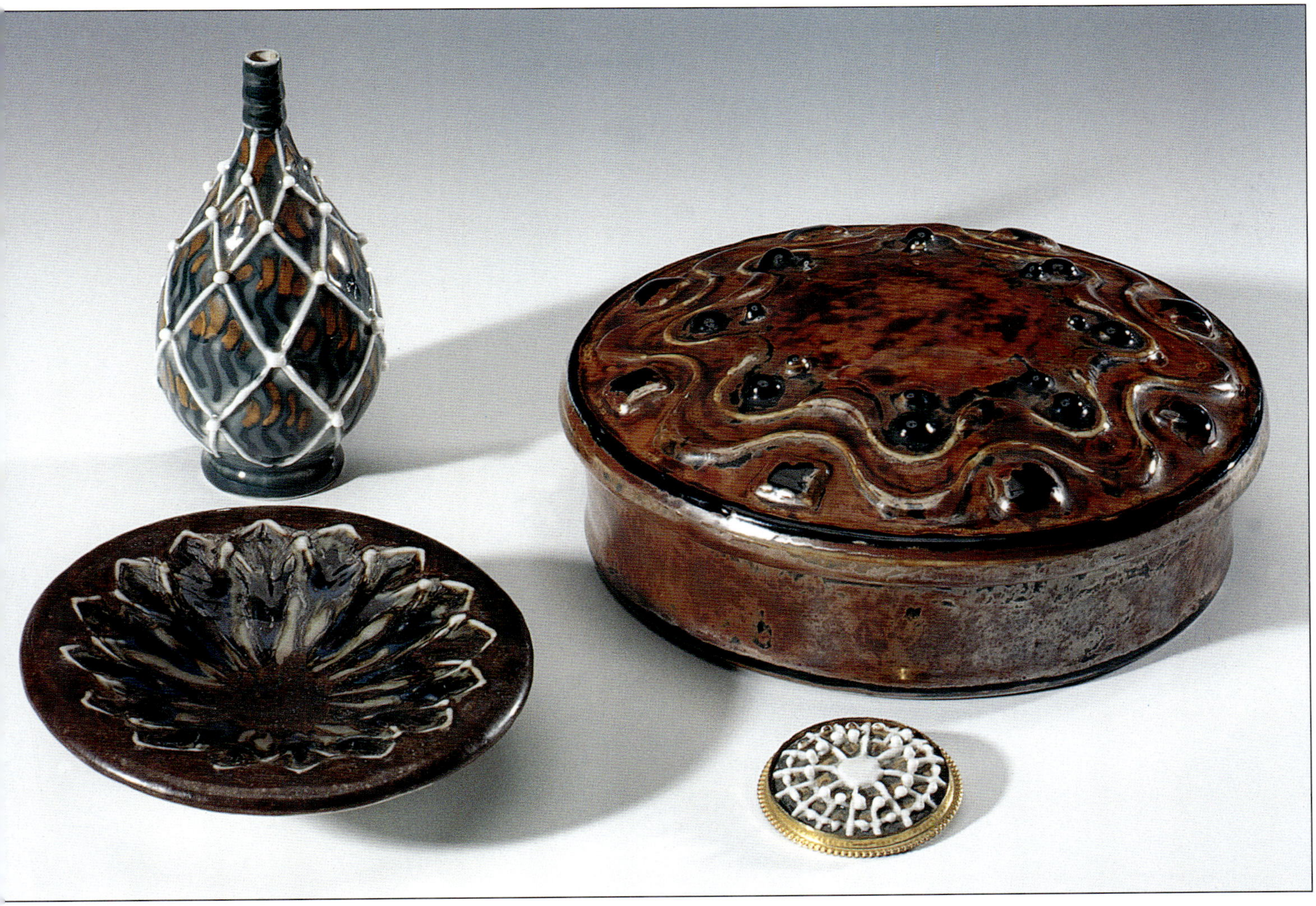

Vase, *Narcisse*, after 1943, marked *L. Lib* (Lucienne Liberge); pendant, 1930-1945; round box, 1930-1945, *Th* painted in black (decoration by Camille Tharaud); ashtray, porcelain mark only. Each less than $500.

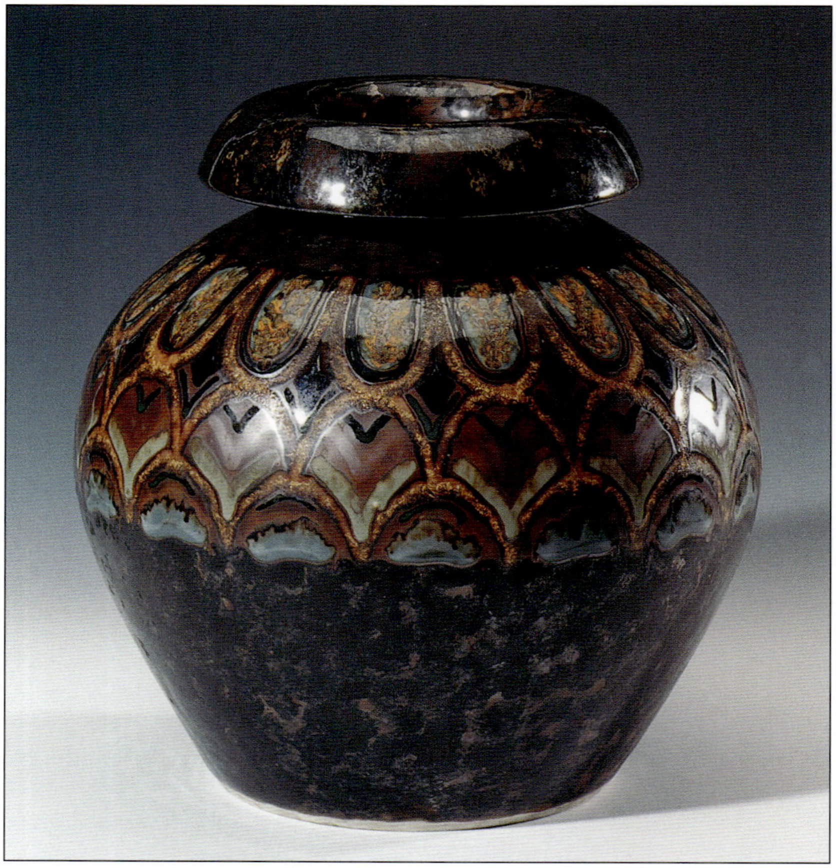

Vase, *Amarante*, shape of Henri Rapin, 1930-1945, marked *S. Lam* (Simone Lam). $500-$1,000.

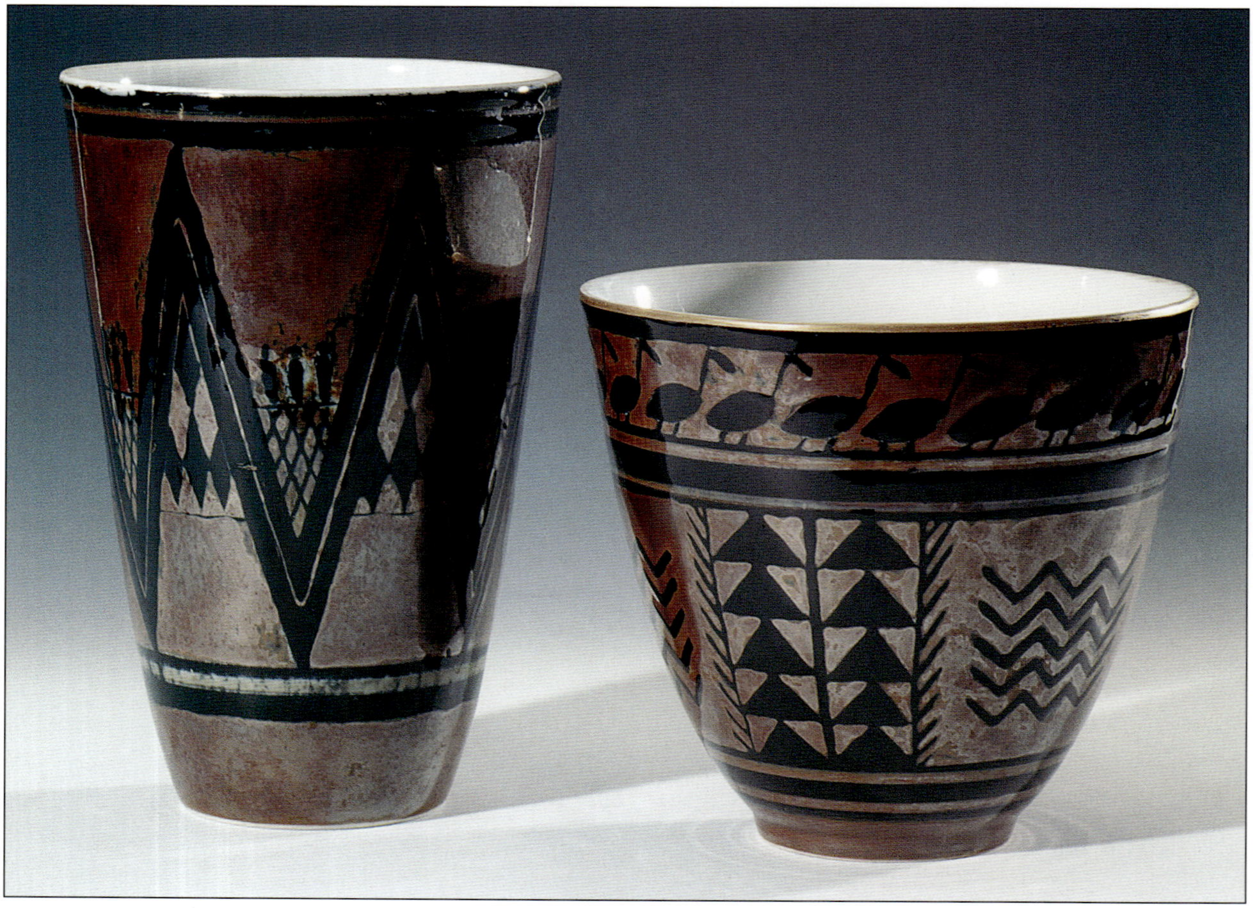

Vases, about 1945, Art Deco design influenced by ancient Iran (Ferrer), marked *L. Lib* (Lucienne Liberge). (Ferrer) Each $500-$1,000.

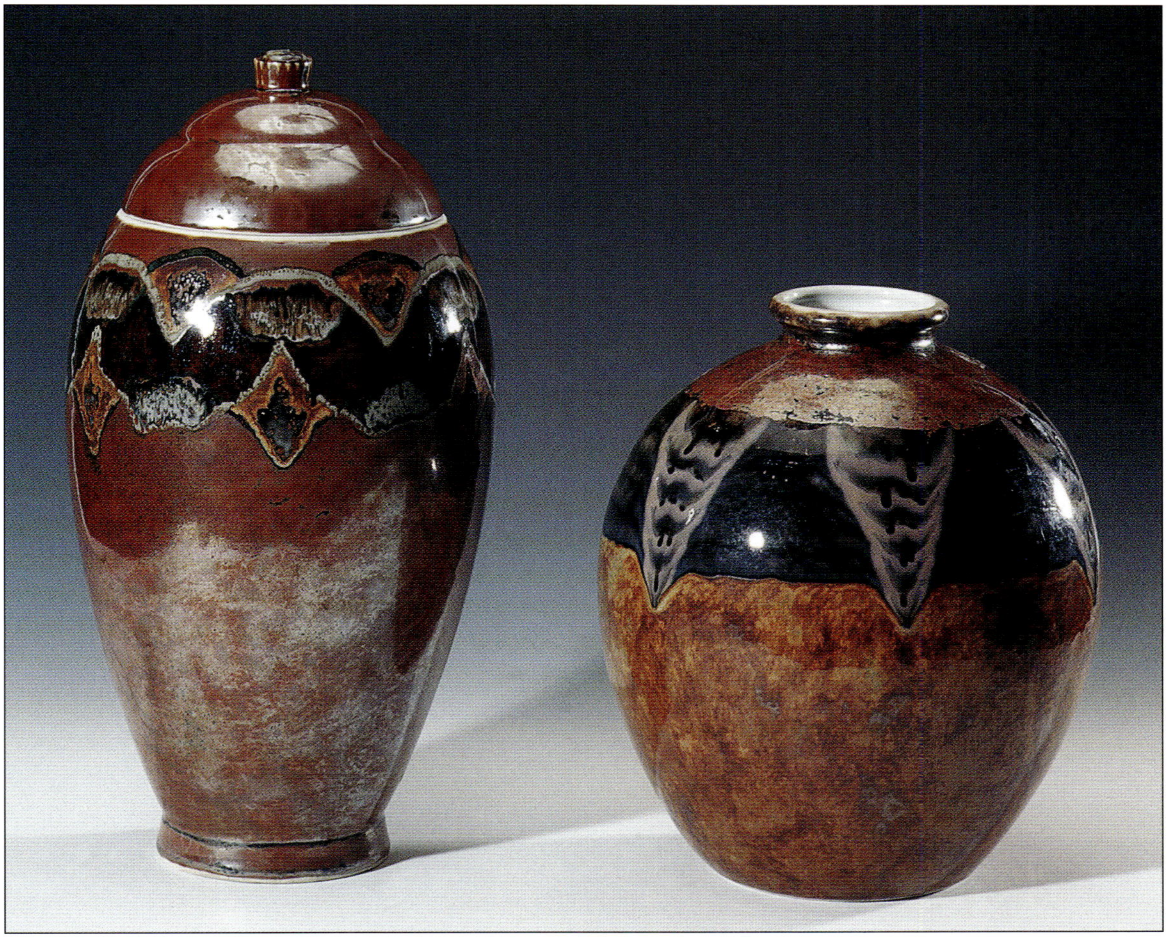

Vases, *Manon*, left, and *Zinnia*, right, both 1930-1945. Each $500-$1,000.

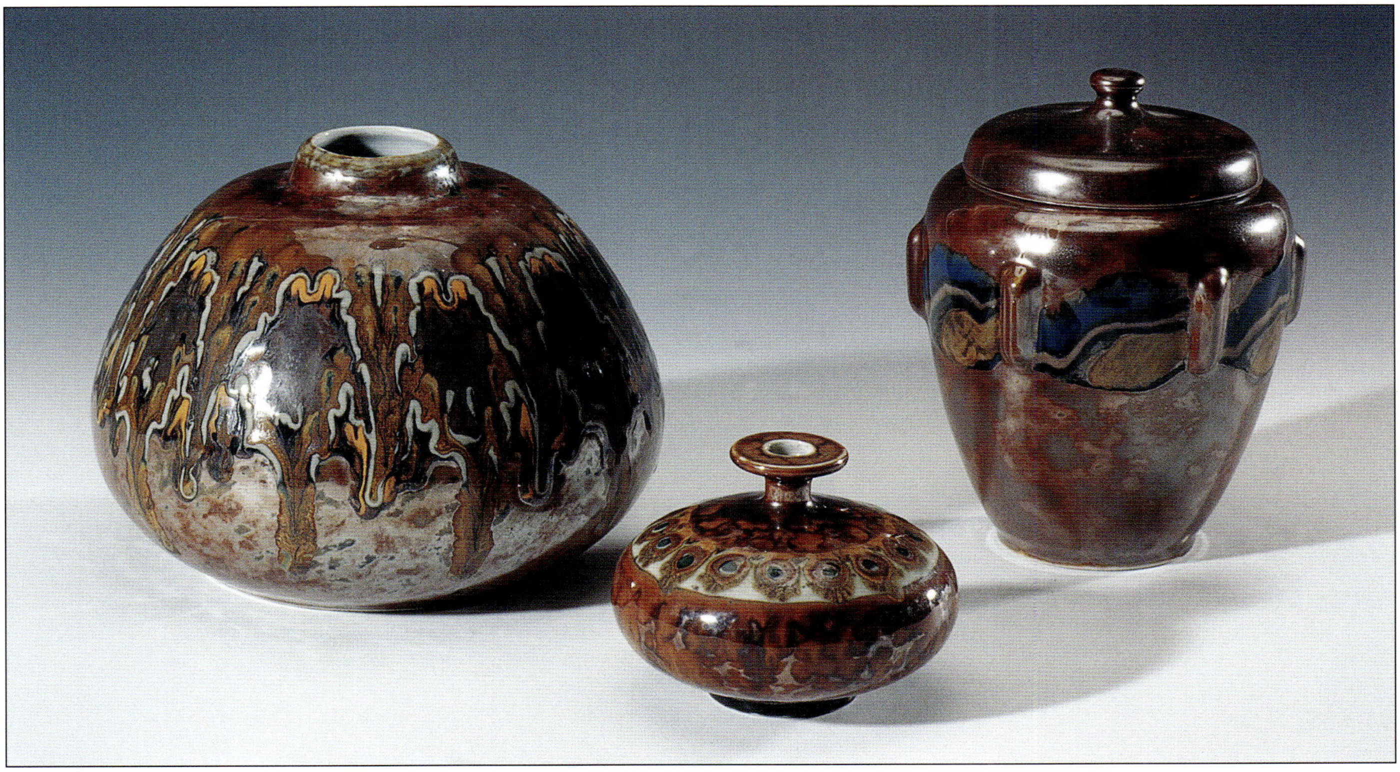

Vase, *Chardon*, left, incised *EL* (Elise), 1930-1945; covered pot, *Lohengrin*, shape of Marcel Goupy; right, marked *JZ* (Joseph Z.), about 1945; and bud vase, *Pivoine*, center, after 1943. Vase and covered pot, $500-$1,000; bud vase, less than $500.

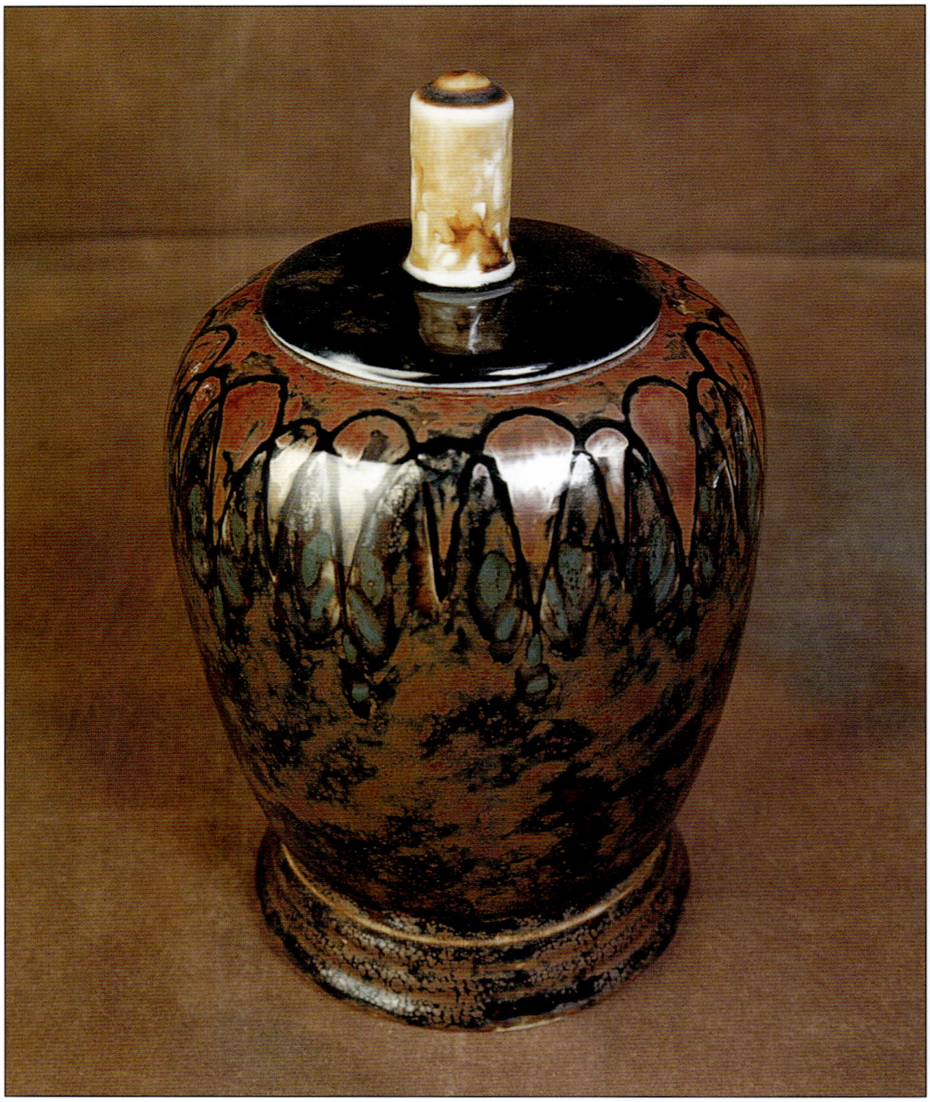

Vase, *Thaïs*, 10.75" high, 1930-1945, signed *L. Lib* (Lucienne Liberge). $1,000-$1,500.

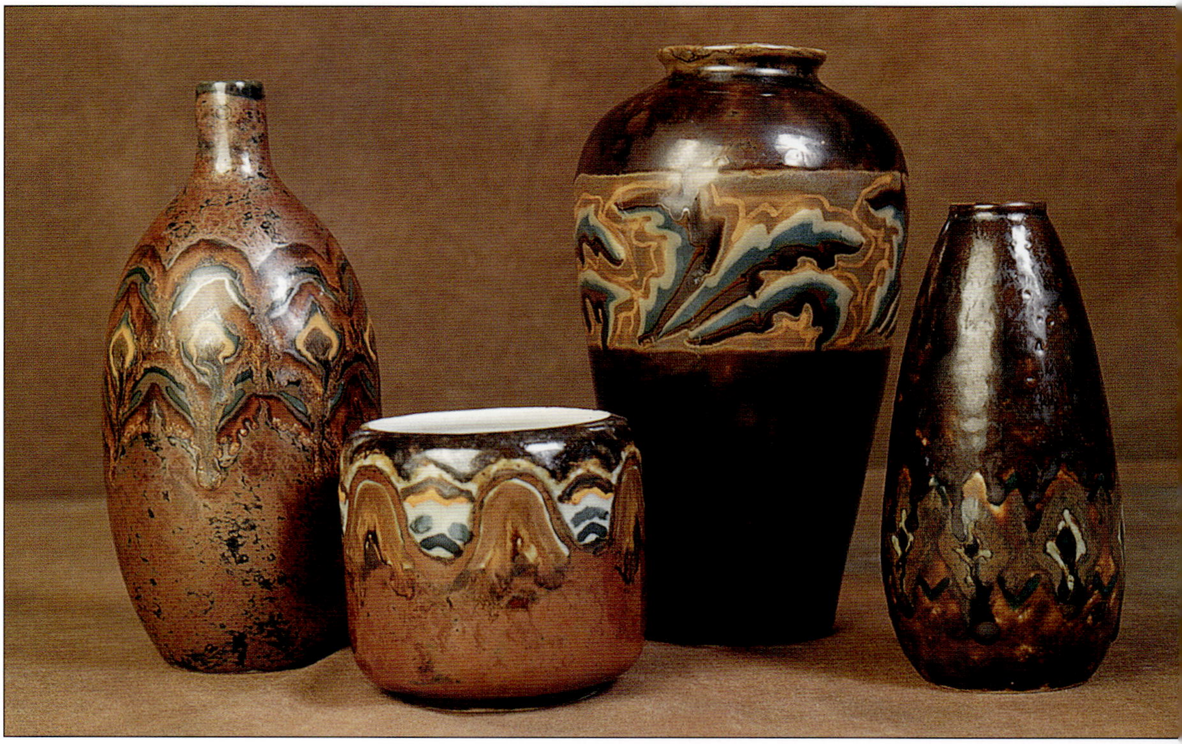

Vases and cup, all 1930-1945, left to right, 8.25" high; 3.5" high; 8.5" high and incised *Y.G.*; and 6" high and incised *Y.P.O.* Left to right, $500-$1,000; less than $500; $500-$1,000; less than $500.

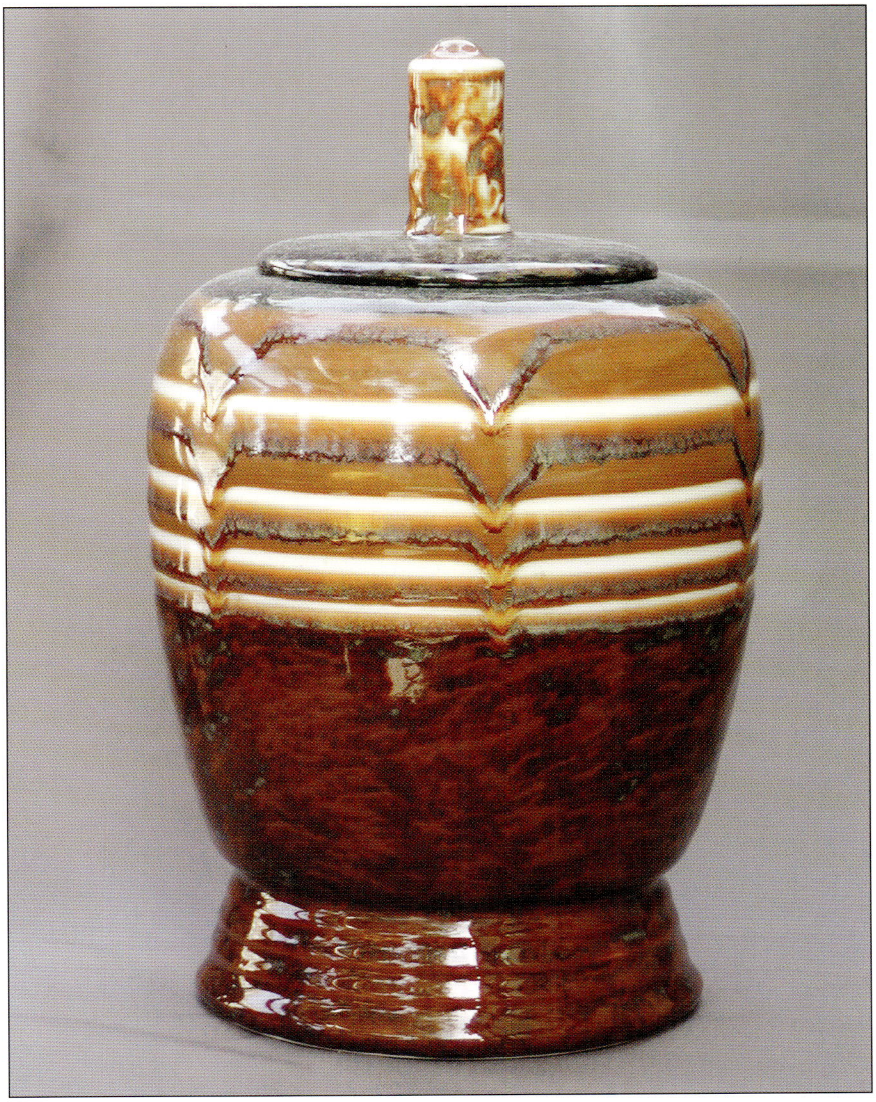

Vase, *Thaïs*, 10" high, *Th* and *HR* incised, 1930-1945. $500-$1,000.

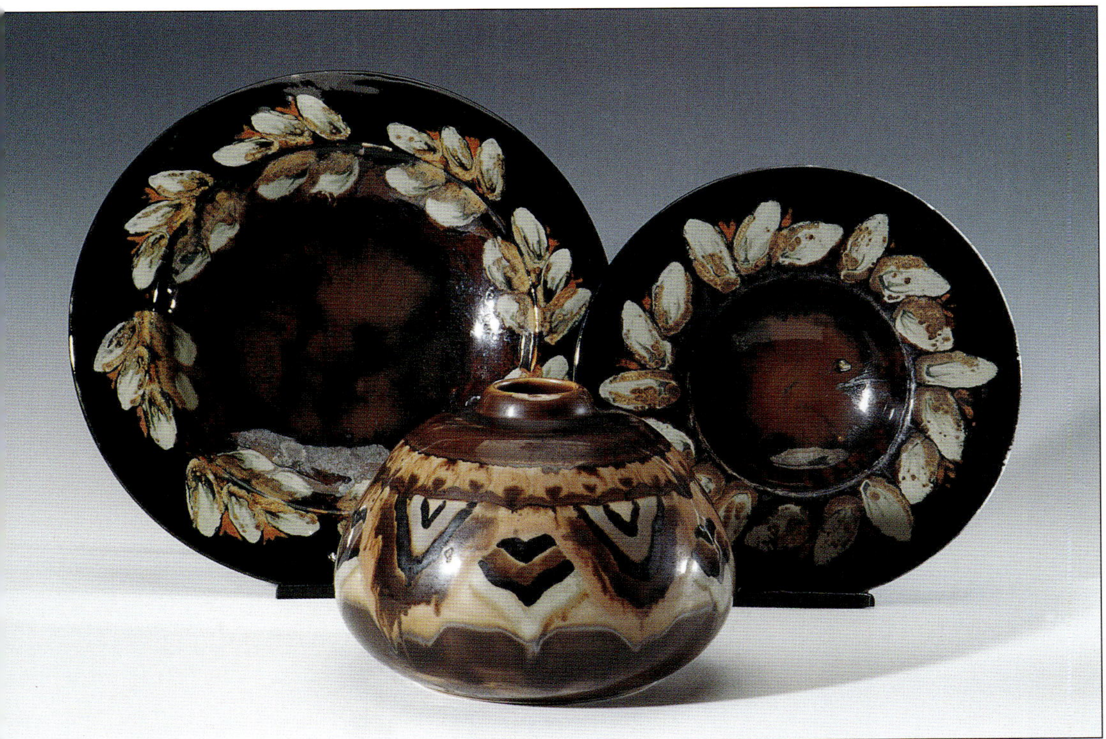

Tray; vase, *Chardon*; and bowl, *Rabat*, marked *OTh*, (decoration by Odette Tharaud). The tray and bowl have a mussel or clam shell motif and the vase a shark's tooth motif. Tray, $500-$1,000; bowl, $500-$1,000; vase, less than $500.

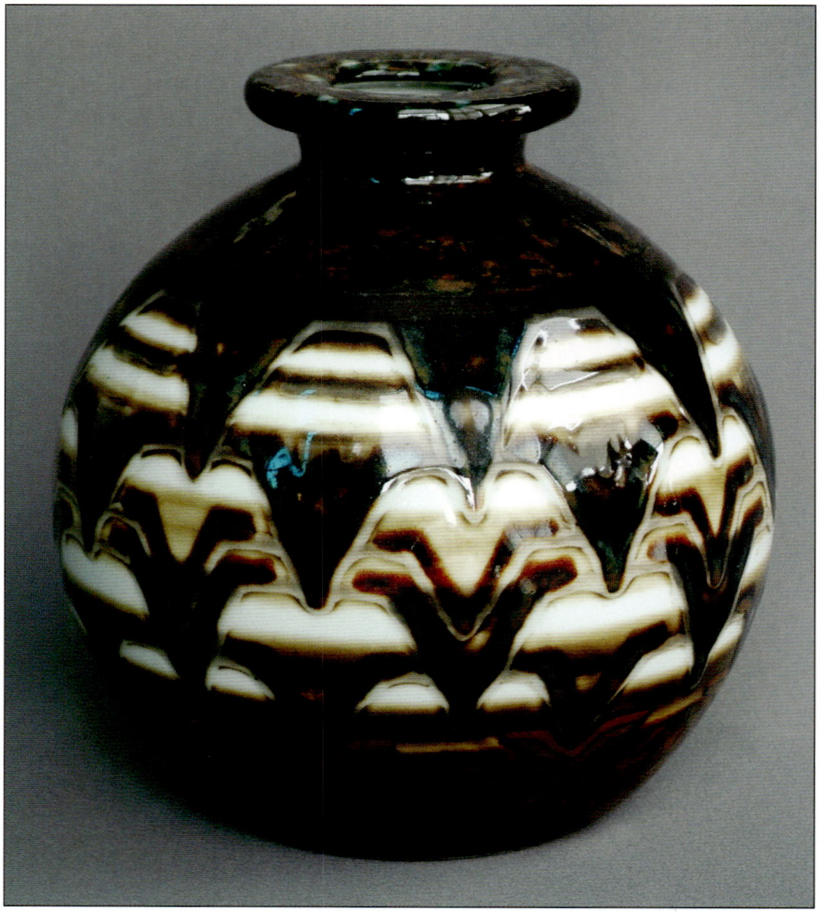

Vase, *Jasmin*, 9.25" high, incised *Th* (decoration by Camille Tharaud), one of the finest examples of the shark tooth design, 1930-1945. $500-$1,000.

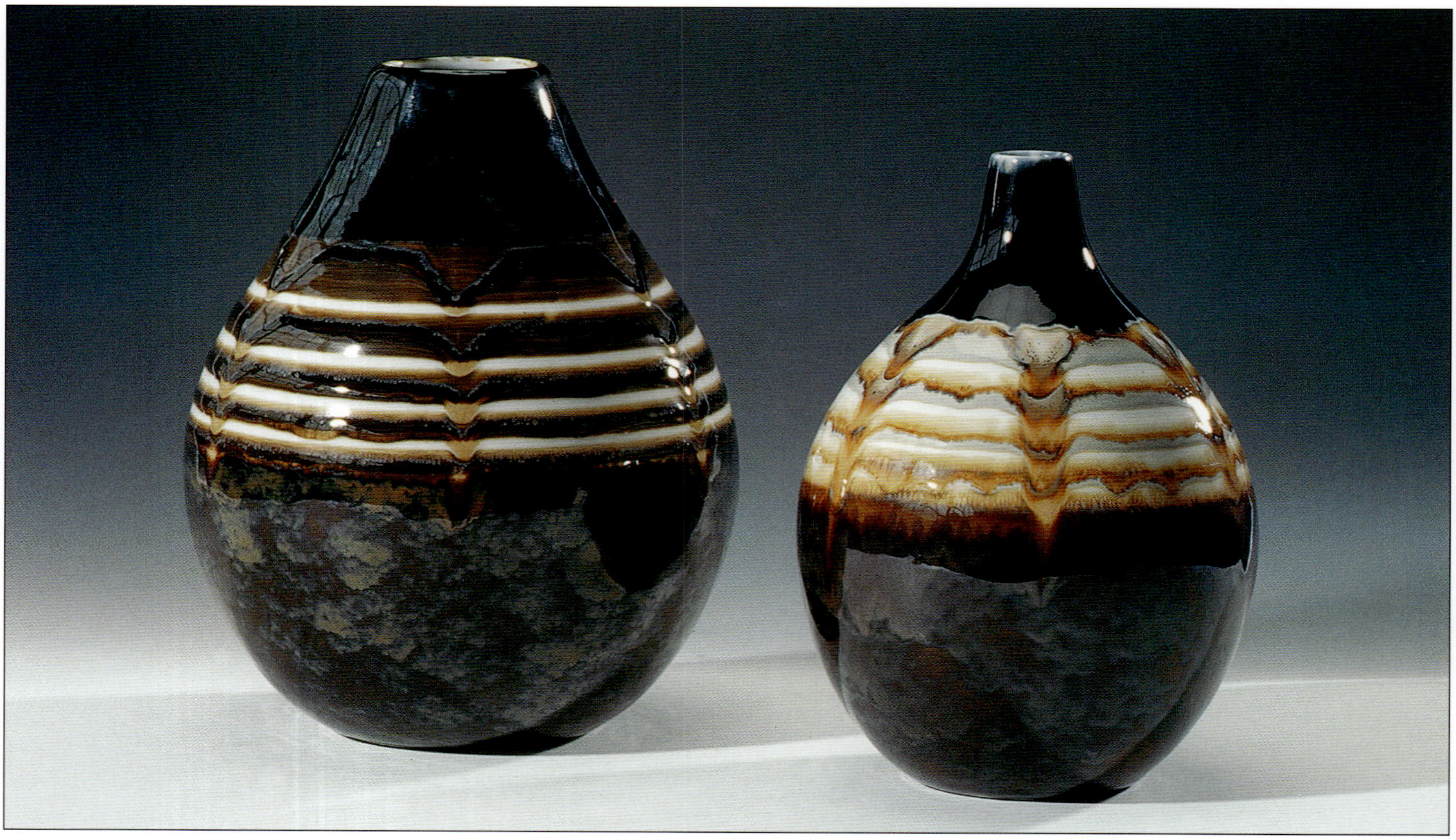

Two vases, 9.5" and 8.5" high, 1930-1945, both incised *Th* (decoration by Camille Tharaud). Left $500-$1,000; right less than $500.

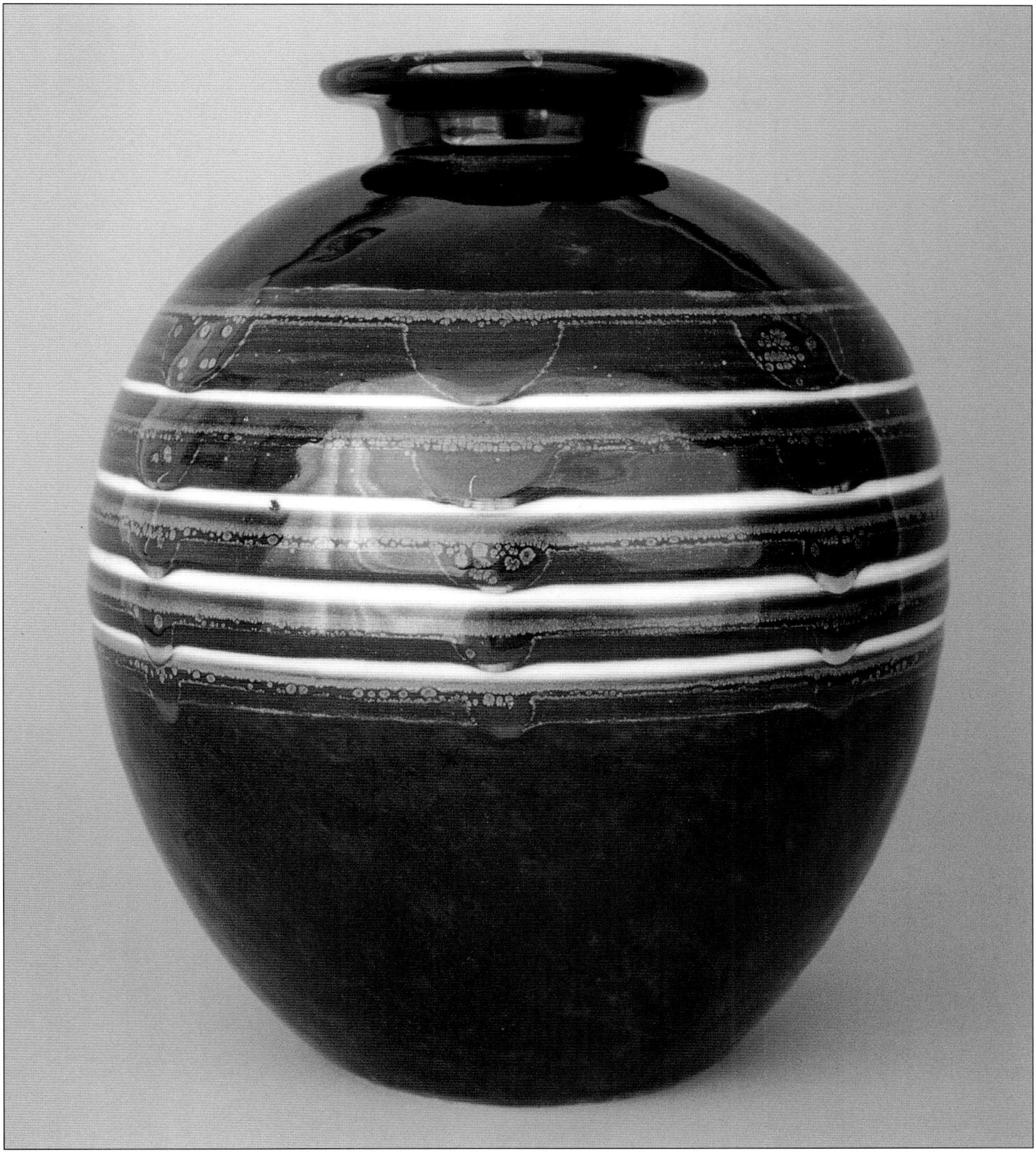

Vase, *Jasmin*, shape of Henri Rapin and decoration of Camille Tharaud, 11" high, 1930-1945, incised marks of Rapin and Tharaud. $500-$1,000.

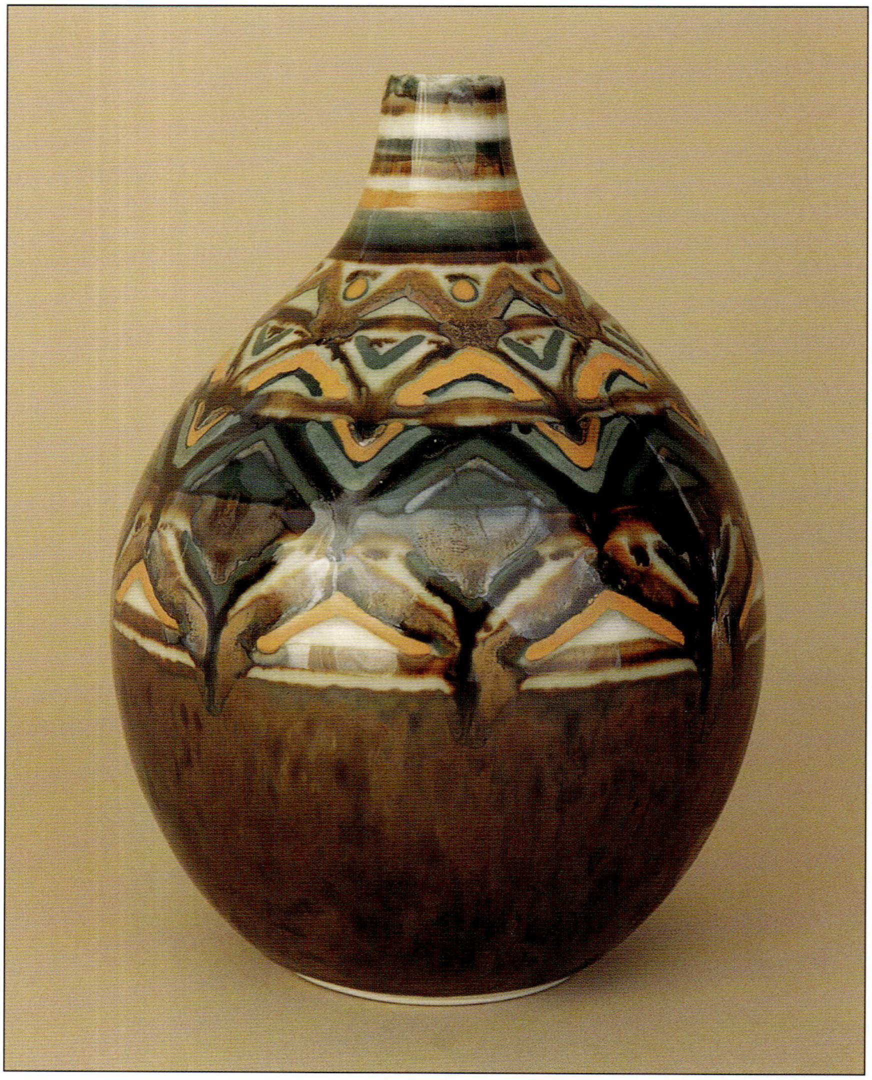

Vase, 8.5" high, 1940-1945, signed *S. Lam* (Simone Lam) in brown. $500-$1,000.

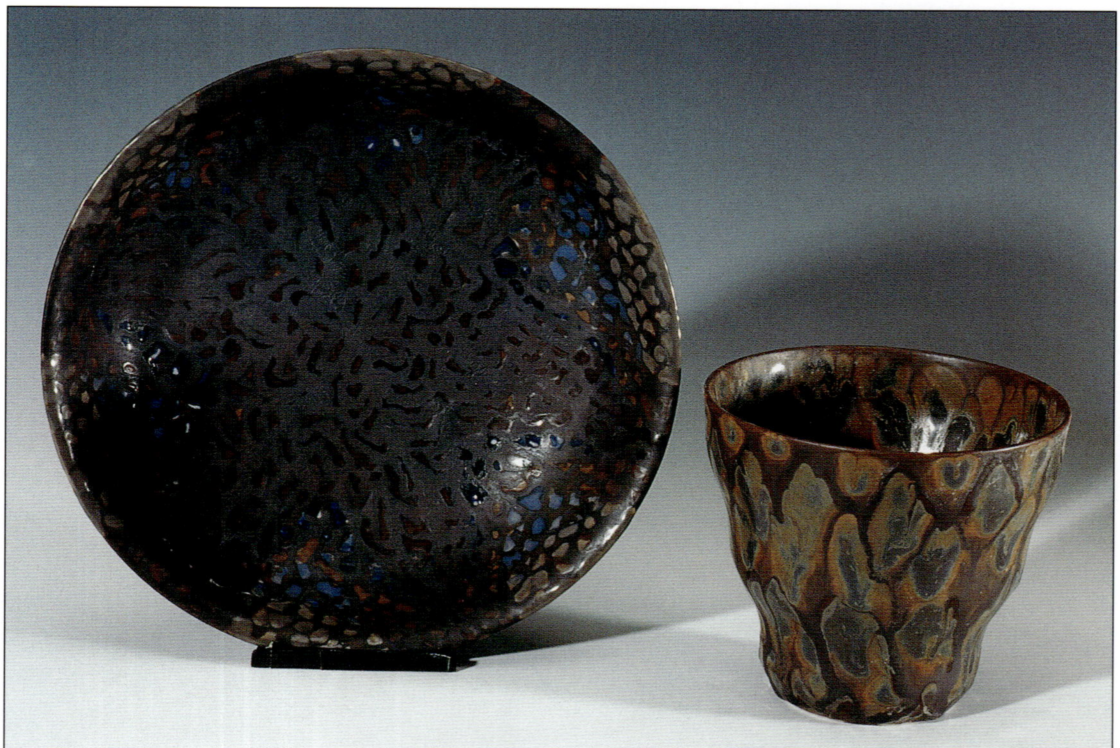

Bowl and vase decorated with lava by Odette Tharaud, bowl marked *3.37* (March 1937). Bowl, $500-$1,000; Vase, less than $500.

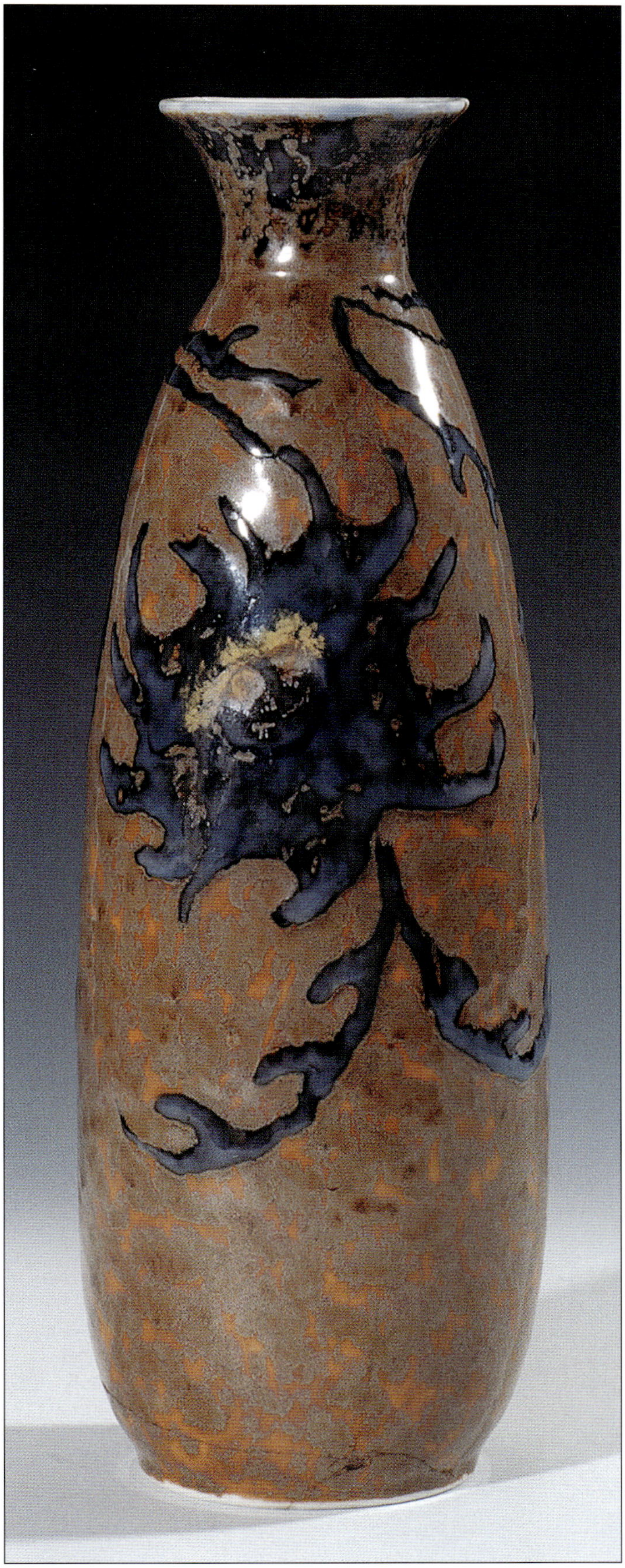

Vase, 13" high, decoration of chrysanthemums superimposed on brown jasper enamel base, Far Eastern inspiration, about 1943. (Ferrer) $500-$1,000.

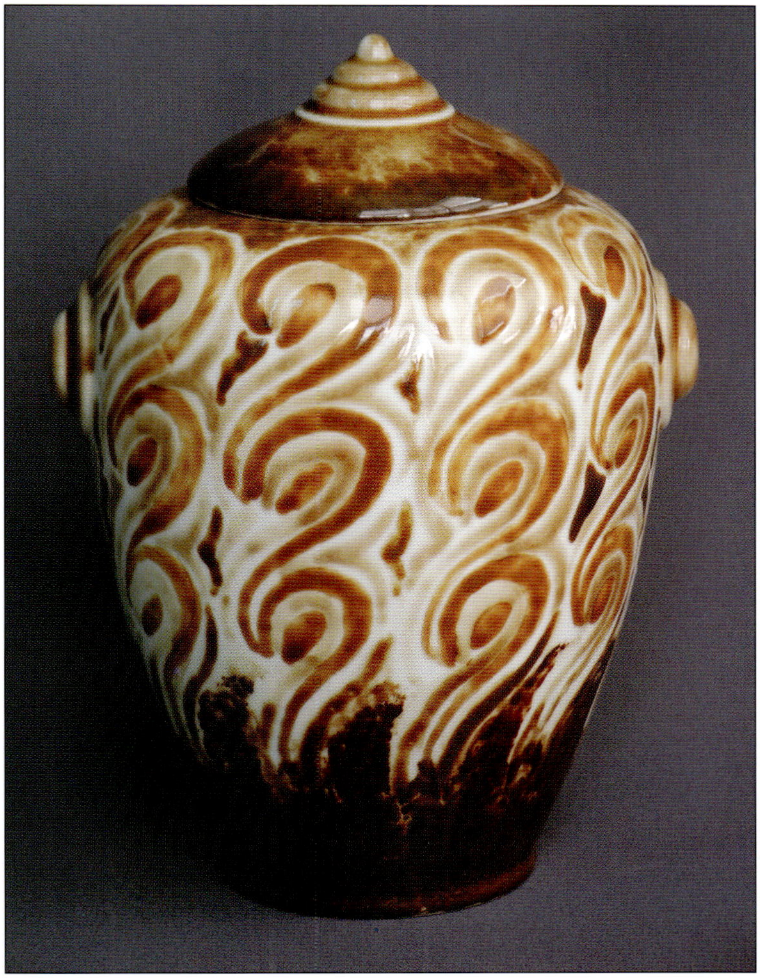

Lidded jar, *Tannhäuser*, shape of Marcel Goupy, rare shape, about 1929. (Ferrer) $500-$1,000.

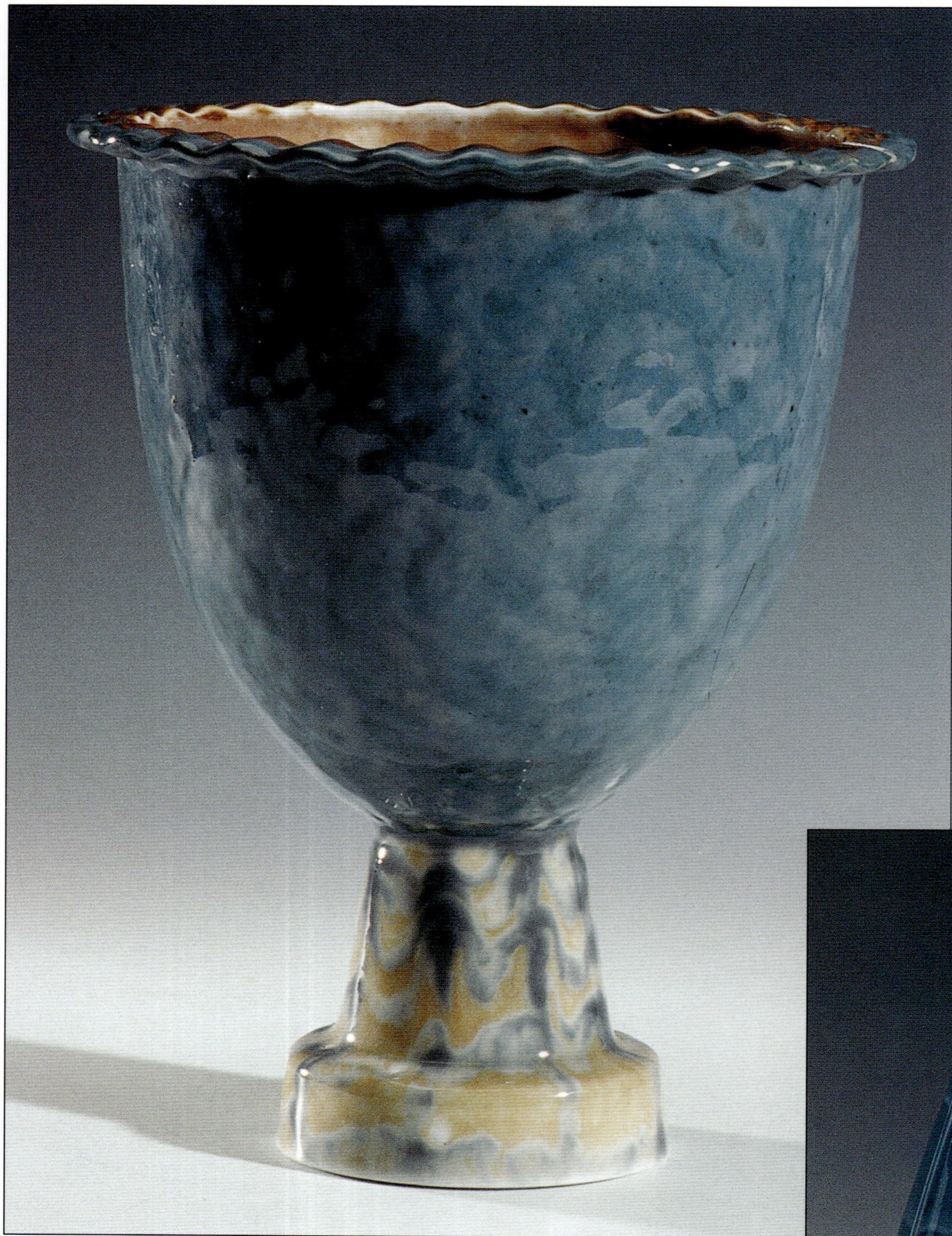

Ostrich egg shaped cup, 9.5" high, 1930-1945. Less than $500.

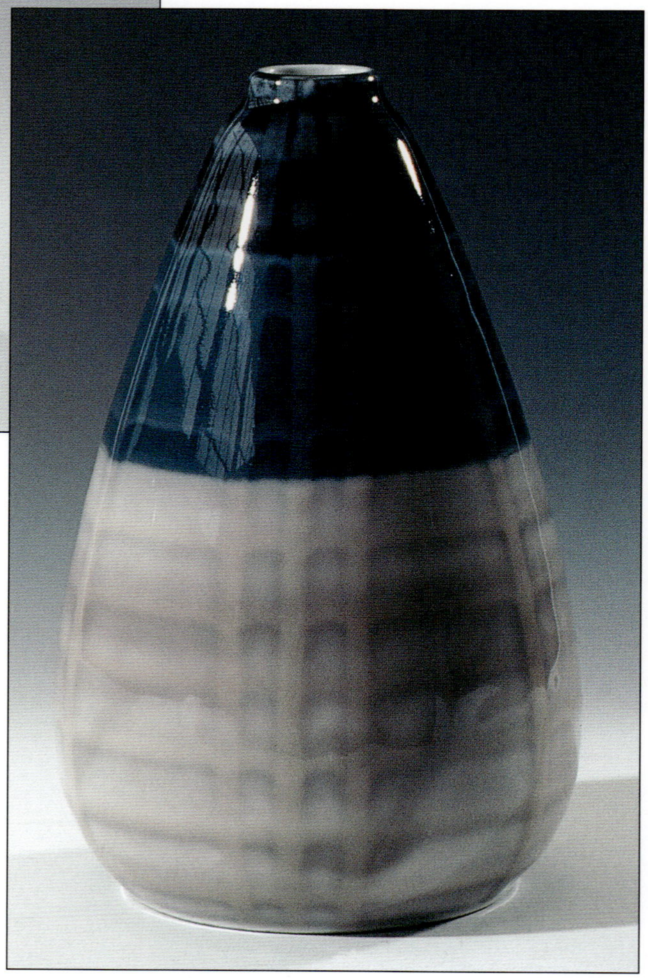

Vase, 7.5" high, 1930-1945. Less than $500.

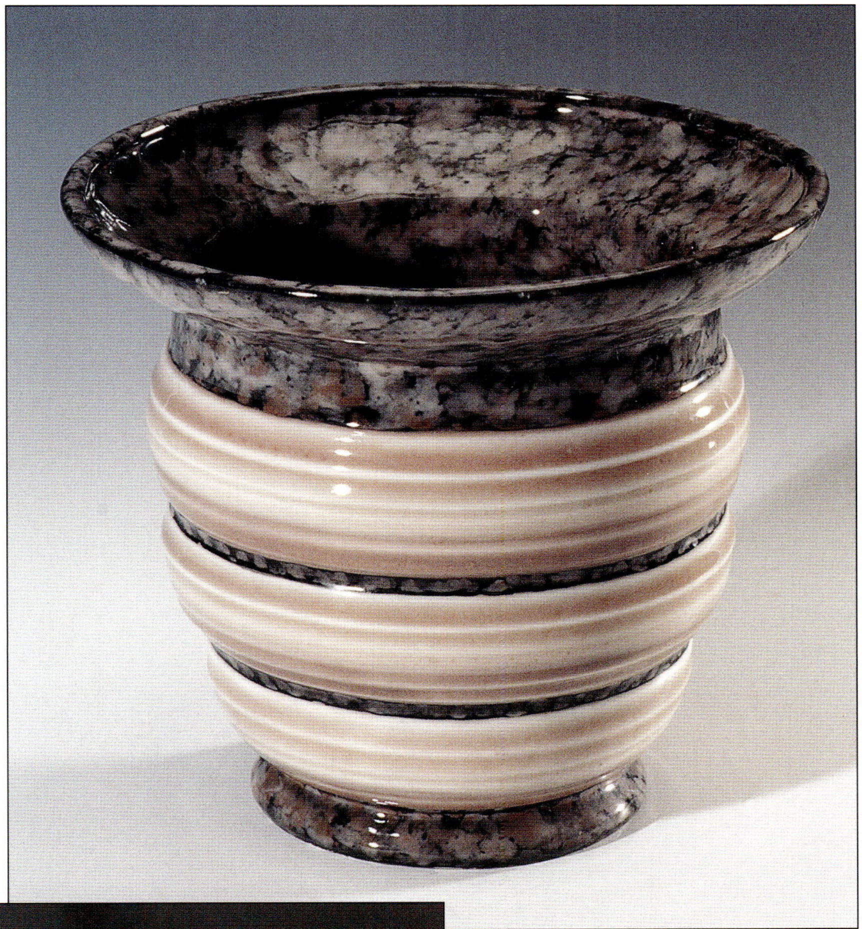

Vase, shape similar to *Genève*, 8" high, marbleized both inside and outside of vase, 1930-1945. $500-$1,000.

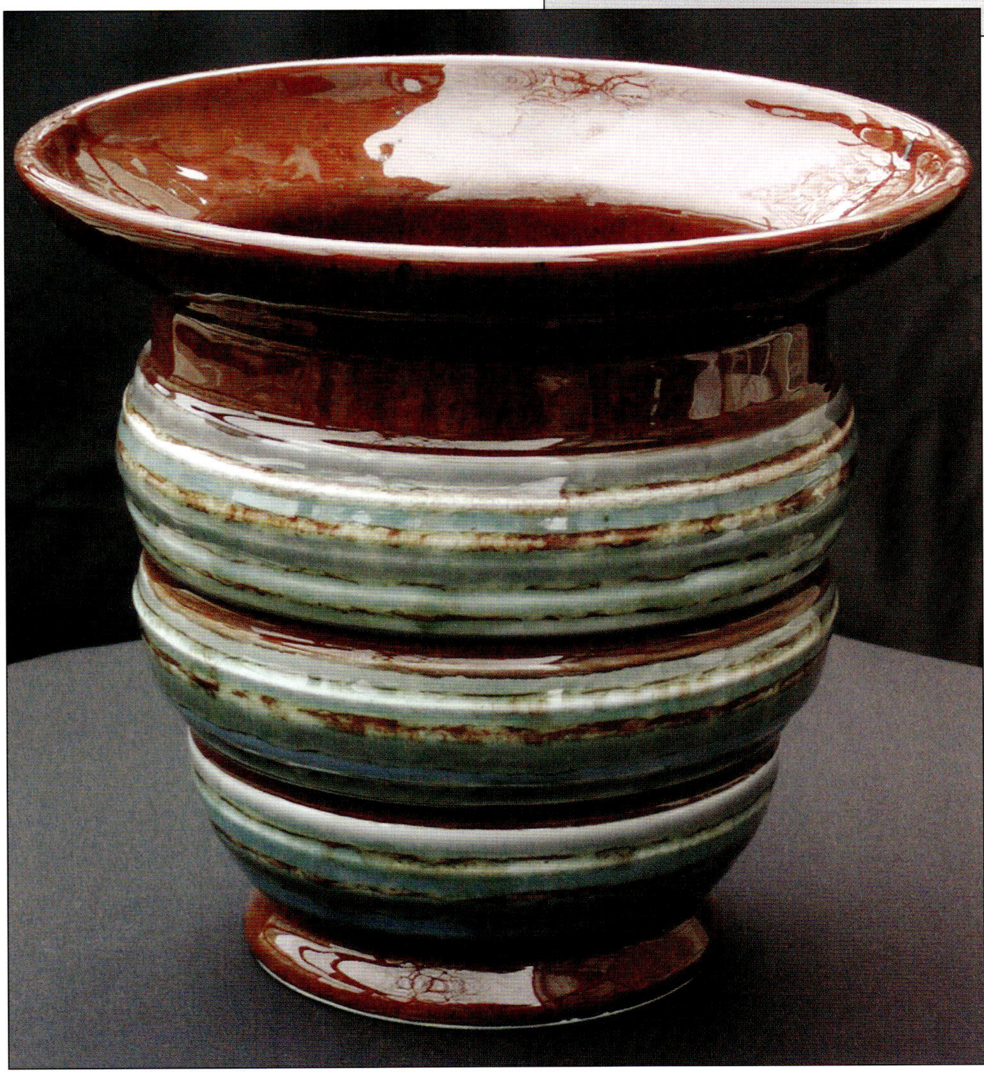

Vase, shape similar to *Genève*, 8" high, 1930-1945. $500-$1,000.

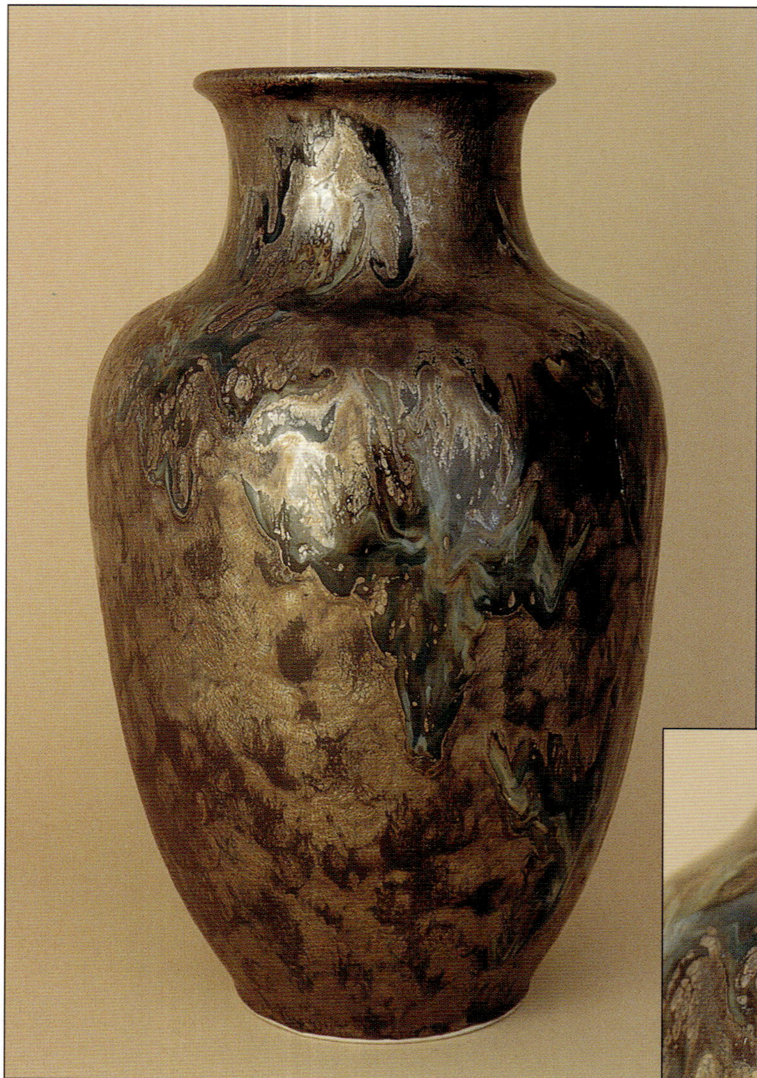

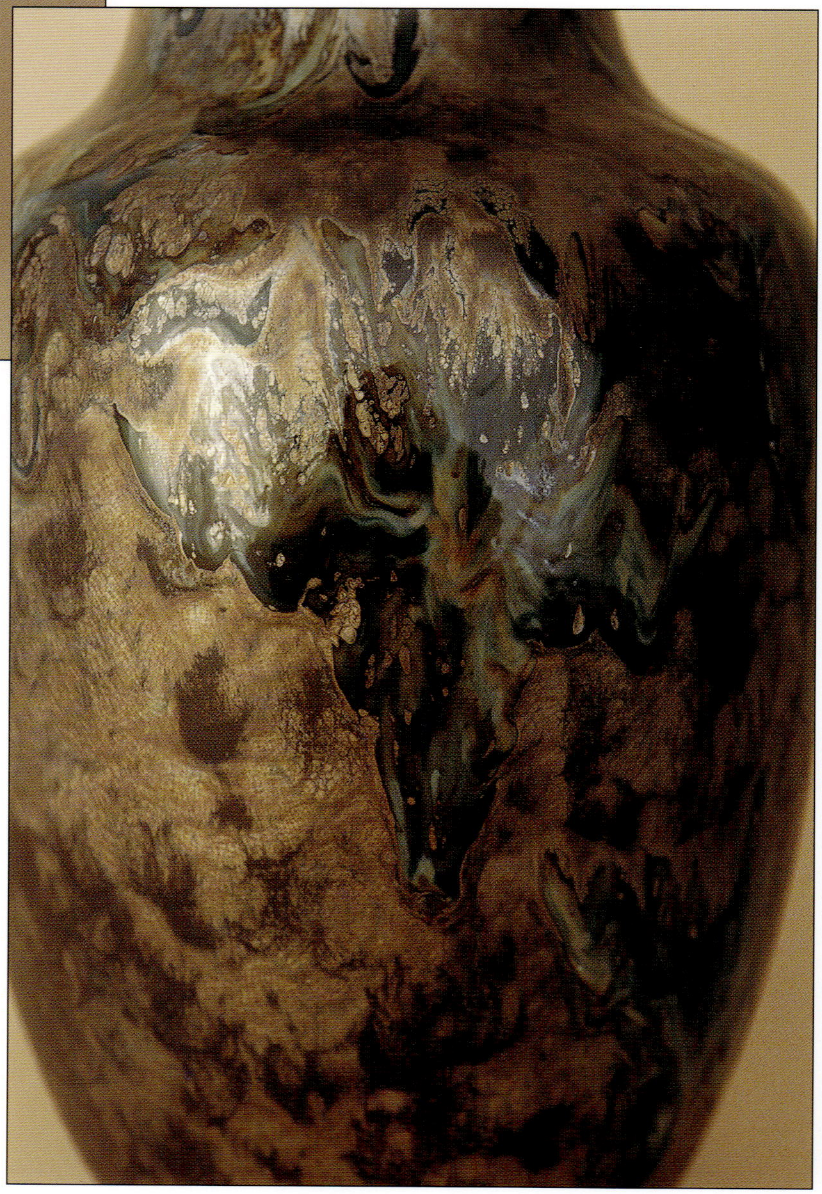

Vase, 14.5" high, 1940-1945, signed, *L. Lib* (Lucienne Liberge). The layering of the enamels containing metallic oxides produce unique colors and effects—what Camille Tharaud called the "effets de matière." The base of the background enamels is wolfram. $500-$1,000.

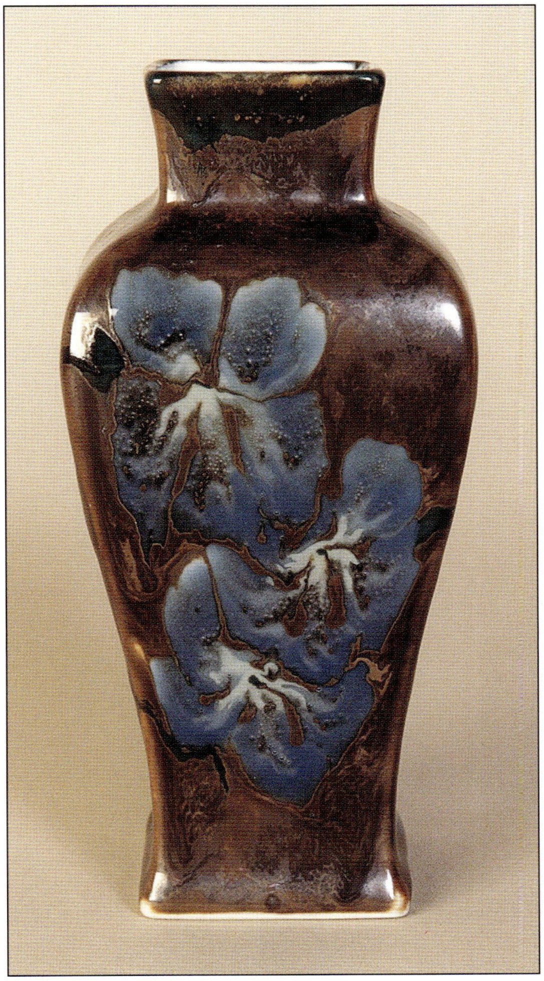

Vase, *Japonais*, 6.5" high, 1930-1945, Japanese inspired decoration, incised *R*. Less than $500.

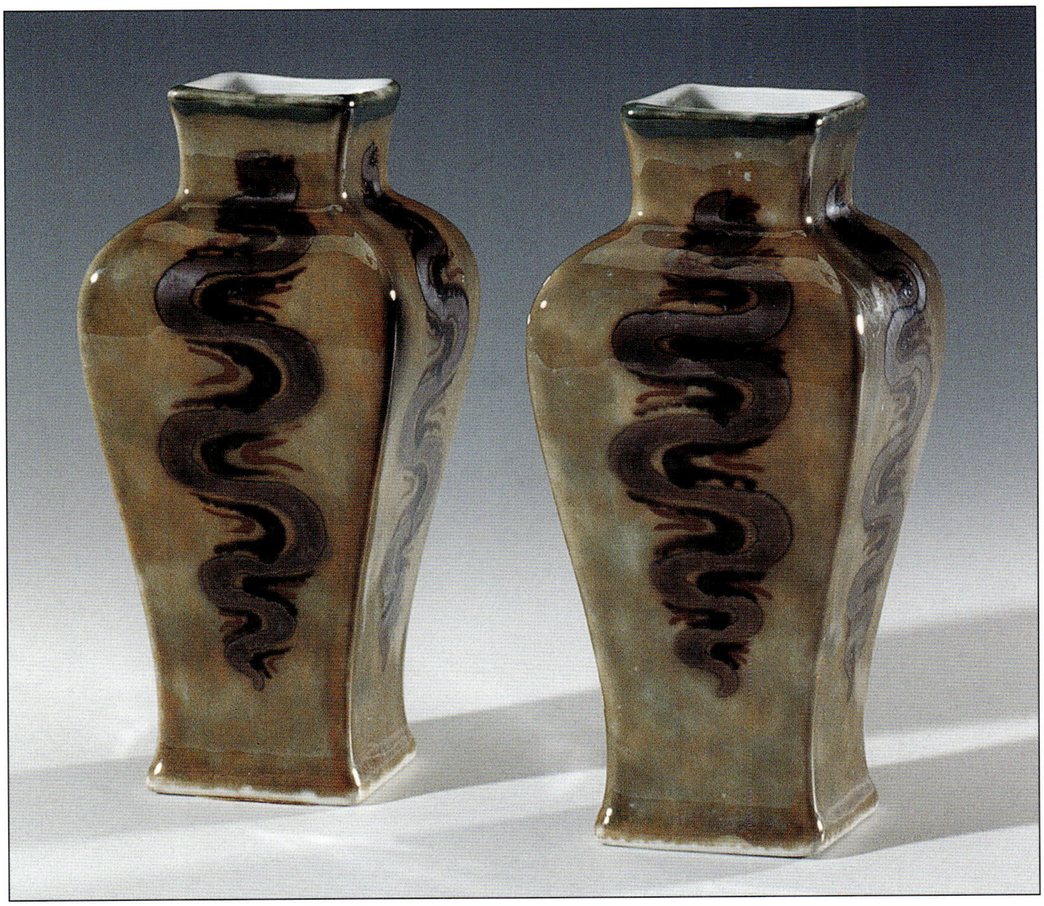

Vases, *Japonais*, 6.75" high, in celadon, marked *M.T.L.* or *M.T.M.* If mark is *M.T.M.*, then it was painted by Marguerite Mouton, one of the premier painters at the Tharaud studio, 1930-1945. Pair $500-$1,000.

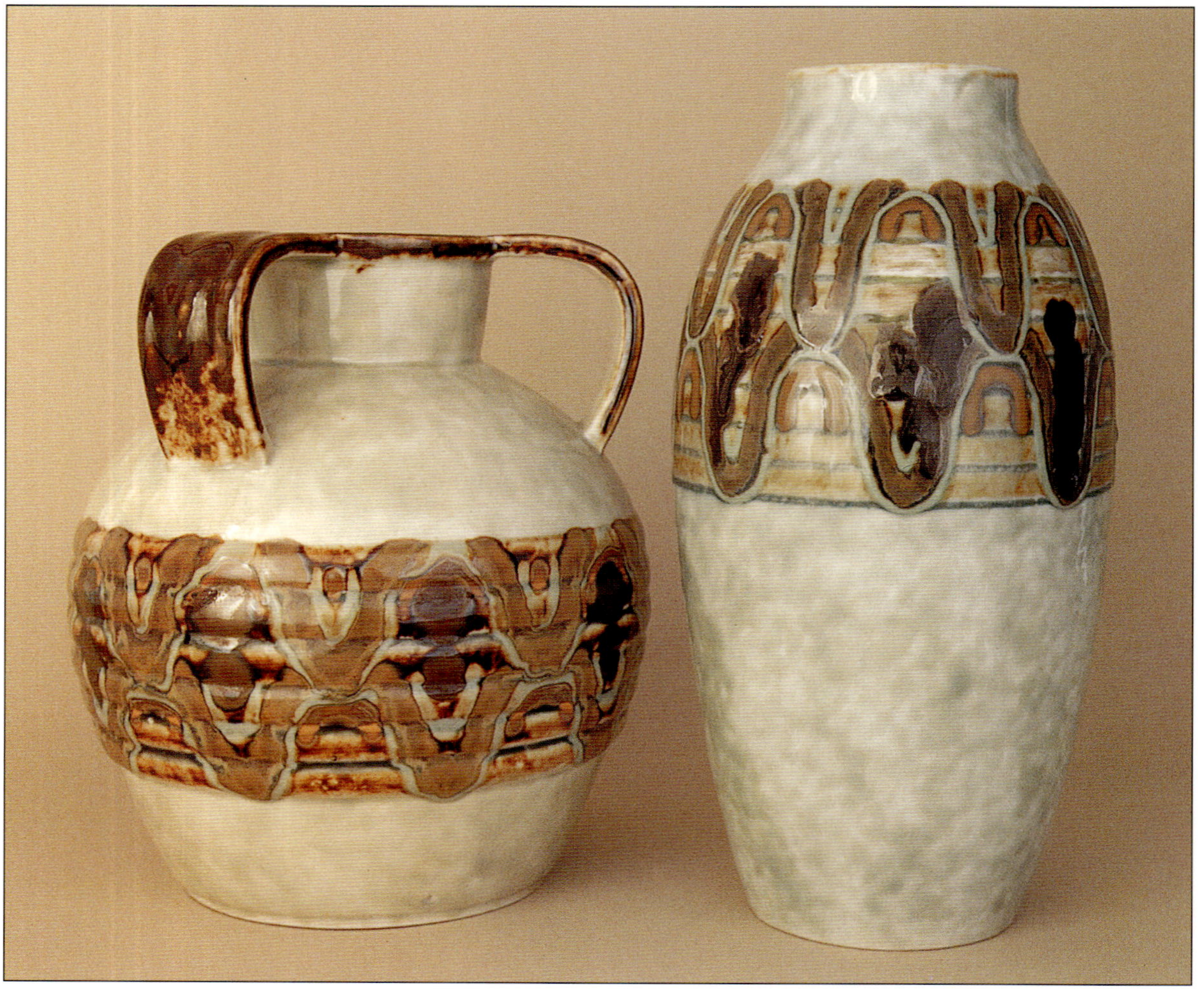

Three-handled jug, *Muflier*, shape by Henri Rapin, 1930-1945, incised mark of Henri Rapin and signed, *L. Lib* (Lucienne Liberge); and vase, 12.4" high, 1930-1945, incised *EL* (Elise L.). Jug, $500-$1,000; vase, less than $500.

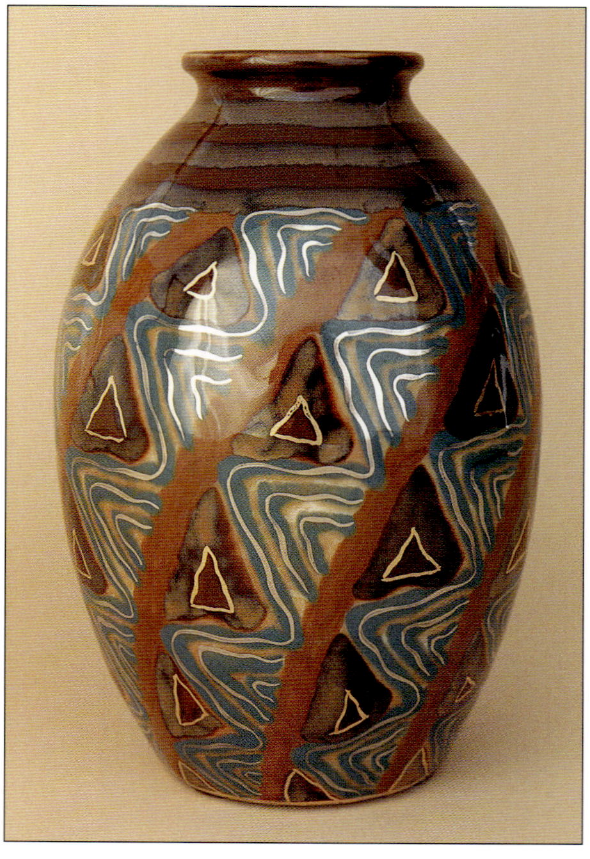

Vase, 9.25" high, 1930-1945. Less than $500.

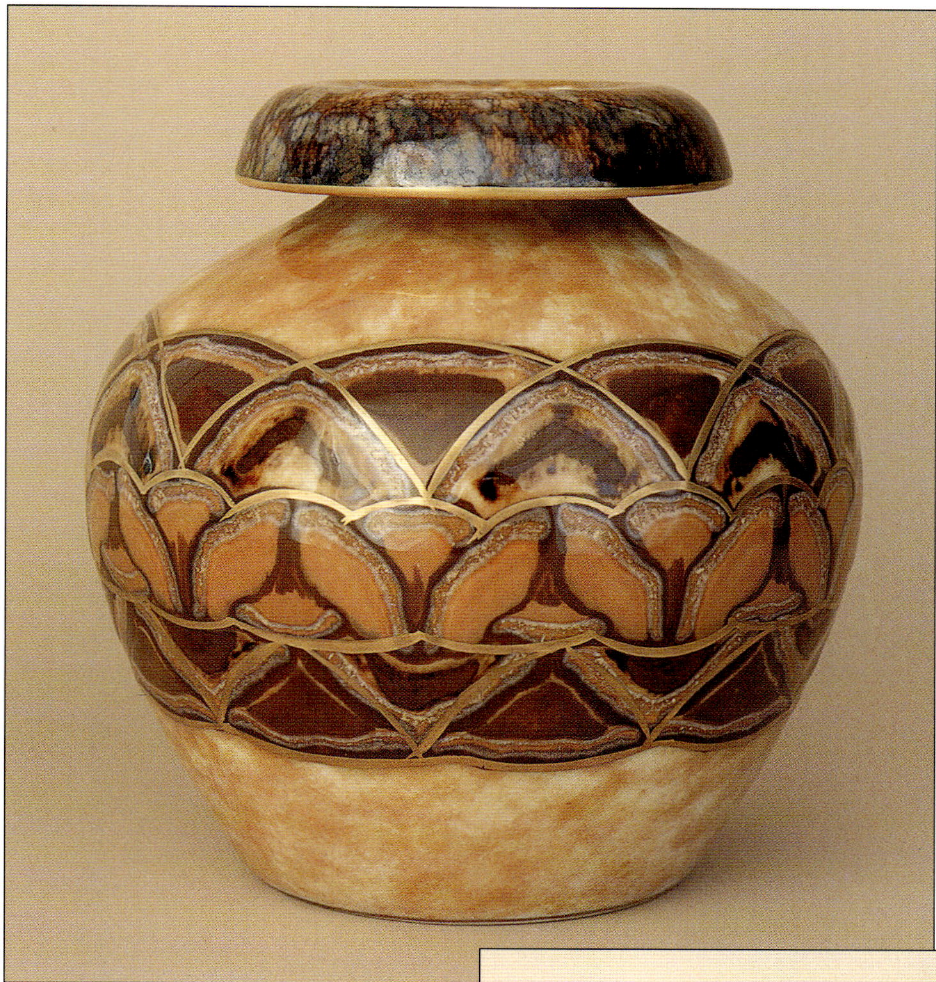

Vase, *Amarante*, 8.75" high, about 1946, incised *JP*. $500-$1,000.

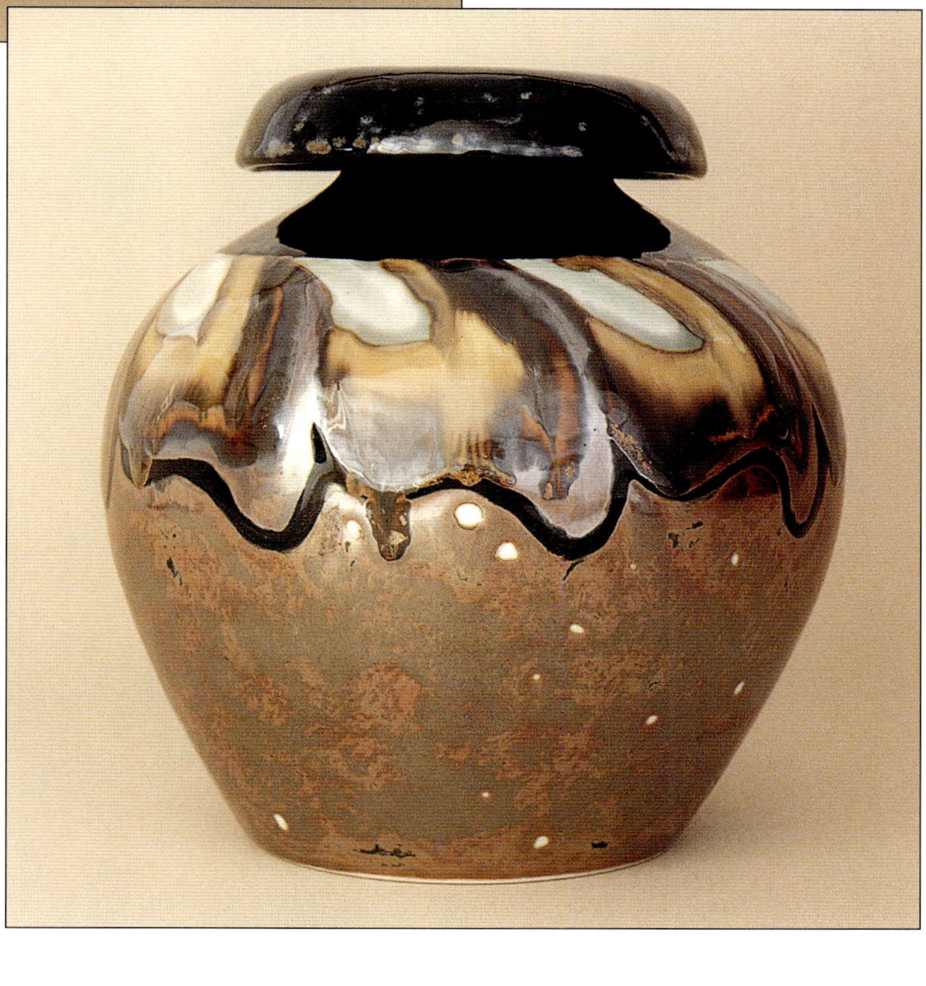

Vase, *Amarante*, 8.5" high, 1930-1945. Note the number of enamel skips, which was one of the difficulties which resulted from the enamels used by Camille Tharaud. Less than $500.

Right:
Vase, *Canna*, 7.5" high, 1930-1945, rare sea decoration with two fish swimming in blue-green water among stylized seaweed. $500-$1,000.

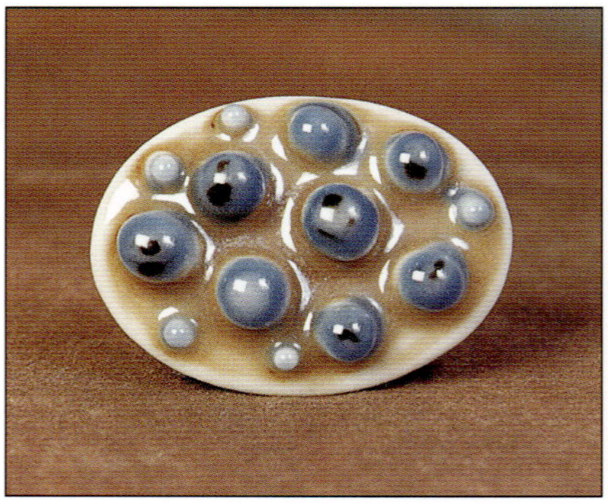

Oval broach, 2" x 1.5", 1930-1945. Many of these pieces were made during World War II because of the scarcity of precious stones and metals for jewelry during the war years. Less than $500.

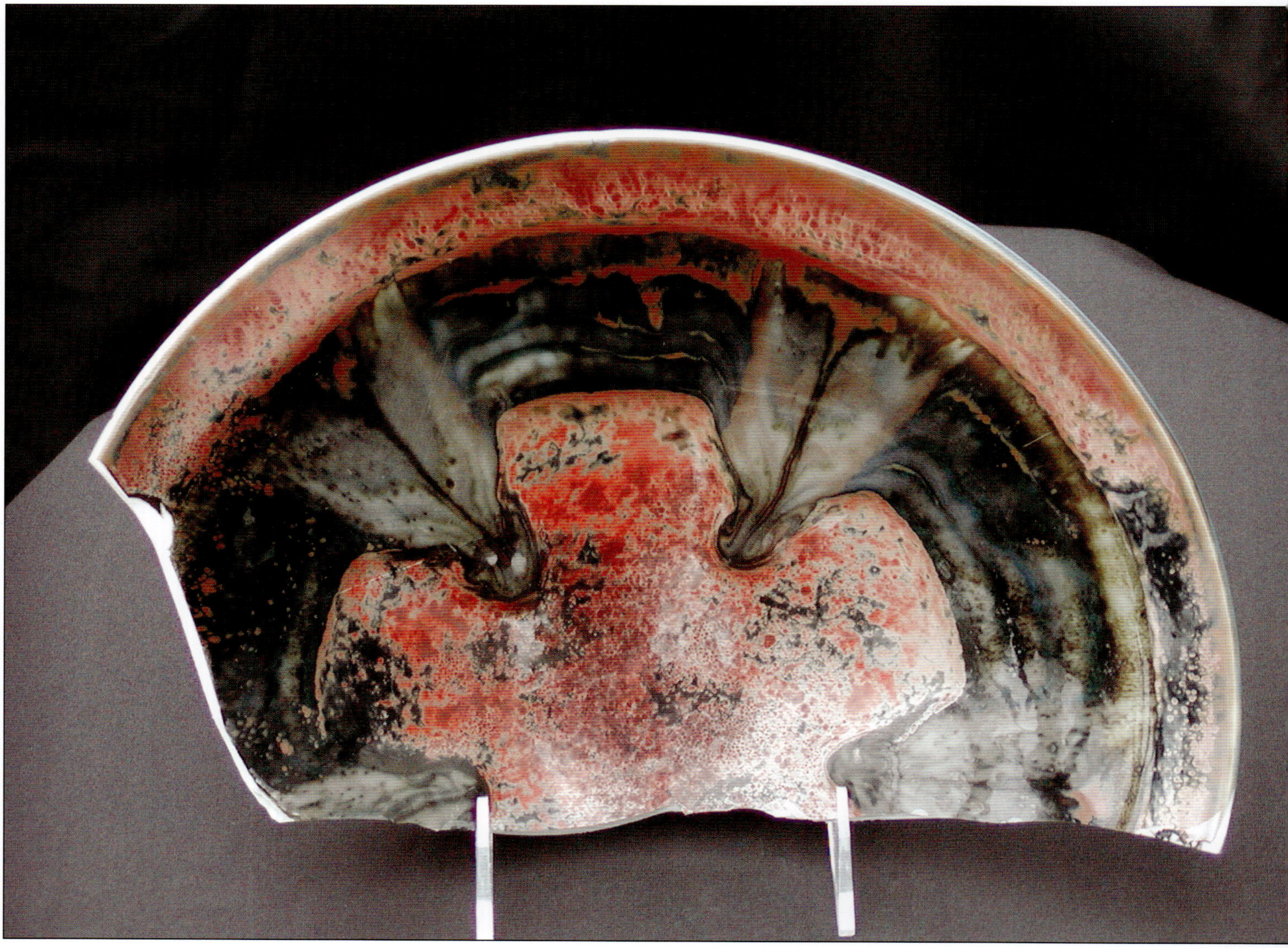

Broken plate, 11.75" in diameter, about 1945, decorated by Lucienne Liberge.

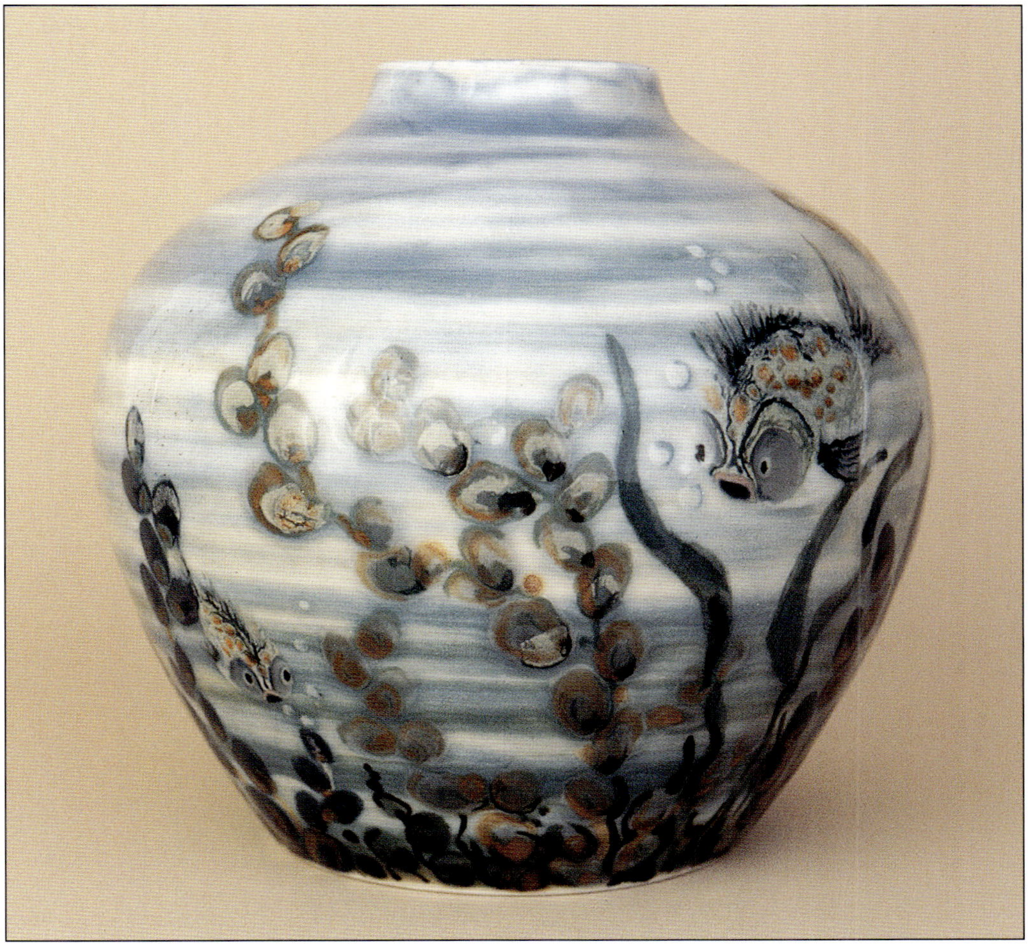

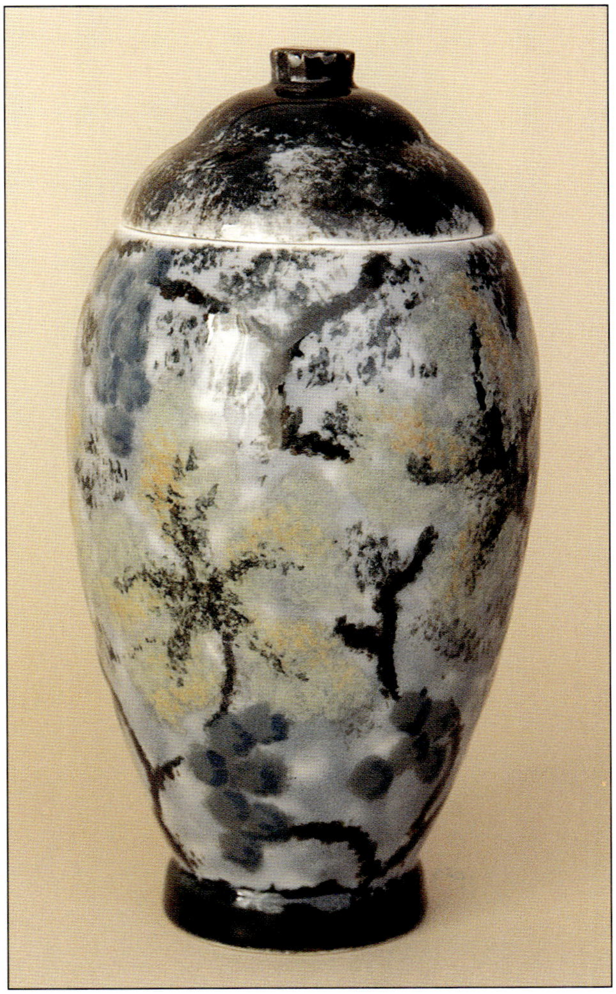

Vase, *Manon*, shape of Henri Rapin, 7.5" high, 1940-1945, designed and painted by Lucienne Lib. Less than $500.

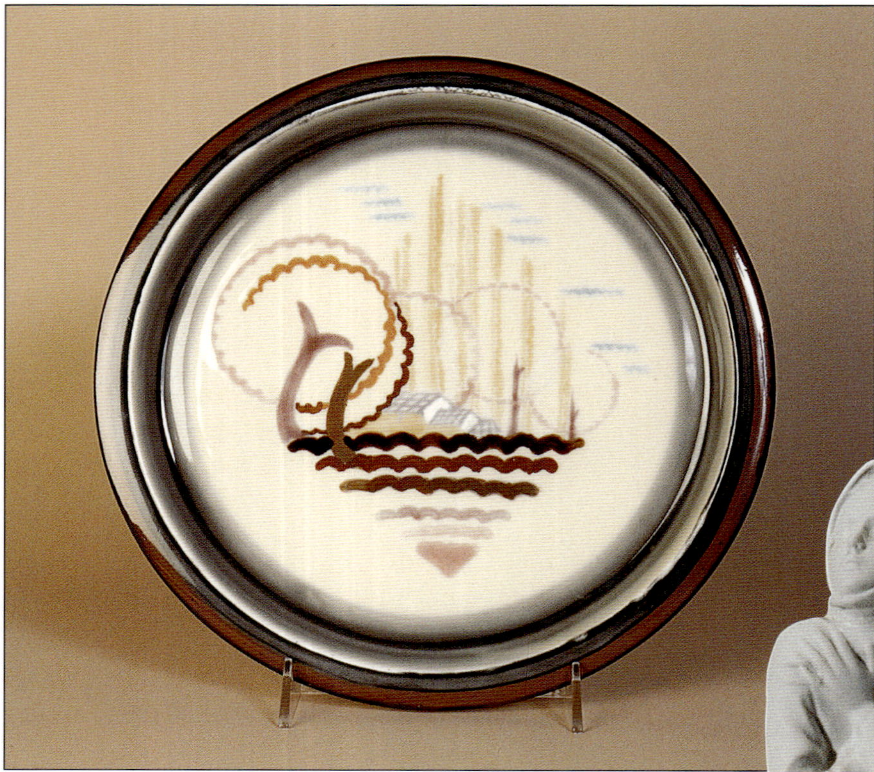

Tray, 11.5" in diameter, 1930-1945. Decoration depicts a fertile farm, with a farmhouse, clouds, strokes for rain, and dark brown hues indicating the richness of the soil. $500-$1,000.

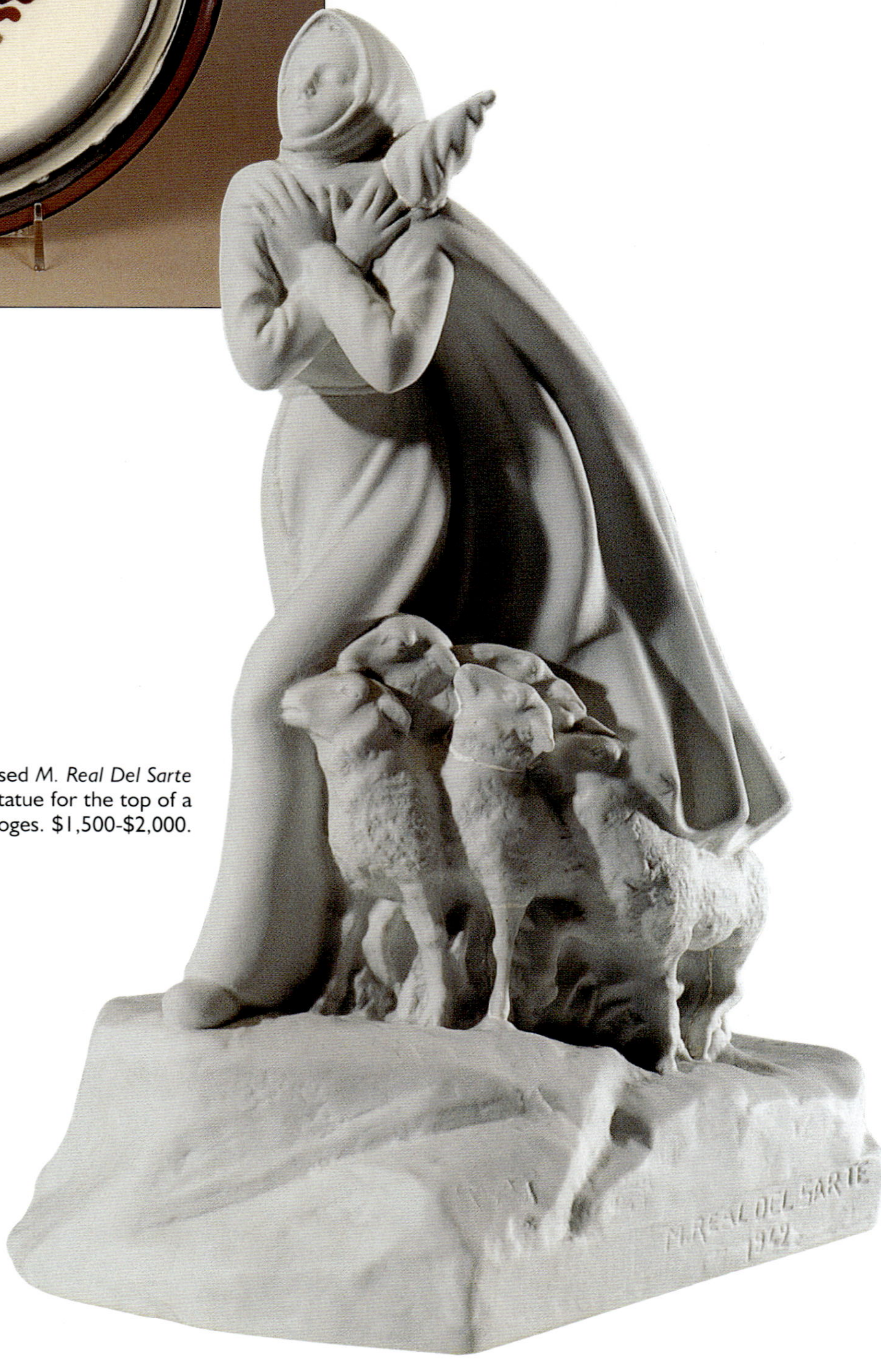

Joan d'Arc, 14" high, incised *M. Real Del Sarte 1942*, prototype for large statue for the top of a department store in Limoges. $1,500-$2,000.

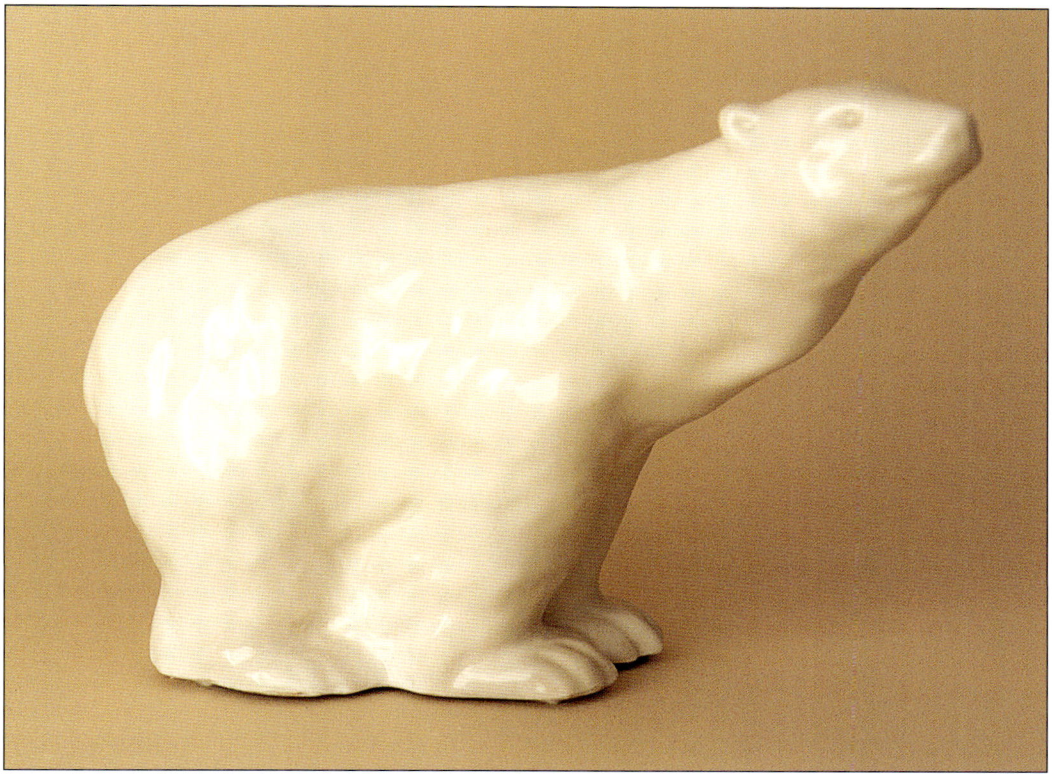

Polar bear, 5.5" high x 8.5", 1930-1945. $500-$1,000.

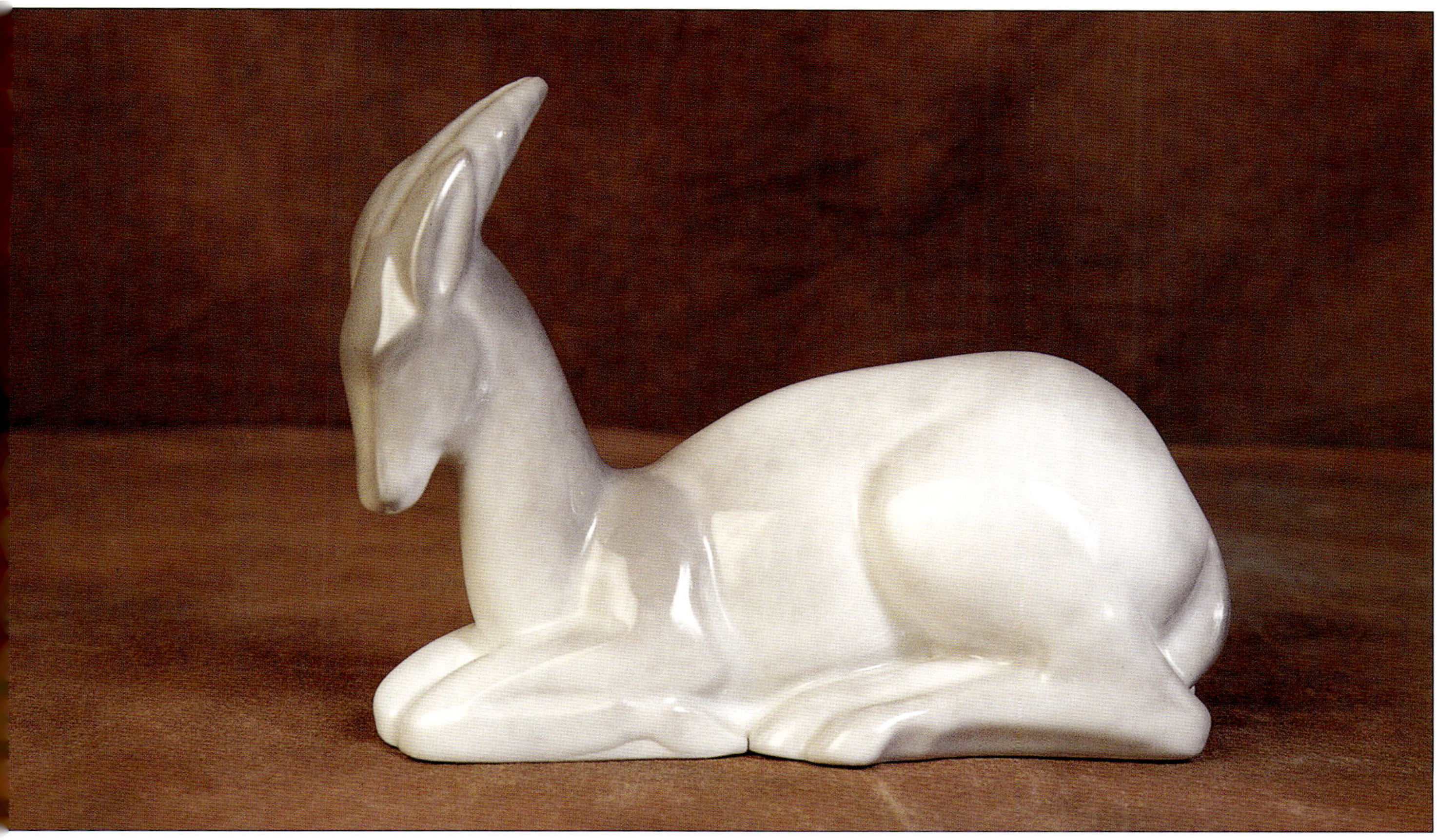

Gazelle, 6.5" high x 8", 1930-1945. $500-$1,000.

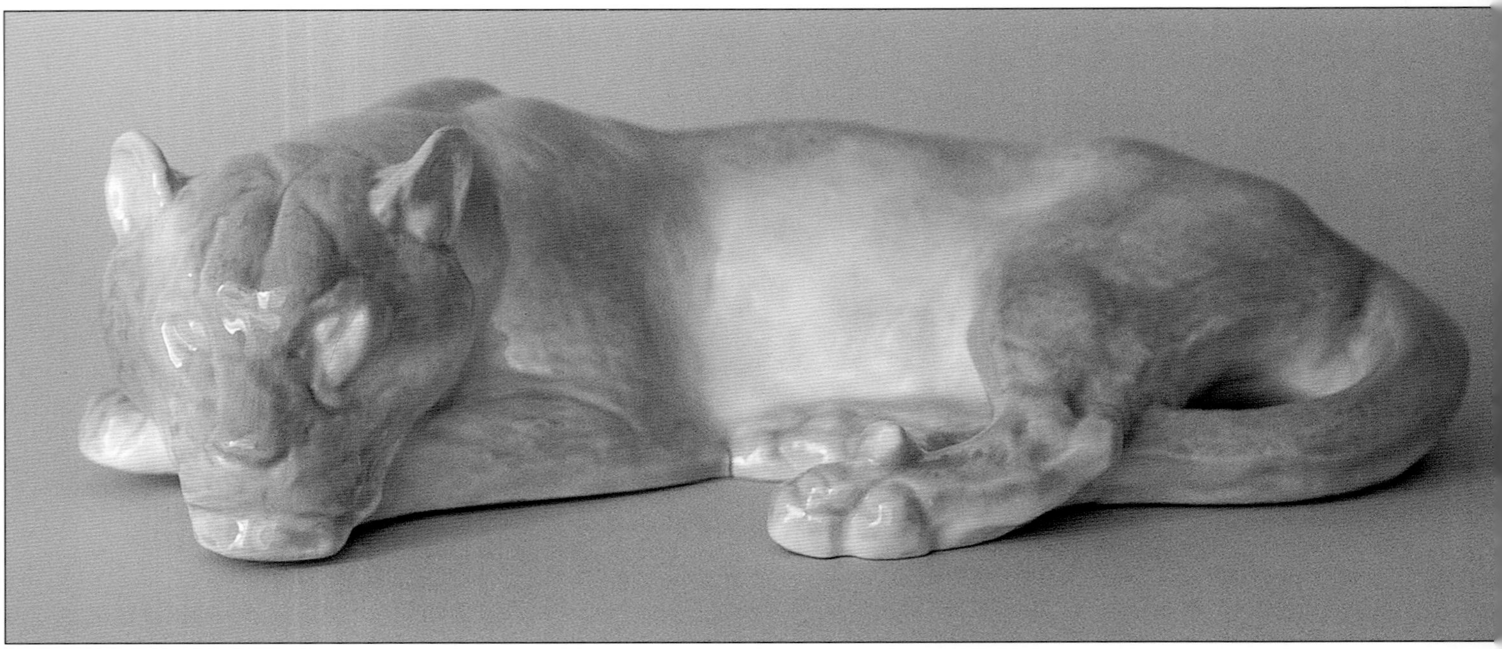

Lioness, 10" x 6", 1930-1945, *sous émail* gray and platinum. $500-$1,000.

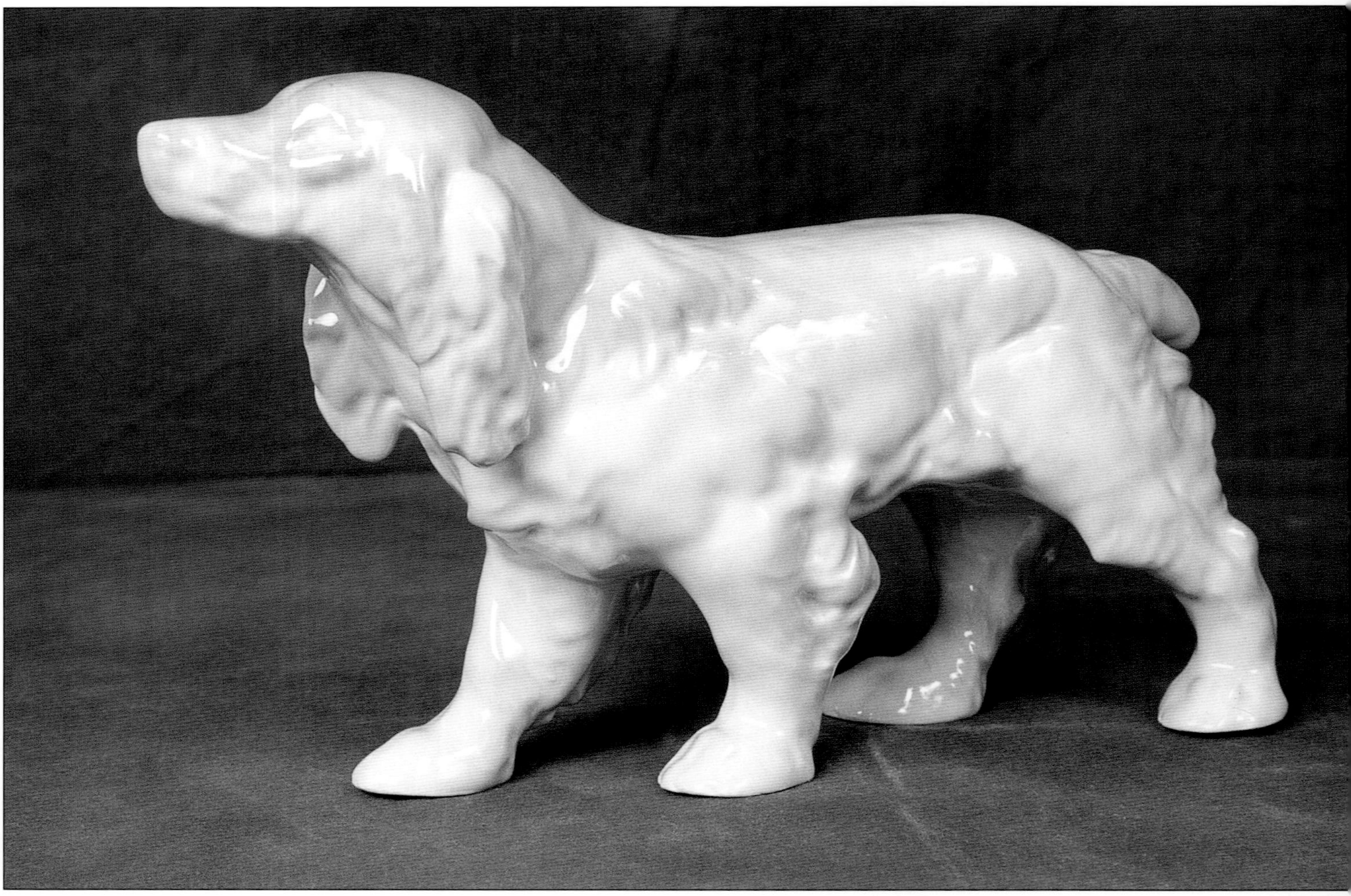

Spaniel, 12" x 7.25" high, 1930-1945. $500-$1,000.

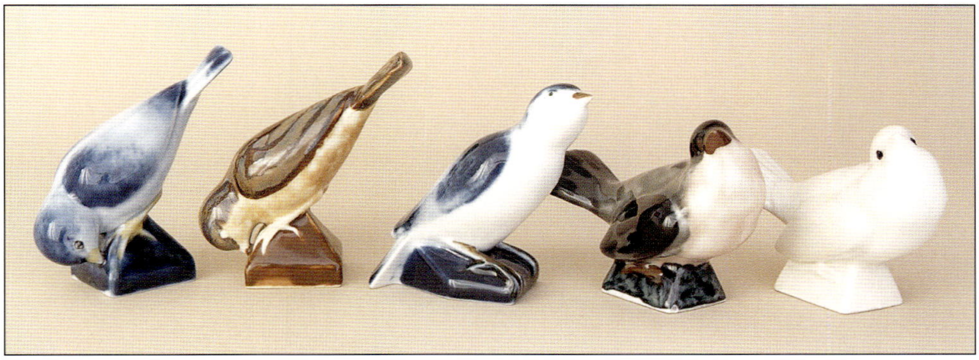

Birds, 1930-1945. Each less than $500.

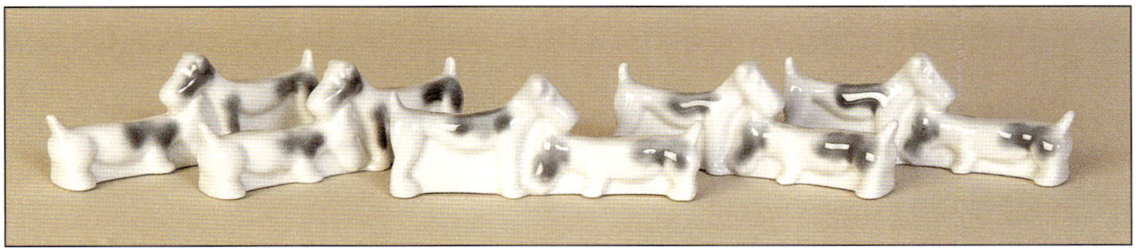

Knife rests, 3.9" x 1.9" high, 1930-1945. Set less than $500.

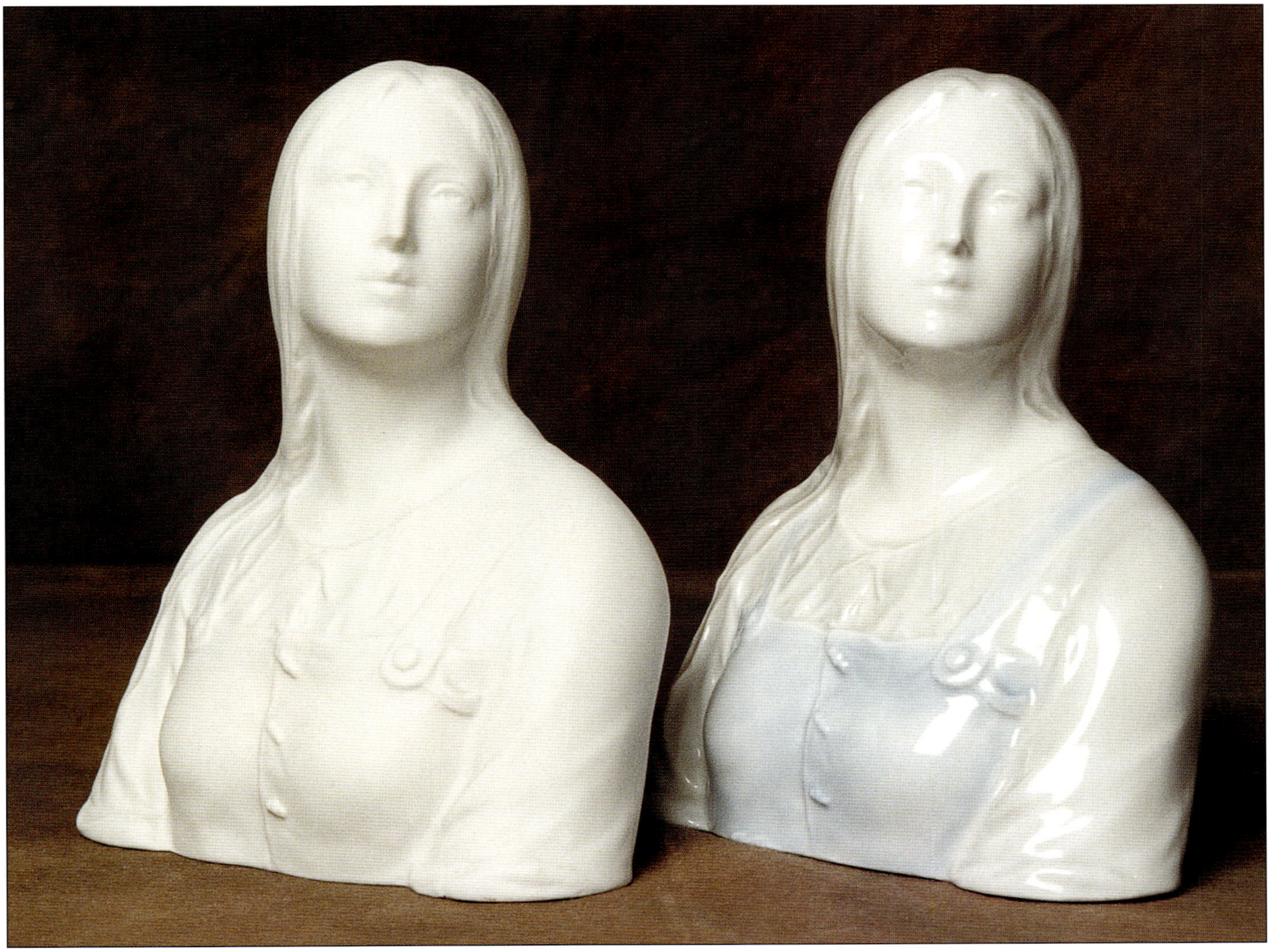

Busts, 7" high, 1930-1945. Left, $500-$1,000; right, $1,000-$1,500.

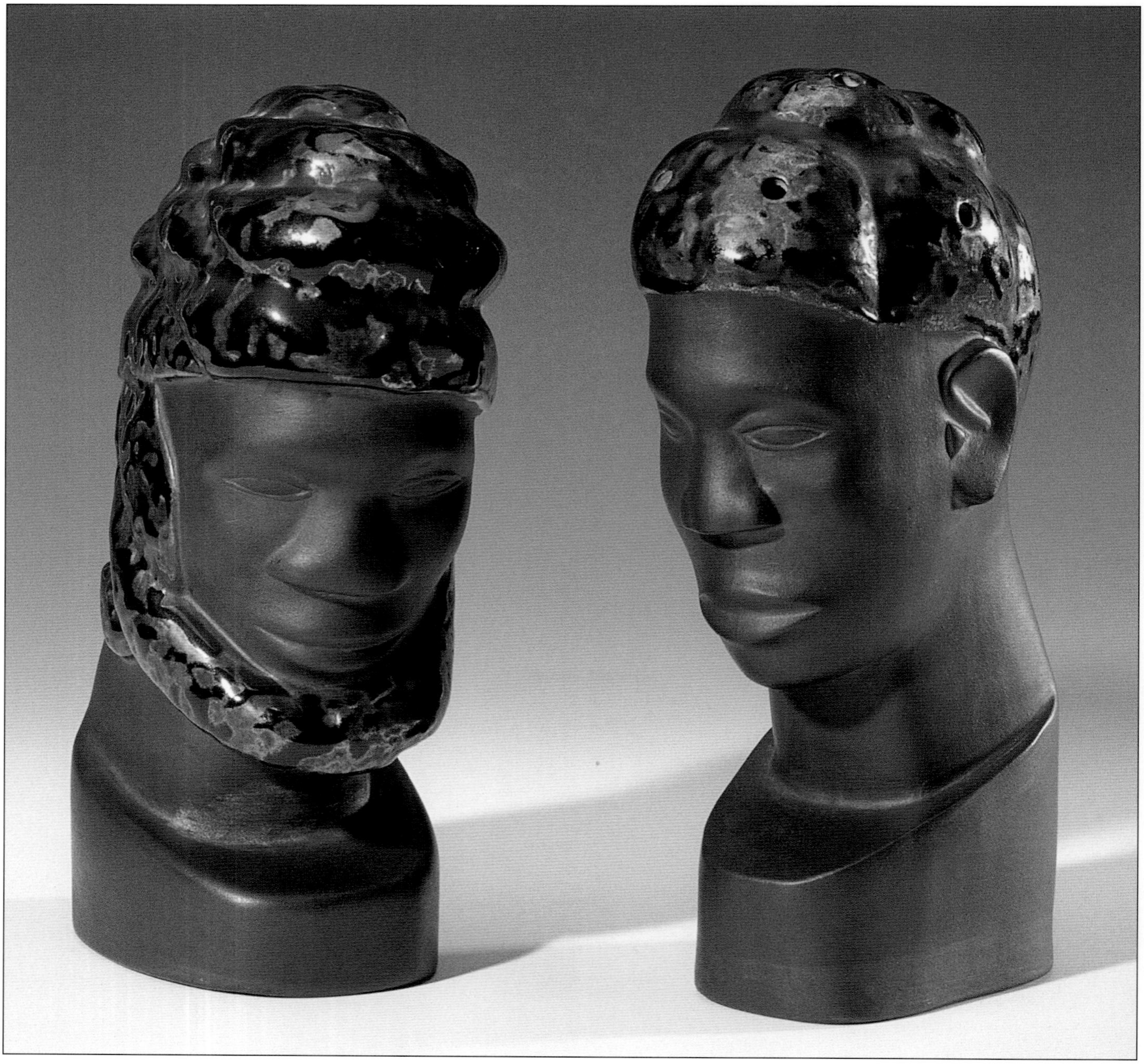

Bookends, very rare, 1930-1945, represent African influence in Camille Tharaud's work. Set, $2,000+.

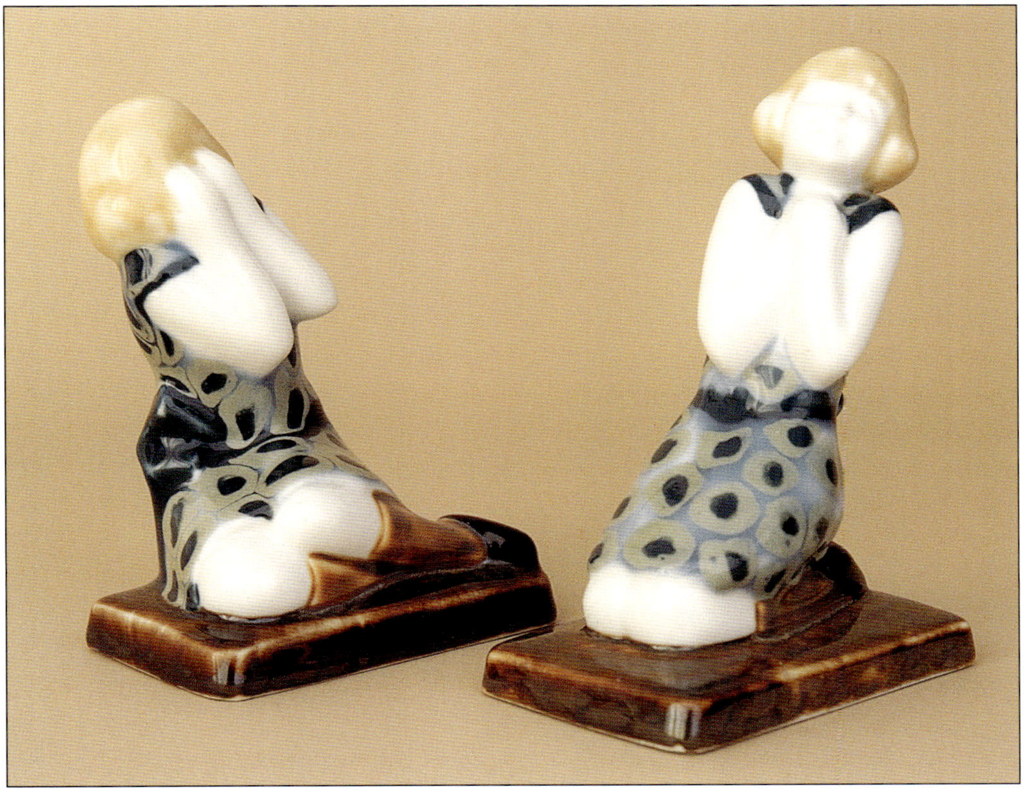

Girl bookends, 5.5" high x 5", 1930-1945. Set, $500-$1,000.

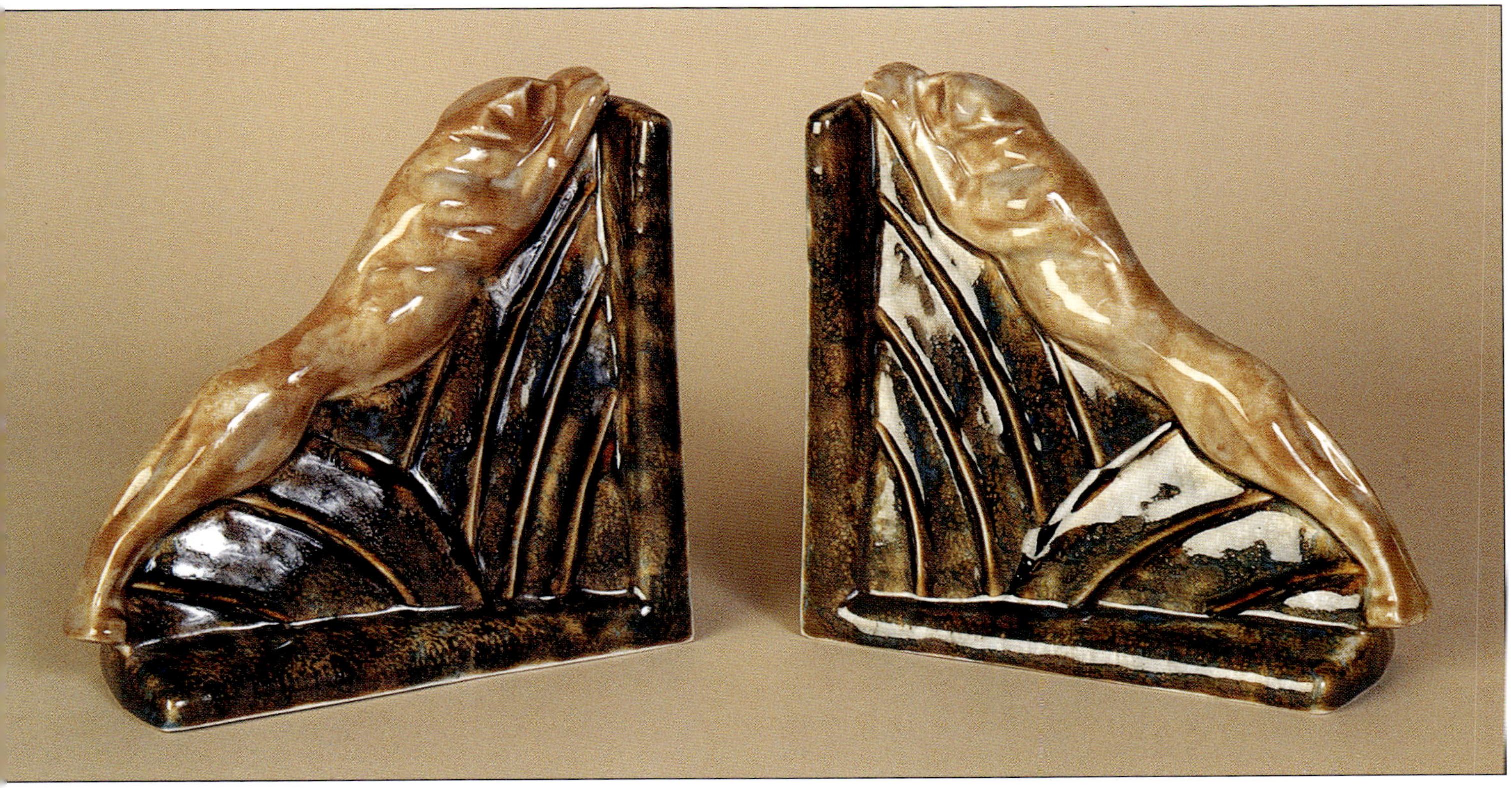

Panther bookends, 7" high x 7.25", 1930-1945. Set, $500-$1,000.

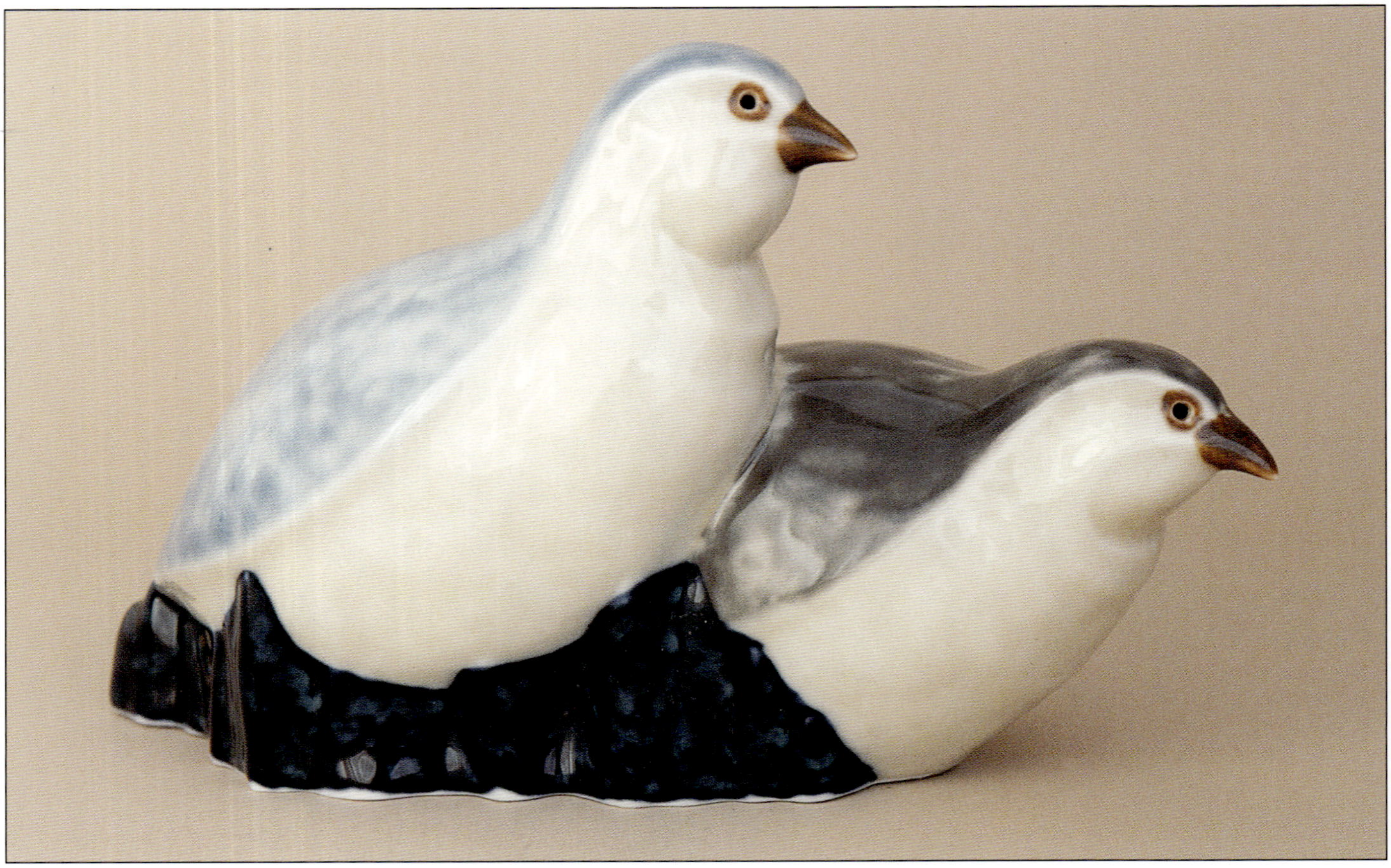

Quail nightlight, 9" x 5.1" high, 1930-1945. $500-$1,000.

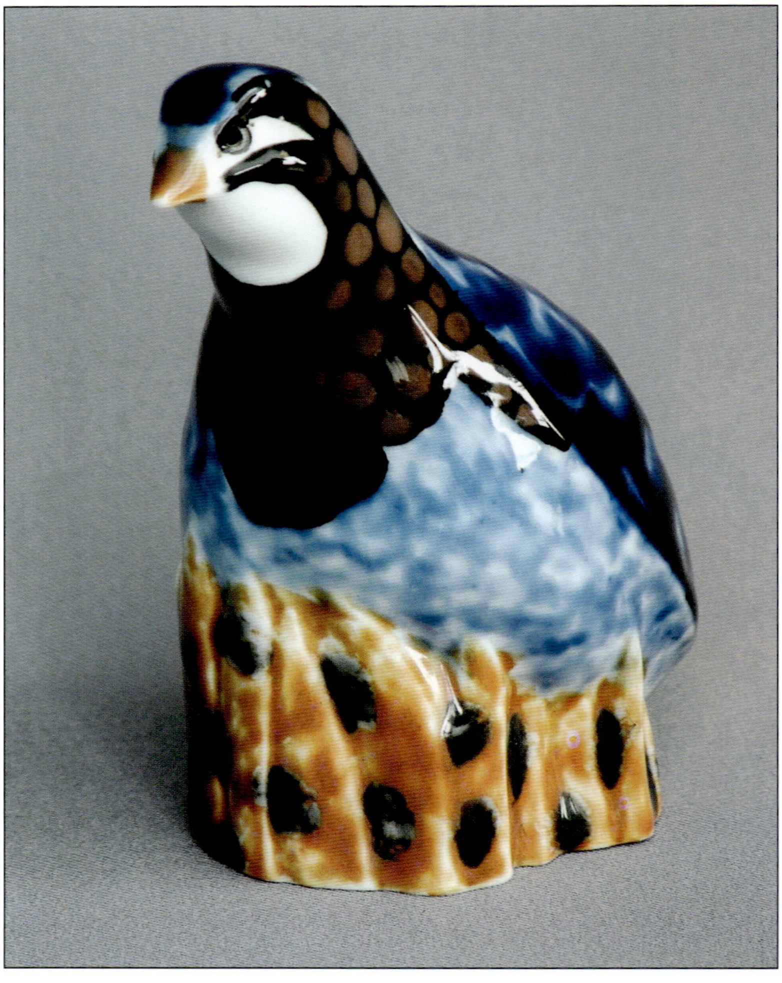

Quail Nightlight, 5.25" high, $500-$1,000.

After 1943

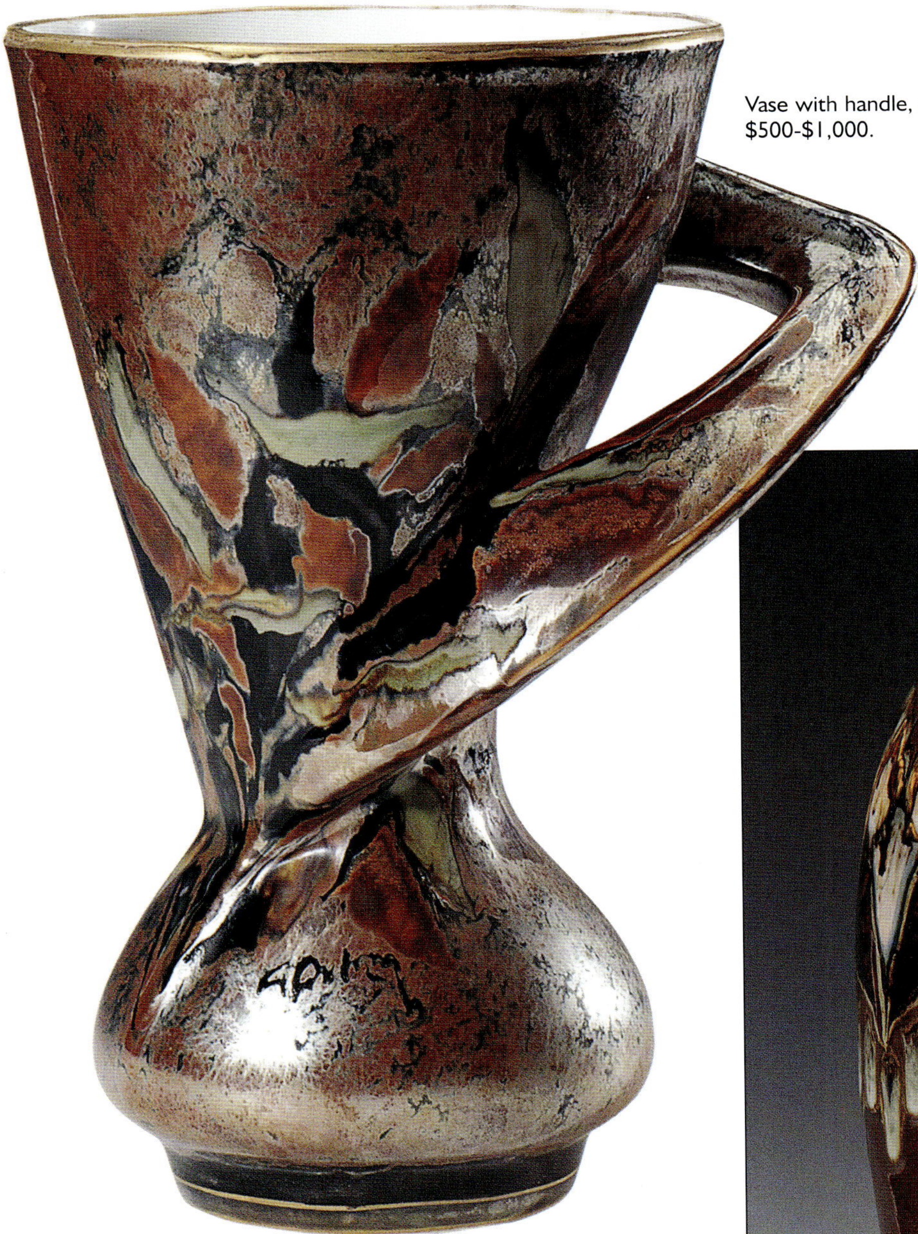

Vase with handle, after 1943. $500-$1,000.

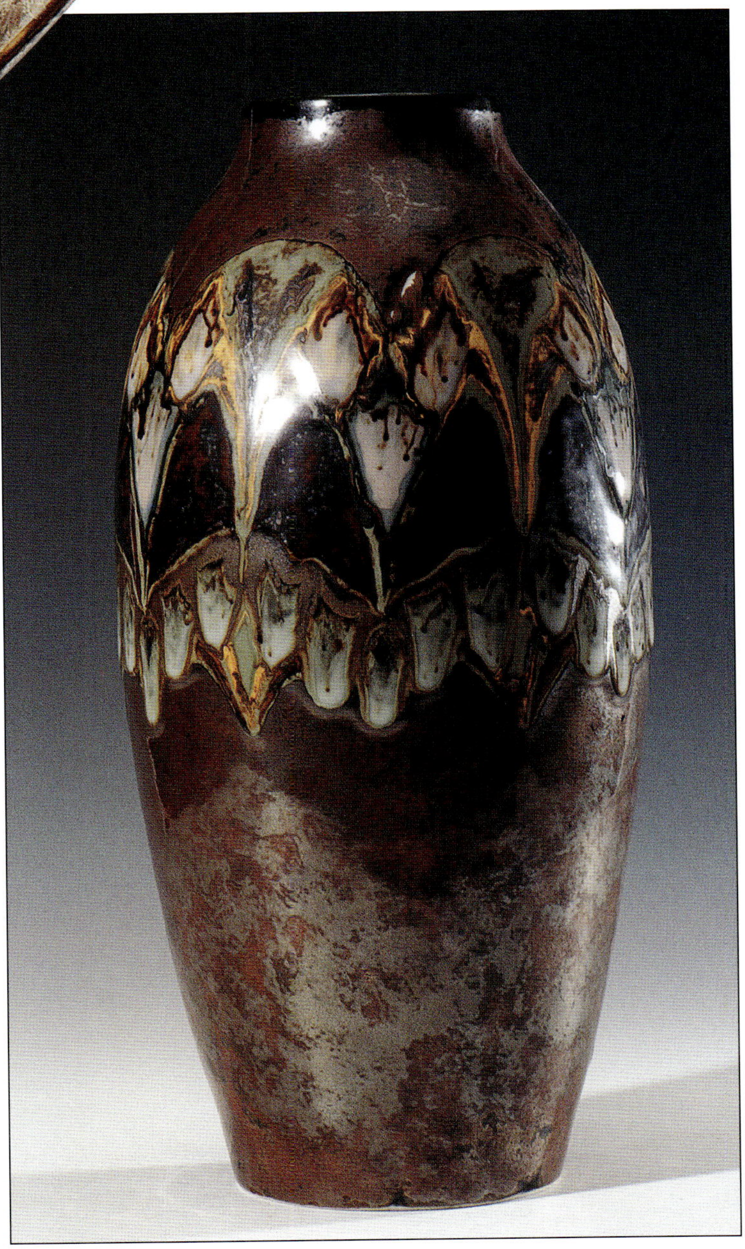

Vase, 15.5" high, after 1943. $500-$1,000.

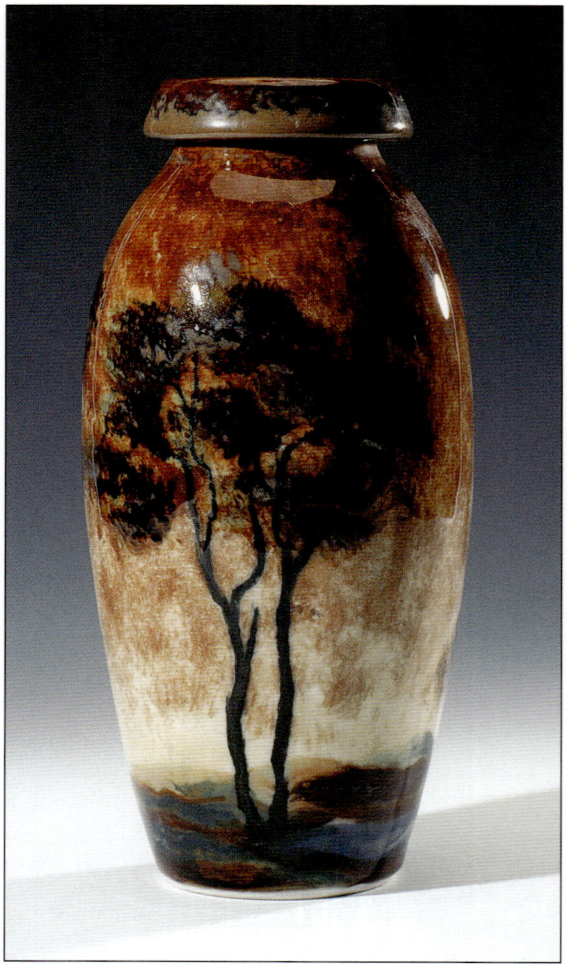

Vase with landscape, after 1943. $1,000-$1,500.

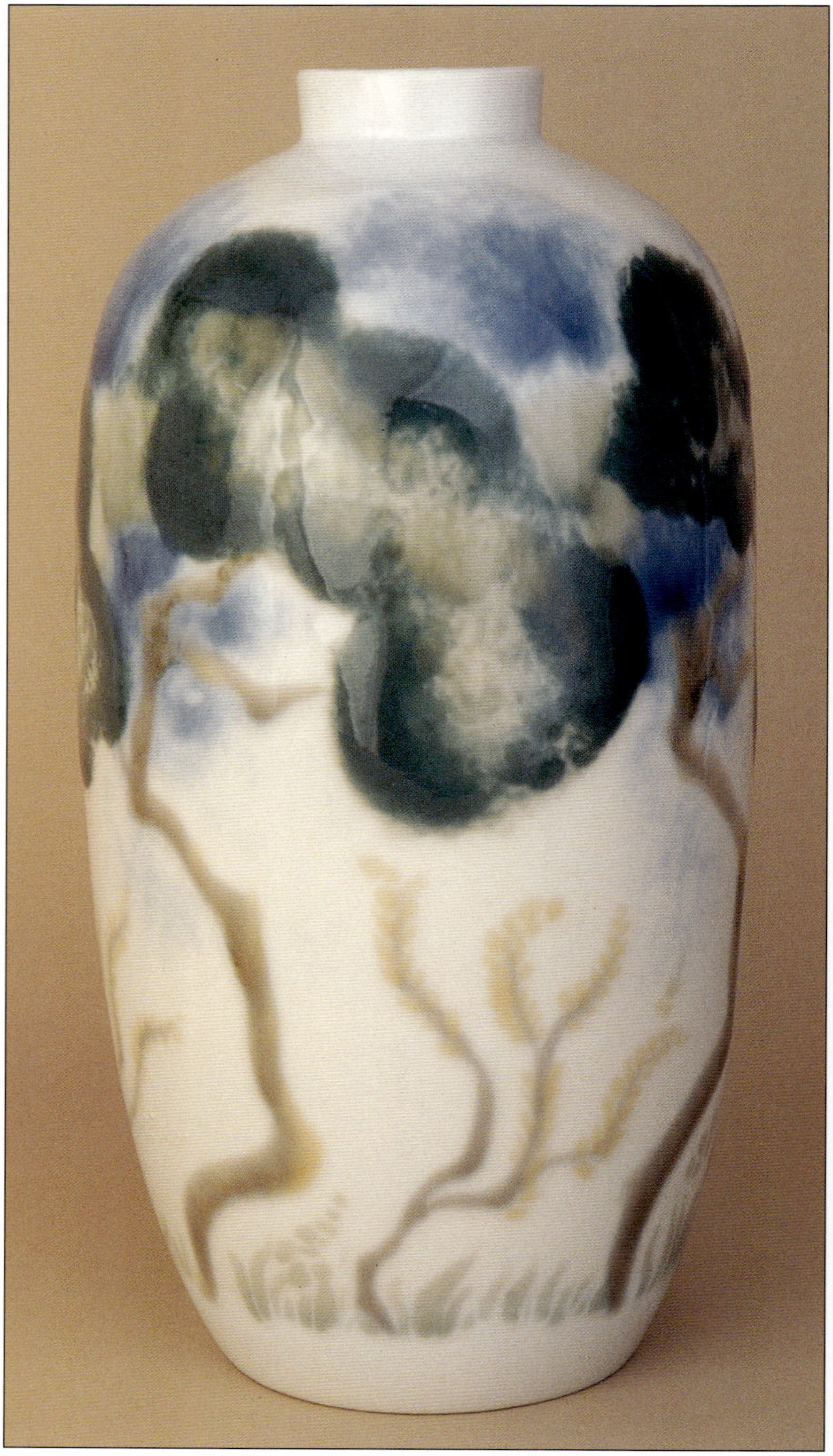

Vase, 12" high, after 1943, rare design of a forest. $500-$1,500.

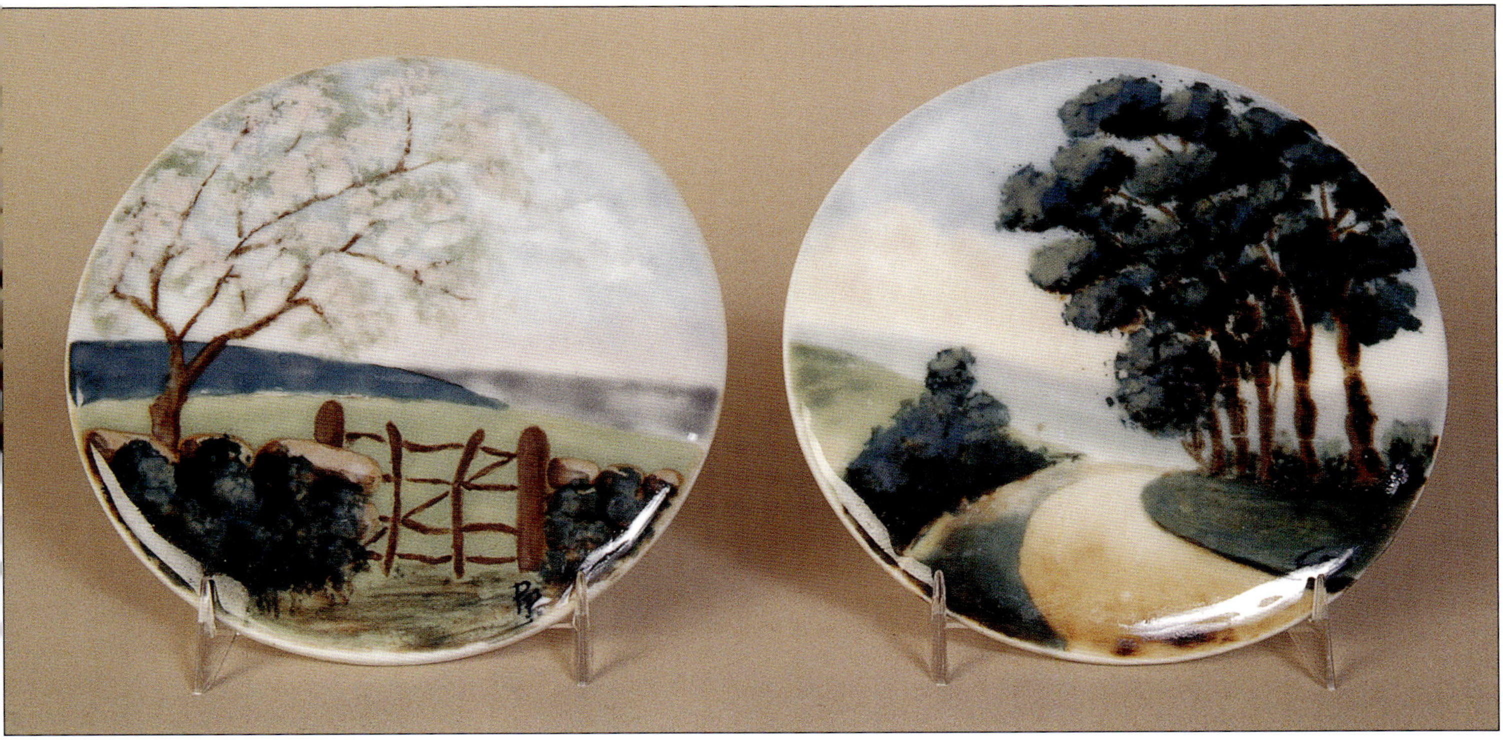

Two plaques, 6.25" in diameter, scenes around Limousin, very popular pieces, created by Andrée Taris, marked *PP* (Paulette P.) and *GD* (Germaine Dufour), after 1943. Each less than $500.

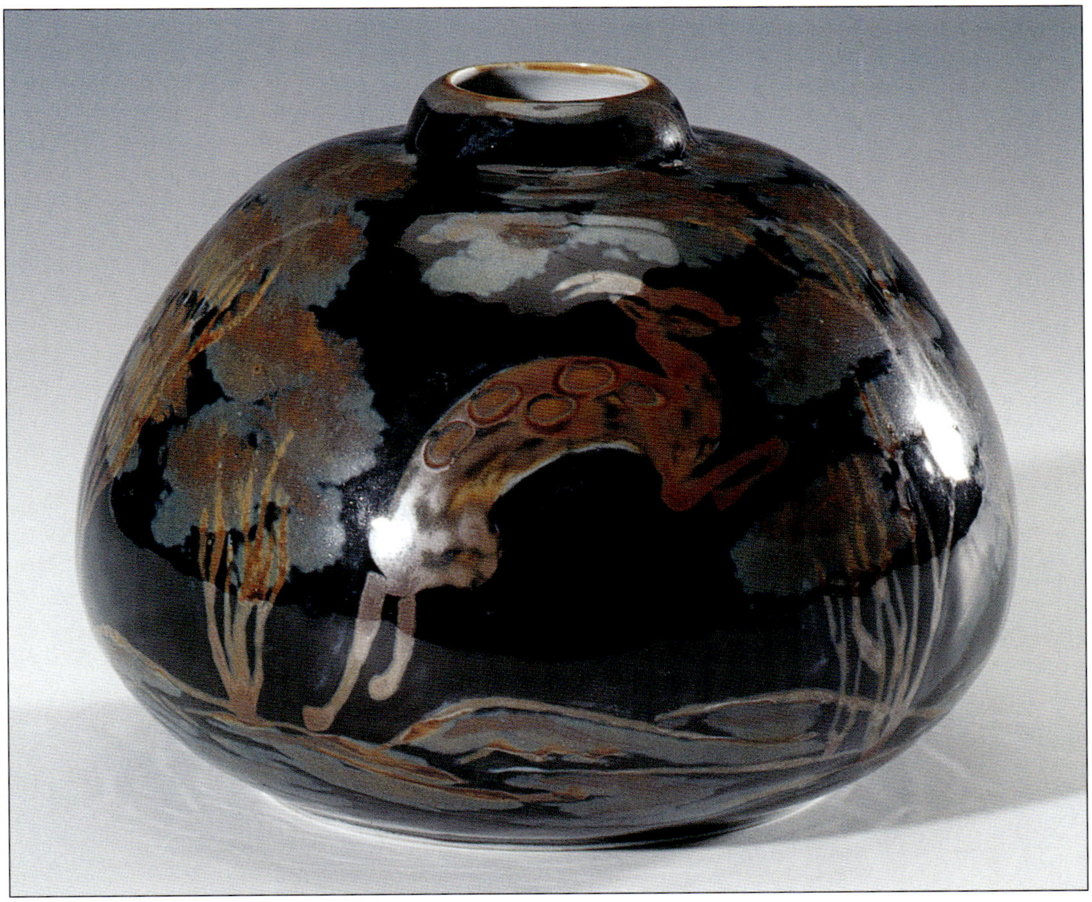

Scenic vase, *Chardon*, with deer in forest, 7" high, after 1943, marked *L. Lib* (Lucienne Liberge). $1,000-$1,500.

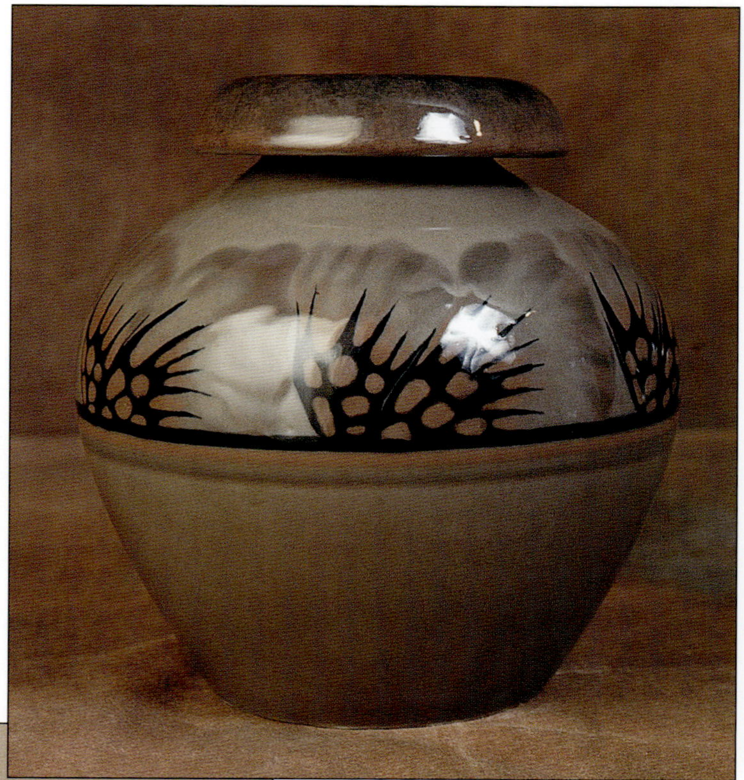

Vase, *Amarante*, shape by Henri Rapin, after 1943. Less than $500.

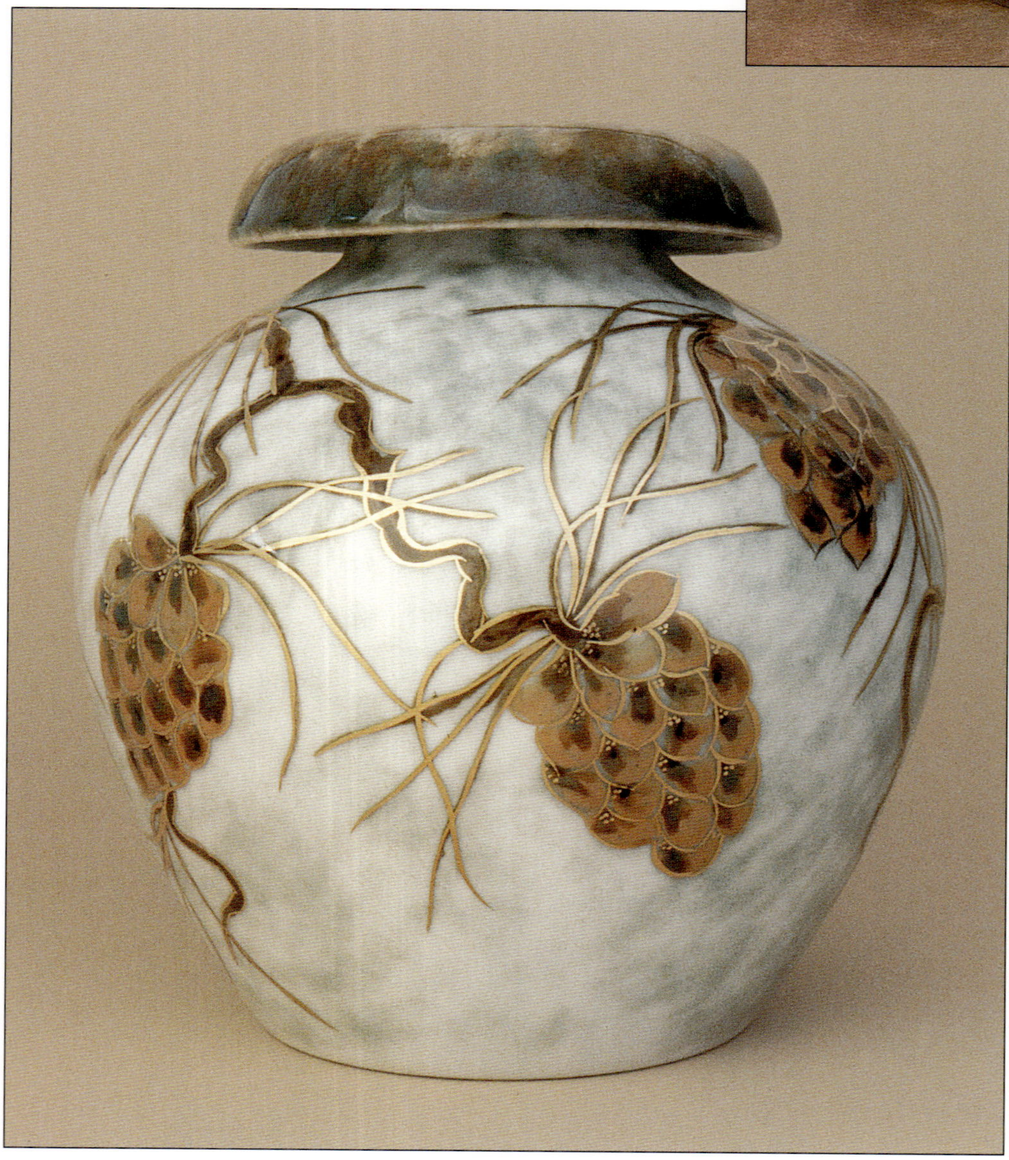

Vase, *Amarante*, 8.25" high, after 1943, incised *MS* (Marguerite S.). Less than $500.

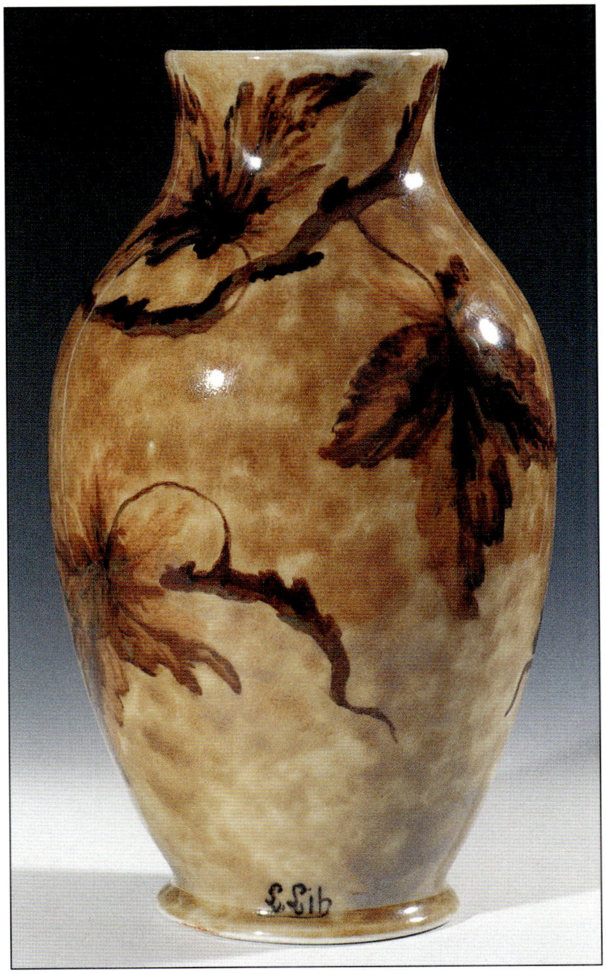

Vase, *Aconit*, decorated with *Feuilles de vigne*, 1940-1945, signed *L. Lib* (Lucienne Liberge). $500-$1,000.

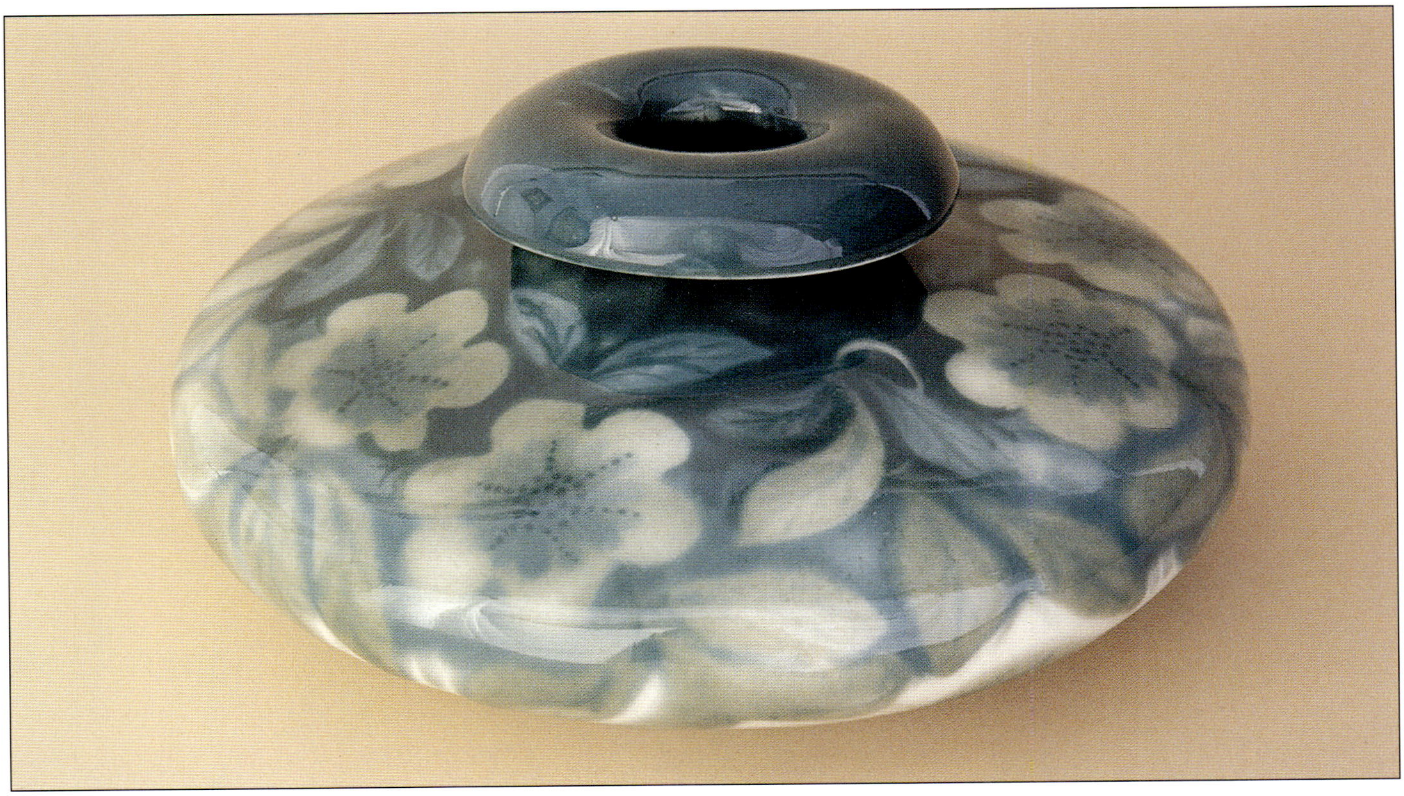

Vase, *Lentille*, 9" in diameter and 4.5" high, after 1943, incised *J de B* (Julienne de Buis), flowers decorated in camaieu green. Less than $500.

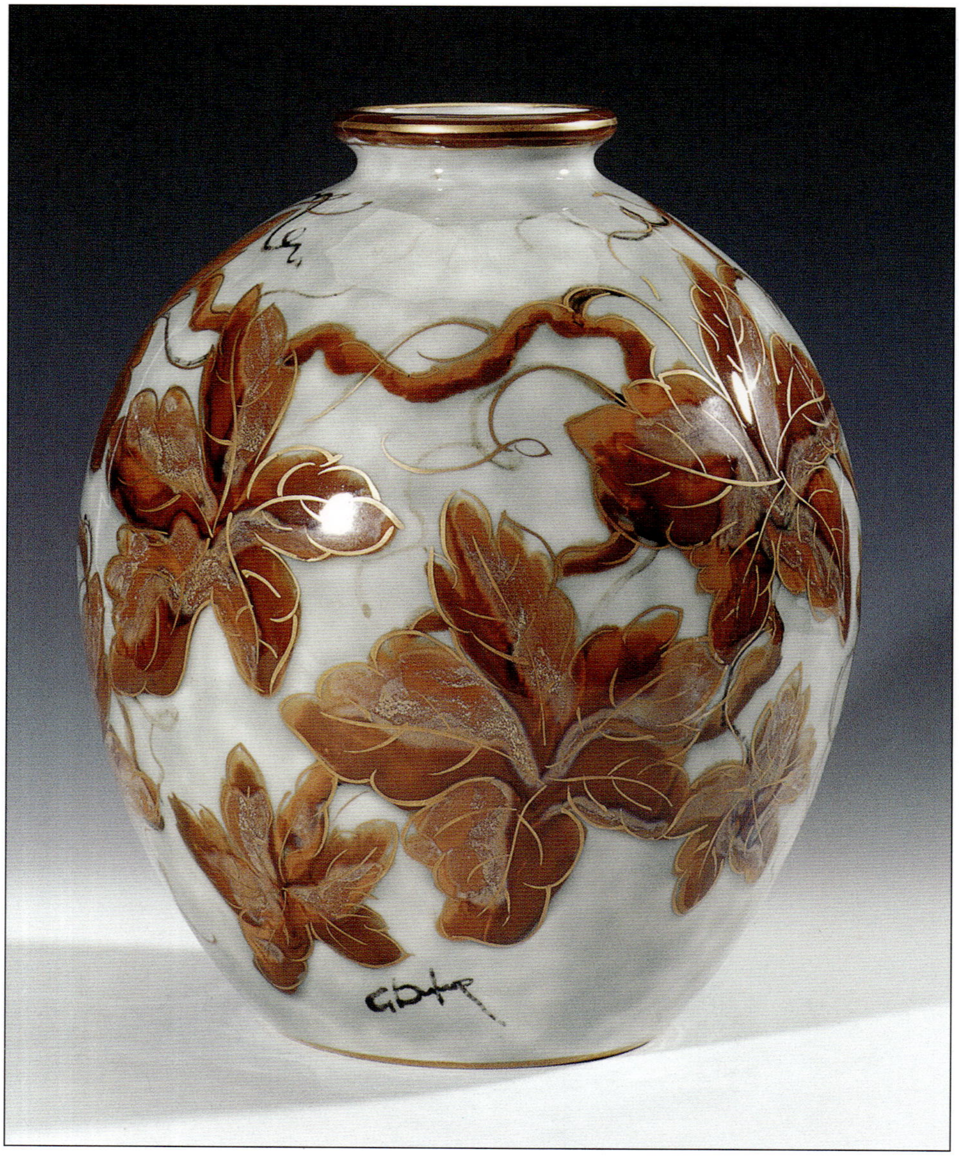

Vase, *Genêt*, decorated with *Feuilles de vigne*, 11" high, signed in black *G.* [Germaine] *Dufour*, the last decorator and manager of the Tharaud studio, from 1943. $500-$1,000.

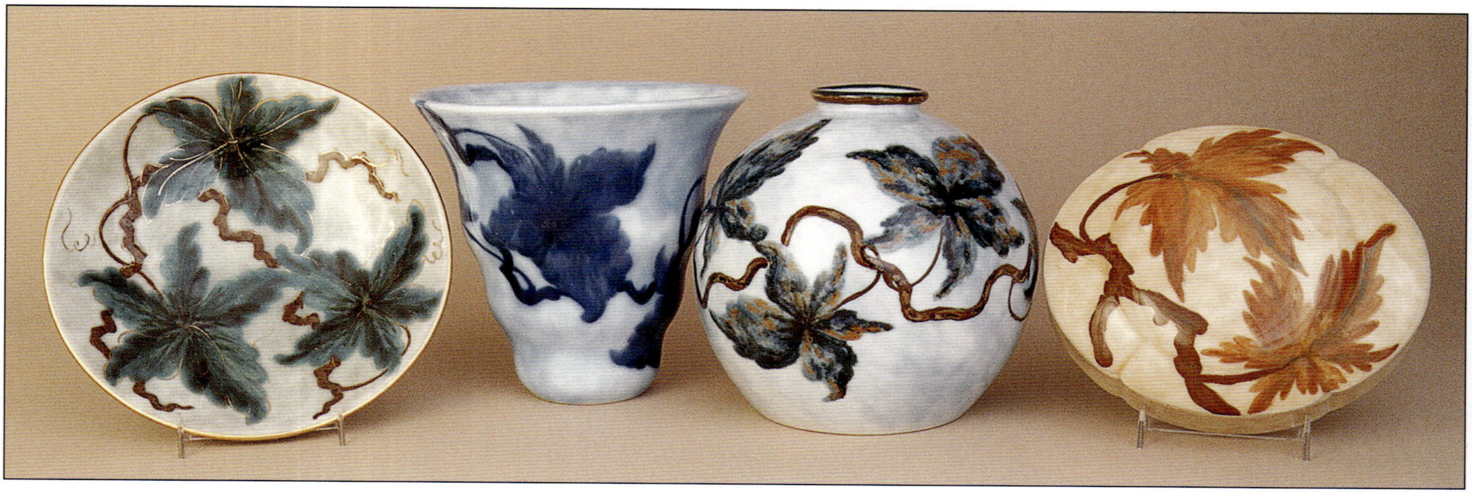

Bowl, 8.6" in diameter x 2.75" high, *Feuilles de vigne,* after 1943, marked in black, *A.M.*; vase, *Genève*, shape by Maurice Dufrène, 7.25" high, *Feuilles de vigne* (blue leaves with emerald highlights) after 1943; vase, 7.5" high, *Feuilles de vigne,* after 1943; and covered box, right, *Feuilles de vigne*, 2.75" high x 7.5" x 6.4", 1930-1945. Each less than $500.

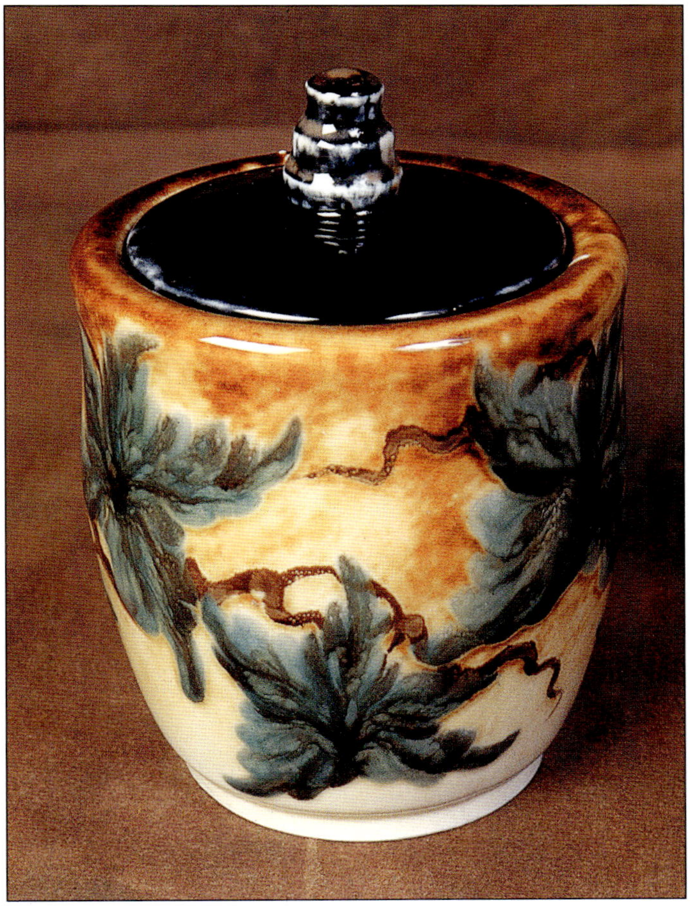

Covered pot, *Camélia*, 7.25" high, mark painted *M.M.* (Monique M.), after 1943. Less than $500.

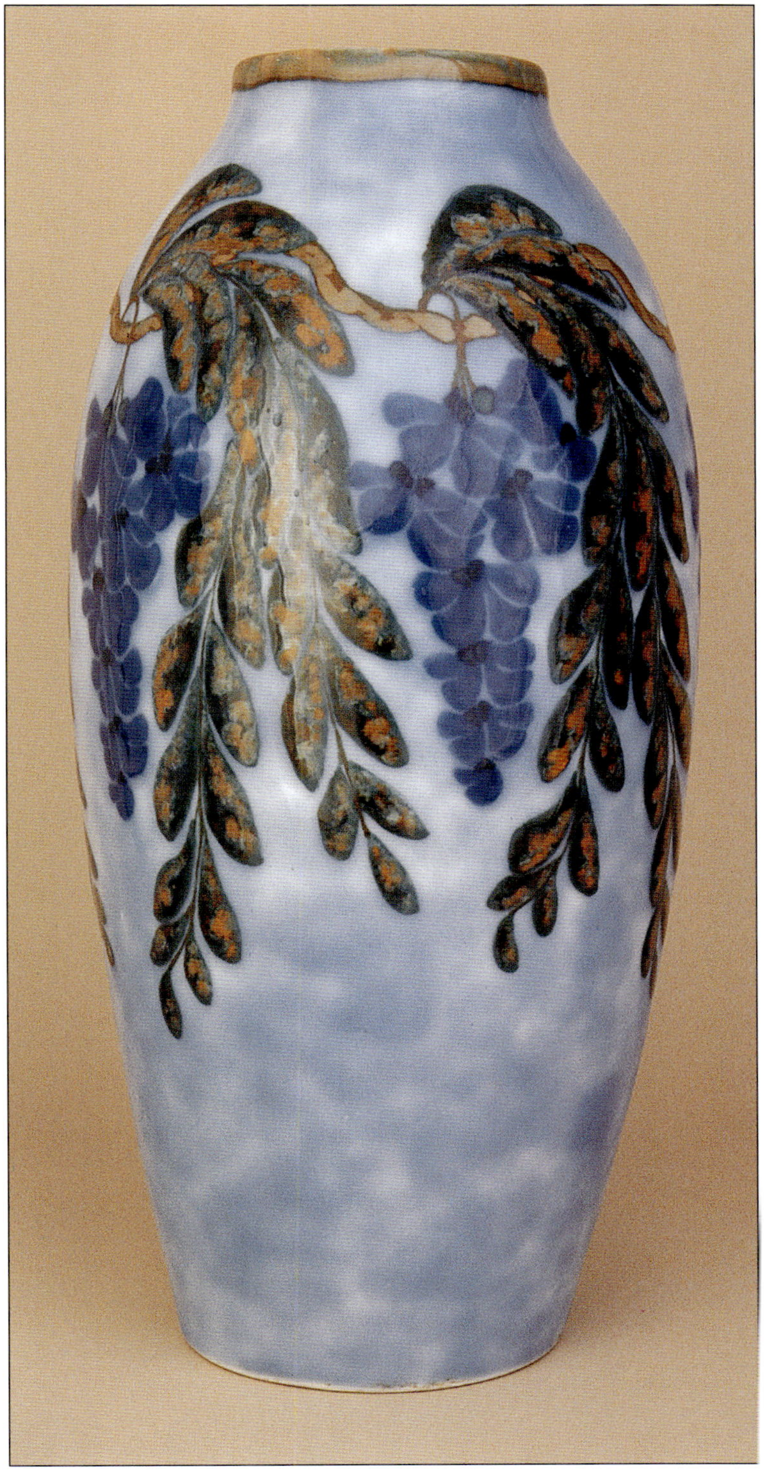

Vase, *Glycines* [wisteria] *et feuillage*, 15.5" high, mark painted *J. de Brito* (Julienne de Brito), after 1943. $500-$1,000.

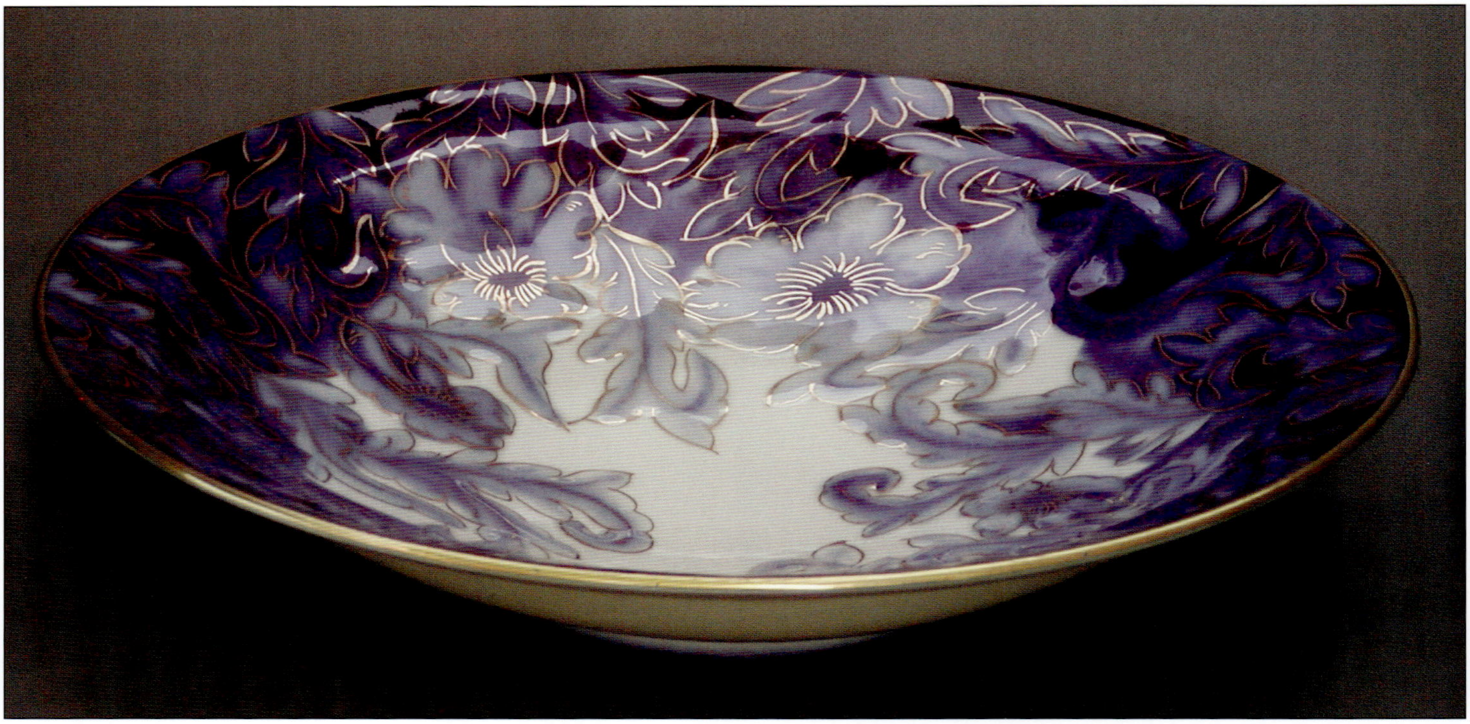

Bowl, 11.75" in diameter, after 1943. Less than $500.

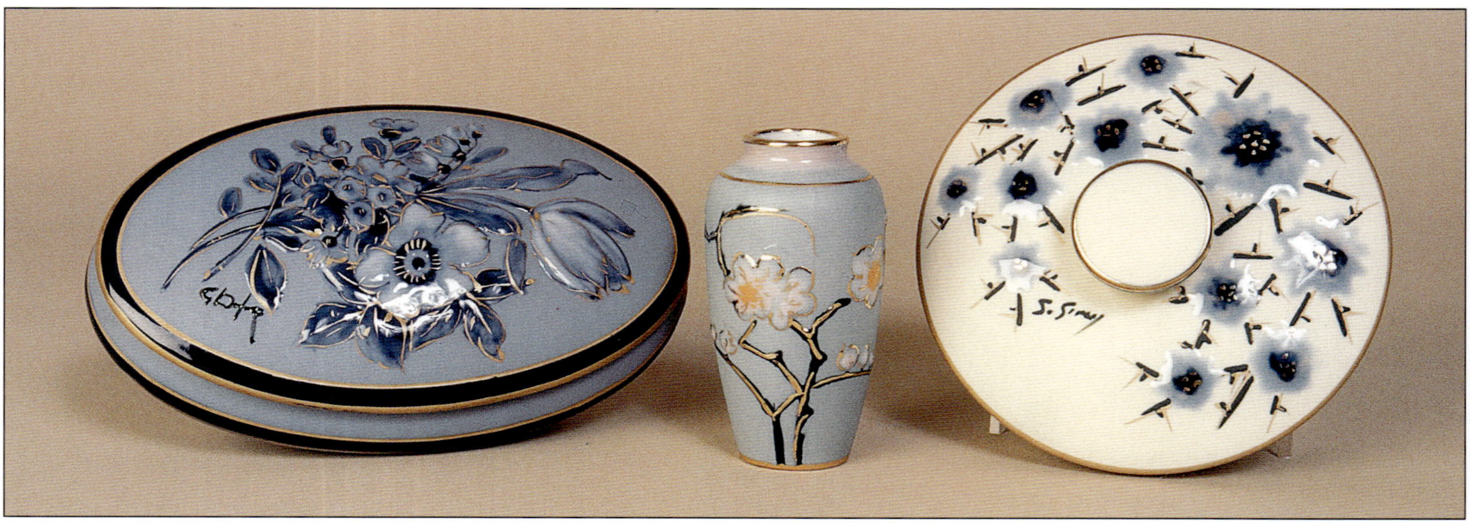

Oval covered box, 6.75" x 4.25", after 1943, signed *G.* (Germaine) *Dufour*, the last decorator and manager of the studio; vase, 3.75" high, after 1943; covered box, after 1943, blue enamel for the flowers is raised, painter's signature in black is illegible. Less than $500.

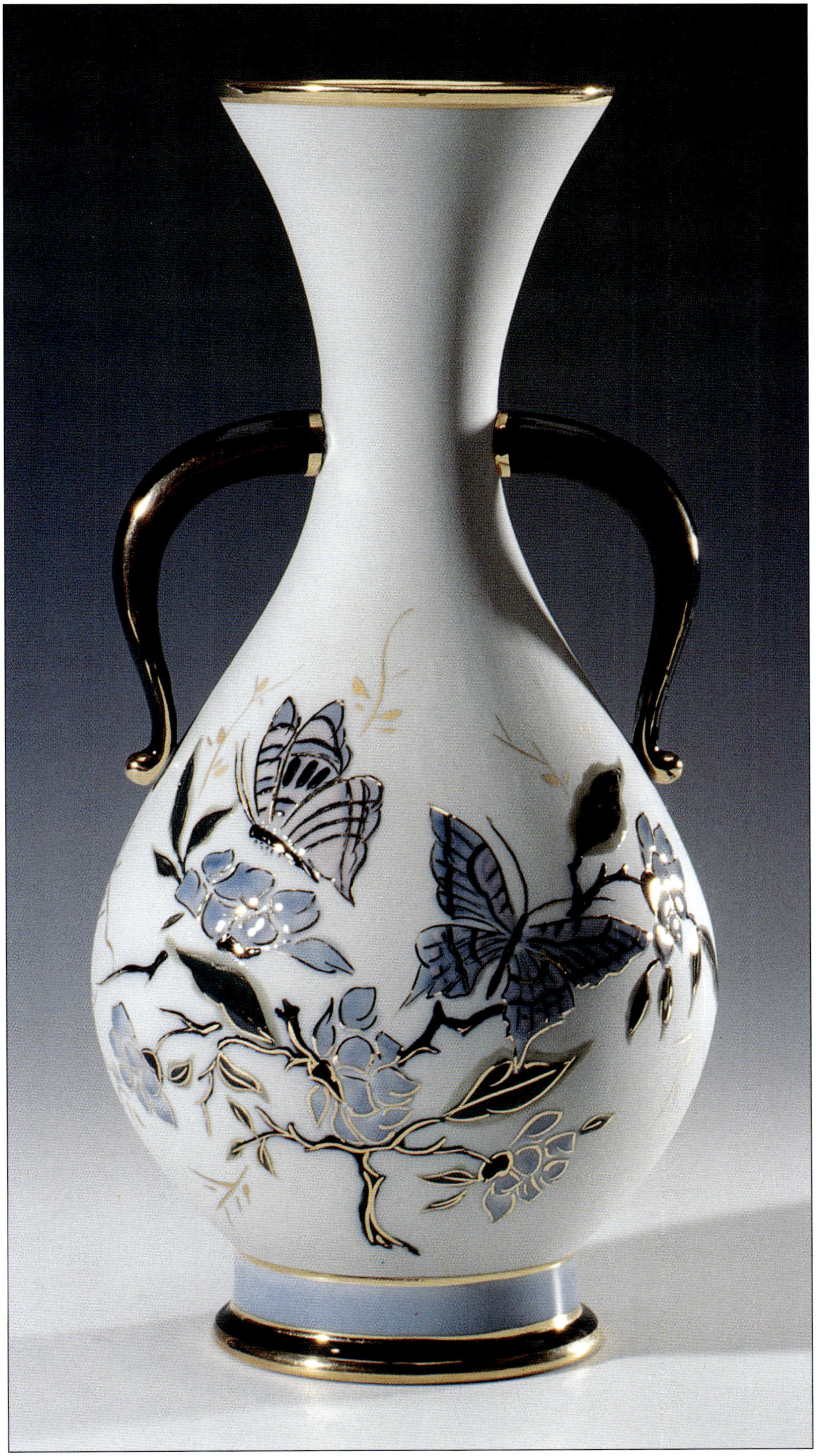

Vase, 13" high, after 1943. Less than $500.

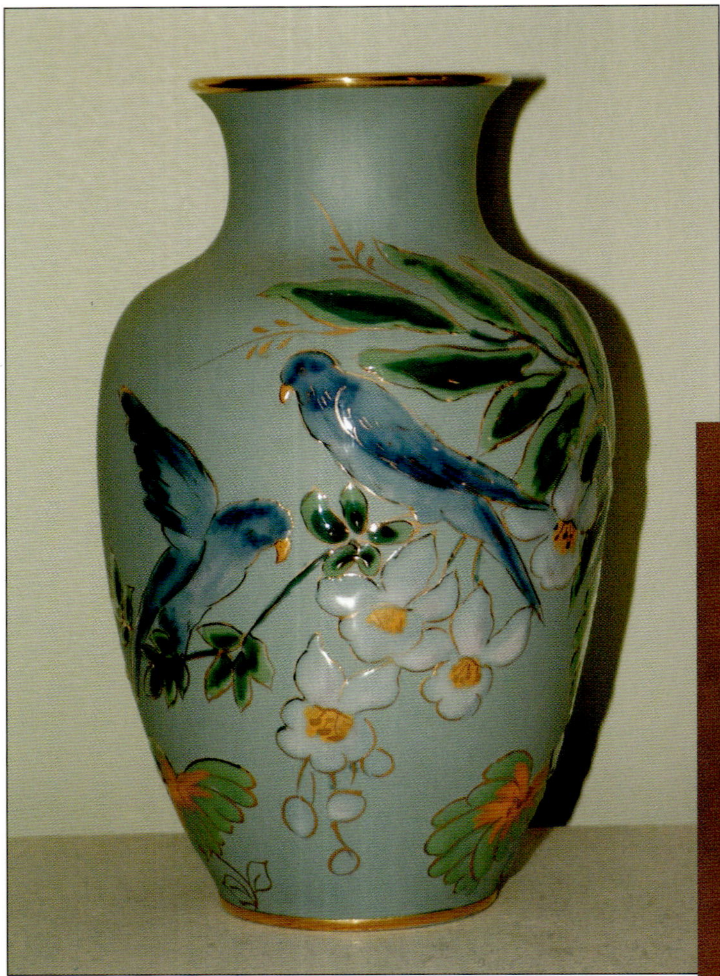

Vase, 8.5" high, enamel, after 1943. Less than $500.

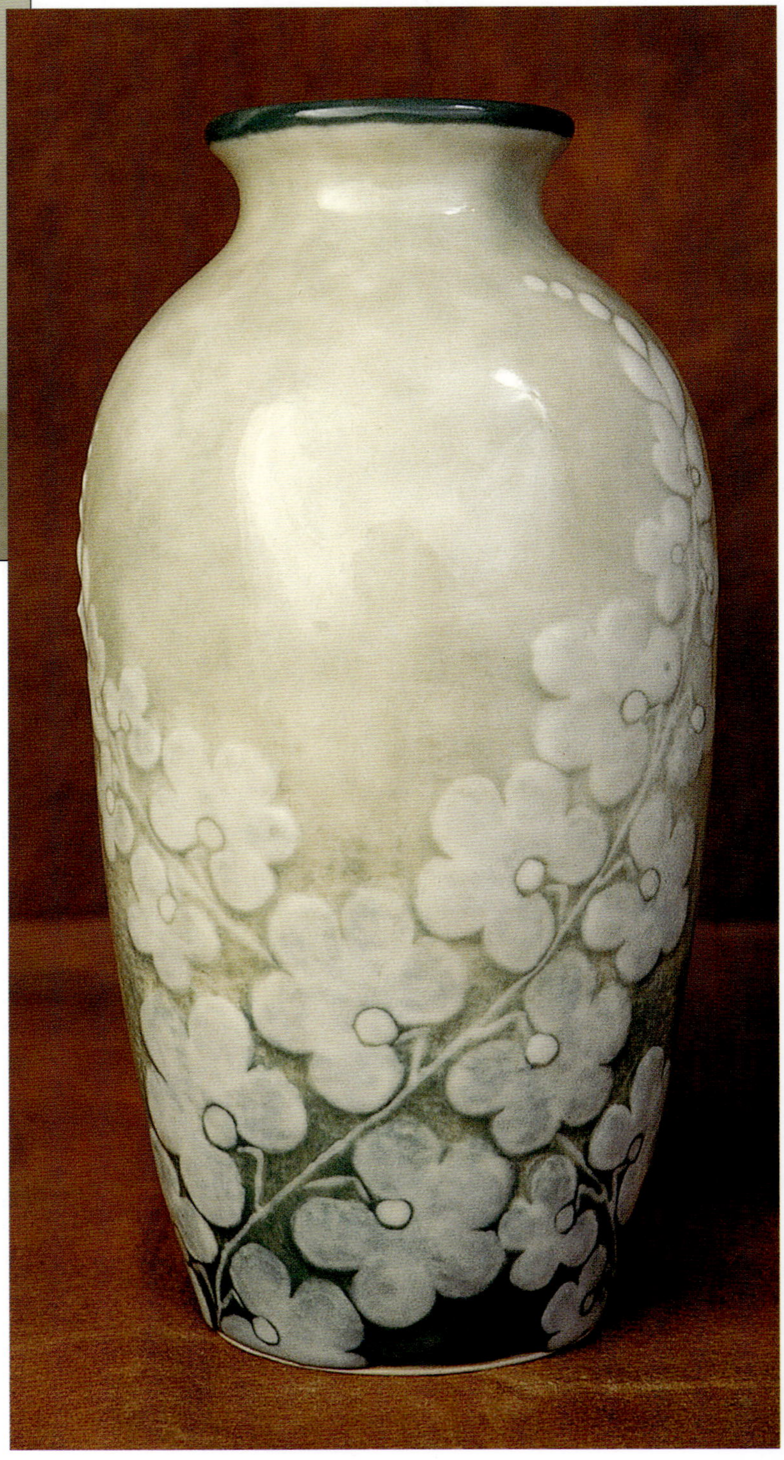

Vase, 10.5" high, after 1943. $500-$1,000.

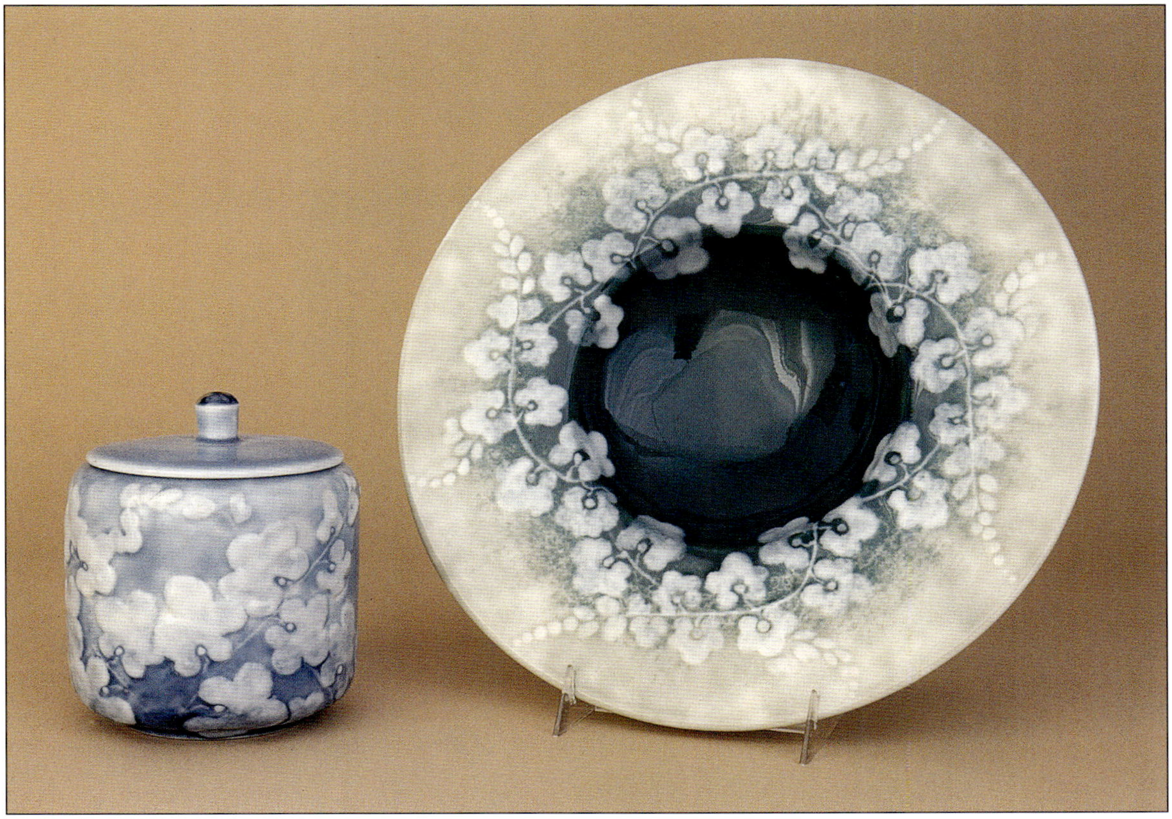

Covered jar, 4.5" high x 3.6" in diameter, after 1943, incised *CN*; right, bowl, *Rabat*, 9.6" in diameter and 2" high, after 1943, signed *A.M.* Each less than $500.

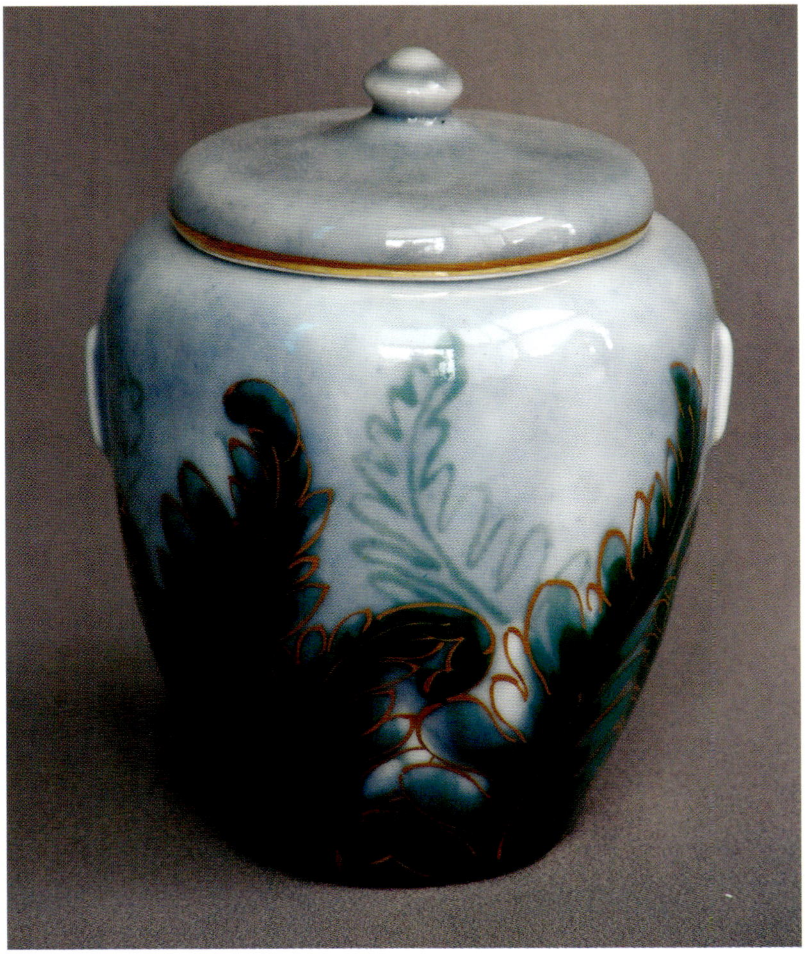

Tobacco Jar, 5.75" high. Less than $500.

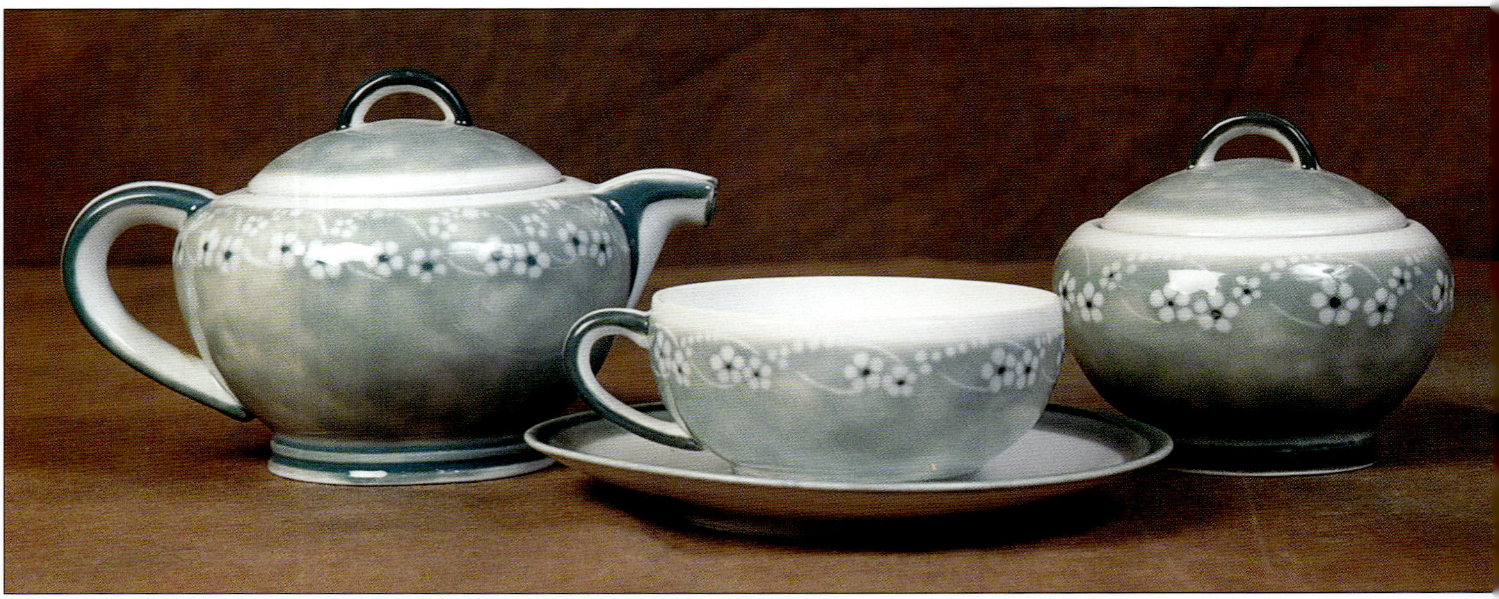

Tea set, after 1943. Less than $500.

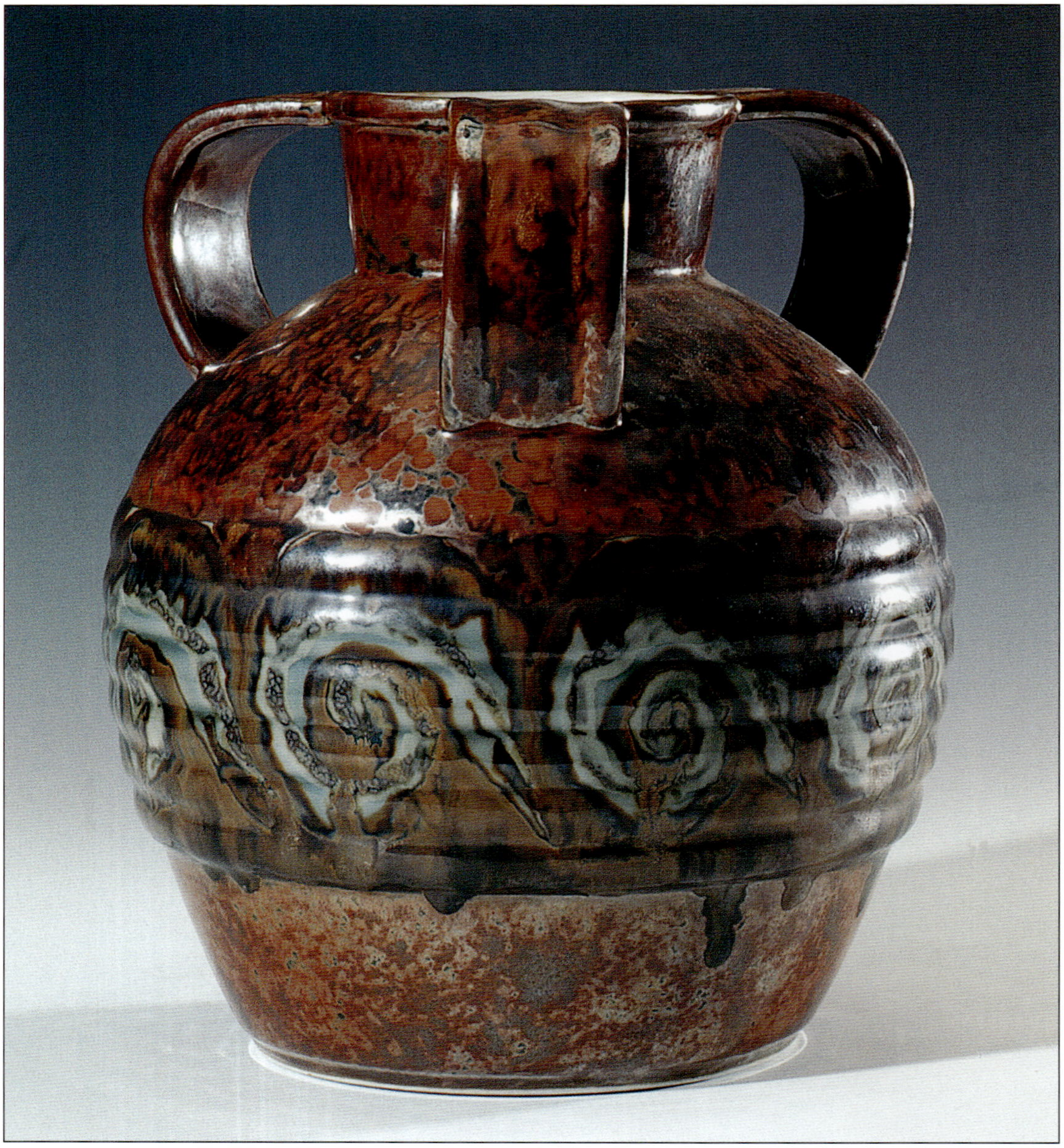

Vase, *Muflier*, 10" high, after 1943. $500-$1,000.

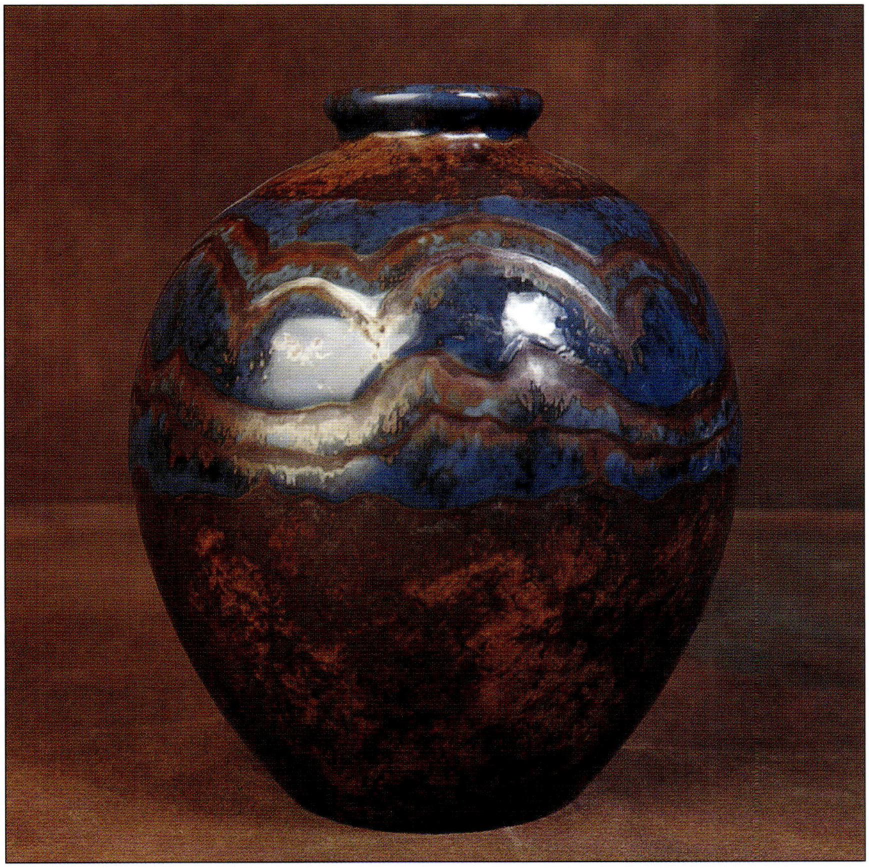

Vase, *Genêt*, 9.75" high, *MAC* and *JS* (Jeanne S.) incised, 1943-1945. $500-$1,000.

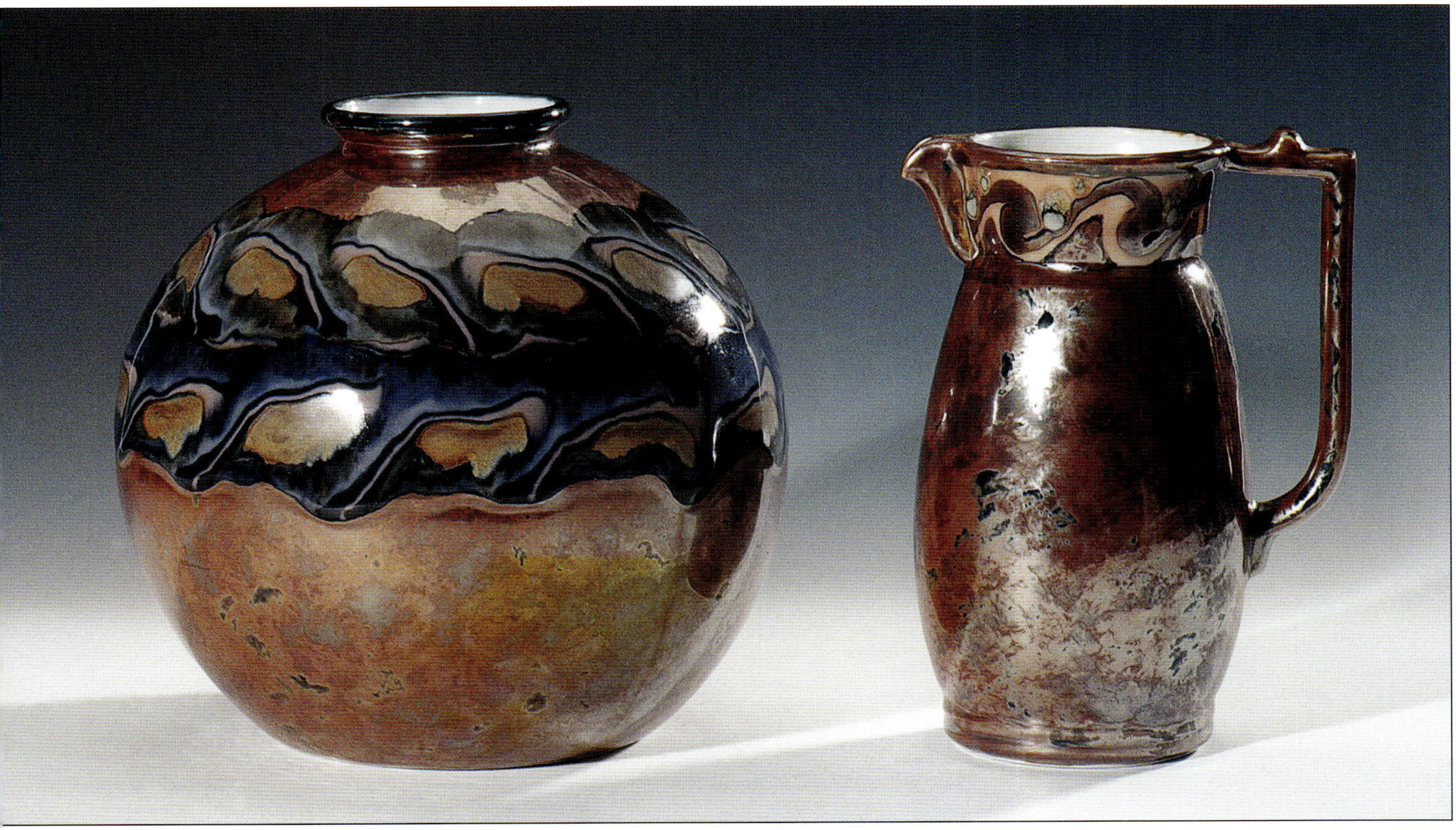

Vase and Pitcher, 9.5" and 8.25" high respectively, vase marked in black *I.A.M.* and pitcher incised *B*, both from 1943. Each less than $500.

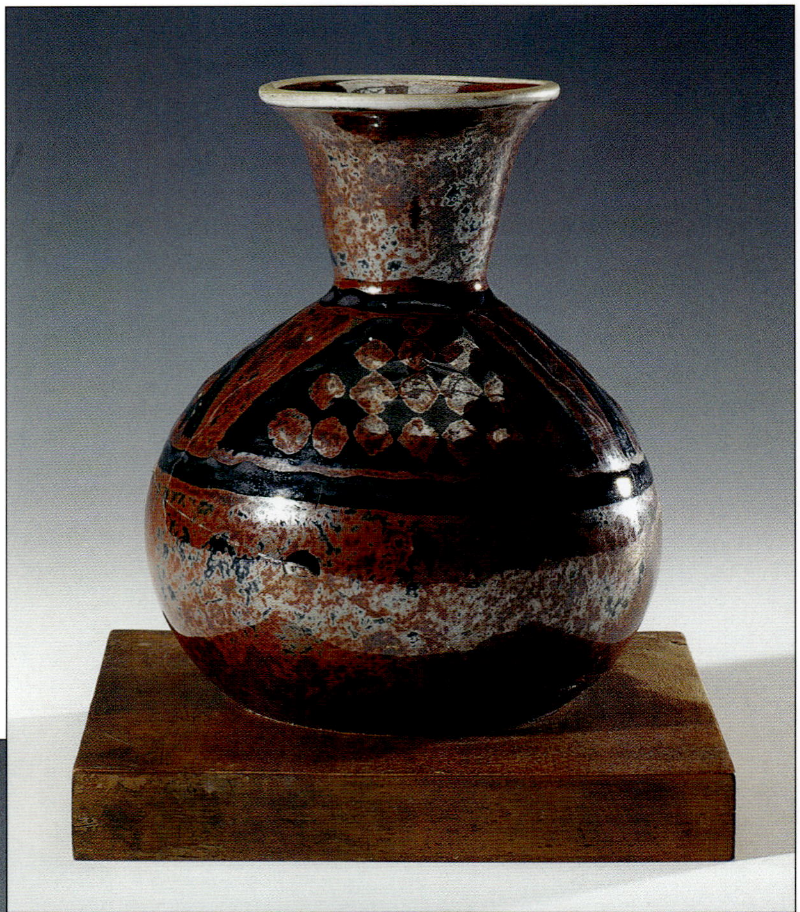

Vase, 7" high, after 1943.
$500-$1,000.

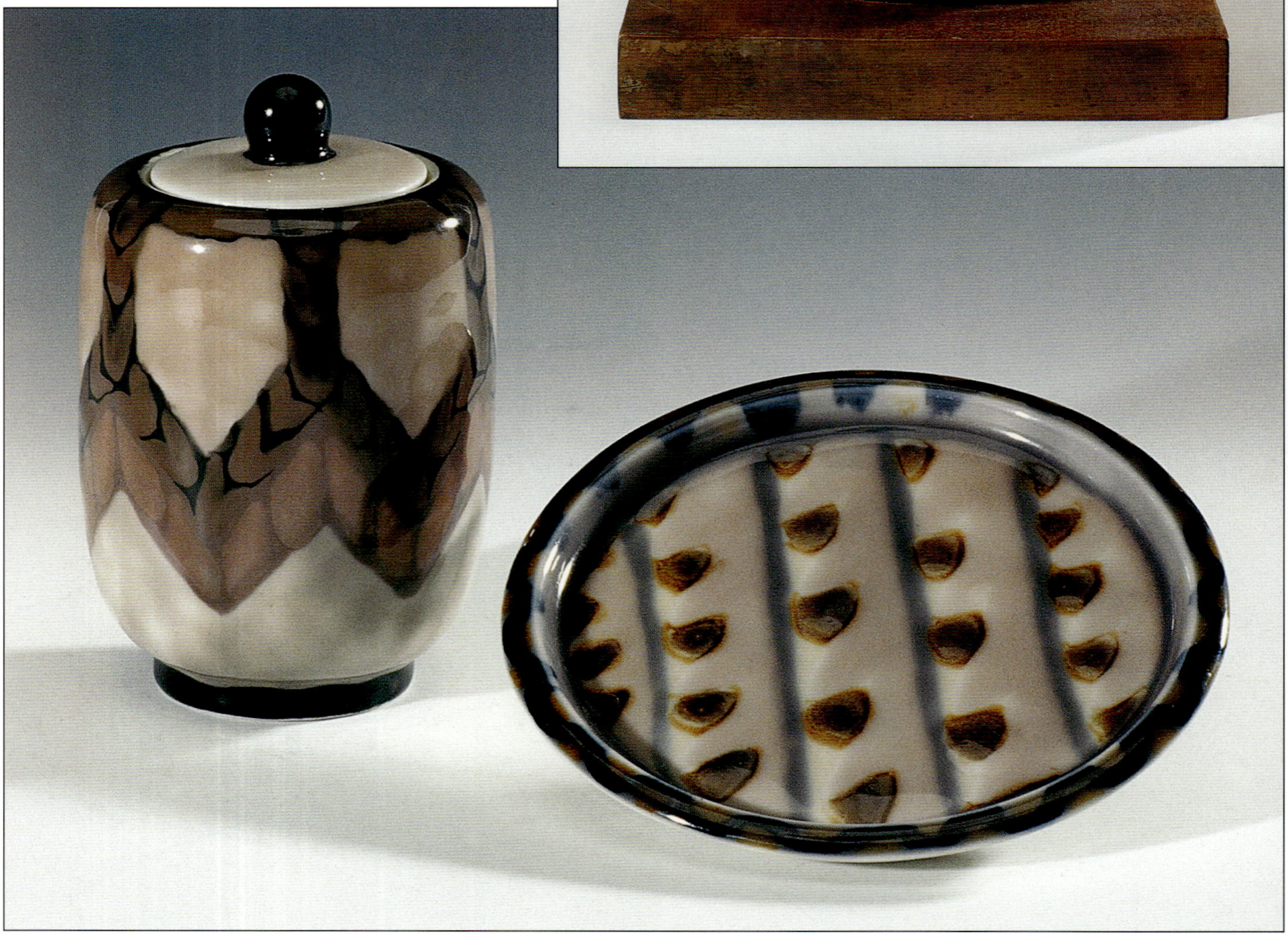

Covered pot, *Werther*, and small plate; pot, 5.5" high, and plate, 6.25" in diameter, both after 1943. Each less than $500.

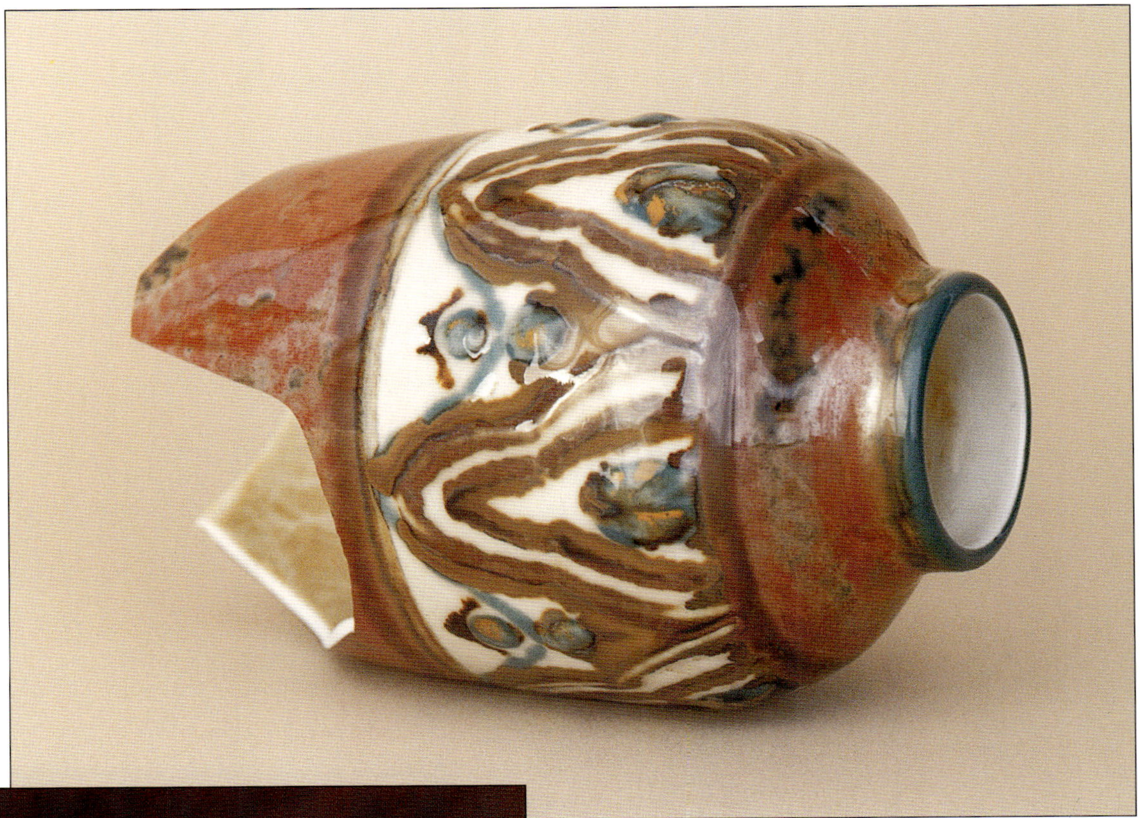

Broken vase, 6.75" high, unusual red color, 1945-1955.

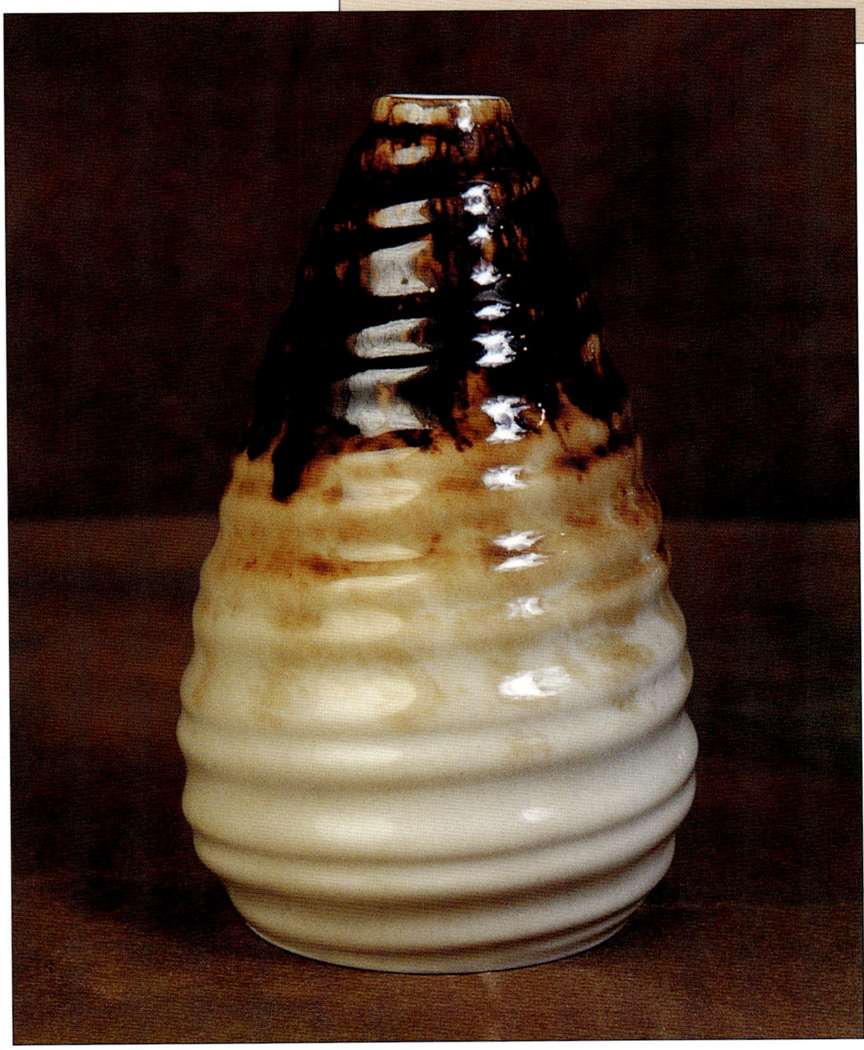

Vase, *Tulipe*, 7.5" high, and incised *GD*, after 1943. Less than $500.

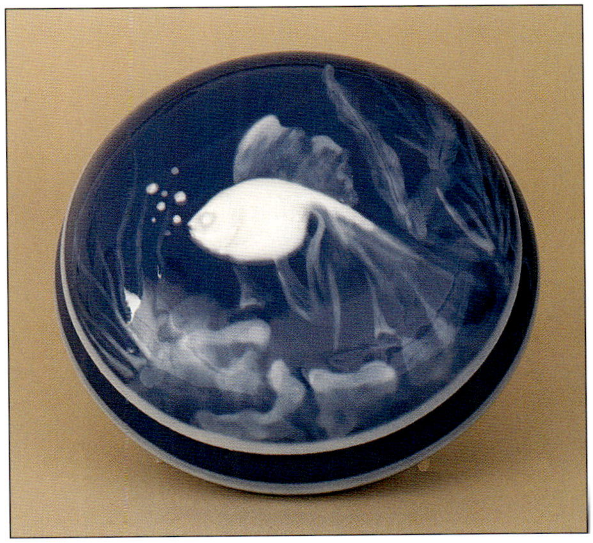

Covered dish, 6" in diameter, after 1943, incised *B*. Less than $500.

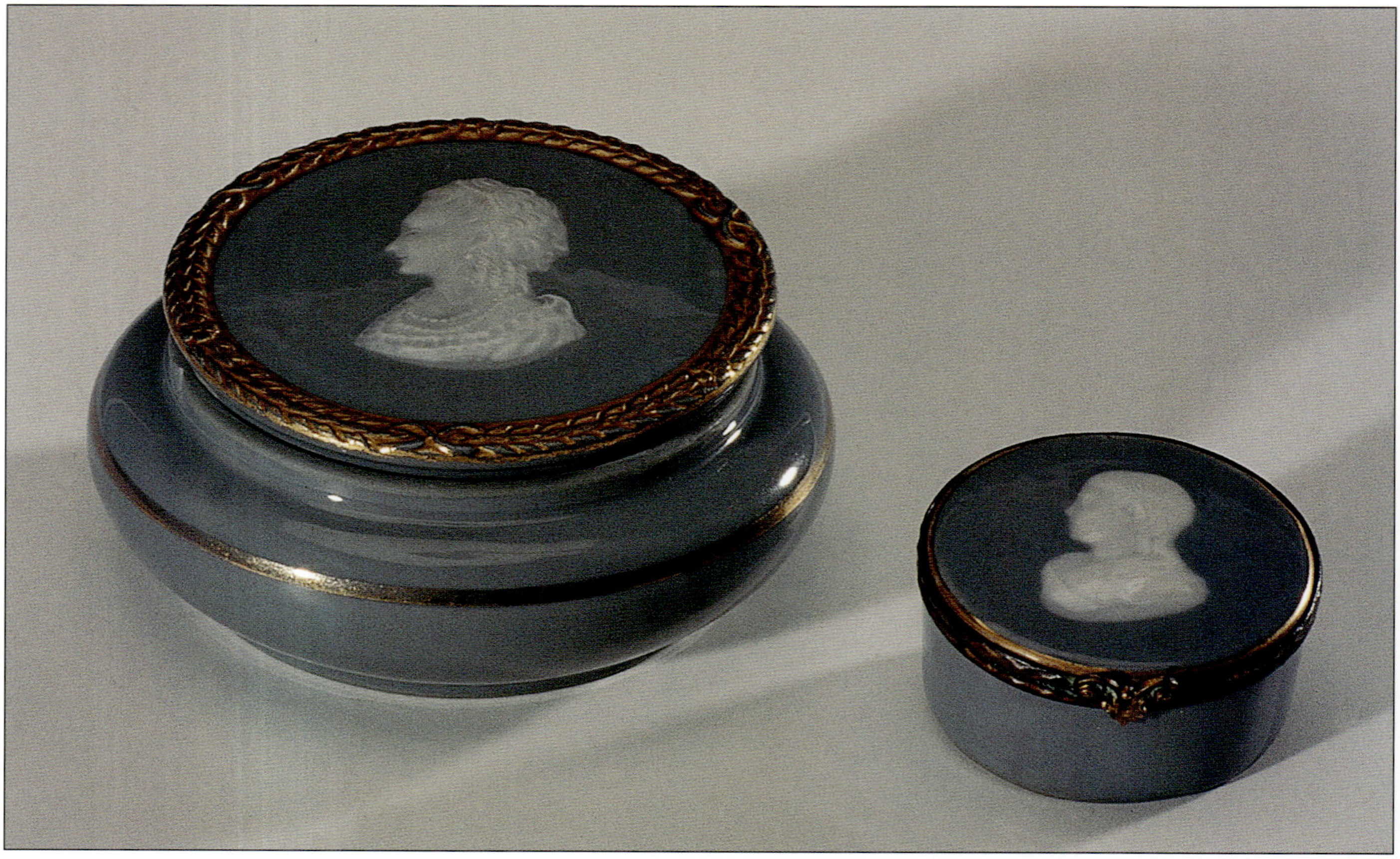

Two covered boxes, 4.25" and 2.25" in diameter, after 1943. Each less than $500.

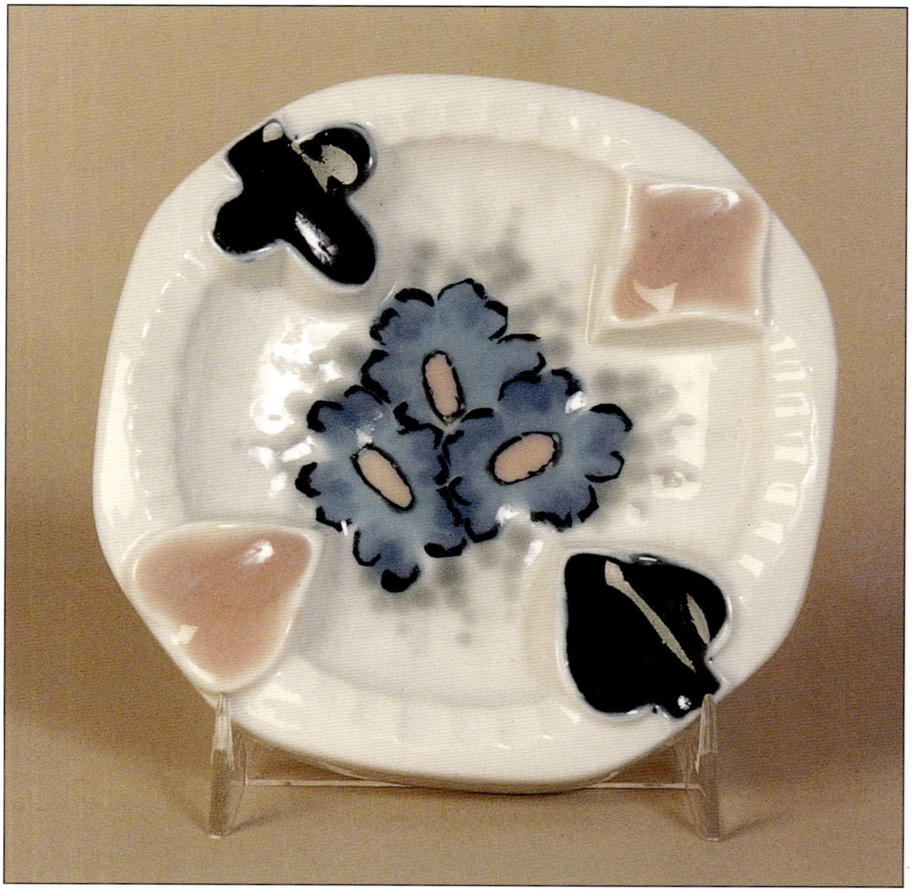

Ashtray, 5.25" in diameter, marked *inauguration Poral juin 1949* and incised *KS*. Less than $500.

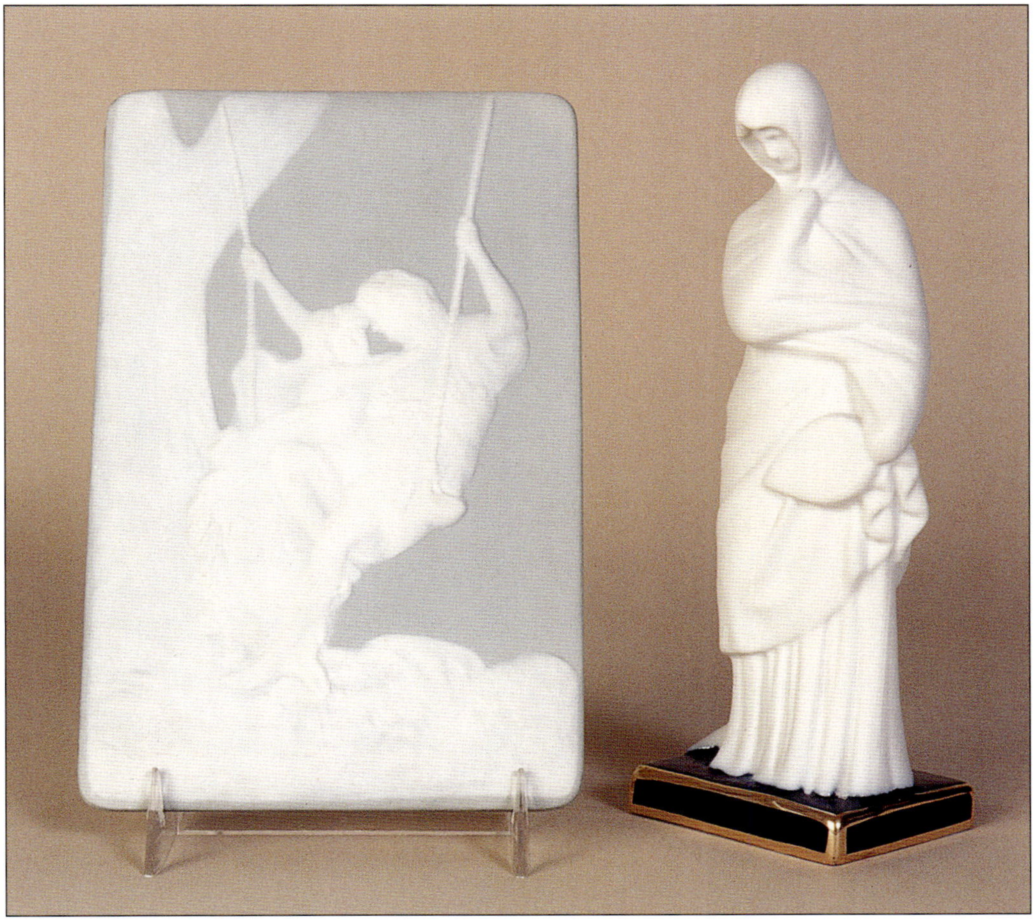

Plaque and nightlight; plaque, 7" x 4.5", matt finish, and nightlight, 7.5" high, bisque finish, both after 1943. Each less than $500.

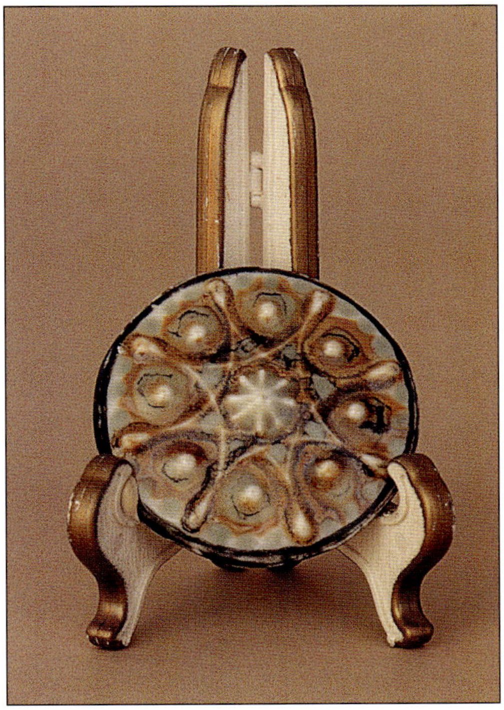

Broach, 2" diameter. Pieces like this were made for jewelry during World War II when precious stones and metals were scarce. Less than $500.

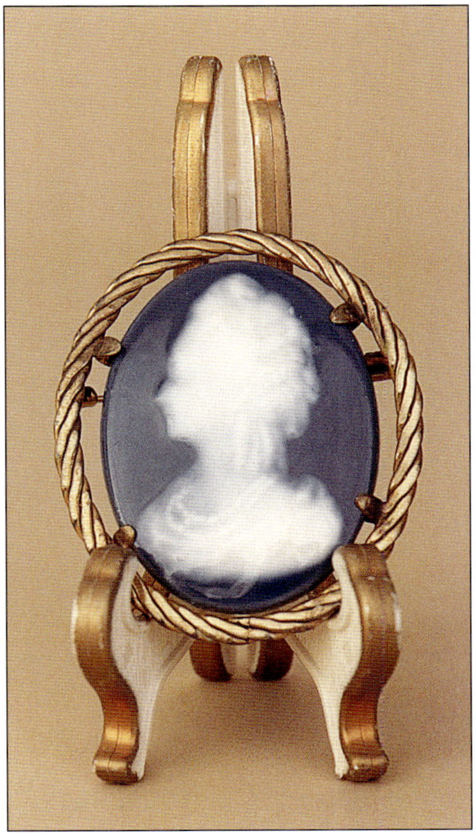

Broach, 2" x 1.4", "pâte sur pâte," probably made during World War II. Less than $500.

Undated Pieces

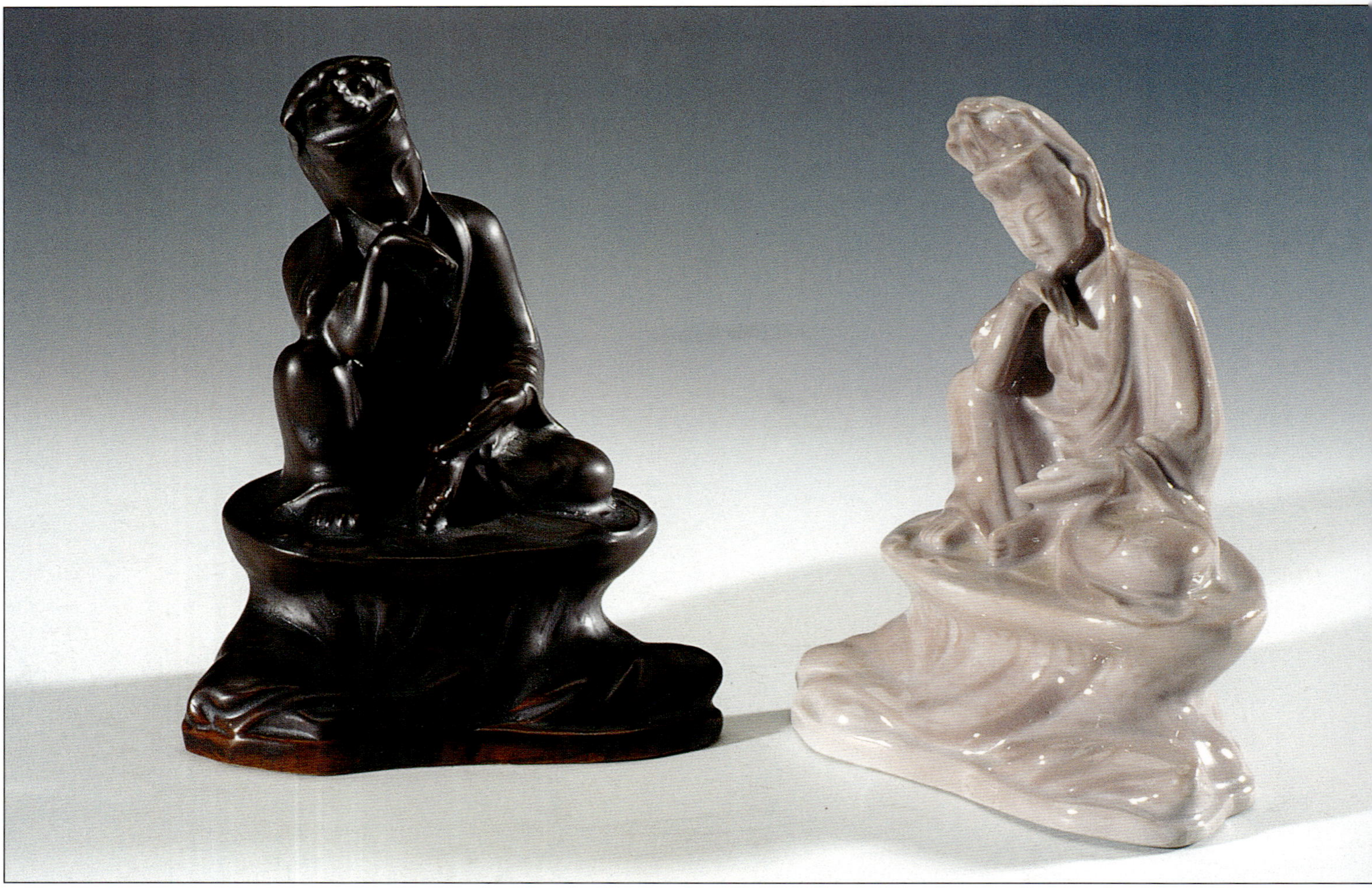

Female Buddhas, 5.5" high. Each less than $500-$1,000.

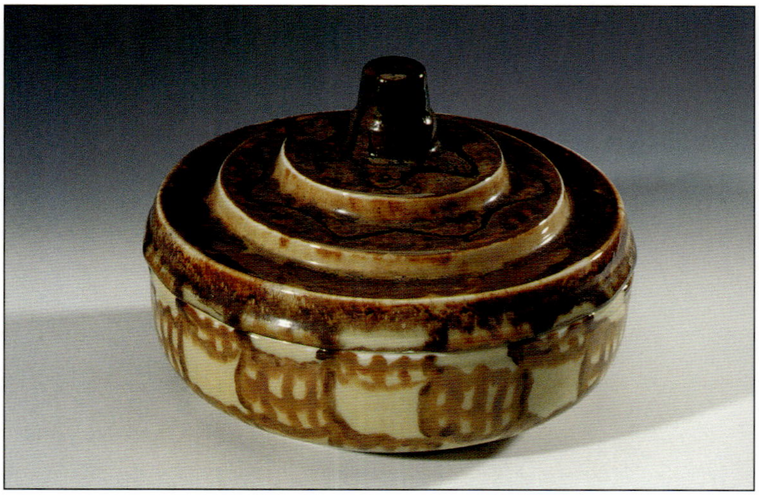

Covered bowl, incised *Th* (decoration of Camille Tharaud). $500-$1,000.

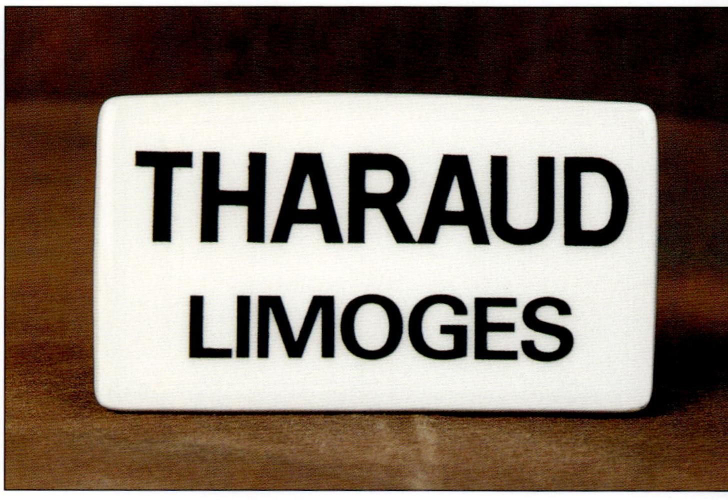

Tharaud store sign. Less than $500.

Color Palettes

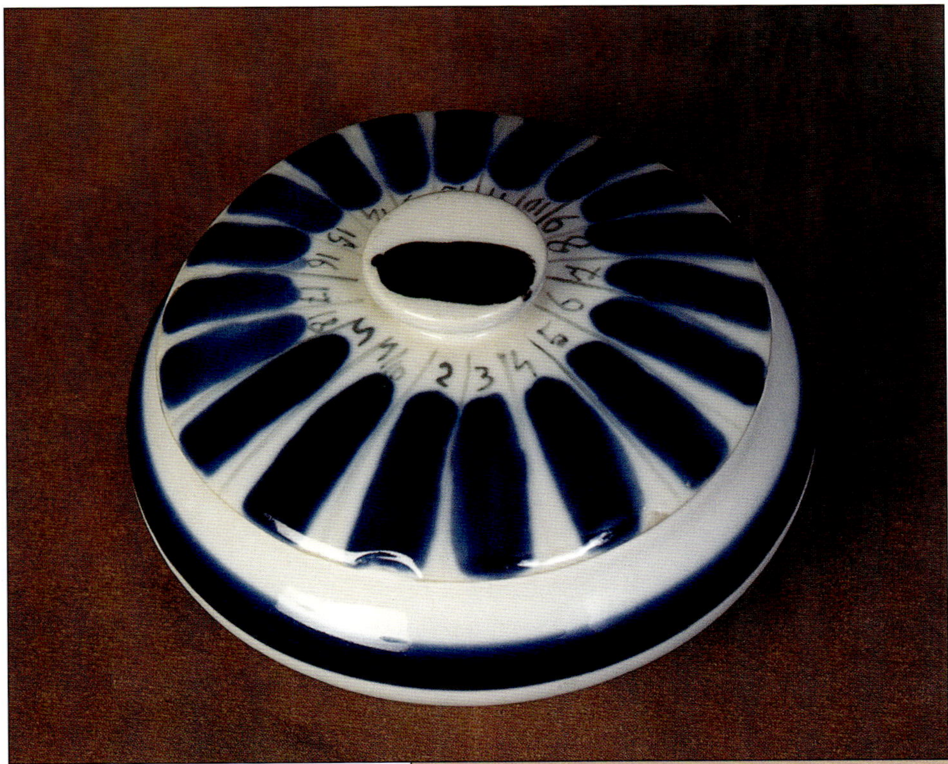

Cobalt Palette. Less than $500.

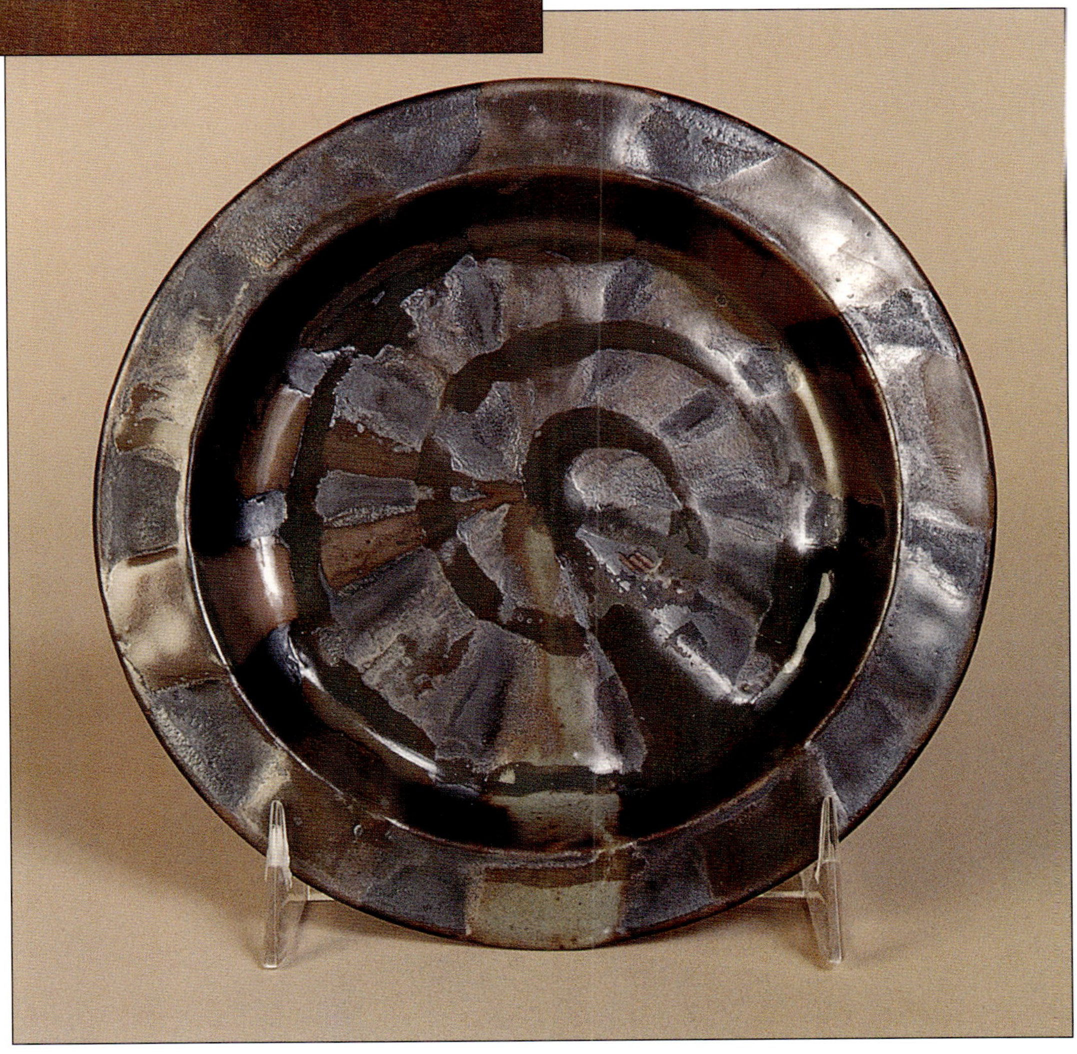

Green Palette, 5.4" in diameter, marked "vert ordinaire." Less than $500.

New Design from Artoria Limoges

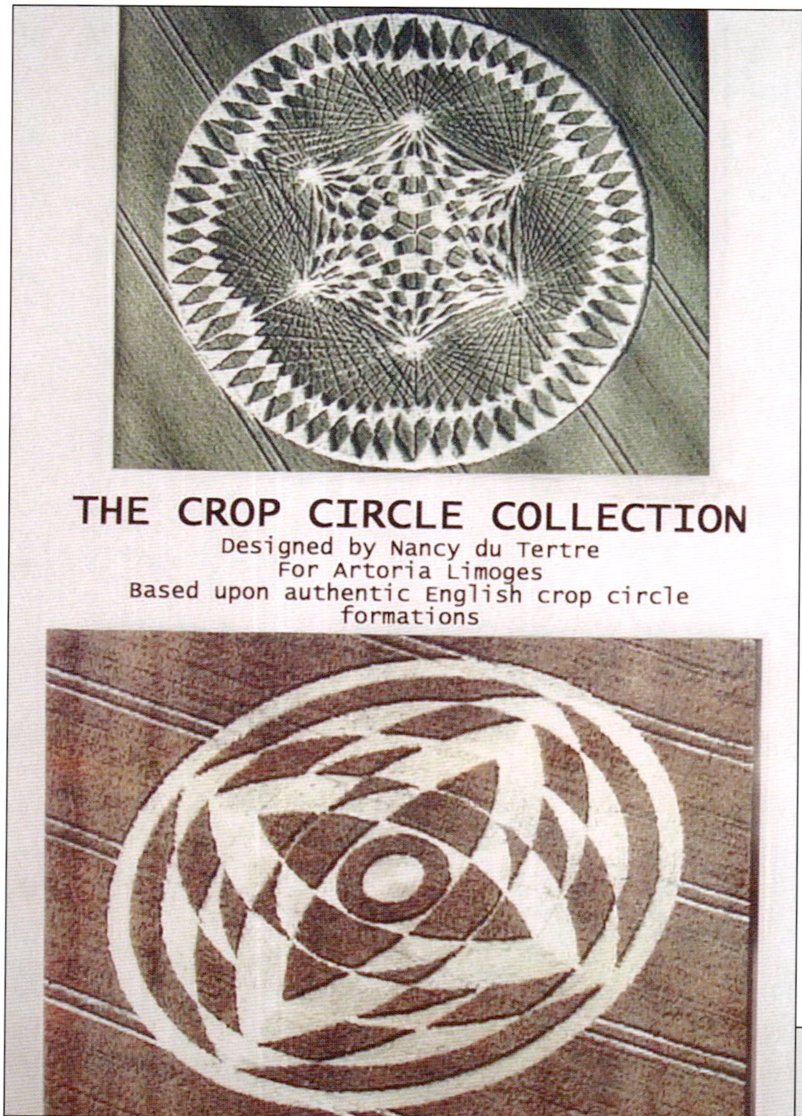

Print of Crop Circle decoration by Nancy du Tetre for Artoria Limoges.

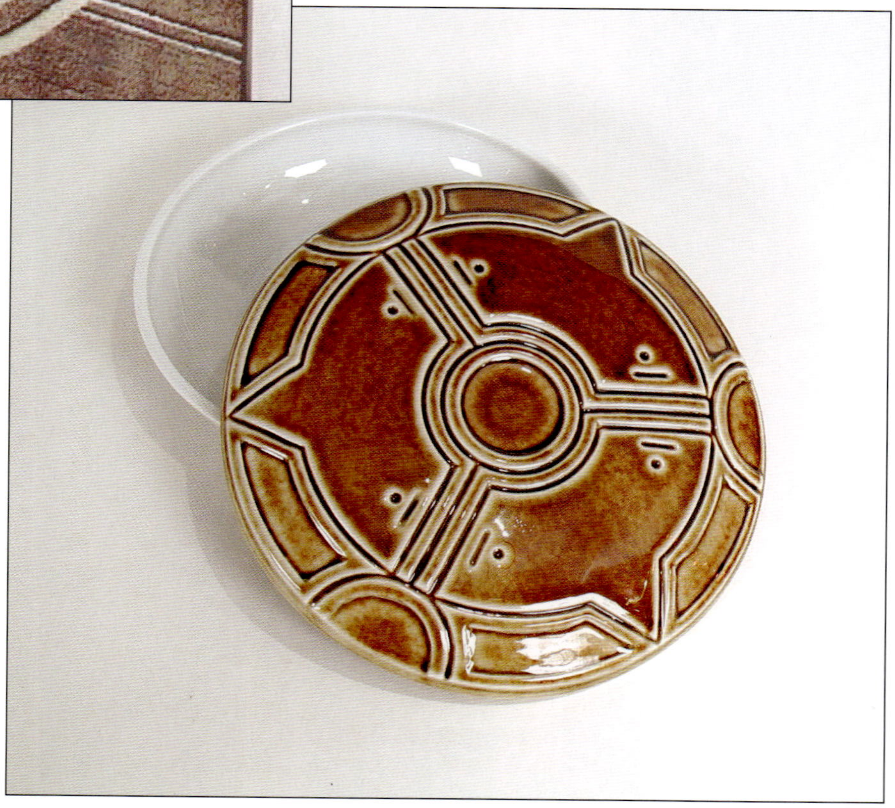

Crop Circle bowl decorated by *grand feu* after the manner of Tharaud. The president of Artoria Limoges, Thierry de Merindol, is the grandson of Camille Tharaud. Less than $500.

Dating of Porcelain and Decorating Marks for Camille Tharaud

Ferrer was able to develop a reliable dating chart using historical documents, records of exhibitions, and conversations with individuals who worked at the studio. The following dating system is based primarily upon Ferrer's work:

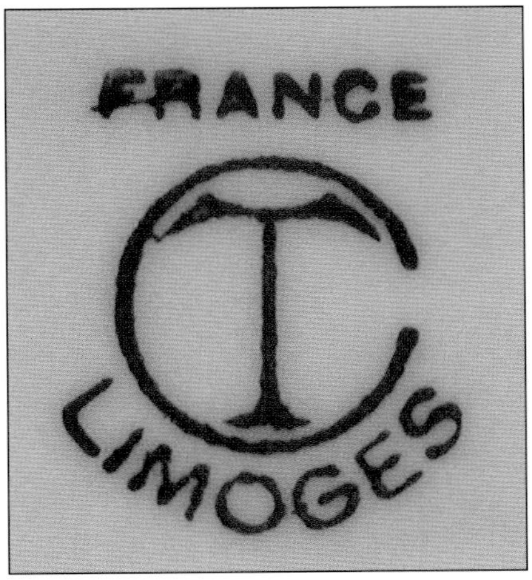

Porcelain mark

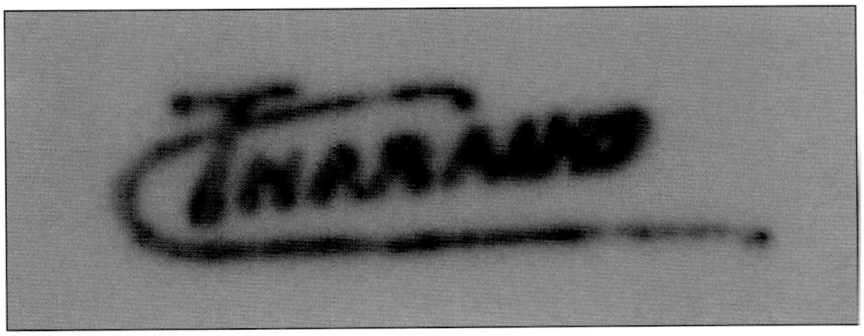

Decorating mark beginning in 1928

1920-1924
Many pieces are unmarked.
Some pieces have only the following marks:
CT

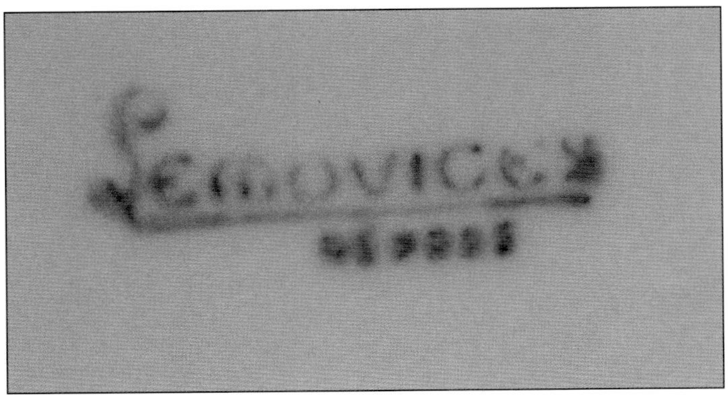

1925-1927 Decorating mark

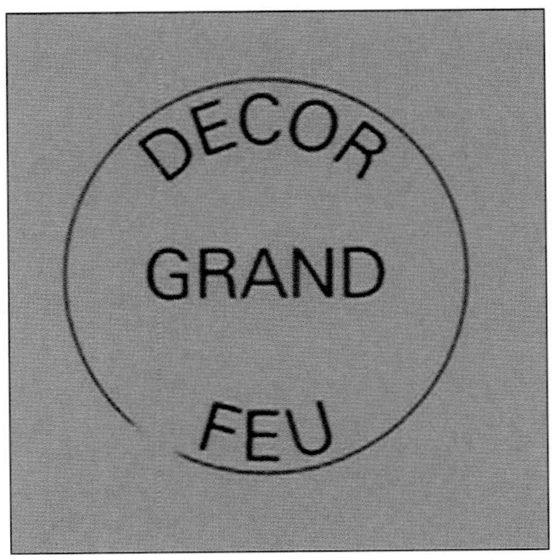

1925-1927

Lémovices in blue	*CT* in green

1928-1930

CTharuad in black	*CT* in green; occasionally in blue or brown

1930-1945

CTharaud in blue	*CT* in green; occasionally in blue or brown

From 1943

CTharaud in blue	*CT* in blue
CTharaud in green	*CT* in green

CTharaud, Made in France, EMAUX GRAND FEU, Décor Main (Pieces made primarily for the US market, according to the Goumot-Labesses.)

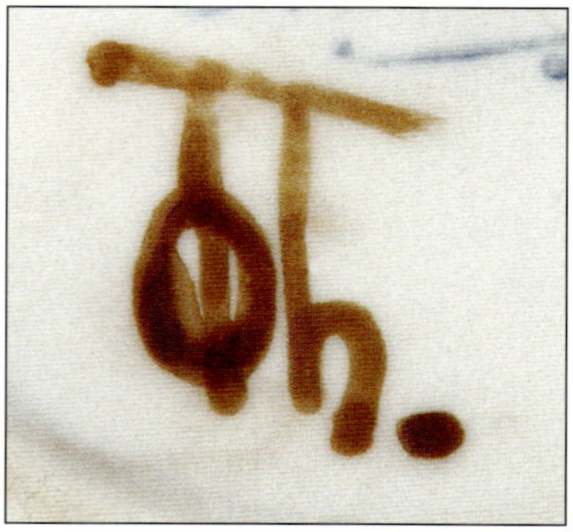

Mark of Odette Tharaud.

Marks of the Artists

Th incised or in color	A decoration of Camille Tharaud
THARAUD incised	Decoration executed by Camille Tharaud
HR incised or in color	A decoration or shape of Henry Rapin
L.J.	Léon Jouhaud (1926-1927)
J.E.	Juliette Geoffroy (1929 or the end of 1930)
R.B. or *René Barlaud*	(1929-1933)
OTh incised or in color	Decoration of or by Odette Tharaud
A. Riff.	Auguste Riffaterre (1929-1935)

Incised marks of Camille Tharaud and Henri Rapin.

Many of the earliest pieces, 1920-1924, made by the Tharaud factory do not have the Tharaud factory decorating mark. Those that are marked often have the names of the Limoges decorators. In 1927, the studio abandoned the *Lémovices* decorating mark, which was replaced by the black *CTharaud* decorating mark.

René Barlaud's decorations were often signed *R.B.* and dated. Pieces that represent the collaboration with Auguste Riffaterre have the marks of both Riffaterre and Tharaud. Odette Tharaud designed and painted many pieces, but few of them were signed because she kept many of them for herself. Pieces with her signature command very high prices.

Many of the unique pieces resulting from *effets de matière* did not have a decorating mark but instead have the incised marks of Tharaud and Rapin.

Tharaud's Architectural Works

Very few Art Deco ceramists ever attempted large ceramic architectural pieces. Throughout his career, Tharaud completed several such pieces. While these works had the effect of mosaics, they were not a repetition of classical mosaics with numerous small squares, but rather mosaics with rectangular or triangular pieces of varying sizes. He brought mosaics back into fashion in the decorative arts. Below is a listing of his architectural pieces:

1929 Decorative panels of friezes, with 1,500 pieces, from patterns by Henri Rapin for the Bénédictins Station in Limoges. The tiles that made up the panels were eventually taken by some of the city's officials.

1931 Fountain, with 3,000 pieces, based on the drawings of Henri Rapin, exhibited at the Exposition coloniale internationale and receiving the grand prize. After the exhibition it was offered to the city of Limoges and installed on a plaza next to the Bénédictins Station.

1933 Clock dial for the Society Général in Limoges, with 600 pieces, from the sketches of Mrs. Marquis, an engineer at Sèvres.

1933-1934 Fountain, also with Mrs. Marquis, for the square in front of the Banque coopérative (now, Banque populaire du Centre) in Guéret in the Creuse region.

1937 Fireplace in collaboration with Lucien Crèlerot at the Exposition internationale des arts et techniques dans la vie moderne, receiving a diploma of honor. This was Tharaud's last architectural piece.

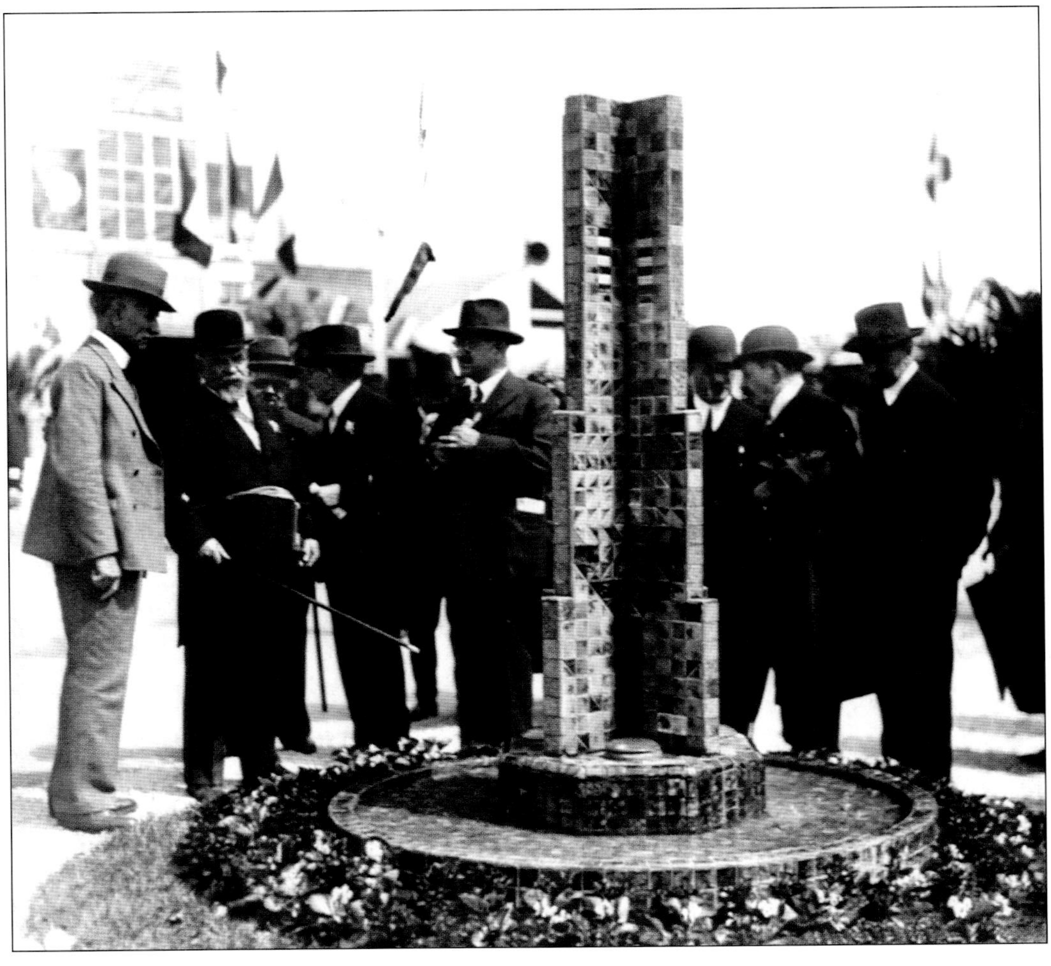

Major Expositions of Tharaud's Work

The progress and acceptance of Tharaud's work was reflected in the many expositions that included his pieces. Below are the most important of these expositions:

1925 Exposition internationale des arts décoratifs industriels et moderns (later termed the Art Deco exhibition), Paris, diploma of honor.

1927 Salon des artistes décorateurs, Paris, sixteen pieces exhibited, second prize from the Society d'encouragement à l'art et à l'industrie.

1928 Salon des artistes décorateurs, Paris, twenty pieces exhibited, first prize from the Société d'encouragement à l'art et à l'industrie.

1929 Salon des artistes décorateurs, Paris.

1929 Salon d'automne, Paris.

1930 Salon des artistes décorateurs, Paris.

1930 Salon d'automne, Paris, grand prize.

1930 Salon de l'automobile, Paris, a prize from the Society d'encouragement à l'art et à l'industrie, and Exposition internationale *L'aéronautique et l'art*, "prime" from the Society d'encouragement à l'art et à l'industrie, and silver medal from the city of Paris. Pieces by Lucien Crèlerot and Eugène Alluaud were presented.

1931 Musée de Sèvres, Exposition *Œuvres des céramistes modernes* (1890-1930), Paris, sixteen pieces exhibited. Tharaud was the only living Limoges ceramist honored at this exposition.

1931 Salon des artistes décorateurs, Paris, silver medal from the Society d'encouragement à l'art et à l'industrie.

1931 Exposition coloniale internationale, Paris, grand prize for the decorative fountain which was based on the drawings of Henri Rapin.

1937 Exposition internationale des arts et techniques dans la vie modern, Paris, grand prize for the body of work. Tharaud's exhibit included dinner services, pieces done by Henri Rapin, goblets designed by Maurice Dufrène, and a series of animals done in collaboration with Robert Lemoine. Pieces from the creative synergy of Tharaud, Henri Rapin, and Tharaud's daughter, Odette, were also exhibited. This exposition reflects the end of the Art Deco movement.

Historical Photographs of the Tharaud Factory and Family Members and Friends

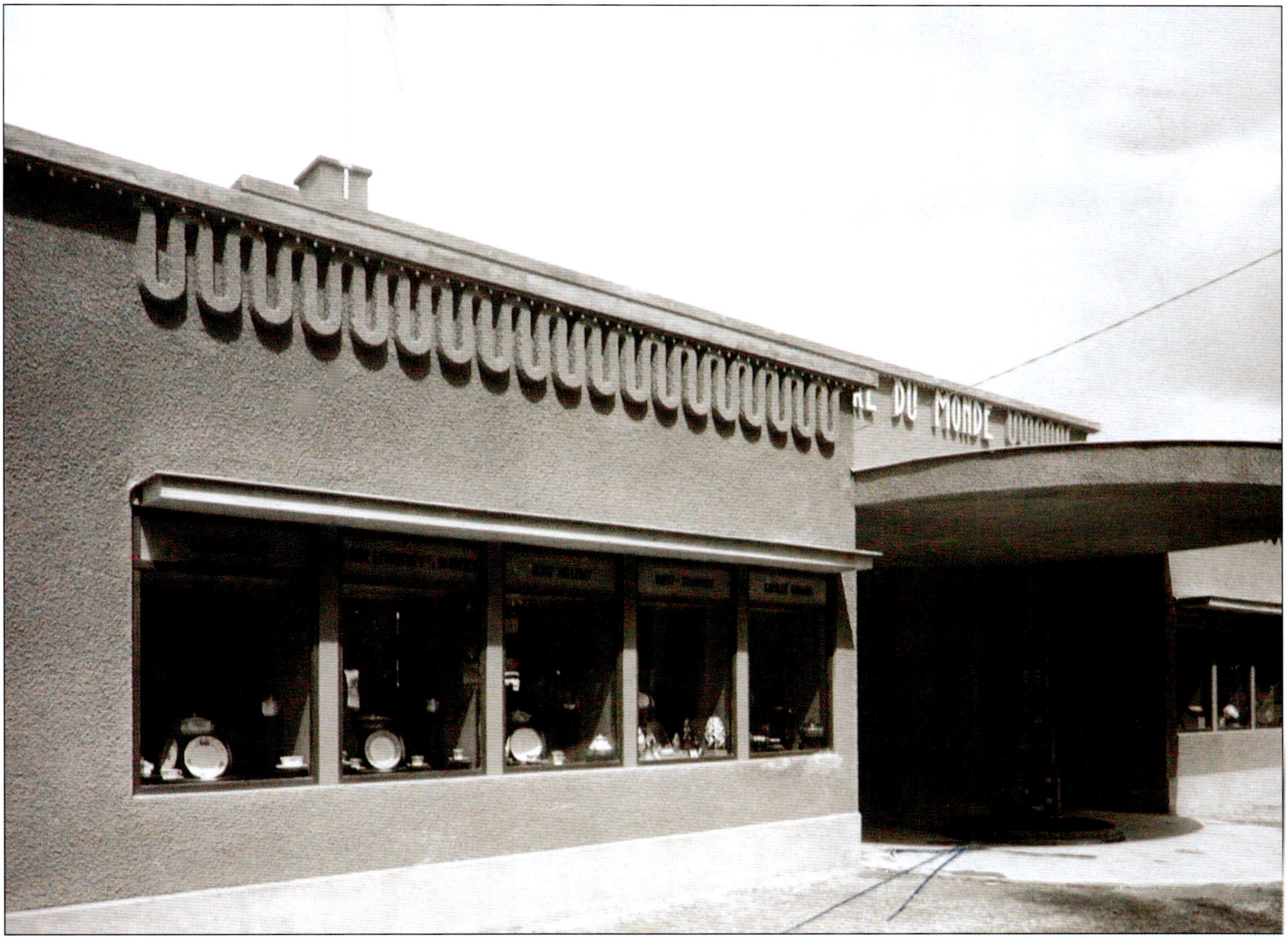

Tharaud showroom.

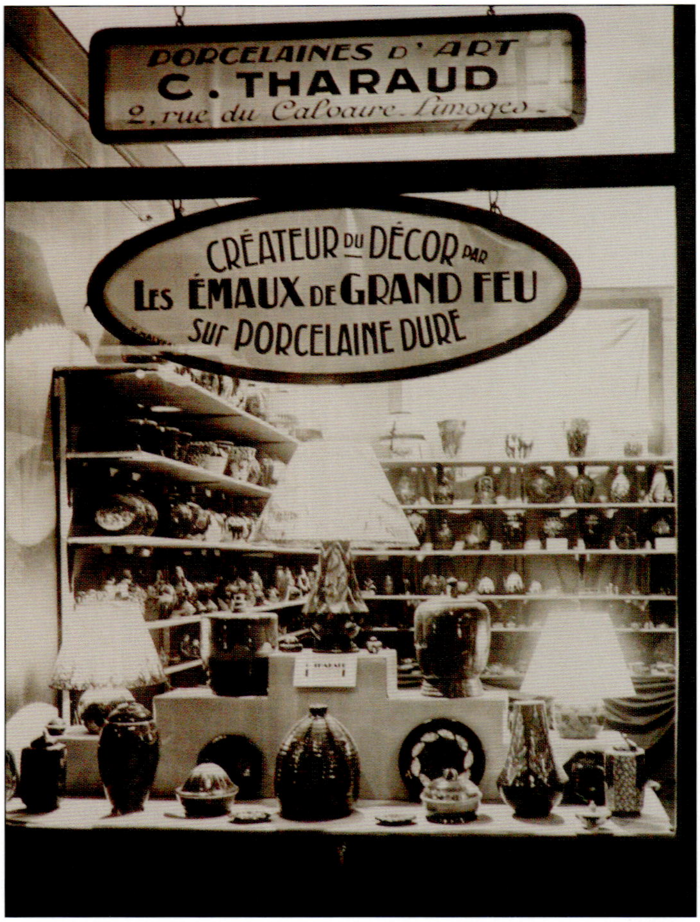

Display of Tharaud's porcelain.

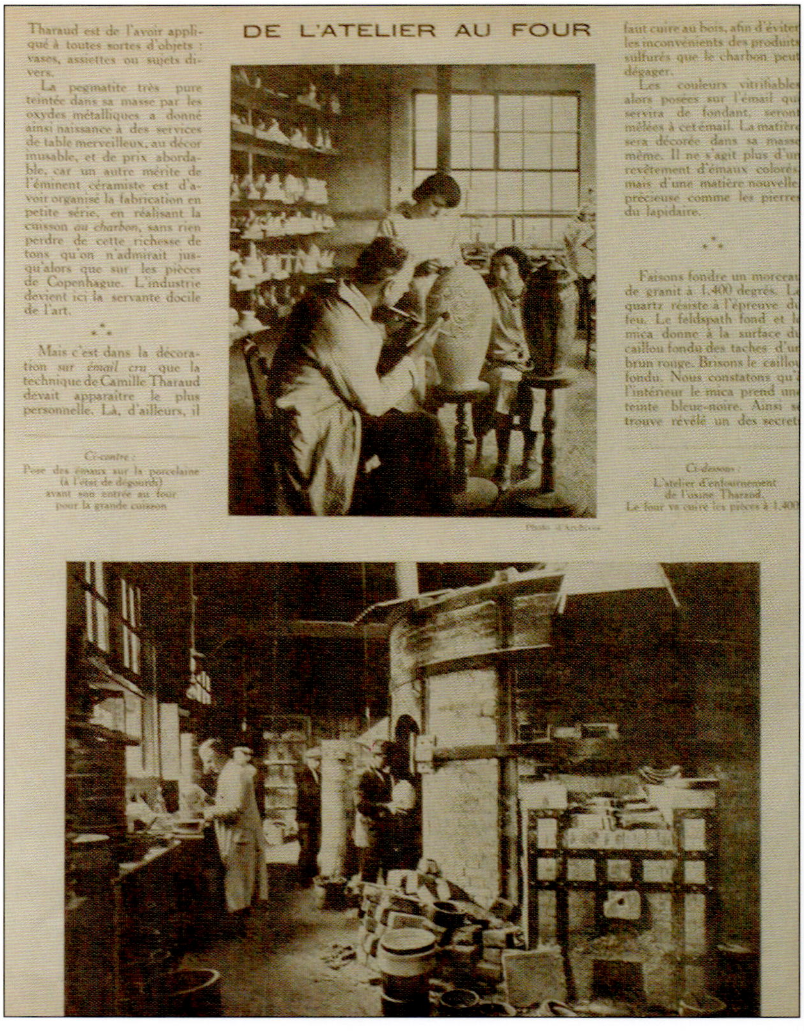

DE L'ATELIER AU FOUR

Tharaud est de l'avoir appliqué à toutes sortes d'objets : vases, assiettes ou sujets divers.

La pegmatite très pure teintée dans sa masse par les oxydes métalliques a donné ainsi naissance à des services de table merveilleux, au décor inusable, et de prix abordable, car un autre mérite de l'éminent céramiste est d'avoir organisé la fabrication en petite série, en réalisant la cuisson *au charbon*, sans rien perdre de cette richesse de tons qu'on n'admirait jusqu'alors que sur les pièces de Copenhague. L'industrie devient ici la servante docile de l'art.

* * *

Mais c'est dans la décoration *sur émail cru* que la technique de Camille Tharaud devait apparaître le plus personnelle. Là, d'ailleurs, il faut cuire au bois, afin d'éviter les inconvénients des produits sulfurés que le charbon peut dégager.

Les couleurs vitrifiables alors posées sur l'émail qui servira de fondant, seront mêlées à cet émail. La matière sera décorée dans sa masse même. Il ne s'agit plus d'un revêtement d'émaux colorés, mais d'une matière nouvelle précieuse comme les pierres du lapidaire.

* * *

Faisons fondre un morceau de granit à 1.400 degrés. Le quartz résiste à l'épreuve du feu. Le feldspath fond et le mica donne à la surface du caillou fondu des taches d'un brun rouge. Brisons le caillou fondu. Nous constatons qu'à l'intérieur le mica prend une teinte bleue-noire. Ainsi se trouve révélé un des secret

Ci-contre :
Pose des émaux sur la porcelaine (à l'état de dégourdi) avant son entrée au four pour la grande cuisson

Ci-dessous :
L'atelier d'enfournement de l'usine Tharaud.
Le four va cuire les pièces à 1.400

Tharaud's workshop.

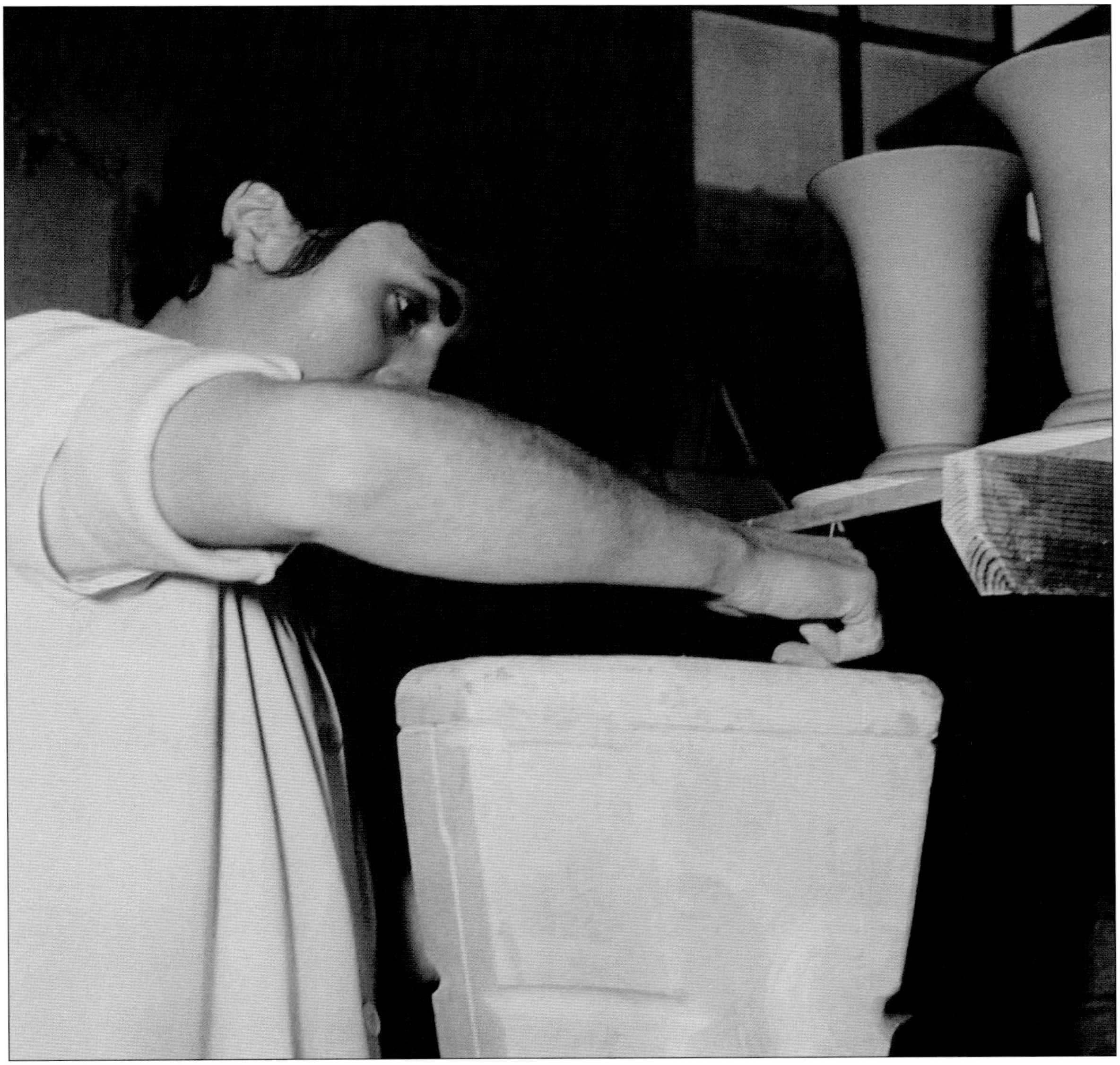

Unmolding a piece of porcelain.

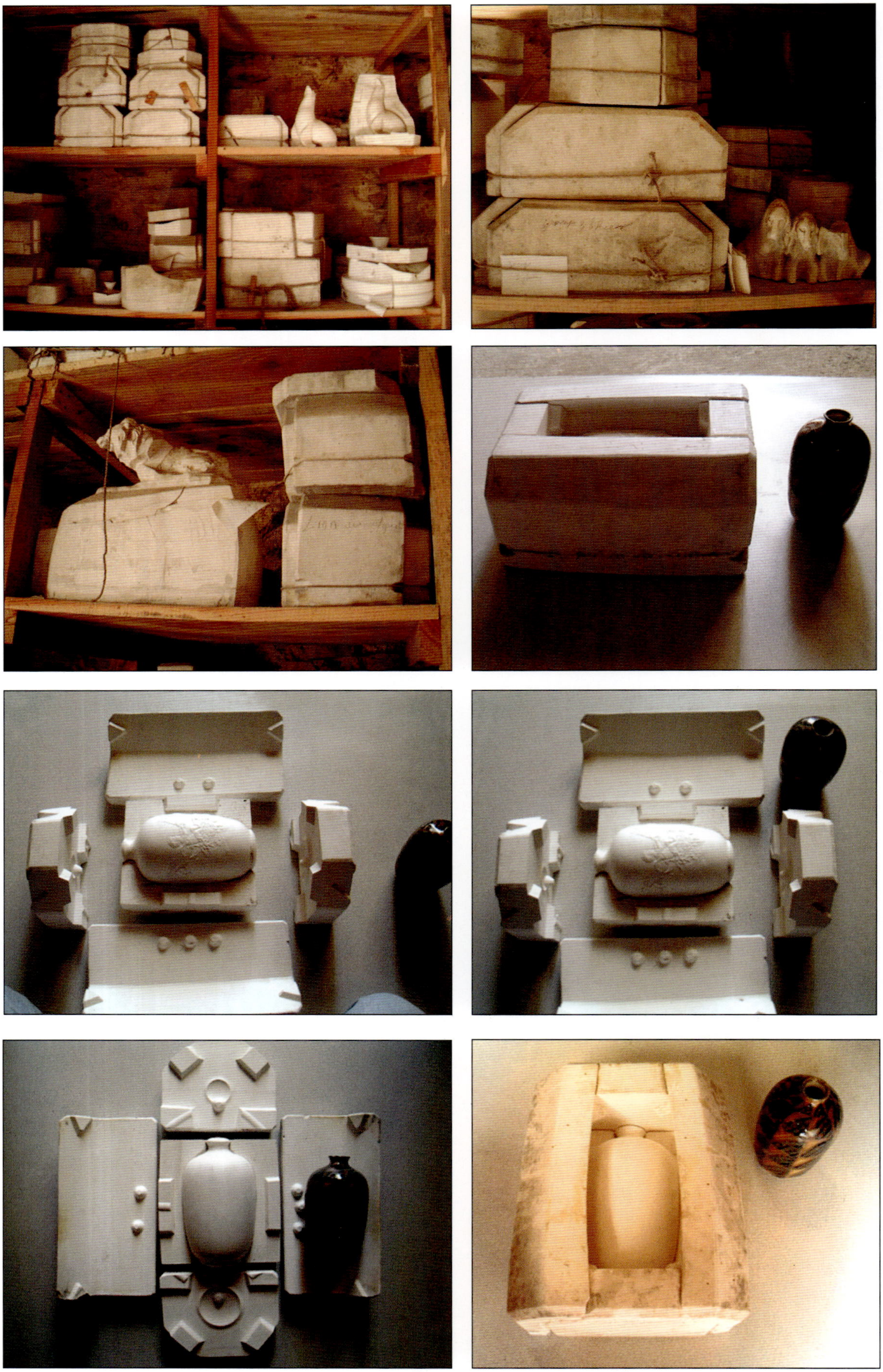

Original Tharaud molds. The Tharaud family still has all of the original Tharaud molds.

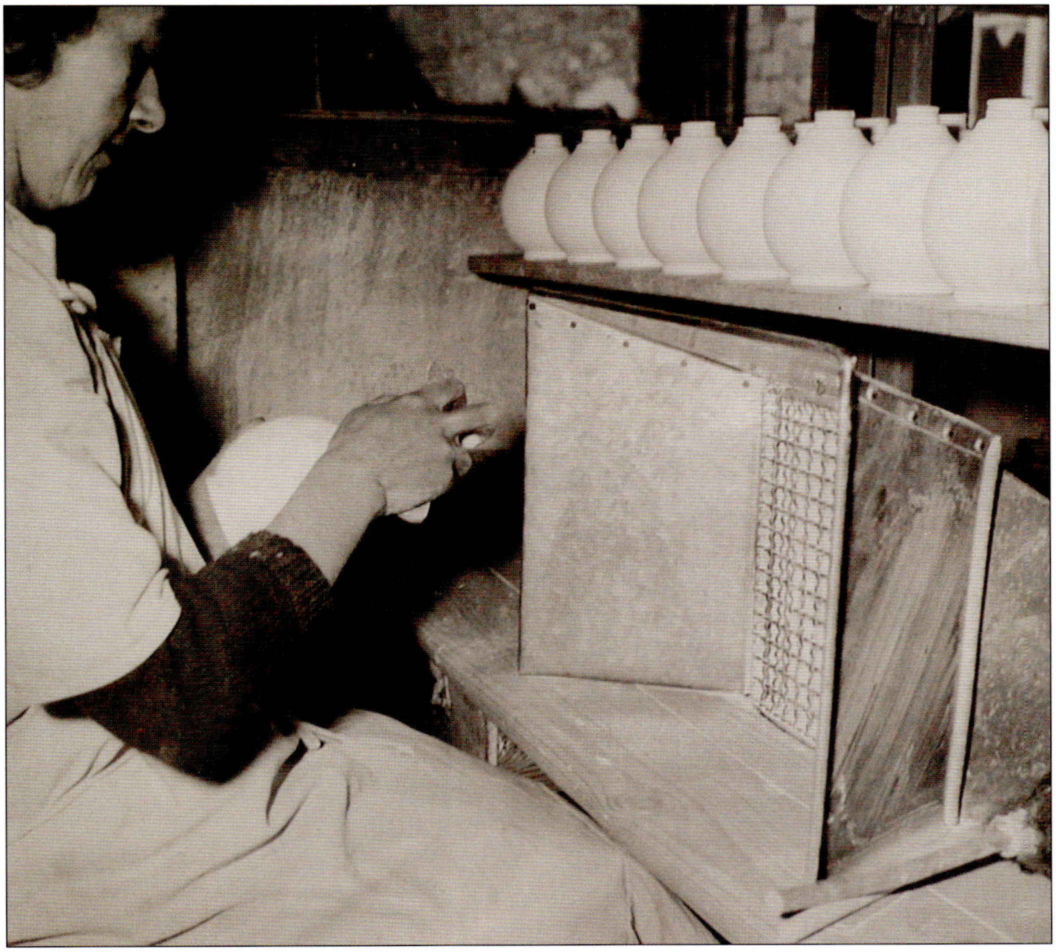

Removing excess clay.

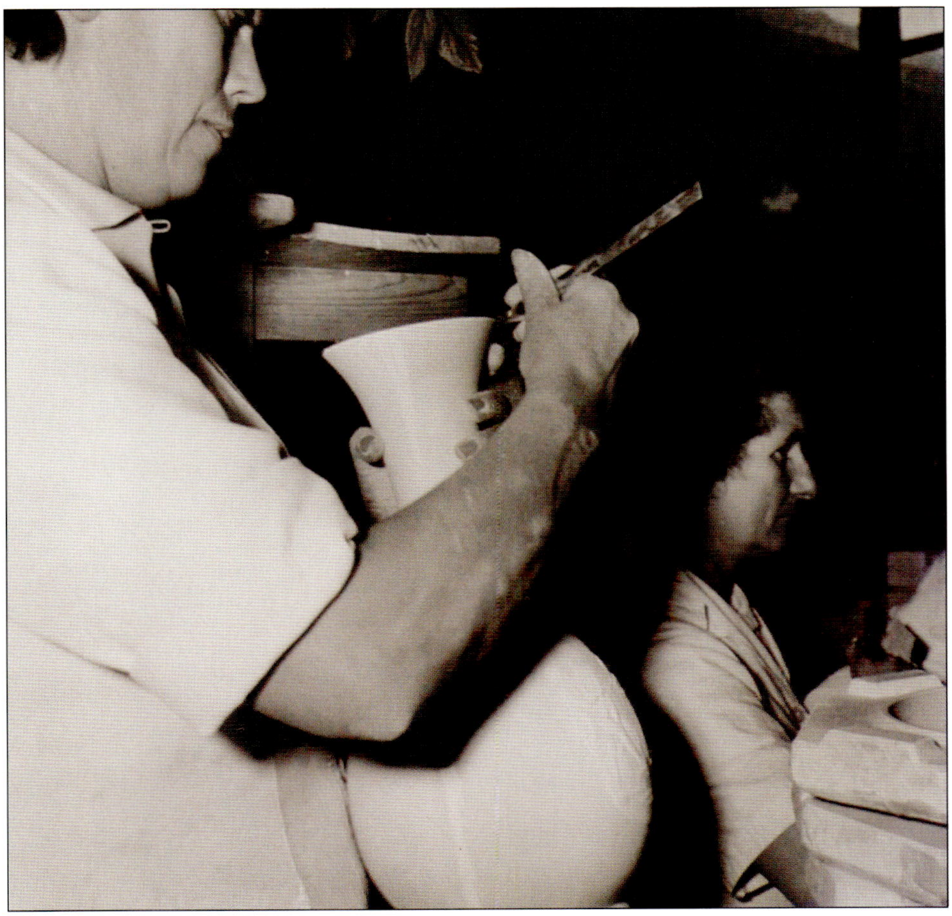

Removing excess clay.

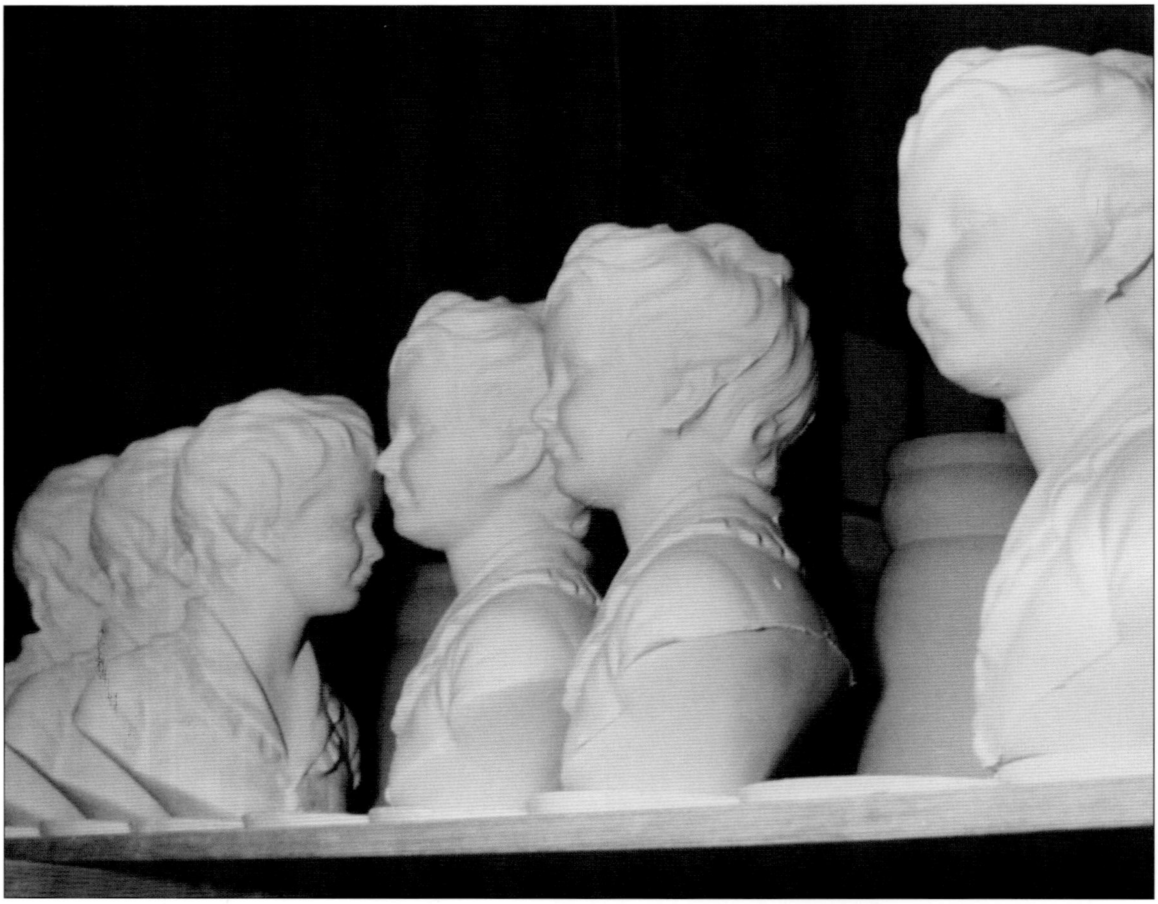

Bisque busts.

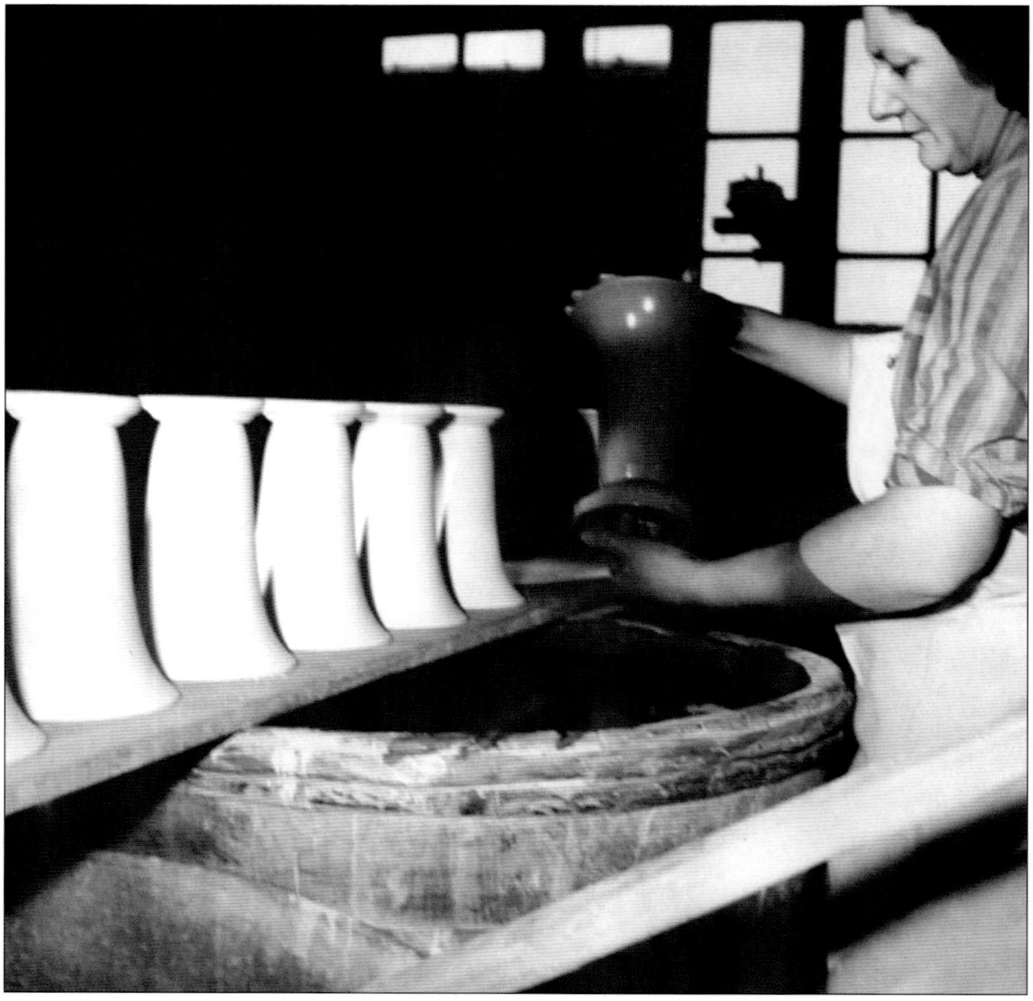

Dipping porcelain in enamel.

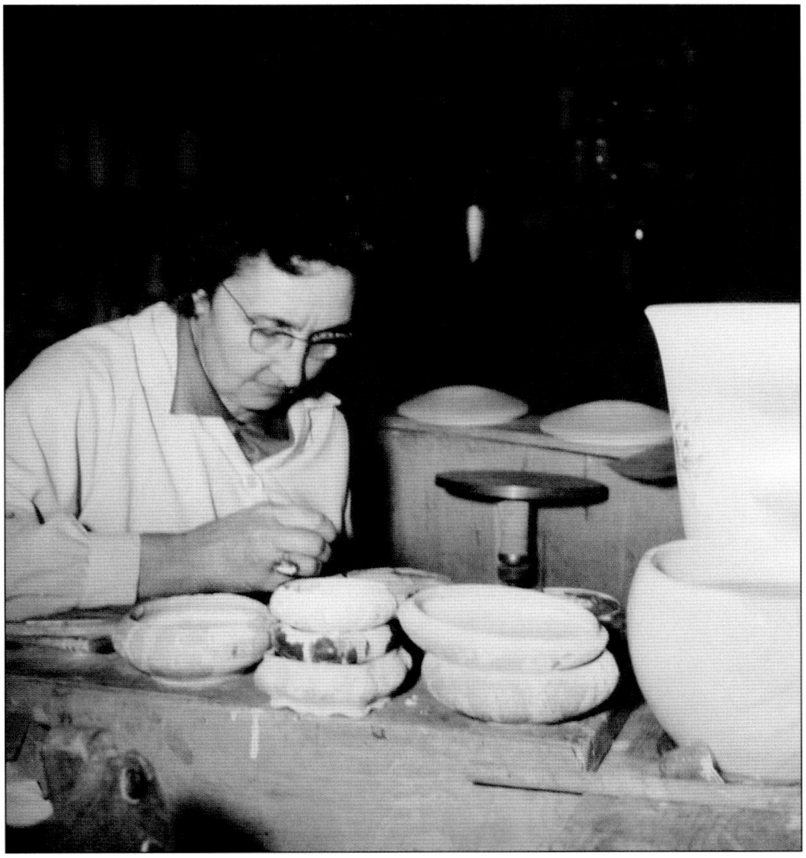

Applying enamel as decoration.

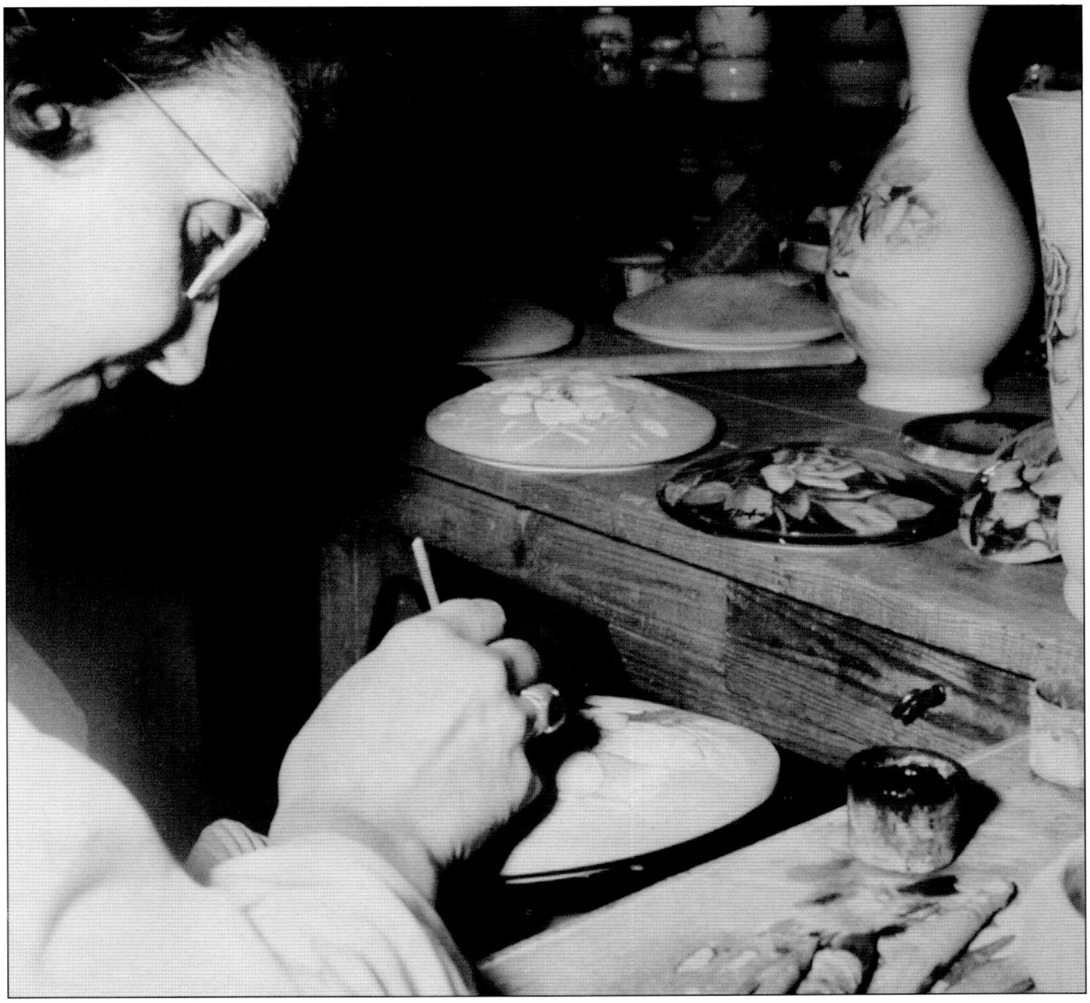

Applying enamel as decoration.

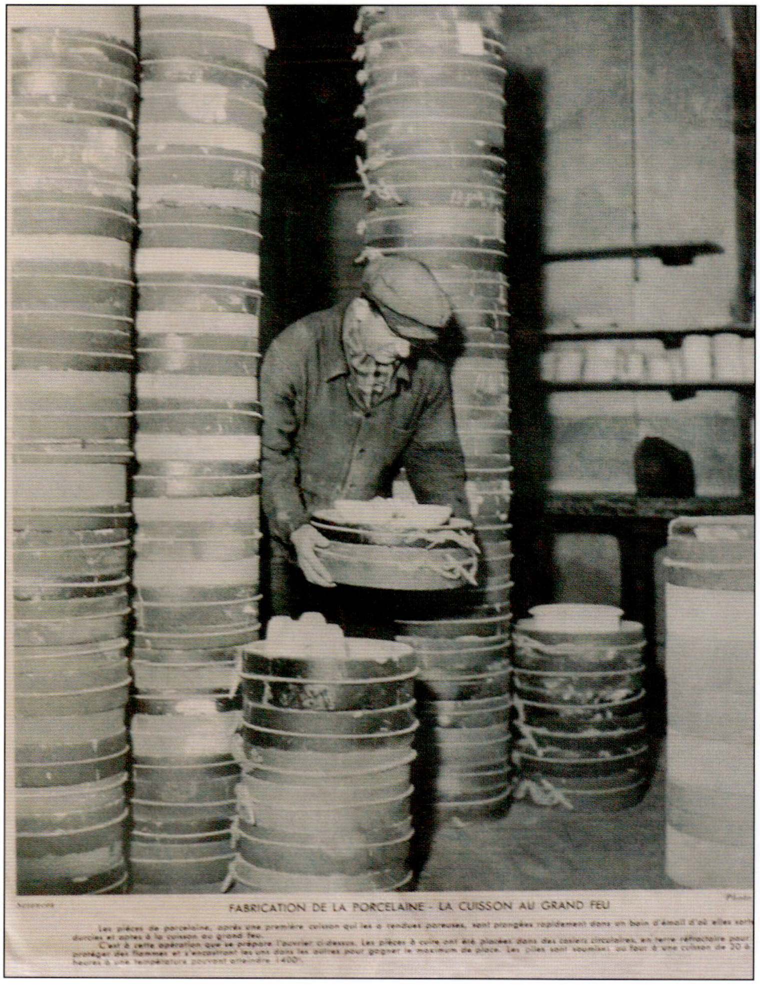

Gazettes for holding porcelain during firing.

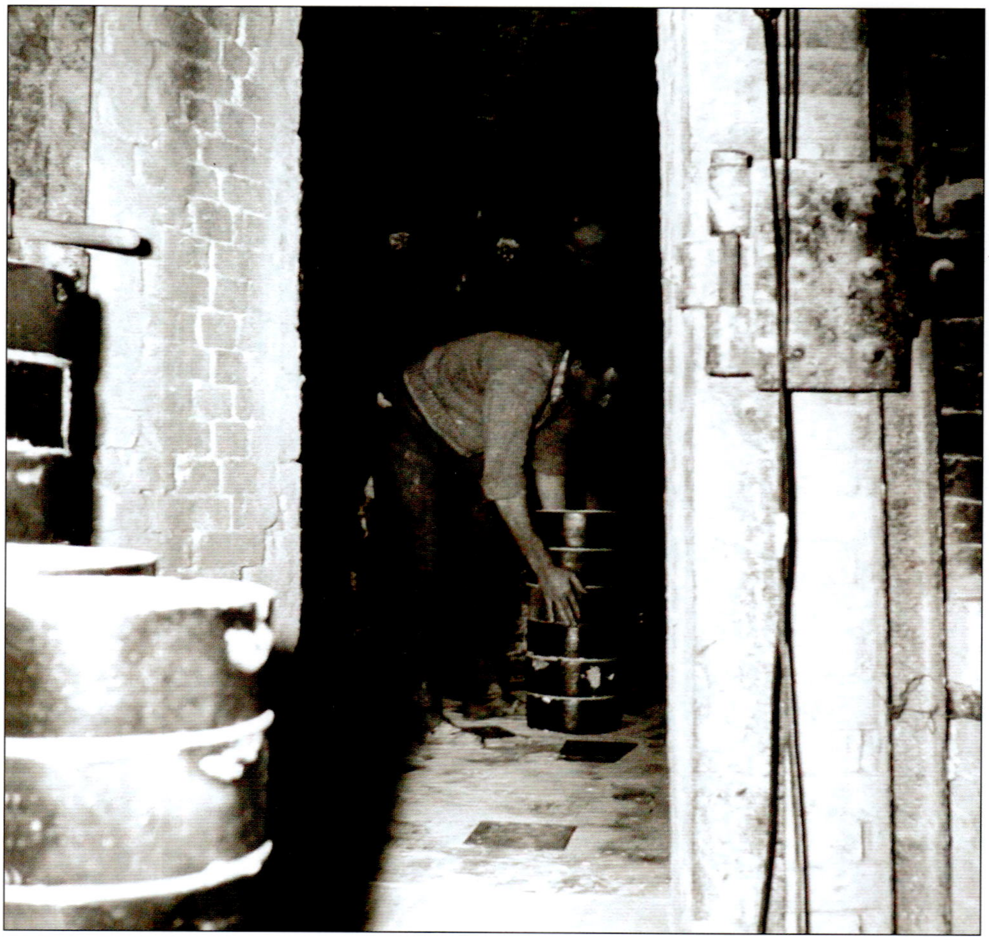

Gazettes.

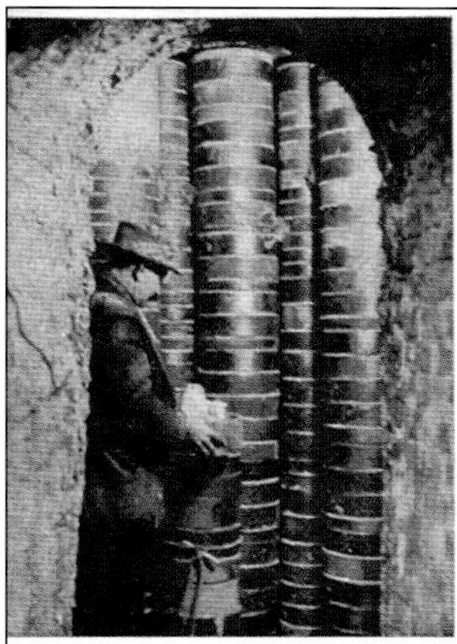

Photo d'Archives

L'homme de four plaçant ses gazettes.
La corde que l'on aperçoit maintient une gazette fendue.
Elle sera enlevée quand la pile sera montée.

des techniques nouvelles. Dans le sous-émail, la matière est *emprisonnée* et elle donnera à la cuisson une teinte différente de celle obtenue en surface. La différence peut d'ailleurs être légère. Ainsi le chlorure d'or donne en *sous-émail* un ton rose saumon et en *sur-émail* un ton lilas voisin du rose pâle. Les jeux de la lumière varieront aussi suivant les deux procédés. De la gelée de groseille posée sur de la crème offrira un ton et un éclat tout autres que ceux qu'on observerait en mélangeant la crème et la gelée.

Premières surprises

La seconde image montre l'application au pinceau, de ces pâtes d'émaux colorés sur un vase de porcelaine dégourdie et déjà recouverte de la couche habituelle d'émail blanc.

C'est sur cette couche (par la décalque) ou sous cette couche (qui l'emprisonnait) que dans une cuisson à part on fixait jusqu'ici le décor simple, peinture légère déjà cuite.

Là, au contraire, ce sont des reliefs puissants, des masses de pâte d'émail, ou *pegmatite* (caillou du Limousin dépouillé de son mica), masses d'émail offertes dans toute leur épaisseur aux jeux de la lumière.

La première fois que Peyrusson, pharmacien qui se livrait à des recherches céramiques, appliqua ces émaux colorés sur l'émail blanc et mince de la porcelaine, il observa un affaissement du relief minéral déposé au pinceau. Au feu, tout cela coulait et on obtenait, certes, un résultat intéressant mais non conforme, et inattendu : c'étaient les *vases flammés*.

Tharaud qui voulait autre chose constata que les colorants augmentaient la fusibilité. Pour conserver le dessin prévu, il remédia à cette fusibilité en ajoutant diverses matières comme le quartz, réalisant ainsi des *émaux synthétiques* résistant au feu comme l'émail pur.

Séries réduites - Emaux profonds

Il put alors sans crainte introduire dans le four que représente la troisième image les objets décorés à l'atelier. Le four allait les lui rendre avec les ornements espérés, et riches d'une matière neuve et somptueuse, décor inusable aux variétés chatoyantes, propres à faire pâlir les bronzes et la vaisselle d'or.

La photo ci-contre montre l'homme de four devant des colonnes de gazette en terre réfractaire empilées dans le globe où joue la flamme renversée du four chauffé au bois, parce que le bois donne plus de richesses aux coloris. Ceux-ci naissent de l'oxydation des poudres minérales déposées sur le vase, oxydation exempte de brutalité grâce aux gazettes protectrices.

Dans le four, de dimensions modestes (dix à douze mètres cubes) on ne fait pas la grande série.

Tantôt en sortent des pièces uniques, tantôt des séries de dix ou cent objets de même forme, encore que le travail de décoration à la main laisse à chacun sa personnalité. La petite série indique une mise au point, une sûreté d'exécution. Elle

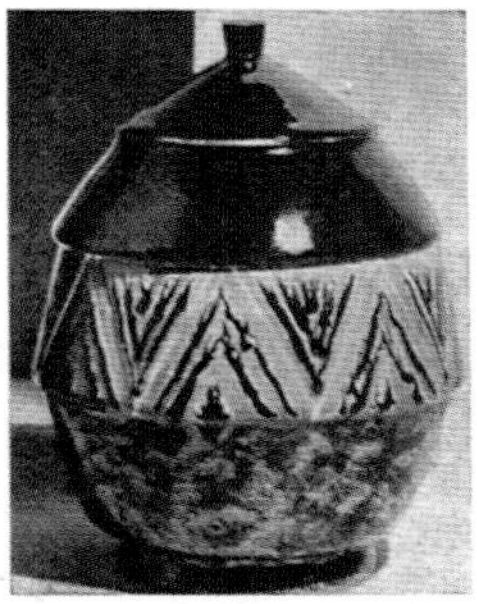

Un vase décoré par Tharaud (forme de H. Rapin).

fait évoluer l'art vers une diffusion plus large sans tomber dans la banalité des reproductions sans mesure.

La dernière image ci-dessus donne un exemple de cette exploration céramique passionnée qui dura un quart de siècle. L'émail en masses, vitrifié par-dessus la couverture d'émail blanc de la forme en porcelaine dure qui constitue le fond refléchissant, est baigné de lumière dans ses couches successives.

Ainsi, au lieu d'avoir des couleurs amorties sous l'émail blanc qui fait écran, on obtient des couleurs vives comme le bleu de four si réputé.

L'œuvre magique du feu naît aux environs de 1.400 degrés, et l'oxydation qui n'est pas limitée comme dans le décor sous-émail d'une pièce de porcelaine livre une pièce vêtue de la robe des pierres naturelles.

EDMOND BLANC.

Gazettes and a vase formed by Henri Rapin and decorated by Tharaud.

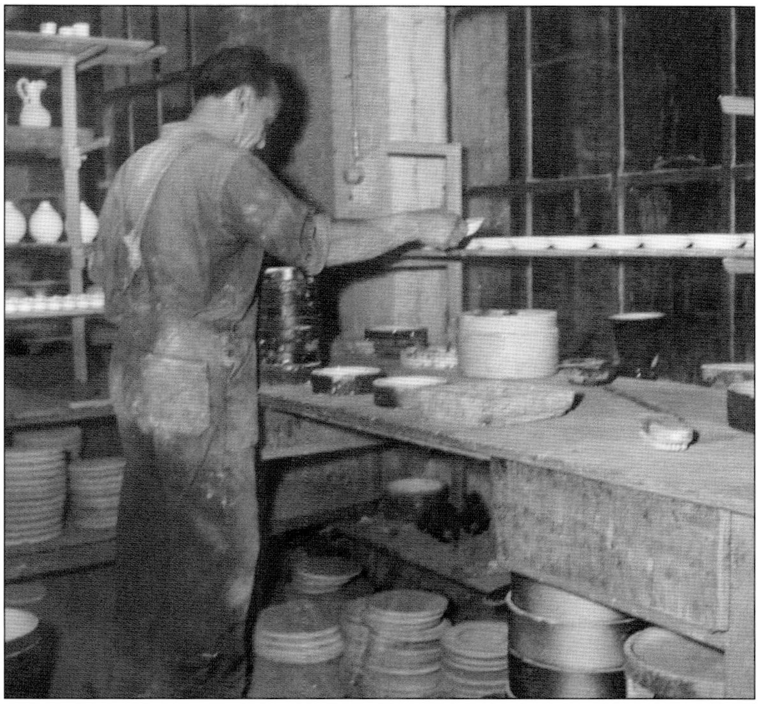

Placing porcelain in gazette before firing.

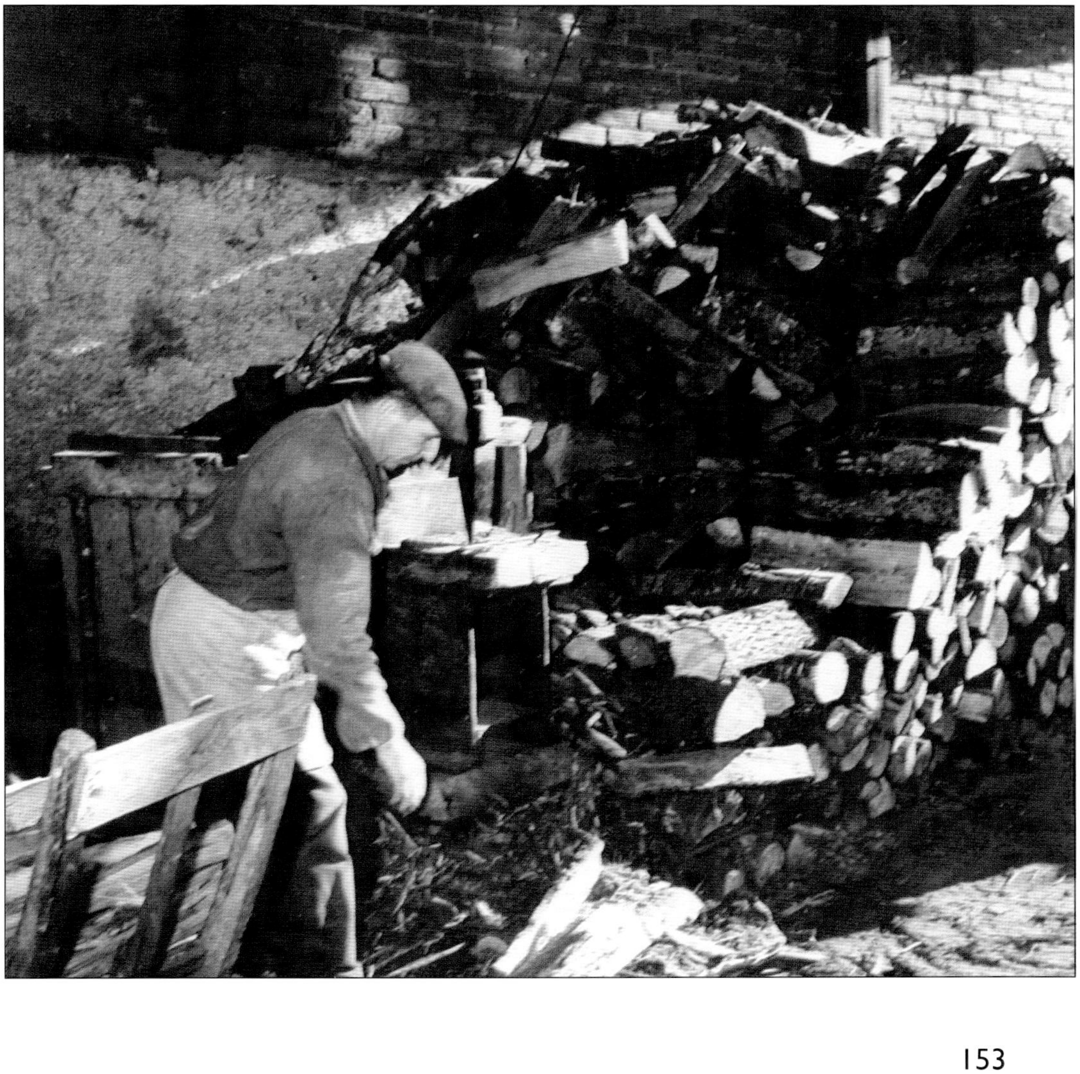

Woodpile.

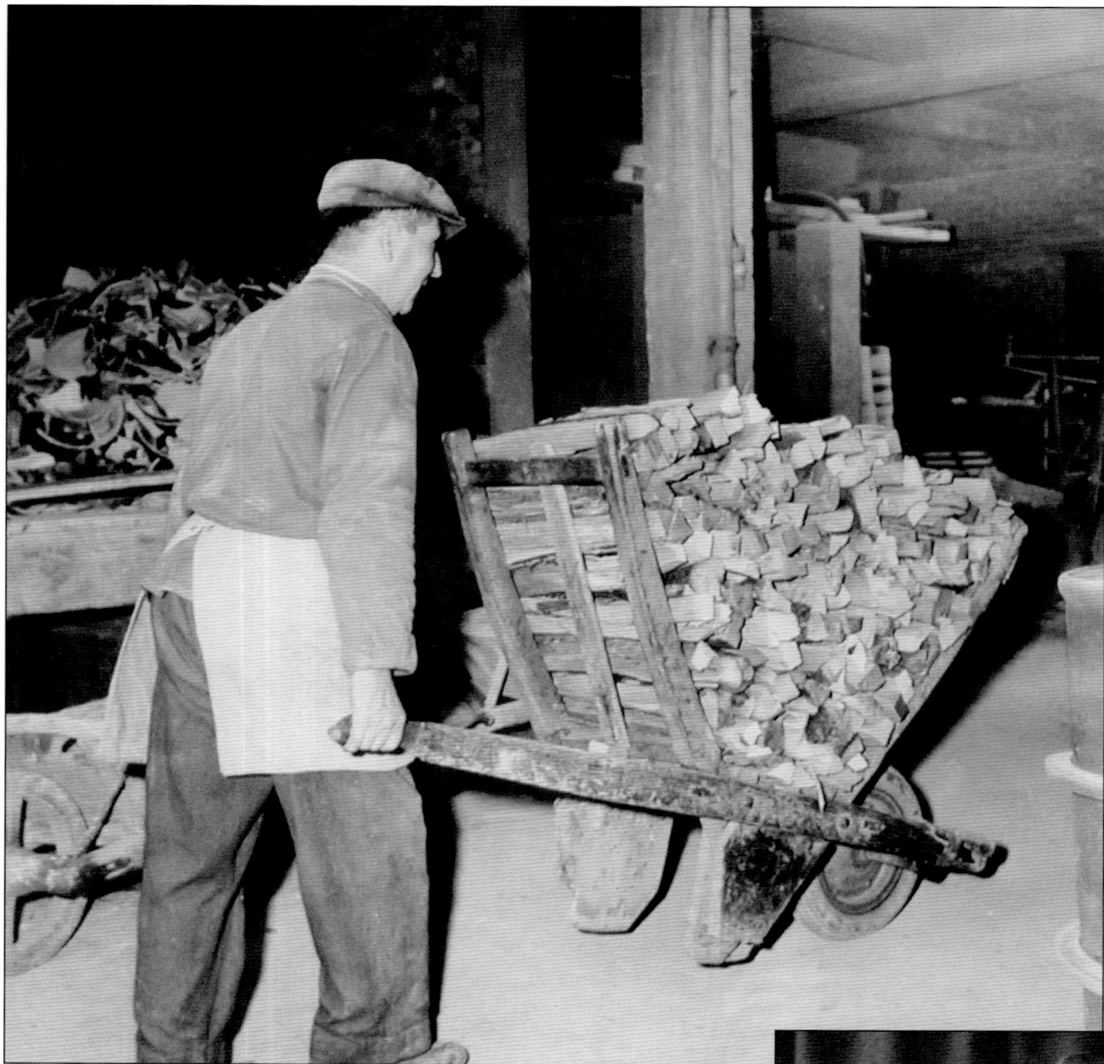

Taking wood to fire the kiln.

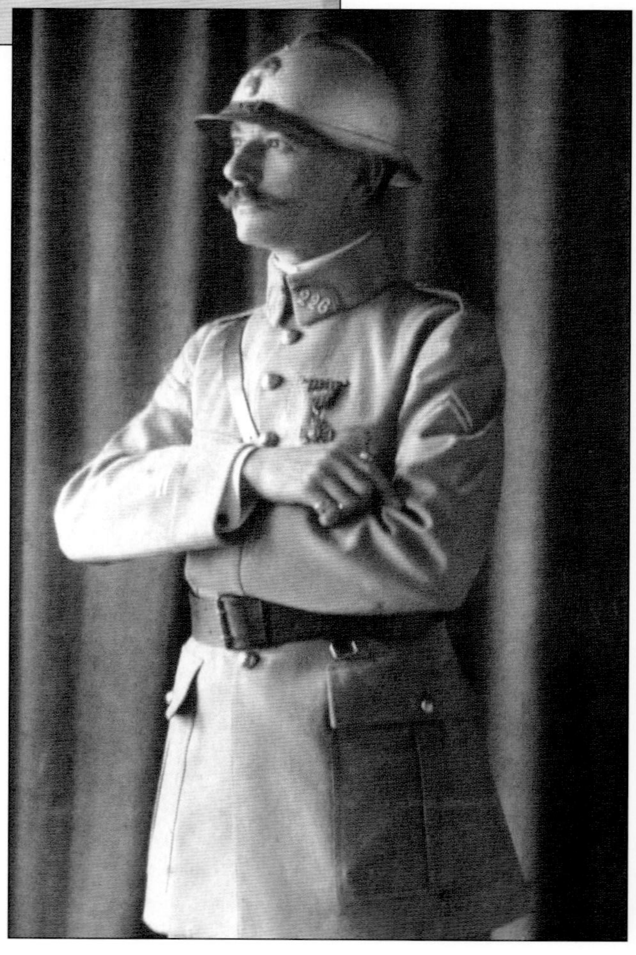

Tharaud in military uniform.

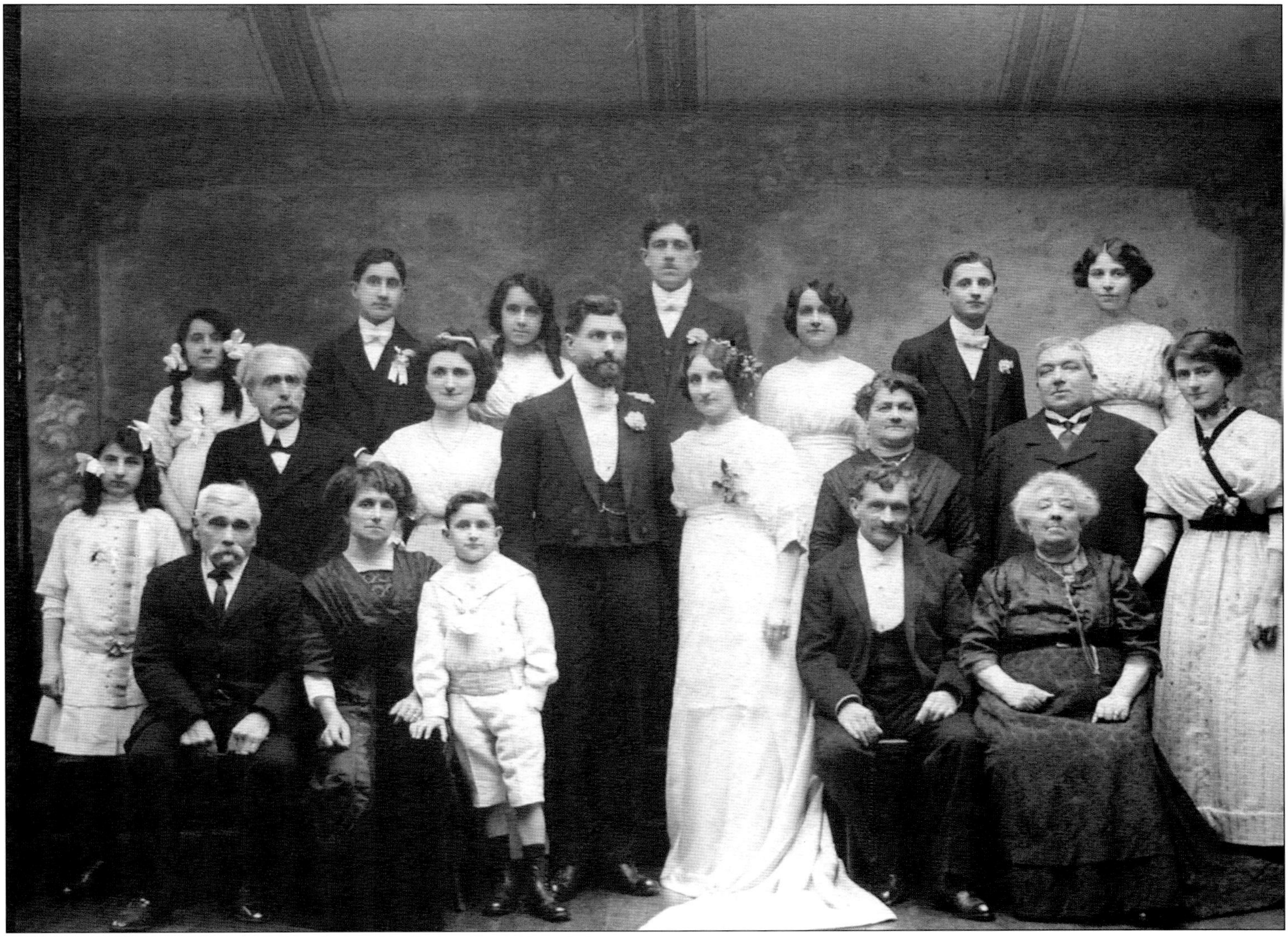

Wedding of Berthe and Camille Tharaud.

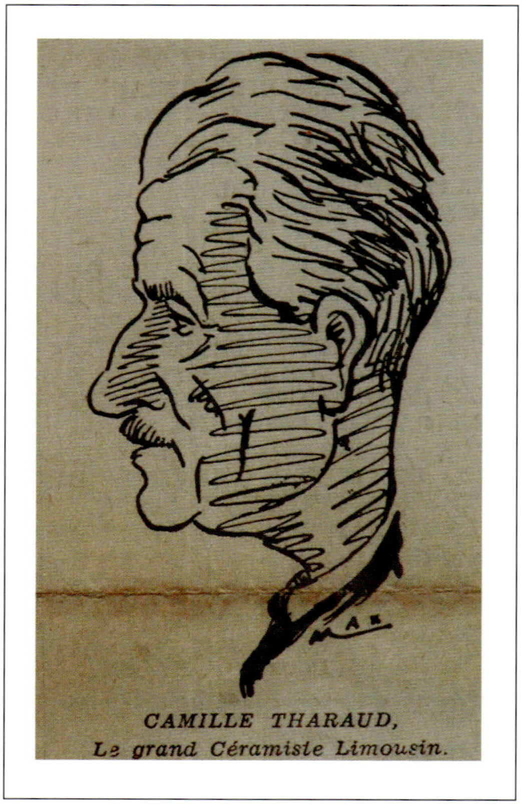

Cartoon of Tharaud, the well known ceramist.

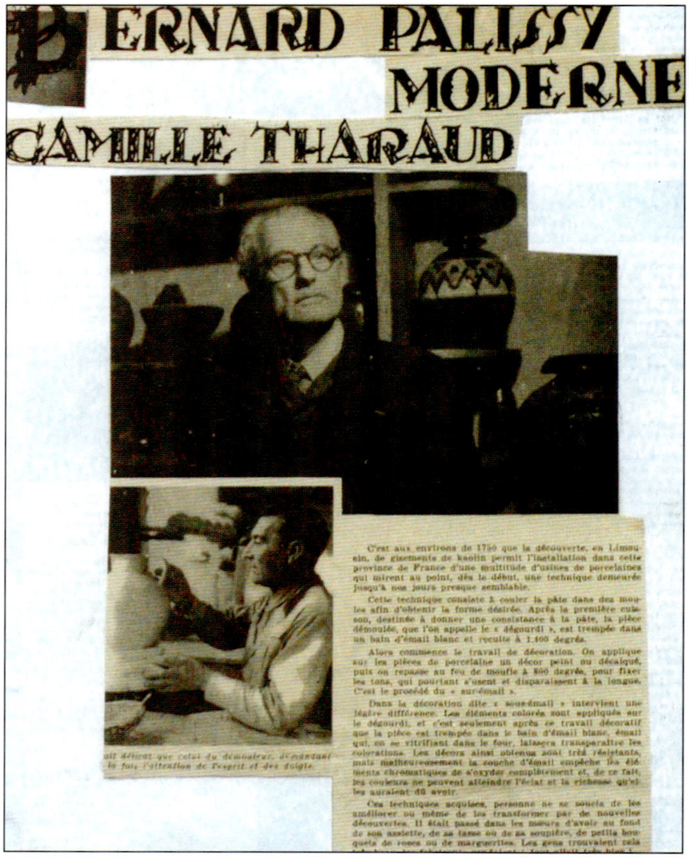

BERNARD PALISSY MODERNE
CAMILLE THARAUD

...ait délicat que celui du démoulage, demandant à la fois l'attention de l'esprit et des doigts.

C'est aux environs de 1750 que la découverte, en Limousin, de gisements de kaolin permit l'installation dans cette province de France d'une multitude d'usines de porcelaines qui mirent au point, dès le début, une technique demeurée jusqu'à nos jours presque semblable.

Cette technique consiste à couler la pâte dans des moules afin d'obtenir la forme désirée. Après la première cuisson, destinée à donner une consistance à la pâte, la pièce démoulée, que l'on appelle le « dégourdi », est trempée dans un bain d'émail blanc et recuite à 1.400 degrés.

Alors commence le travail de décoration. On applique sur les pièces de porcelaine un décor peint ou décalqué, puis on repasse au feu de moufle à 800 degrés, pour fixer les tons, qui pourtant s'usent et disparaissent à la longue. C'est le procédé du « sur-émail ».

Dans la décoration dite « sous-émail » intervient une légère différence. Les éléments colorés sont appliqués sur le dégourdi, et c'est seulement après ce travail décoratif que la pièce est trempée dans le bain d'émail blanc, émail qui, en se vitrifiant dans le four, laissera transparaître les colorations. Les décors ainsi obtenus sont très résistants, mais malheureusement la couche d'émail empêche les éléments chromatiques de s'oxyder complètement et, de ce fait, les couleurs ne peuvent atteindre l'éclat et la richesse qu'elles auraient dû avoir.

Ces techniques acquises, personne ne se soucia de les améliorer ou même de les transformer par de nouvelles découvertes. Il était passé dans les mœurs d'avoir au fond de son assiette, de sa tasse ou de sa soupière, de petits bouquets de roses ou de marguerites. Les gens trouvaient cela

Article comparing Palissy and Tharaud as modern ceramists and as innovators in enamels.

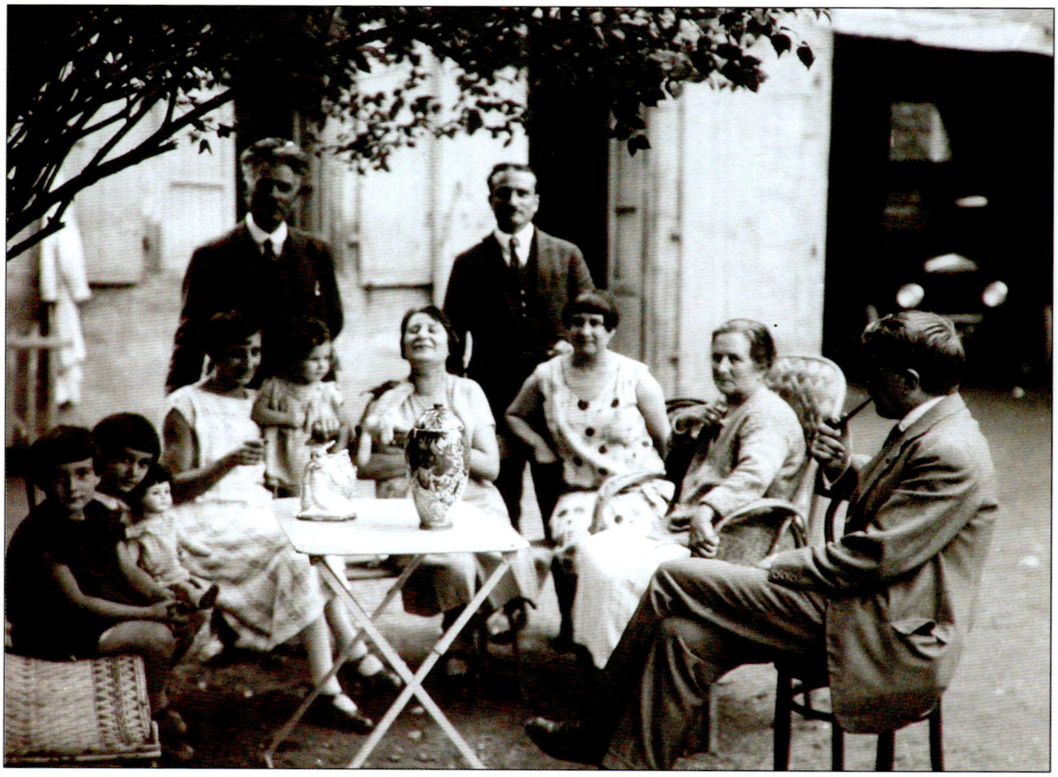

Interior court of the Tharaud factory; from left to right, Colette, the daughter of Louis Menigault; Odette Tharaud; Berthe Tharaud with daughter Nicole and Camille Tharaud; Mr. and Mrs. Menigault; Mrs. Rapin; mother of Camille Tharaud; and Henri Rapin.

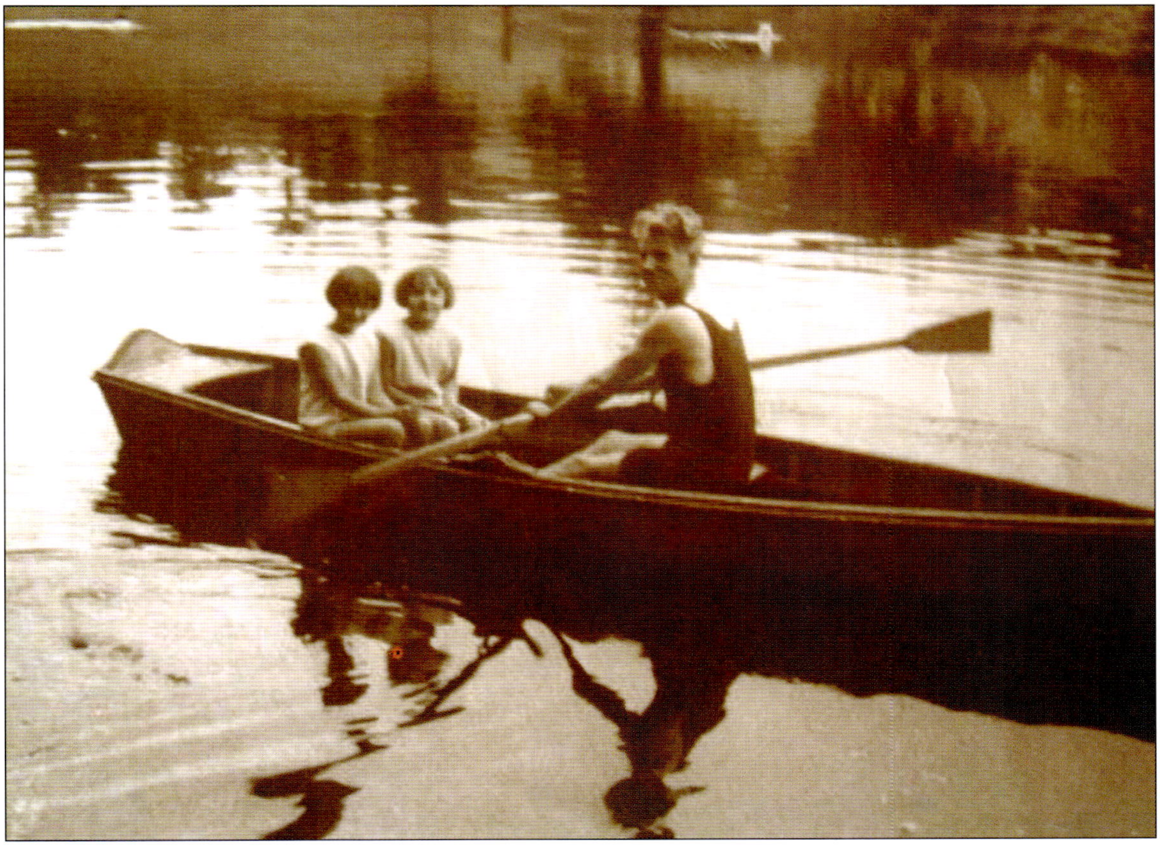

Camille Tharaud with his daughters, Odette and Nicole.

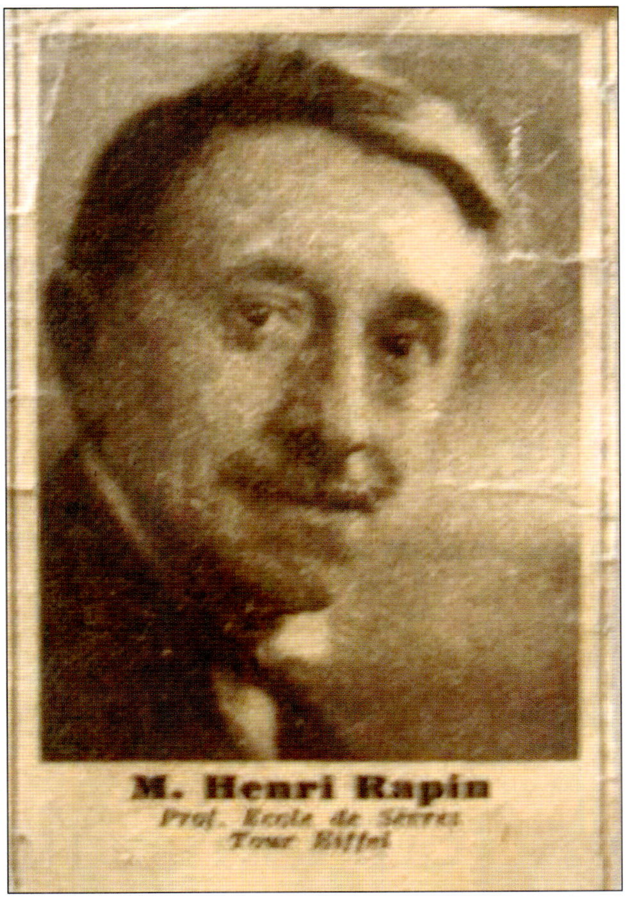

Henri Rapin.

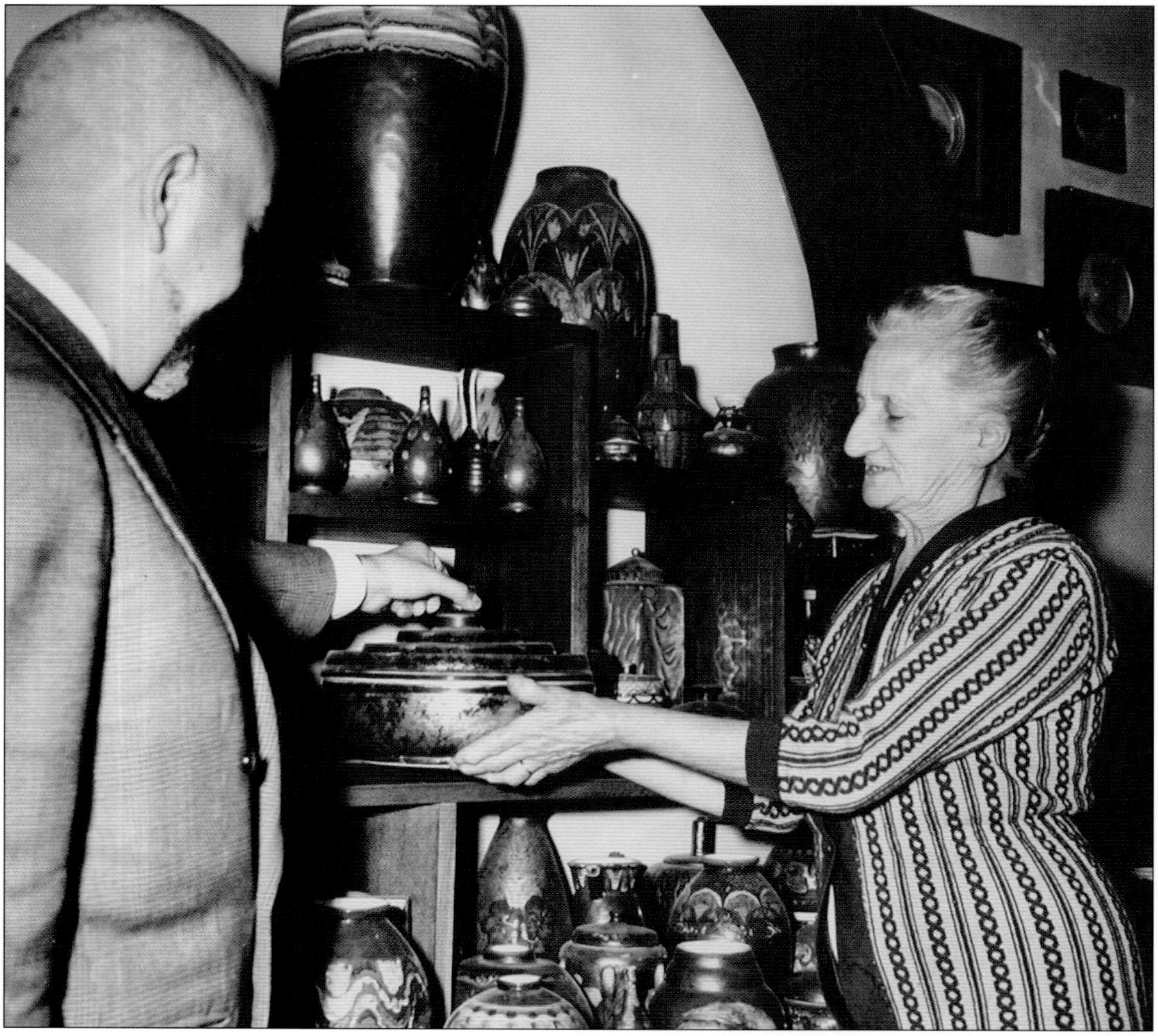

Berthe Tharaud.

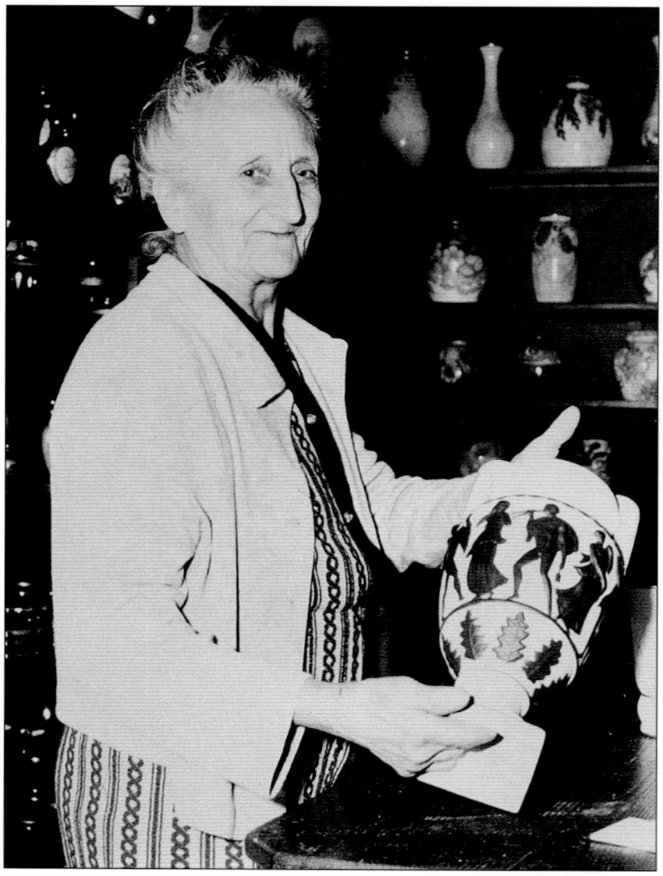

Berthe Tharaud.

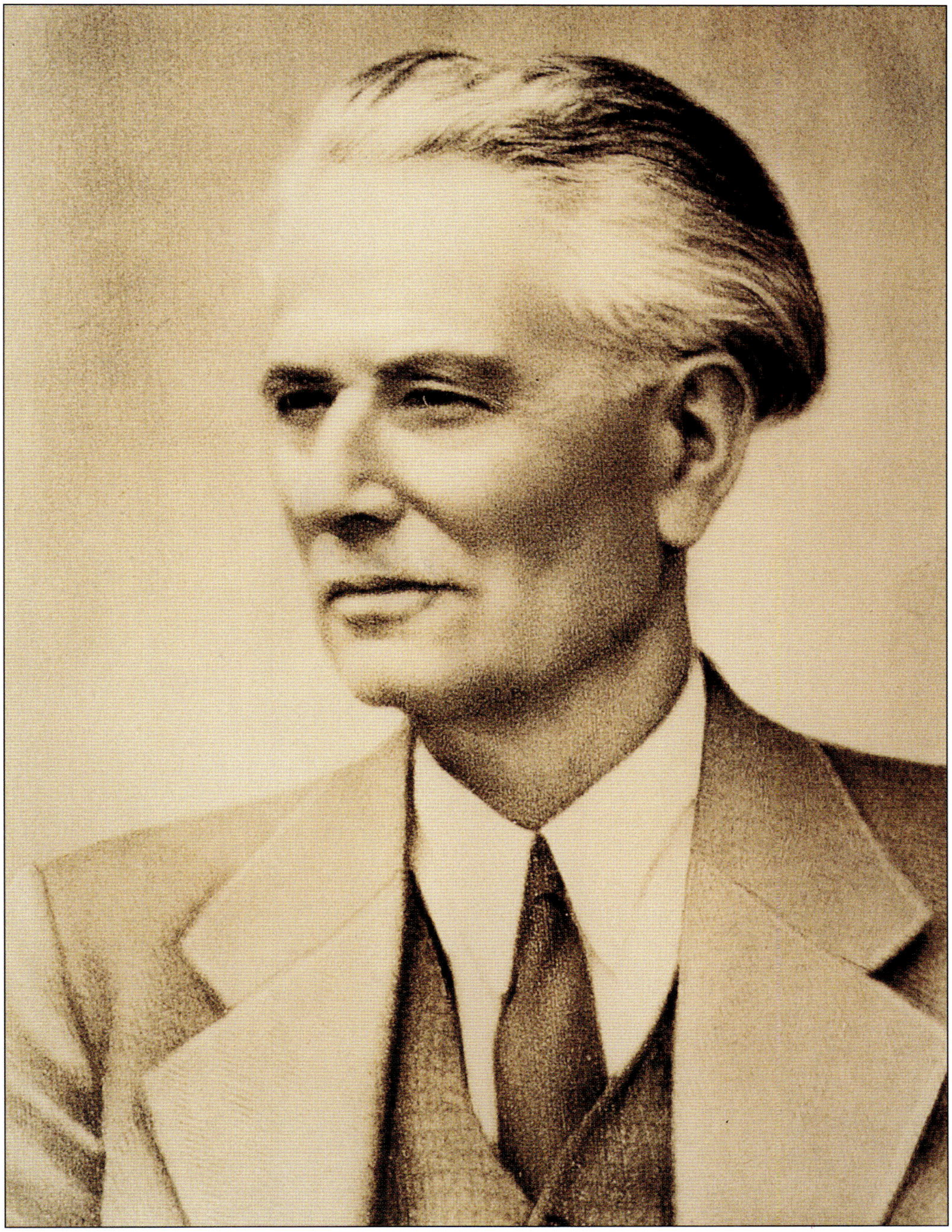

Camille Tharaud.

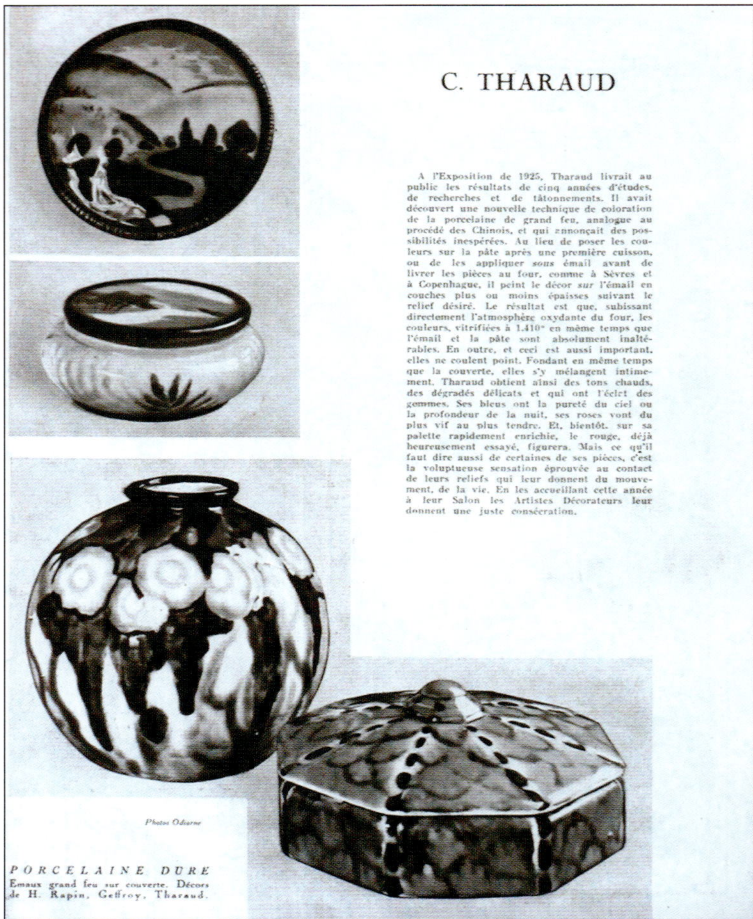

C. THARAUD

A l'Exposition de 1925, Tharaud livrait au public les résultats de cinq années d'études, de recherches et de tâtonnements. Il avait découvert une nouvelle technique de coloration de la porcelaine de grand feu, analogue au procédé des Chinois, et qui annonçait des possibilités inespérées. Au lieu de poser les couleurs sur la pâte après une première cuisson, ou de les appliquer *sous* émail avant de livrer les pièces au four, comme à Sèvres et à Copenhague, il peint le décor *sur* l'émail en couches plus ou moins épaisses suivant le relief désiré. Le résultat est que, subissant directement l'atmosphère oxydante du four, les couleurs, vitrifiées à 1.410° en même temps que l'émail et la pâte sont absolument inaltérables. En outre, et ceci est aussi important, elles ne coulent point. Fondant en même temps que la couverte, elles s'y mélangent intimement. Tharaud obtient ainsi des tons chauds, des dégradés délicats et qui ont l'éclat des gemmes. Ses bleus ont la pureté du ciel ou la profondeur de la nuit, ses roses vont du plus vif au plus tendre. Et, bientôt, sur sa palette rapidement enrichie, le rouge, déjà heureusement essayé, figurera. Mais ce qu'il faut dire aussi de certaines de ses pièces, c'est la voluptueuse sensation éprouvée au contact de leurs reliefs qui leur donnent du mouvement, de la vie. En les accueillant cette année à leur Salon les Artistes Décorateurs leur donnent une juste consécration.

Photos Odiarne

PORCELAINE DURE
Emaux grand feu sur couverte. Décors de H. Rapin, Geffroy, Tharaud.

Tharaud pieces exhibit at the 1925 Exposition internationale des arts décoratifs industriels et moderns, Paris. In summary the article says that Tharaud's work represents the results of five years of study and research and of trial and error. He discovered a new technique for color at high fired temperatures, which was similar to the Chinese process. Instead of painting pigments directly on the pastry under the glaze after the first firing—like Copenhagen and Sèvres, Tharaud paints directly on the glaze in thick coats according to the decoration. The pastry and the glaze are totally stable, and they are vitrified at the same time at 1410° which results in subtleties in the decoration.

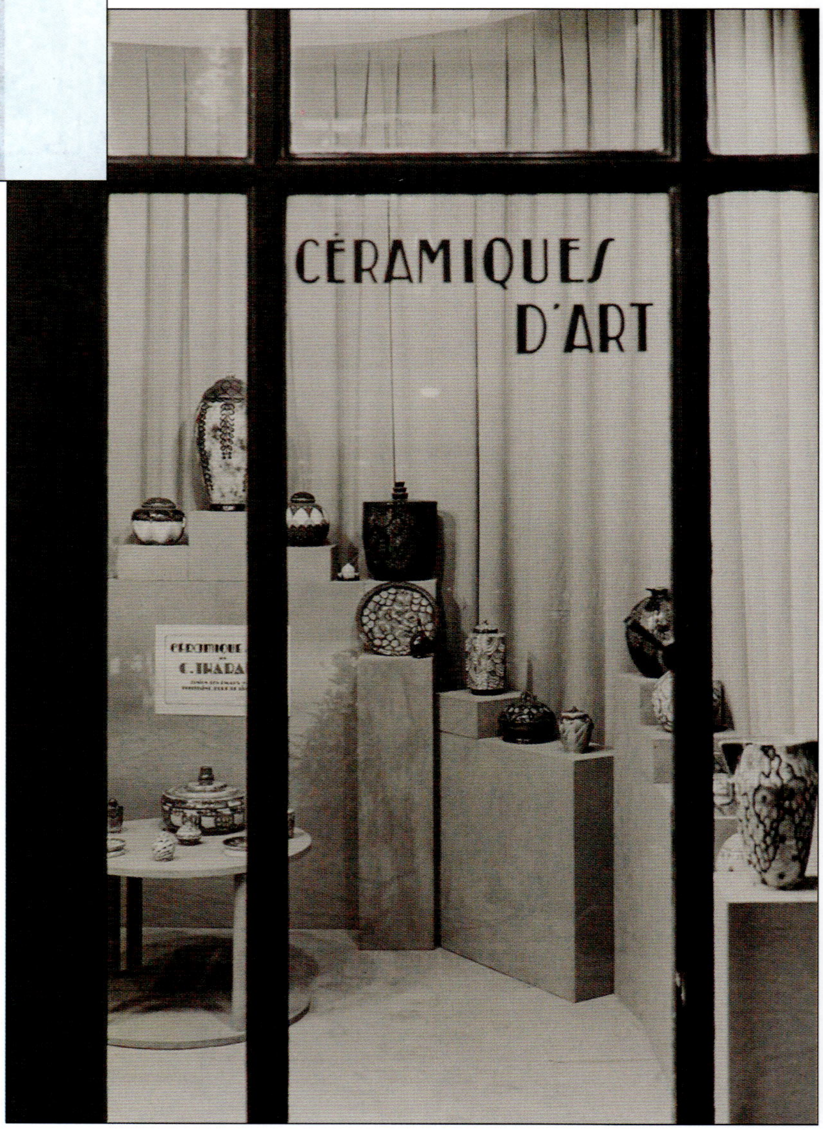

Tharaud's booth at Art du Feu Fair in Paris, which no longer exists.

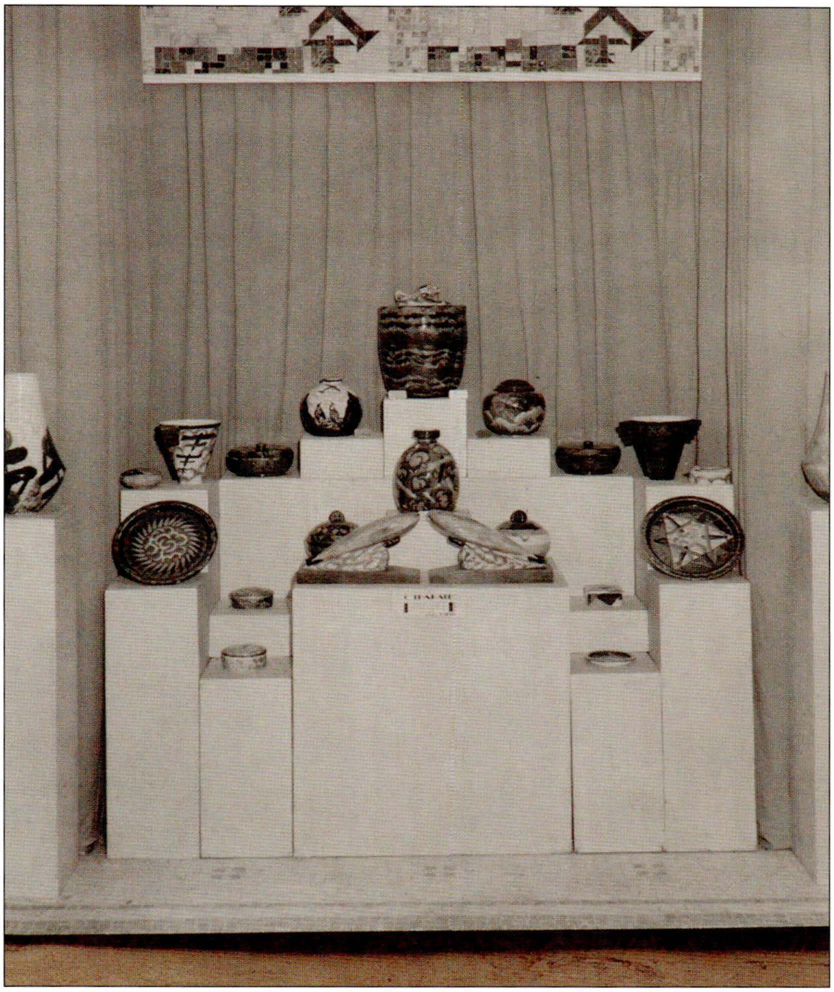

Pieces exhibited at the 1930 Aeronautics Exposition, Paris.

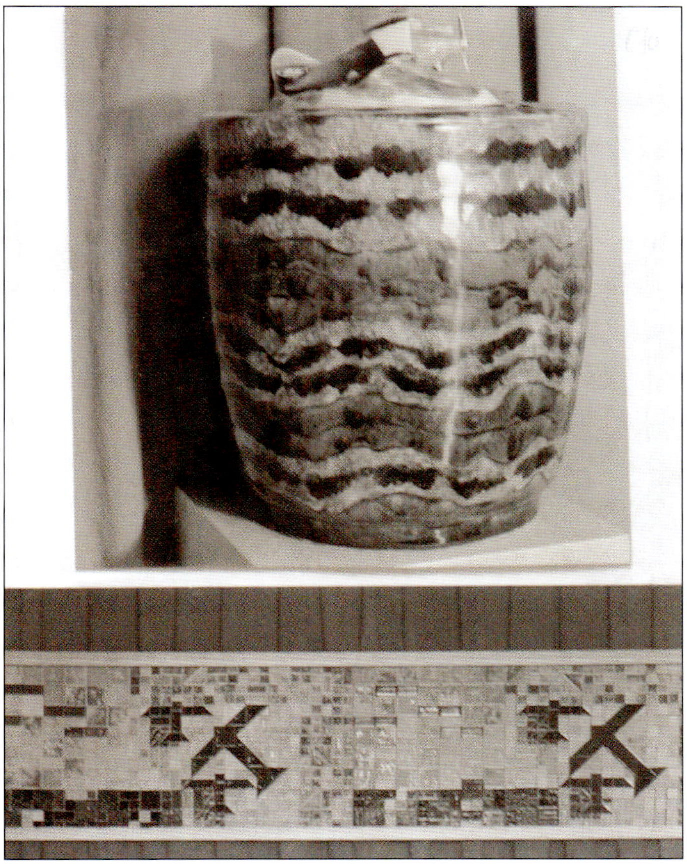

From the 1930 Aeronautics Exposition, Paris.

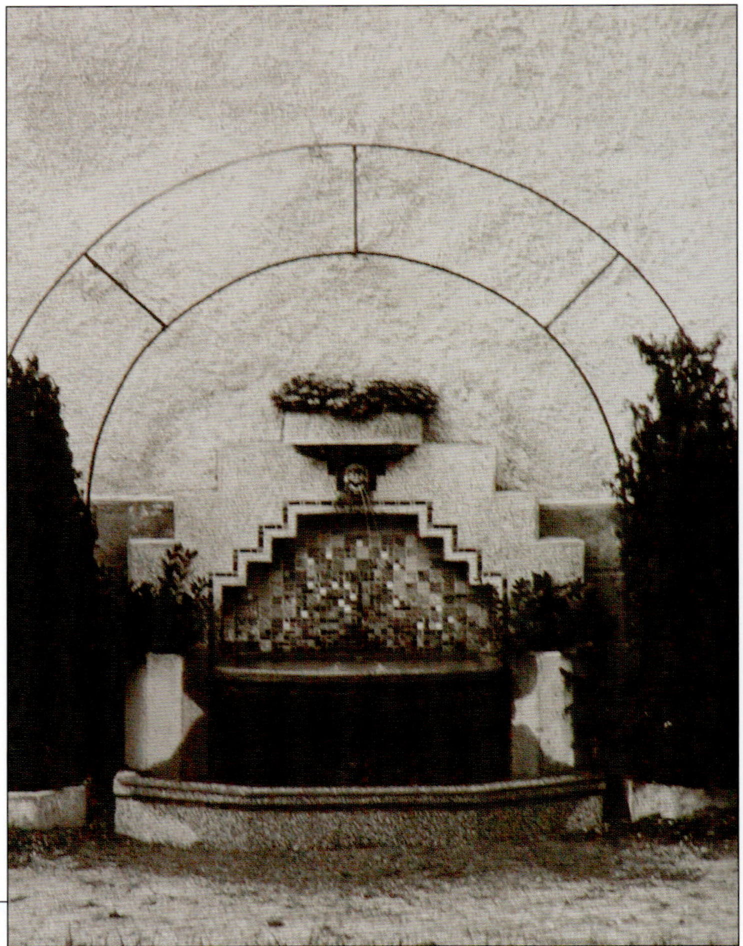

Fountain for the Banque coopérative, 1934.

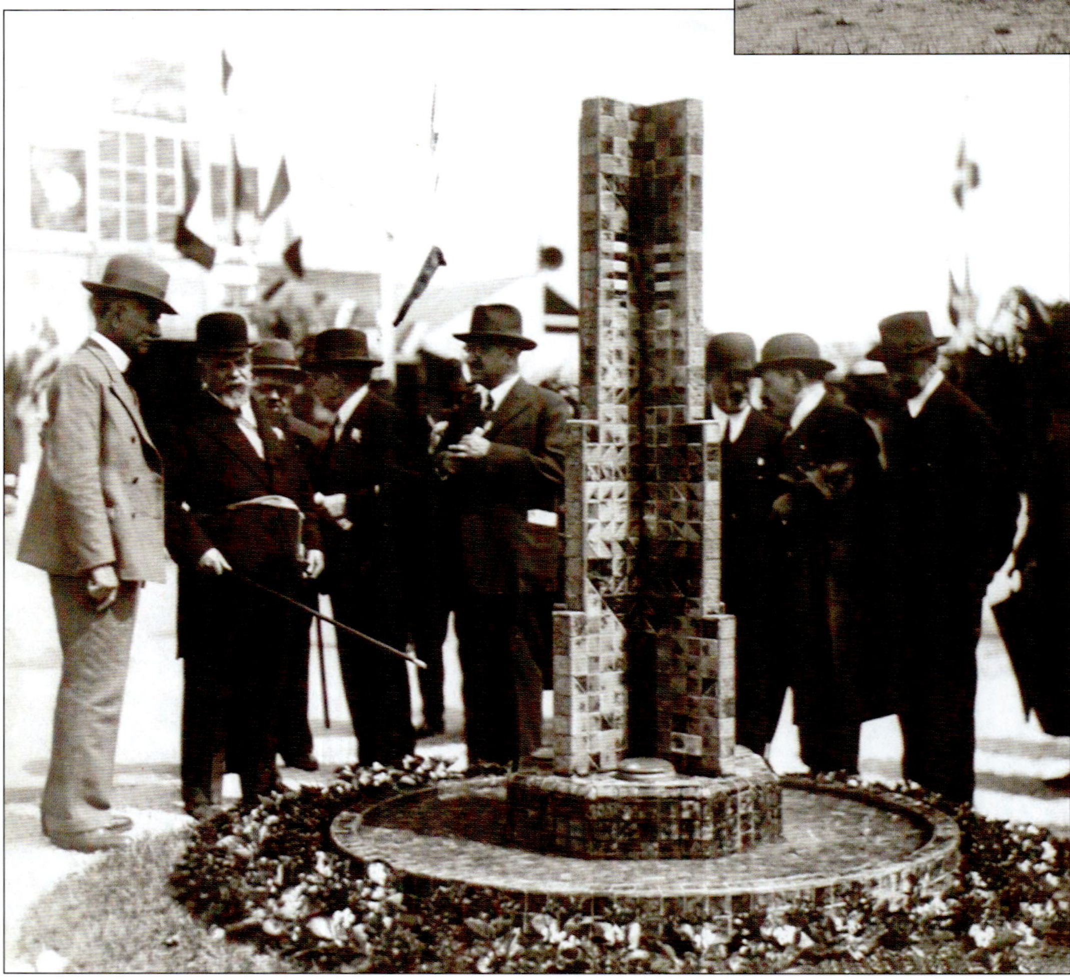

Fountain exhibited at the 1931 Colonial Exposition, Paris.

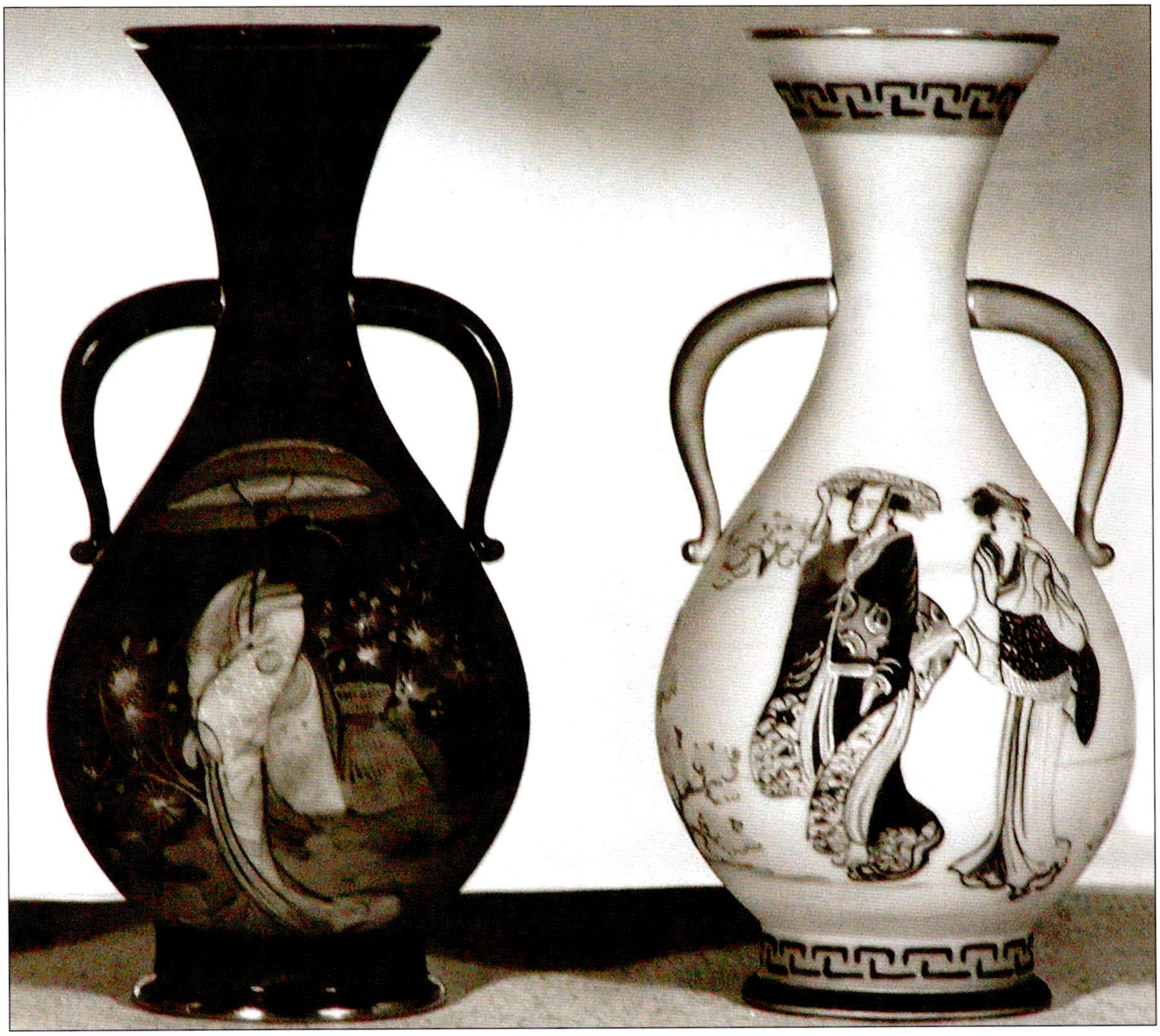

Two unusual Tharaud vases.

Other Art Deco Ceramics

Camille Tharaud, of course, was not the only porcelain company in Limoges and elsewhere that produced Art Deco designs. We have included Art Deco designs by other Limoges companies that are representative of this period. Included also are ceramic pieces made for the Paris retailer that are typical of French Art Deco designs. Of special significance are the photographs of nearly all of the Art Deco dinnerware patterns made by the Limoges firm, Gérard, Dufraisseix, Abbot (GDA), now Royal Limoges. This is the first time that these patterns have been published, and they represent a broad spectrum of Art Deco design in Limoges.

Robj

Any discussion of Art Deco ceramics in France must include Robj, because of the success of its fanciful and humorous ceramic objects. Robj was a retailer, and not a manufacturer, and it commissioned companies in Limoges and elsewhere to produce ceramics. Robj became famous for its design competitions. Major design competitions in ceramics and porcelain were held in 1927, 1928, and 1929, and pieces were awarded prizes. Robj often ordered objects semi-finished—"they are then coloured by low firing at the decorator's studio, where they also be 'personalized' and given the appropriate finish." (Brega)

Robj was founded by Jean Born during the first decade of the twentieth century. After Born died in a car accident, Lucien Willemtez took over the management of Robj and the firm began its most successful period, beginning in 1922 and continuing until the retailer closed in 1931. The major ceramic objects were nightlights, perfume lamps, liqueur bottles, ashtrays, inkwells, and bookends.

It is clear that many of the porcelain liqueur bottles and other objects were made by Limoges companies, since some of the objects still retain a Limoges porcelain mark and some of the same blanks were sold directly by the Limoges companies with their own decorating marks. When we are certain that the blank was made by a Limoges company, we identify it as from Limoges. For many of the Robj porcelain objects, however, it is not possible to identify the original manufacturer. Nevertheless we have included many Robj pieces because they are wonderful examples of the French Art Deco period.

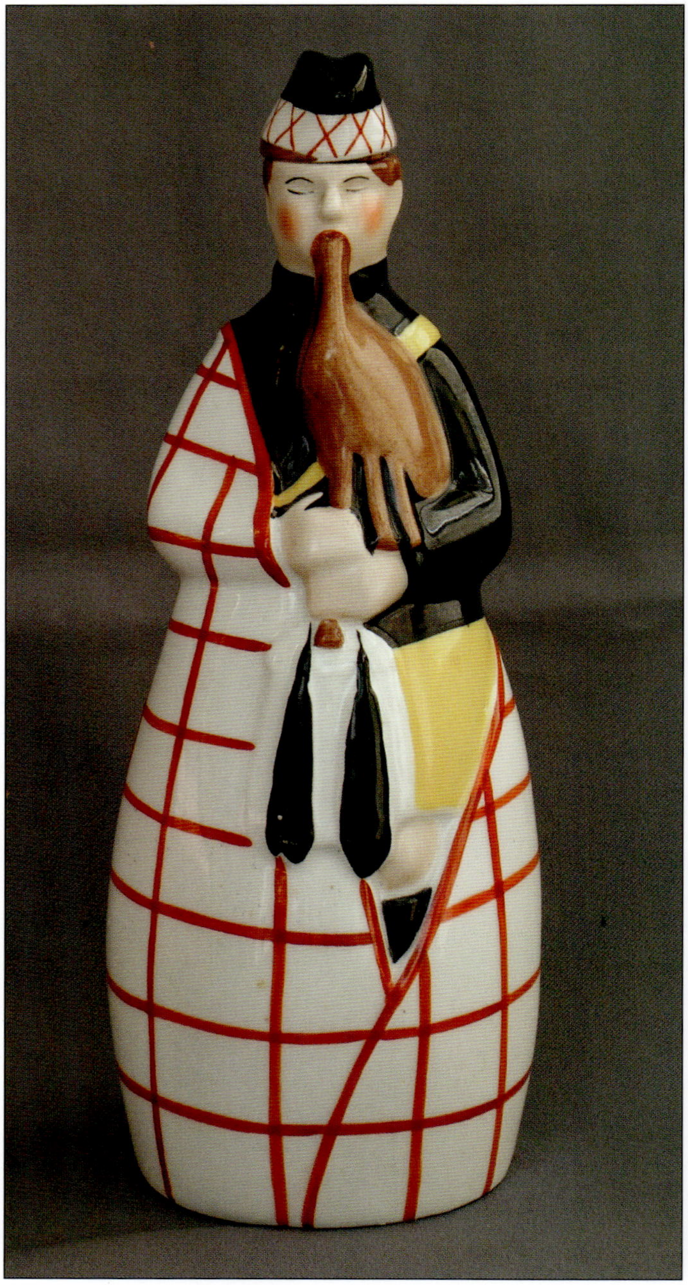

Bagpipe Player flask, also called the Scotsman, 10" high. Less than $500.

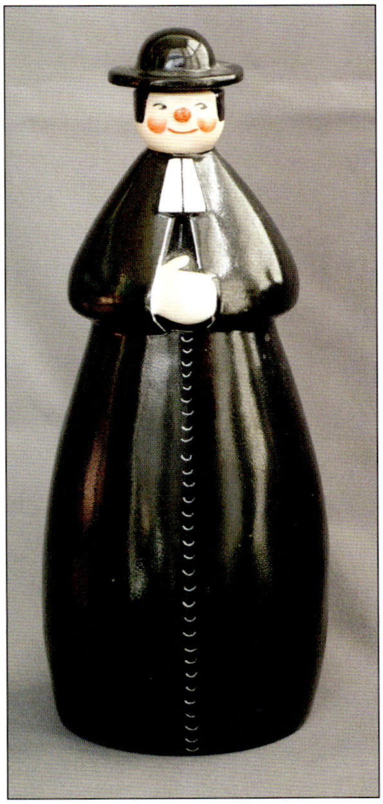

Benedictine flask, 10.25" high, figure dressed as Benedictine monk, the origin of Benedictine liqueur, made in Limoges. Less than $500.

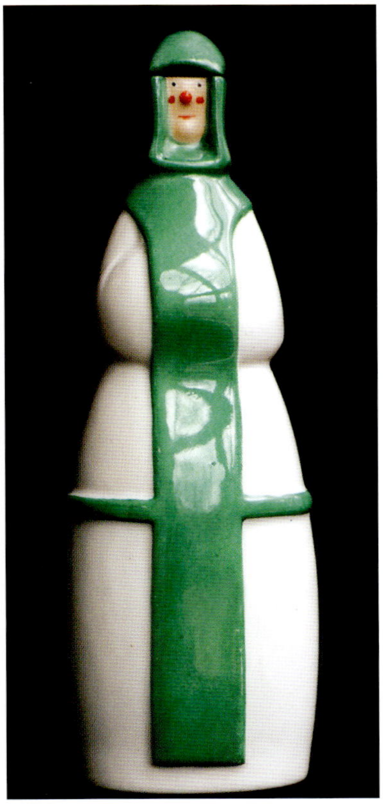

Chartreuse, 10" high, dressed like a Carthusian monk, where chartreuse originated. $1,000-$1,500.

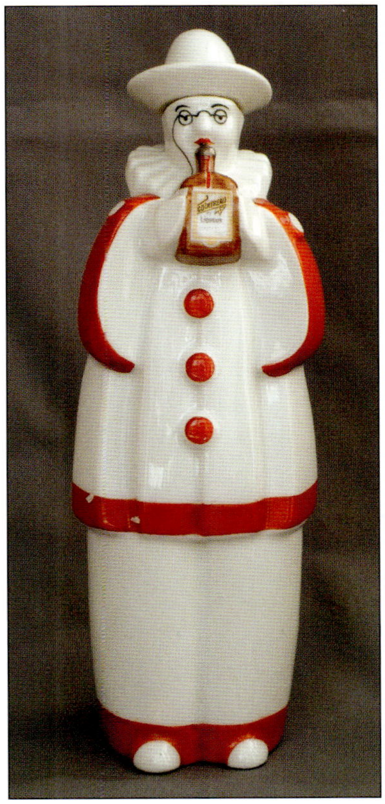

Cointreau flask, 10.25" high; marked, creation de Robj Paris pour Cointreau liqueur, Angers, made in France. $1,000-$1,500.

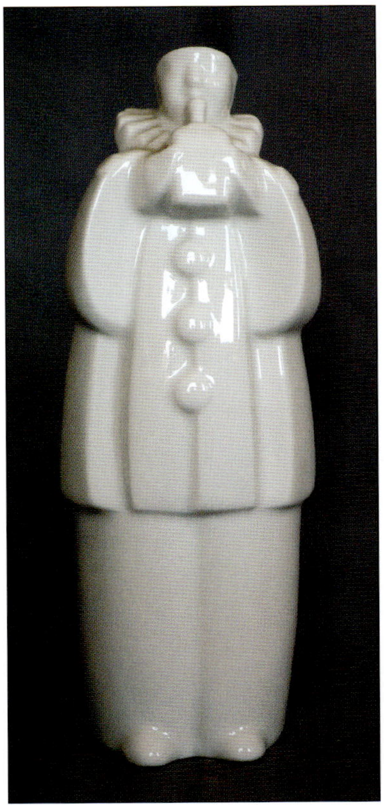

Blank for Cointreau, made by GDA and located in Royal Limoges museum.

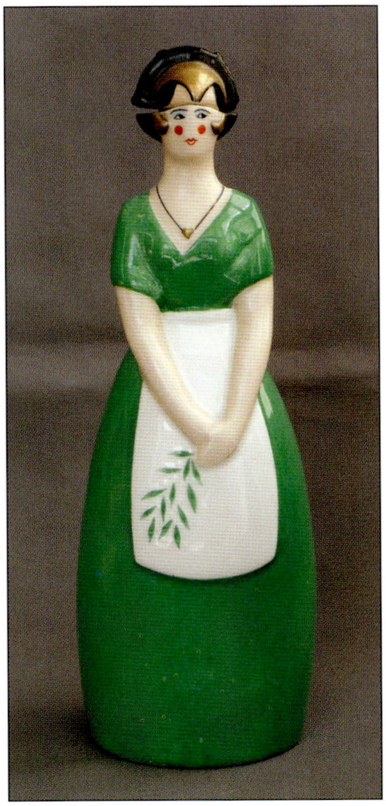

Cusenier flask, "Genièvre" de Cusenier, 10.5" high, Cusenier SA is located in the Languedoc-Roussillon region of France. Less than $500.

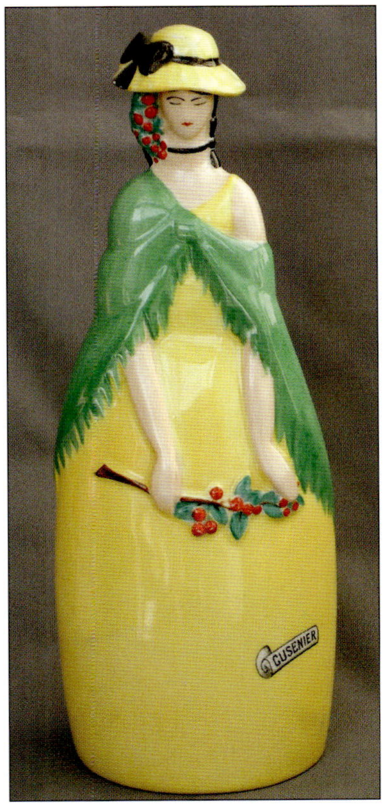

Cusenier flask, 10.75" high. $1,000-$1,500.

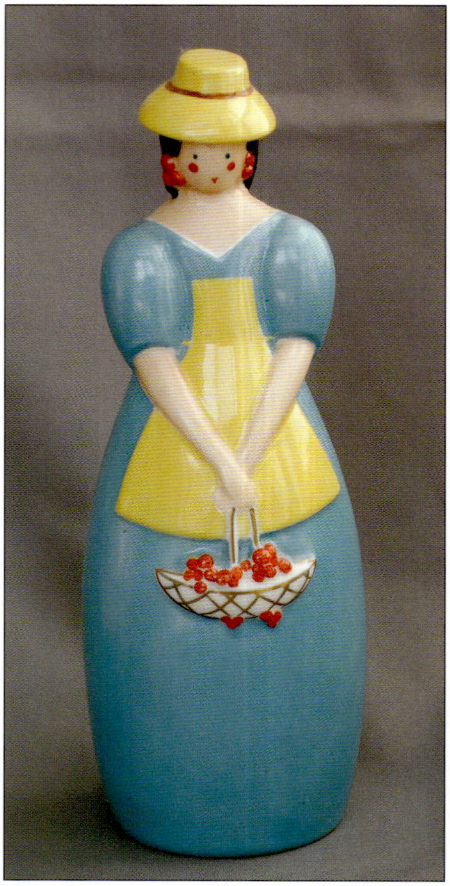

Guignolet flask, 10" high, lady in typical dress of Alsace, the origin of the dark cherries, guignes, (in lady's basket) from which guignolet is made, blanks made by Michelaud in Limoges. $500-$1,000.

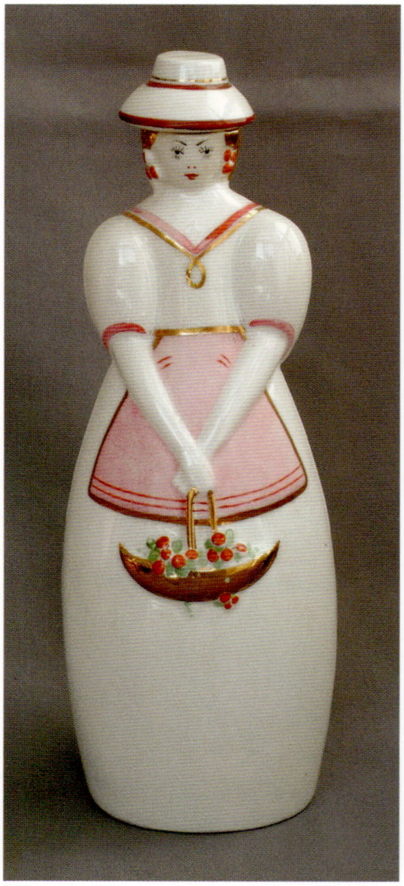

Flask, 10" high, not marked Robj; marked on back, Tangerine liqueur by Roger fils of Bordeausc, made by Michelaud in Limoges. Less than $500.

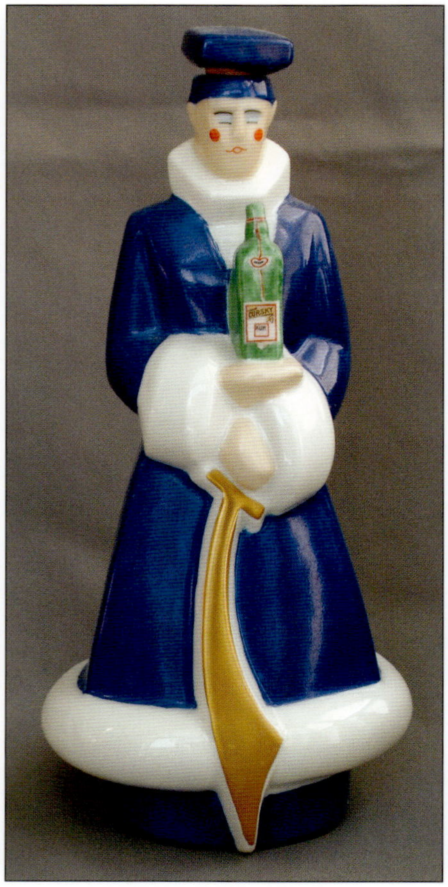

Kummel Cursky de Cointreau flask, 10.75" high; marked, creation de Robj Paris pour le Kummel Cursky de Cointreau, Angers, made in France. $1,000-$1,500.

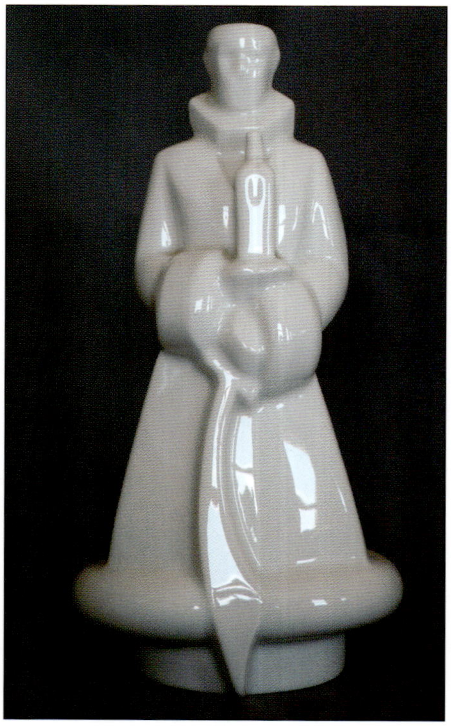

Blank for Kummel Cursky de Cointreau, made by GDA and located in Royal Limoges museum.

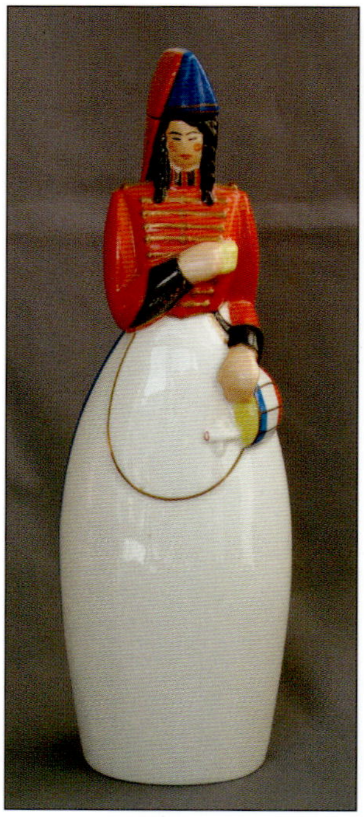

La Cantiniere flask, 12" high. La Cantiniere is the name of a pretty young lady who cooks for soldiers—a camp waitress. $500-$1,000.

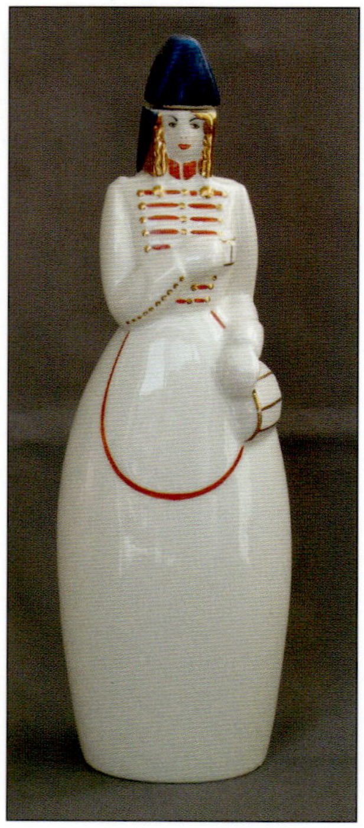

Flask, 12" high, same shape as La Cantiniere, not marked Robj, marked Michelaud, in Limoges. Less than $500.

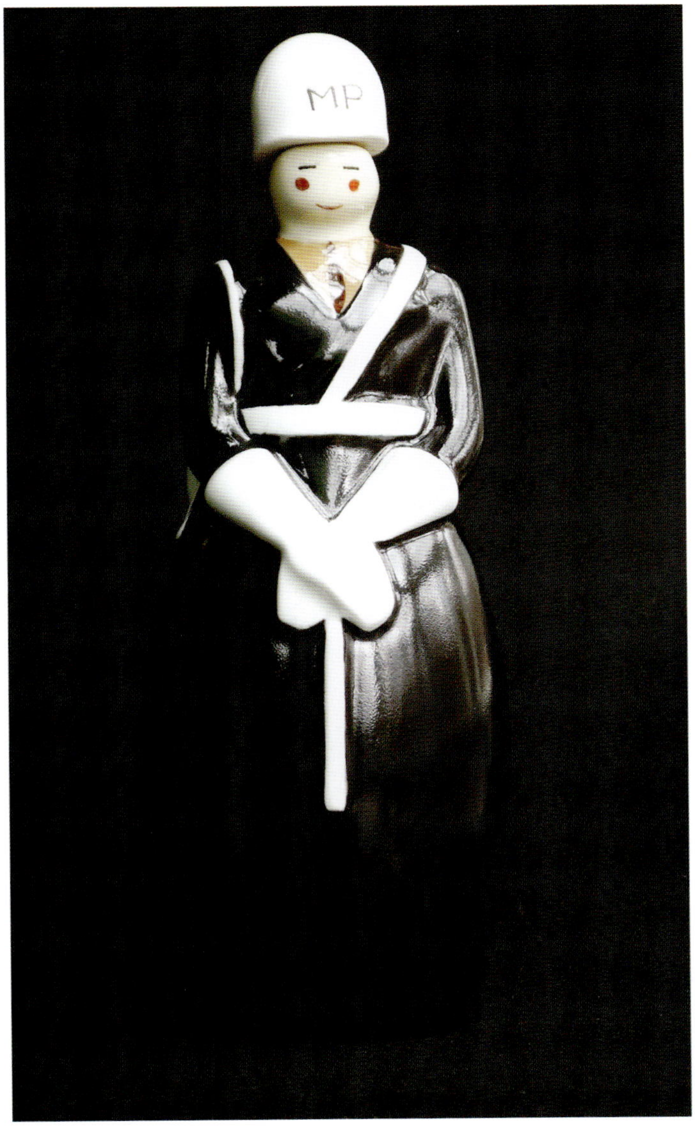

Military Police, 10.25" high. $1,000-$1,500.

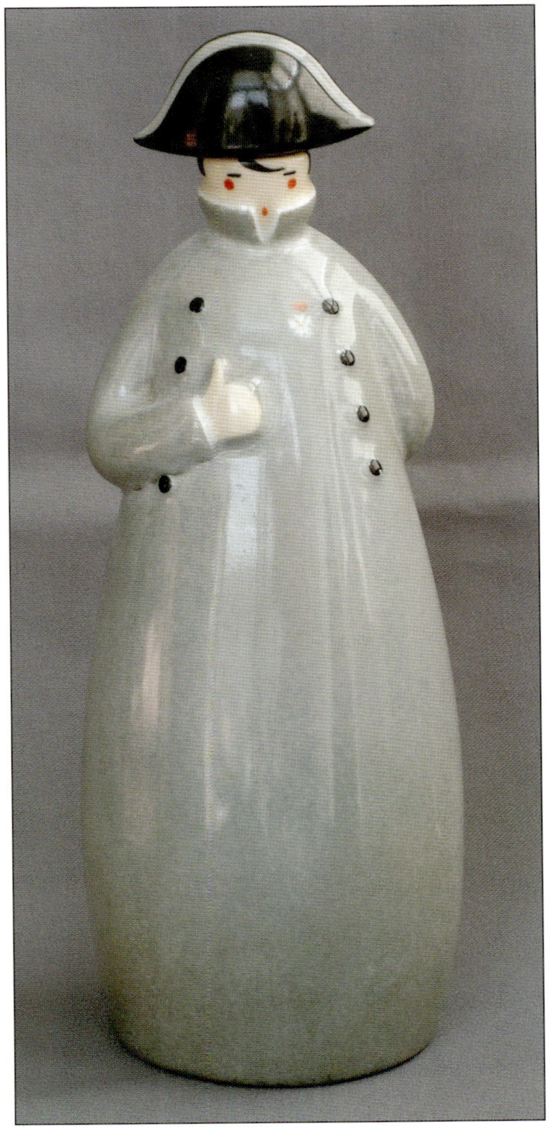

Napoleon flask, 10.25" high, made in Limoges. Less than $500.

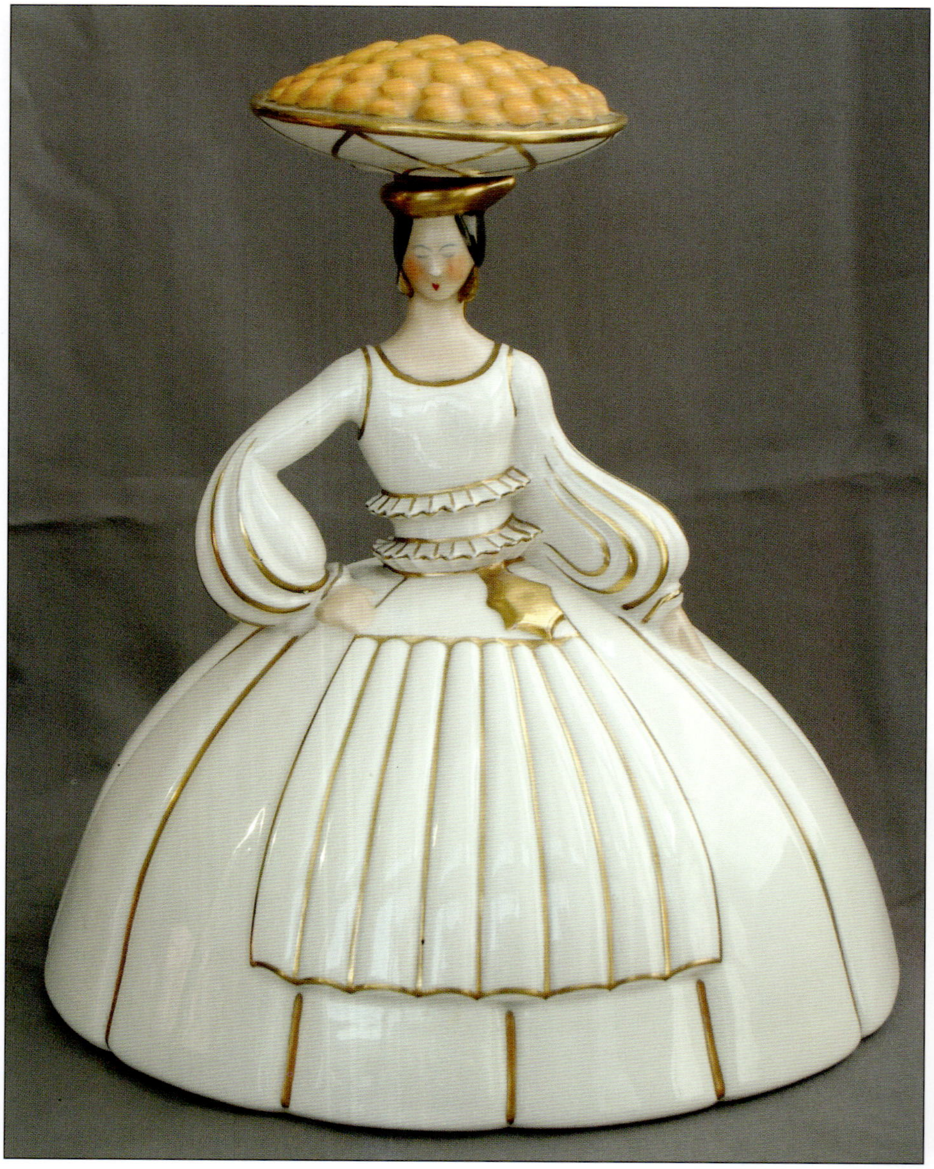

The Orange merchant flask, 11" high x 9.75" diameter at base, probably held Curaçao, an orange based liqueur. $3,000+.

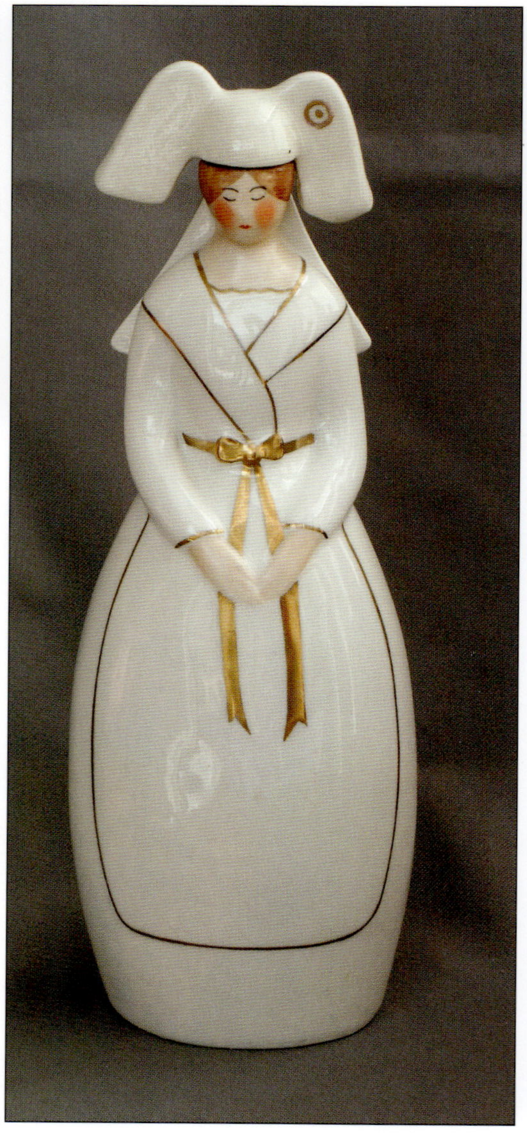

Prunelle flask, 10" high, figured dressed in an Alsacienne (Alace-Lorraine) costume. Prunelle is any variety of wild plums, which indicates that this flask held a plum based liqueur, made in Limoges. $500-$1,000.

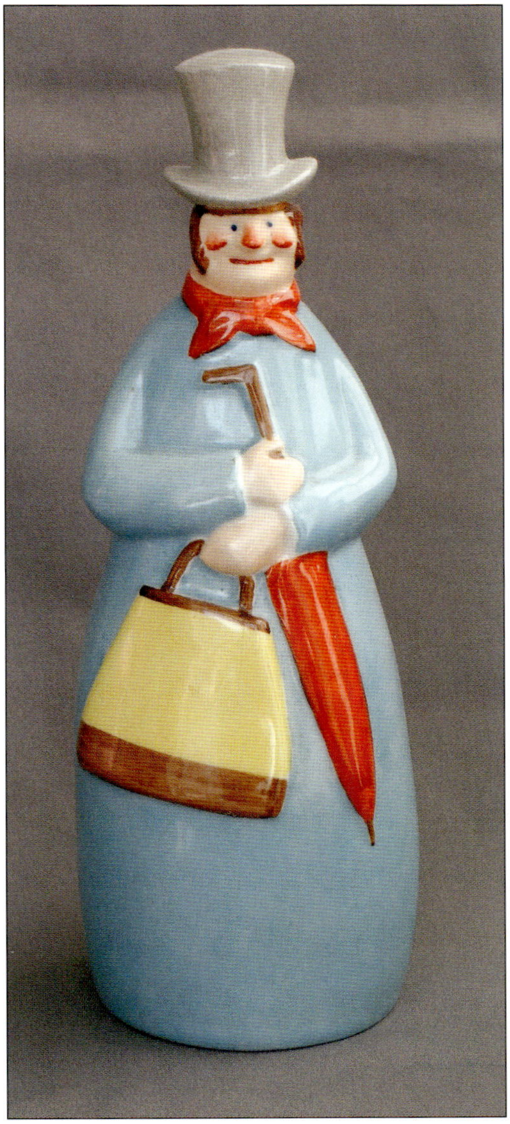

Raspail flask, 10" high, often referred to as the "Englishman," although Raspail was actually a French chemist and politician who died in 1879, a famous boulevard in Paris is named after Raspail, made in Limoges according to d'Albis. Less than $500.

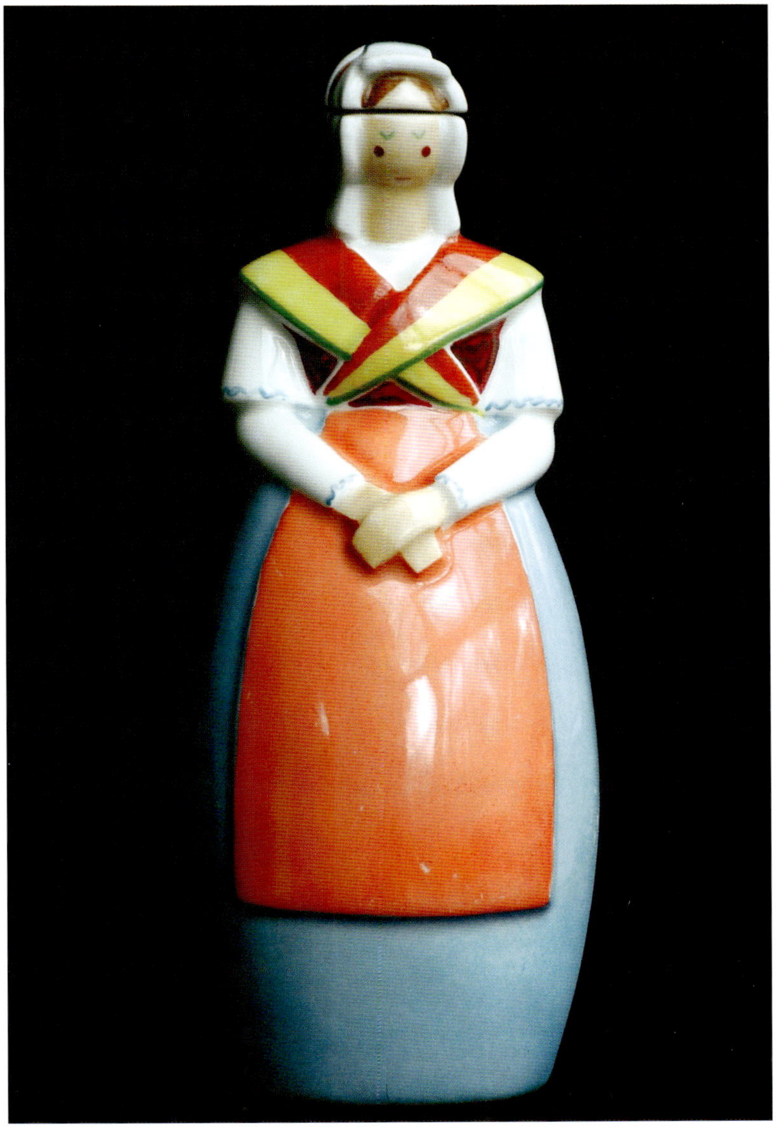

Revolutionary Farmer, 10.5" high, made in Limoges. $1,500-$2,000.

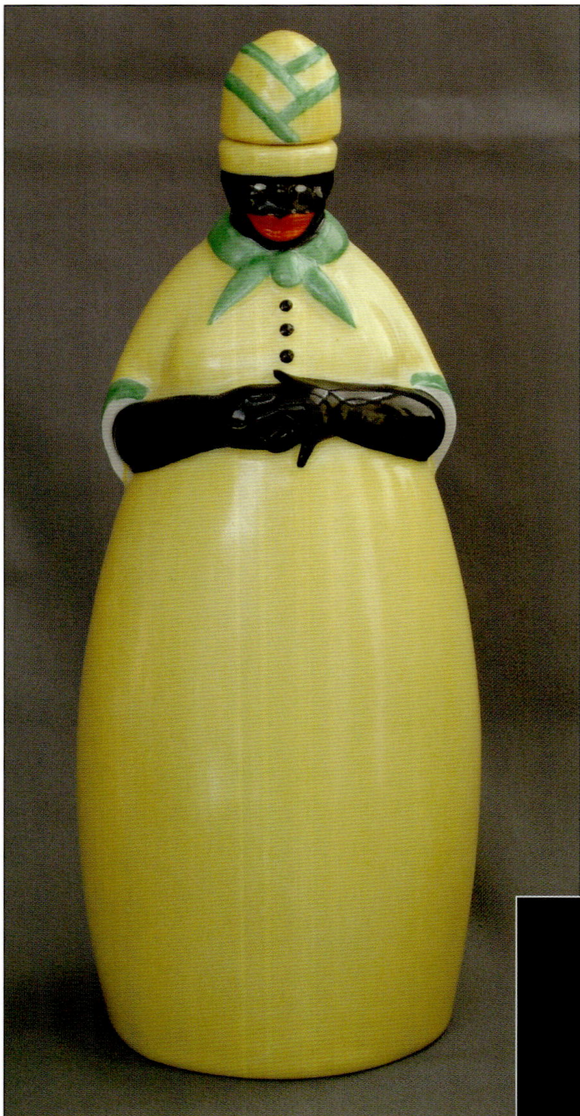

Rum flask, 10.5" high, figured dressed in costume from Martinique, a former French colony and the source of rum imported in France, made in Limoges. $500-$1,000.

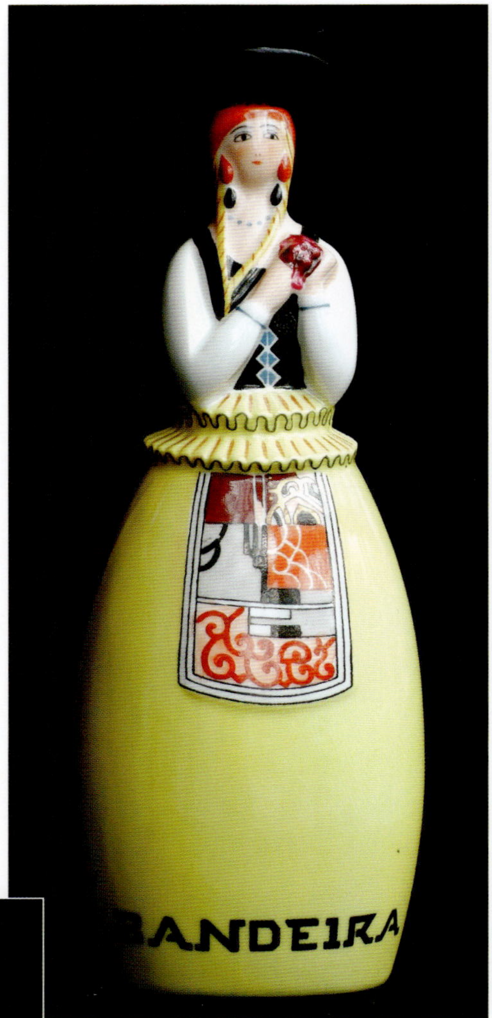

The Spaniard, 10.25" high. $1,500-$2,000.

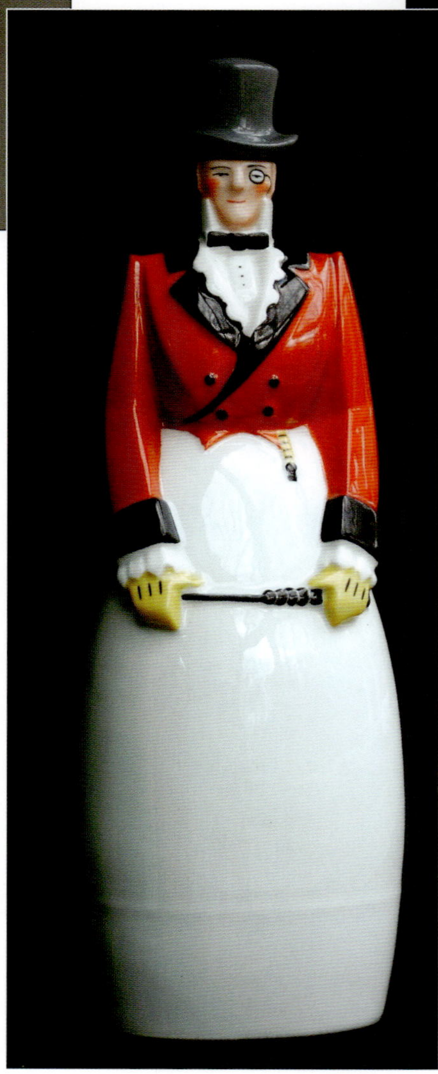

The Tamer, 12" high, a music box on bottom of flask. $2,000-$2,500.

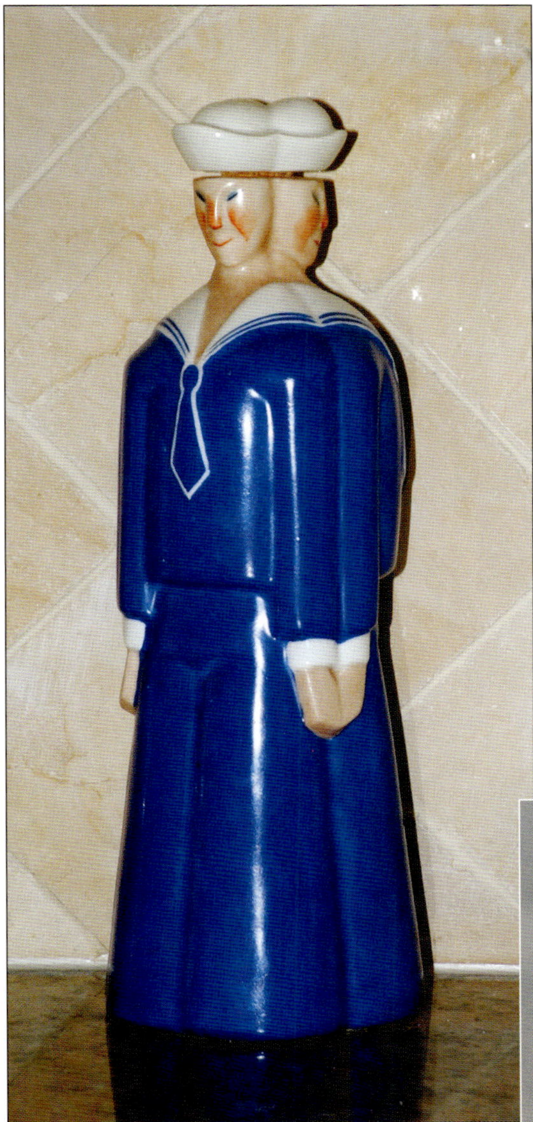

Three sailors flask, 11" high. $2,000-$2,500.

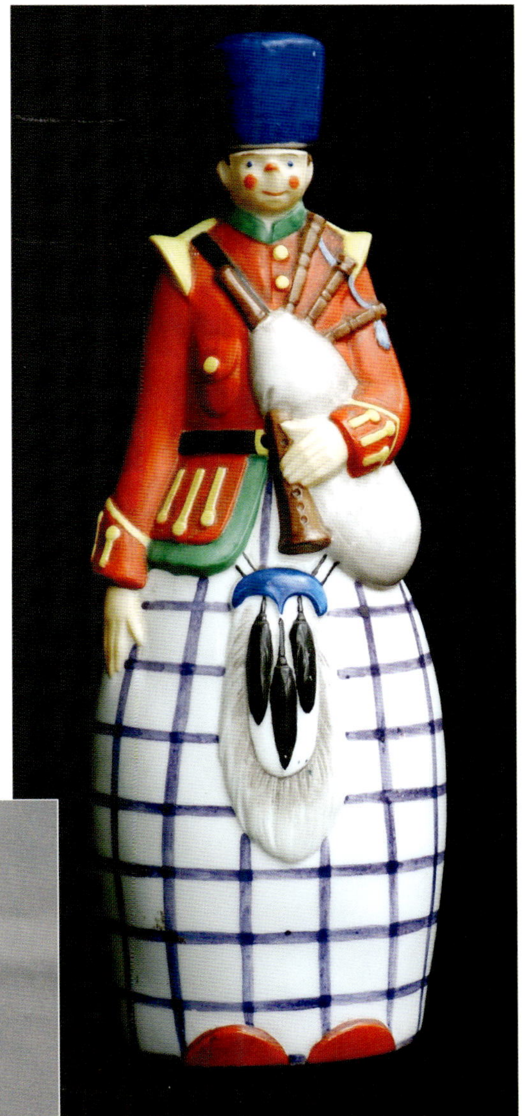

Unidentified Man, 9.5" high. $1,500-$2,000.

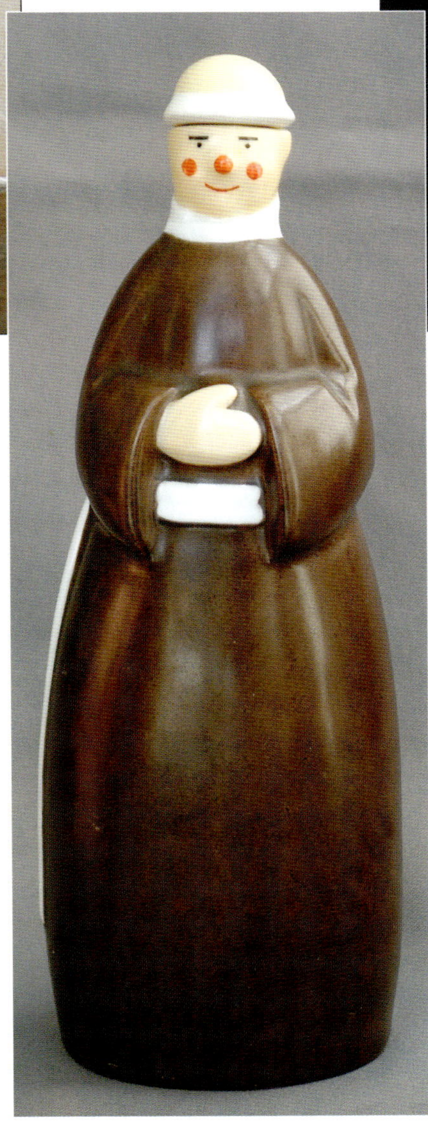

Flask, 10.5" high. Less than $500.

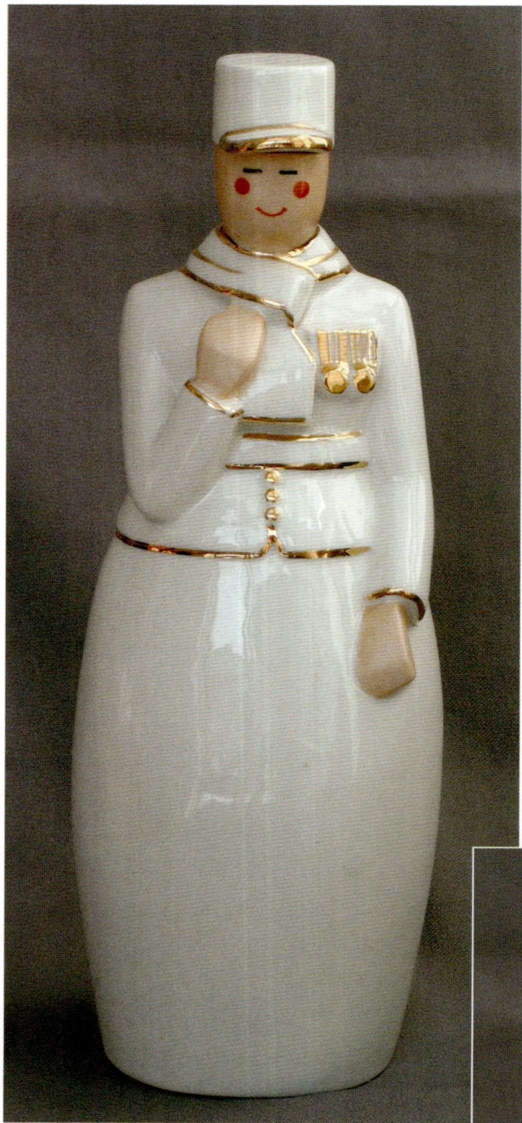

Flask, 10.5" high. Less than $500.

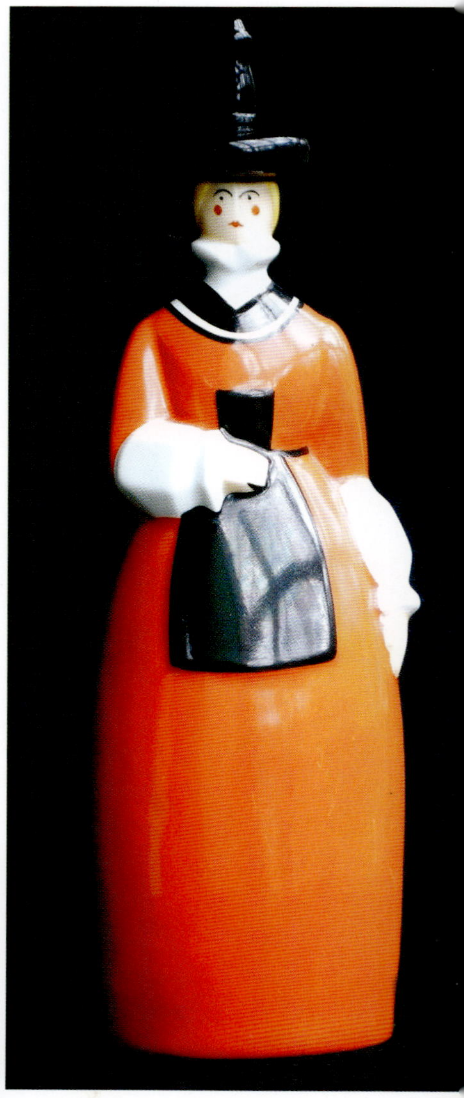

Vodka flask, 10.75" high. $1,000-$1,500.

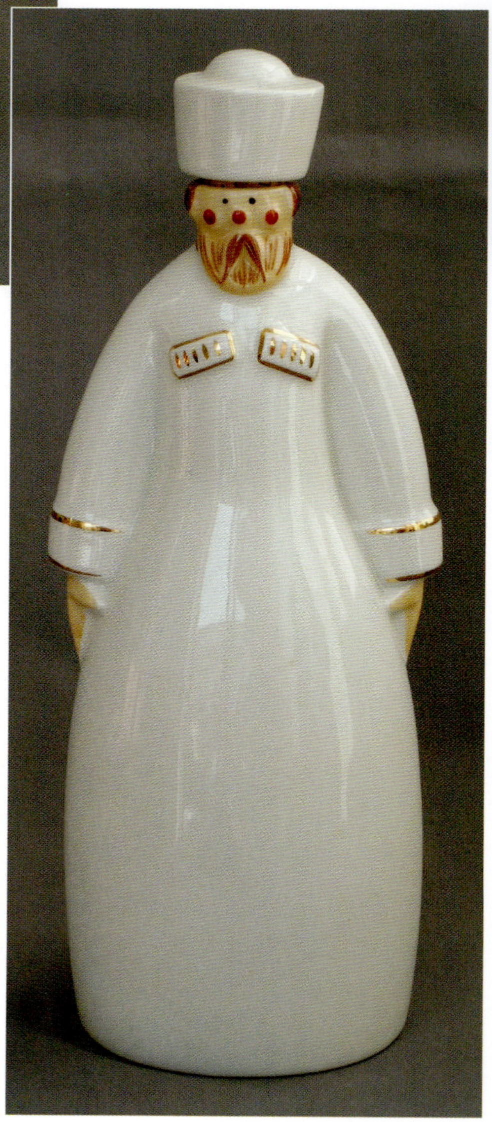

Vodka flask, 10.4" high. Less than $500.

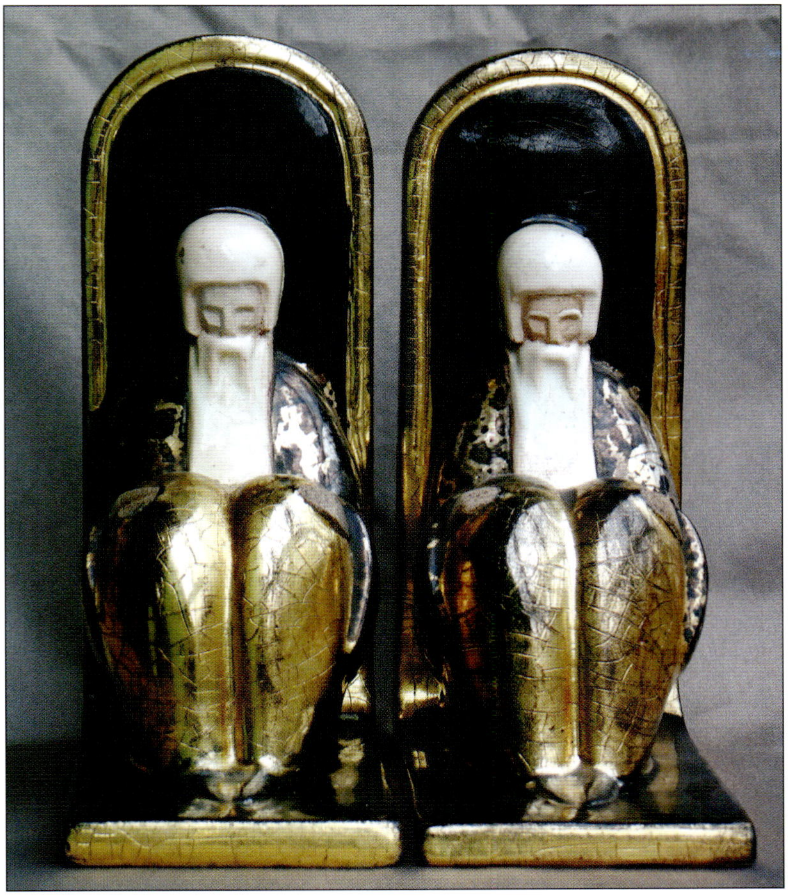

Bookends, 7.25" x 4". $1,500-$2,000.

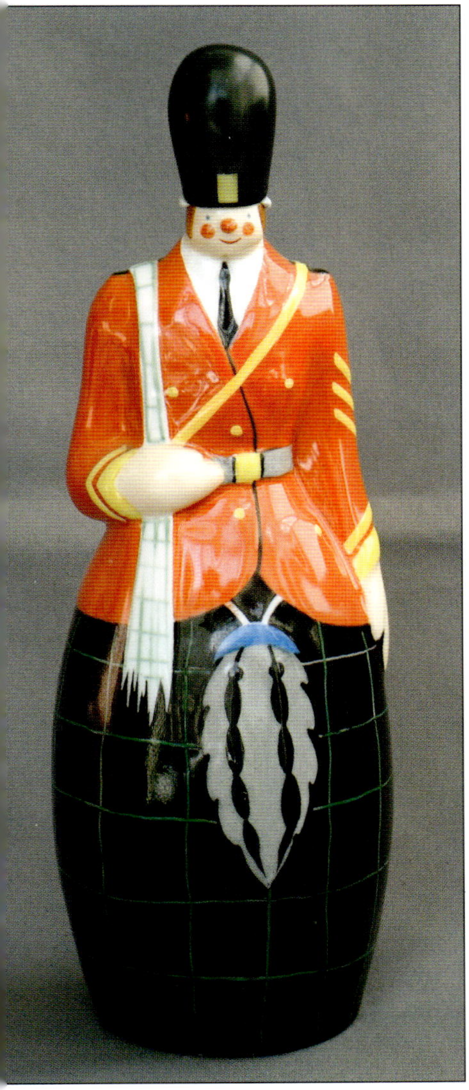

Scotsman, 10.75", figure dressed in costume for Scotland, the main distiller of whiskey. $500-$1,000.

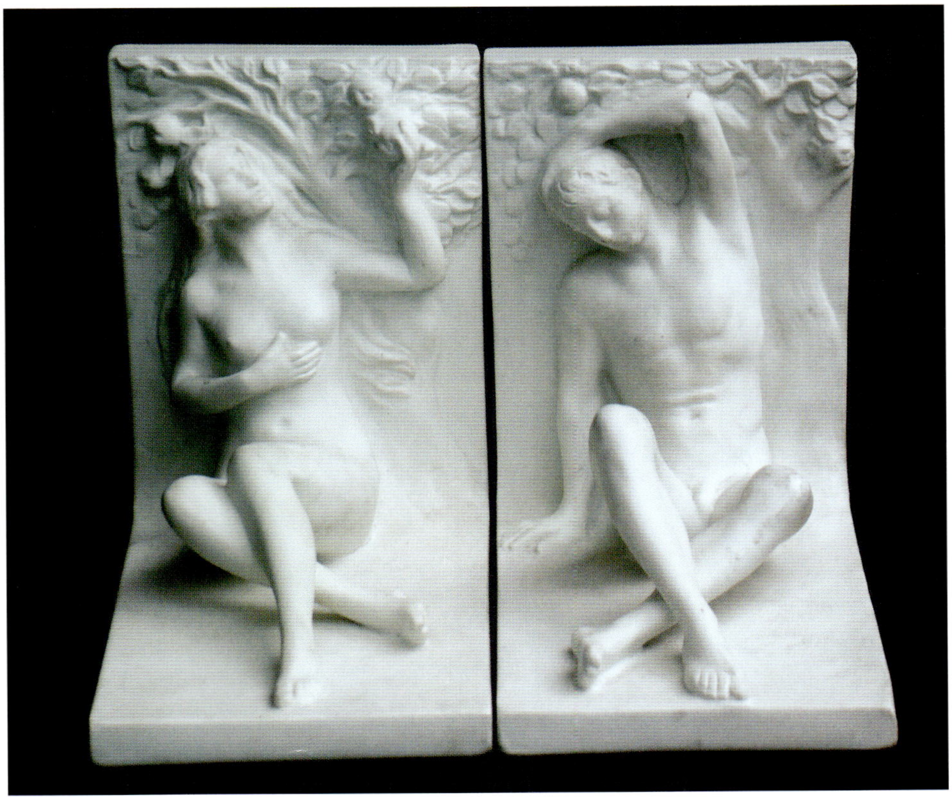

Adam and Eve bookends, 6" x 6". $1,500-$2,000.

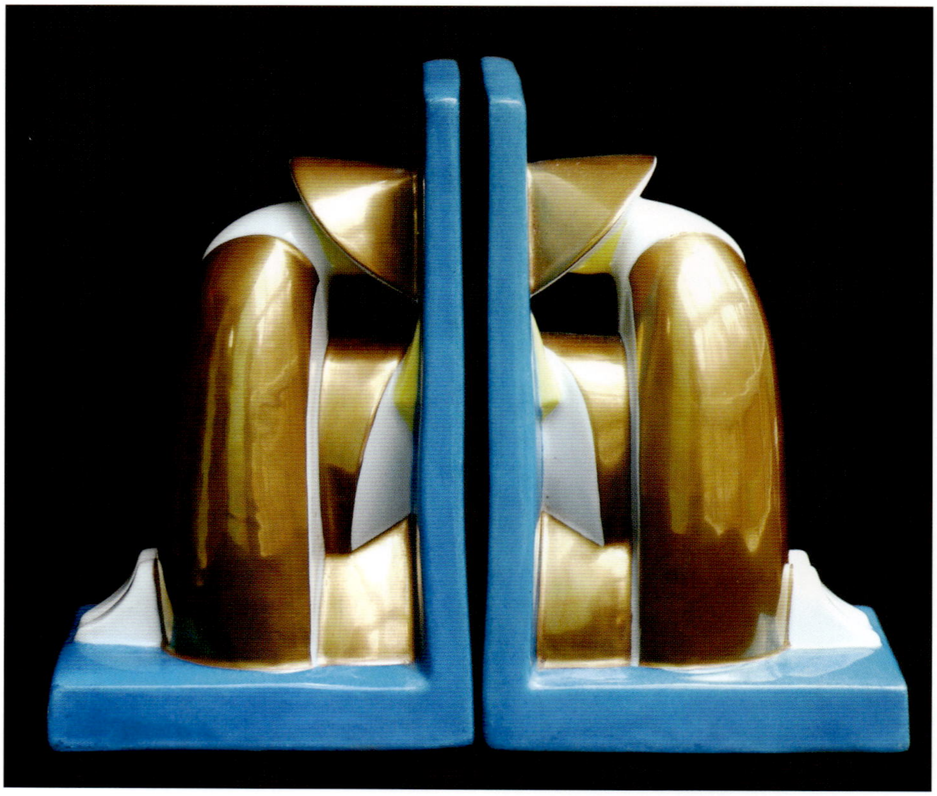

Two Confucian disciples in prayer bookends, 7" x 4". $1,500-$2,000.

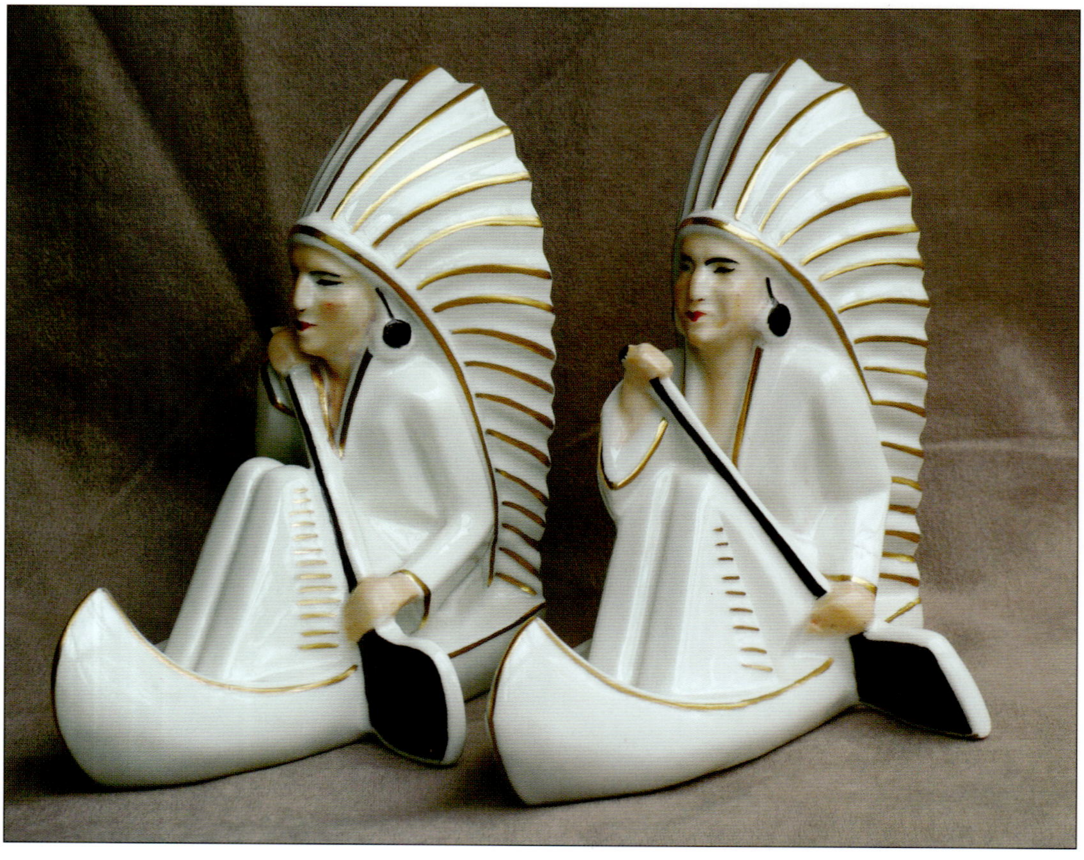

Indian bookends, 6" x 4.75". $1,000-$1,500.

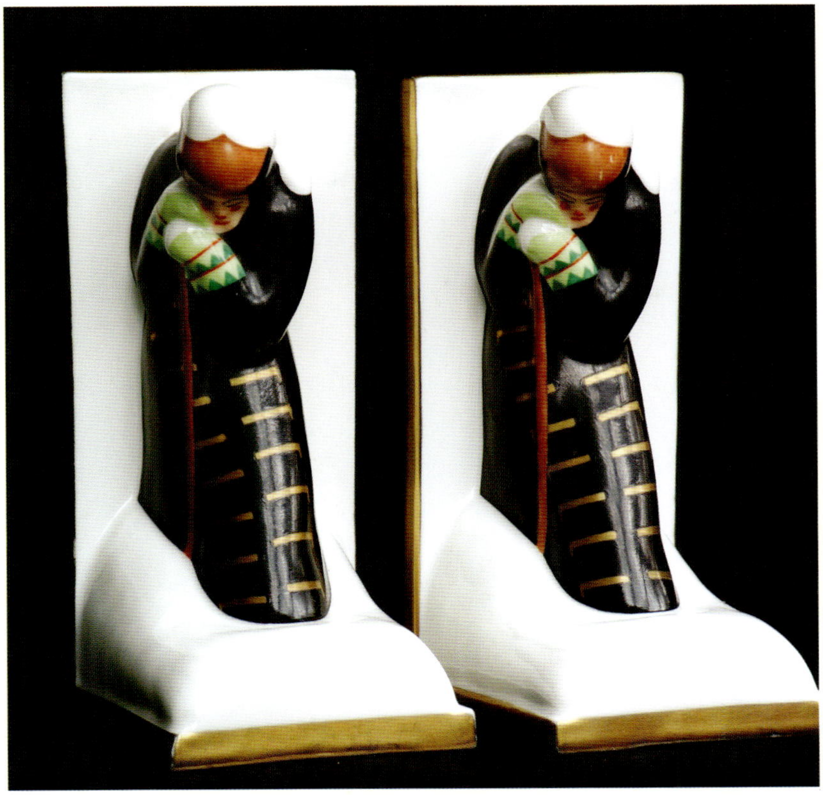

Men in snow bookends, 6.5" x 3" x 2.5". $1,500-$2,000.

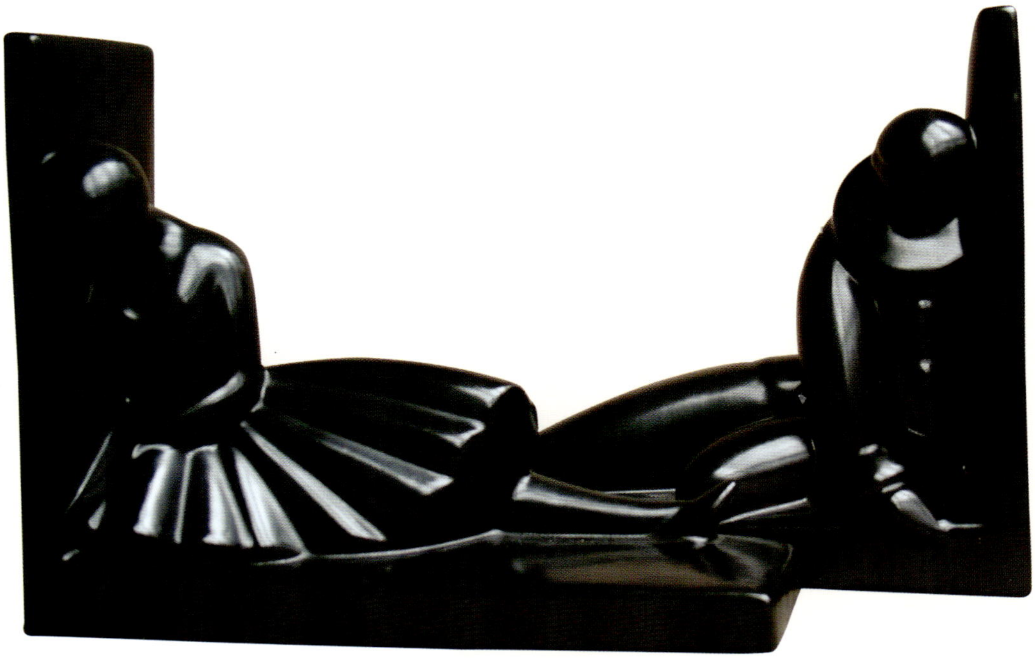

Pierrot bookends, 5.5" x 7". $1,000-$1,500.

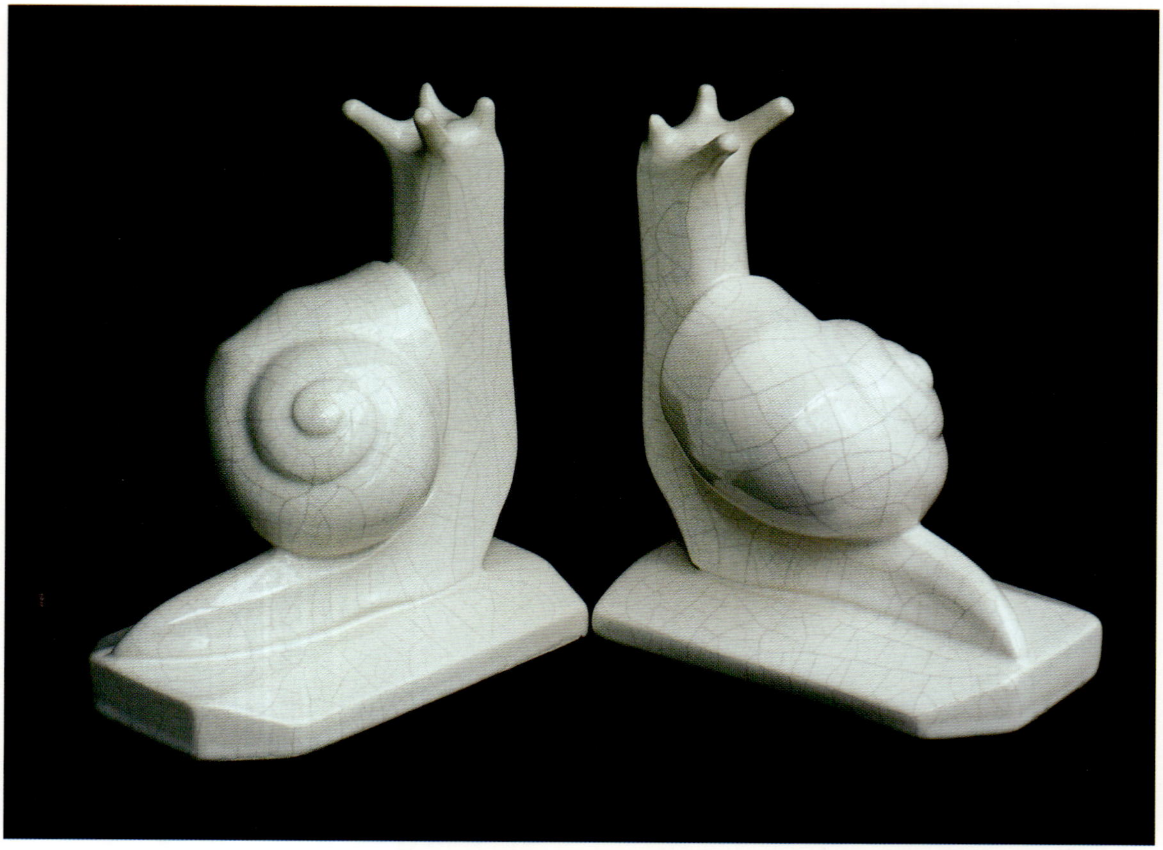

Snail bookends, 6" high. $500-$1,000.

Train bookends, 6" x 5.5". $5,000-$5,500.

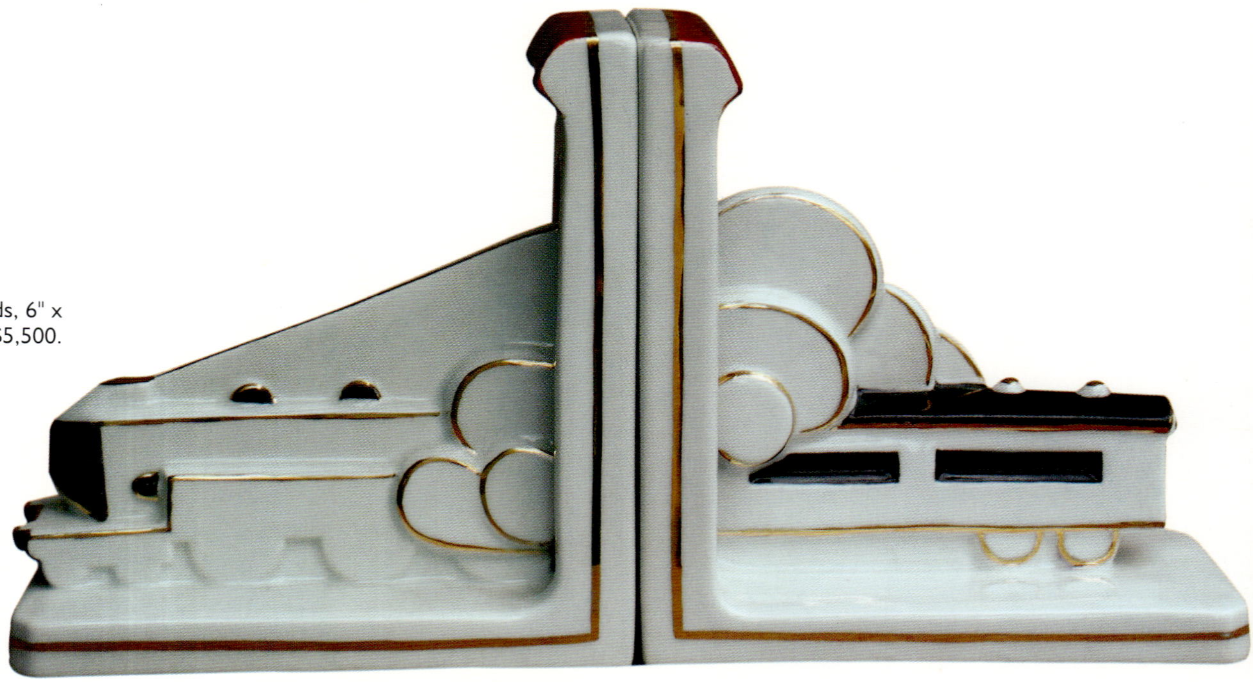

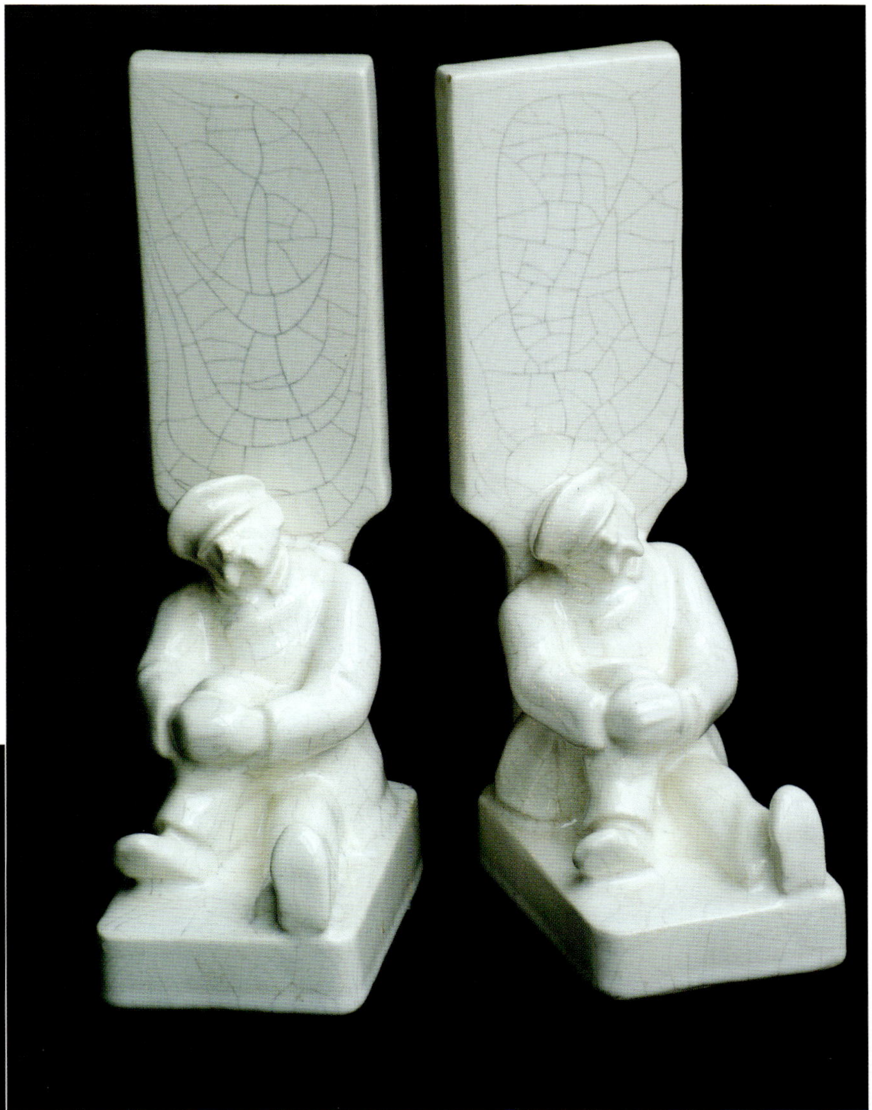

Tramp bookends, 7.25" high. $1,000-$1,500.

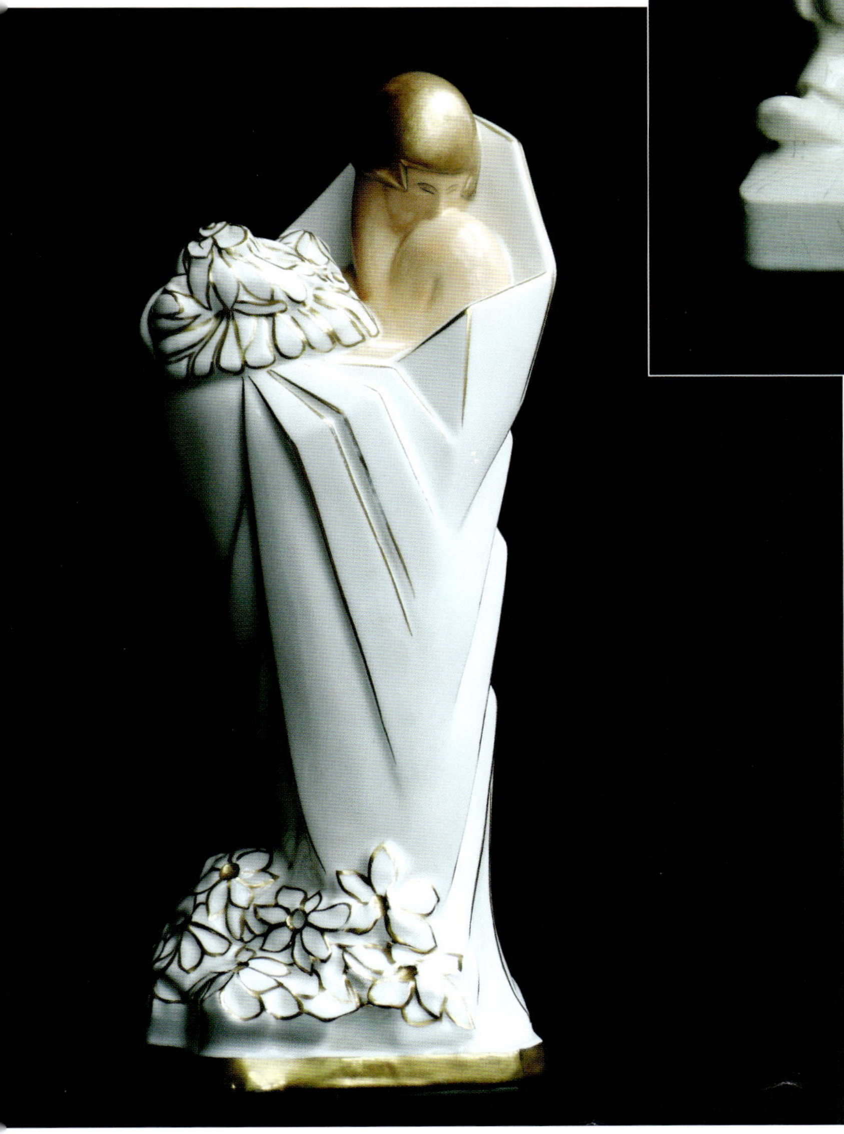

Draped lady, 12.5" high, perfume lamp, plaster model made by Jean Courtebassis. $2,000-$2,500.

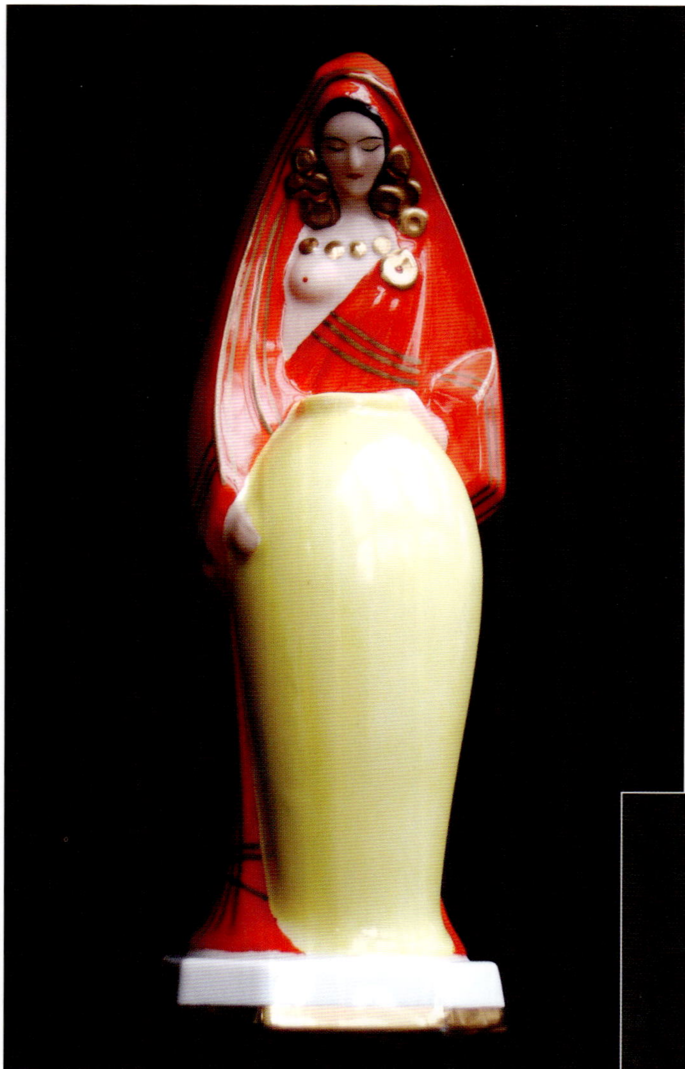

Nightlight, 8.25" high.
$500-$1,000.

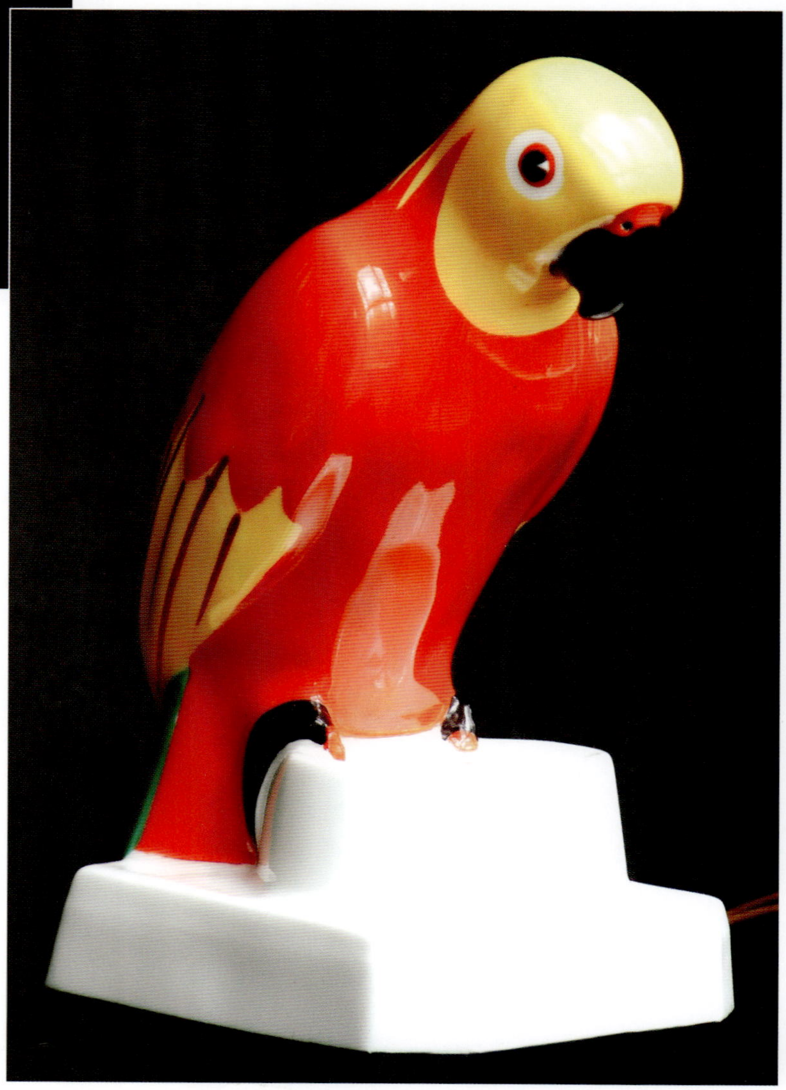

Parrot inkwell, 7" high.
$1,000-$1,500.

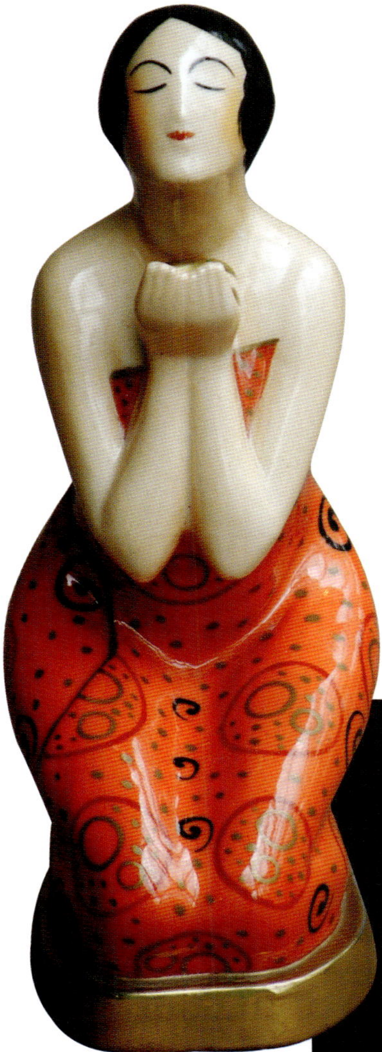

Perfume nightlight, 7.25" high. $2,000-$2,500.

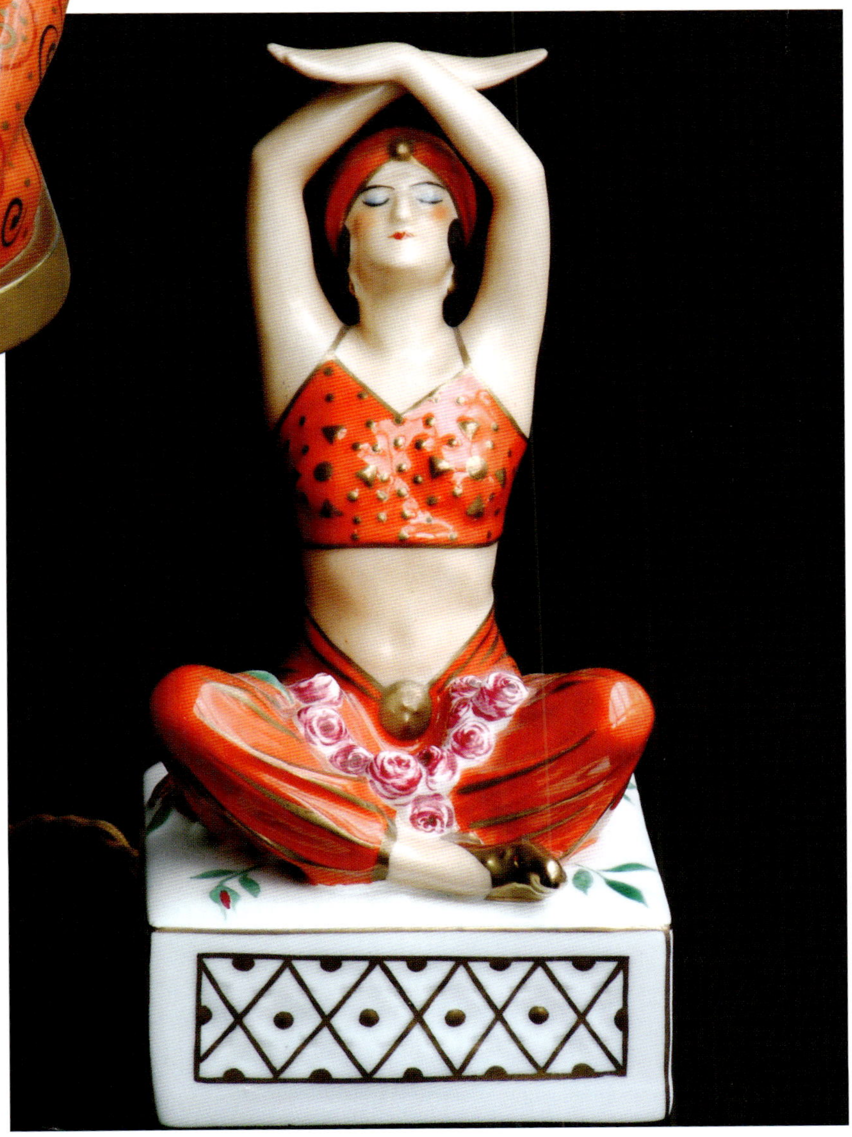

Perfume Nightlight, 7.75" high. $1,500-$2,000.

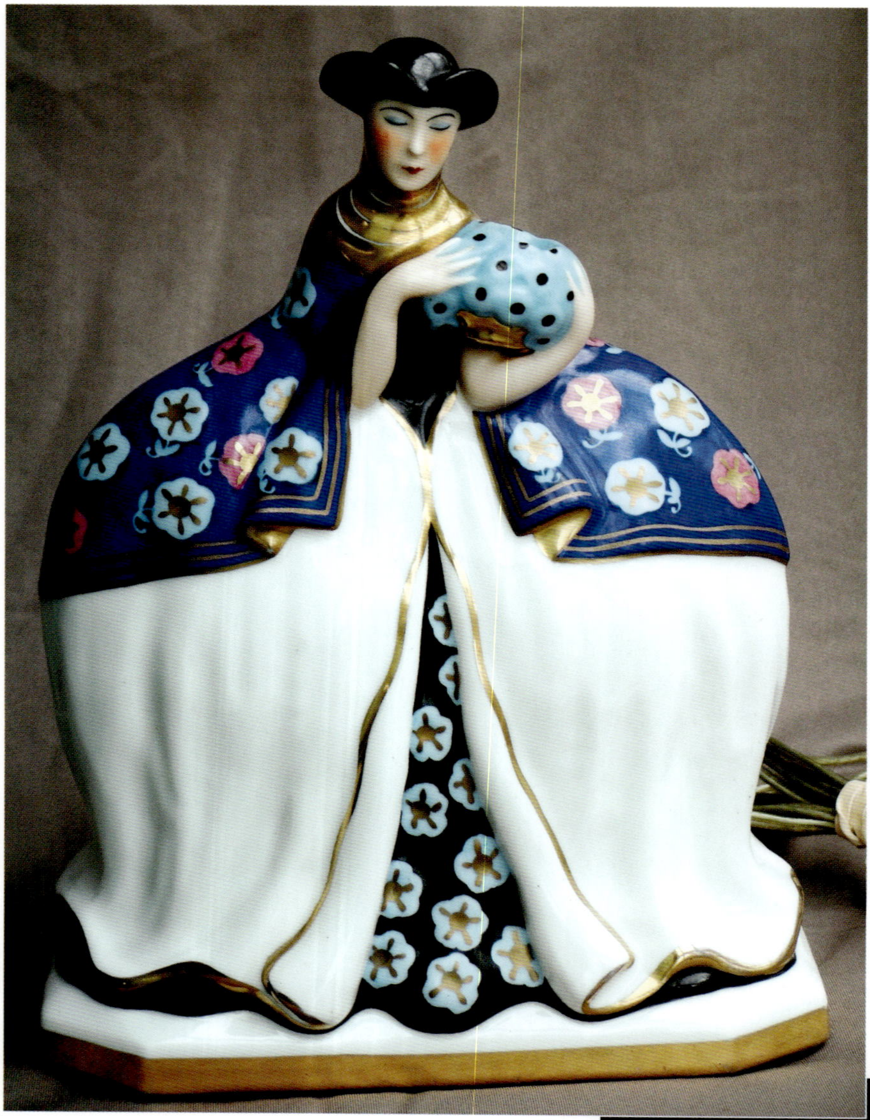

Venetian lady nightlight, 11.25" high. $2,500-$3,000.

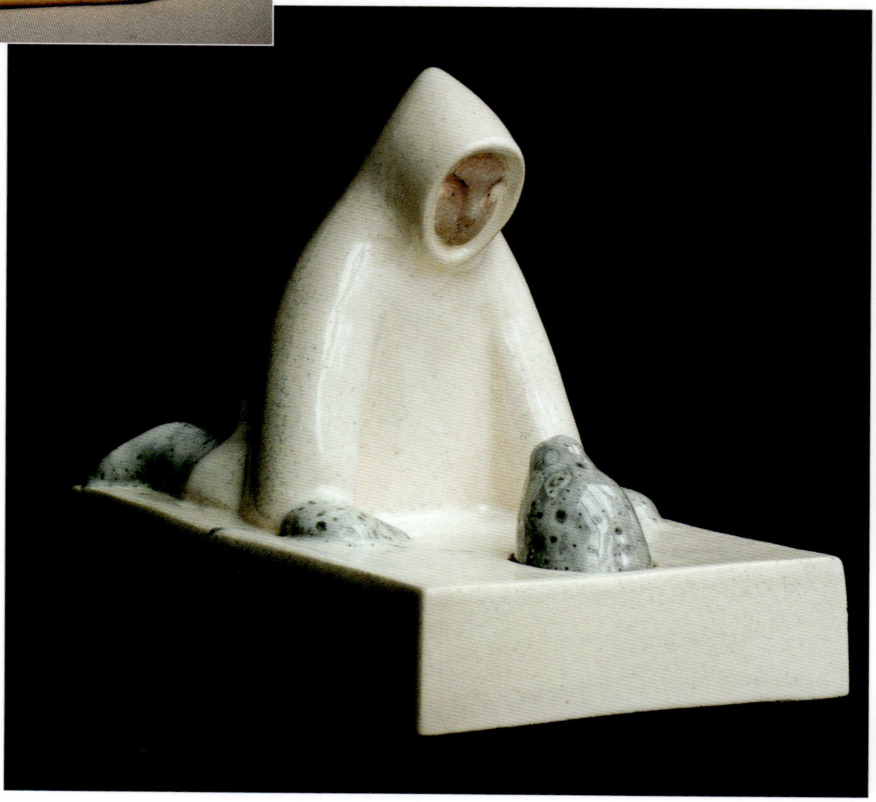

Eskimo Inkwell, 6.5" high x 7.5" x 4.5". $2,000-$2,500.

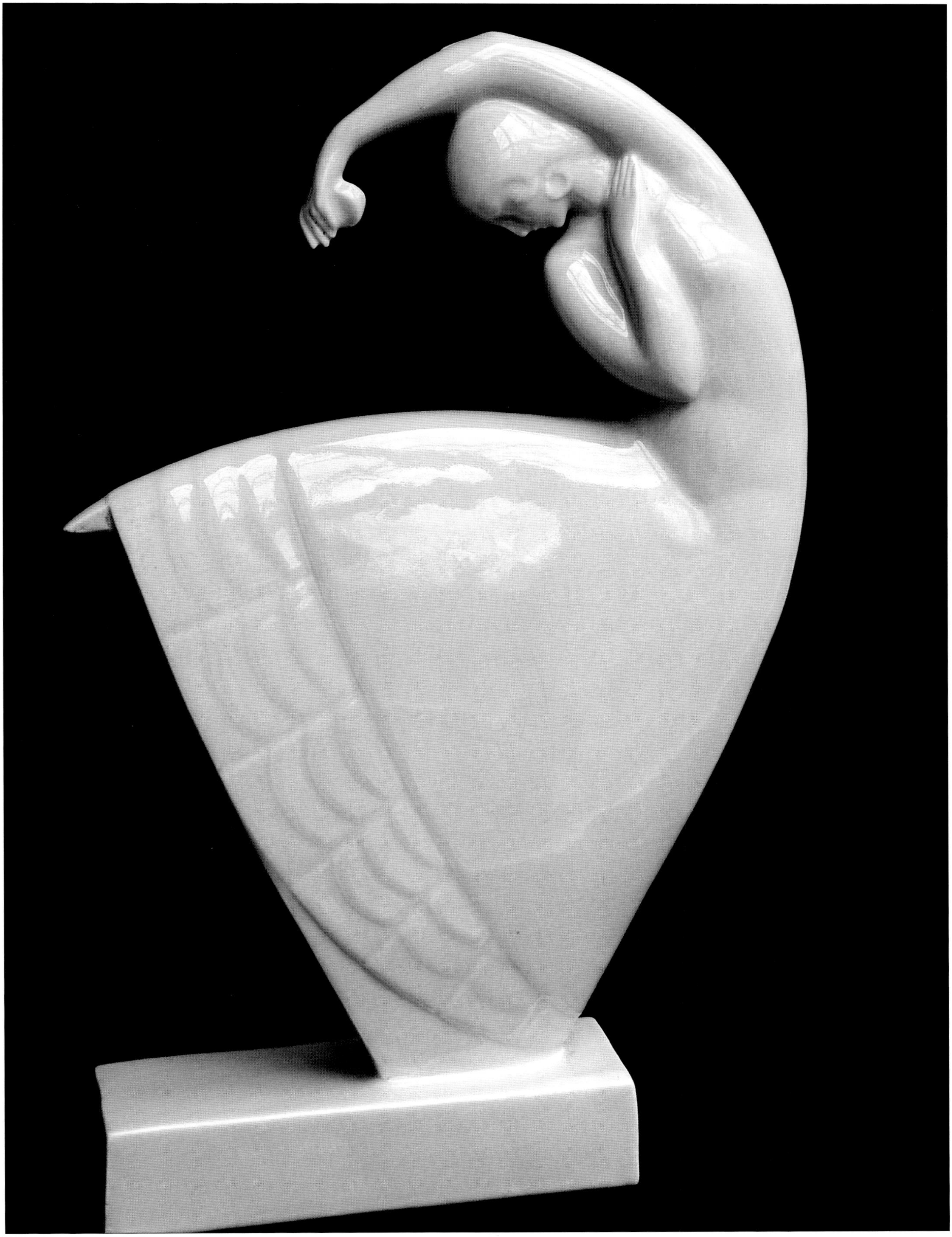

Female dancer, 15" high, mark of Guerbe, made by Villeroy & Boch. $2,000-$2,500.

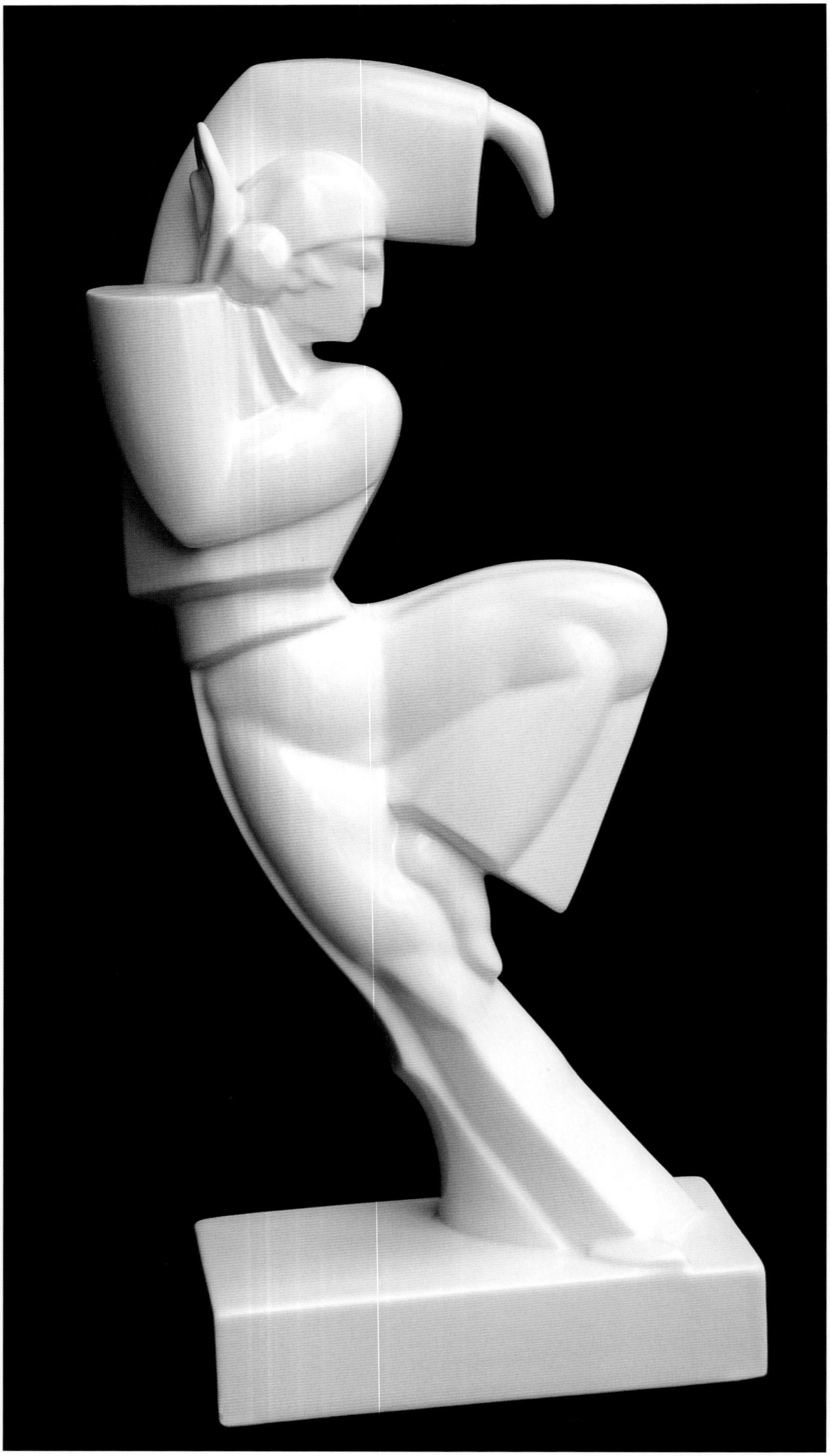

Spanish dancer, 17" high, mark of Margerie, made by Villeroy & Boch. $2,000-$2,500.

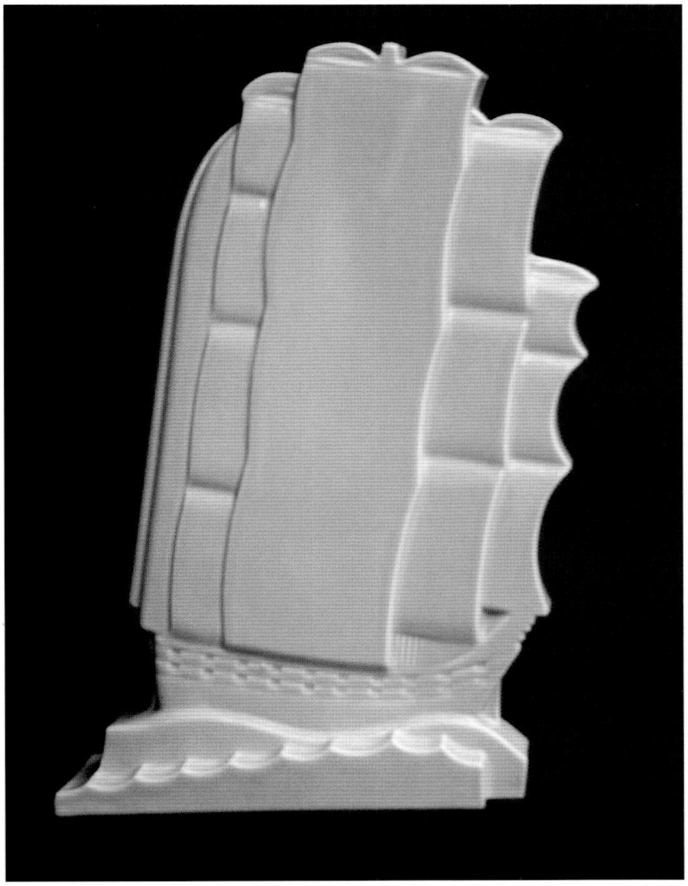

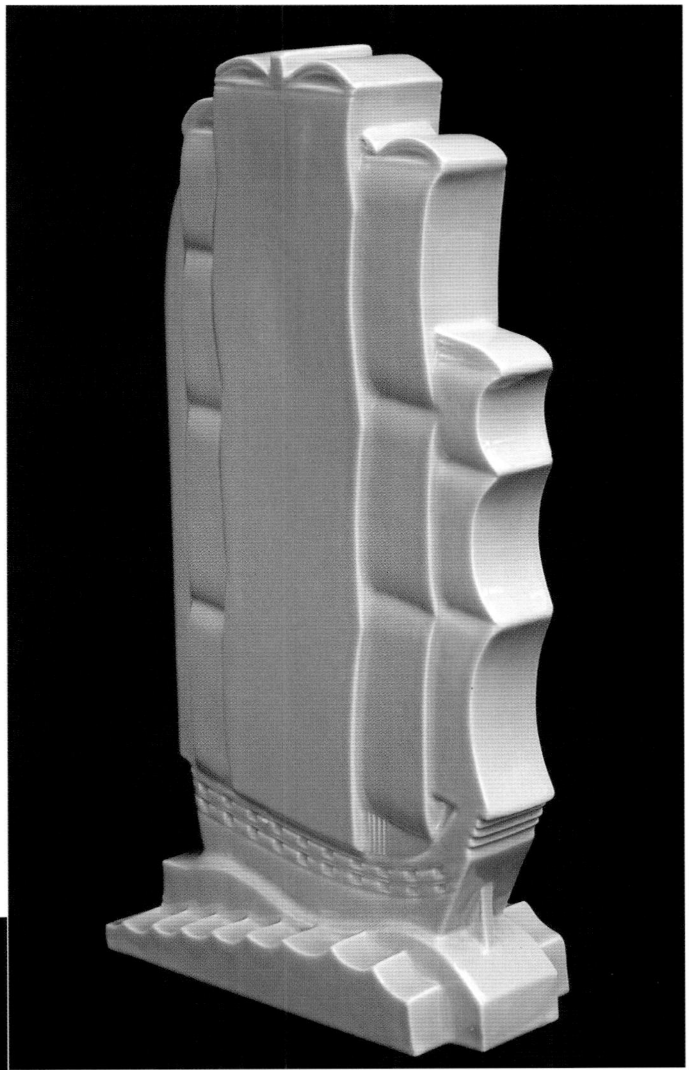

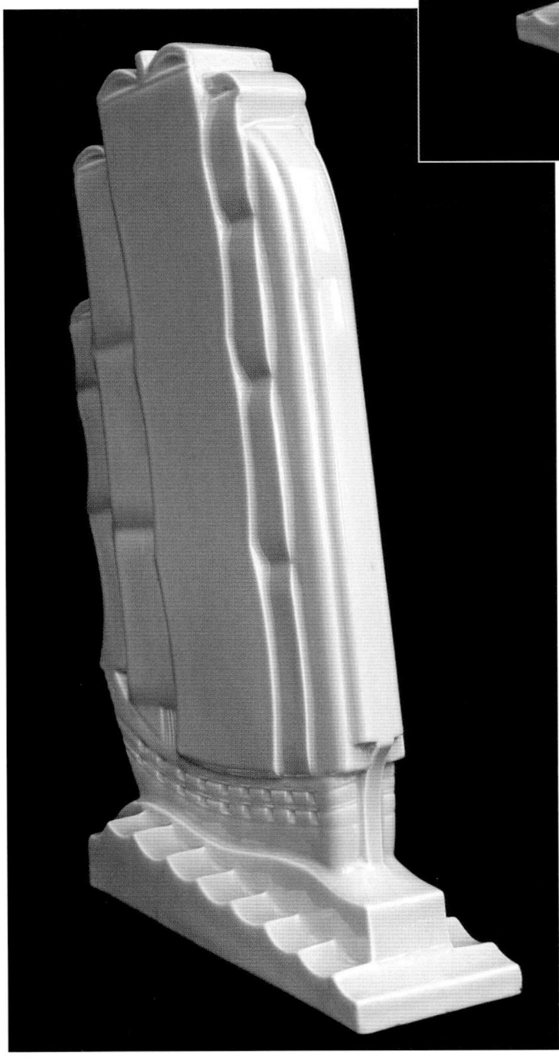

Frigate, 17" high, won first prize in Robj's second contest, plaster model made by Feuerstein, Villeroy & Boch. $1,500-$2.000.

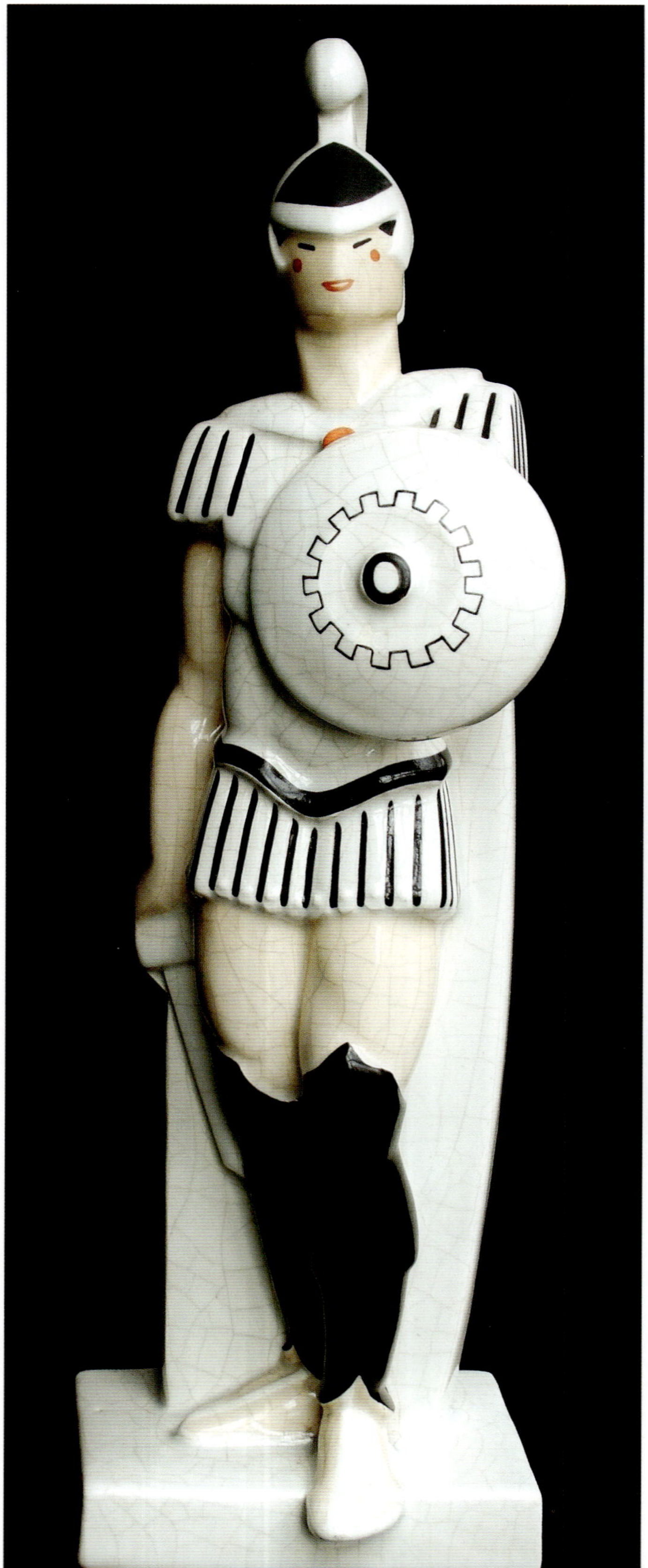

Greek warrior, 15" high, mark of Hache. $2,000-$2,500.

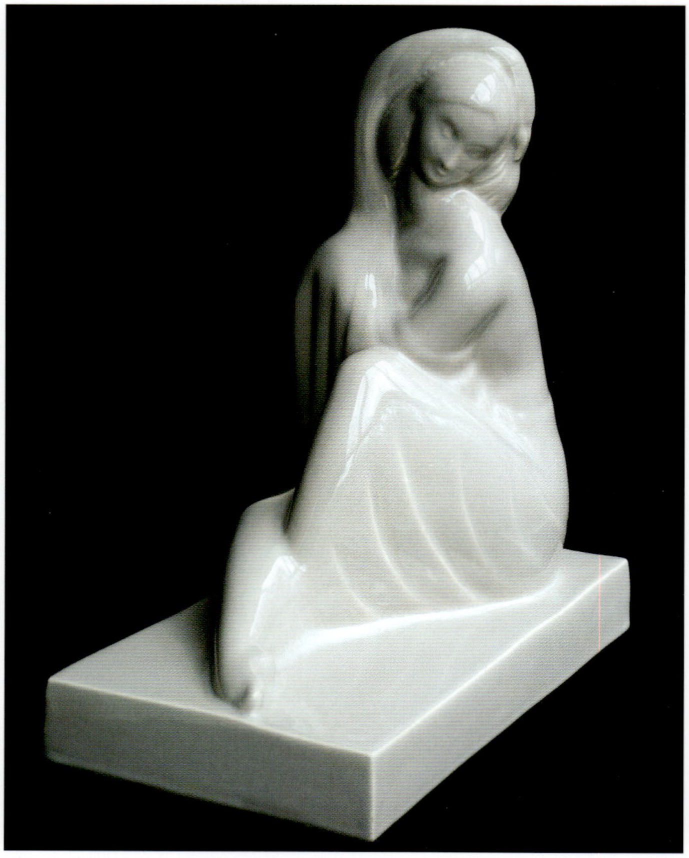

Woman figurine, 10.75" high. $1,000-$1,500.

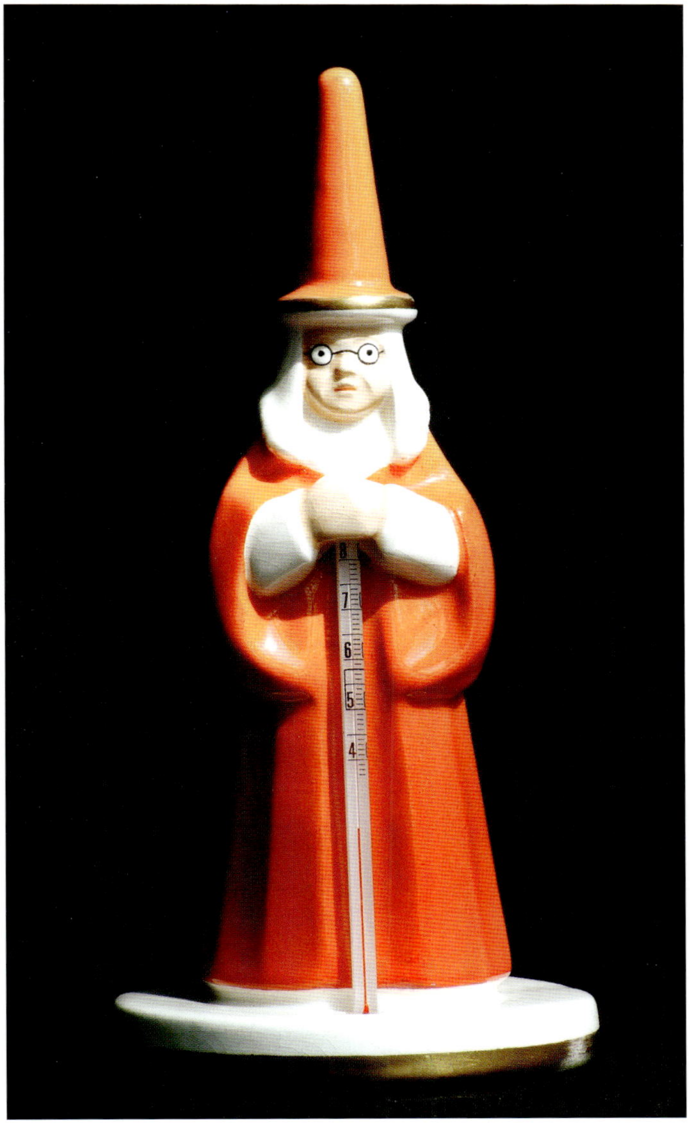

The Doctor thermometer, 9.5" high. $1,500-$2,000.

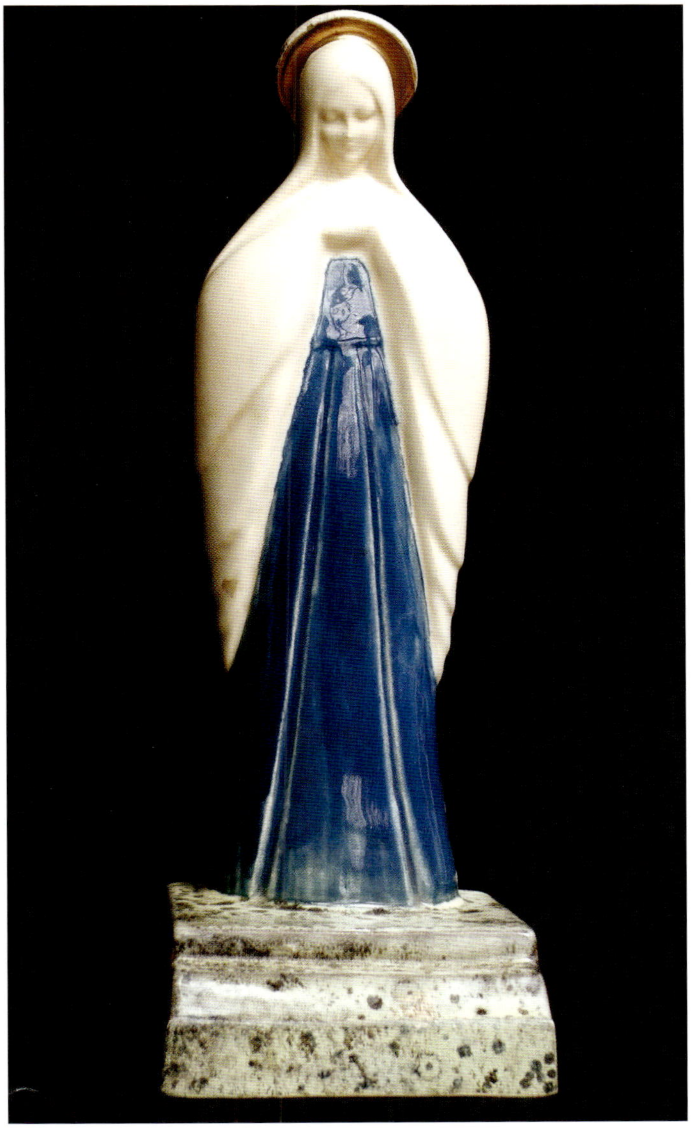

Virgin Mary, 13" high. $500-$1,000.

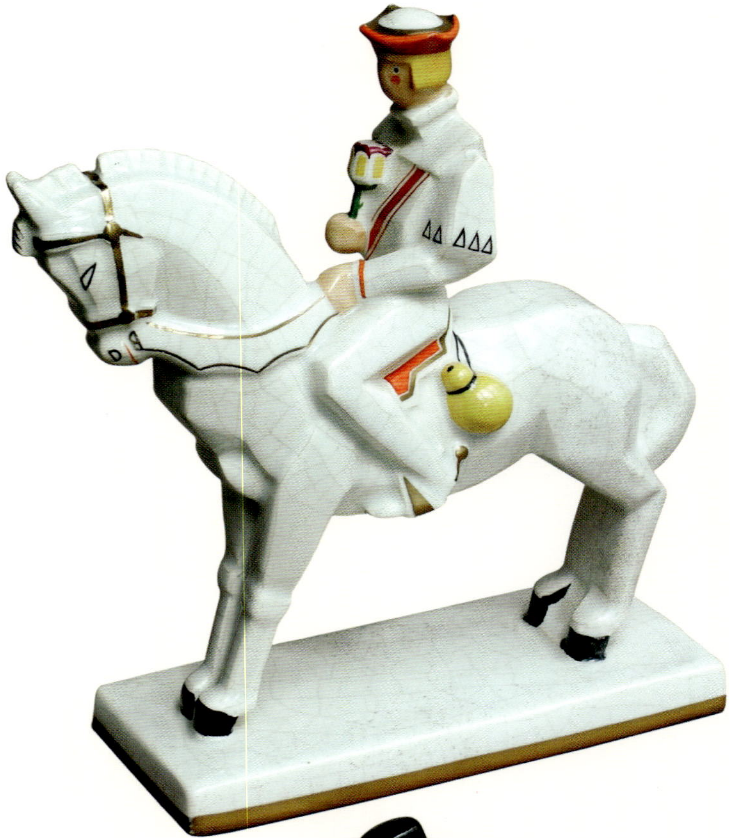

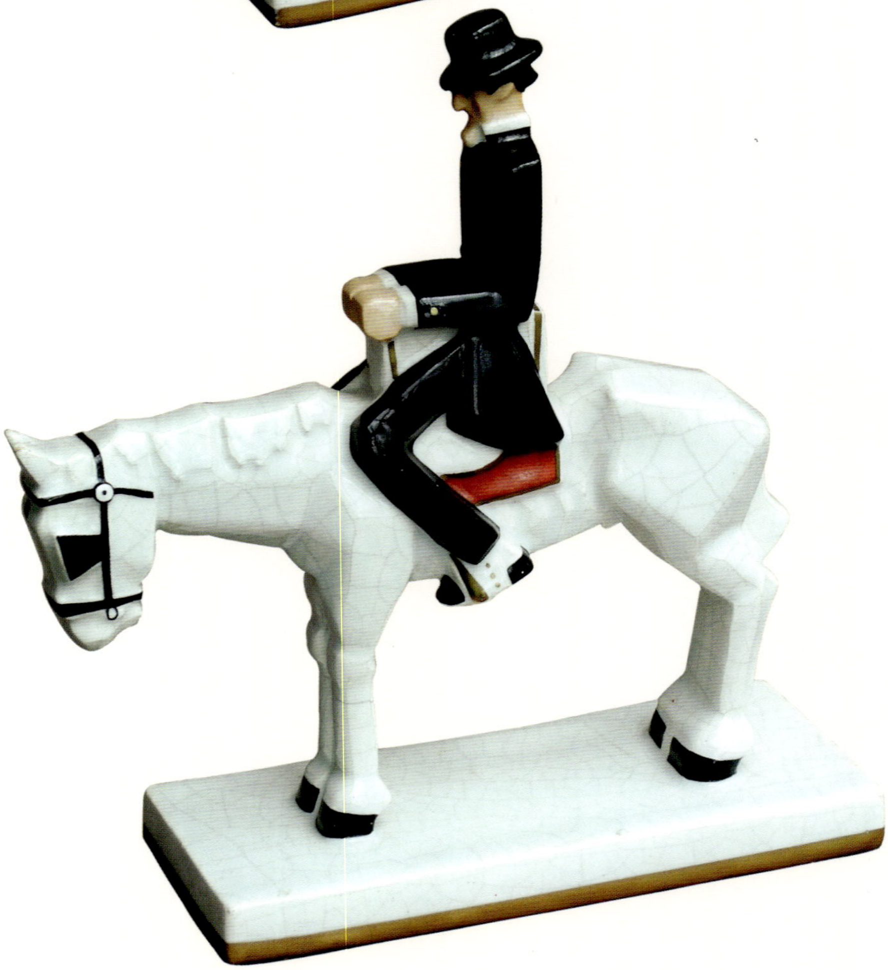

Giglio, left, 9" high, and Taxis, right, 9" high, two of three figures in a story and play, *King Pausole*, written by Pierre Louÿs. $1,000-$1,500 each.

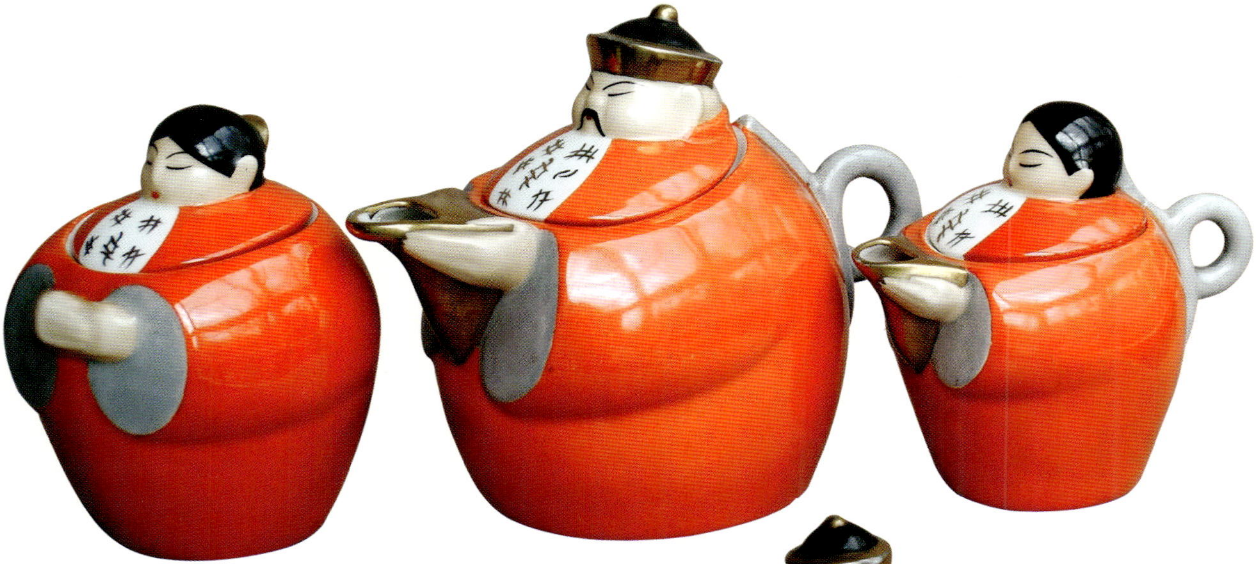

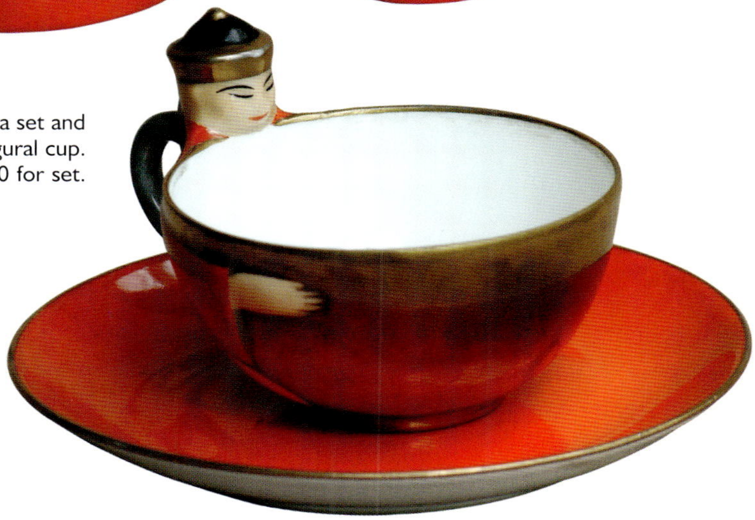

Asian figural tea set and matching Asian figural cup. $5,000-$5,500 for set.

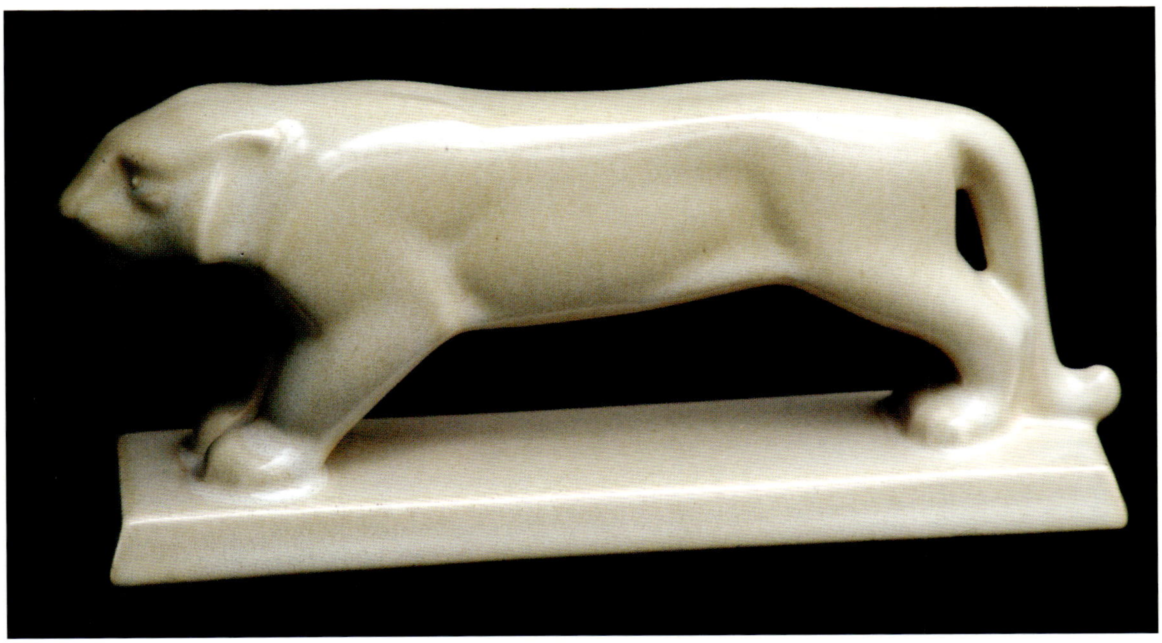

Animal figurine, 5" x 2.5". Less than $500.

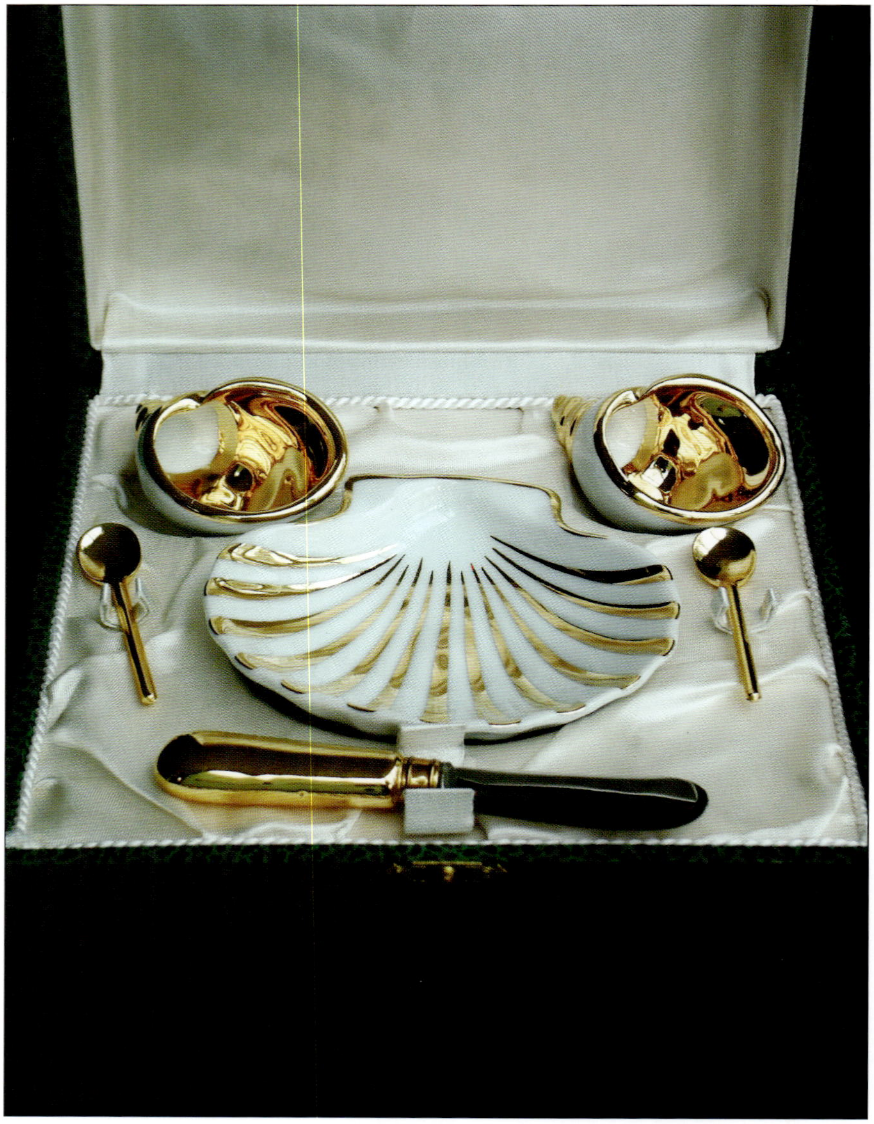

Salt, pepper, and condiment set. $500-$1,000.

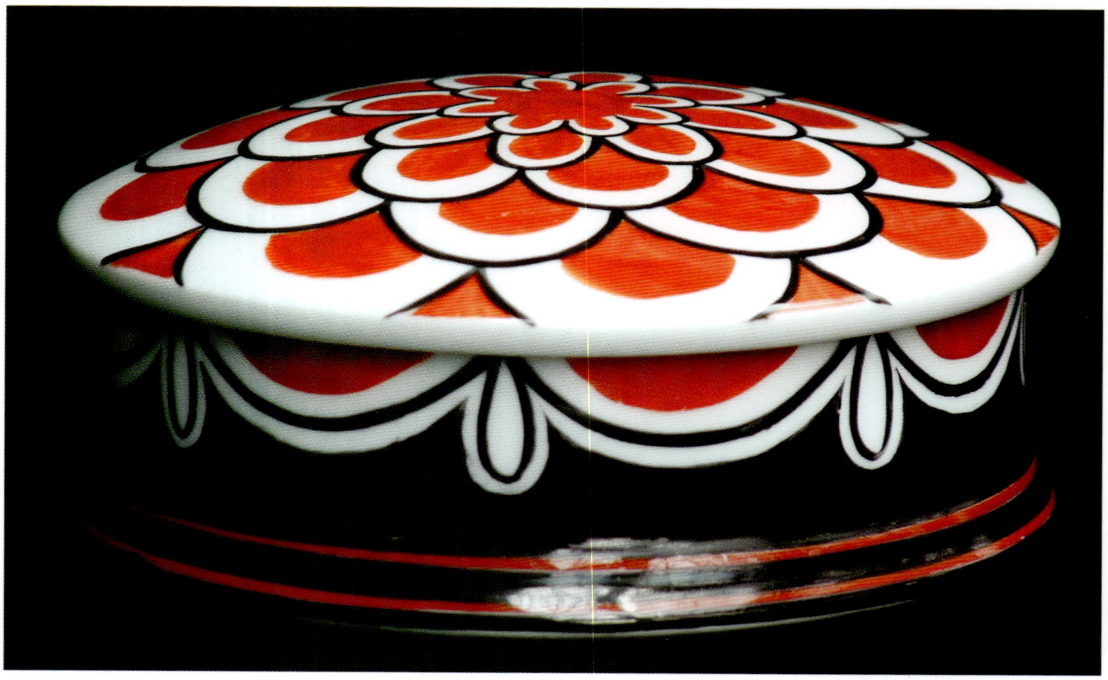

Powder Box, 5" in diameter. $1,500-$2,000.

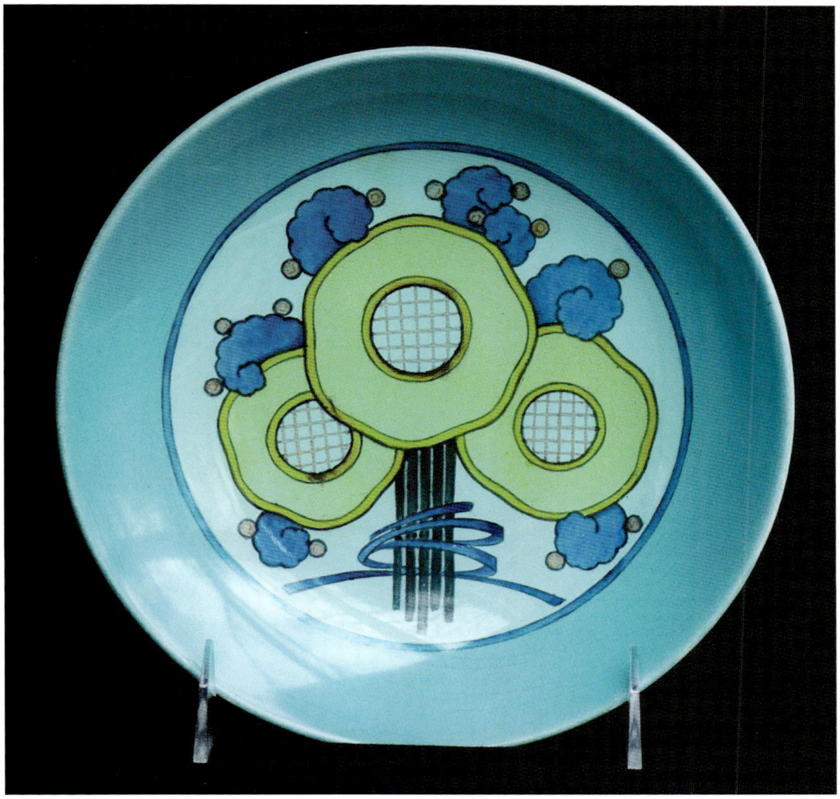

Two bowls, 7.5" in diameter, M. Gevaert, artist; made in Luxembourg. Less than $500 each.

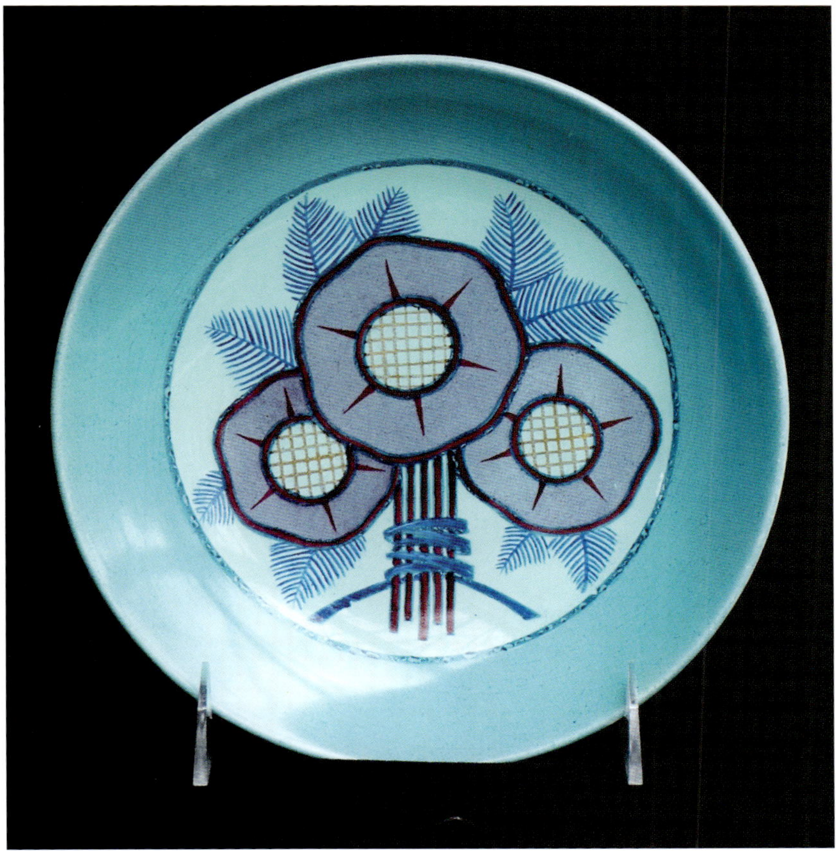

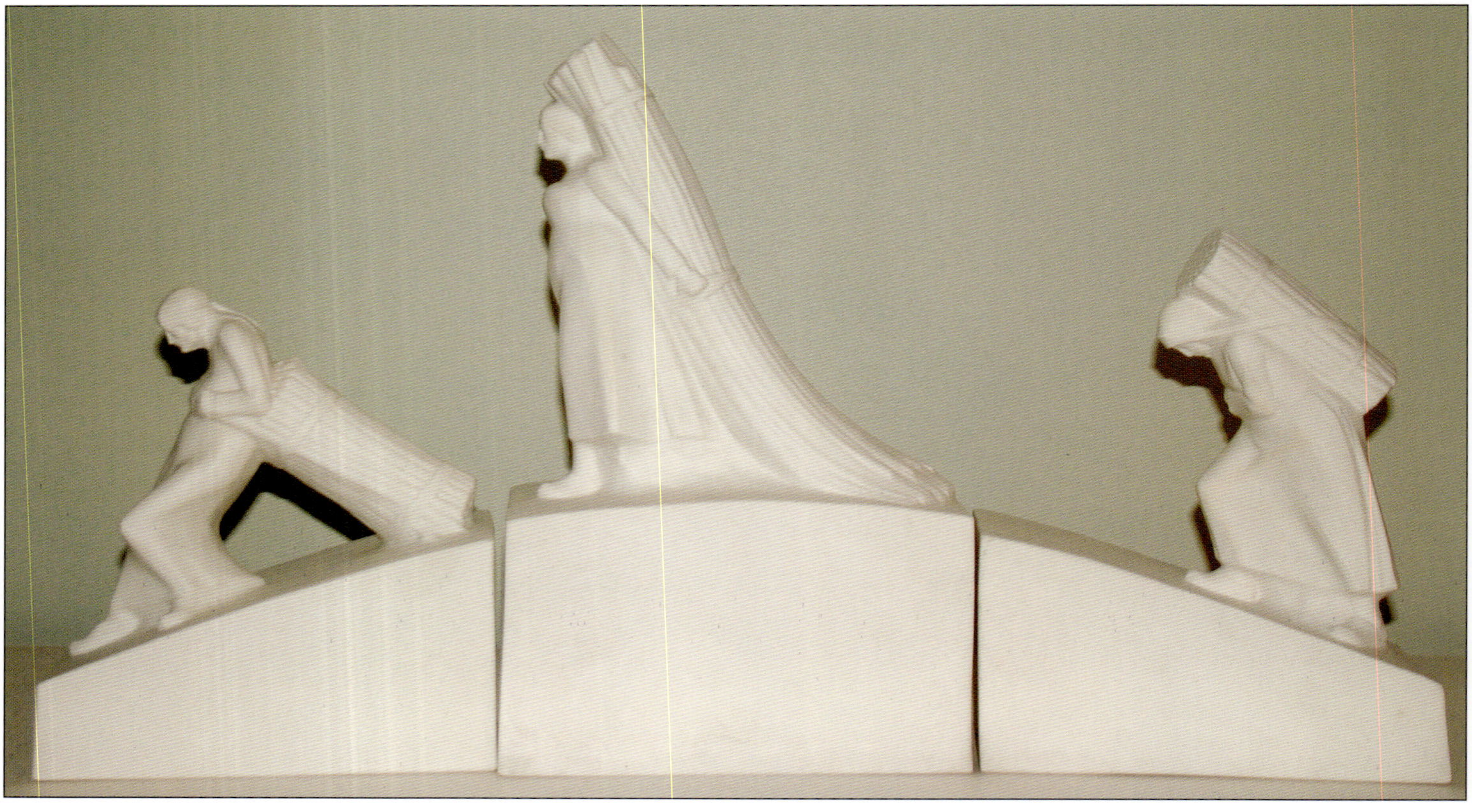

Life's Path of the Harvest Woman, Sèvres, Artist [Raoul] Mabru impressed, only 20 sets made, won second prize in first Robj contest in 1927. $5,000+.

Édouard Marcel Sandoz (1881-1971)

Édouard Marcel Sandoz captured the essence of Art Deco design and colors in the porcelain animals that he designed for Théodore Haviland, Porcelaine de Paris, Sèvres, and Richard-Ginori. In addition to porcelain, Sandoz also produced animals in wood, bronze, and stone. His Art Deco porcelain tea and coffee sets (1916-1917) won him international recognition, and two of the pieces he designed for Porcelaine de Paris, *Vase Poisson-Chat* and *Chat Debout*, were included in the 1925 Exposition internationale des arts décoratifs industriels et moderns in Paris. Sandoz's animal figurines were highly popular in his day, and they have continued to be highly popular today. (McCready)

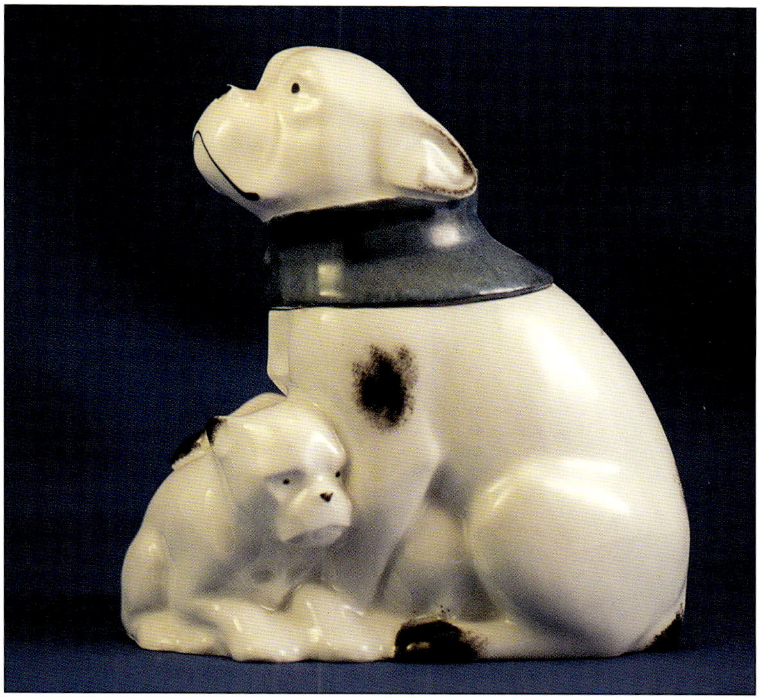

Bulldog bonbonnière, T. Haviland. $500-$1,000.

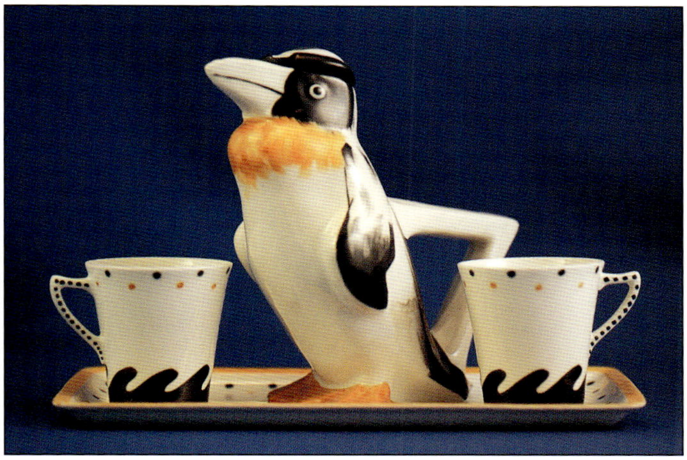

Tête-à-tête Penguin Service, T. Haviland. $1,500-$2,000.

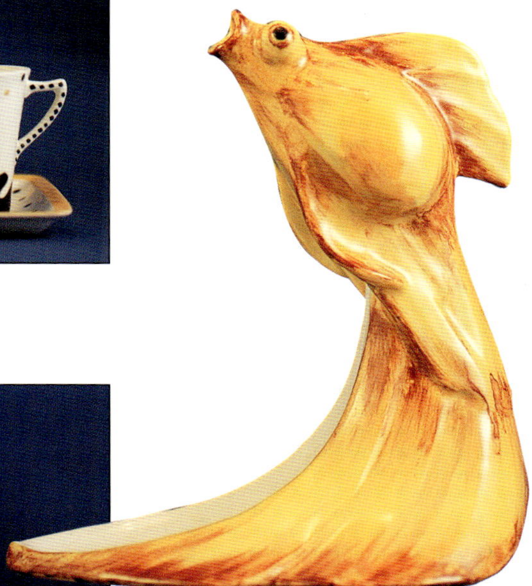

Chinese fish. T. Haviland. $1,000-$1,500.

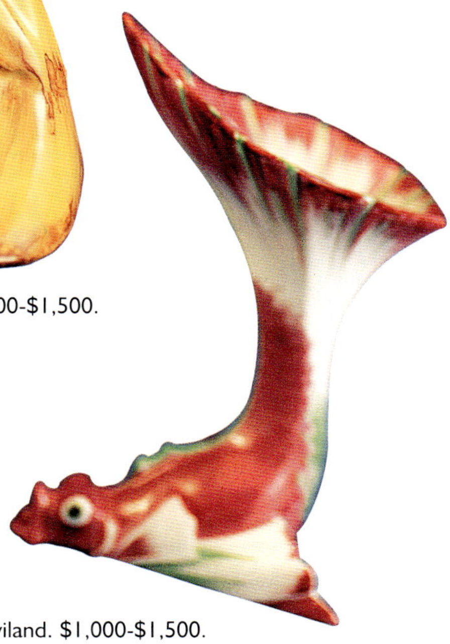

Fish Vase, T. Haviland. $1,000-$1,500.

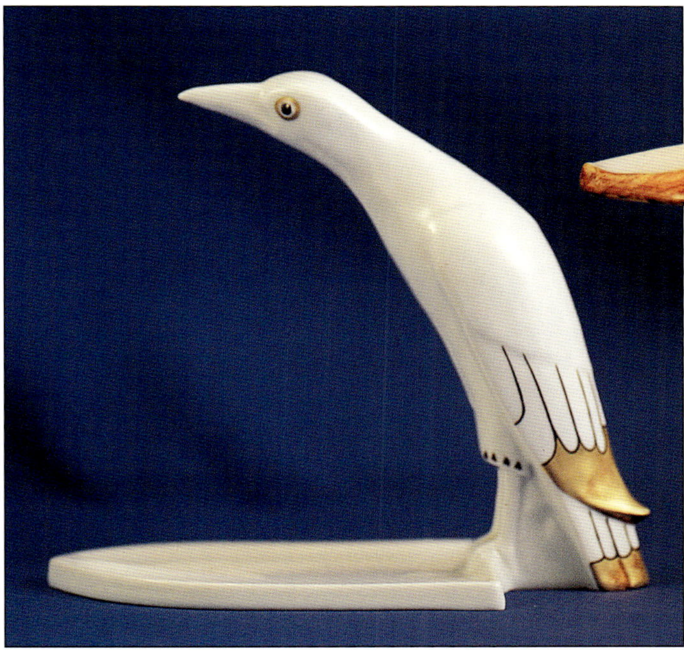

African blackbird "change/key tray," T. Haviland. $500-$1,000.

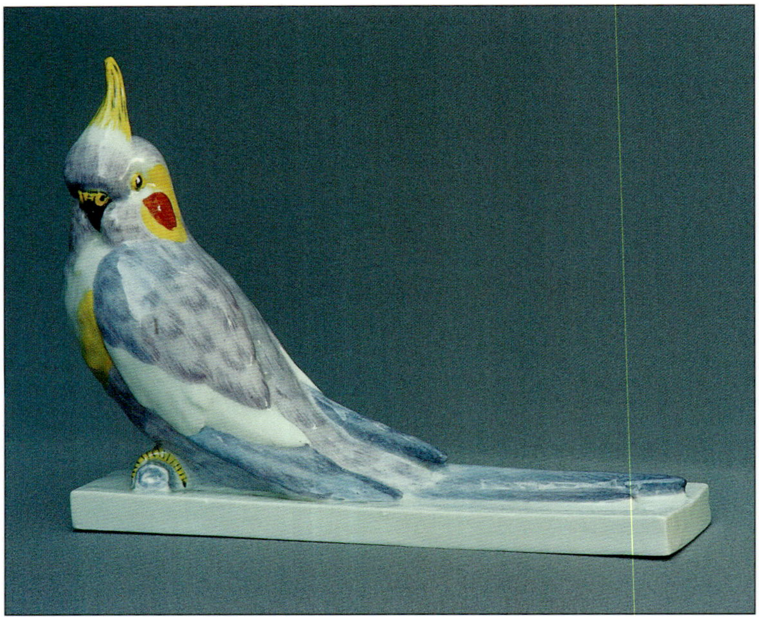

Parakeet figurine, Porcelaine de Paris, $1,000-$1,500.

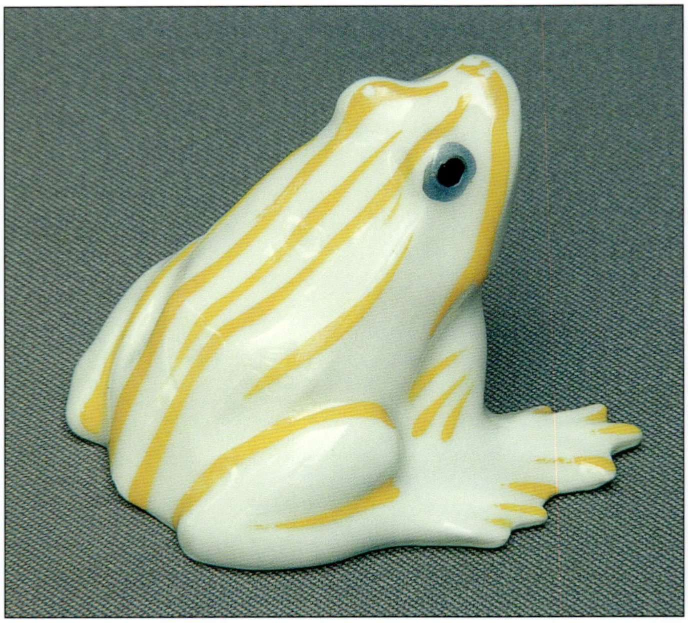

Frog salt shaker, T. Haviland. Less than $500.

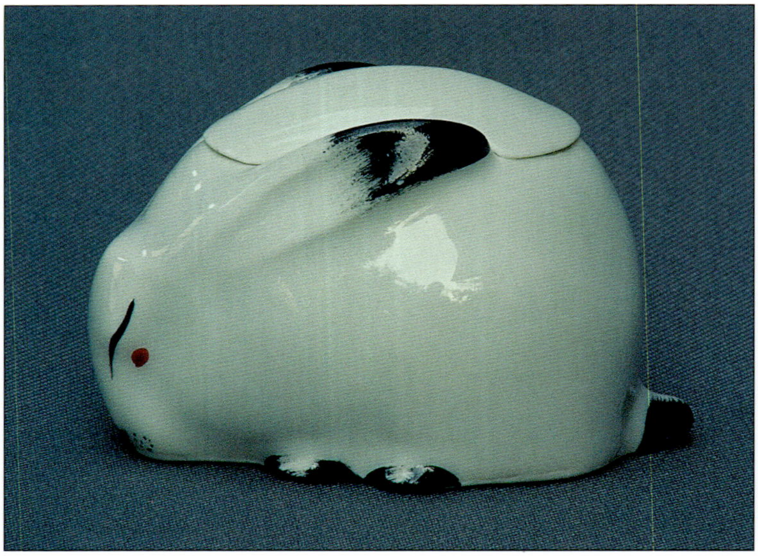

Rabbit mustard cup, T. Haviland. Less than $500.

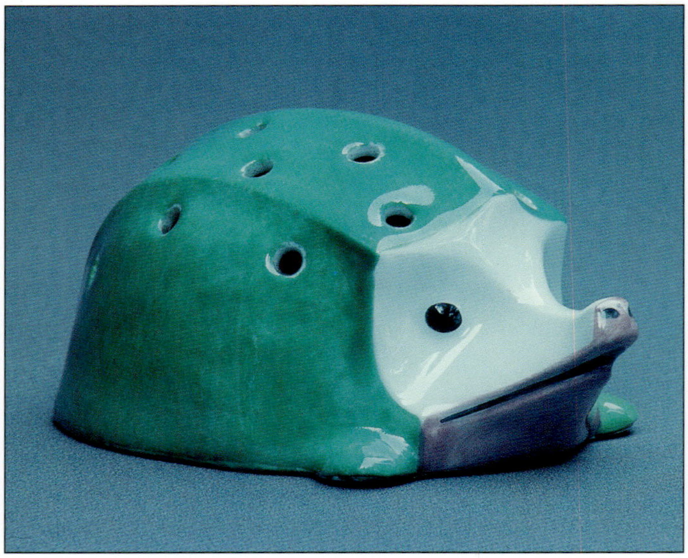

Hedgehog flower stand, T. Haviland. Less than $500.

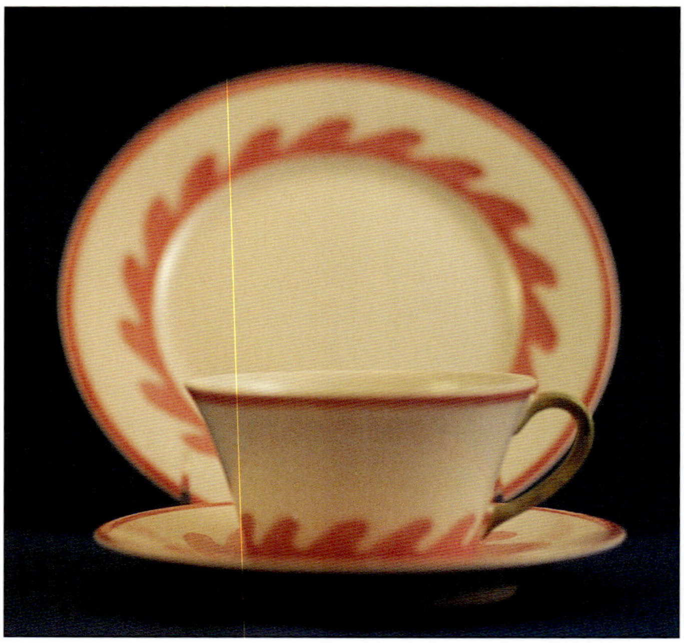

Cup, saucer, and plate, T. Haviland. Less than $500 for cup and saucer and less than $500 for plate.

Suzanne Lalique

Suzanne Lalique was the daughter of the famous glassmaker, René Lalique. An artist in her own right, Suzanne Lalique began exhibiting her works in the Salons of Paris. She did paintings and drawings and worked in other mediums as well—glass, porcelain, and textiles. She was commissioned by Sèvres and Théodore Haviland and others to develop designs for porcelain. She decorated for T. Haviland from 1928 to either 1931 or 1933. Most of her designs were done on celadon and ivory porcelain, which was fashionable during the Art Deco period. (*Haviland Collectors Inernationale Foundation Quarterly Newsletter*, March 2002)

Below are examples of different Suzanne Lalique patterns for T. Haviland.

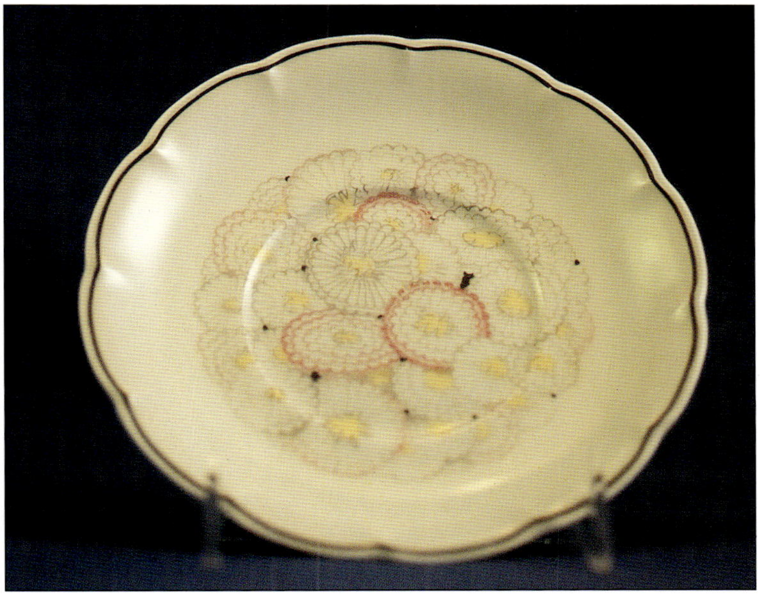

Saucer. Less than $500.

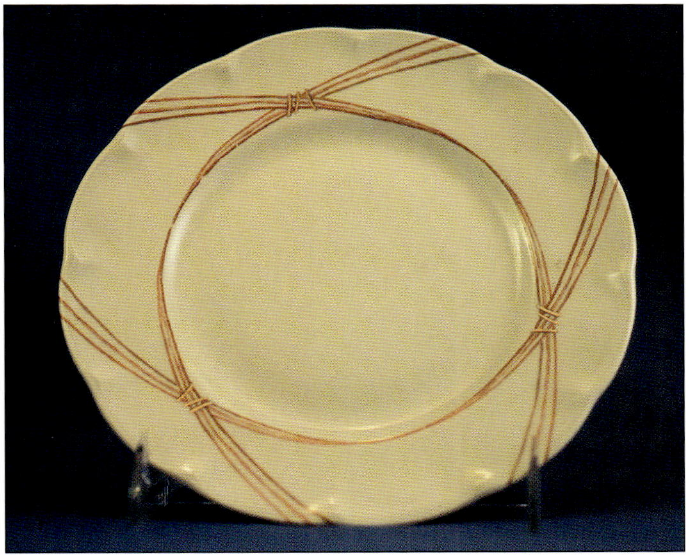

Plate. Less than $500.

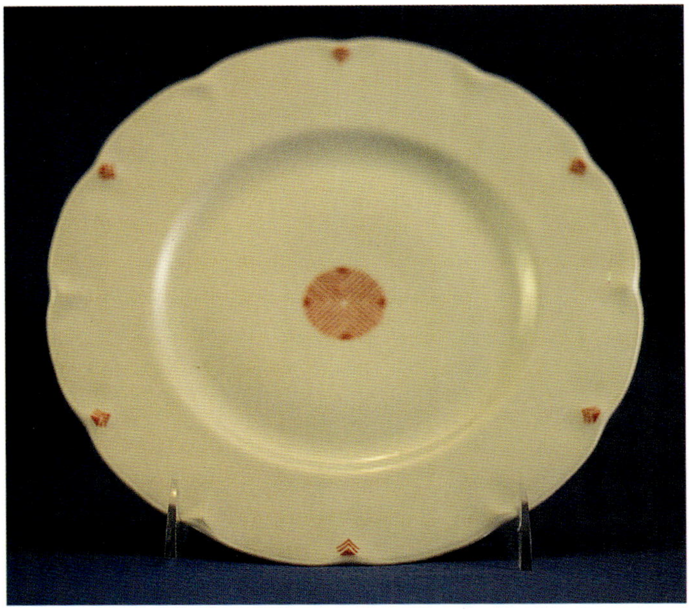

Plate. Less than $500.

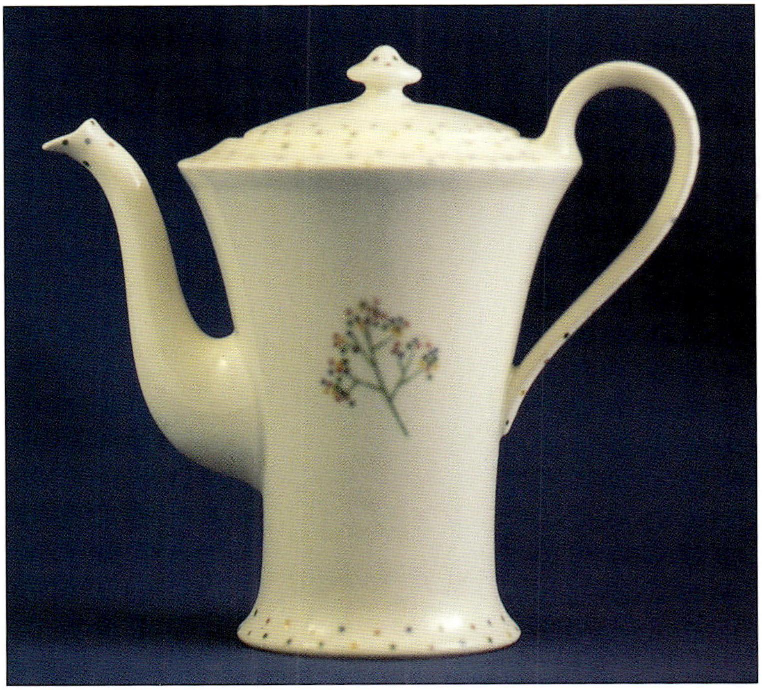

Coffee pot. $500-$1,000.

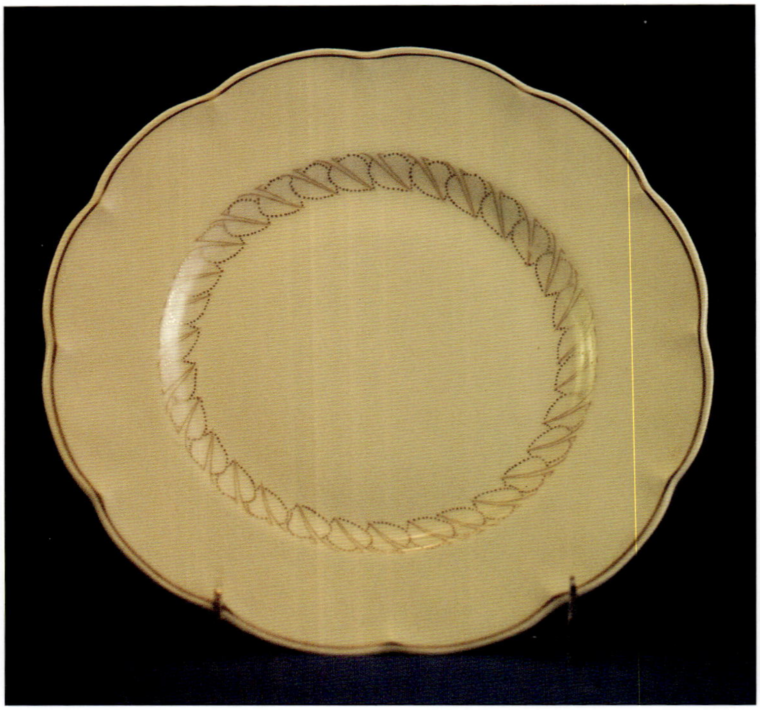

Plate. Less than $500.

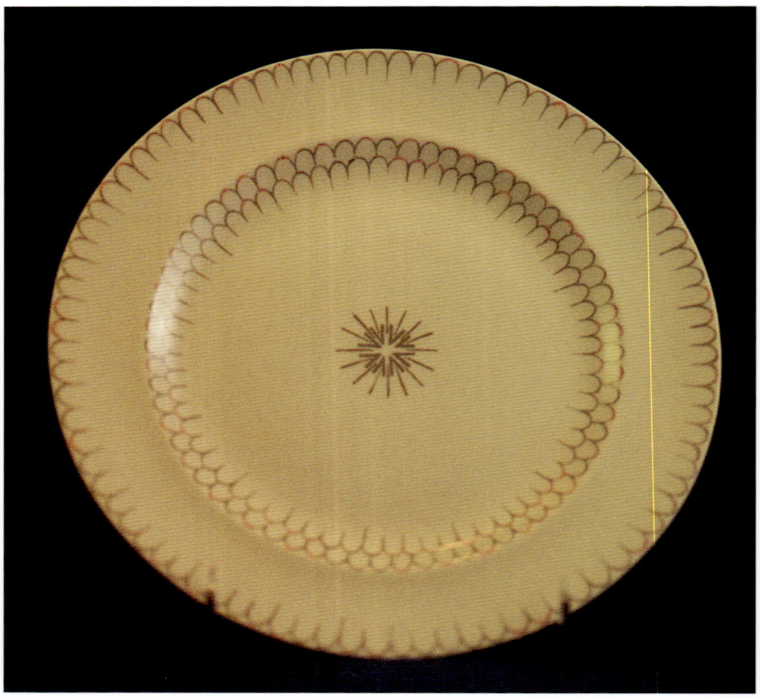

Plate. Less than $500.

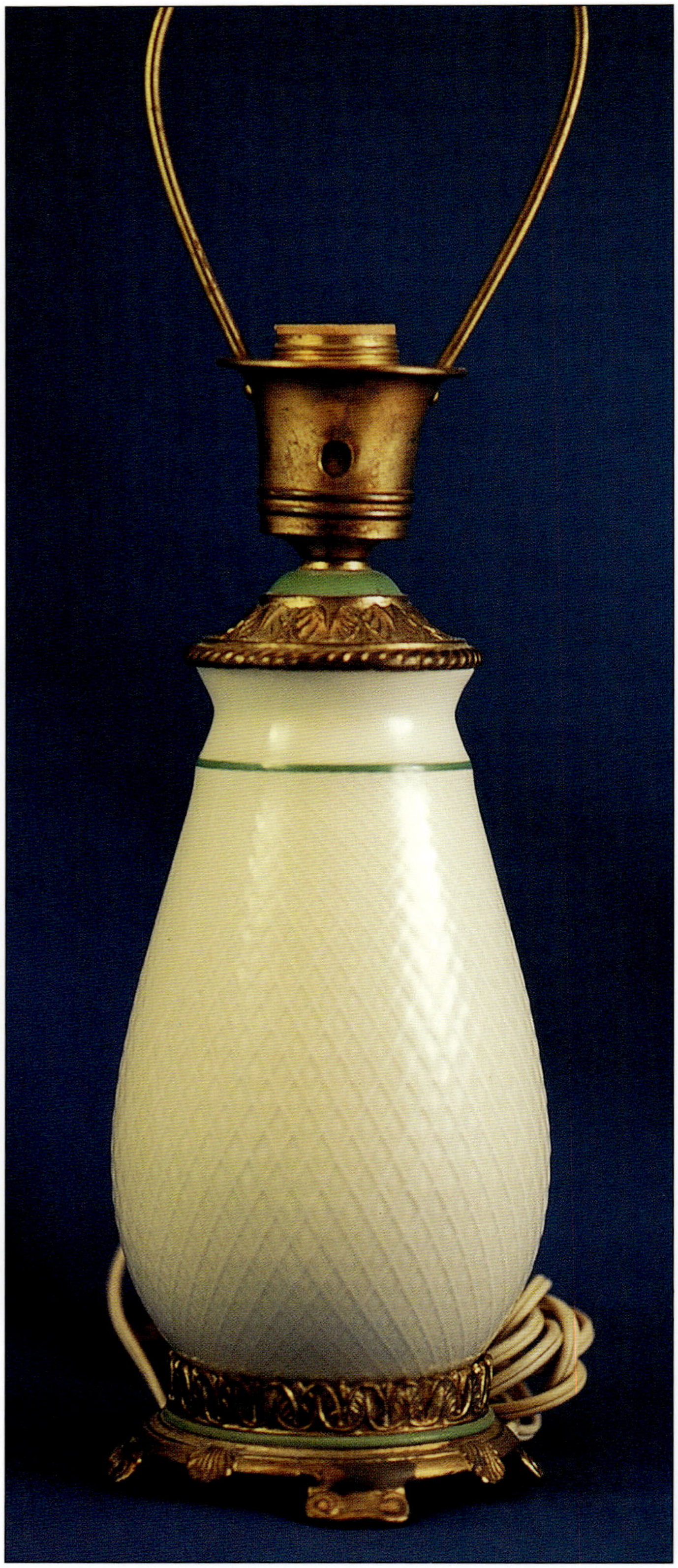

Lamp. $500-$1,000.

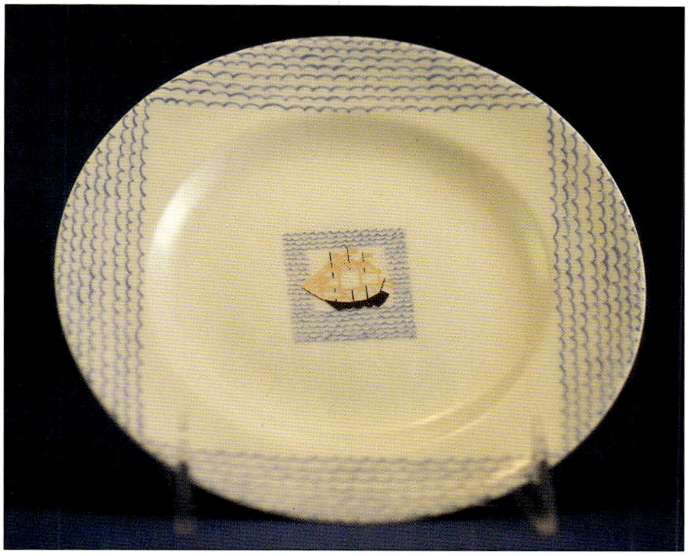

Plate. Less than $500.

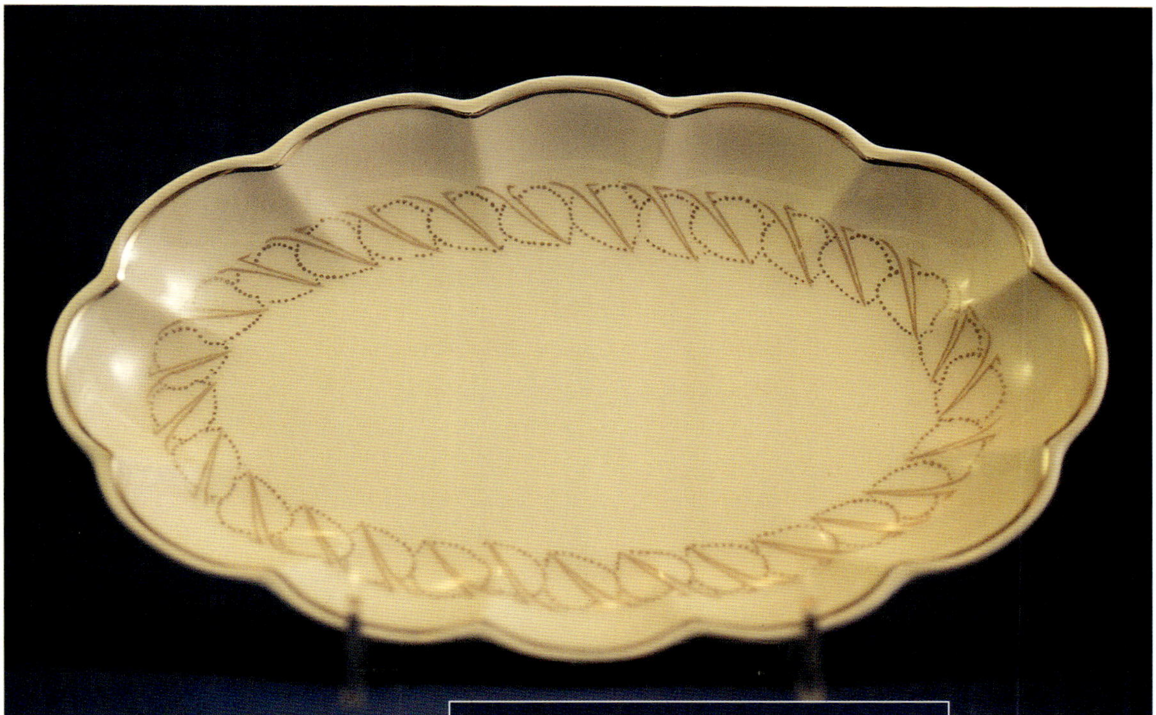

Relish tray. Less than $500.

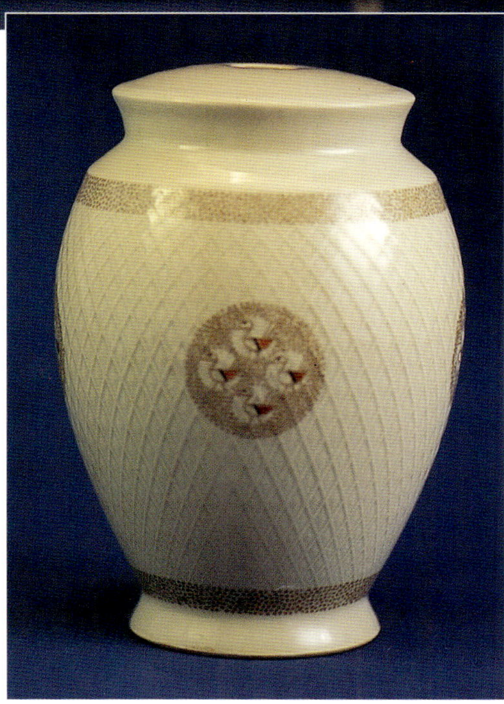

Lamp. $500-$1,000.

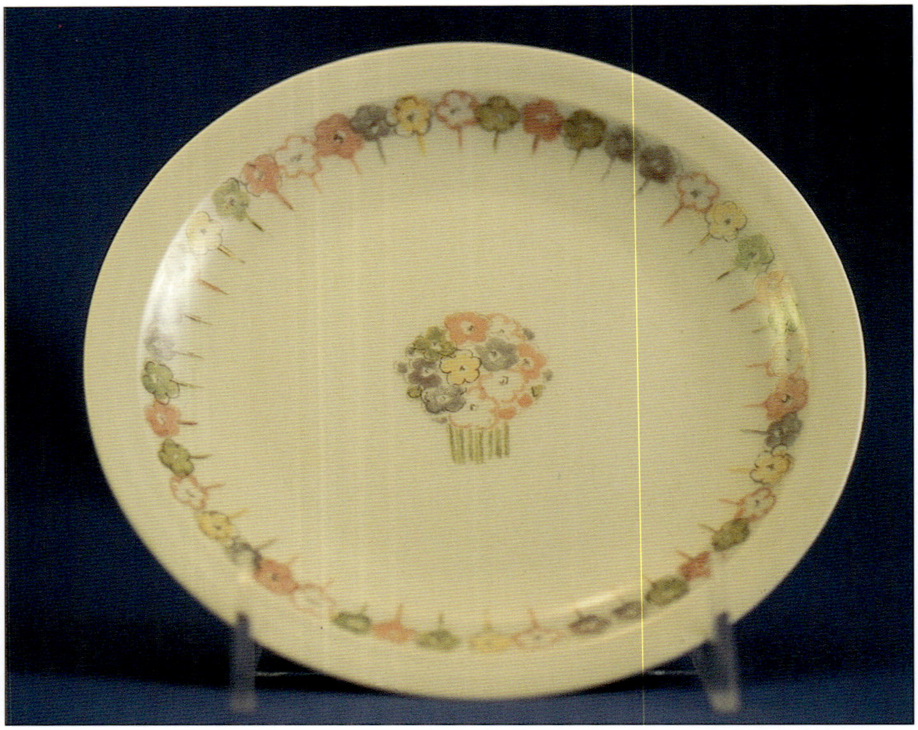

Bowl. Less than $500.

Plate. Less than $500.

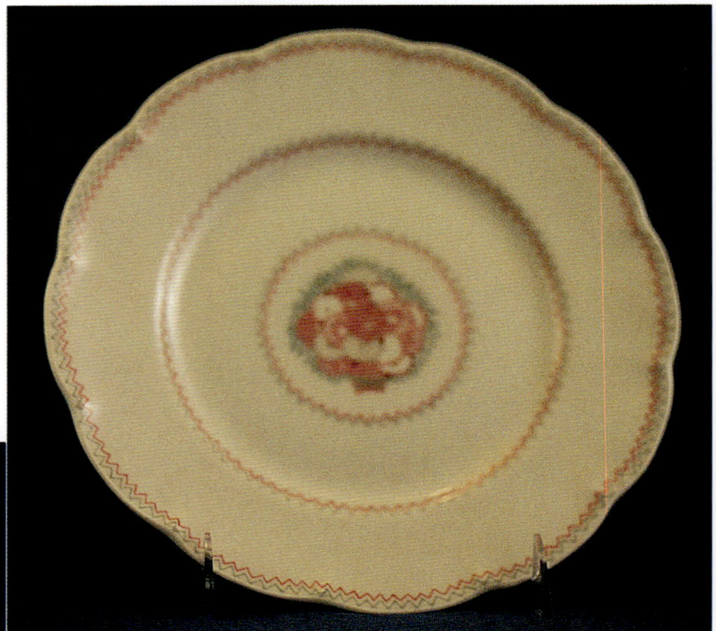

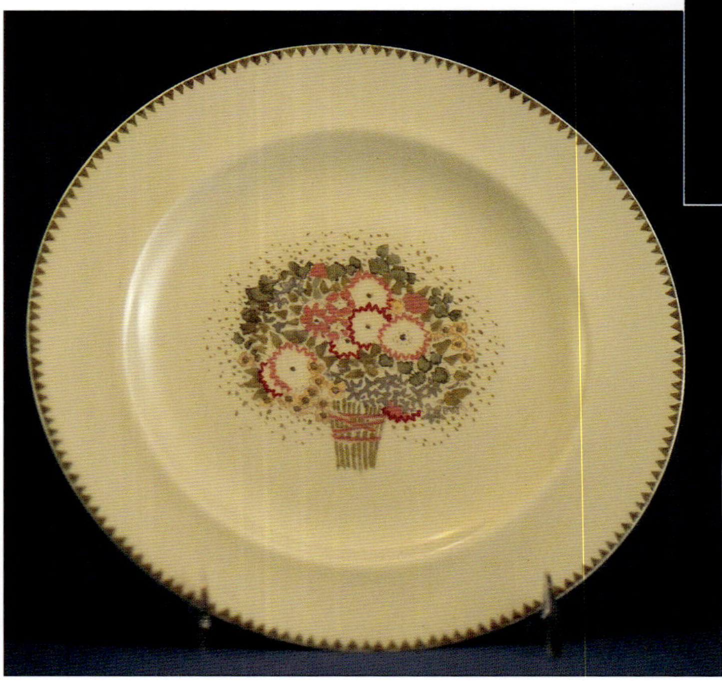

Plate. Less than $500.

Royal Limoges

Royal Limoges, a manufacturer and decorator of porcelain, has a long history in Limoges with origins from the original François Alluaud and Charles Field Haviland companies. The old Gérard, Dufraisseix, Abbot (GDA), and A. Lanternier companies are now part of Royal Limoges. The current factory has been modernized by Lionel Delaygue, who is the president and who has been very helpful to us in the preparation of this book.

Léon Jouhaud (1874-1950)

Léon Jouhaud was a ceramist and painter in Limoges, and he experimented extensively in the development of enamels. Based upon his talents, he was made the artistic leader at Gérard, Dufraisseix, Abbot in 1920. He was introduced to Camille Tharaud by Françis Chigot, and Jouhaud and Tharaud later became collaborators. He had a broad interest in porcelain. In his collaboration with Tharaud, he worked with Tharaud on the technical details of the firing process and the enamels and on artistic designs. Pieces decorated by Jouhaud for Tharaud are signed L.J. He also designed many Art Deco shapes, and he became an influential artist of the Art Deco period in Limoges.

Below are shapes and designs of Jouhaud from the Art Deco period that are in the Royal Limoges museum.

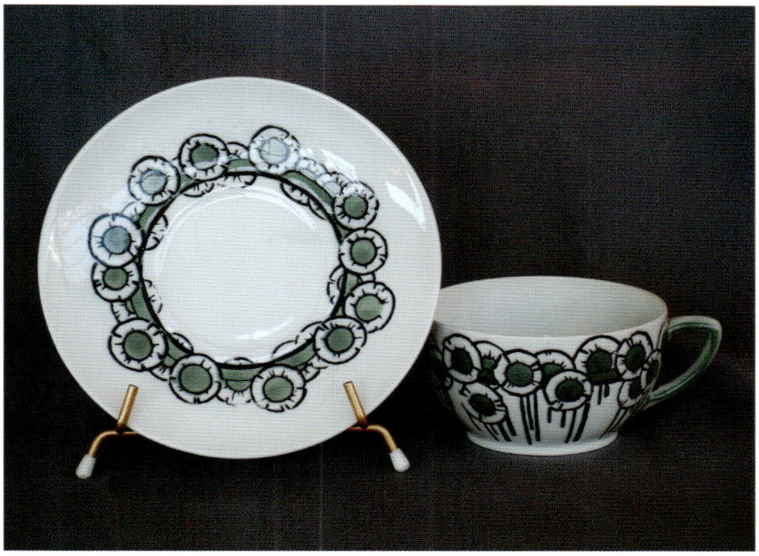

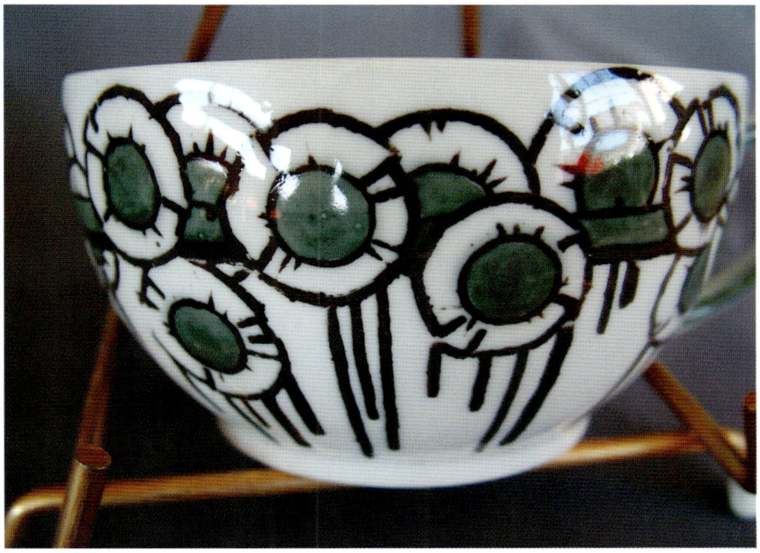

Decoration by Léon Jouhaud.

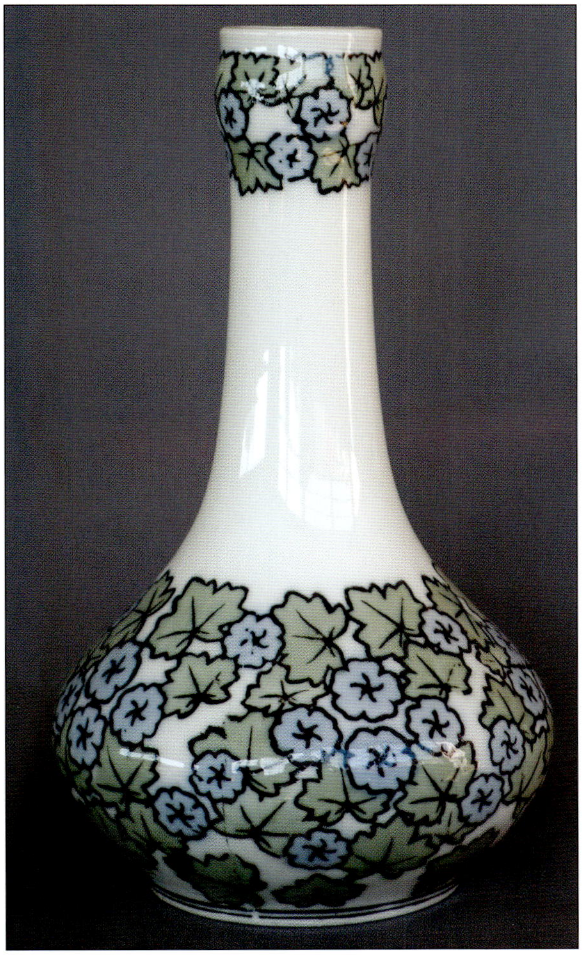

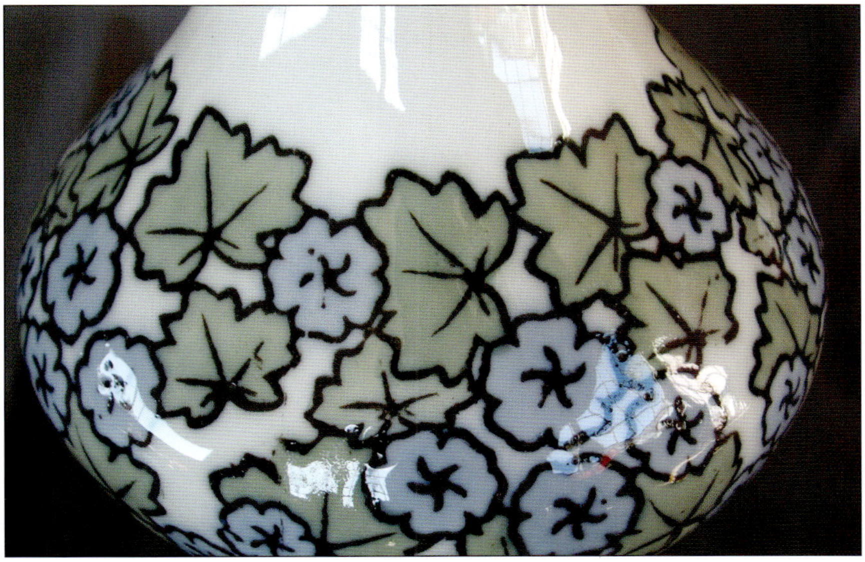

Decoration by Léon Jouhaud.

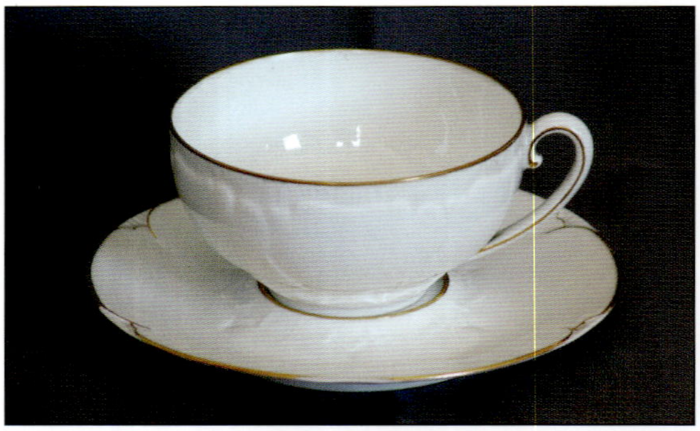
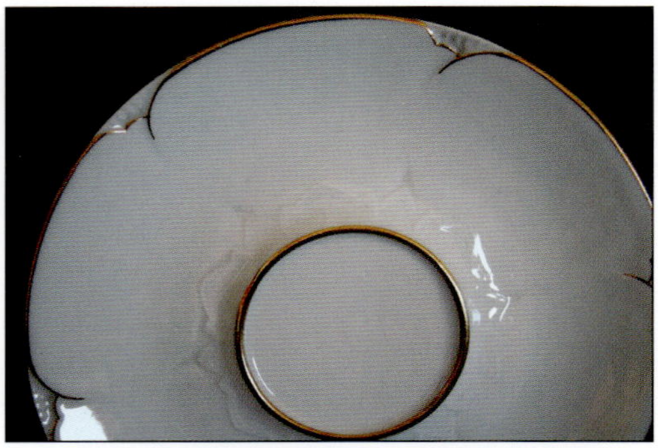
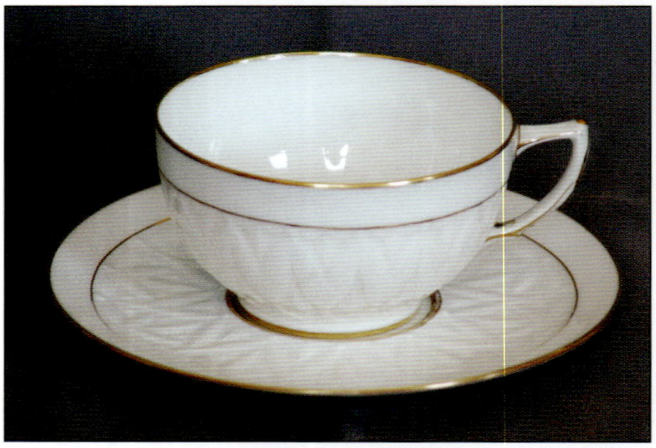
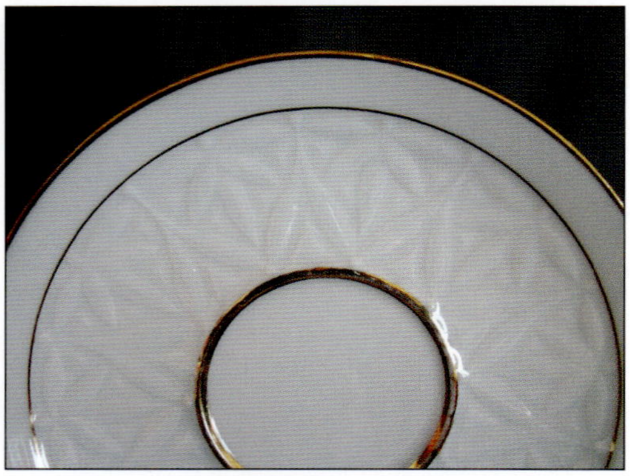
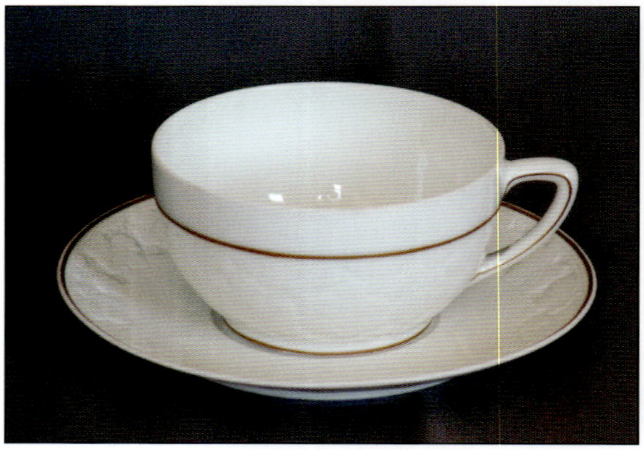
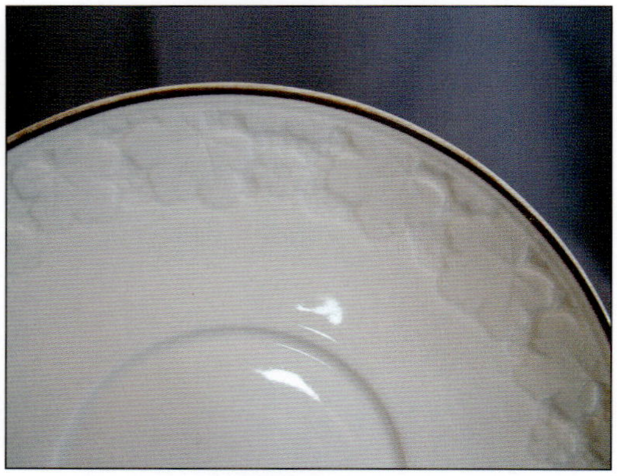
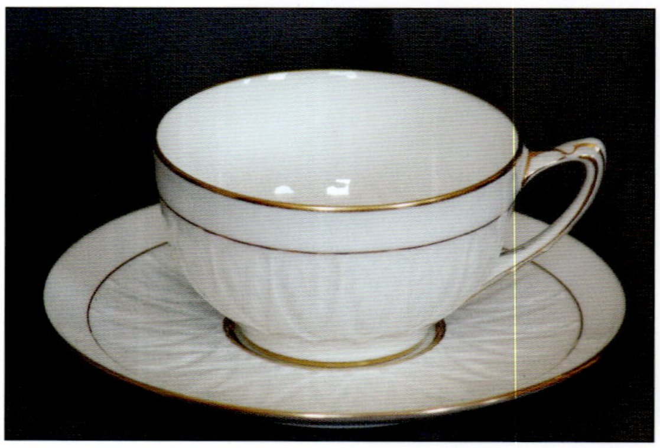
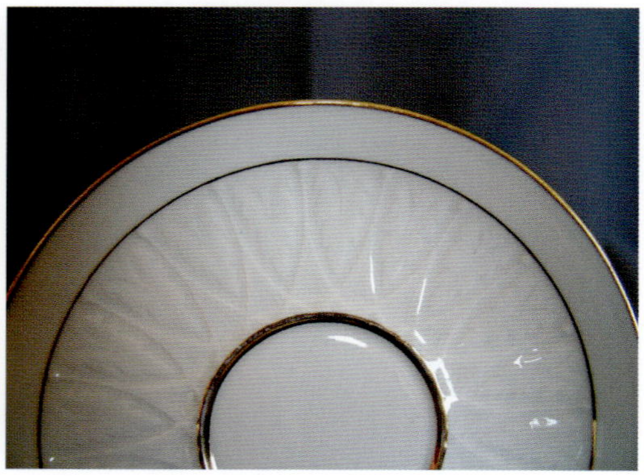
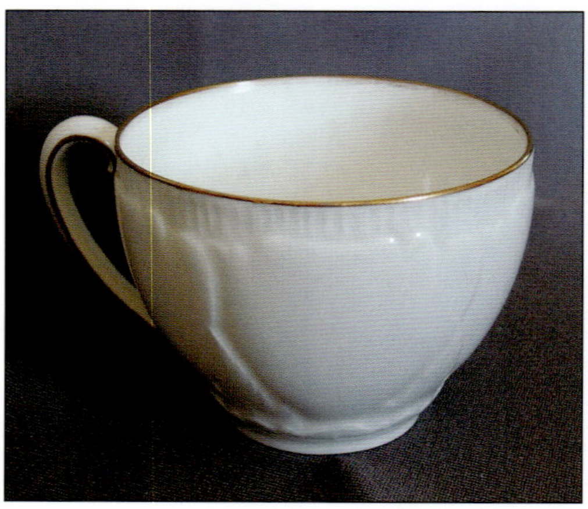

Shapes designed by Léon Jouhaud (Lionel Delaygue).

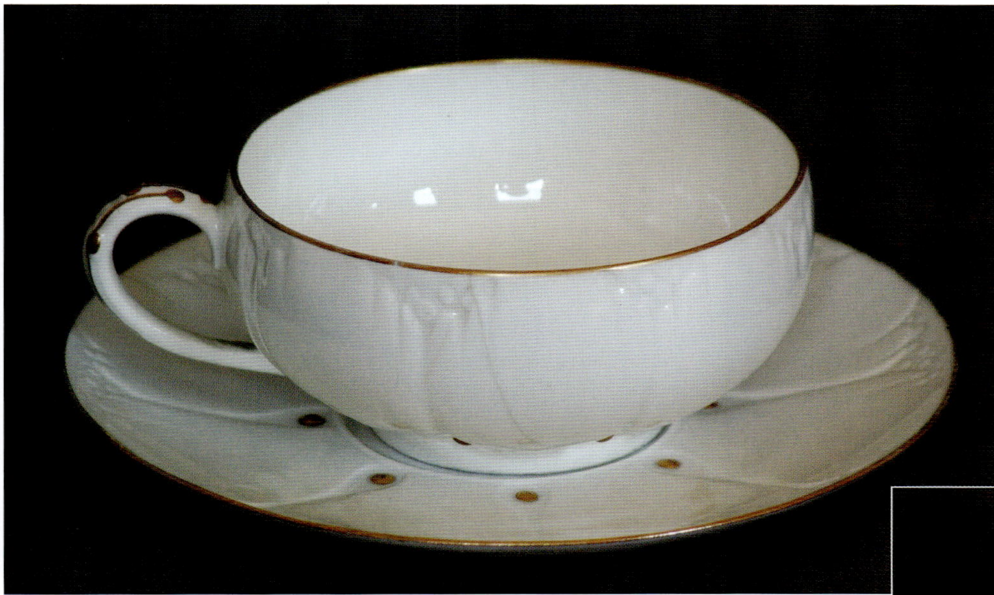

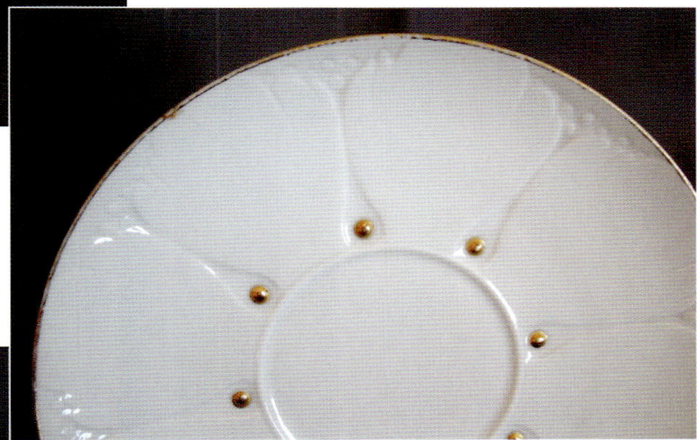

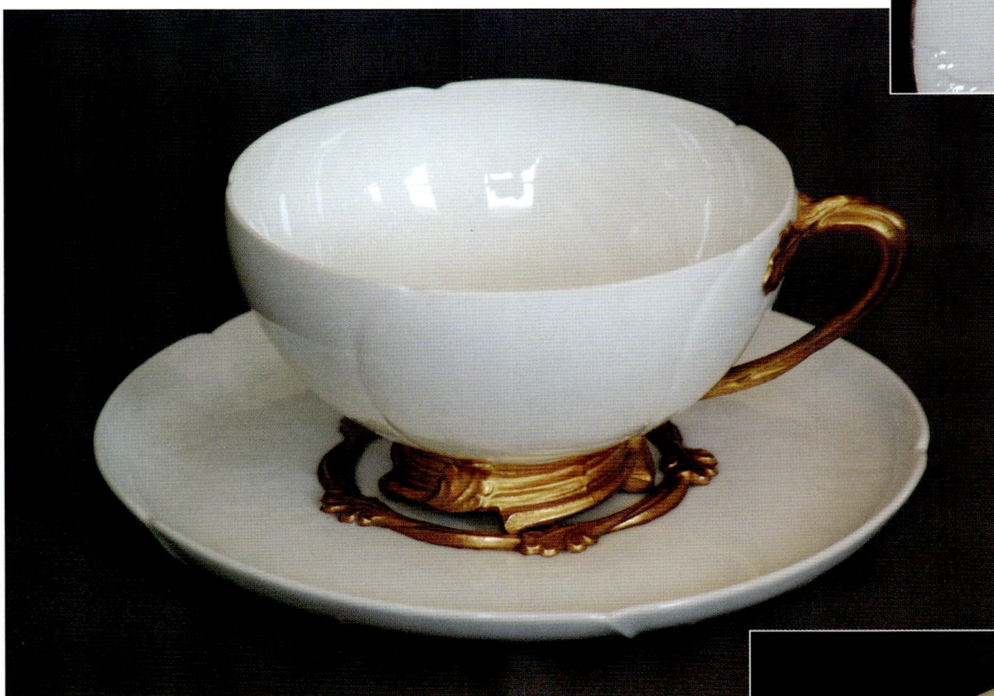

Shapes possibly designed by Léon Jouhaud (Lionel Delaygue).

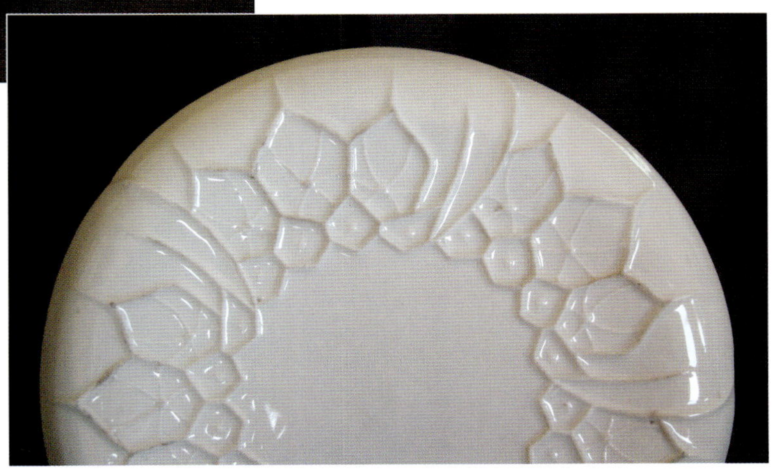

Other Art Deco Pieces in Royal Limoges Museum

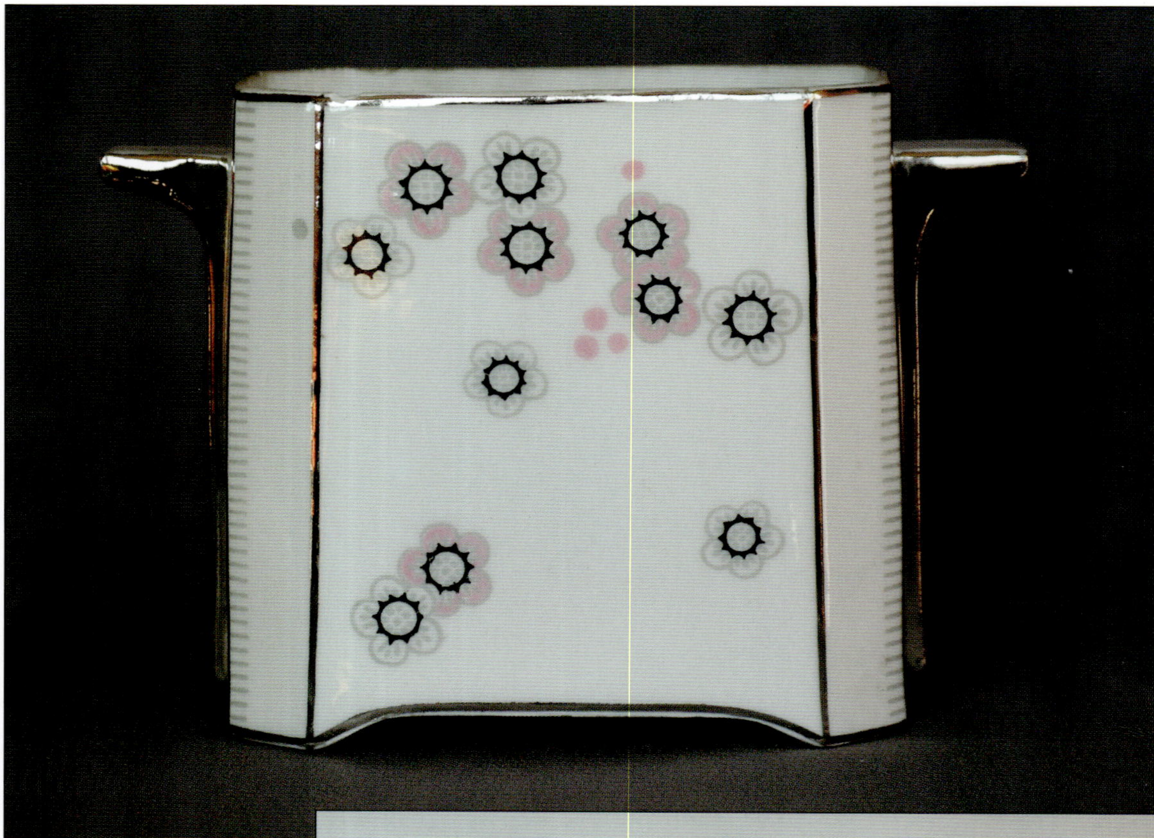

A. Lanternier, shape *Astra*.

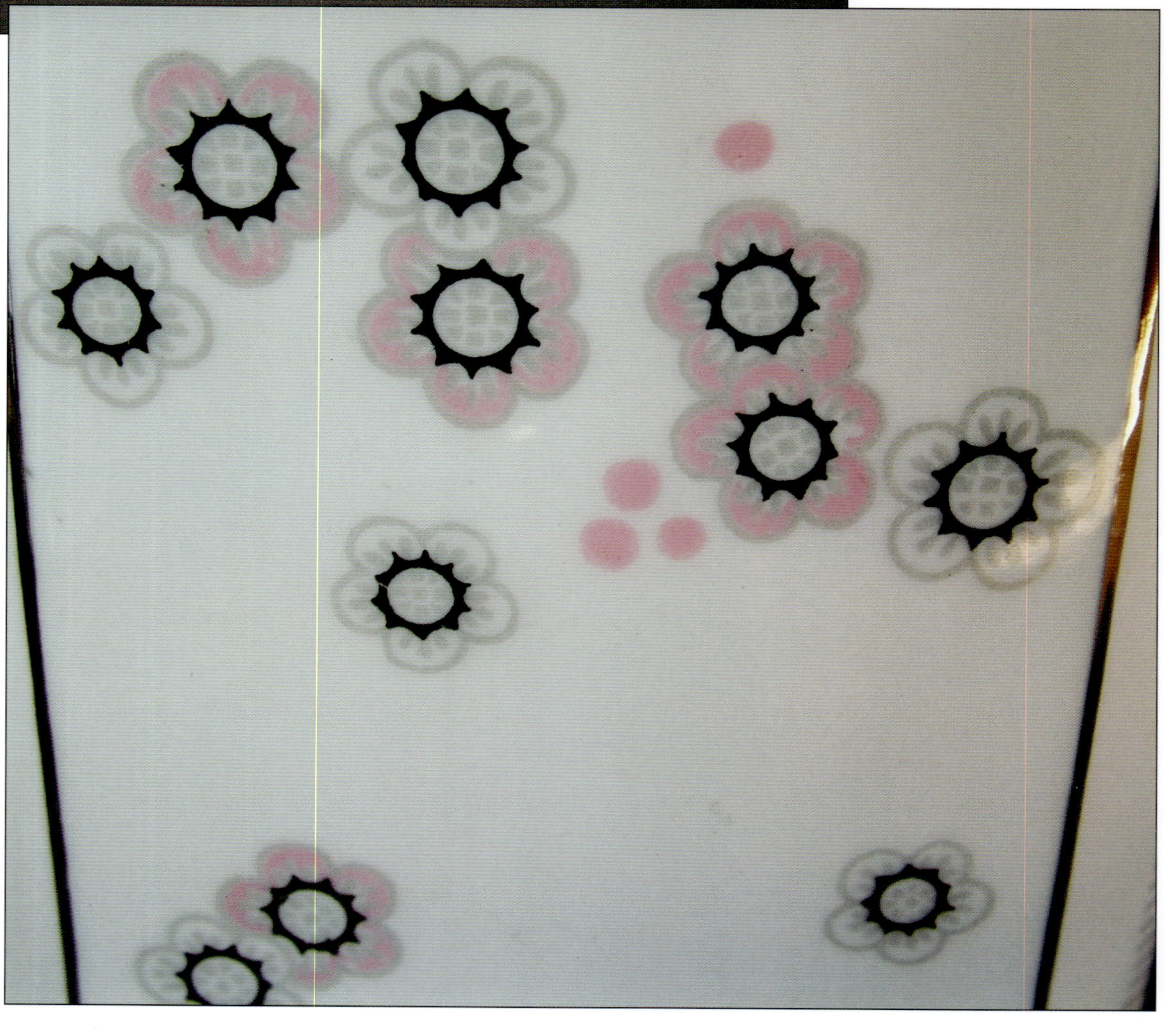

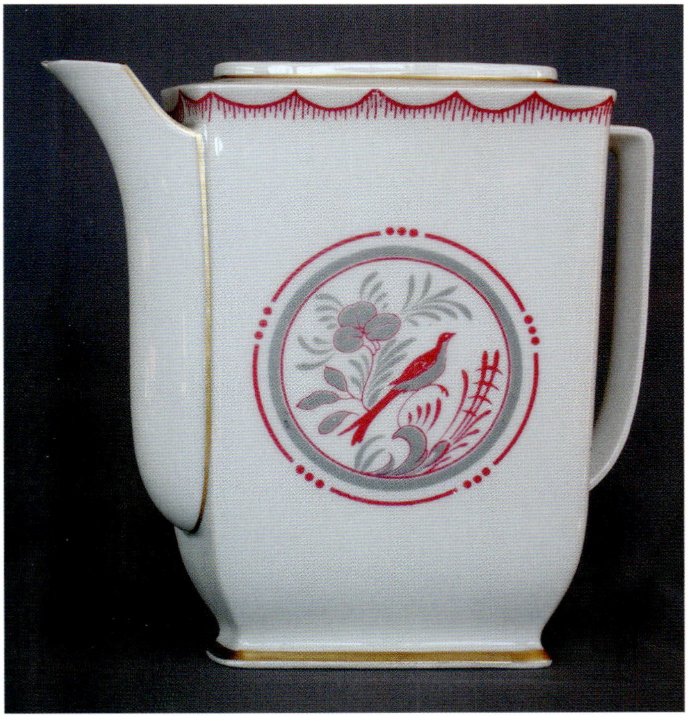

A. Lanternier.

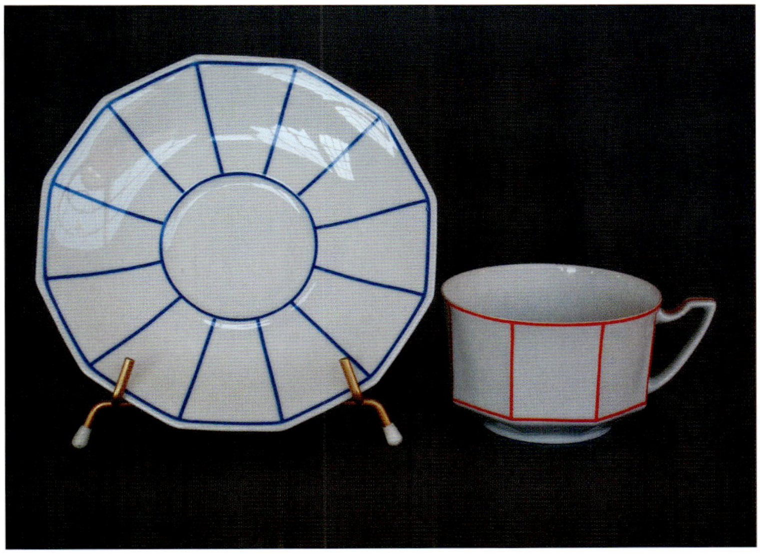

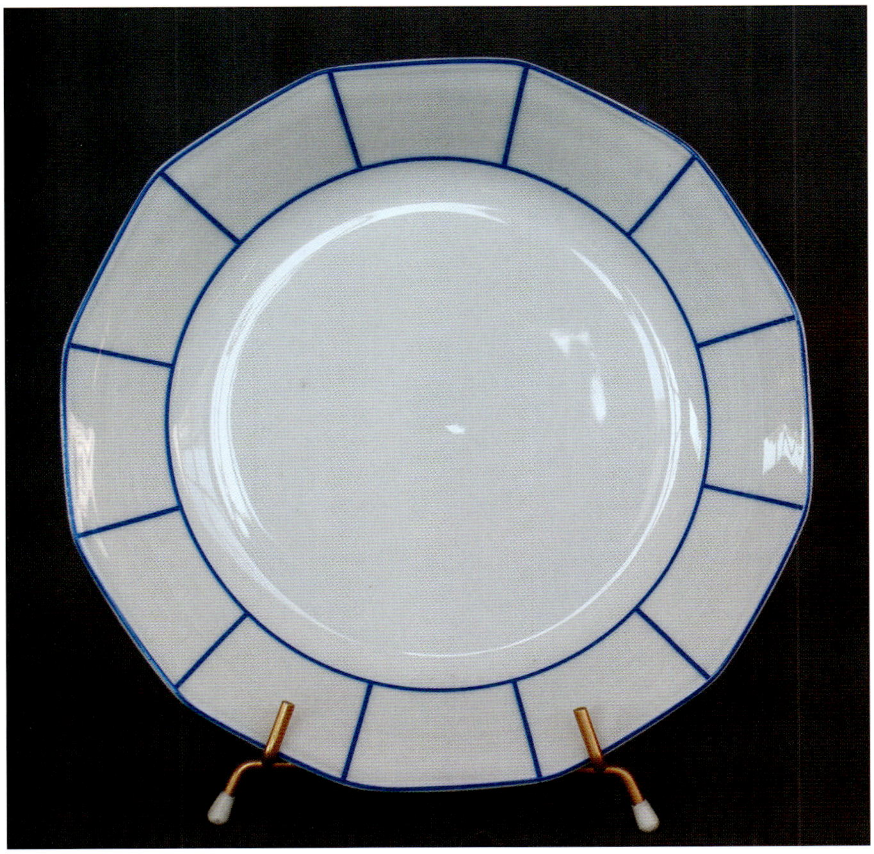

A. Lanternier, design with blue lines won the gold medal at the 1931 Exposition coloniale internationale, Paris.

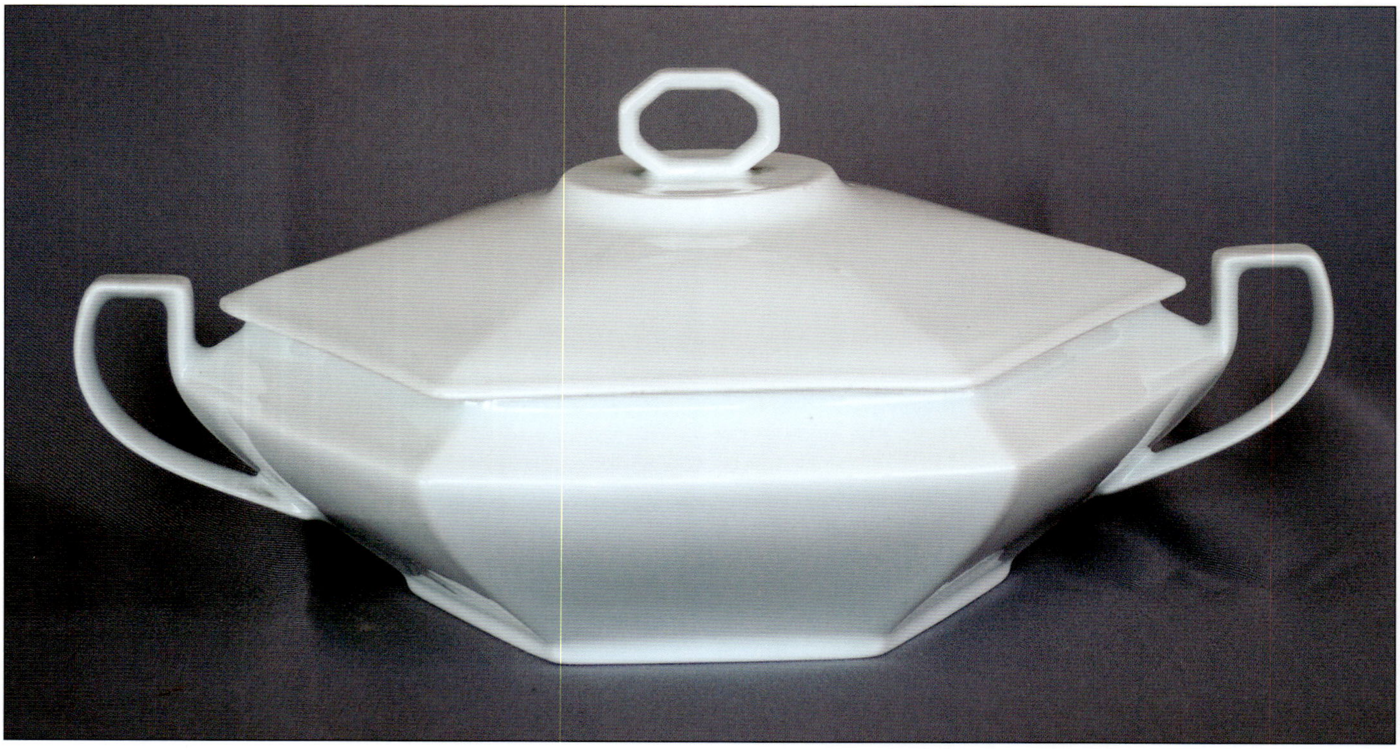

Covered Vegetable Bowl.

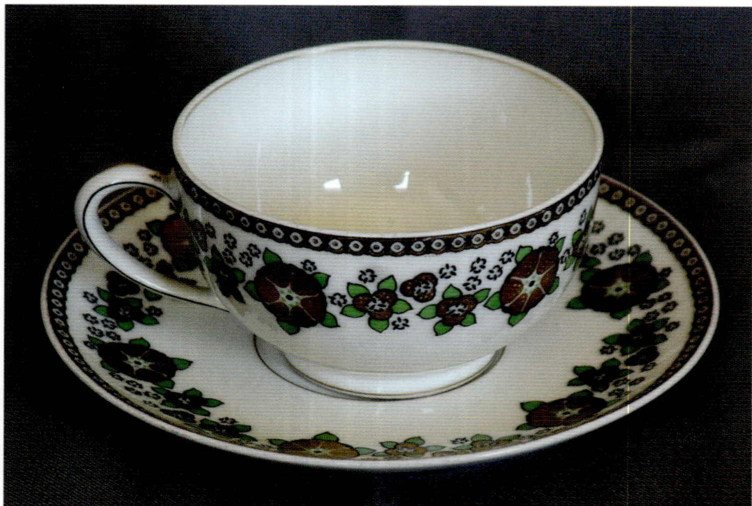

Marked GDA.

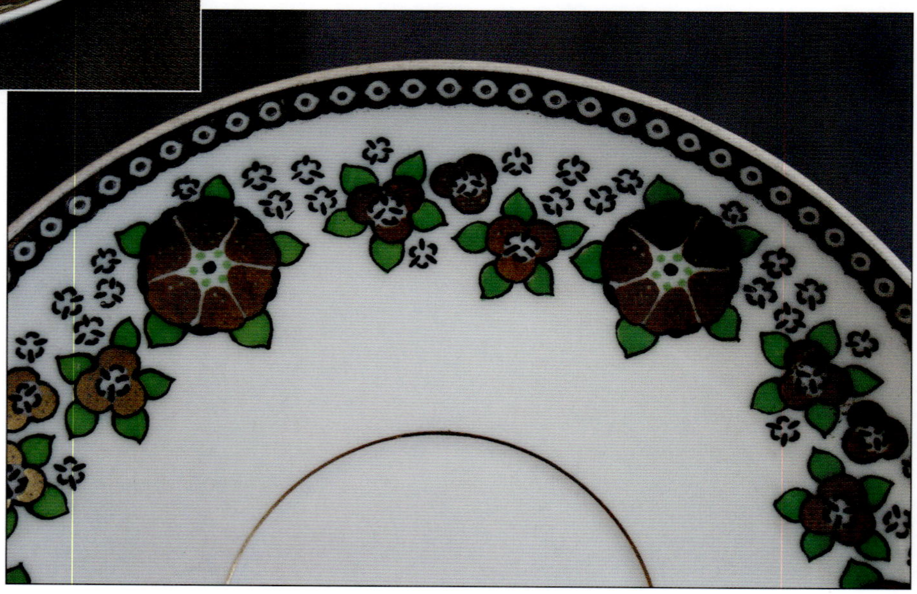

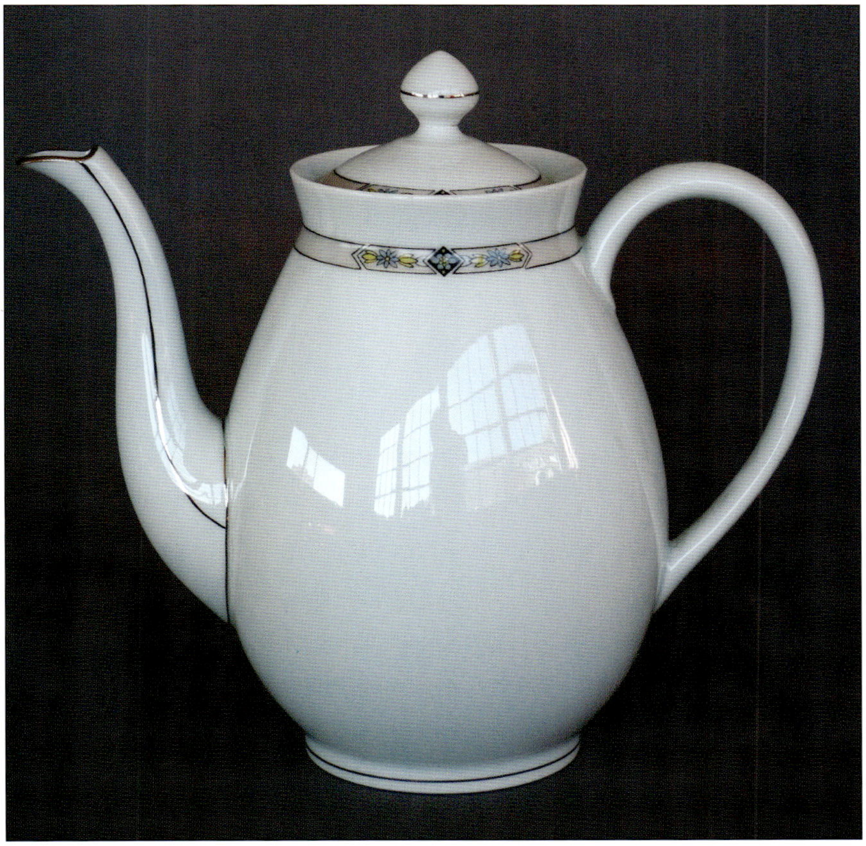

Coffee pot, Harmony shape, decoration of Granville/Diamant.

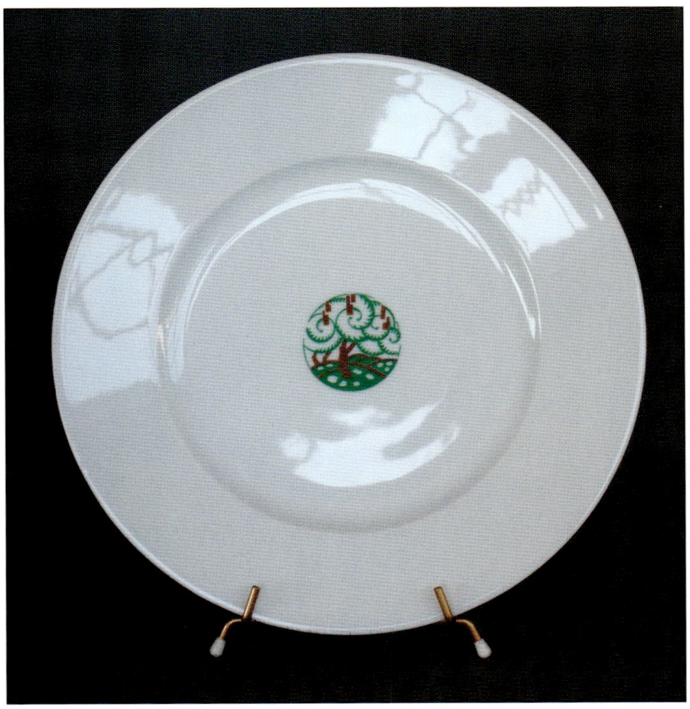

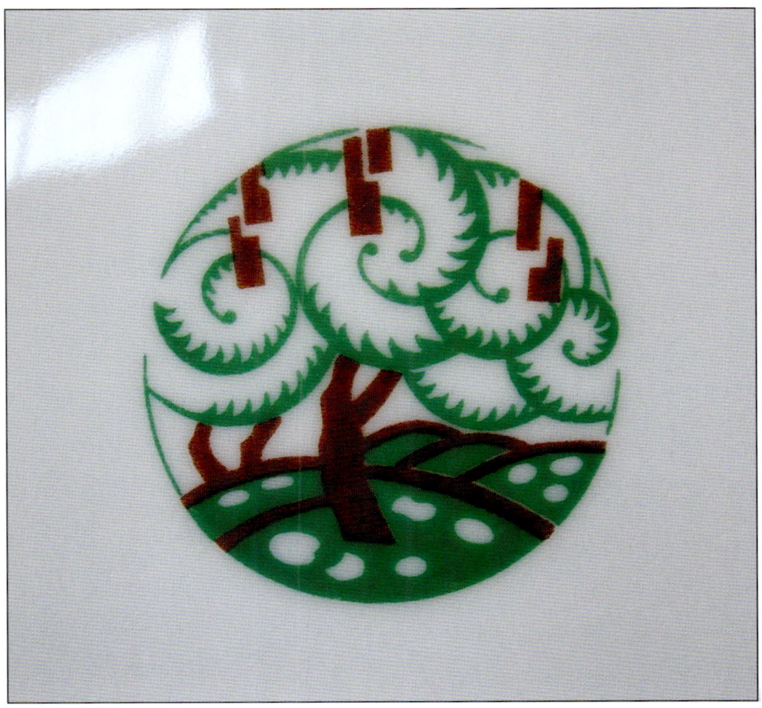

A. Lanternier.

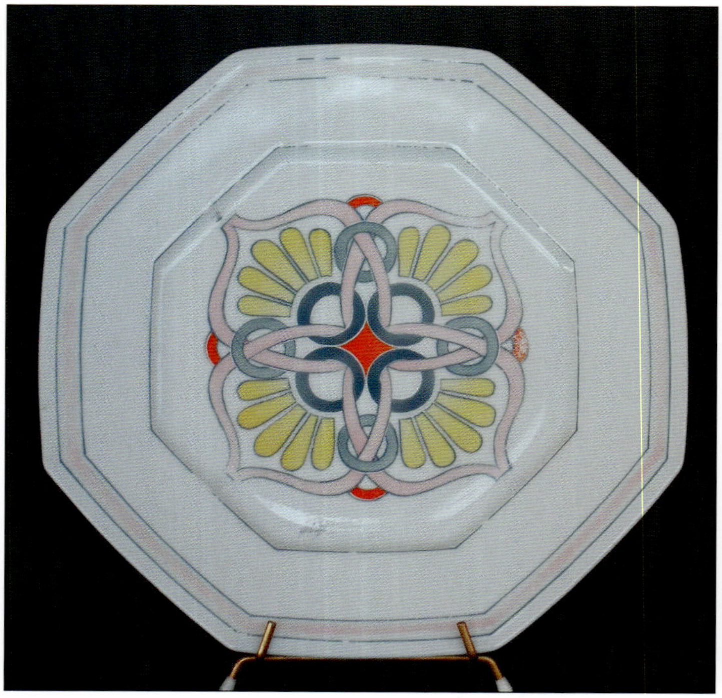

A. Lanternier.

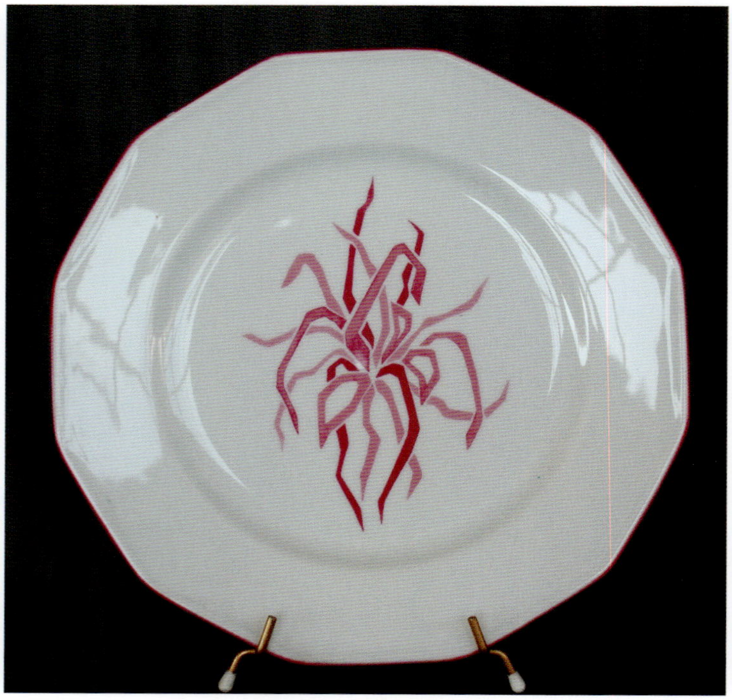

Art Deco shaped plate but pattern is more modern, A. Lanternier.

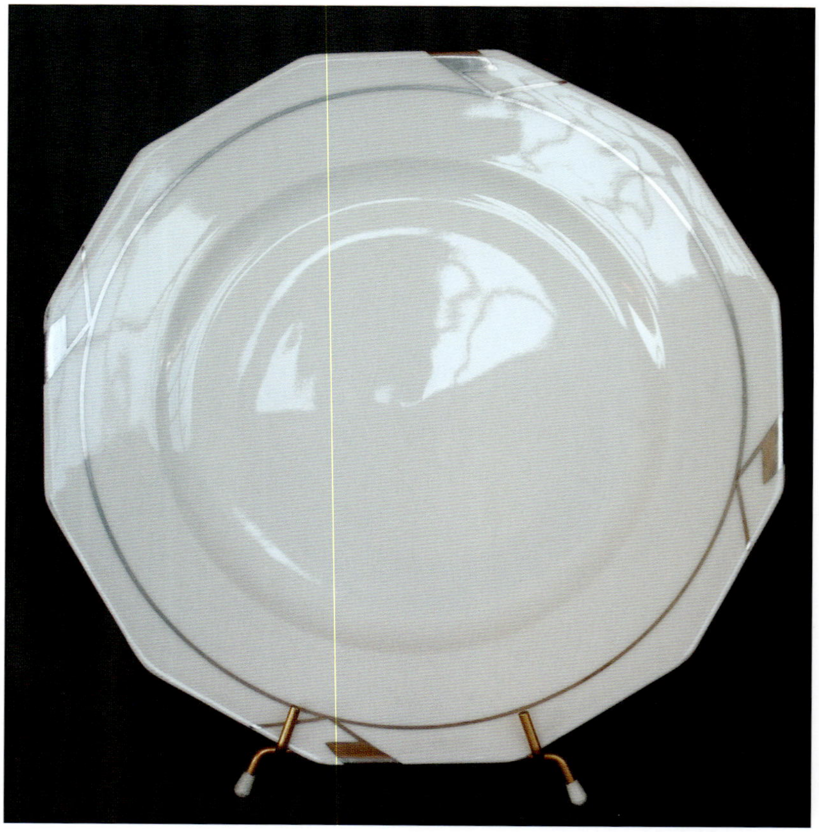

Art Deco shaped plate but pattern is more modern.

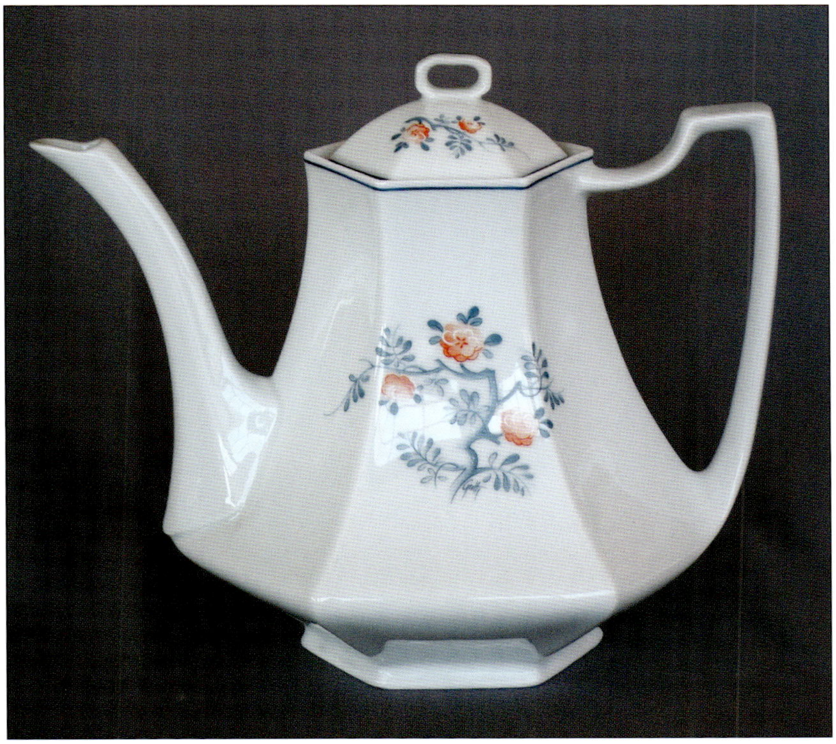

Coffee pot has an Art Deco shape but the pattern is more modern, A. Lanternier.

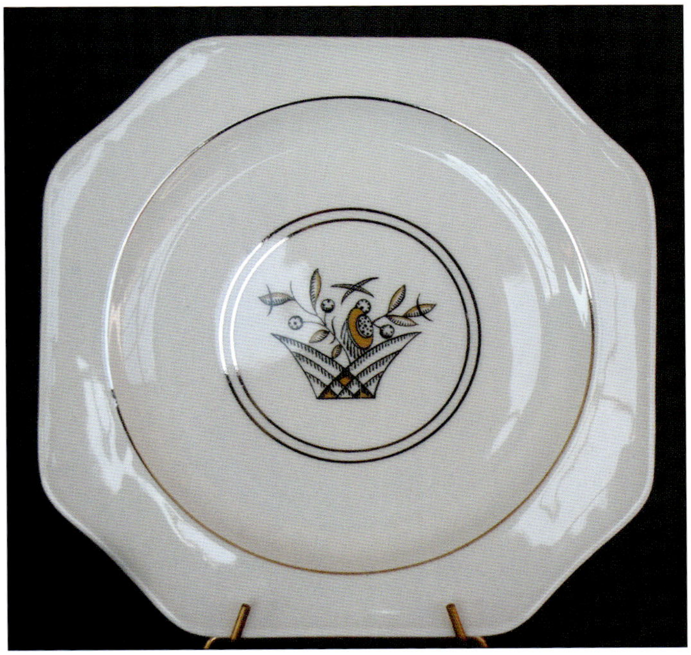

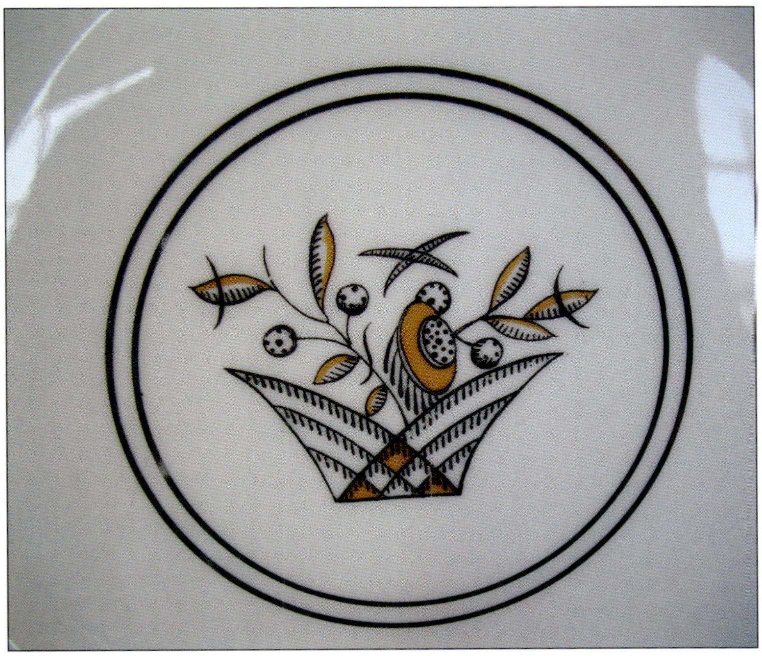

Shape of plate is Astra and the decoration is Fanny, A. Lanternier.

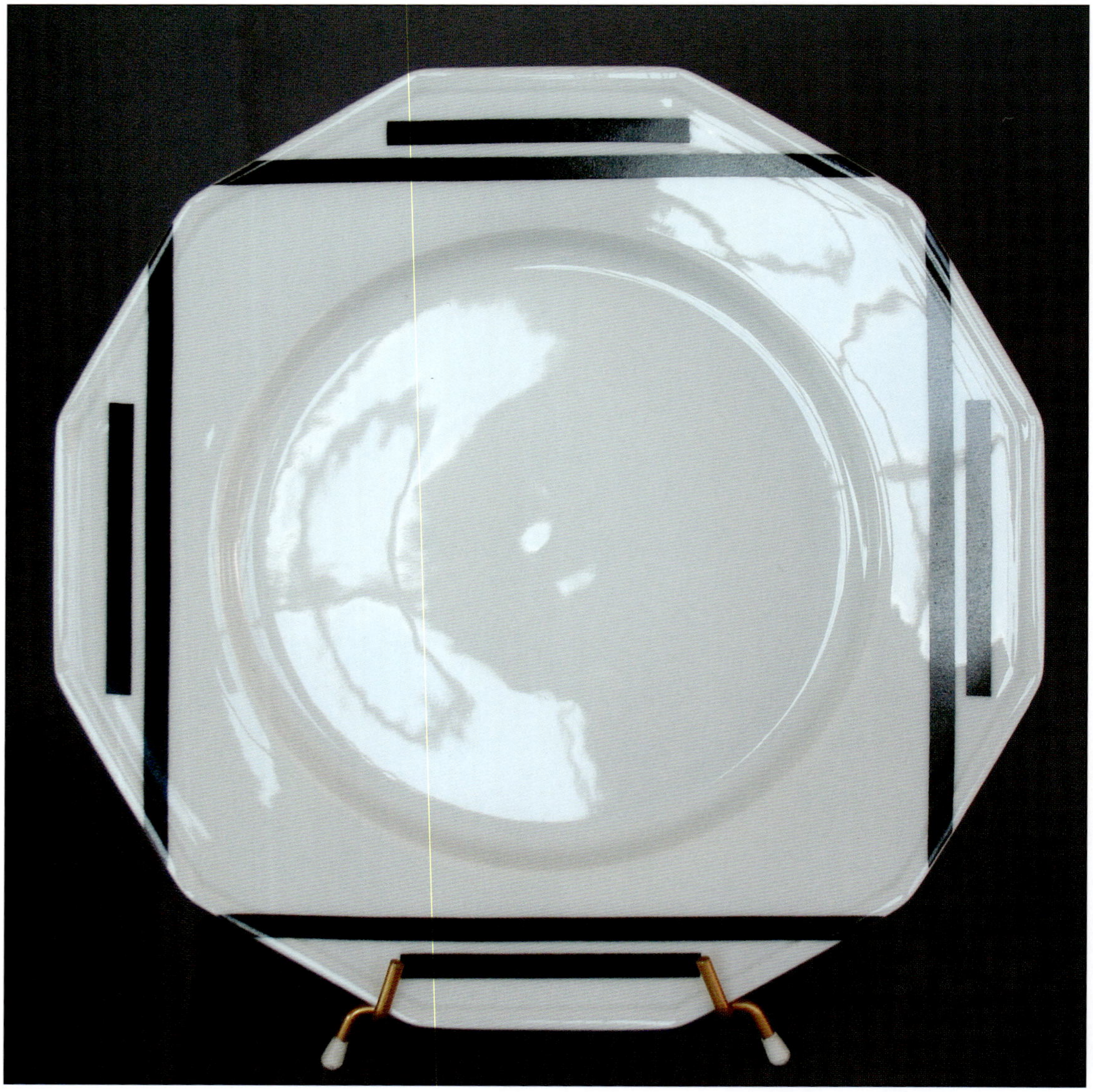

A. Lanternier.

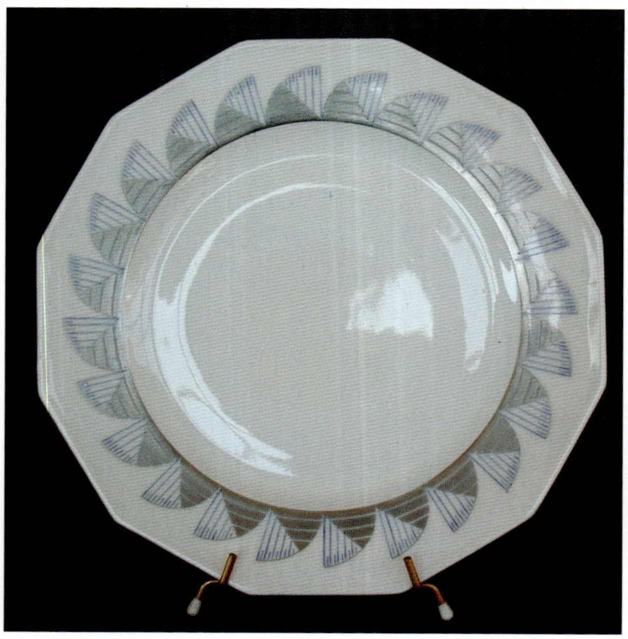

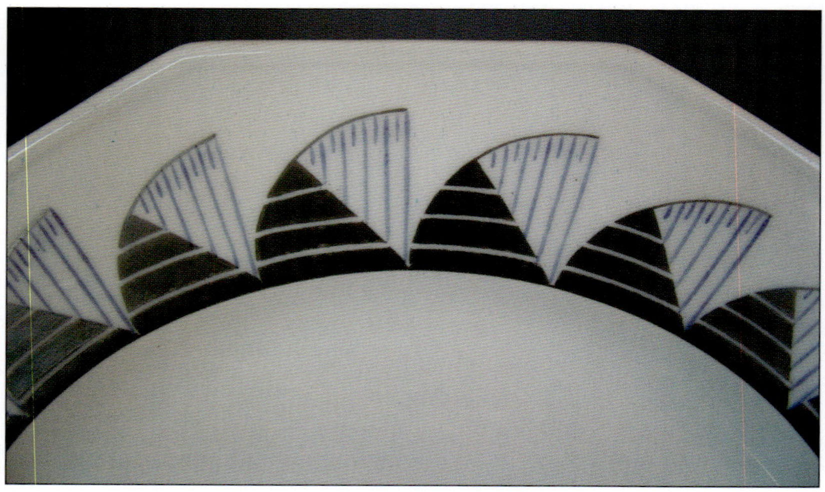

Pronounced Art Deco pattern.

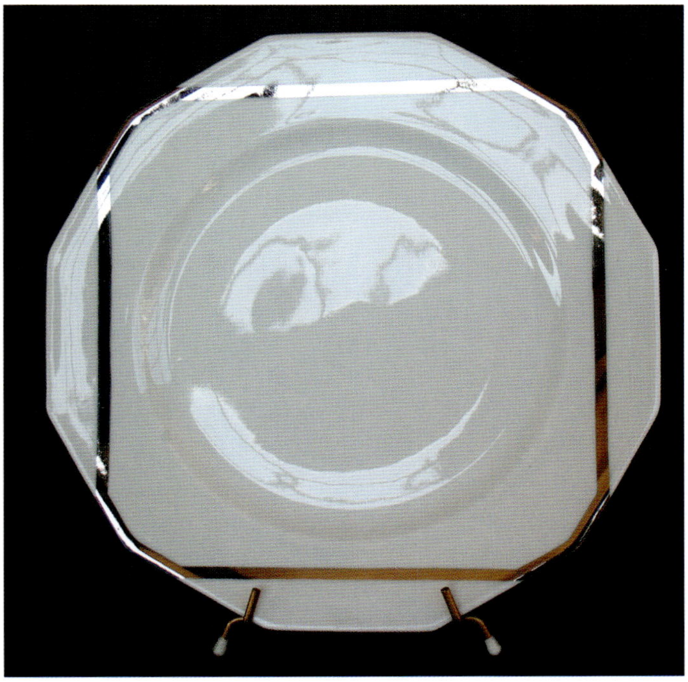

Bold square pattern, A. Lanternier.

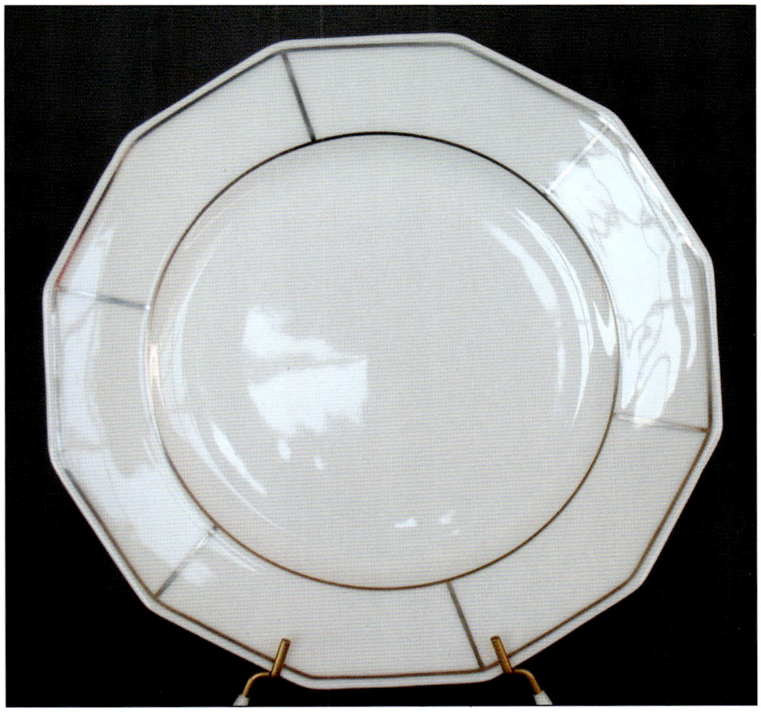

A. Lanternier.

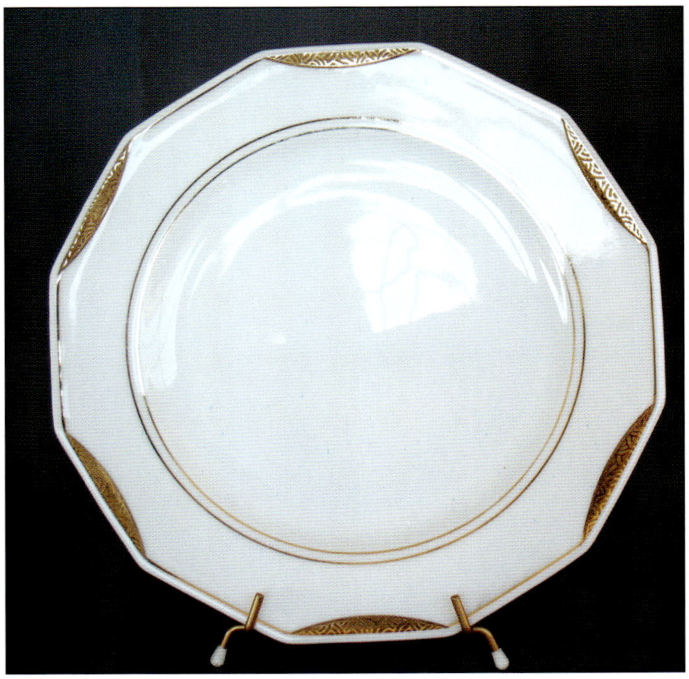

Shape is Rouen and pattern is Eclipse.

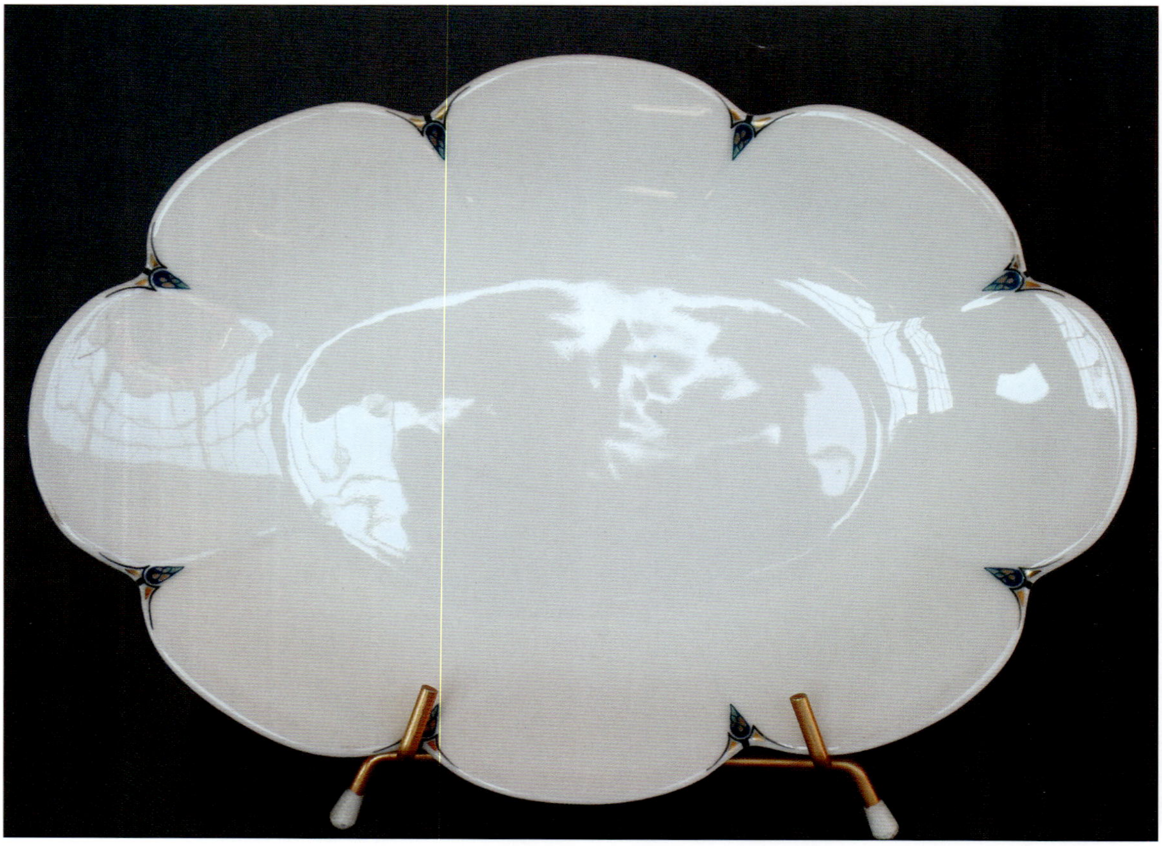

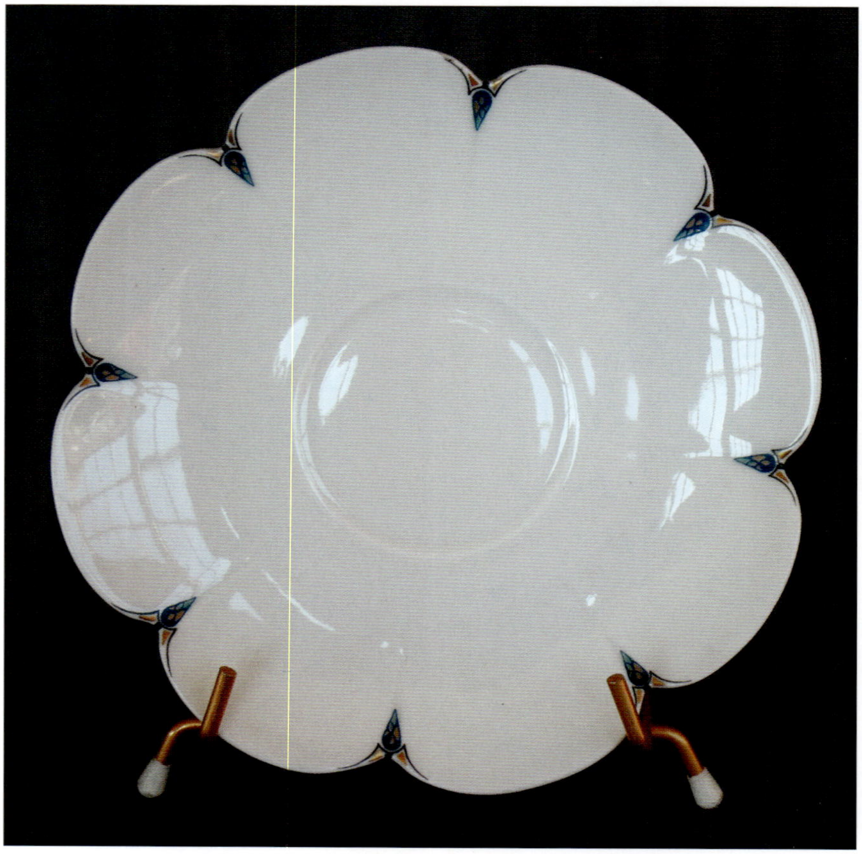

Pattern is named Apollo and design won a prize at the 1925 Exposition internationale des arts décoratifs industriels et moderns, Paris, GDA.

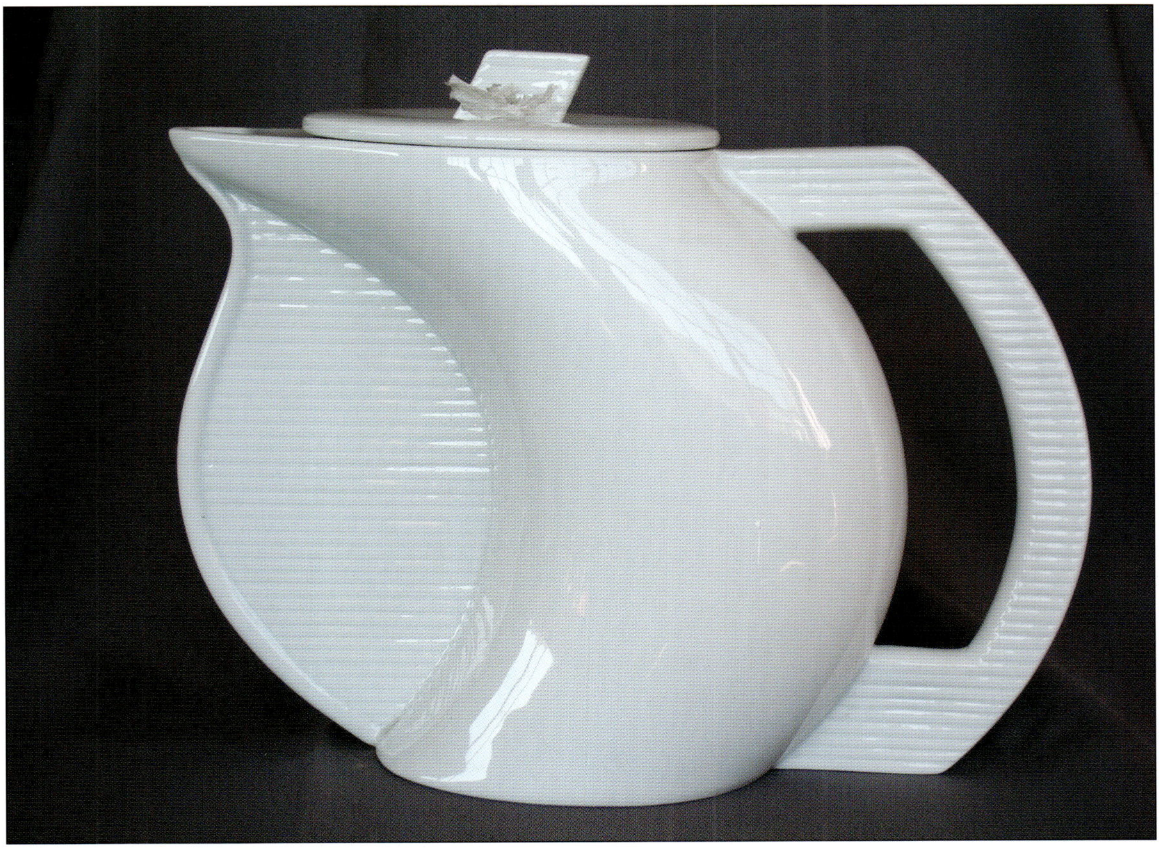

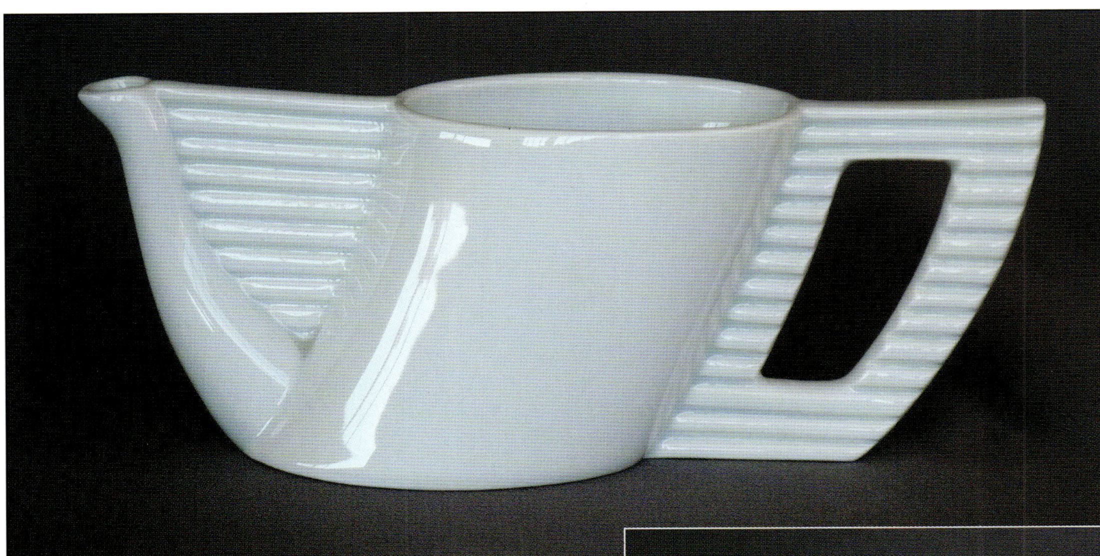

Art Deco design made for the World Cup, Royal Limoges.

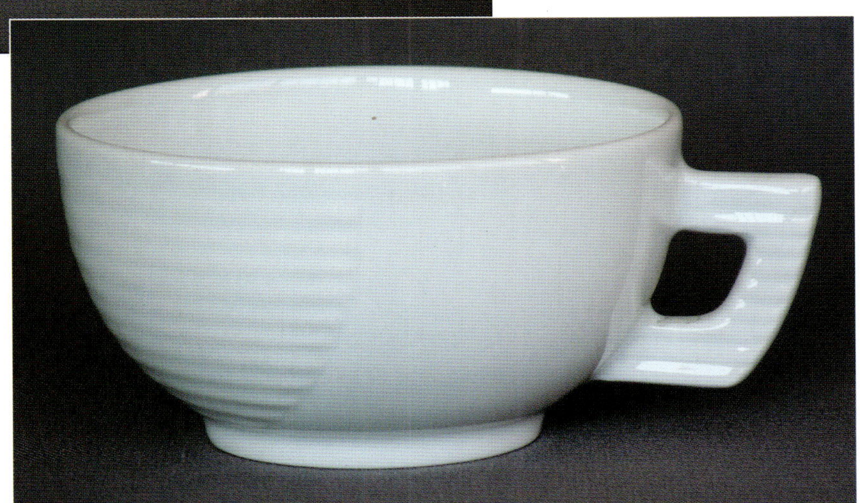

Art Deco Patterns from the GDA Design Book

All of these Art Deco patterns were made by GDA for dinnerware. These patterns comprise one of the most complete Art Deco collections for a major Limoges company.

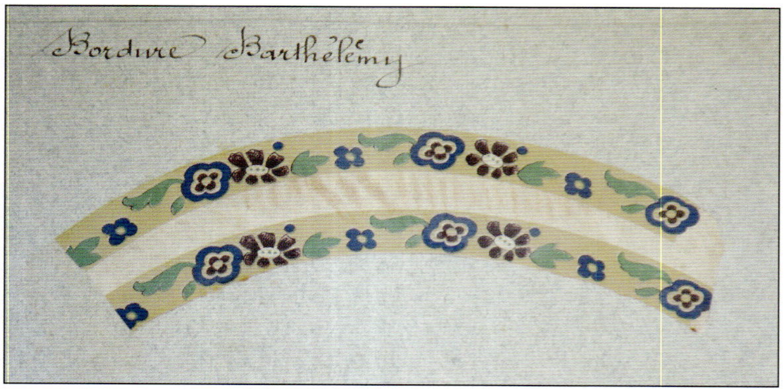

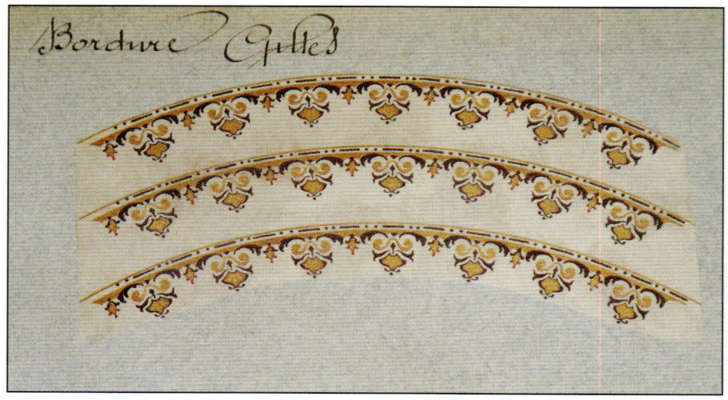

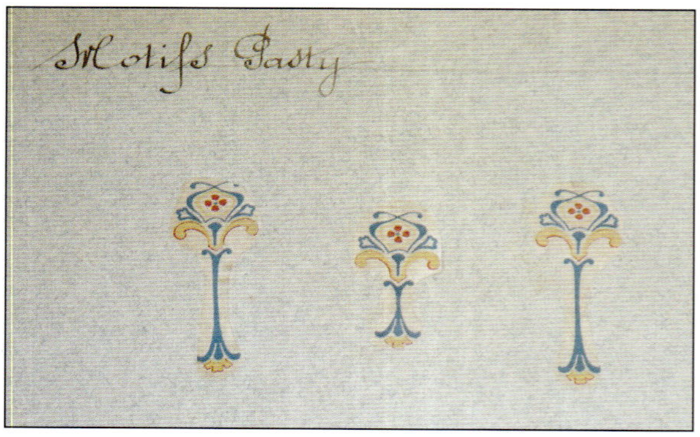

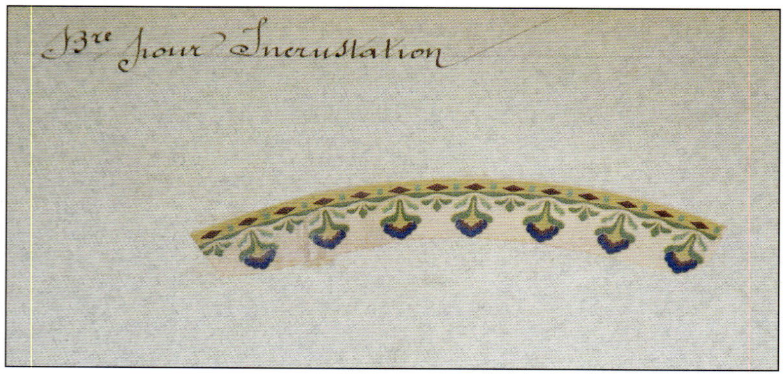

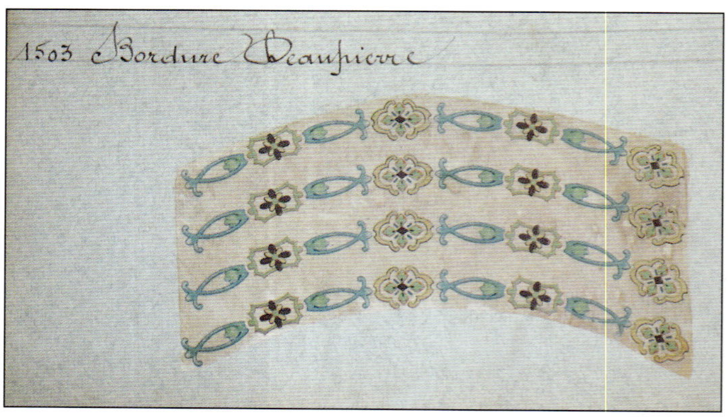

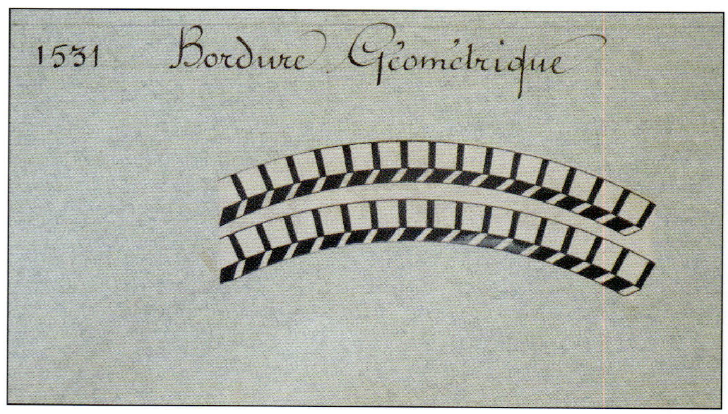

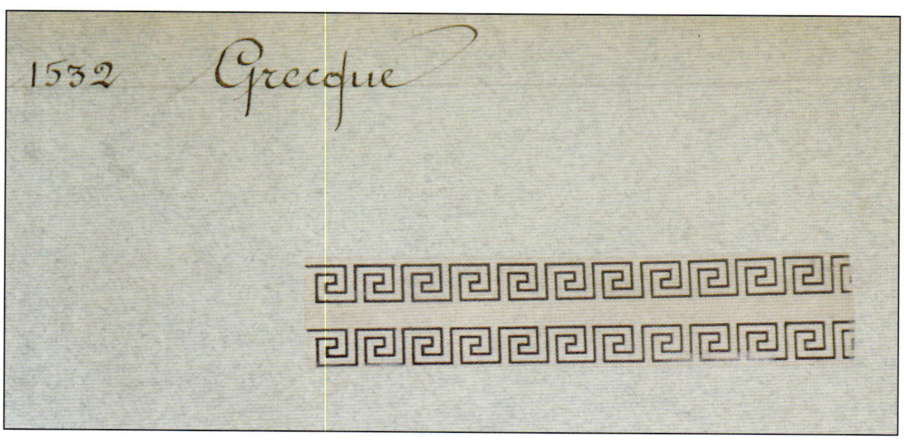

1644.- Motifs Charleville

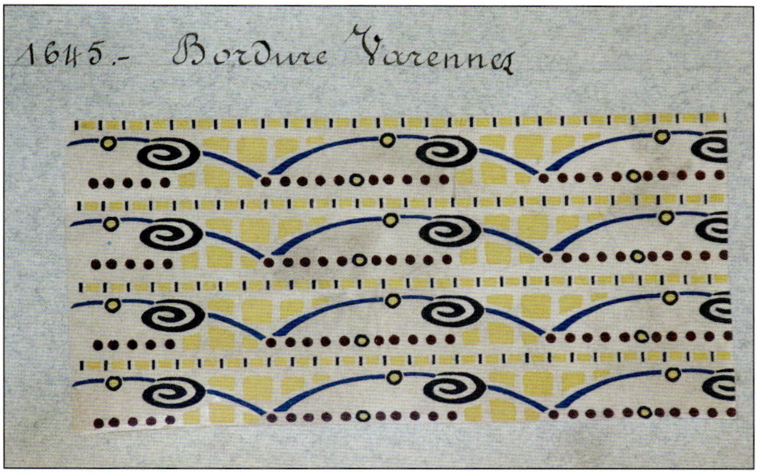
1645.- Bordure Varennes

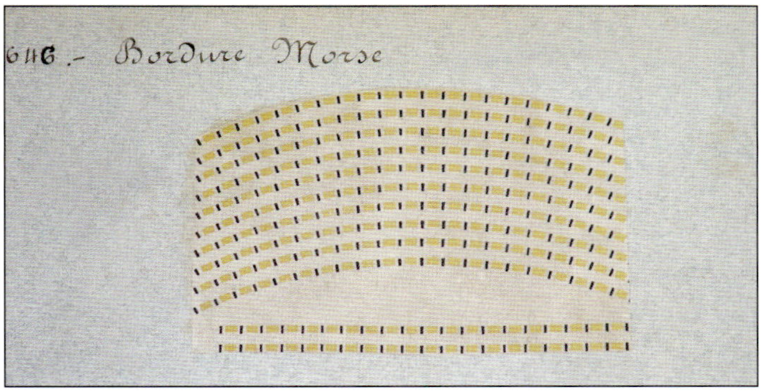
646.- Bordure Morse

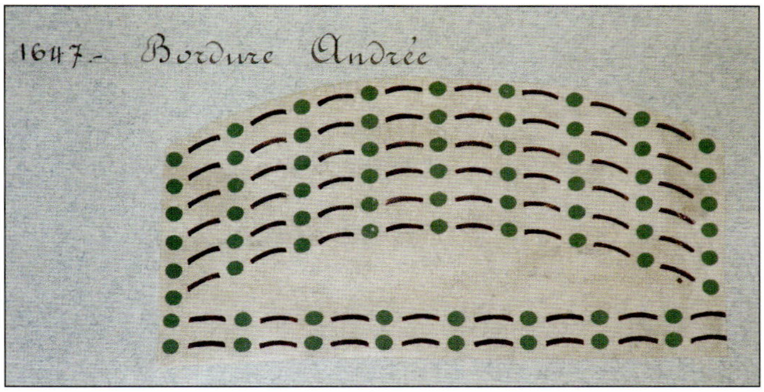
1647.- Bordure Andrée

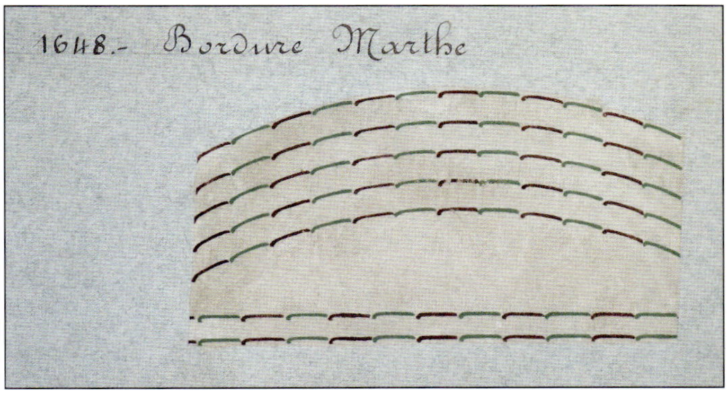
1648.- Bordure Marthe

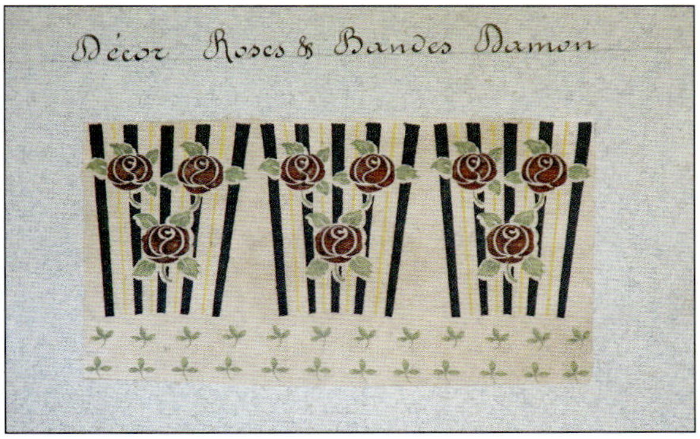
Décor Roses & Bandes Damon

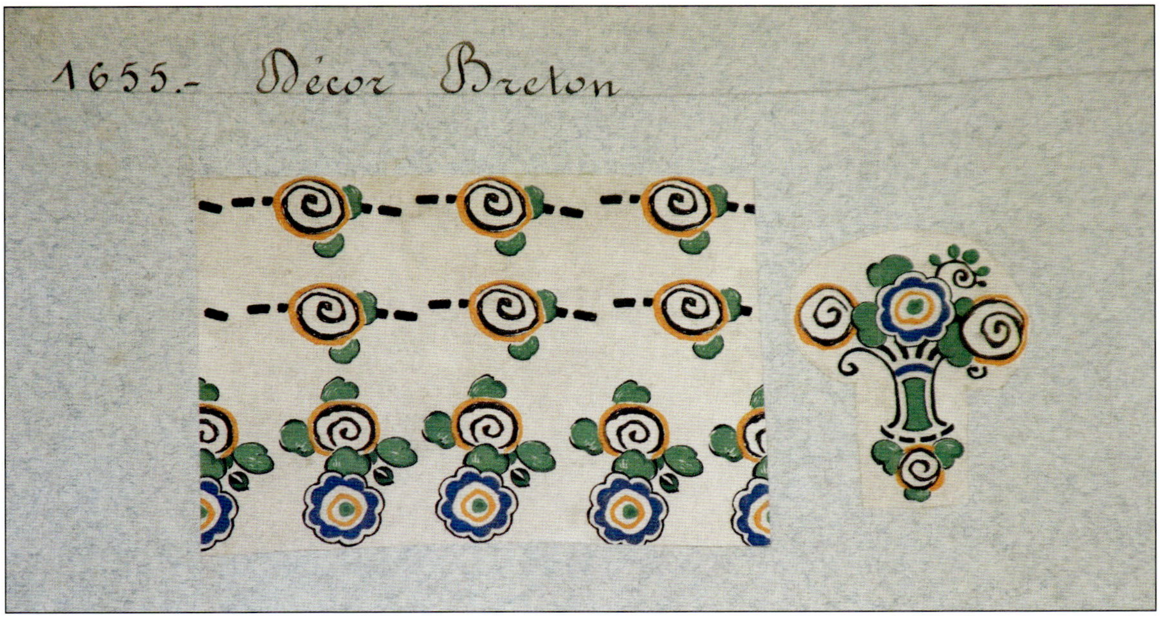
1655.- Décor Breton

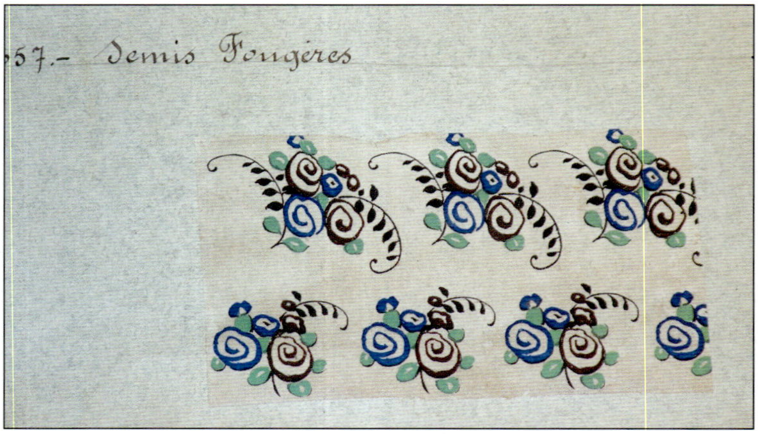
57.- Demis Fougères

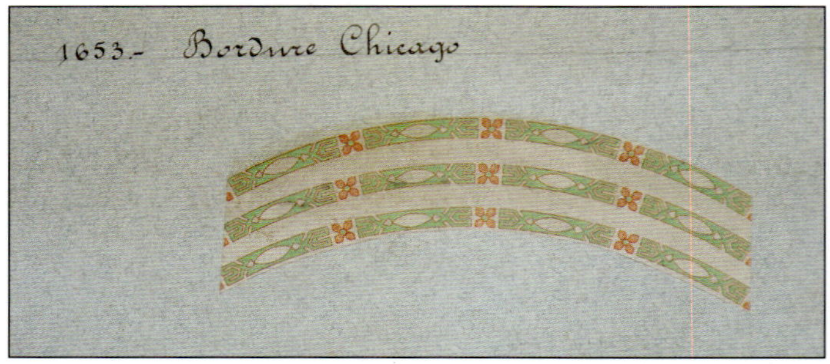
1653.- Bordure Chicago

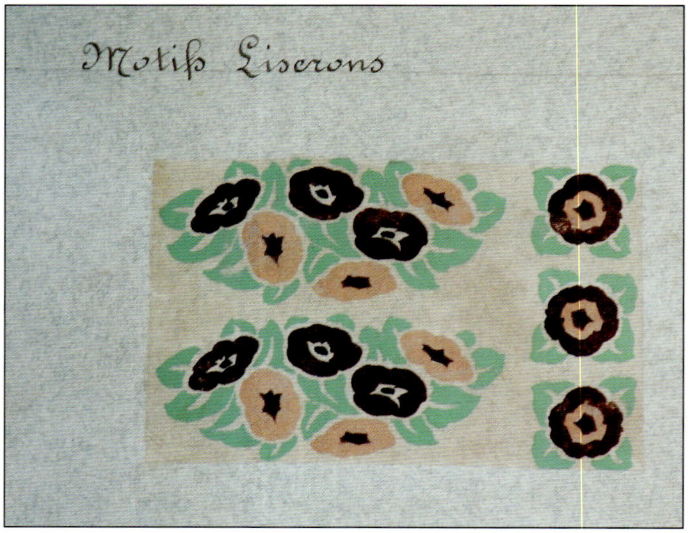
Motifs Liserons

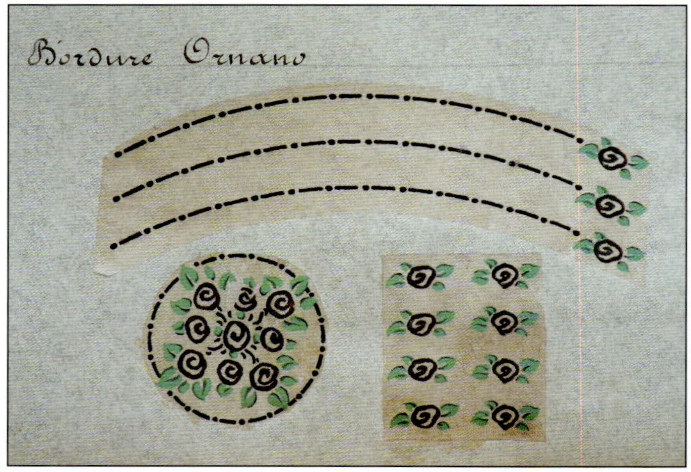
Bordure Ornano

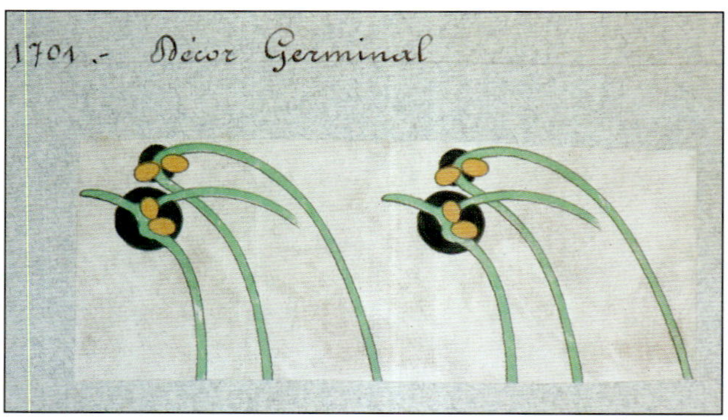
1701.- Décor Germinal

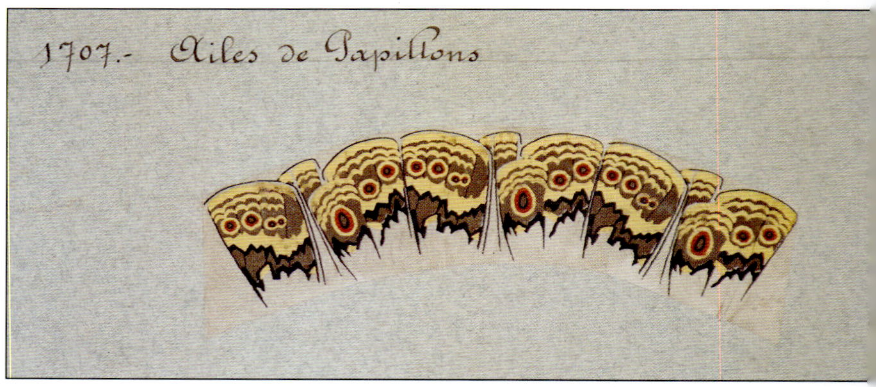
1707.- Ailes de Papillons

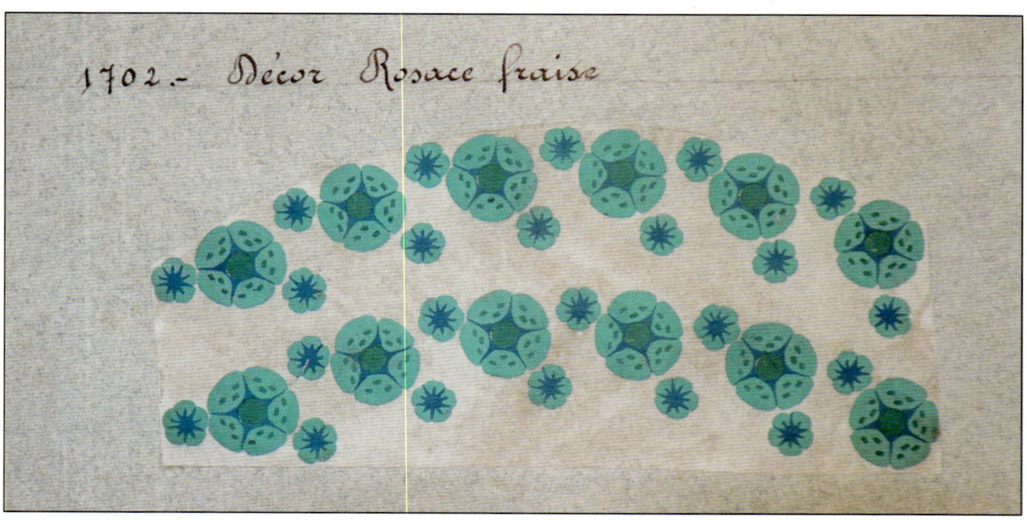
1702.- Décor Rosace fraise

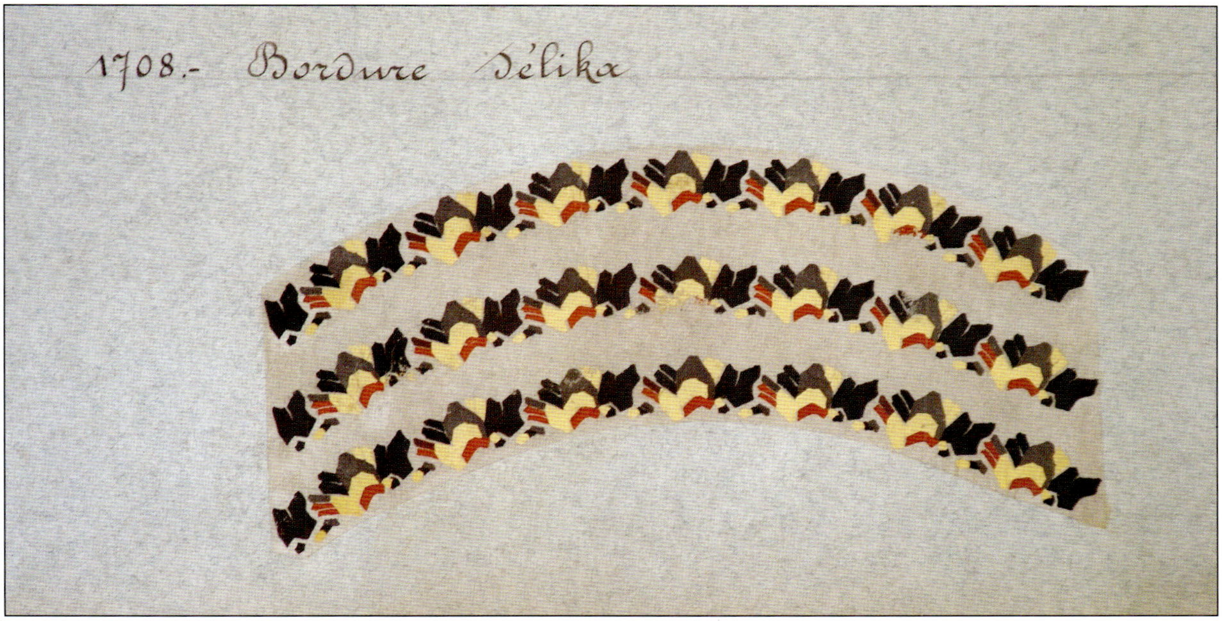
1708.- Bordure Délika

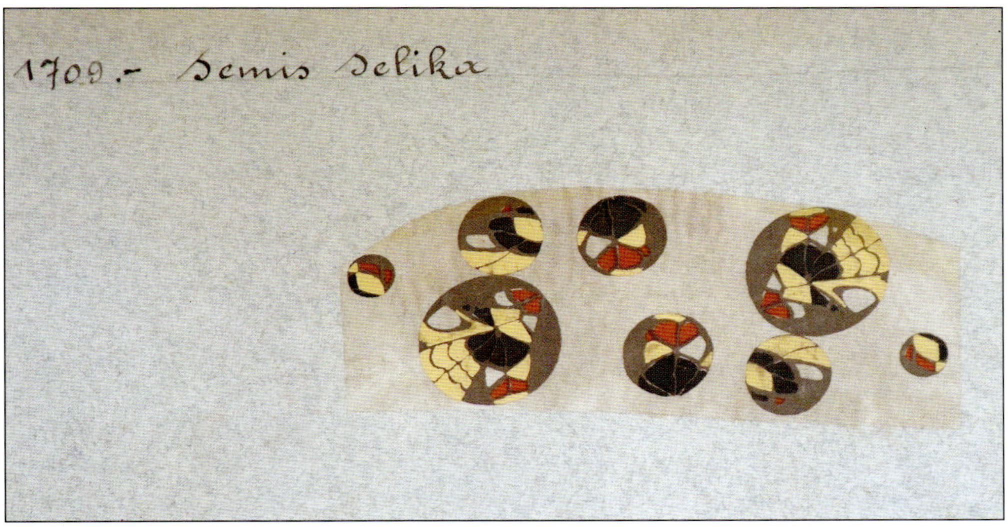
1709.- Semis Délika

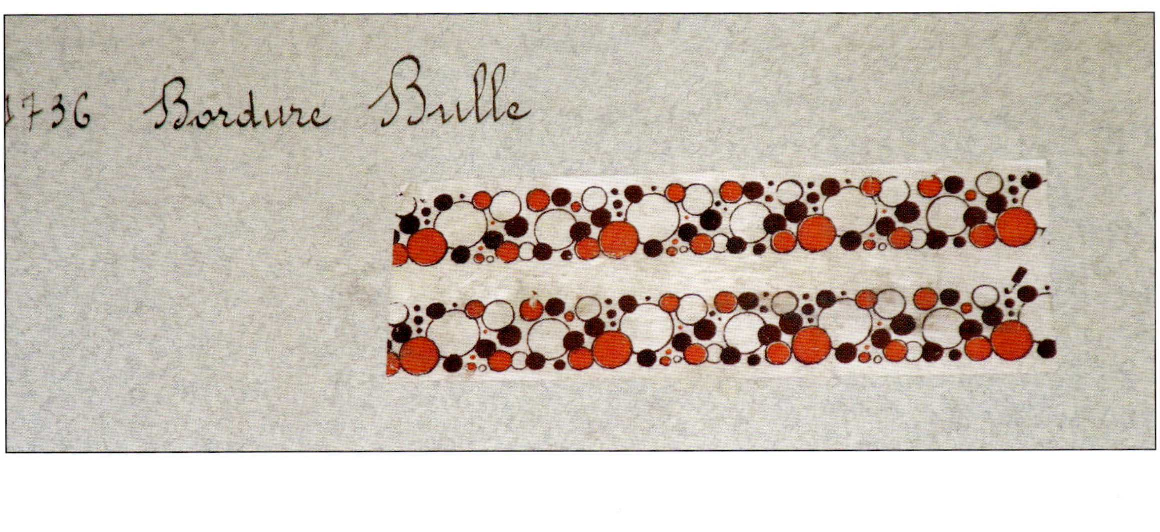
1736 Bordure Bulle

Selected Other Limoges Art Deco Porcelain

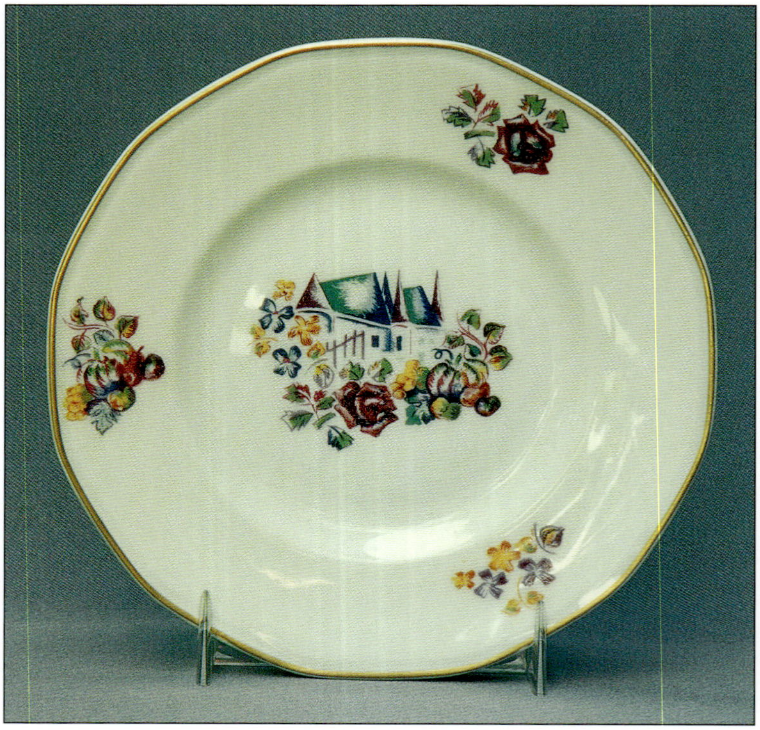

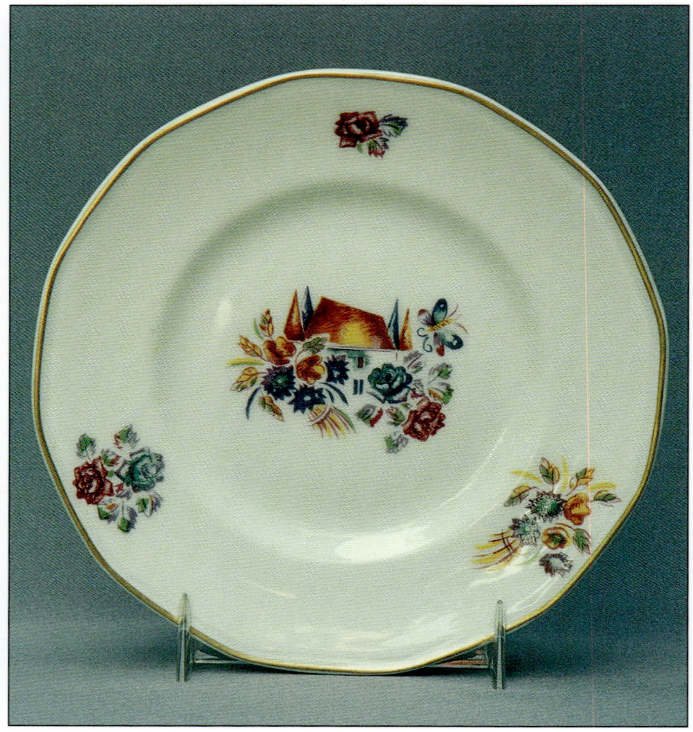

Plates, Jean Dufy for T. Haviland. Less than $500 each.

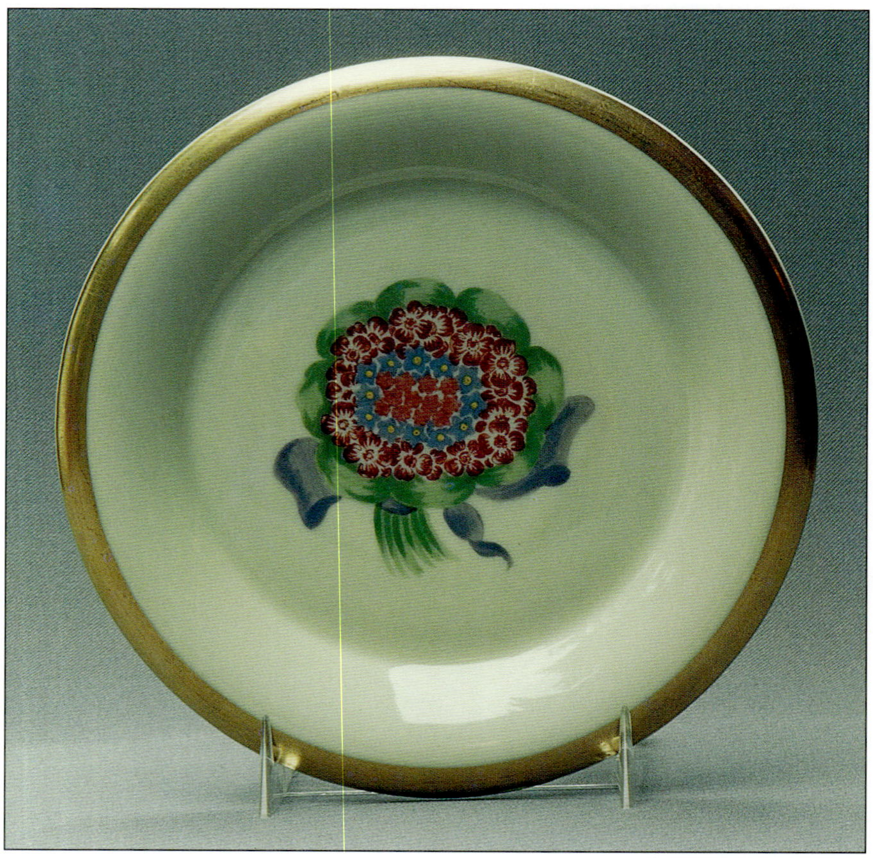

Plate, design by Marcel Goupy on *Orsay* ivory blank designed by Goupy, from a 19th century Chinese shape. (d'Albis). Less than $500.

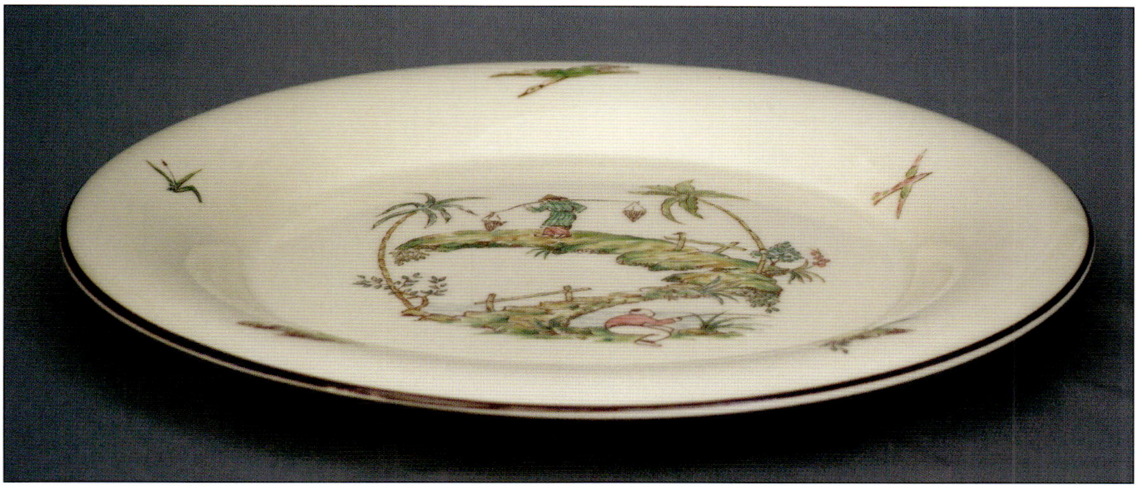

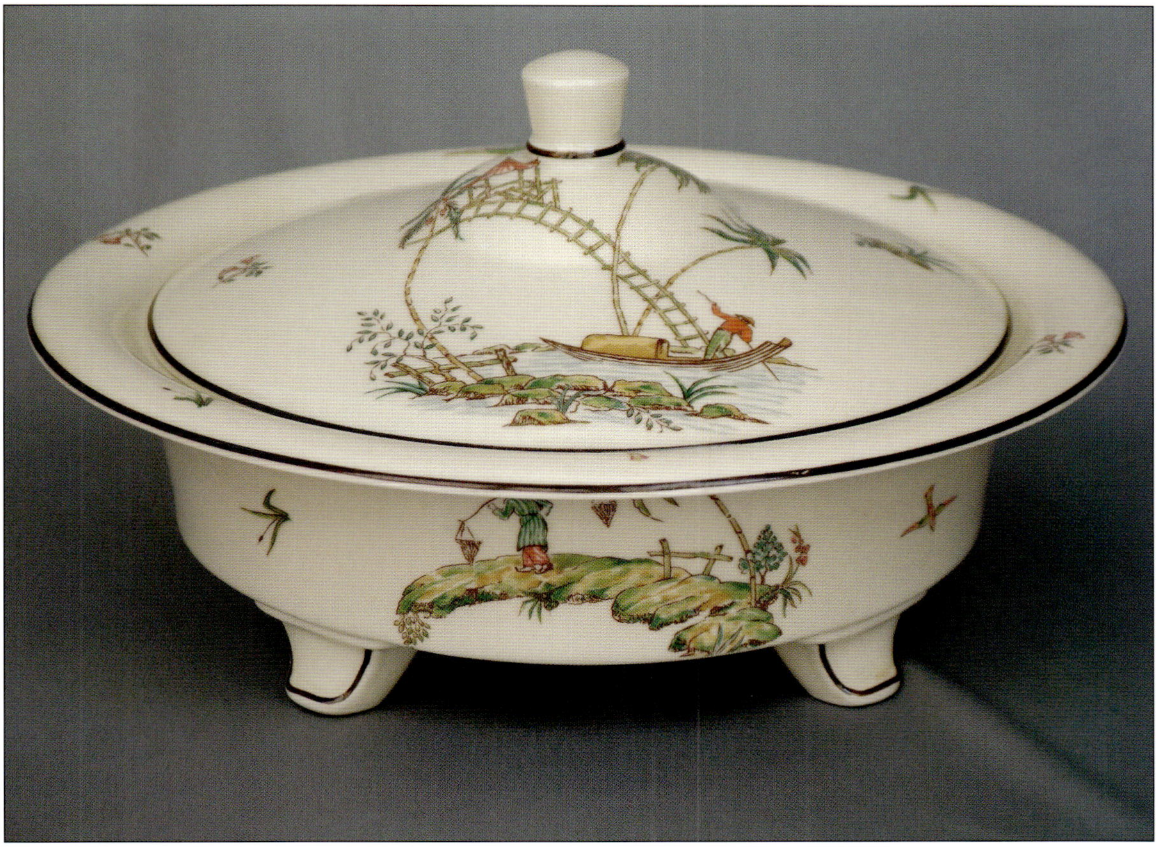

Plate, covered vegetable bowl, and tea set, Pillement pattern on *Orsay* ivory blank designed by Marcel Goupy, from a 19th century Chinese shape, T. Haviland. Each less than $500.

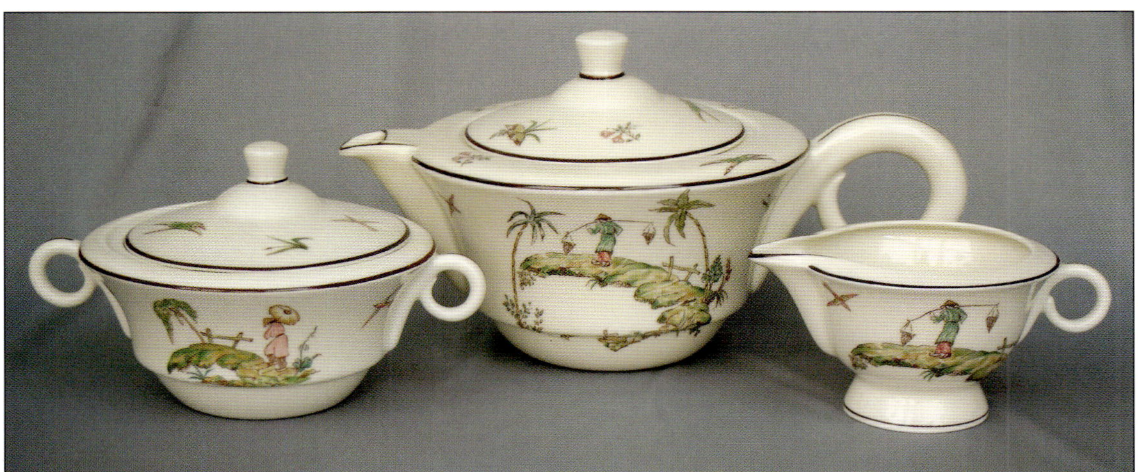

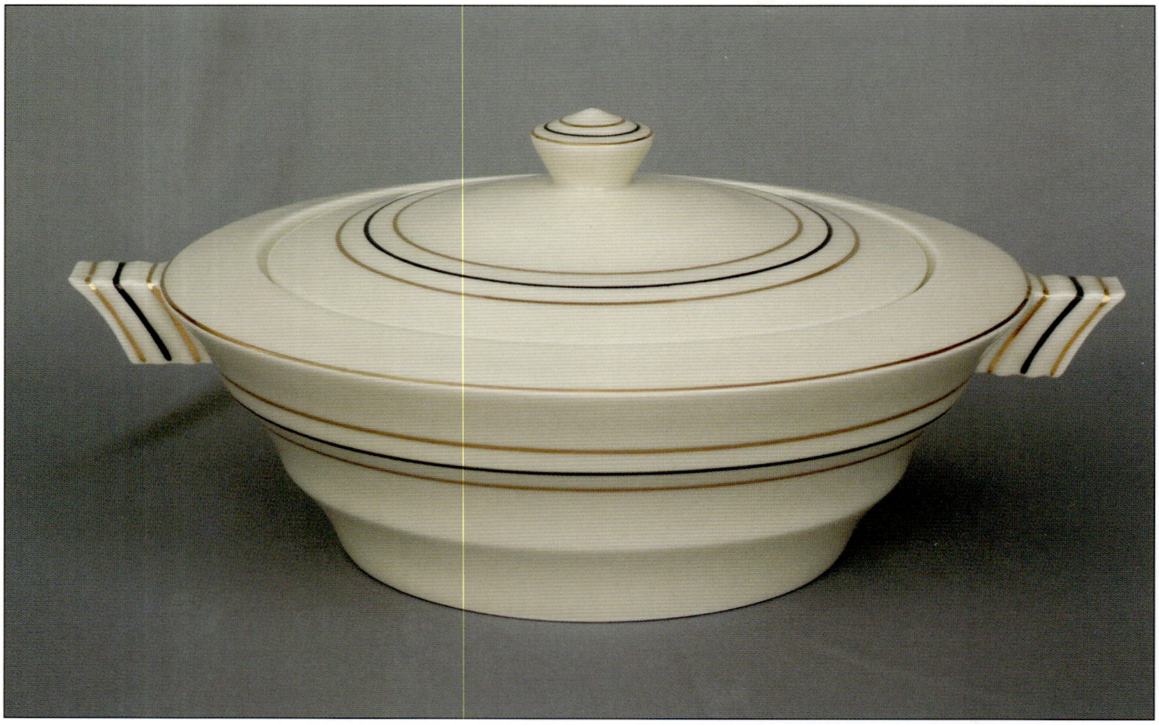

Covered vegetable. Ritz pattern, T. Haviland. Less than $500.

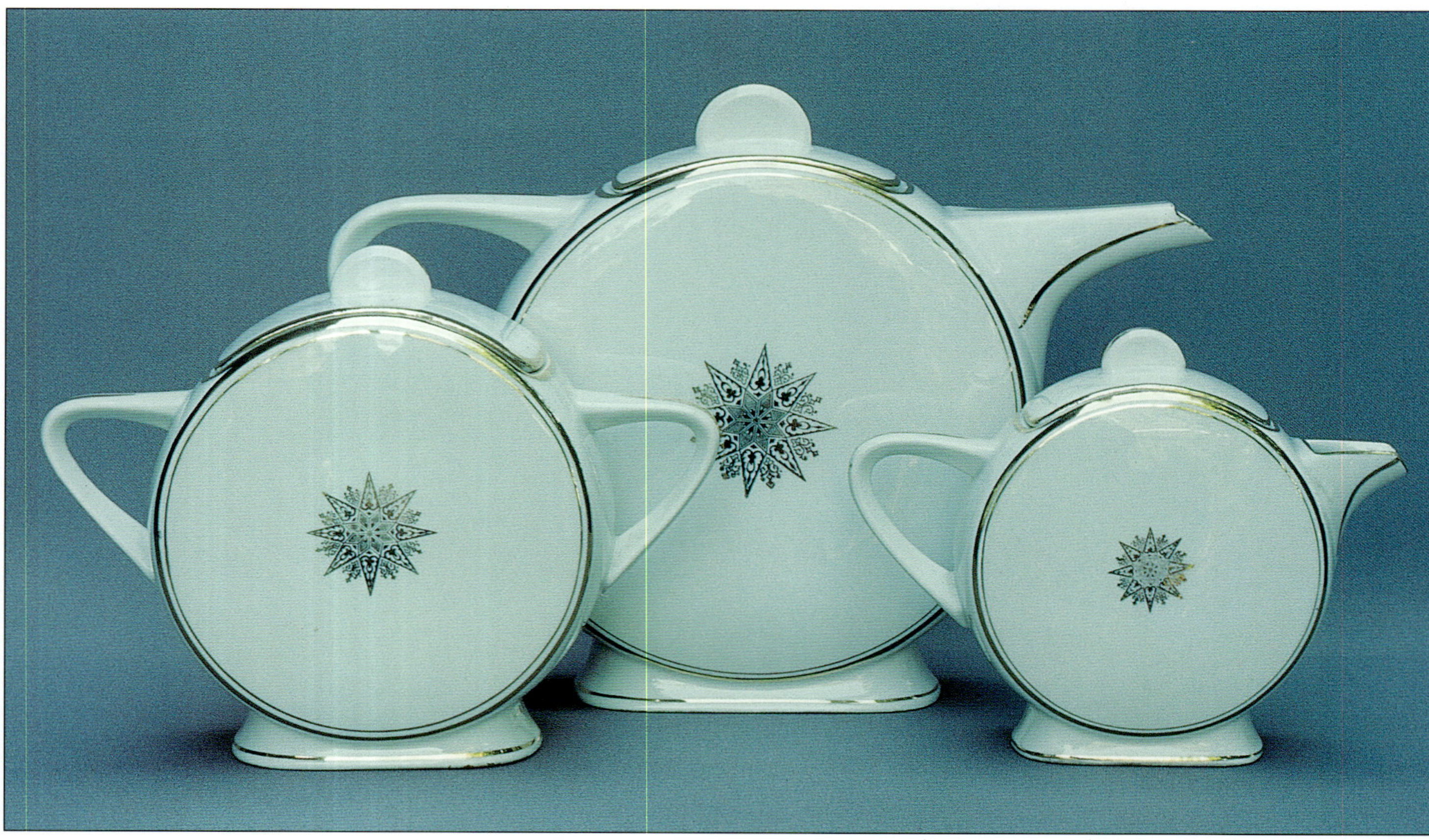

Tea set, Touze, Lemaître & Blancher. Less than $500.

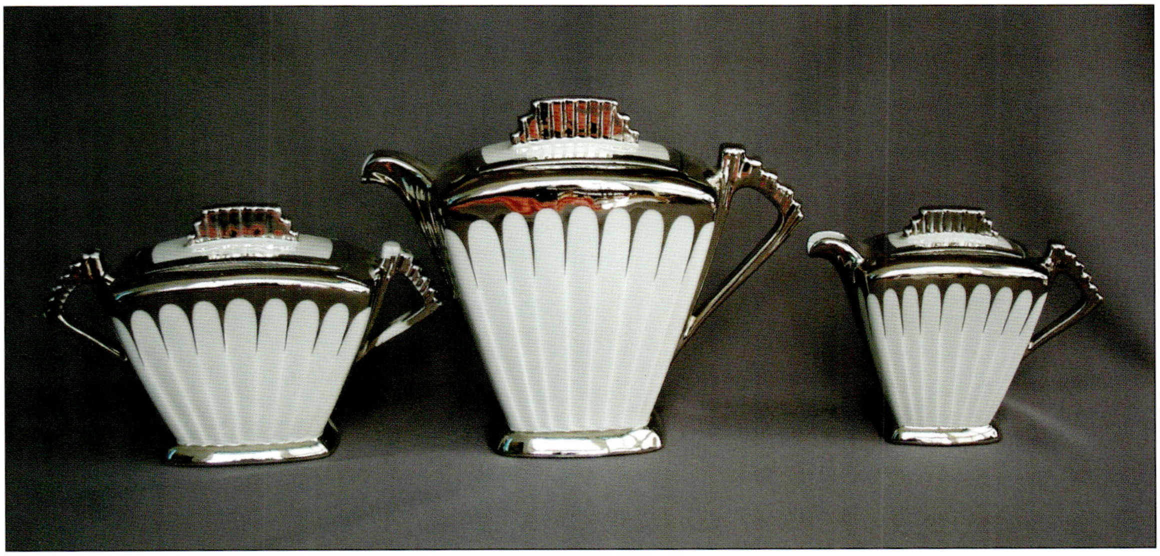

Coffee Set, blanks made by Descottes, Reboisson & Baranger, and set decorated by Jacomart & Cie/244 et 248/rue Léon Gambette/Lille. Less than $500.

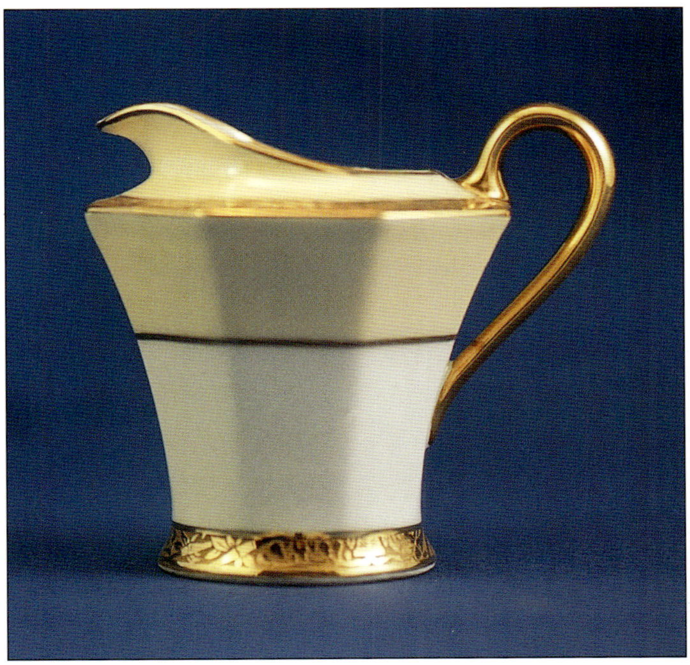

Creamer, T. Haviland. Less than $500.

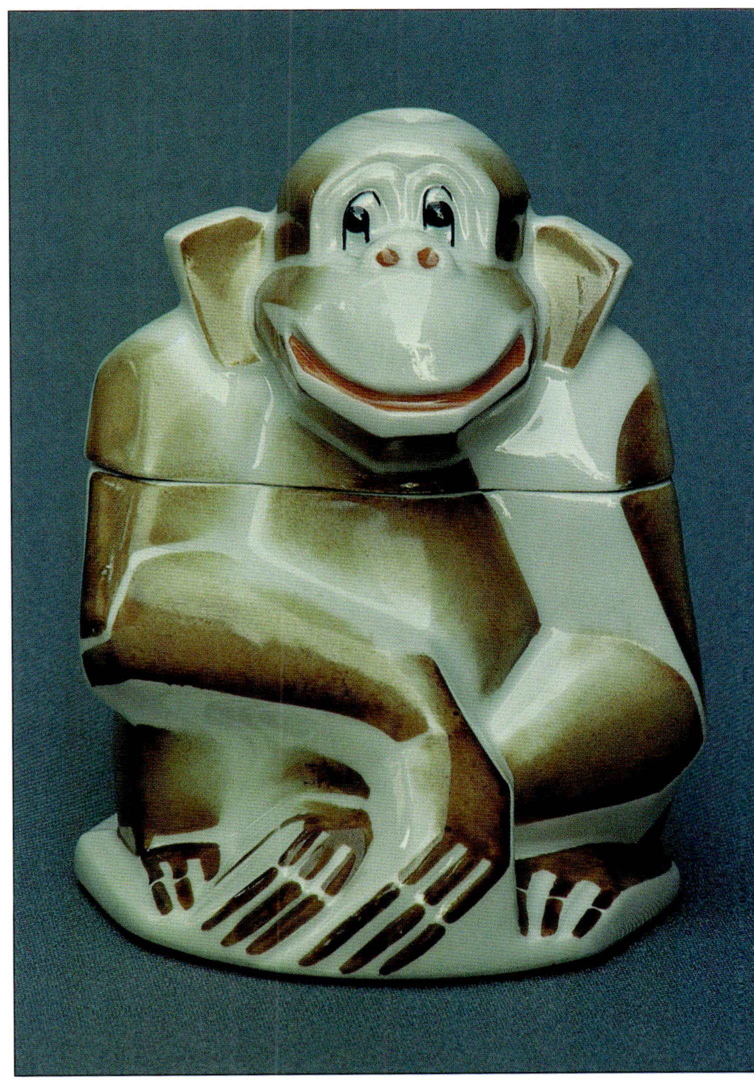

Monkey box, possibly A. Lanternier. Less than $500.

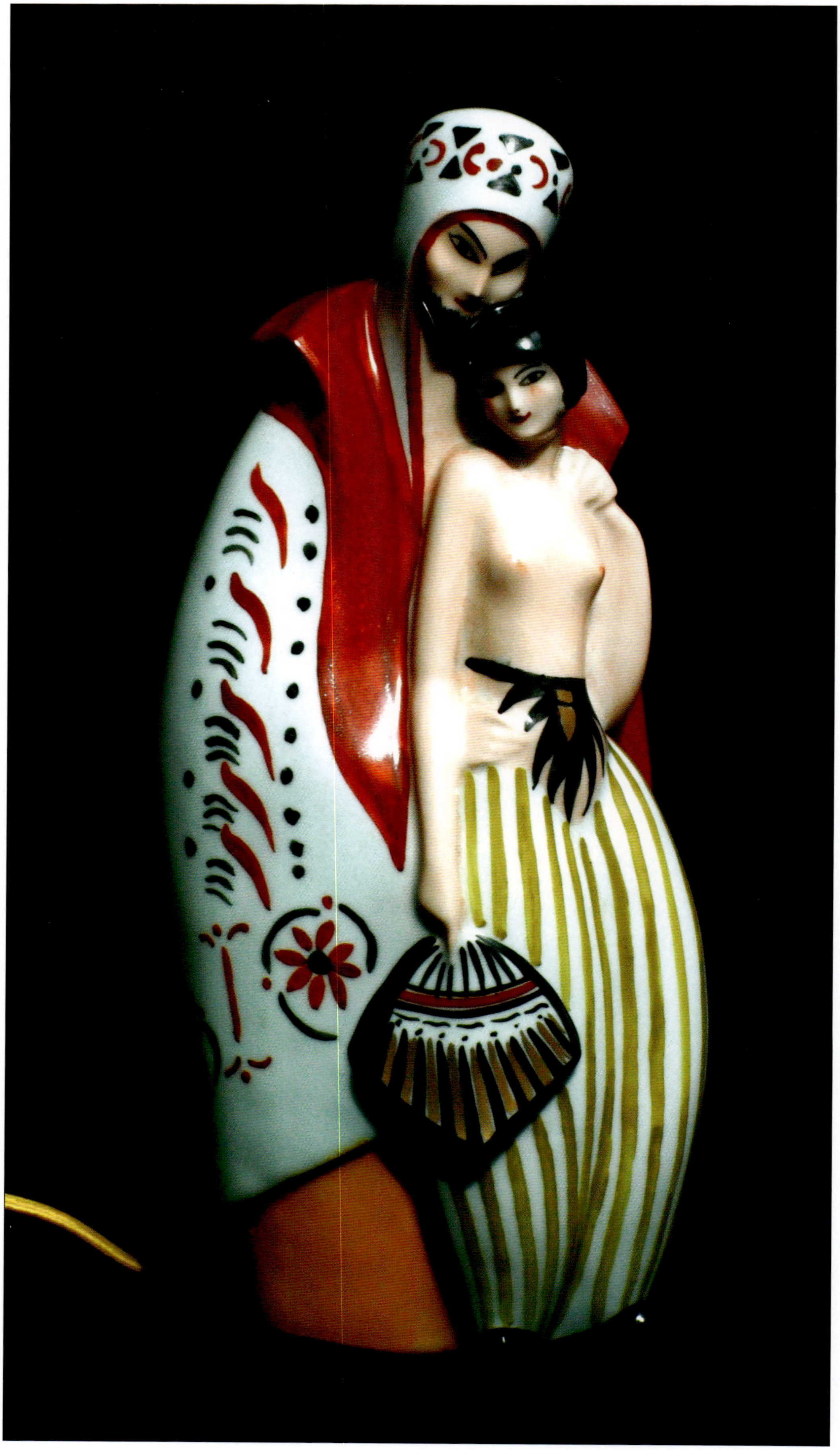

Perfume lamp, 13" high, Arabian couple. $500-$1,000.

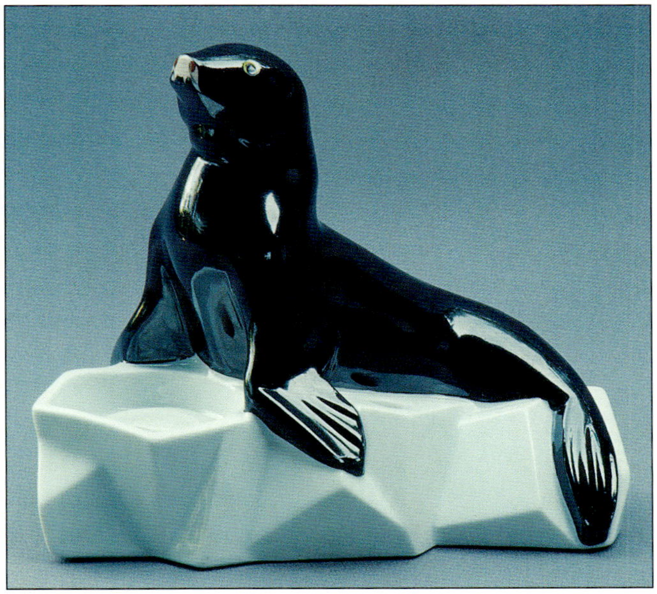

Inkwell, possibly A. Lanternier. Less than $500.

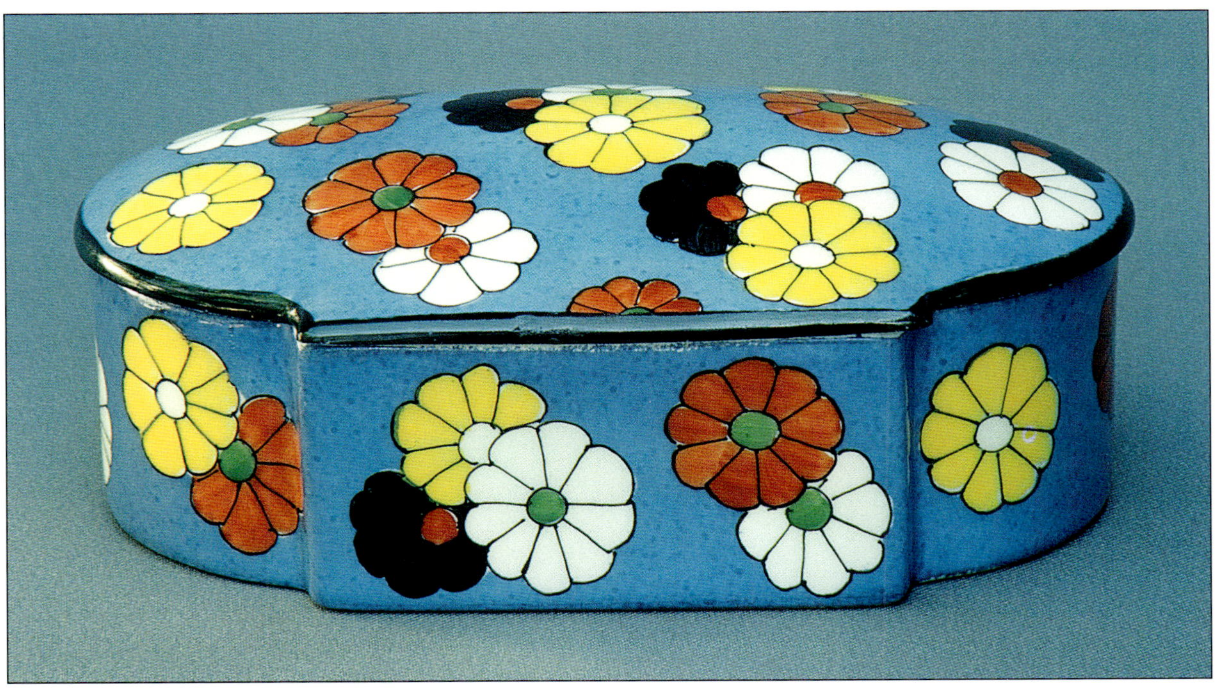

Dresser box, L. Michelaud. Less than $500.

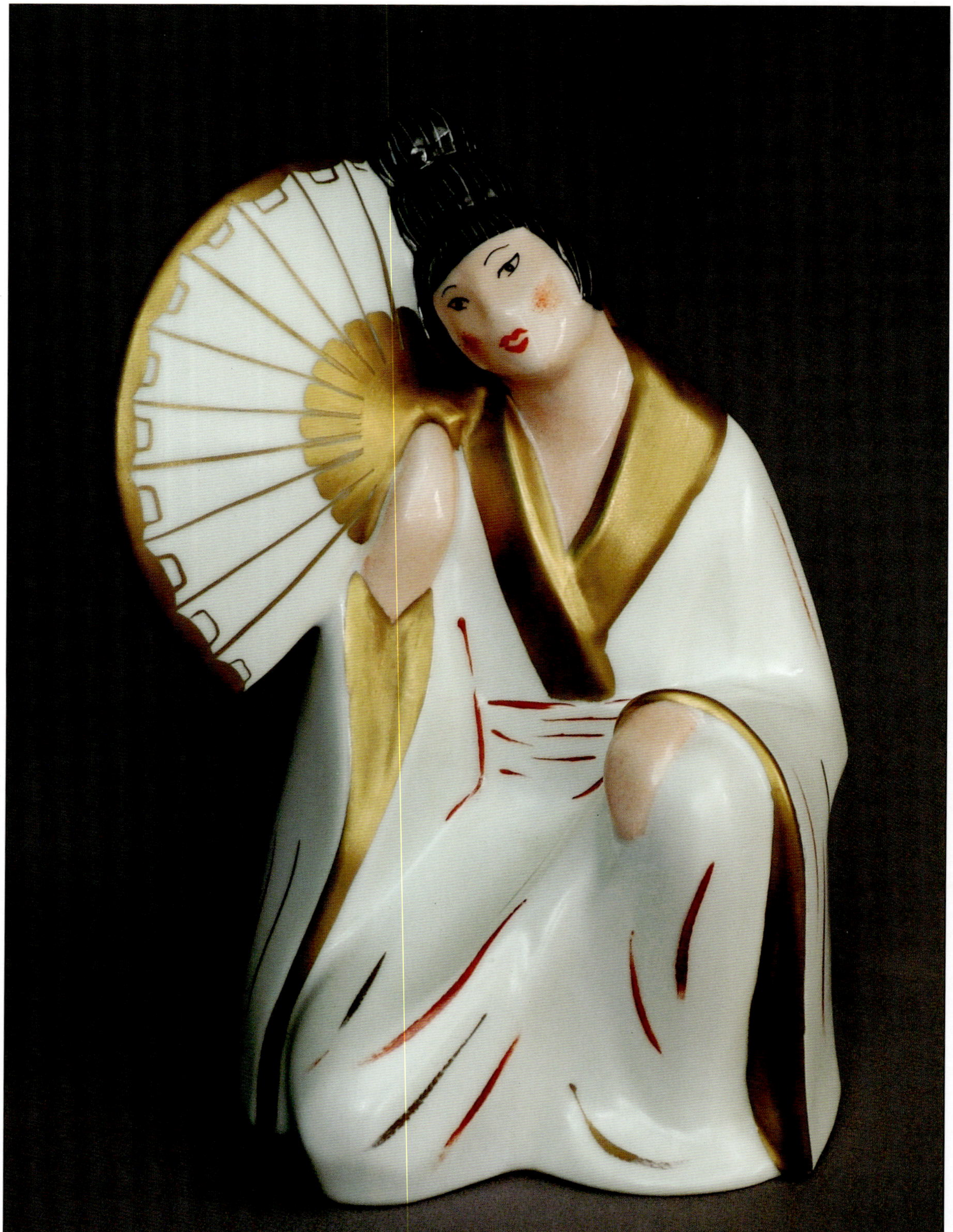

Geisha nightlight. Less than $500.

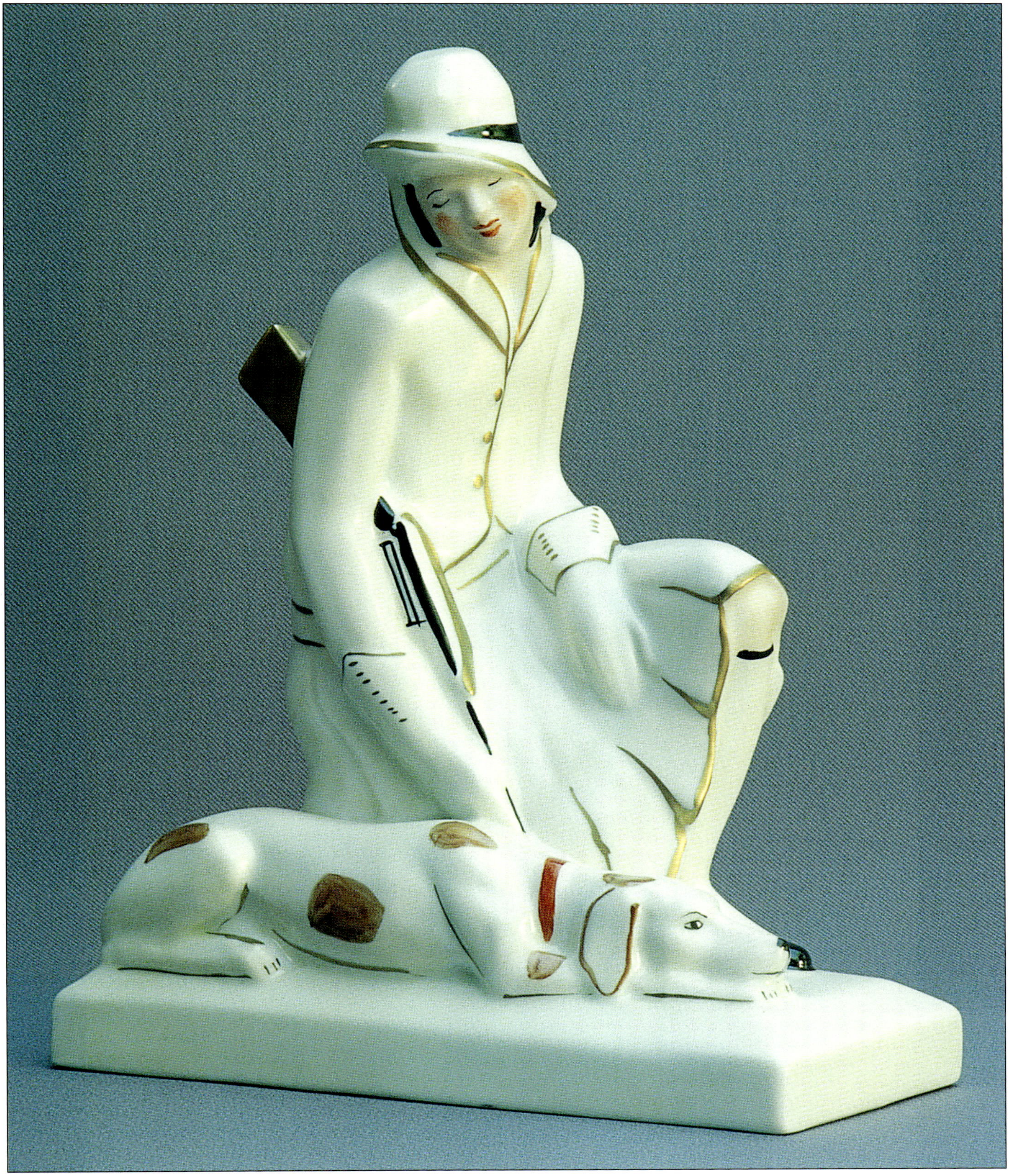

Nightlight. Less than $500.

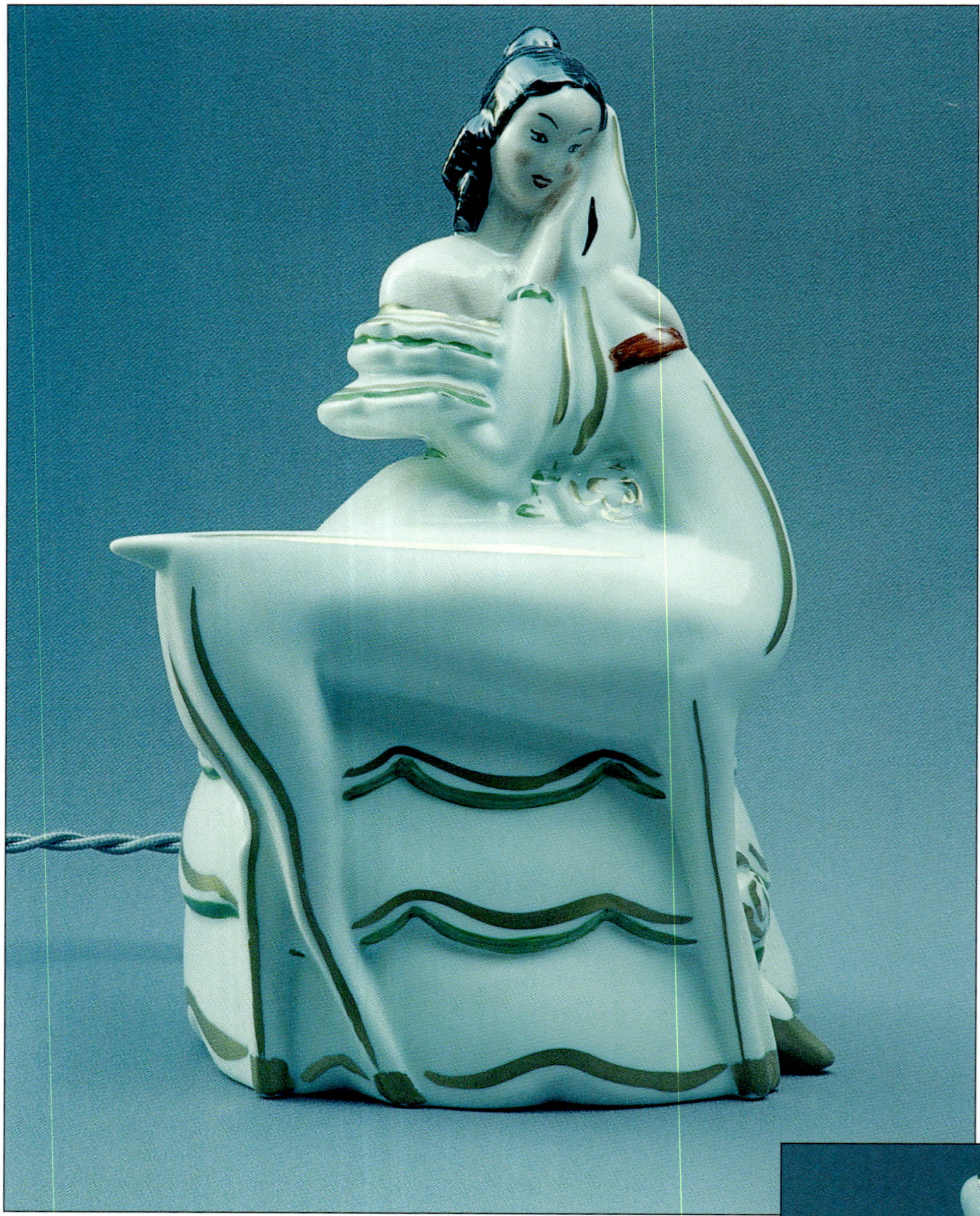

Nightlight. Less than $500.

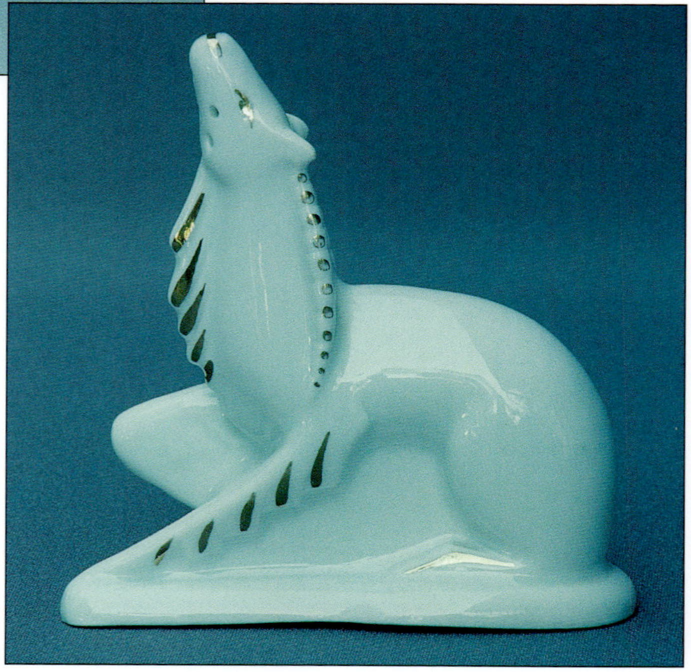

Salt shaker. Less than $500.

Selected Bibliography

d'Albis, Jean. *Haviland.* English translation by Laurens d'Albis. Paris: Dessain et Tolra, 1988.

d'Albis, Jean, and Céleste Romanet. *La Porcelaine de Limoges*. Paris: Sous le Vent, 1980.

Art Deco Painting and Design. London: Grange Books, 1998.

Arwas, Victor. *Art Deco.* Revised Edition. New York: Harry N. Abrams, Inc., 1992.

Brega, Vanna. *Robj Paris: Le Ceramiche: 1921-1931*. Italy: Leonardo Periodici, 1995.

Cameron, Elisabeth. *Encyclopedia of Pottery and Porcelain: 1800-1960*. New York: Facts on File Publications, 1986.

"La Céramique Régionale." *Les Échos des Industries d'Art,* (May 1927).

Champigneulle, Bernard. "La Porcelaine de Limoges." *L'Art Vivan,* (September 1927).

Chavance, René. "Le 19ème Salon des Artistes Décorateurs." *Les Échos des Industries d'Art,* (June 1927).

Chefs-d'Oeuvre de la Porcelaine de Limoges. Paris: Réunion des Musées Nationaux, 1996.

Les Échos des Industries d'Art, (November 1927).

Edouard Marcel Sandoz: de La Sculpture a La Porcelaine. Paris: Réunion des Musées Nationaux, 1999.

Edward, Alfred W. *Art Deco Sculpture & Metalware*. Atglen, Pennsylvania: Schiffer Publishing, Ltd., 1996.

Ferrer, Jean-Marc. *Camille Tharaud: L'Art de la Porcelaine de Grand Feu.* France: Lucien Souny Éditeur, 1994.

Goumot-Labesse, Albert and Odette, Panazol, France, Interview, May 20 and 21, 2003.

Hannum, Hurst and Robert S. Blumberg. *Brandies and Liqueurs of the World.* Garden City, New York: Doubleday & Co., Inc., 1976.

Malaureille, Patrick. *Craquelés: Les Animaux en Céramique, 1920-1940*. Paris: Massin Éditeur, 1993.

Mannoni, Edith. *Porcelaine de Limoges*. Paris: Massin Éditeur, n.d.

Marcilhac, Félix. *Édouard Marcel Sandoz: Sculpteur, Figuriste et Animalier, 1881-1971*. Paris: The Éditions de L'Amateur, 1993.

McConnell, Kevin. *Collecting Art Deco*. Atglen, Pennsylvania: Schiffer Publishing, Ltd., 1990.

McCready, Karen. *Art Deco and Modernist Ceramics*. London: Thames and Hudson Ltd., 1995.

Meslin-Perrier, Chantal. *Musée National Adrien Dubouché: 100 Ans d'Architecture et 10 Ans d'acquisitions*. Paris: Éditions de la Réunion des Musées Nationaux, 2000.

_____. *The National Museum Adrien Dubouché, Limoges*. Paris: Musées et Monuments de France, 1992.

Meslin-Perrier, Chantal, and Marie Segonds-Perrier. *Limoges: Deux Siècles de Porcelaine*. Paris: Les Éditions de L'Amateur, Réunion des Musées Nationaux, 2002.

Meslin-Perrier, Chantal, and J. P. Gratien. *La Porcelaine de Limoges*. Rennes, France: Éditions Quest-France, 1998.

Mobilier et Décoration, December 1929.

Rambosson, Yvanhoé. *Mobilier et Décoration*, April 1930.

La Renaissance de l'Art Français et des Industries de Luxe, 1929.

La Renaissance de l'Art Français et des Industries de Luxe, 1930.

Segonds, Jean-Claude. *Les Créations en Porcelaine de Limoges: D'Édouard Marcel Sandoz*. Italy: Hermé, 1995.

Sollar, Fabien. "Salon des Artistes Décorateurs." *Les Échos d'Art,* (June 1931).

Taboury, F. *Revue Générale du Centre-Quest.* (December 1929)

Weisberg, Gabriel P. *Art Nouveau: Bing*. New York: Harry N. Abrams, Inc., 1986.

For additional citations on the works of Camille Tharaud, see the bibliography in Ferrer's book.

Index

This index is organized into three main categories—names of Tharaud shapes; artists, painters, collaborators and companies; and expositions. Sometimes we have only the initials or part of the initials of the Tharaud studio painters/decorators, and there are a few instances where we are unsure of the letters in the initials. Nevertheless, we have included all of the initials found on the Tharaud pieces in this book, hoping that if any of the initials are incorrect, someone will be able to identify and correct them in the future.

Artists, Painters, Collaborators, and Companies

Names of Tharaud Vessels

Expositions

(For a more complete list of Expositions, see chapter on Major Expositions of Tharaud's Work.)

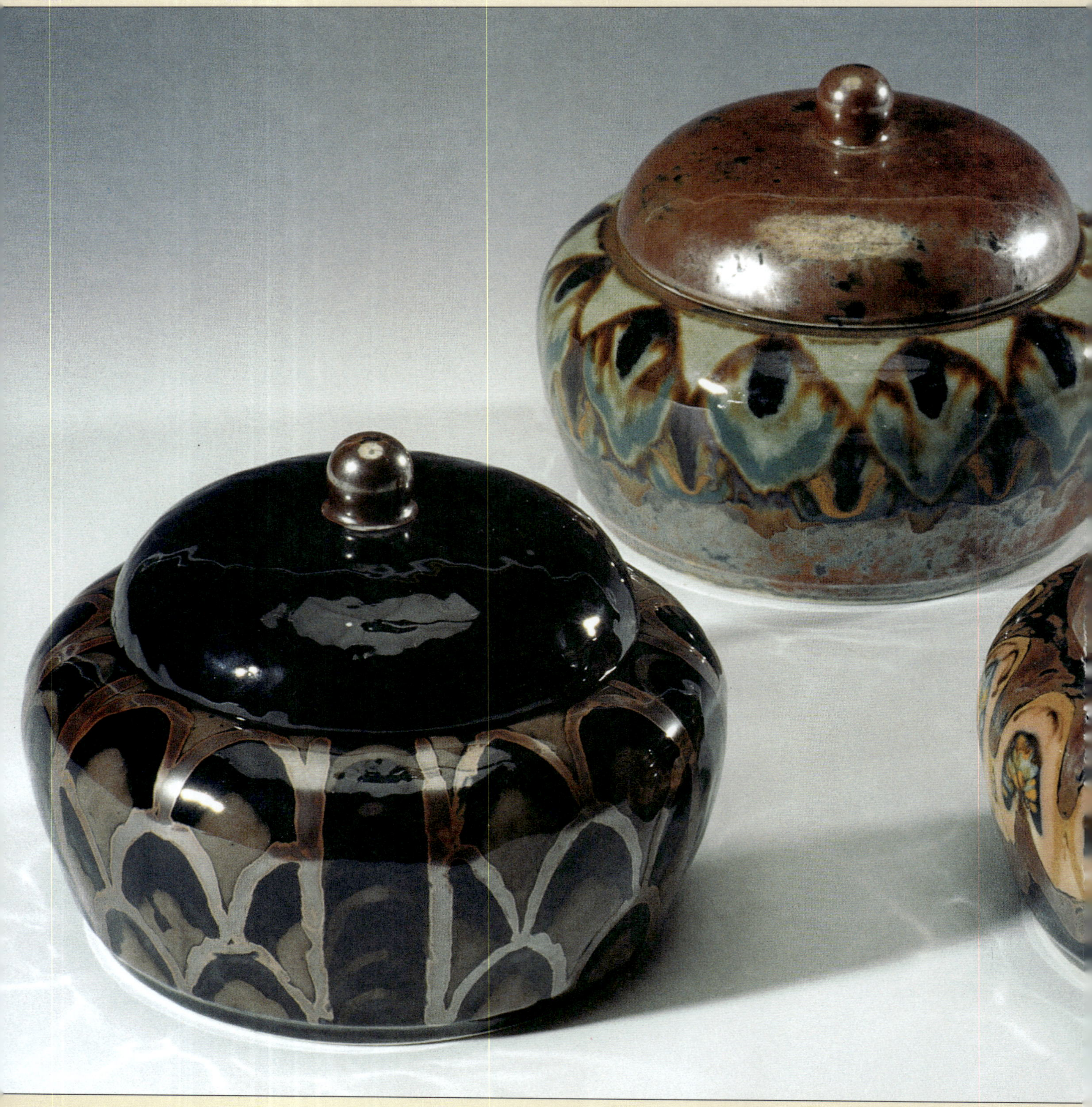